DATE DUE

NOV 1 2 2012		

Deaf People
Around the World

Deaf People Around the World:

Educational and

Social Perspectives

*Donald F. Moores and
Margery S. Miller,* Editors

Gallaudet University Press   *Washington, D.C.*

Gallaudet University Press
Washington, DC 20002

http://gupress.gallaudet.edu

© 2009 by Gallaudet University

All rights reserved. Published 2009

Printed in the United States of America

Library of Congress Cataloging-in-Publication Data

Deaf people around the world : educational perspectives / Donald F. Moores and Margery S. Miller.

   p. cm.

   Includes index.

   ISBN 978-1-56368-410-4 (alk. paper)

   1. Deaf—Social conditions.   2. Deaf—Education.   3. Deaf—Psychology.   I. Moores, Donald F.
II. Miller, Margery Staman, 1945–

   HV2380.D428 2009

   371.91′2—dc22

                                    2008046137

∞ The paper used in this publication meets the minimum requirements of American National Standard for
Information Sciences—Permanence of Paper for Printed Library Materials, ANSI Z39.48-1984.

For Kip Lee Miller and Tige Justice Miller

Contents

Preface

THE MOTIVATION for this book developed over a long period of time, and we attribute that lengthy development to several factors. First among them has been the opportunity for us, both together and separately, to visit a wide range of countries to participate in and present at conferences, observe in schools, visit universities, discuss research, conduct workshops, and visit clubs for the Deaf. Our experiences around the world with both Deaf and hearing colleagues have been uniformly pleasant and informative. Visits we made to clubs for the Deaf have been particularly gratifying. There was always more ease of communication with deaf signers if we did not share a language than there was with hearing speakers if they did not speak English and we did not speak their language. Of course, many people have noted this phenomenon.

Each of us has had tenure of more than 20 years at Gallaudet University, another source of international exchange. During that time, Gallaudet hosted two Deaf Way conferences in which thousands of Deaf individuals came together from around the world to share their arts and experiences. As the only liberal arts college for Deaf people in the world, Gallaudet serves as a magnet on an international scale. In addition to participating in in-service training for professionals from other countries, we have taught and advised deaf and hearing undergraduate and graduate students from all six continents. We first met some of the contributors to this book when they were students, predoctoral fellows, postdoctoral fellows, researchers, and fellow faculty members. In this way, we have been able to develop an appreciation of the commonality that defines deaf people around the world combined with the uniqueness of each national identity.

A final major influence has been Moores' role of editor of the *American Annals of the Deaf.* The *Annals* has always had international contributors, including Alfred Binet in 1910, but their numbers were relatively small. This situation started to change in the 1990s, when the Joint Annals Administrative Committee directed the editor to increase the number of articles from outside of the United States and Canada. The results were apparent by the turn of the century, and by 2008, approximately 40% of all manuscript submissions to the *Annals*—and subsequent publications—have come from international sources. The contact with these authors has been gratifying, and relationships are on a first-name basis, even without the opportunity to actually meet face to face. In fact, many of the contributors to this text have published in the *Annals.*

It may be said that there is a worldwide Deaf community and, as we have noted, the ease of communication among deaf individuals with different sign languages has long been a subject of discussion. We hope that this book helps to address in a larger way some of the shared developmental, social, and educational issues facing Deaf people around the world as filtered through the prism of unique national, regional, ethnic, and racial realities.

REPRESENTATIVE COUNTRIES

At present, the United Nations recognizes more than 200 countries. Our goal was to have contributions from as wide a geographic area as possible, representing ranges of economic development and varying histories of educational and social services for Deaf citizens. We also wanted to include countries with small, medium, and large populations. We received recommendations from colleagues around the world for countries and possible contributors. Because space limitations called for no more than 30 chapters, a small minority of the possible total number of countries, we faced some difficulty in coming up with a final list. There were concerns about limiting the number of chapters on European countries, where education of the deaf began. We are completely aware that two, three, or more texts could be developed using contributions from other countries, and we encourage colleagues to do so.

We decided that there should be chapters on the three countries with the world's largest populations: China, India, and the United States. We also wanted to include chapters on countries with high rates of ethnic and racial diversity. Brazil, South Africa, and the United States were obvious candidates, although racial and ethnic diversity is increasing in several countries. After that, it was a matter of including countries with varying characteristics within defined geographic areas. Almost everyone contacted agreed to participate, and we are gratified by their enthusiasm and unique insights.

FORMAT

The goal was to provide a common framework for each chapter while at the same time allowing flexibility to accommodate the tremendous diversity in the different countries. Thus, we suggested the following common topics:

1. History
2. Current academic placement
3. Communication modes in schools
4. Sign languages
5. Curriculum and the extent to which it matches schools for hearing children
6. Status of Deaf adults, including those in teaching
7. Special laws
8. Secondary and postsecondary opportunities
9. Preparation of special personnel—teachers, psychologists, therapists, etc.
10. Current developments and trends

The Deaf and hearing contributors represent an outstanding group of scholars with resultantly strong opinions on the current situation in their individual countries. No attempt was made to modify their positions, and we are delighted with their contributions.

ORGANIZATION

As may be seen in the table of contents, the text is divided into five major sections: Asia/Pacific, the Middle East and Africa, Europe, North and South America, and International Developments. Each section has from four to seven chapters of roughly equal length and is designed to include countries of different sizes and different levels of development.

The section on international developments has wider multinational perspectives across at least two continents and includes the International Committee on Sports for the Deaf and the World Federation of the Deaf, two global organizations administered by international Deaf leaders.

AUDIENCE

We developed this book, keeping in mind a potential worldwide audience of Deaf and hearing readers, both professional and lay. In addition to practicing professionals, an important audience consists of Deaf and hearing college students around the world who are preparing for careers as teachers, school and clinical psychologists, school counselors, interpreters, social workers, and speech and language therapists. Another audience for this book is parents of Deaf children who might not be aware of the rich histories of Deaf communities and their accomplishments and who may also be unaware of their rights and ability to shape the education of their children. A relatively new potential audience consists of general education teachers and other educational personnel. As noted in many of the chapters, there is a strong international movement for inclusion of Deaf children in regular classrooms. General education personnel usually have had no training in the education of deaf students but are now expected to provide quality education to a child who may be the only Deaf child in the school—a unique and very challenging situation. Finally, the general public is another important audience. There has been a groundswell of interest in deafness and national sign languages across the world. Many of the countries have formally recognized their national sign languages as official languages. The United States does not have an official sign language, but enrollment in high school and college American Sign Language classes makes it one of the most popular languages selected for study. In addition, numbers of hearing parents are using signs with their hearing babies in the belief that the practice will enhance cognitive and communicative development.

Acknowledgments

WE OWE a debt to so many people over the course of our careers that it is impossible to enumerate everyone. We want to acknowledge the contributions of the authors who contributed to this text. Their expertise and commitment will be obvious to the reader. Each one faced a difficult task in condensing large amounts of information into very limited space, and we applaud their success and appreciate their cooperation. Even though we know some only by e-mail, we are friends for life!

We were fortunate to have the support and counsel of Ivey Pittle Wallace of the Gallaudet University Press from the time we developed a proposal for this book through the inevitable pitfalls that an undertaking of this nature entails to final completion. We were also fortunate to have the services of Deirdre Mullervy, who handled the technical editing of the manuscript with her usual tact, patience, and skill. We appreciate the assistance of Melanie (Chrissy) Lafferty, a graduate student in the Department of Exceptional Student and Deaf Education at the University of North Florida, who provided invaluable help at various stages of the process. Finally, to all of the Deaf mentors, colleagues, students, researchers, and friends who have enriched our lives and to whom we owe a debt of gratitude—thanks.

Asia/Pacific

Deaf Education and the Deaf Community in Australia

Desmond Power

AUSTRALIA IS the only island continent. Its indigenous people have lived here for at least 40,000 years, having traveled from Asia via land and water crossings. It is known that they use signs during periods when speech is tabooed (e.g., during mourning for women and initiation for men) and also while hunting (Kendon, 1988). It is known that in some communities, hearing and deaf people also use signs for general communication. Indigenous deaf people in north Queensland use a mixture of Australian Sign Language (Auslan) and indigenous signs in everyday communication. The system is known locally as "Ailan" (Karen Fayd'Herbe, personal communication, July 9, 2008; Cathy Nixon, personal communications, July 9, 2008).

The population of Australia in 2007 is a little more than 20 million. Despite the popular image of Australia's outback, the large majority of Australians live close to the coast in the state capital cities, several of which have a population of more than 1 million, Sydney being the largest with close to 4 million. Australia is a multicultural nation. Apart from the indigenous people, 77% of the people were born in Australia and 23% in another country, mostly the United Kingdom or New Zealand, with significant groups from other European countries and Asia. The official language is English, but significant groups of people use many other languages (of which Auslan, or Australian Sign Language, is officially one; see Lo Bianco, 1987), mostly at home and within their own communities.

Despite several probes around the Australian coast by Dutch, Spanish, and Portuguese traders to the East Indies, European settlement was established by the British after Captain James Cook's voyage of exploration of the east coast in 1770. After the American Revolution, the British Government needed somewhere else to send its convicts and chose Botany Bay (near the site of present-day Sydney), and the "First Fleet" of convicts and their guards settled at Sydney Cove in 1788. The settlement fell on very difficult times in the early years, but gradually life improved, and the country began to be explored and other settlements established, not only near Sydney but also in other places around the country. Numbers of "free settlers" gradually arrived and took up farming and ranching sheep and cattle. A huge boost to the economy and the population came with the gold rushes beginning in the 1850s. Australia is now a developed nation with an economy based on mineral and agricultural exports as well as manufacturing.

Deaf history in Australia may be considered to begin with the arrival of the Second Fleet of convicts and guards in 1789. One of the convicts on that fleet was Betty Steel, who had been convicted of stealing a watch in London and sentenced to 7 years transportation (Branson & Miller, 1995; Carty, Neale, & Power, 1997). She lived for a time in Sydney and was eventually freed, but died quite young in 1794. Her tombstone was discovered during excavations for new buildings in Sydney in 1991.

Several other Deaf people arrived as free settlers in the early 19th century. Notable among them was "deaf and dumb" John Carmichael, an engraver and artist, who had attended the Edinburgh Institute for the Deaf and Dumb and had arrived in Australia in 1825. His motive for emigrating is not known. He became well known in Sydney and engraved some of Australia's first maps and postage stamps.

Of particular importance to the development of the Australian Deaf community and the education of its deaf children were John Pattison, Frederick J. Rose, and Sister Mary Gabriel Hogan. Pattison and Rose were Deaf men from Scotland and England, respectively, and Sister Mary Gabriel was a Deaf nun from Ireland. They established the first three schools for the Deaf in Australia: in 1860, Pattison in Sydney and Rose in Melbourne and, in 1875, Sister Mary Gabriel in Newcastle, New South Wales, with the first Catholic school for deaf girls (and younger boys). Schools followed in all the other Australian states and all were well established by the beginning of the 20th century. The Irish Christian Brothers established a school for deaf boys in Sydney in 1925. Unlike some other countries (notably the United States), these schools (except for the Newcastle Catholic school and another Catholic school outside Melbourne) were in capital cities, so from their founding were both day and residential (for children from rural areas). The non-Catholic schools were founded as "charitable institutions" funded by public subscriptions and donations and did not become state schools until well into the 20th century. They, like their counterparts in the United States and elsewhere, played an important role in establishing the Deaf community and in developing Auslan (a descendant of British Sign Language).[1]

In the schools, reactions to the Milan Congress declaration of "Eviva la parola" ("Long live speech") was not speedy. Gradually, however, Deaf teachers disappeared from the schools, even though in most cases the "Combined Method" operated, with signing and fingerspelling being widely used as well as speech, though often, preschool and early grades were oral, with signing being introduced in the later years (the "Combined System").

The schools continued pretty much along these established lines until the great increase in the number of deaf children as a result of the rubella epidemics of the 1940s, which led to an "oral revival" after a visit of Sir Alexander and Lady Irene Ewing from the oralist Manchester University program in 1950. Because of parent pressure, this visit led to the establishment of several new oral schools, itinerant teacher services for deaf students in regular classes, an increase in the number of special units in regular schools, and the initiation of specialist training for teachers of the deaf. Basically, the school system has remained unchanged since that time, except for the changes in modes of communication to be outlined below.

EDUCATIONAL PROVISIONS

Australia has a mixture of public and private schools; about half of the children of school age are in each category. Most of the private schools are religiously affiliated; there are large Catholic, diocesan-based systems. The states and territories (six states and two territories) are the adminis-

---

1. Australian sign linguist Trevor Johnston created the name Auslan. A dictionary (Johnston, 1998) and an online source of Auslan signs is available at Auslan Signbank (http://www.auslan.org.au/).

trators of the public school systems (in effect, they are very large school districts). With the exception of the two Catholic schools for deaf students and itinerant teacher services, there are few private services for deaf students, the most notable exceptions being an outreach early intervention program, preschools, schools (one oral and one bilingual bicultural), and an itinerant teacher service run by the Royal Institute for Deaf and Blind Children in Sydney, New South Wales.

There are early intervention programs in all state capital cities and a number of regional areas. They are, with rare exceptions, orally oriented. In some states, they are administered by Departments of Health and in others by Departments of Education. They provide both onsite and home-visiting services for deaf children and their families. The role of these programs has become much more central since the widespread adoption of Universal Newborn Hearing Screening programs in all states.[2] Since the inception of these programs, the age of diagnosis and hearing aid fitting has dropped dramatically from older than 2 years to younger than 1 year for severely and profoundly deaf infants. This development has led to a proliferation of oral early intervention programs and more "mainstreaming" of deaf students.

A large majority of Australia's deaf children are mainstreamed into regular classes in preschools, elementary schools, and high schools (about 86% overall; Hyde & Power, 2004; Power & Hyde, 2003). Most of them receive support from an itinerant teacher of the deaf (ranging from a once-a-semester checkup to up to five visits per week). The large majority of these students are educated through oral-only methods, though a small but growing number of them have some degree of support from a signing interpreter (increasingly Auslan, but mostly Australasian Signed English;[3] see MacDougall, 1988). A number of recent court cases have reinforced the providing of Auslan interpreting in regular settings (Komesaroff, 2007).

Most other deaf students are in groups of classes (often called "Units" or "Facilities") of deaf children in a regular elementary or high school. In these units, there will be differing degrees of integration into regular classes, with the deaf students accompanied by their teacher of the deaf, who will interpret and tutor the deaf students on the content of the lesson. Some units attempt very little social or academic integration and are in effect "mini schools for the deaf" that happen to be sited on a regular school campus.

Most traditional state day/residential schools for the deaf, with the exception of the Victorian College for the Deaf (actually a K–12 school) in Melbourne and the elementary Mosman Park School for Deaf Children in West Australia, have been closed down over the last 20 years. The students from the closed schools have mostly been moved to the units mentioned above. However, as also mentioned above, an early intervention program, a preschool, and three day schools have been established privately by the Royal Institute for Deaf and Blind Children in Sydney.

In earlier days (until the 1970s) when only the state schools in the capital cities were available, very few deaf students received an education beyond Grade 9 level. It was believed that deaf boys and girls were destined for trades and other lower skilled occupations, and they were trained and schooled with that end in mind. Numerous reports over the years noted the low literacy and numeracy levels of the graduates of the traditional schools. Nowadays, all deaf students in regular or special schools or units follow the local state curriculum quite closely,

---

2. See, for example, the program in Queensland at http://www.health.qld.gov.au/healthyhearing.

3. *Australasia* is the term commonly used when considering Australia and New Zealand together. The two countries are closely linked but are not a political union.

and academic levels appear to have improved, giving access for some graduates to higher education and more skilled professions.

It is important to note the role of Australian Hearing—originally known as the National Acoustic Laboratory—in the education of deaf students in Australia. After founding the National Acoustic Laboratory to assist deafened veterans after World War II, the national government soon expanded its role to provide free hearing aids and services to government pensioners and deaf children. From a large number of "hearing centres" throughout Australia, it diagnoses deafness in infants and children as well as provides, fits, and maintains their hearing aids until they turn age 21. This service has been particularly important in allowing children with residual hearing to access speech and listening for development and learning.

The most widely used cochlear implant (the "Nucleus") was developed and is manufactured in Australia, and implantation of children has become widespread. It is estimated that up to 90% of profoundly deaf and a large number of severely deaf children are wearing implants, many receiving them before the age of 2 years, an age that is rapidly decreasing as Universal Newborn Hearing Screening takes effect around the nation. The national government service Australian Hearing does not supply implants as it does hearing aids, but it does (along with early intervention programs and schools) provide communication training and audiological assessment before and after implantations, maintenance and repair services for eligible children with implants, and speech processor upgrades "to ensure that all eligible children have access to the latest advances in cochlear implant technology." Increasingly, under the management of "Auditory-Verbal" early intervention programs, almost all implanted children proceed to attend regular schools, and there is a certain degree of controversy about whether this plan leads to the most advantageous placement for some of them. Few implanted children have access to signing, whether Australasian Signed English or Auslan.

A special problem in rural Australia is the high prevalence of chronic middle ear disease (mostly otitis media) in indigenous children, with its resultant health and educational problems. Numerous projects have attempted to address this problem, but it has proved quite intractable over a long period. Some success in managing its health and educational implications has been reported. Higgins (1997) has recommended a set of strategies for addressing the problem in schools and communities, and resources have been produced for teachers (Low Incidence Support Centre, 1997; Sherwood & McConville, 1994). A concerted health and educational effort is required if the problem is to be brought under control.

Communication in Schools

Given the history and demography of Australian schools for the deaf outlined above, the majority of Australian deaf students are educated orally at the present time because of their presence in hearing-speaking classes at regular schools. Some units for deaf students are also oral, but most use Simultaneous Communication in speech and Australasian Signed English. A small but increasing number use a bilingual-bicultural approach with Auslan.

There was a period in the 1960s and 1970s when Cued Speech was in vogue, especially in the Catholic programs. It was eventually superseded by an entirely oral approach in those programs. As it became clear in the late 1960s that, for severely and profoundly deaf students, the prevailing "pure oral" approach was not helping many deaf students learn, there was a confused period when services cast about for a better approach. Some Deaf people recount having used several approaches. One Deaf friend tells the story of how her hearing mother did not know what to make of it, "One week I was oral, then I was using Cued Speech, then I was allowed to fingerspell, then I was signing in English!" Her story, though somewhat embellished, points to an unsettled period. Eventually, with the growing awareness of "Total Communication," methods settled down in the 1970s to the use of Simultaneous Communication in speech and Australasian Signed English until the advent of a number of bilingual-bicultural programs using Auslan in the 1980s. Probably the majority of signing programs in regular school units still use Australasian Signed English, although no national data are available.

Now, there are bilingual-bicultural programs using Auslan as their signed communication in every Australian state. Some (e.g., the Claremont Project in Tasmania[4] and the Toowong State School program in Queensland[5]) use a "co-enrollment" approach (Kirchner, 2004) whereby deaf and hearing students are in the same classroom, doing the same work and being cotaught by a regular teacher and a teacher of the deaf. Queensland in 2008 has instituted a policy of bilingual-bicultural education for all signing students and Griffith University is providing training in Auslan and bilingual-bicultural pedagogy for its teachers.[6] Other bilingual programs (e.g., the Victorian College for the Deaf[7] and the Thomas Pattison School in New South Wales[8]) are freestanding schools for the deaf. Deaf children with disabilities, especially those with severe or profound intellectual impairment, physical impairment, or both, are educated in special schools for such children, usually with major curriculum and teaching processes adapted to their needs.

A recent arrival, mainly in early intervention programs, has been the so-called Auditory-Verbal Therapy Method. This unisensory approach insists that the deaf child as far as possible use only audition, with as little access to vision as feasible (i.e., no speechreading and gesture; signing is a complete anathema).[9] This approach is now widely used in Australia in early intervention and some preschool programs.

Curriculum

As noted above, the states and territories are the "school districts" in the Australian education system, which means that each state and territory develops its own curriculum that is mandated for state schools. In most states, it is compulsory for private schools to follow the state curriculum and this requirement is reinforced by most pupils undertaking a state-based Grade 12 school exit assessment. There has recently been some agitation for a national curriculum and school-leaving examination, especially in literacy, mathematics, and science, but "states rights" means that such a curriculum will be very slow arriving, if it occurs at all.

All services for deaf students who do not have other special learning needs follow, as far as possible, the curriculum of those students' state or territory. The state curricula cover the usual

---

4. For more information, see http://www.aceinfo.net.au/resources/ADD_FOLDER/ADD_listings/ADDclaremont.html.

5. For more information, see http://www.toowongss.qld.edu.au/bilingualprogram.

6. See http://education.qld.gov.au/studentservices/staff/workshops/auslan.html.

7. For more information, see http://www.vcd.vic.edu.

8. For more information, see http://www.ridbc.org.au/services/hi_schoolaged_tps.asp.

9. For an example, see http://www.listen-up.org/oral/a-v.htm. For early intervention, see Simser (1993) and Pollack (1985); for school age, see Stone (1983); for a counterview, see Power and Hyde (1997).

school subjects familiar in the developed Western world: literacy and numeracy, science, social and environmental studies, health and physical education, languages other than English (including Auslan in several states), information technology, and the arts. Typical is that of the state of Queensland.[10]

Until quite recently, Deaf people did not achieve high levels of schooling, especially in literacy. This lack of achievement excluded them from many occupations, and men were concentrated in trades such as carpentry and building, French polishing, shoemaking, automobile bodywork and related jobs, as well as process work in factories. Women became seamstresses, copy typists, cleaners, and housewives. In recent years, as we have seen in discussing postschool opportunities, Deaf people have had much better access to further education, and there is now a large number of women and men Deaf professionals: lawyers, teachers, accountants, scientists, psychologists, audiologists, and many others (Punch, Hyde, & Power, 2007), although there are concerns that Deaf people are still not getting "a fair go" when seeking employment and in obtaining opportunities for promotion (Miers, 2006). More still needs to be done in this respect.

Postsecondary Opportunities

Australia has three types of postsecondary education institutions: universities, Technical and Further Education (TAFE) colleges, and private colleges (these last specialize mainly in business, tourism, and hospitality; few deaf students attend them). Only three of the 41 universities are private foundations; the remainder are government funded (state and federal) but legislated by the states (except for the Australian National University in Canberra, established under federal government legislation). All are self-governing. The TAFE colleges are state based and federally and state funded.

The TAFE colleges provide certificates and diplomas in numerous areas, including business, engineering and mechanics, tourism and hospitality, trades, adult education, and paraprofessional courses of many kinds (nursing and child care among them). The colleges also provide short-term periods of study for students who are apprenticed to a master tradesman and are learning "on the job." A number of TAFE colleges have specialist services for supporting deaf students, and one or more in each state offers Auslan interpreter training and Auslan courses. All colleges would have a generic "disabled student service" that would provide some interpreting (if interpreters can be found!), note-taking, and (sometimes limited) tutorial support for deaf students. A large number of deaf people have been able to benefit from attendance at TAFE colleges and have been able subsequently to enter the workforce in steady employment in many of the areas mentioned above.

For many years, few deaf students entered universities, and they usually found little or no support for or understanding of their learning needs. No funds were available for any support; for example, if a student required interpreting, he or she would often have to pay for it out of pocket (Rumsey, 1999). This circumstance began to change at approximately the time of the International Year of the Disabled in 1981 and as Deaf people and educators of the deaf began to press for more opportunities for Deaf people to be educated beyond school. The federal government introduced regulations that funded "A Fair Chance for All," and a

---

10. See http://education.qld.gov.au/curriculum.

number of state and federal antidiscrimination acts made the community and the universities more aware of the rights of people with special needs. As a result, support programs began to be implemented for them. Most universities provide support for deaf students through their generic disabled student programs.

An early impetus for the establishment of support programs was the desire of the Deaf community and many educators of the deaf to enable Deaf people to become teachers of the deaf themselves; particularly as the use of signing in schools and units became more widespread. (Since the World War I period, there had been very few Deaf teachers of deaf students in any Australian school for the deaf.) The earliest program of this type was established at a Brisbane teachers college in 1985, and after a series of mergers, this program—the "Deaf and Hearing Impaired Student Support Program" of Griffith University in Queensland—has since grown into one of the largest and most comprehensive of its type in an Australian university. This program provides interpreting, note-taking, FM hearing aids (and other technology if required), tutorial support, and access to the regular university personal, vocational, and other counseling and advice services for deaf undergraduate and graduate students across a wide range of degrees, including education, psychology, business, science, law, graphic arts, visual arts, creative arts, and information technology (Punch et al., 2007). In 2004, the university graduated its first Deaf PhD, and it is fitting that the thesis was on an aspect of Australian Deaf history (Carty, 2005). Research into aspects of interpreting at the tertiary level is emerging (Napier, 2002; Napier & Barker, 2004).

Sign Language

Sign language—a 19th-century variety of British Sign Language in its southern and northern (Scots) dialects—was brought to Australia by deaf free settlers from about 1830 on. It has adapted itself to the Australian environment since that time, although there is still a good deal of overlap between British Sign Language and Auslan. Both use two-handed fingerspelling. The Catholic schools brought Irish Sign Language, which was used in their schools until the 1950s. There are a few Irish signs that have entered into Auslan, but no significant community of Deaf people now uses Irish Sign Language in Australia. In recent years, because Australian Deaf people have traveled and studied in the United States, a number of American Sign Language signs have made their way into Auslan, especially the technological, science, mathematics, and other vocabularies that have been adopted for use in schools and higher education.

Auslan is recognized in the *National Policy on Languages* (Lo Bianco, 1987) and *The Australian Language and Literacy Policy* (Dawkins, 1991) as a CLOTE (Community Language Other Than English; see also Power, 2001):

Deaf Australians have evolved Sign Language to meet their communication needs. Australian Sign Language is considered to be a language in the same sense as verbal languages[11] and consequently is to enjoy the same status. For children who use sign language, it is recognized that this is their language of initial learning. For the deaf, access to services and equity in opportunity generally require acknowledgement of their need for interpreting services and for education using the appropriate language systems. . . . The deaf consider

---

11. More accurately, "vocal" languages; sign languages are, of course, just as "verbal" as spoken ones.

Australian Sign Language to be their community language and desire that they be acknowledged as a community group with a distinctive language. This acknowledgment implies
services and educational provisions which mirror those made for other [Non-English
Speaking Background] communities. (Lo Bianco, p. 76)

It is now increasingly recognised that signing deaf people constitute a group like any
other non-English-speaking language group in Australia, with a distinct sub-culture
recognised by shared history, social life and sense of identity, united and symbolised by
fluency in Auslan. . . . Auslan is an indigenous language, having developed from British
and Irish sign languages brought to Australia. . . . Auslan could be made extensively available to deaf students in schools, colleges and universities. (Dawkins, 1991, p. 20)

Support for bilingual-bicultural education (although that term was not at that time widely
used in Australia) could also be found:

Research overseas supports the value of bilingual education in the national language and
the first language (a sign language) for deaf children too. Like other children speaking
another language who are also learning the national language, deaf children in bilingual
programs apparently master the national language and the regular curriculum more quickly
than children in monolingual programs. (Dawkins, 1991, p. 52)

These recognitions of Auslan as a community language of equal status to spoken ones and of
Deaf people as a community similar in many respects to other non-English speaking communities did much to awaken public awareness of the characteristics, aspirations, and needs
of the Deaf community and strengthened their (eventually successful) lobbying efforts for
better interpreting services, more captioned television, telephone relay services, and similar
supports.[12] The *National Policy on Languages* considered increased interpreting availability, for
example, to be "an aspect of service provision . . . rather than a welfarist program for the disadvantaged" (Dawkins, 1991, p. 164).

Interpreting has emerged as a profession in Australia, growing out of the earlier service
orientation of welfare workers from Deaf societies. As in many other parts of the world,
there is a desperate shortage of personnel to meet all interpreting needs as Deaf people enter
higher education, become better educated, and enter the professions and business (Napier,
Bontempo, & Leneham, 2006; Orima Research, 2004; Ozolins & Bridge, 1999). The
National Accreditation Authority for Translators and Interpreters accredits Auslan and spoken language interpreters at two levels—Paraprofessional and Interpreter. The majority of
Auslan interpreters are accredited at the Paraprofessional level, and there is concern about
the large number of unaccredited interpreters, especially in school settings. A professional
association is well established: the Australian Sign Language Interpreters Association,[13]
which lobbies for better recognition, conditions, and training for Auslan interpreters. The
Commonwealth Government also funds the National Auslan Booking Service,[14] which
provides and arranges free interpreting services for medical and paramedical appointments
nationwide.

---

12. At the time of writing (February 2008), there was only one limited video relay service operating in Australia.
13. See http://www.aslia.com.au.
14. See http://www.nabs.org.au.

THE DEAF COMMUNITY

As mentioned above, Deaf people played an important role in the early history of the Deaf community in Australia. This role was not limited to education. The British system of "missions" to Deaf people (with a strong focus on Protestantism) was imported into Australia in the second half of the 19th century, and several Deaf men and women played important roles as "Superintendents" and "Missioners" in the early days (Carty, 2005). Around the turn of the century, hearing people (some of them Codas, or children of deaf adults) began to assume control over what came to be called "Deaf Societies," and this control continued until well into the 20th century. It was only in the 1980s that some Deaf people again assumed significant roles in "managing their own affairs" (Carty, 2005), and now, roles in the societies are filled by Deaf people.

The societies were quite paternalistic in their orientation to services and Deaf people until well after World War II. They employed people known as "Welfare Officers" (almost all of them hearing, again, some Codas) who acted very much in a welfare support role with respect to any difficulties Deaf people might be having in the hearing community. The support they provided included interpreting for medical, legal, personal (e.g., helping with income tax returns), and social needs and difficulties, and it is from this group that professional interpreting began to emerge as a separate profession in the 1980s.

Sport has always been a major focus of interest for the Australian Deaf communities. Interstate rivalries in a number of sports go back to colonial days. Sporting carnivals became the source of many Deaf romances and marriages as well as sports competition. Deaf Australians have been active on the world sports scene, strongly supporting the Deaflympics (the Summer Games were held in Melbourne in January 2005) and supplying a president (John Lovett) to the Comité Internationale des Sports des Sourds. The Deaf Sports Association[15] is active in organizing and promoting sports at all levels, including the Australian Deaf Games held every 3–4 years in states on a rotating basis. Several Deaf athletes have represented Australia at international levels in the Olympic and Commonwealth Games, the best known being 1992 Olympic Deaf decathlete Dean Smith, swimmer Cindy-Lou Fitzpatrick, and skier Andrew Swan who was dual Winter Deaflympics gold medal winner and the first non-European to win a skiing gold medal.

Religion has played a major part in the lives of Australian deaf people. As mentioned above, the orientation of the Deaf societies was often Protestant, and their senior staff members were sometimes called "Missioners" to the Deaf. In more recent years, the societies have largely relinquished this role because the major churches have appointed chaplains to the Deaf community, some of them being deaf themselves.

In common with Deaf people in many countries, Australian deaf people have been active in Deaf Theater, both at local amateur levels and professionally. The professional Australian Theatre of the Deaf,[16] funded by a consortium of government and business supporters, has for more than 25 years staged major productions in Sydney and tours extensively to both deaf and hearing schools. Deaf TV is not so well developed, but there is a "Deaf TV" program on a community channel in Melbourne that broadcasts a weekly show, and "SignPost" broadcasts

---

15. See http://www.deafsports.org.au.
16. See http://www.ozdeaftheatre.com.

every two months in Sydney and is shortly to be extended to other capital cities. Both use Auslan as their communication medium, and screenings are also subtitled. Deaf Australia (formerly the Australian Association of the Deaf and renamed in 2007) is lobbying to obtain a regular Deaf TV program on national television.[17]

A number of groups have been organized over the years to represent the interests of Deaf people. Some of these, particularly in the first half of the 20th century, were in reaction to the well-intentioned but paternalistic control over the affairs of Deaf people by the then hearing-dominated Deaf Society in each state; the Australasian Deaf and Dumb Association was founded in 1903 but collapsed in the 1920s, and in 1932, the Australian Association for the Advancement of the Deaf was started ("The AAAD is of the Deaf, by the Deaf, for the Deaf") but it disappeared in late 1930s (Carty, 2005). There was then a long gap until the present peak body of deaf people, the Australian Association of the Deaf (now Deaf Australia) was started:

Deaf Australia Incorporated (formerly the Australian Association of the Deaf (AAD)) is the leading national body in Australia for Deaf people who use Auslan (Australian Sign Language). Deaf Australia represents the views of Deaf people, provides information to the Deaf and wider communities, facilitates improved access to information and services, and liaises with the Australian Government and relevant industry leaders and service providers to ensure that Deaf people are accepted, respected and included in the Australian community. Deaf Australia is managed by Deaf people who are actively involved in promoting, reserving, informing and supporting the ongoing development of the Australian Deaf community, its language and cultural heritage. Deaf Australia believes that Deaf people belong to a linguistic minority group and are disadvantaged by a lack of access to communication, education and services. It is our goal to reverse this inequality and to empower Deaf people through full access and self-determination in an equal world. (Deaf Australia, 2008)

Deaf Australia is very active in representing the views of deaf people to governments and the hearing community.[18] It has been particularly successful in advocating for improved educational opportunities and the introduction of bilingual-bicultural approaches, advancing Deaf people's access to telecommunications as well as establishing a TTY relay service, captioned television, and interpreting. Deafness Australia is an active member of the World Federation of the Deaf (WFD), and the XIII World Congress of WFD was organized by ADD and held in Brisbane in 1999.

Australia has a TTY relay service (Australian Communication Exchange; ACE) that is available nationwide 24 hours per day, 365 days per year ("We connect anyone with everyone") and is funded by the Commonwealth Government.[19] ACE grew out of a previous Deaf community relay organization and Deafness Resources Australia. It was the first relay service in the world to provide a dedicated emergency services contact number.

In 2008, Deaf Australia established an "Auslan Shop" (both online[20] and with a Sydney shop) that "will sell materials in Auslan, and about Auslan, Deaf culture, Deaf history, interpreting, education, etc." It has also established the "Auslan Endorsement System" that guarantees that sale items meet certain standards.

---

17. See http://www.users.fl.net.au/~aad/info/ndtv1.php.
18. See http://www.deafaustralia.org/au.
19. See http://www.aceinfo.net.au.
20. See http://www.auslanshop.com.au.

As mentioned above, the Australian Association of the Deaf was active in lobbying for extended availability of captions on television, and their work in part led to the establishment of the Australian Caption Centre.[21] Founded originally to provide captions for television (and still active in that capacity), the Australian Caption Centre is now also a diversified media access company providing language services, audio description, and other media services. All news, current affairs, and prime-time free-to-air television has been captioned since 2001 (news since 1996), and 70% of free-to-air programs will be captioned from 6:00 a.m. to midnight by 2007. Pay television has agreed to caption 25% of programs on 40 channels by 2009.

A debate has been taking place over the number of signing Deaf people in Australia. Hyde and Power (1992) estimated that there were approximately 15,000 signing Deaf adults and children in 1992, and this figure was generally taken as accurate until challenged by Johnston (2006a). There was an exchange of views on this matter in a special issue of *Sign Language Studies* (Carty, 2006; Hyde, Power, & Lloyd, 2006; Johnston, 2006a, 2006b). The dispute appears to be a matter of point of view about who uses sign language. Johnston argues for considerably fewer signers than was previously assumed. He also predicts a likely considerable diminution in their numbers in the future because of increasing numbers of children with cochlear implants who are educated orally without access to signing and decreasing numbers of deaf children being born, a result of genetic engineering and similar technologies.

Johnston is probably correct if one wishes to count only "native," fully fluent users of Auslan who would be of use and interest to sign linguists (admittedly, a significant group whose loss would be greatly regretted), but Hyde and colleagues and Carty argue that one needs to take a wider view of what the term *signer* means. They state that there are many users of Auslan and other kinds of sign (e.g., Signed English) who would not meet Johnston's strict criteria but who consider themselves to be members of the signing Deaf community and culture. Carty, for example argues that "late signers" who come to signing after an oral education and regard signing as an important aspect of their social and cultural lives should be counted among users of Auslan. Power, Power, and Horstmanshof (2007) found that 33% (possibly even 45%) of the members of the "hardcore" Australian Association of the Deaf (now Deaf Australia) had been educated orally and came later to signing. There is also some evidence of this form of identity conversion to either a Deaf or a bicultural identity within the data of a recent study of deaf and hard of hearing graduates of the Griffith University Deaf and Hearing Impaired Student Support Program over the last 20 years (Punch et al., 2007). A recent study conducted by Access Economics (2006) on the economic effect of deafness in Australia chose to use a median estimate of 10,000 for the number of Deaf community members. The debate is unresolved, and further research is required to determine the matter.

Preparation of Special Personnel

Professionals working in deafness-related areas other than medical specialties include teachers, speech pathologists, audiologists, social workers, psychologists, psychiatrists, and others. All of these professionals are graduates of university programs (most hold 4-year bachelor degrees, but in many cases, they hold additional graduate qualifications in their field or a

---

21. See http://www.auscap.com.au.

related one). Regrettably, with the exception perhaps of teachers, very few of these professionals who work with Deaf people can sign and, consequently, have to rely on interpreters. This situation is not a satisfactory one, especially in sensitive areas, and it does not appear to be easily resolved. A major infusion of government funding would be required to improve the situation.

CURRENT DEVELOPMENTS AND TRENDS

Contradictory trends are currently evident in relation to deafness and the rights and aspirations of Deaf people in Australia. The major current trend as far as childhood deafness is concerned is the rapid pace at which the age of diagnosis is lowering, the result of widespread Universal Newborn Hearing Screening programs. Most children with hearing loss are now diagnosed before they reach the age of 1 year, fitted with an auditory aid (which, for almost all profoundly and many severely deaf children, increasingly is a cochlear implant), and enter an early intervention program. This early diagnosis and intervention is leading to placement in regular schools and lack of access to signing. At the same time, because of a strong push toward inclusion, increasing numbers of children are receiving interpreting support in regular classes. Exact numbers are not known, but classroom interpreters appear to be using a mixture of Australasian Signed English and Auslan. Recent court cases have reinforced the right of signing students to Auslan interpreting in preference to Signed English (Komesaroff, 2007).

At the same time as education is moving toward a largely oral communication mode, there is increasing awareness of the Deaf community as a linguistic and cultural minority with the rights that being such a minority implies for recognition and services such as interpreting, captioning, relay services, and the like. Whether the size and vitality of the Deaf community in Australia can be maintained in the face of the trends outlined above, as noted by Johnston (2006a), remains to be seen.

Like many Deaf communities around the world, Australian Deaf people have taken eagerly to electronic text communication. They have long used TTYs, telephone relay services, and fax, but are now more likely to rely on Short Message Service and e-mail as well as to browse the Web for topics of interest (from deaf and hearing sources) (Power & Power, 2004; Power et al., 2007). It seems that this communication access is opening up the "Deaf World" to Australian Deaf people in ways that have not previously been possible, with effects that have yet to be seen. In fact, it may well be not only making them more aware of themselves as *Australian* Deaf people but also allowing them to enter the "global Deaf community" (see Breivik, 2005).

REFERENCES

Access Economics. (2006). *Listen hear! The economic impact and cost of hearing loss in Australia.* Melbourne: Cooperative Research Centre for Cochlear Implant and Hearing Aid Innovation and the Victorian Deaf Society. Retrieved July 3, 2008, from http://www.audiology.asn.au/pdf/ListenHearFinal.pdf

Branson, J., & Miller, D. (1995). *The story of Betty Steel: Deaf convict and pioneer.* Petersham, NSW: Deafness Resources Australia.

Breivik, J-K. (2005). *Deaf identities in the making: Local lives, transnational connections.* Washington, DC: Gallaudet University Press.

Carty, B. M. (2005). *Managing their own affairs: The Australian Deaf community during the 1920s and 1930s.* Unpublished PhD thesis, Griffith University, Queensland. Retrieved July 3, 2008, from http://www4.gu.edu.au:8080/adt-root/public/adt-QGU20060123.131332/index.html

Carty, B. M. (2006). Comments on "W(h)ither the Deaf community?" *Sign Language Studies, 6,* 220–225.

Carty, B. M., Neale, J., & Power, D. (1997). *Deaf studies program: P–7. (Video Unit 3: Deaf people in the past in Australia).* Brisbane: Language Australia Centre for Deafness and Communication Studies, Griffith University.

Dawkins, J. (1991). *Australia's language: The Australian language and literacy policy* (and *Companion Volume*). Canberra: Australian Government Publishing Service.

Deaf Australia. (2008). *Deaf Australia: Description.* Retrieved October 10, 2008, from http://www.accc.gov.au/content/index.phtml/itemId/289169/fromItemId/815972/quickLinkId/816530/whichType/sng

Higgins, A. H. (1997). *Addressing the health and educational consequences of otitis media among rural school-aged children.* Townsville, Queensland: Australian Rural Education Research Association.

Hyde, M. B., & Power, D. J. (1992). The use of Australian Sign Language by Deaf people. *Sign Language Studies 75,* 167–182.

Hyde, M. B., & Power, D. J. (2004). The personal and professional characteristics and patterns of work of itinerant teachers of the deaf and hard of hearing in Australia. *Volta Review, 104,* 51–68.

Hyde, M. B., Power, D. J., & Lloyd, K. (2006). Comments on "W(h)ither the Deaf community?" *Sign Language Studies, 6,* 190–202.

Johnston, T. (1998). *Signs of Australia: A new dictionary of Auslan (the sign language of the Australian deaf community).* North Rocks, New South Wales: North Rocks Press.

Johnston, T. (2006a). W(h)ither the Deaf community: Population, genetics and the future of Australian Sign Language. *Sign Language Studies, 6,* 137–173.

Johnston, T. (2006b). Comments on "W(h)ither the Deaf community?": Response to comments. *Sign Language Studies, 6,* 225–243.

Kendon, A. (1988). *Sign languages of aboriginal Australia: Cultural, semiotic, and communication perspectives.* New York: Cambridge University Press.

Kirchner, C. J. (2004). Co-enrollment: An effective answer to the mainstream debacle. In D. Power & G. Leigh (Eds.), *Educating deaf students: Global perspectives* (pp. 161–174). Washington, DC: Gallaudet University Press.

Komesaroff, L. (2007). Denying claims of discrimination in the Federal Court of Australia: Arguments against the use of native sign language in education. *Sign Language Studies, 7,* 360–386.

Lo Bianco, J. (1987). *National policy on languages.* Canberra: Commonwealth Department of Education.

Low Incidence Support Centre. (1997). *Otitis Media: What every teacher should know.* Brisbane: Queensland Department of Education.

MacDougall, J. (1988). The development of the Australasian Signed English system. *The Australian Teacher of the Deaf, 29,* 18–36.

Miers, K. (2006). Giving Deaf people a fair go. *AAD Outlook, 15*(8), 2.

Napier, J. (2002). University interpreting: Linguistic issues for consideration. *Journal of Deaf Studies and Deaf Education, 7,* 281–301.

Napier, J., & Barker, R. (2004). Accessing university education: Perceptions, preferences, and expectations for interpreting by deaf students. *Journal of Deaf Studies and Deaf Education, 9,* 228–238.

Napier, J., Bontempo, K., & Leneham, M. (2006). *Sign language interpreting in Australia: An overview.* Retrieved July 3, 2008, from http://aslia.com.au/c/aslia/pub/stories/PDF/GeneralDocs/VIEWS2006.pdf

Orima Research. (2004). *Supply and demand for Auslan interpreters across Australia*. Canberra: Department of Family and Community Services. Retrieved July 3, 2008, from http://www.facs.gov.au/disability/auslan-report/Auslan_Interpreter_Report_with_Attachments.pdf

Ozolins, U., & Bridge, M. (1999). *Sign language interpreting in Australia*. Melbourne: Language Australia.

Pollack, D. (1985). *Educational audiology for the limited-hearing infant and preschooler* (2nd ed.). Springfield, IL: C. C. Thomas.

Power, D. J. (2001). Deafness and sign language in government policy documents 1983–1990. In J. Lo Bianco & R. Wickert (Eds.), *Australian policy activism in language and literacy* (pp. 279–292). Canberra: Language Australia.

Power, D. J., & Hyde, M. B. (1997). Multisensory and unisensory approaches to communicating with deaf children. *European Journal of Psychology of Education*, *12*, 449–464.

Power, D. J., & Hyde, M. B. (2003). Itinerant teachers of the deaf and hard of hearing and their students in Australia: Some state comparisons. *International Journal of Disability, Development and Education*, *50*, 385–402.

Power, M. R., & Power, D. J. (2004). Everyone here speaks TXT: Deaf people using SMS in Australia and the rest of the world. *Journal of Deaf Studies and Deaf Education*, *9*, 333–343.

Power, M. R., Power, D. J., & Horstmanshof, L. (2007). Deaf people communicating via SMS, TTY, relay service, fax and computers in Australia. *Journal of Deaf Studies and Deaf Education, 12,* 80–92.

Punch, R., Hyde, M., & Power, D. (2007). Career and workplace experiences of Australian university students and graduates who are deaf or hard of hearing. *Journal of Deaf Studies and Deaf Education*, *12*, 504–517.

Rumsey, C. (1999). Australia. In H. W. Brelje (Ed.), *Global perspectives on the education of the deaf in selected countries* (pp. 1–30). Hillsboro, OR: Butte Publications.

Sherwood, J., & McConville, K. (1994). *Otitis Media and aboriginal children: A handbook for teachers and communities*. North Sydney: Board of Studies NSW.

Simser, J. (1993). Auditory-verbal intervention: Infants and toddlers. *The Volta Review, 95*, 217–219.

Stone, P. (1983). Auditory learning in a school setting: Procedures and results. *The Volta Review, 85*, 7–13.

Deaf Education and the Deaf Community in China: Past, Present, and Future

Kathryn Johnson, Richard Lytle, and Jun Hui Yang

DEAF AND HEARING American and Chinese professionals have been working together since 1999 to empower change in China's system of deaf education. Through these years of collaboration and partnership, an expanding and empowering network that is built on *guanxi* has been evolving. *Guanxi,* a key concept in Chinese culture, characterizes several societal relationships. In some instances, it describes a personal connection between two people. In other instances, it can also represent a network of contacts on which an individual can call when something needs to be done and through which he or she can exert influence on behalf of another. In addition, the concept can describe a general understanding between two people in which one is aware of the other's wants and needs and will take them into account when the one decides her or his course of future actions that concern or could concern the other. The relationships formed by guanxi are personal and are not transferable. Through guanxi, a deeply rooted, foundational level of understanding has developed and continues to evolve, one that shapes the depth and breadth of the context and culture of China for deaf individuals who live there.

DEAF EDUCATION AND THE DEAF COMMUNITY IN CHINA: AN HISTORICAL PERSPECTIVE

A review of the history and current developments in the deaf community and in education for deaf children in China is enhanced when discussed in the context of modern Chinese history and events in deaf communities elsewhere in the world. Many of the developments in deaf education and deaf people's place in society parallel changes in Chinese society and government. Although the first half of the 19th century witnessed the establishment of many schools for the deaf in the United States and in Europe, there are no recorded developments in deaf education in China for this time period. In the United States, many of these new schools were being founded by deaf leaders and had many deaf teachers. It is not until the latter quarter of the 19th century that we see the first documented establishment of a school for the deaf in China.

During the 19th century, many in China looked to the West for new ideas, but often, these new ideas were accompanied by Western imperialism. When the Emperor tried to stop the importation of opium, Britain went to war to force the continued drug trade. After the Opium War in 1842, China was forced to accept a Western presence in key Chinese cities along the coasts. Along with this "treaty" of forced openness and trade, missionaries came into the country. Two American missionaries working in China at this time attended the 1880 International

Congress on Deafness in Milan, Italy. After the Milan congress, the Rev. Charles Rogers Mills and his wife, Annette Thompson Mills, returned to China where, in 1887, they established the first documented school for the deaf and blind in China, the Chefoo School for the Deaf in Dengzhou, Shandong (Piao, 1992, 1996; Dai & Song, 1999, cited in Yang, 2002).

Education for children with disabilities such as deafness did not exist in any systematic or formal manner before the missionaries arrived. These children were viewed as burdens to their family and to society, and the cost-benefit of educating them was deemed negligible.

The Chefoo School promoted the oral methodology and trained hearing people to become teachers of deaf children. A few years after the founding of the Chefoo School, another school for the deaf opened in Shanghai. This school, established by a French Catholic Church, used the French Manual Alphabet. The school continued until 1952 (Dai & Song, 1999, cited in Yang, 2002). In 1914, the first school for the deaf founded by Chinese was established in Hangzhou by a man with a deaf son. The deaf son later became a teacher at this school and elsewhere in China (Dai & Song, 1999, cited in Yang, 2002). Many of these early schools for the deaf continued to have strong Christian evangelical orientations.

Since the establishment of the first school for the deaf by American missionaries, the oral approach has continued to be the dominant approach promoted by Chinese governments and by educators in China (Yang, 2002). However, everyday practice in schools for the deaf has long entailed the use of Sign Supported Chinese (SSC) and Chinese Sign Language (CSL). Even today, the Chinese government policy officially supports oral rehabilitation as the preferred approach to teaching deaf children, though there is increased recognition and support of schools and projects that use Sign Supported Chinese or Chinese Sign Language for some deaf children.

During the first half of the 20th century, China experienced tremendous political upheaval, beginning with the end of the imperial dynasties in 1906. There were periods of weak central government and terrible suffering and struggle. Much of the progress in education during this period was left to individual or small family initiatives.

One example was the Wushan School for the Deaf in Hangzhou, founded in 1931 and the first school for the deaf started by deaf Chinese people (Dai & Song, 1999, cited in Yang, 2002). This school, like many of the early schools for the deaf, provided a strong academic curriculum comparable with that provided to hearing children. As was the case in the United States before the implementation of oralism, these schools employed many deaf teachers (Yang, 2002). During this period before the birth of the People's Republic of China under the Communists in 1949, it is estimated that 21 schools for the deaf were founded by Deaf Chinese.

In 1934, Yu Dafu, a famous Chinese writer, visited the Wushan School for the Deaf and wrote to Yu Shufen, a deaf teacher, "When deaf people hear by reading the text, and mute people speak by writing it down, none of them will be deaf-mute anymore." That is to say, when deaf people are educated, they can accomplish anything (Yang, 2002). This quotation precedes by more than 50 years the better known quotation that "deaf people can do anything, except hear" popularized by Dr. I. King Jordan, Gallaudet University's first Deaf president in 1988.

In 1949, after many years of civil war, the People's Republic of China was created under the leadership of Mao Zedong. At this time, only 42 schools for the deaf, serving about 2,400 students, were known to exist in China, leaving the majority of deaf children in China with no access to an education (Piao, 1992). Many of these schools were private institutions that were absorbed into the public school system during the 1950s.

With the advent of a strong central government under Mao Zedong and the Communist Party, schools became a central component of the party's efforts to unify the country in spirit and thought. There was no longer room for individual initiatives in education, including those by deaf people. Significant advances were made in providing universal education and literacy to millions of Chinese children during the early years of the People's Republic of China. However, the education of children with disabilities did not become a priority until 30 years later.

In 1953, the government-led China Deaf Welfare Organization was established in Beijing. In 1954, a national conference on the teaching of the Chinese language in schools for the deaf concluded that oral teaching was still the best practice (Yang, 2002). Unlike the United States, China did not have a national organization founded by and run by deaf people. Consequently, there exists no Chinese deaf organization that challenges the national policy in an organized, strategic manner. Today's China Deaf Association is a quasi-governmental organization with nominal deaf leadership that is run under the auspices of the China Disabled Persons' Federation (CDPF). Although oral teaching dominated government policy, in 1959 the Ministry of Education encouraged the standardization of "Deaf Sign Language" (Yang, 2002). However, to date, Chinese Sign Language has not been standardized, a situation that continues to challenge the education system (Johnson, 2003). Great variation in sign language continues to exist between regional areas such as Shanghai and Beijing.

In 1955, Zu Zhengang (aka Norman Zsu) became the first deaf Chinese person to matriculate at Gallaudet College where he received a BA degree in sociology. His attendance at Gallaudet was funded by Yale University. Zu returned to China in 1956 and taught at the Shanghai Technical School for Deaf Youth and Shanghai School Number 1 for the Deaf. During this same time period, a medical catastrophe occurred that drastically increased the number of deaf children in China. Although Western medicines had been introduced, there was a general lack of knowledge about how best to use them. Consequently, many children suffered from overinoculation of antibiotics for fever. The result of this state of affairs was a new generation of deaf individuals. Some families had two or three children affected by this process, all of whom became deaf or hard of hearing (Johnson, 2003).

By 1965, China had "266 schools for Deaf and/or blind, with more than 23,000 students and 4,000 teachers and staff" (Piao, 1992, cited in Yang, 2002, p. 14). Beginning in 1967 and continuing for the next 10 years, the Cultural Revolution disrupted education across China. Schools closed and teacher education and research ceased. China literally closed its doors to the outside world. No new knowledge entered and no new knowledge of what was happening within China exited. By 1976, only three more schools for the deaf had been established (Piao, 1992, cited in Yang, 2002). During this time period, hundreds of thousands of deaf children had no access to education.

As the Cultural Revolution ended in China, advancements in deaf education began to emerge. The nation's first national sign language studies conference occurred in Beijing in 1979 (Yang, 2002). An outcome of this conference was the publication of revised sign language books. In 1980, the Office of Special Education was established within the Chinese Ministry of Education. In 1983, the China Language and Hearing Rehabilitation Center was established in Beijing (Yang, 2002). This institution continues to lead the country in government-sponsored research and development promoting an oral-only educational philosophy (Johnson, 2003). In 1984, an experimental television captioning program was approved by the government. In 1985, the government-sponsored China Association for the Deaf and Blind recommended that special education be included in the 9-year compulsory education plan provided to all Chinese students. That same year, the first special education teacher training school was established in Nanjing. During 1985–1988, progress continued to be made within deaf education. By 1988, CDPF and the China Deaf Association had been established. CDPF is China's lead policymaking organization for deaf individuals (Yang, 2002). During the 1970s and 1980s, much of China's educational leadership, including deaf education, came from exchanges with the Soviet Union.

In 1986, Yang Jun Hui became the first deaf student admitted into a regular education program in modern China. That same year, Beijing Normal University became the first teacher training institution to offer a special education major. Even today, prospective teachers of the deaf study in generic special education programs. There are still no universities offering a specialization in deaf education.

In 1988, China's first special education college for students with disabilities was established in Changchun. Many deaf students study there, but they are limited in their educational choices, with many majoring in art-related subjects. Recently, a few of these Changchun graduates were admitted to Gallaudet University. Since 1988, three more special education colleges have been established, but all have curricula for deaf students that are limited to art, cooking, and computer graphics. Students who are physically disabled but not deaf have the option to study in all the academic disciplines at these universities.

In the late 1980s, sign language interpreting of the news first appeared along with limited open captioning of television programs. Unfortunately, the interpreters were not trained in Chinese Sign Language and used Sign Supported Chinese; therefore, many in the deaf community could not understand them (Johnson, 2003). Open captioning, however, has provided a huge, though unintended, benefit to deaf people, even though it was actually designed to provide television news and entertainment to the millions of Chinese who spoke a language or dialect other than Mandarin. Everyone in China shares the same written form of the language.

In 1990 under the leadership of Deng Pufang, China enacted the Law of the People's Republic of China on the Protection of Disabled Persons (Zhang, 2000). It was the first law to address the rights of individuals with disabilities. The law did not address the specific needs of deaf individuals such as accommodations or equal access but categorized their needs in conjunction with those of individuals with disabilities. This law provided a "charity approach" to disability policy, where the attitude and view of loving and taking care of the disabled was embedded. Throughout China, there still existed great discrepancies on the implementation of the law (Johnson, 2003). During the 1980s and early 1990s after China opened its doors to the world, international collaborations resumed with visits by faculty members from Gallaudet University and the National Technical Institute for the Deaf, leaders of several U.S. schools for the deaf, members of the World Federation of the Deaf, and faculty members from universities in the United Kingdom (Yang, 2002). Even though these exchanges mostly involved deaf and hearing people who used sign language, China's policies and practices continued to focus primarily on oral communication (Johnson, 2003). Only recently have there been long-term, sustainable collaborations that are affecting the acceptance of Chinese Sign Language as a legitimate language.

The old adage that seeing is believing did not hold true in China; many Western deaf individuals who had PhD degrees and prominent positions visited and discussed the potential of deaf individuals in China and left, having had no effect on changing the belief that deaf Chinese are capable of the same achievements. It was not until deaf Chinese students attending Gallaudet University's China Study Abroad program began coming back to China that Chinese hearing *and deaf* people started to believe the *deaf Chinese individuals* also could achieve great things. The people of China had to see *deaf Chinese,* not deaf Westerners, to shift their belief system.

Though China and the United States both enacted significant laws in 1990 focusing on the rights and needs of people with disabilities,[1] the outcomes and implementation of the two laws were and continue to be very different (Meyer, 2002). In China, as in the United States, there has been movement toward mainstreaming or inclusion for children with disabilities. Some schools for the deaf have been closed or consolidated in China, with more and more deaf children being taught in the public schools. However, few of these students receive any support services, and there are no sign language interpreters in the schools. Hence, there is not a high level of success for these students.

Suring this same time period, Piao Yongxin, Fang Junming, and Zhang Ningsheng, all professors known for their scholarship in special education, became leading scholars in the area of deaf education. Significant contributions were made by these individuals through their research and writings focusing specifically on the needs, education, and capabilities of deaf individuals. The first international awareness and publications concerning deaf education in China emerged through the efforts of Professor Zhang as he collaborated on research and publication with David Martin of Gallaudet University (Johnson, 2003; Martin, Craft, & Zhang, 2001).

The challenge with the research during this time was that, although great advancements were made in the United States in understanding sign language development and its validity as a language (Wilcox & Peyton, 1999) as well as its use in the education of the deaf, few discussions of these advancements were translated into Chinese. Therefore, there was, and still is, extremely limited access to research completed outside of China. The negative effect of this isolation is that, in some instances, Chinese research is just beginning to study that which was already researched, validated, and proved in the United States and European countries. An example of this situation is a research question from a Chinese article that asked, "Are deaf children capable of the same cognitive abilities as hearing children?" That question was posed in the mid-1990s in China, long after the answer was known in the United States. However, with the rapid growth of the Internet and requirement of English in schools and universities, access to new international knowledge and research is occurring among the deaf and hearing populations.

In 1999, Partners in Education (PIE), a grassroots educational reform effort in China, founded by Dr. Richard Lytle, was established with deaf and hearing Chinese and American

---

1. In the United States, see the Americans With Disabilities Act (Pub. L. No. 101–336), and in China, see PRC Law on the Protection of Persons with Disabilities.

faculty, staff members, and students at Gallaudet University assisting with the efforts. This international collaboration began as an opportunity to improve deaf education in China. In 2000, with the support of the Shaanxi Educational Commission and its Foreign Affairs Director, Mr. Sun Jianning, PIE hosted a China–United States conference in Xi'an. Together, deaf and hearing people participated in developing plans for improving their cities and schools. This event was the first national conference in China to include deaf people in discussions about deaf education. This inclusion occurred thanks to PIE's guidelines, which required the contingent from each participating city to have equal numbers of deaf and hearing members. In 2002, PIE hosted a leadership training program for 25 deaf and hearing Chinese participants, including school principals and government leaders, at Gallaudet University. These leaders also attended the Deaf Way II Conference. This shared experience had a profound effect on both the deaf and hearing Chinese participants. The opportunity provided new knowledge and constructs about what deaf individuals are fully capable of achieving. The goal was to have this knowledge and shift in beliefs transfer back to China. These deaf and hearing Chinese partners continue to meet together to further reforms in their schools and communities, but knowledge and attitudinal paradigm shifts are a process that take many years.

The years 2002 through 2006 brought significant changes to PIE as it transitioned and evolved from an educationally focused initiative to broad efforts comprising increased employment opportunities, policy alternatives, and improved social-cultural values toward deaf individuals. With this transition, PIE evolved into Partners in Excellence for International Development. In January of 2007, Partners in Excellence officially became a nonprofit organization whose mission is as follows:

Global Mission Statement
People working together to improve:
  • education
  • employment
  • economic development
  • participation
  • access to society

by and for deaf and hard of hearing people by partnering in a cross-cultural model of development that is empowering and self-sustaining. (Partners in Excellence, n.d.)

This historical summary provides an understanding of the growth and development of educational opportunities for deaf individuals in China. As PIE came to realize, the interconnectedness of education to employment and the influence of national policy and social-cultural values on both cannot be dismissed. The historical time line provided a linear approach to understanding the history of deaf education and rights in China. In discussing the present state of affairs in the next section, that linear approach now shifts to an interconnected, systems approach.

UNDERSTANDING THE ECONOMIC, EDUCATIONAL, POLITICAL, AND SOCIAL-CULTURAL SYSTEMS OF INFLUENCE ON DEAF PEOPLE IN CHINA IN 2007

The content in this section is based on the research, work, and experience of the chapter authors during the last 10 years of working with deaf education, employment opportunities, policy development, and societal-cultural traditions and values toward deaf individuals in China. Few articles are written in English on the topic of deafness in China. However, two research dissertations were recently completed that focused on deaf issues in China. The first was Johnson (2003), a dissertation on the current challenges and issues confronting deaf education and empowerment in China and strategies for overcoming these challenges. The second was Yang (2005), a dissertation on the status of deaf education and deaf teachers in China. A third publication of significance was done by Biggs (2004) on bilingual education in China. Biggs work was supported by UNICEF in Beijing, and focused on the development of a bilingual program in Tianjin. This publication emphasized the positive impact upon deaf children's learning through participating in a bilingual education, but also highlighted the challenges confronting the replication and sustainability of this model on a national level.

The combination of these two research studies and publication, in conjunction with the work of PIE during the last 10 years, has opened the door of knowledge to the Western world *and to deaf individuals in China* on the current status of deaf rights and education in China. For deaf individuals in China, the realization that, "outside" of China, deaf individuals have rights, abilities, and access to education and careers beyond what had ever been imagined in China created dialogues, discussions, and debates within deaf communities across China on how these possibilities could be achieved within the country. The Internet has become the mode of communication for the Deaf community, with chat rooms, blogs, and Web sites that promote dialogue and discussion on these issues. This discussion is also allowing for critical reflection and dialogue of the current policies and the roles and responsibilities of the CDPF. The CDPF is stated as having three functions: 1) "represent the interests of people with disabilities in China and help protect their legitimate rights; 2) provide comprehensive and effective services to disabled people; and, 3) commissioned by the Chinese government to supervise affairs relating to people with disabilities in China" (International Labour Organization, n.d.). With new policies and international influence on disability rights, the functions of the CDPF will gain significant relevancy for developing strategic plans for implementing the new policies.

Reliable, up-to-date information on the demographics, etiology, and additional disabilities of deaf and hard of hearing children and adults in China is difficult to find. A 2003 United Nations Children's Fund (UNICEF) study estimated that 10% of the population (more than 120 million people) had a hearing loss. In December of 2006, The Second China National Survey on Disability was completed by the CDPF. This survey documented that the "hearing impaired" population consists of 20.04 million people in China (China Disabled Persons' Federation, n.d.).

This number represents the deaf and hard of hearing population across China. As with the national distribution of rural and urban populations and the discrepancies of wealth and poverty among the general population, the lived experience of being deaf varies greatly depending on where one resides. Many of the challenges and barriers that exist within the world of deafness on a national level have great similarities, but the divide between the rural and urban deaf experience in economic and educational opportunities is wide and deep. This section will illuminate the economic, educational, political, and social-cultural circles of China within which deaf individuals function, providing comparative perspectives and examples between the rural and urban situations.

China's Economic System and Its Circle of Influence and Understanding

Currently, China is taking a leadership role in the interconnected, interdependent global economy. However, poverty remains a growing concern. According to the World Bank's China Country Partnership Plan (2007), 40% of the poor in China, defined as living on less than $1.00 per day, are those with disabilities. This statistic illuminates the low employment rates for individuals with disabilities. For a deaf individual in China, the challenges of finding sustainable employment have been doubly complicated with the recent transition from state-owned businesses to jointly or wholly owned foreign businesses. This shift in ownership has had a drastic effect on the job market for many deaf individuals in China who were hired in state-owned enterprises that were abiding by the disability hiring quota established by the Chinese government "that requires all public and private employers to reserve no less than 1.5% of jobs for persons with disabilities" (International Labour Organization, n.d.). Businesses also have the option to pay government fines if this quota is not respected. Some businesses find it easier to pay the quota than to hire disabled individuals, which also contributes to decreased employment opportunities for deaf individuals.

An example of this trend is in the rural area of Jiujiang, where the deaf community has reported that more than 98% of the deaf population is now unemployed and trying to live on the monthly stipend of 100 RMB (about US$10) per month, provided by the city government (He, personal communication, 2004). Needless to say, this financial challenge for deaf individuals has led to an increased negative social perception of deaf individuals and their ability to contribute to the economic development of China. It is not uncommon to see deaf individuals prohibited and sometimes banned from entering businesses and local establishments because of this negative social perception (Johnson, 2003).

Within the urban areas, employment also remains a challenge for deaf individuals, even though, in urban areas, a child who is deaf is much more likely to receive an education. However, it is the quality and type of education that they receive that perpetuates poverty and unemployability among the majority of deaf adults. The national oral language policy has led to a reduced and watered-down curriculum where huge amounts of time are spent working on oral language skills. The reality is that the high majority of deaf students rarely attain functional speech even after years of speech and hearing therapy. Chinese is a tonal language, and a deaf individual's inability to hear the tones greatly challenges the ability of expressive and receptive skills (Biggs, 2004; Johnson, 2003). The emphasis on an oral type of education and limited curriculum and course offerings contributes to few options within the secondary and higher education programs for deaf students in China. Therefore, deaf students in China are limited in their postsecondary options, with the majority of students who choose postsecondary options attending technical programs. These programs offer an extremely limited curriculum in limited major areas of studies. Typically, students may major in computer programming, cooking, or art. These limited careers options allow for only narrow and severely restricted options for employment.

A second negative effect on employability is the hearing population's limited social perception of what individuals who are deaf can contribute to the economic development of China and what capabilities a deaf individual has to productively work in a hearing world. This negative social perception is highly affected by the lack of certified interpreters in China and by the lack of means by which deaf individuals might communicate with the hearing world. Advances in telephones, especially mobile cell phones, offer a means for deaf individuals to attain freedom of communication through limited text messaging. The deaf community is now interconnected in a manner that was unheard of only 5 years ago, but although it has greatly increased the level of independence for the deaf community, it has not increased employment options. Technology that enhances employability for deaf individuals in a country like the United States is still virtually unheard of and inaccessible to the deaf population in China. Ironically, many of the products that deaf individuals take for granted on an international level are manufactured and produced in China, but are not available for purchase by, or even affordable to, the deaf community in China. A vibrating alarm clock, a flashing fire alarm, a video relay and the products needed to support it, the Sidekick, and the Blackberry—all are inaccessible to deaf individuals in China. Without certified interpreters and access to innovative technologies and tools that enable communication and independent living, huge barriers in independence and communication still exist between the hearing and deaf worlds.

Still today, individuals with disabilities, be they physical or mental, are prohibited from entering typical colleges and universities in China. A physical exam is required for entrance, and if one does not pass this exam, then one is automatically disqualified from admission (Johnson, 2003). However, a few top deaf students from the technical programs have been admitted to universities in the United States. Up to this date, three deaf individuals, all women, have attained their PhD in the United States. The potential contribution they hold for providing leadership and advice on reforming deaf education in China is immense, but the social stigma of the limited capabilities of being deaf prohibit them from attaining employment in China. These individuals have remained in the United States or Europe to seek employment commensurate with their doctoral degrees due to a lack of professional opportunities in China. The fact that they are deaf trumps any educational degrees they may receive outside of China. Therefore, to this date, not one Chinese student educated outside of mainland China has returned, except Norman Zsu in 1956. This fact demonstrates that the model of international development that funds individuals to come to the United States to study and attain higher educational degrees to benefit their country is limited in its influence and impact when there is nothing for them to go back to. Nonprofit organizations and foundations that provide individual funding or scholarships may learn from this example. Taking this reality into consideration when funding international development projects that are based on individual opportunities would benefit from assistance support programs for re-entry of the individuals into the home country.

China's Educational System and Its Circle of Influence and Understanding

Underpinning the challenge of employment in China is the quality of deaf education programs and national oral policy for deaf schools. Five national bilingual programs have been established by nonprofit and international organizations in China. These programs hold immense potential for affecting national policy because the research that is being collected on the progress of children within them demonstrates the true capabilities and abilities of deaf children who are instructed in their first language, Chinese Sign Language. The language, knowledge, and intellect of these children are surpassing all expectations (Biggs, 2004; Lytle et al., 2006).

One such school, Tianjin Number One School for the Deaf in Tianjin, China, is developing a national model program. This model is being accomplished through the collaboration and support of UNICEF in Beijing, the Tianjin Number One School for the Deaf, and the Tianjin Hearing Rehabilitation Centre. These partnerships are offering workshops, trainings, and professional development for teachers and parents across China. Two current initiatives of this partnership are an early childhood program and an interpreter training program, one of the first in China (Biggs, 2004). The language and cognitive development of the deaf children in the program who have access to a visual language parallels the language and cognitive development of hearing children.

A main priority of this school, and a significant contributor to its success, is the inclusion of teachers who are deaf. A broad negative effect of the national oral language policy is the belief that deaf individuals are not capable of becoming teachers of the deaf because they are unable to teach oral language skills. It is true that these individuals cannot teach oral language, but they *can* teach and model sign language (Biggs, 2004; Johnson, 2003). It is greatly hoped that the efforts of this committed group of teachers, administrators, and parents, along with those of the other bilingual programs, will influence national policy to be inclusive of sign language, not just on paper, but in practice. The brand new school in Tianjin opened its doors in December 2006. Not only is this school providing a model bilingual program, but it is also a model building that has built in technology that meets the needs of deaf students. Examples of this are flashing fire alarms and lights for the students. This school program in Tianjin reflects a model educational opportunity for students in an urban area of China.

Within the rural communities of China, education varies greatly. Often, students who are deaf, if they are in school at all, are in programs that educate children with other disabilities such as blindness or developmental disabilities. In these environments, best practices for educating the child who is deaf are rarely known or implemented. Teachers are normally taught in general special education university programs and have received no special training for teaching students who are deaf. Chinese Sign Language is often not used in instruction, and educational progress is limited. Some teachers, after being in a school for a period of time, may use Signed Supported Chinese in their teaching, but this is often not understood by the students (Biggs, 2004; Johnson, 2003; Yang, 2006). It is not uncommon for students who are deaf in these programs to display unproductive behavior because they have limited abilities to communicate effectively. This again contributes to negative social perceptions of deaf students.

One model program eventually intended for the rural areas was developed in Jiujiang under the guidance and expertise of a principal who was deaf himself. Although the school is limited in its financial resources, it has made great progress in the education and success of its students. Many of the students enrolled in this school had no prior access to education. Within the kindergarten room, small and simple with boxes as chairs, 5-year-olds sit next to 20-year-olds, both experiencing their first days in school. In the eyes of the 20-year-olds one can see no shame—only pride that they are finally learning how to count and read. The conflicting irony of this situation is that this school is in the same city that has the 98% unemployment rate among the deaf adults of the community. It is hoped that as the education of the deaf students improves, so will the employment opportunities for the next generation.

A challenge that exists within both the rural and the urban special education systems is the lack of qualified teachers (Biggs, 2004; Johnson, 2003; Pang & Richey, 2006; Yang, 2006). Within deaf education, teacher training programs have not yet developed courses or training on how to educate deaf children. The bilingual programs are attaining research that documents the benefits of having deaf teachers whose first language is Chinese Sign Language. However, the teachers within these programs have not yet achieved the full status or benefits of hearing teachers, as they lack the certification from an approved teacher training program. This lack of certification is interconnected to the lack of certified interpreters. Deaf individuals have very limited opportunities and access to the teacher training programs that do exist. The complexities of this are embedded within the political and economic arenas and social/cultural values and attitudes (Johnson, 2003; Yang, 2006). The development of teacher training programs with a specific focus on preparing teachers to teach deaf children would benefit from parallel development of opportunities for deaf individuals to partake in the programs. The issue of qualified teachers is very critical and essential element for successful educational reform in both rural and urban areas.

China's Political System and Its Circle of Influence and Understanding

The lack of a national policy that addresses deaf people's specific language and communication needs contributes to the employment and educational challenges facing the deaf community. On May 15, 1991, the Law of the People's Republic of China on the Protection of Persons with Disabilities was enacted by President Yang Shangkun (Zhang, 2000). However, the language of the law is permeated with the medical model of disability in which the goal for rehabilitation is to "fix" what is wrong with the individual. (Wrigley, 2006) An example of this approach is found in Article 22, which states, "Ordinary institutions of preschool education shall admit disabled children who are able to adapt themselves to the life there" (China Disabled Law, 1999). For deaf individuals, that statement means that those who are able to adapt themselves by "hearing enough" will be allowed access to this education. Nevertheless, two other articles within this law have held a more hopeful promise for deaf individuals: Article 25 states that "teachers of special education and sign language interpreters shall enjoy allowances for special education" (China Disabled Law, 1999) and Article 26 states that "governmental departments concerned shall organize and support the research and application of Braille and sign language" (China Disabled Law, 1999). However, in reality, these two articles have made little, if any, significant contribution to improving the education, employment and lives of deaf individuals.

This policy was revised on July 1, 2008, with language that seeks to reflect the rights of the disabled internationally. This was done in preparation for the Paralympic Games that were held in China in September of 2008. With China hosting the Paralympics in 2008 and the Special Olympics in the fall of 2007, a new awareness of the abilities of disabled individuals is taking hold. Khalid Malik, the UN Resident Coordinator in China, was quoted as saying, while at the Paralympics opening ceremonies, "People with disabilities exemplify the best of the human spirit. There are no people with disabilities, but people with different abilities. Their rights shall by no means be ignored, disrespected or not fulfilled" (Paralympic Games, 2008). The challenge remains, however, on shifting the national policies from a "charity model" of love and protection to a "human rights" model (Kambovski & Deanoska, 2007). CDPF, the organization established to oversee implementation of the law, has an immense challenge confronting it in implementing the revisions of the law. This quasi-government organization in the past has tended to perpetuate the disabilities of individuals rather than promotes their abilities (Kohrman, 2005). An organizational paradigm shift to reflect the revised law is in process. A major challenge with this organization is that the government-appointed leadership does not adequately represent the deaf population. Members of the deaf community believe that their "voice" is not represented or heard within CDPF (Johnson, 2003). Without influence or an ability to contribute to strategies and new policies, limitations and barriers to education and employment are a challenge for the deaf community.

Another recent policy that holds great potential for impacting deaf education in China is the United Nations Convention on the Rights of Persons with Disabilities. This convention was put into entry on May, 3, 2008. China was among the first to sign this convention and ratified it on August 1, 2008 (United Nations Convention, 2008). The Convention, and in wider context the concept of protection of the rights of persons with disabilities, is based on eight principles as follows:

1. Respect for inherent dignity, individual autonomy including the freedom to make one's own choices, and independence of persons;
2. Non-discrimination;
3. Full and effective participation and inclusion in society;
4. Respect for difference and acceptance of persons with disabilities as part of human diversity and humanity;
5. Equality of opportunity;
6. Accessibility;
7. Equality between men and women;
8. Respect for the evolving capacities of children with disabilities and respect for the right of children with disabilities to preserve their identities. (Kambovski & Deanoska, 2007)

Within this convention, there exists language that is specific to the communication and educational needs of the deaf community. The following articles exemplify this:

Countries are to promote access to information by providing information intended for the general public in accessible formats and technologies, by facilitating the use of Braille, sign language and other forms of communication and by encouraging the media and Internet providers to make on-line information available in accessible formats (Article 21). (United Nations Convention, 2008)

States are to ensure equal access to primary and secondary education, vocational training, adult education and lifelong learning. Education is to employ the appropriate materials, techniques and forms of communication. Pupils with support needs are to receive support measures, and pupils who are blind, deaf and deaf-blind are to receive their education in the most appropriate modes of communication from teachers who are fluent in sign language and Braille. Education of persons with disabilities must foster their participation in society, their sense of dignity and self worth and the development of their personality, abilities and creativity (Article 24). (United Nations Convention, 2008)

Ratifying this convention is only the first of many steps; implementing the articles in a strategic manner on a national basis will be the challenge. The concept of a linguistic identity for the deaf community, as exemplified within the language of the convention, will require Chinese society to also make an immense paradigm shift in social-cultural values and political leadership. If these two particular articles are to be taken seriously, in conjunction with the full U.N. convention, strategic plans for reforming education for all children with special needs will be critical, inclusive of teacher preparation programs.

China's One Child Policy has also had an effect on disabled children. This policy has resulted in a disproportionate number of males to females; the World Bank (2007) estimates that there are 137 males to every 100 females in the rural areas and 119 males to every 100 females in the urban areas. The policy has also increased parents' desire to ensure that their one child be "perfect." This One Child Policy has specific consequences for the child who is deaf. Although deafness is difficult to identify at birth, desperate parents may choose to abandon a child who is identified as being deaf between the ages of 2 and 3 due to the lack of support services, financial assistance, and educational opportunities. The one benefit of this policy is that parents who do choose to keep the child who is deaf commit great amounts of time, energy, and resources for this one child to receive the best education and life path possible. Unfortunately, all too often, these precious resources are spent on finding a "cure" for deafness—everything from acupuncture to cochlear implants. Very few resources exist for parents of young children who are identified as being deaf. Those that are available tend to reflect the national policy of oralism and offer preschool programs that emphasize hearing and speech rehabilitation, with limited emphasis on language and cognitive development (Lytle et al., 2006; Johnson, 2003).

These three policies illuminate the challenges that confront deaf individuals in China but also the hope. Policy language on paper does not yet coincide with implementation of the laws or with the social perceptions, values, constructs, and beliefs. A commitment by the government to provide the funding support necessary to implement the new policies is emerging within the political leadership.

China's Social and Cultural System and Its Circle of Influence and Understanding

The discussion of the social and cultural values with respect to deaf individuals and the deaf community is a critical one. Values and beliefs are foundational to the education system, economic opportunities, and policy development. Before the early 1980s, the definition of disabilities referred to *can fie* (the handicapped and useless) (Zhang, 2000). Only recently has this definition of disabilities shifted to "*can ji ren*," which means "persons with disabilities" or "disabled persons" (Zhang, 2000). This shift in language evolved through a shift in social attitudes. A leader in this shift was Deng Pufang, the son of a significant political leader Deng Xioping and disabled himself, who strongly promoted a new image of abilities and set forth a new paradigm for the disabled population. This new paradigm, however, tended to focus on the physically disabled, the disability that was visible to the common eye, and still represents a charity model focused on "loving and caring for the disabled." A new paradigm for the hidden disability of deafness remains absent.

Currently, through the work of UNICEF, PIE, and Tianjin Hearing Rehabilitation Centre, founded upon the UN Convention on the Rights of Persons with Disabilities, great efforts are being made for influencing social values, attitudes, and beliefs toward individuals with disabilities. The effort is influencing a more positive approach to respecting disabled individuals for who they are and what they are capable of truly contributing to the overall growth and development of China. Through the development of public service announcements and a 5-year Communication Strategy Plan for promoting the abilities of individuals with disabilities, hopefully another dramatic shift in attitudes will occur in society. That possible shift holds potential for then influencing policy changes and implementation of these, educational reforms, and employment opportunities because it is foundational to all three. The first public service announcements are promoting the abilities of deaf individuals and the advantages of sign language and have been created by PIE, in partnership with UNICEF, the Tianjin Hearing Rehabilitation Centre, and CDPF. The full effect of these announcements may take years to measure, but the promotion of sign language, done throughout the announcements, may significantly influence the national oral language policy and may lead to a policy that is more open to sign language. Fully understanding the foundational effect of social and cultural values on educational, economic, and political environments is critical for any effort or organization that seeks to empower a disenfranchised population on an international level.

A NEW PARADIGM AND PROCESS FOR EMPOWERMENT THROUGH PARTNERSHIPS

Within China, Communism still prevails. With this form of government, a priority is to maintain social order and structure. Therefore, the idea of "empowering" a group or a community that has a common identity such as deafness is essentially prohibited and banned. Through years of working with the deaf community in China, the authors of this chapter have learned that the process of empowerment is relative to the context and culture, *but is not culturally or morally relativistic.* Empowerment relative to the context and culture is a process of evolving individualism, collectivism, and rights that challenge the current cultural social and moral values toward individuals whose human rights have been challenged. As with the influence of knowledge and research from "outside" of China that has lead to discussions, dialogues, and debates by means of the Internet, the process of empowering a "disempowered" community takes years of discussions, dialogues, and debates. In addition, the process of empowerment is not isolated to the disempowered minority group but also affects and influences those in power. In the case of the deaf community, those in power represent the hearing hegemony and leadership. Both groups, deaf and hearing, are in need of being empowered to influence others to shift from a "charity model" to a "human rights" model of development.

PIE is working in collaboration and partnership with the deaf and hearing community in China on this process. We have learned that dialogue alone leads to nothing. Modeling and living the core values of our organization contribute to greater influence. These core values respect the intellect and ability of the deaf population on an international level, regardless of what country one resides within. Through these core values, an unwritten rule exists that no meeting, dialogue, or discussion will be held without the input and participation of deaf individuals. Through this means, the deaf community is given a "voice" that is otherwise unheard in China. We also have learned that empowerment is interconnected within the economic, educational, political, and social-cultural systems of China. It is only through working through all systems and circles of influence that sustainable, influential change will occur.

Numerous challenges and barriers exist in China for individuals who are deaf. With the raised awareness of the rights of disabilities on an international level through China hosting the Special Olympics (October 2007), the Olympics (August 2008) and the Paralympics (September 2008) all within one year, new opportunities are rapidly emerging for the disabled, inclusive of the deaf population, in China. These three international events, when united with the signing and ratifying of the UN Convention on the Rights of Persons with Disabilities by the Chinese government this year, demonstrates a strong commitment from the leadership of China to take action and promote greater awareness and acceptance of the abilities of individuals with disabilities. Through this commitment and promotion of awareness, educational equity and advancement should occur. Through this means greater employment opportunities for individuals who are deaf should expand. Finally, through improved educational opportunities and increased employment, the social cultural values toward individuals who are deaf should also shift to attitudes of acceptance and full value as human beings. International organizations and foundations are being summoned to action to effect positive change for China's disabled population. The window of opportunity for making a change and contributing to a paradigm shift is now. In closing, a famous Confucius quote states, "The journey of a thousand miles begins with the first step" (Confucius, 2008). The first step has been taken for promoting the rights and education of individuals who are deaf in China and the journey has begun . . .

Authors' Note

For more information on how to contribute to the rights, education, and empowering process for the deaf community in China, please visit www.partnersinexcellence.org.

References

Biggs, C. (2004). *A bilingual and bicultural approach to teaching deaf children in China.* Beijing: UNICEF.

China Disabled Law. (1999). *PRC Law on the protection of persons with disabilities.* Retrieved September 21, 2008, from http://www.cdpf.org.cn/english/info_01.htm.

China Disabled Persons' Federation. (n.d.). *Communique on major statistics of the second national sample survey on disability.* Retrieved July 15, 2008 from http://cdpf.org.cn/old/english.top-7.htm.

Confucius, (2008). Retrieved September 21, 2008 from http://www.quotationspage.com/quotes/Confucius/.

International Labour Organization. (n.d.). *Facts on people with disabilities in China.* Retrieved September 21, 2008 from http://www.ilo.org/public/english/region/asro/beijing/download/factsheet/disabilities.pdf.

Johnson, K. (2003). *Deaf education in China: 2002–2020.* Unpublished doctoral dissertation, University of Minnesota, St. Paul.

Kambovski, V. & Deanoska, A. (2007). Legal analysis on the existing Chinese legislation on children with disabilities vis-à-vis the UN convention on the rights of persons with disabilities. Draft manuscript. Beijing, China: UNICEF.

Kohrman, M. (2005). *Bodies of difference: Experiences of disability and institutional advocacy in the making of modern China.* Berkeley: University of California Press.

Lytle, R. R., Johnson, K. E., & Yang, J. H. (2005/2006). Deaf Education in China: History, Current Issues and Emerging Deaf Voices. *American Annals of the Deaf, 150*(5), 457–469.

Martin, D., Craft, S., & Zhang, N. S. (2001). The impact of cognitive strategy instruction on deaf learners: An international comparative study. *American Annals of the Deaf, 146*(4), 366–378.

Meyer, H. D. (2002). *Culture and the framing of disability in the United States and Asia.* Paper presented at the annual conference of the Council for International Exchange of Scholars. Orlando, FL.

Pang, Y. & Richey, D. (2006). The development of special education in China. *International Journal of Special Education, 21*(1), 77–86.

Paralympic Games. (2008). *Press conference: Career development of people with a disability in China.*

Retrieved September 21, 2008 from http://paralympic.beijing2008.cn/news/pressconference/livewebcast/n214591555.shtml.

Partners in Excellence (2008). *Partners in Excellence Mission Statement.* Retrieved September 21, 2008 from http://www.partnersinexcellence.org/PIEweb/pie_mission_statement.htm.

Piao, Y. (1992). *Teshu jiaoyu gailun [Introduction to special education].* Beijing, China: Huaxia Press.

United Nations Convention. (2008). *UN convention on the rights of persons with disabilities.* Retrieved September 21, 2008 from http://www.un.org/disabilities/convention/conventionfull.shtml.

Wilcox, S. & Peyton, J. (1999). *American sign language as a foreign language.* Retrieved September 21, 2008 from http://www.cal.org/resources/digest/ASL.html.

World Bank. (2007). *China and the world bank: A partnership for innovation.* Washington, DC: Author.

Wrigley, O. (1996). *The politics of deafness.* Washington, DC: Gallaudet University Press.

Yang, J. H. (2002). *A chronology of deaf education in China.* Unpublished manuscript. Gallaudet University, Washington, DC.

Yang, J. H. (2006). *Deaf teachers in China: Their perceptions regarding their roles and the barriers they face.* Unpublished dissertation. Washington, DC: Gallaudet University.

Zhang, E. (2000). *The protection of rights of people with disabilities in China.* Retrieved on September 21, 2008 from http://www.disabilityworld.org/01_07/china.shtml.

Postsecondary Education for Deaf People in China

Patricia A. Mudgett-DeCaro and James J. DeCaro

CHINA IS a developing country with a large population, moving very quickly on many fronts to become a modern, international player in the global marketplace (Dahlman & Aubert, 2001). This growth has occurred within the context of a progressively more market-driven economy with a strong central government. In present-day China, education at all levels has assumed a central role as a tool for advancement and modernization. In the mid-1990s, science, technology, and education were put at the forefront of development policy and given a leading role in driving change (Dahlman & Aubert, 2001). Overriding all of this development is the challenge of simultaneously allocating limited resources on so many fronts in a rapidly changing society.

Concurrent rapid growth and transition is taking place with respect to improvement in the lives of people who are disabled. This change is part of the country's far-reaching goal of realizing an increasingly humane civilization. The desire and will to achieve such improvement is strong. The official Web site of Shanghai indicates that serving people with disabilities is an important undertaking because it is a "sign of a civilized and progressive society and an important part of a perfect social security system" (Shanghai Municipality WWW Site, 2002). Similarly, Fang (2001) suggests that the development of special education is a sign of social and economic strength and represents a civilized society. The country's commitment to achieving these ends is evidenced by the fact that China is different from other developing countries in its very high literacy levels and the numbers of deaf people educated at the elementary level (Callaway, 1999).

It is illustrative to review some statistics with respect to the education of deaf people as a way to demonstrate the progress being made. In the fall of 2004, there were approximately 20.57 million deaf or hard of hearing people in China. In 1988, less than 6% of deaf children were educated in primary school. By 2004, in less than two decades, more than 80% of deaf children were educated at the compulsory level, which comprises 9 years of education, roughly covering primary and junior middle school levels.

Legislation with respect to education for disabled people is relatively recent in China. The first law establishing educational institutions for disabled people was passed in 1951; however, further progress was slow until after 1978, in large part a result of the Cultural Revolution. In 1982, the state officially accepted the responsibility for special education of disabled people, and in 1986, this responsibility was passed along to local governments (Liu, 1998).

On March 15, 1988, the government established the China Disabled Persons' Federation (CDPF), largely because of the influence of Deng Pufang, the son of Deng Xiaoping. Deng Pufang is himself disabled and uses a wheelchair. The mission of CDPF "is to protect human rights of persons with disabilities so as to enable them to participate in society with equal status and opportunities and share the cultural and material achievements brought about by the socio-economic development" (China Disabled Persons' Federation and the Work for Persons With Disabilities in China, March 1998, p. 2). The specifics of representation for any one disability group are dealt with on the local level. Thus, the CDPF is a federation of single-disability organizations, including the Chinese Association of the Deaf (CAD), established in 1956 as the only official organization for people who are deaf. CAD has local associations in all provinces and some large cities, and each is a member organization of the CDPF ("Eastern Red," 1998).

The CDPF organized and drafted the *Law of the People's Republic of China on the Protection of Disabled Persons*, which was codified on December 28, 1990—a significant turning point in the history of people with disabilities in China. The CDPF also promoted and participated in the formulation of the *Regulations on the Education of Persons with Disabilities* and the *Regulations on the Labour and Employment of Persons with Disabilities* (China Disabled Persons' Federation and the Work for Persons with Disabilities in China, 1998). This set of laws and regulations represented an important step toward the goal of including people with disabilities in education and society.

Individuals with disabilities are well represented within the structure of the CDPF. For example, more than half the membership of policymaking bodies and two thirds of advisory committee members must be disabled (Callaway, 2000). Although Deng Pufang has made it clear that the CDPF must consult with disabled people and its membership before making policy, some have indicated that the deaf community and organizations, representing all individuals, need a greater voice in policy ("Eastern Red," 1998). However, the Beijing Deaf Association and the Tianjin Deaf Association are quite proud of the advances their cities have made in equalizing opportunities for deaf people, and the Tianjin Deaf Association president is quoted as saying, "TDA is an important bridge between the Deaf community and hearing people. . . . Many people depend on TDA to fight for their rights" ("Eastern Red," p. 19). Significantly, the tenth *5-Year Plan of the People's Republic of China* (Li DongMei, CDPF, personal communication, December 1, 2006) established as a goal the full use of organizations of disabled people and calls on the nation to strengthen disabled people's organization, thus clearly demonstrating the government's recognition of the importance of these organizations.

The CDPF has direct responsibility for decisions with respect to education for disabled people, backed by laws passed in 1992 and 1994, the latter establishing a legal requirement for government at all levels of society to undertake this responsibility. As a part of this responsibility, the CDPF has established rehabilitation centers around the country for deaf students in preschool through Grade 7. The function of these centers is to improve speech so as many deaf students as possible will have the oral skills to enter mainstream hearing schools. Students who cannot speak well enough to enter the mainstream attend schools for the deaf.

The CDPF is also responsible for representing the needs of disabled people to the central government and for implementing the central government's 5-year plans. The ninth 5-year plan (1996–2000) focused on improving compulsory deaf education for Grades 1 through 9. The tenth 5-year plan (2001–2005) shifted the focus to improving preschool and upper secondary school deaf education and set a goal of mainstreaming 25% of deaf students by the end of the plan. The eleventh 5-year plan (2006–2010) added tertiary deaf education while maintaining the focus on other levels of education (Li DongMei, CDPF, personal communication, December 1, 2006).

CHINESE PHILOSOPHIES AND TRADITIONAL VALUES

Changes and improvements in any society occur within the cultural, economic, religious, governmental, and historical contexts of the country itself. Fundamental traditional, Chinese cultural values (for example, humanitarianism, respect and care for the disabled) and ancient philosophies such as Buddhism and Confucianism are critical for understanding the changes occurring in deaf education in China, and are specifically noted in Chapter I, Article 7 of the 1990 *Law of the People's Republic of China on the Protection of Disabled Persons*. Some traditions are very helpful and support the goals of equality for deaf people in education and work. Some, however, may unintentionally limit achievement of these goals. The following discussion highlights some important traditional cultural values that influence the level to which deaf people are included in Chinese society.

Social harmony and balance are very important in Chinese society. Confucianism stresses harmony and conformity within mainstream society (Lin, 2002). There is a strong focus on developing together as a group or society as well as on working together toward group or societal goals. "Building up a good social ambience with equality, fraternity and harmony" is a goal that is stated for people with disabilities (Shanghai Municipality WWW Site, 2002). Further, the core curricula of schools for the deaf identify as required components moral training as well as knowledge about society and social skills (Callaway, 1999).

Individuals who are disabled are often regarded as "ill" and, accordingly, are considered responsible for doing what is needed to improve themselves (Lin, 2002). The 1990 *Law of the People's Republic of China on the Protection of Disabled Persons* reflects Confucian philosophy when it states that "disabled persons should display an optimistic and enterprising spirit, have a sense of self-respect, self-confidence, self-reliance and make contributions to societal construction" (Article 10, p. 5). Further, the law indicates that disabled persons should actively take part in training programs for their recovery, strengthen their ability for self-care and work skills, and take individual responsibility to do everything possible to improve themselves. As a part of this strong belief in individual responsibility for self-improvement, Chinese culture places great value on lifelong education. However, it should be noted that the stress on social harmony and conformity often makes it difficult for a person who is disabled to request special accommodation (Lin, 2002).The Chinese education system has an obligation to address the individual needs and personal development of students through accommodation (Wu, 2002).

Similarly, society bears certain responsibilities. The greater society is expected to encourage individuals to grow and develop as whole, well-rounded persons. Confucian philosophy encourages rewarding of personal achievement, and to this end, Chapter I, Article 12 of the 1990 *Law of the People's Republic of China on the Protection of Disabled Persons* states that it is the responsibility of governments and departments to award disabled persons who have been successful. The World Federation of the Deaf ("Eastern Red," 1998) notes that although this recognition is excellent, most of the role models highlighted are oral deaf adults and may therefore be unrealistic models for many deaf students.

Strong family and community responsibilities, along with deep respect for authority and elders, are also very important Chinese societal values. Families have a very strong responsibility to care for members who are disabled, and parents have significant input and influence with respect to a disabled person's life, including education and work. Because Confucian teachings stress conformity and behavior control, many families work very hard to make their deaf child as "normal" as possible, especially in light of China's one-child policy (Callaway, 2000). In the case of a deaf child, the search for normalcy often results in parents seeking possible cures rather than seeking alternative ways for this child to learn and grow. In support of parents, the tenth 5-year plan set a goal to train 80,000 parents by 2005 with respect to caring for their disabled child. This same plan indicates that families are responsible for purchasing hearing aids but also stipulates that they can be obtained for free if the family cannot afford to do so.

All these beliefs and values as well as others are an important part of the Chinese cultural context. The challenge is to make significant changes in the welfare of people who are deaf while working within this established system of beliefs. In recent decades, particularly in Western societies but also worldwide, the medical view of deaf people in society as well as the linkage of deaf people to people with disabilities in general have been brought into question. The debate continues around the world; however, the emerging view, buttressed increasingly by laws, supports recognition of deaf people as capable citizens who, if given access and accommodation through sign language, aural-oral habilitation, and education, are able to take charge of their own lives and affairs. Educated Chinese deaf people and members of the Chinese educational establishment are well aware of these trends and the changes occurring within and outside of China. A continued discussion of these issues will lead to positive and constructive change to achieve what China refers to as modernity and an advanced society.

TERTIARY DEAF EDUCATION

From the early days of deaf education in China until the early 1950s, the schools for the deaf used the manual, oral-aural, and combined methods of communication (Fromkin, 1975; Johnson, 2003; see also Johnson, Lytle, & Yang, this volume). During the 1950s, there was a shift to a predominantly oral approach combined with fingerspelling and written language, with signs used as a backup in cases where students failed to understand. Education itself, including deaf education, was seriously impeded between 1966 and 1976 during the Cultural Revolution. A government act of March 15, 1996 (Callaway, 2000), established sign language as the official language of deaf people to be used in education of deaf children in schools for the deaf. This act also encouraged research with respect to documenting and unifying Chinese Sign Language, work that had begun in 1959 (Callaway, 2000). The CAD has been heavily involved in this work. However, for the most part, the sign system that is used is actually sign-supported Chinese (Callaway, 1999).

Shanghai established the first upper-secondary technical program for deaf students in 1954 with primarily vocational programs ("Eastern Red," 1998). The first upper-secondary program to offer academic and college preparation was established in 1993 by Nanjing and the CDPF, which was part of the ninth 5-year plan. Most of the students attending this school were prepared for entry into the Technical College for the Deaf of Tianjin University of Technology. As of 2002, there were still only five upper-secondary programs for deaf students in the country (Sun & Hu, 2002), but a CDPF administrator indicated that by 2003, there were 21 such programs enrolling a total of 1,351 deaf students.

More than 80% of the deaf students are now receiving the 9 years of compulsory education. CDPF figures as of July 20, 2004, state that there are 1,700,000 deaf children receiving compulsory education, 52% mainstreamed in regular classes and 48% in special schools or special classes, with no statistics with respect to whether or not those who are mainstreamed tend to be more hard of hearing (Nie, personal communication, July 20, 2004). With respect to language modality, Martin, Hussy, Sicoli, and Zhang (1999) noted that signs were traditionally seen as a tool to use when communication was not successful, particularly in the early grades, but that more signs were used in middle school classes. Most schools provide the core subjects along with moral training and social skills education, and many texts used in these schools have been developed by the National Education Commission for Schools for the Deaf, with others developed in Shanghai and some schools using mainstream textbooks (Callaway, 1999). Students who attend mainstreamed schools receive the standard education with standard textbooks, but receive minimal or no extra support in learning (Callaway, 1999; Johnson, 2003; Martin et al., 1999).

Johnson (2003) warns, however, despite this remarkable progress, "With the well-intended goal of providing education to the majority of deaf and hard of hearing students, an evaluation into the quality of education . . . is in need. The focus has been on quantity, i.e., getting more students into the schools" (p. 34). The World Bank (Dahlman & Aubert, 2001) similarly mentions a need for education in general to redirect the focus to improving the quality of the educational system. They recommend that the role of the Ministry of Education needs to shift from a tightly regulated system to one that ensures the quality and equity of all of the institutions of higher education. Nonetheless, the fact that students are now in schools is the critical first step.

In 1985, legislation was passed that opened the doors of colleges to students with disabilities. Special education at the postsecondary level is identified as the education of deaf, blind, and mobility impaired individuals; however, in most cases the postsecondary programs began with deaf education, in part because deaf education had a longer history. The first tertiary educational program admitting deaf students was established at Changchun University in 1987. Two majors were available to students—Chinese traditional painting and arts/crafts. Chinese Sign Language interpreters from the local school for the deaf were hired, and college faculty learned Chinese Sign Language (Yang, personal communication, September 15, 2003).

In 1991, Tianjin Technical College for the Deaf was established at Tianjin University of Technology and offered the first 3-year program for technology majors. Since then, one more national university program for deaf students has been established at Beijing Union University. Further, several local college programs have been established in Nanjing and Shanghai (Sun & Hu, 2002). The number of tertiary programs has increased rapidly as provinces have established such programs. In addition, one associate degree program in Hangzhou, Zhejiang, has been expanded to a bachelor-level program (Yang, personal communication, March 28, 2005).

Currently, there are not enough upper-secondary school programs for deaf students, but ambitious current goals are being set to establish them as quickly as possible across the country. Sun and Hu (2002) found that the numbers of secondary students preparing for college are fewer than the numbers expressed in enrollment goals of college programs serving deaf students. Because school options are primarily vocational in nature, with computer programming a recent addition, career options tend to be limited for deaf students (Martin et al., 1999).

College programs for deaf students independently develop their respective entrance tests for deaf students. As a result, there is great variety in test content and level of difficulty (Sun & Hu, 2002), and many secondary deaf programs focus intensively on preparation to pass the tests to the detriment of learning foundational skills. There is great pressure to prepare for all these tests because there is no standardized college entrance test for the deaf students.

In contrast, only very few deaf individuals are able to pass China's national university entrance exams, which are taken by other students aspiring to attend university, and if they do pass, there is minimal support or accommodation provided (Johnson, 2003). Yu and Zhang (2003), studying mainstreamed college students, recognized this dilemma and recommended that support services and assistance strategies be provided to deaf students in mainstream tertiary education.

Colleges for deaf students currently offer a limited set of majors. Ta Ta (2000) writes that Chinese deaf students attending university in the United States called for a greater range of majors to be offered in China for deaf students to pursue. The CDPF has recognized this challenge and is "asking the special institutions of higher learning to offer more specialties according to the local market demands with consideration of the character of the disabled students" (Nie, personal communication July 20, 2004).

EVALUATING TERTIARY EDUCATION

In 2002, the Postsecondary Education Network-International (PEN-International) undertook a series of interviews with a wide variety of individuals involved in some way with tertiary deaf education in China. The purpose was to collect and synthesize ideas that might result in recommendations for the improvement of tertiary deaf education and provide helpful data for the eleventh 5-year plan of the People's Republic of China (2006–2010).

This research was funded by PEN-International, which has been supported since 2001 by grants totaling more than US$9 million from The Nippon Foundation of Japan. PEN-International is a multinational program that strives to improve the postsecondary education of men and women who are deaf around the world—primarily in developing countries. PEN-International is a partnership of universities and colleges in China, the Philippines, Thailand, Japan, Russia, South Korea, and the United States. PEN-International is housed at the National Technical Institute for the Deaf at Rochester Institute of Technology, Rochester, New York. The authors of this chapter served as the principal investigators of this study.

It was critical as part of this research to collect the opinions of a wide variety of individuals who had connection to, or knowledge of, tertiary education for deaf individuals. A total of 38 individuals were interviewed: (a) 11 administrators or their representatives from college programs serving deaf students; (b) 6 administrators from schools for the deaf; (c) 3 CDPF government administrators; (d) 7 college faculty members (6 hearing and 1 deaf); (e) 3 deaf teachers at the precollege level; (f) 3 deaf college alumni; and (g) 5 deaf college students. In total, there were 12 deaf and 26 hearing interviewees. The goal was to obtain as many different perspectives on a similar topic as possible.

The interviewers raised the following critical issues or topics during the interviews:

- Perception of deafness and deaf people
- College entrance

- Accommodations
- Communication
- Majors and program offered
- Employment

Perceptions of Deafness and Deaf People

The respondents were not asked directly about perceptions of deaf people, but offered their opinions in the course of the interview with respect to their perceptions of deaf people's abilities and capabilities along with explanations for these judgments. Nearly every hearing person interviewed, especially administrators, referred to achievements in terms such as the "extraordinary successes of deaf students."

Perceptions and attitudes have a direct effect on the decisions individuals make with respect to what is and what is not "suitable" for people who are deaf. Thus, the perception that deaf people are strongly visual led, in part, to the almost universal programming in visual arts at the college level. Even computer-related majors are often focused on graphic design. It was actually quite difficult to discuss the topic of other fields with some of the interviewees because a question about other majors was almost uniformly interpreted as meaning "other applications of artistic abilities." Likewise, perceptions with respect to communication abilities appear to have led to an emphasis on various majors that do not require spoken communication. In addition, the majority of administrators expressed the view that hearing individuals needed to help deaf students develop social interaction skills and often planned for this to occur.

Among most hearing interviewees, the perception that deaf students are weak at abstract thinking further limits the availability of certain majors. Their expectations with respect to deaf students' abilities in fields other than those that use concrete applications of skills are low, which means that they may discourage students who are excellent in other fields and at abstract thinking from pursuing studies in fields other than art and computing. It should be noted that there are some significant differences between the responses of deaf and hearing interviewees—for example, with respect to expectations, concepts of suitability, variety of majors, and the role of successful alumni. For example, where hearing individuals felt that deaf students were weak in abstract thinking, deaf respondents argued that low expectations in precollege programs meant that students were not challenged to learn and practice abstract thinking skills.

College Entrance

As mentioned earlier, deaf students who desire to continue their education must take a college entrance examination that is different from the exam administered to hearing students. Each college program for deaf students designs its own college entrance test, administers the test, and admits deaf students independently. As a result, there is great variety in test content and level of difficulty (Sun & Hu, 2002).

Precollege preparation certainly makes entrance exams challenging, and there are calls for a national textbook that may help to standardize the education—and, therefore, the entrance exams—over time. However, some have suggested adopting a more diverse set of criteria for college entrance rather than rely on the entrance exam as the only measure of college entrance. For example, an art portfolio in addition to the exam might be used as one possible measure. Some form of precollege transition program other than simply offering study and practice for the exam might be helpful in better preparing students not only for their academic studies but also for study skills and social interactions. Accommodations for mainstream programs, currently not affordable, are nonetheless a critical step toward precollege preparation and entrance exams.

Accommodations

Accommodations provided for students vary across each of the colleges for students who are deaf. It is worth noting that administrators, faculty, and deaf individuals emphasized the need for visual learning methods, but not everyone agreed on what visual learning methods should mean in practice.

A wide variety of possible support services usually are available, including communication access, tutoring, and speech and audiological services. However, there is considerable variation among colleges, particularly with respect to communication in the classroom. Support services for a mainstream class are rarely discussed, are seen as too expensive, or are judged unworkable for various reasons. Collaboration between colleges within China and outside the country would be a useful way to search for accommodations that might be feasible. Most administrators expressed the opinion that their hearing faculty signed "well enough." In contrast, however, those deaf students interviewed overwhelmingly indicated that improving faculty members' signing ability was their top priority with respect to communication and that although some hearing faculty sign, most do not sign fluently. Likewise, although administrators often mentioned that most tutoring is provided by faculty, students indicated that they received most of their tutoring from other students, deaf classmates, or "good-hearted" hearing students.

As for teaching methods, all respondents supported increased use of multimedia technologies despite some obstacles, and several faculty members have used very creative new approaches to teaching their classes. There was recognition that simplification of texts or curricula can pose a danger of lowering expectations and limiting the possible achievement of those who are able to do more. Likewise, requiring additional courses should be based on need, established through individual assessment, because additional courses could be a waste of time for the best students.

Colleges are conducting considerable experimentation. Research and collaboration on the effectiveness of these experimental approaches would be helpful. The opinions of deaf individuals is an essential and critical aspect of research and program design. Support services for a mainstream class are rarely discussed, seen as too expensive, or judged unworkable for various reasons. Collaboration between colleges within China and outside would be a useful way to search for accommodations that might be feasible.

Communication

Communication is particularly complex in China. Students come to tertiary-level education programs from all over China, where both spoken and sign language dialects differ widely.

The traditional view has been that signs are useful if oral communication is not successful. However, this view has changed in various ways over time.

There is ongoing debate with respect to the use of various forms of communication, but as one student says, "I (use) both sign languages . . . Signed Chinese for class (and sometimes use voice and speech with teachers), and CSL [Chinese Sign Language] to communicate, to chat with people. If I meet hearing people then I write back and forth." As in the United States, most deaf individuals are competent in the use of multiple communication approaches; however, the deaf respondents in this study overwhelmingly indicated that the ability to sign was the number-one priority and preference for them in communication.

None of the colleges has an actual communication policy, and the government has not provided guidelines in this regard. It is also clear that there is a different emphasis and focus between (a) deaf individuals, who strongly emphasize the need for quality sign language to improve access to information, and (b) most of the administrators, for whom it was a lesser priority and who had a tendency to feel that the faculty signed well enough. Faculty members themselves were said to be highly motivated to learn to sign well, but in general, hearing individuals stressed the need to use multiple communication methods in class to meet the needs of the variety of students present. Only one college offered sign language classes; others encouraged faculty to learn from students or books. Evaluation of faculty sign skills was usually carried out by hearing individuals, although one college solicits deaf opinions informally, and another asks deaf students for their evaluations.

Majors and Programs Offered

The majority of college programs for deaf students are 2-year programs, and many have been established recently. Several programs were so new that they did not yet have graduates at the time of this study. Only three of the colleges offered 4-year bachelor degree programs for deaf students. All of the programs are self-contained, meaning none of them are mainstreamed, although all are situated on a campus with hearing students. As mentioned earlier, because of the underdevelopment of upper-secondary programs for deaf students, many of the deaf students attending these colleges are coming, with gaps in foundational knowledge, straight from a "middle school" education to a college program. These gaps, of course, place strong limits on the programs that can be offered at a college. It was not clear whether this situation applies to deaf graduates of mainstreamed upper secondary programs, given that approximately half of the deaf students were educated in the mainstream classes with hearing students.

For a number of reasons, some majors are considered more suitable for deaf students than others. Most deaf students are steered into art or computer science because these fields require visual acuity. Fortunately, art and computer majors have been successful in finding jobs after graduating. Deaf students' lack of foundational knowledge is also cited as a reason for limiting access to other majors. In addition, low expectations and stereotypes with respect to abilities play a role.

The current focus on improving high school education opportunities for deaf students will hopefully be a factor in expanding college programming over time. Deaf students reported that they would like to have more choices of majors, but they are concerned about finding work. College administrators acknowledge the fact that market demands are changing, and all of the administrators participating in this study believed that it is possible to increase the number and type of majors offered to deaf students, although many suggestions were still within the arts and computer areas. With the strong desire of deaf students and possible changes in employer demands, change will certainly occur over time.

Employment

The greatest concern of deaf students, college administrators, and faculty members relates to employment. One student leader told us, "Many people are very worried about finding a job when they graduate." The number of individuals seeking employment in China is huge, which makes the job market highly competitive for all individuals, whether deaf or hearing. The number and types of majors offered in colleges and universities is based partly on national employment need and partly on local needs. Majors offered in rural areas may differ from those offered in urban locations. Students, deaf and hearing, select majors with an eye to employment.

A variety of barriers can make it difficult for deaf graduates to find work: attitudes and lack of knowledge with respect to deafness; lack of student experience; intense competition; and a gap between what colleges teach and what employers want. Faculty members can play a significant role in preparing students for the workplace, including counseling them about the communication challenges they will face on the job and how these issues might be resolved. College administrators and the CDPF have a responsibility to show employers the abilities of deaf men and women, not only through the media but also within nurturing school-work partnerships. Further, more and more universities are consulting with big companies to seek advice and counsel with respect to curriculum, in an effort to decrease the gap between what colleges teach and what businesses need from the graduates.

Recommendations

Overall, the two authors of this chapter were most impressed with the number of interesting and creative ideas being discussed and implemented in China as it strives to offer post-secondary education to people who are deaf. The following is a summary of the recommendations derived from the interviews. These authors realize that once their study is subject to wide scrutiny, some recommendations will be adopted as is, others will be adapted, and still others will be rejected.

IMPROVE THE QUALITY OF EDUCATION. China has achieved great success in ensuring that most deaf children receive compulsory education, and the country is establishing secondary schools and tertiary programs very rapidly. There is now a need to emphasize ways to improve the *quality* of this education.

DIVERSIFY AND INCREASE THE NUMBER OF MAJORS BEYOND ART AND COMPUTERS. Almost every deaf individual interviewed expressed the desire for a greater choice of majors. Some deaf students have gone to other countries so they could receive an education in a variety of fields not available to them in China.

CREATE ACCESS TO MAINSTREAM COURSES AND PROGRAMS. A number of individuals thought that deaf students could succeed in mainstream courses and programs, including distance learning, if there were ways to overcome the barriers and obstacles to access within these programs.

IMPROVE PRECOLLEGE EDUCATION. Underdeveloped precollege programs were often cited as a serious limitation to the success of deaf students in college. China has few upper-secondary school options for deaf students; however, the middle schools are working very hard to prepare deaf students for college because students often go directly to college from these schools. It is important to note that most faculty and administrators at the postsecondary level could not visualize how to be helpful in improving precollege education other than by raising entrance requirements and providing guidance and practice for the entrance exams.

ESTABLISH PARTNERSHIPS WITH EMPLOYERS. There is a great deal of competition for jobs throughout China. Deaf students lack opportunities to acquire work experience and are often ill prepared to enter the work force because of a gap in information and skills between what colleges teach and what employers need. Involving potential employers in discussions about curriculum in postsecondary educational could help reduce the gap between schooling and the needs of industry.

INCREASE OPPORTUNITIES FOR STUDENT LEADERSHIP DEVELOPMENT. Currently, student leaders appear to have minimal responsibilities in college. Their primary focus is on arranging social events and passing on ideas to teachers and administrators. Suggestions for increasing student leadership were mentioned:

IMPROVE COMMUNICATION COMPETENCIES. Each college approaches communication differently, and none has a communication policy. Most hearing individuals, administrators, and faculty considered the sign skills of faculty to be "good enough," yet almost every deaf student interviewed said that faculty sign communication skills need to improve.

FORM PARTNERSHIPS WITH DEAF INDIVIDUALS AND ORGANIZATIONS TO SOLICIT FEEDBACK, TO ADVISE, AND TO INCREASE DIALOGUE WITH RESPECT TO OPINIONS AND GOALS.

WORK TO CHANGE PERCEPTIONS ABOUT DEAF PEOPLE. Real strides are being made in China in this regard as deaf graduates enter society and the workplace and demonstrate their abilities to be successful, but more work needs to be done. Future efforts will need to illustrate and stress what deaf people "can do," using successful deaf people as role models (being careful to include successful role models who are profoundly deaf and who primarily use sign language).

CONCLUSION

China has placed great value on bringing people who are deaf into society, and the country is moving very quickly to make this inclusion a reality. With each governmental 5-year plan, ambitious goals are set with respect to expected progress. China is facing all the same challenges that have been faced around the world in the education of people who are deaf, but the country is dealing with the challenges on a much larger scale.

China is striving diligently to find solutions to these challenges that are in harmony with its culture and society. The country has displayed a refreshing willingness to explore solutions implemented in other countries in an effort to systematically determine which are appropriate for adoption or adaptation in China.

Addressing all the recommendations expressed in this chapter would be a daunting task indeed. The resources required to do everything suggested here would be enormous to say the least. In addition, achieving some recommendations will be dependent on achieving other prerequisite recommendations. For example, as the quality of education is improved, as more graduates who are deaf are successful in the workplace, and as teacher preparation programs for deaf people are established, a critical mass of deaf experts and of teachers will become available to colleges and will likely play important roles in further change.

The recommendations presented here were presented to the CDPF in 2006, and Deng Pufang, chairperson of the federation and son of former Premier Deng Xioaping, pledged his personal support and that of the CDPF in addressing the recommendations. As a result, a series of activities are currently under way to educate interpreter educators so the number and quality of interpreter training programs are increased in China. Further, efforts are under way to increase the number of postsecondary education institutions serving deaf people in China.

In conclusion, this chapter chronicles the myriad creative suggestions for improving post-secondary education for people who are deaf in China that were gleaned from interviews with administrators, faculty members, government and CDPF officials, deaf students, and deaf community members.[1] It also includes a few relevant suggestions and ideas offered by the two authors of this chapter. The two authors of this chapter were most impressed with the number of interesting and creative ideas being discussed and implemented in China as it strives to offer postsecondary education to people who are deaf.

REFERENCES

Callaway, A. (1999). Considering sign bilingual education in cultural context: A survey of deaf schools in Jingsu Province, China. *Deafness and Education International*, 1(1), 34–46.

Callaway, A. (2000). *Deaf children in China*. Washington, DC: Gallaudet University Press.

China Disabled Persons' Federation and the Work for Persons With Disabilities in China. (1998). Beijing, China: China Disabled Persons' Federation.

Dahlman, C. J., & Aubert, J.-E. (2001). *China and the knowledge economy—Seizing the 21st century*. Washington, DC: The World Bank.

Eastern red. (1998, June). *WFD News*, 16–19.

Fang, J. (2001). Report of a series of experimental studies on sensory impaired children. *Chinese Journal of Special Education*, 1(29), 1–4.

Fromkin, V. A. (1975, September). Language training of the Deaf in the People's Republic of China. *The Linguistic Reporter*, 3.

Johnson, K. E. (2003). Deaf education in China: 2002 to 2020. *Dissertation Abstracts International*, 64(2), 957B. (UMI No. 3117543).

Law of the People's Republic of China on the Protection of Disabled Persons. (1990, December 28). Beijing, China: Huaxia Publishing House.

Lin, A. (2002, August). *Chinese philosophies and public attitudes towards deaf people*. PowerPoint presentation, 8th Asia-Pacific Congress on Deafness, Taipei, Taiwan.

Liu, Y. (1998). On improvement and development of legislation on education for disabled people in China. *China Journal of Special Education*, 4(20), 5–9.

---

1. Anyone wishing to view the entire report may download it from http://www.pen.ntid.rit.edu/newdownloads/resources/documents/other/CDPT_report_2006/chinarpt06.pdf.

Martin, D. S., Hussey, L., Sicoli, D., & Zhang, N. S. (1999). Removing barriers and building bridges: American deaf interns teaching Chinese deaf children. *American Annals of the Deaf, 144*(3), 281–288.

Shanghai Municipality WWW Site. (2002). Notice of the municipal government on approval of the tenth five-year (2001–2005) plan for undertakings of Shanghai disabled people. Posted in English and retrieved October 6, 2008, from http://www.pen.ntid.rit.edu/pdf/SGCN-20020519.pdf

Sun, J., & Hu, Z. (2002). Issues in the independent enrollment of some colleges for the deaf students in China. *Chinese Journal of Special Education, 1*(33), 28–32.

Ta Ta. (June 2, 2000). Deaf students call for equal treatment. Posted in English and retrieved October 6, 2008, from http://www.pen.ntid.rit.edu/pdf/cd-20000602.pdf

Wu, L. (2002). Education for deaf students: Respecting education and studying emotional quotient theory. *Chinese Journal of Special Education. 1*(33), 41–44.

Yu, S., & Zhang, N. (2003, December). *Optimized strategies of support-assistant-system in the post-secondary education included people with disabilities*. Paper presented at the Academic Conference of China Special Postsecondary Education Institute, Nanjing, China.

Deafness in India

Madan M. Vasishta

INDIA IS the world's largest democracy, with a population of more than 1 billion people. The country accounts for 2.4% of the world's land area but has 16% of the world's population and is the largest country in the Indian subcontinent. India is the home of one of the oldest civilizations in the world and is diverse ethnically (72% Aryan, 25% Dravidian, 3% Oriental). Hindus (82%) and Muslims (12%) make up the most of Indian population, with Christians (2.3%), Sikhs (1.9%), and Buddhists (less than 1%) contributing to the religious fabric of India. This diversity in ethnicity and religion has resulted from invasions from various parts of the world since before Alexander the Great. India finally became independent in 1947 after about 150 years of British rule. Therefore, India's education system is heavily influenced by British traditions. There are 22 official languages, with Hindi and English being the main national languages.

India is mainly a rural country. According to the 2001 census, about 285 million (27%) people live in urban areas and the remaining (73%) in rural areas. The literacy rate has been rising rapidly during the 20th century and has now reached almost 65% for the total population. The literacy rate for men (75%) is higher than for women (54%).

India is one of the fastest growing economies and is presently the world's fourth largest economy. The effect of this burgeoning economy, however, is not felt much in rural areas, where more than 260 million people (only somewhat fewer than the entire United States population of 300,000,000) live below the poverty line.

HISTORICAL BACKGROUND

Despite the size of India, very little research has been conducted or shared in the area of deafness. Miles (2000) compiled a historical bibliography on education of children who are handicapped in South Asia and found only a few citations related to deafness and the education of children who are deaf over a span of 4,000 years. Miles pointed out that, until the 20th century, deafness was considered a punishment for sins of earlier incarnations. People who were deaf were not allowed to inherit property by law until the beginning of the 20th century (Miles, 2001). With the prevalence of such beliefs, it is not surprising that Indian society does not make deaf education a priority.

Like many Asian and African countries, education of deaf children in India was first started by Catholic missionaries. There is very little information available about earlier schools for the deaf in India. This brief review of history of schools for the deaf is mostly based on an annotated bibliography by Miles (2000), which is sketchy. Additional information about founders of these schools, funding sources, curricula, methodologies, and roles of the deaf in these schools will help provide a wealth of information not only from a historical perspective but also from education and societal perspectives.

The first school for the deaf opened in 1885 in Bombay (Hull, 1913), followed by the opening of a school in Calcutta in 1893 (Banerji, 1904a) and another in Palamcotta in 1896 (Swainson, 1906). In 1903, there were an estimated 70,000 children who were deaf in India. Of these, only 52 (or .07%) were enrolled in the three schools (Banerji, 1904a). This figure of 70,000 is grossly underestimated because the present number of deaf people is about 10 million. Because the majority of the Indian population resides in villages, it is understandable that many deaf people were excluded from this estimate.

The number of schools for the deaf increased sporadically during the 20th century, reaching a reported high of 73 in the 1960s, but decreasing to 70 in the 1970s (Brill, 1986). It appears, however, that what had been stated as the actual number of schools was only an estimate. In 1974, the All India Federation of the Deaf reported the existence of 117 schools for the deaf (Bhat, 1975). The first research-based information on schools for the deaf was compiled in 1999 by the Ali Yavar Jung National Institute for the Hearing Handicapped (NIHH) and was published in a directory format. The directory includes information about 431 schools (Ali Yavar Jung National Institute for the Hearing Handicapped, 2000). Most (330) of the schools are very small in size and are operated by nongovernment organizations. Three government-operated schools are large. Each of these schools has about 550 students. The total number of students attending other schools is not available because information in the directory is sketchy. However, estimates based on past trends and an increase in the number of educational programs suggest that only about 0.5% of students who are deaf attend a special program. About 4.5% of deaf students are estimated to be in regular schools without any support such as interpreters, note-takers, tutors, or counselors. The remaining 95% receive no formal education. If we consider that 30% of the population is of school age, then the number of school age children who are deaf in India could be 3,000,000. The number of children who are deaf and who are receiving an education in the programs listed in the NIHH directory may be about 15,000.

CURRENT ACADEMIC PROGRAMS

As mentioned earlier, a very small portion of deaf children actually attend any program for the deaf. Randhawa (2005) found that most of the deaf students were in primary grades. There was sharp decline in enrollment after the fifth grade. The number of deaf students in Grades 5 through 8 was less than 22% of the total number of students in Grades 1 through 5, suggesting that about 78% of deaf students drop out of school after elementary education. Adenwalla (1999) also indicated that very few deaf students finish high school. There are no formal colleges for the deaf. Adenwalla (1999) believes that a "miniscule" number of deaf students attend university or college.

Communication Modes in Schools

Until 1978, it was generally believed that there was no Indian Sign Language (ISL). Banerjee (1928) compared signs used in three schools for the deaf and concluded that gestures used in each school were different. He believed that signing started in India in the 18th century, but its use was strongly discouraged because signing was believed to impede learning to read. Madan Vasishta sent a questionnaire in 1975 to heads of the 117 schools for the deaf in India. Almost all the respondents agreed that there was no ISL. They did, however, acknowledge that deaf children used some kind of "collection of gestures" (Cross, 1977). Vasishta, Woodward and De Santis (1981) found that ISL is a language in its own right and is indigenous to the Indian subcontinent.

There is a paucity of research done on education of deaf children and signing in India. Educators in India have been compelled to depend on texts and research findings published in Western nations. Immanuel, Koenig, and Tesni (1998) compiled a book containing 19 chapters on deafness in India. Of the 46 references listed in the bibliography, not a single citation is from an Indian author; all are European or American. Given the numbers of individuals who are deaf in India and the vast differences in Eastern and Western cultures, it is imperative to research ISL and the education of Indian children who are deaf rather than rely on Western resources.

In Randhawa's study (2005), most principals of schools for the deaf (75%) claimed to follow either "Total Communication" or an oral approach in educating deaf children. However, 96% of responding teachers claimed to use gestures or signs while teaching in the classroom. Randhawa concluded that there are no formal policies and that schools claim to be oral even when signs are used in classrooms.

The NIHH started ISL classes for interested people in 2001. Both deaf and hearing people attended, and these classes were also offered in the regional centers operated by the NIHH in four other cities. Paradoxically, however, students in NIHH's own teacher training programs are not required to attend these classes.

The interest in use of ISL is on the rise as is indicated by the number of inquiries received by Ishara, a nongovernment agency providing ISL classes to the public (personal communication with the coordinator of Ishara, July 2007).

The Curriculum Used in Schools for the Deaf

Almost all schools for the deaf are required to use the syllabi approved for hearing children in the state. There are no special books available for deaf children. The use of these state-approved and required textbooks depends on the individual school. Some schools use them with a few students and some do not use them at all. Most teachers (60%) believe that deaf students should not be required to use these books (Randhawa, 2005). Teachers do not develop their own materials to meet the needs of children because they do not have training or resources available.

Secondary and Postsecondary Opportunities

India does not have a college for the deaf, and no support system for deaf or hard of hearing students is provided by any university. Therefore, it is logical to assume that the few deaf students who manage to attend regular colleges and universities do it without interpreters or notetakers. No data are available on the number of deaf or hard of hearing students attending postsecondary institutions.

The NIHH directory breaks down the number of students attending schools by gender only. There are no data on the number of students attending or graduating from high school. Of the 431 schools listed in the directory, only 40, or 9%, offered high school level classes. It is safe to assume that the number of deaf children finishing high school is extremely small.

Status of Deaf Adults

No research on deaf adults has been conducted. The following information is based on the author's personal experience and communication with other deaf people. The status of deaf adults in Indian society can be considered deplorable. As mentioned earlier, deaf people in India were not allowed to inherit property until the 20th century (Miles, 2000). Legally, they are allowed to inherit property now; however, actual inheritance depends on the deaf person's family. In a joint family, the deaf person gets only subsistence and not equal privileges.

Very few deaf people married in the past. With the arranged marriage system prevalent in India, marriage depended on parents' means. Rich parents married off their deaf child to hearing girls or boys from poorer families. Marriage of two deaf individuals was unheard of until the 1960s. At present, at least in cities, marriage of two deaf people is becoming a norm. In rural areas, where deaf people seldom or never meet other deaf people, the choice is still dependent on parents. No wonder more than 98% of children in Randhawa's study have parents who are both hearing.

Deaf people are not admitted to teacher training programs because the curriculum in these programs heavily emphasizes the teaching of speech. Nevertheless, there are few teachers of the deaf who are deaf themselves, and these teachers typically are employed as vocational teachers (Randhawa, 2005).

The government has reserved 1% of central government jobs for deaf people. However, there is no proof that this quota is ever met. It is generally believed that a few deaf people are employed as peons and in other lower level jobs. Recently, three deaf people scored very high on the prestigious competition for Indian Administrative Service. All three were bypassed when their deafness was known. The newly founded National Association of the Deaf led huge rallies in New Delhi, and the government was forced to offer jobs to the three deaf candidates (http://timesofindia.indiatimes.com/articleshow/322772.cms).

Special Laws

The first major law affecting disabled people was the Rehabilitation Council of India (RCI) Act of 1992. This act coordinates "training of rehabilitation professionals." The RCI plays a major role in regulating the training of teachers and other professionals in India and provides funding for curriculum development and in-service training. The RCI was further strengthened when, in 1995, the government passed sweeping legislation, the Persons With Disabilities Act. This act is similar to the Americans With Disabilities Act of 1990 and could have a major effect on education, training, and employment of disabled people, including deaf people. However, its implementation is slow and funding for it is limited. It is cited at most professional conferences and government publications, but deaf people know very little about it.

In summary, India has needed legislation for providing support for disabled people, including deaf people. However, despite efforts of advocacy agencies, little progress has been made in implementing whatever legislation has been voted into law. As reported by Hyde in the chapter on inclusion in this volume, the provincial governments and nongovernment agencies do not have the requisite funding to implement these acts.

PREPARATION OF SPECIAL PERSONNEL

In India, most teachers of children who are deaf were trained in schools for the deaf as journey-men apprentices until the 1950s when formal training programs began to emerge. Compara-tively, the first teacher training program in the United States was established in 1873 at Boston University ("Programs for training teachers," 2001). In India, at present, there are 41 pro-grams that offer training in deaf education. Of these programs, 31 offer diploma courses in education of children who are deaf, and they are available to high school graduates. Eight programs offer a bachelor of education degree, and only two programs have a master's level degree. Some programs are based in larger schools for the deaf while others are part of a formal teacher training program operated by universities and colleges. The RCI, the agency that oversees and monitors all training in special education, approves these programs.

Most of the course work in these programs is based on general education, special educa-tion, and deaf education curricula used in England and the United States. The author of this chapter interviewed several chairpersons of training programs in India by phone and e-mail. All of them indicated that the few textbooks and assigned readings required in teacher train-ing programs are published abroad and do not include any information about individuals who are deaf or about the education available in India. Instead, the curricula details information about Gallaudet and Clerc in the United States as well as leaders in deaf education in Europe. There is no mention of S. N. Banerji, J. N. Banerji, Kali Das Bhattacharya, and other indi-viduals who pioneered education of the deaf in India!

Western books on education of children who are deaf do not have information indigenous to India. Key questions and information specific to this population need to be addressed and shared with Indian educators and Western educators of children who are deaf: Are the eti-ologies of deafness in India similar to those in the United States and other countries? Does the standardization of ISL influence learning by children who are deaf, especially when there are more than 400 spoken languages of which 22 are official languages (Vasishta, 1978, 1981, 1987; Zeshan, 2000)? Does the joint family system, practiced for centuries in India, affect a child's socioemotional development compared with the nuclear family system in the West? Can oral methods succeed in a country where the cost of a good hearing aid is more than the annual per capita income? There is a dire need for textbooks that can be used in teacher train-ing programs and that can begin to address, if not answer, such questions.

In addition to teachers, there are several programs that prepare speech pathologists and audiologists. These two disciplines are not yet specialized, and the same academic degree covers both speech and audiology. At present, two programs offer speech and audiology degrees at the master's level, and another 12 are offered at the bachelor's level.

No programs exist to prepare other specialized personnel such as psychologists (school or clinical), social workers, and counselors of any kind. There are a few psychologists who work with deaf people, but they have no special training or knowledge of sign language. Accord-ing to Dr. Smitha Huddar, a professor at NIHH, some professional training programs now include some information on disabled children if a candidate plans to work with special chil-dren. However, this focus is on all disabilities, not on deafness itself.

CURRENT DEVELOPMENTS AND TRENDS

Education and rehabilitation of deaf people is making progress along with the Indian economy and the recognition of needs and services for the disabled population by the government. More and more traditionally oral schools have started to show interest in using sign language with some, if not all, of the student body.

There is a heavy emphasis on full inclusion of all disabled children. The recent passage of Sarva Sikhsa Abhiyan ("Education of All Children") by the central government does not include the providing of special education. Instead, it emphasizes inclusion of all disabled children in regular classrooms. This law can be called a partially funded mandate. The state governments have limited resources to implement these requirements (Hyde, this volume).

With the limited information available, it is difficult to predict future trends in education of the deaf in India. However, the author's personal communication with educational leaders and visits to various schools across the country indicates that the pendulum is slowly swinging toward recognition of ISL and its role in education. Two schools (Bajaj Institute of Learning in Dehradun and the Indore School for the Deaf) have formally announced that they are following a bilingual model of education. The bourgeoning economy and the government's interest in disabled children's education lead us to expect steady progress in education of deaf children in India during the next decades.

REFERENCES

Adenwalla, D. (1999). Education of the deaf in India. In W. Brejli (Ed.), *Global perspectives on the education of the deaf in selected countries* (pp. 191–204). Hillsboro, OR: Butte Publications.

Antia, S. D. (1979). Education of the hearing impaired in India: A survey. *American Annals of the Deaf, 124*(6), 785–789.

Ali Yavar Jung National Institute for the Hearing Handicapped. (2000). *Directory of rehabilitation resources for persons with hearing impairment in India.* Bombay: Author.

Banerjee, H. C. (1928). The sign language of deaf-mutes. *Indian Journal of Psychology, 3,* 69–87.

Banerji, J. N. (1904a). Mr. T. Venkata Rao, Mysore. *The Messenger* (Belfast), *7*(4), 57–58.

Banerji, J. N. (1904b). [Notices of Publications] Majumdar, Mohini Mohan, 1904, Muk-shiksha (Education of the Deaf and Dumb) Calcutta. *American Annals of the Deaf 59*(4), 390–391.

Banerji, J. N. (1907). Calcutta School for the Deaf. *The Messenger* (Belfast), *8*(10), 173–174.

Bhat, R. L. (1975). *Services for the deaf in India.* New Delhi: All India Federation of the Deaf.

Brill, R. (1986). The Conference of Educational Administrators Serving the Deaf: A history. Washington, DC: Gallaudet University Press.

Cross, J. (1977). Toward a standardized sign language for India. *Gallaudet Today, 8*(1), 26–29.

India. School for the Deaf, Palamcottah (Editorial). (1931). *The Teacher of the Deaf, 29,* 133.

Hull, E. R. (1913). *Bombay mission-history with a special study of the Padroado question: Vol. 2. 1858–1890.* Bombay: Examiner Press.

Immanuel, S. P., Koenig, C., & Tesni, S. (Eds.). (1998). Listening to sounds and signs: Trends in deaf education and communication. Bangalore: Christoffel-Blindenmission and Books for Change.

Jepson, J. (1991). Some aspects of the deaf experience in India. *Sign Language Studies, 73,* 453–459.

Miles, M. (2000). Studying responses to disability in South Asian history: Approaches personal prakrital and pragmatical. *Disability and Society, 16,* 143–160.

Miles, M. (2001). Signs of development in deaf south and south-west Asia: Histories, cultural identities, resistance to cultural imperialism. In Alison Callaway (Ed.), *Deafness and development.* Bristol, U.K.: University of Bristol, Centre for Deaf Studies.

Swainson, F. (1906). *Report of the Deaf and Dumb and Industrial School . . . for 1905.* Palamcotta, India: Church Mission Press.

Parasnin, I., DeCaro, J., & Raman, M. (1992). Attitude of teachers and parents in India. *American Annals of the Deaf, 141*(4), 302–308.

Programs for training teachers. (2001). *American Annals of the Deaf, 146*(2), 184.

Randhawa, Surinder P. K. (2005). A status study of special needs schools for the deaf and identification of intervention areas. Unpubl. PhD thesis. Indian Institute of Technology, Roorkee, India.

Vasishta, M. M., Woodward, J. C., & De Santis, S. (1981). *An introduction to Indian Sign Language: Focus on Delhi.* New Delhi: All India Federation of the Deaf.

Vasishta, M. M., Woodward, J. C., & De Santis, S. (1985). An introduction to the Bangalore variety of Indian Sign Language. Washington, DC: Gallaudet Research Institute.

Vasishta, M. M., Woodward, J. C., & De Santis, S. (1987). Indian [sign languages]. In J. V. Van Cleve (Ed.), Gallaudet encyclopedia of deaf people and deafness (Vol. 3, pp. 79–81). New York: McGraw-Hill.

Vasishta, M. M., Woodward, J. C., & Wilson, K. L. (1978). Sign language in India: Regional variation within the deaf. *Indian Journal of Applied Linguistics, 4*(2), 66–74.

Zeshan, U. (2000). *Sign language in Indo-Pakistan: A description of a signed language.* Philadelphia, PA: John Benjamins.

Educating Deaf and Hard of Hearing Students in New Zealand

Connie Mayer, Christine Miller, and Ian Cocks

NEW ZEALAND, also known as Aotearoa, Land of the Long White Cloud, is a country of 4 million people, with a deaf and hard of hearing population of approximately 6,000.[1] The predominant cultural groups are New Zealand European, or Pakeha (68%); Maori, the indigenous peoples of New Zealand (14.6%); Asian (9.2%); and Pasifika (6.9%)[2] (Statistics New Zealand, 2006). The population is concentrated in the North Island with more than a quarter of the total population living in the metropolitan Auckland area. Therefore, even though it is geographically small in size, there are areas of the country that are remote and sparsely populated, creating challenges in providing equal access to education services for all deaf and hard of hearing learners.

The official languages of the country are English, Maori, and New Zealand Sign Language (NZSL). NZSL was added to this list when it was recognized as an official language under the New Zealand Sign Language Act of 2006. There is no distinct Maori sign language, although there are many Maori signs, and as Maori Deaf people have become more aware of their distinct identity (Smiler & McKee, 2007), signs and translations have been developed to express Maori cultural concepts.[3]

Education is a national responsibility, and the Ministry of Education (Te Tāhuhu o te Mātauranga) provides leadership and direction to all national sectors in this regard. The ministry is a core government agency that supplies policy advice to the government for all aspects of education from early childhood through postsecondary, including employment-related education and training. It is also responsible for the delivery of education advisory services and early childhood development through contractual arrangements with other agencies as well as for the providing of direct specialist services to children and young people with special education needs, including those with hearing loss.

As is true in many other countries, the education of deaf and hard of hearing children in New Zealand has undergone many changes and shifts in pedagogy and philosophy over time, particularly with respect to language and communication approaches. And as is also typical, there has been a general move from exclusively oral approaches to educating deaf and hard of hearing children to approaches that incorporate the use of signed language, including both signed forms of English and NZSL.

---

1. In New Zealand, the terms *hard of hearing* and *hearing impaired* have typically been used interchangeably.
2. *Pasifika* refers to the peoples of the Pacific Islands.
3. For further information on this point, see www.nzsign.co.nz.

53

HISTORY OF DEAF EDUCATION IN NEW ZEALAND

The first teacher of the deaf in New Zealand was Miss Dorcas Mitchell, a teacher who had arrived from a deaf school in England. Beginning in 1870, in Charteris Bay near Christchurch, she taught the four deaf children of Reverend R. R. Bradley, in addition to tutoring a number of private pupils (Townshend, 1993). It was noted that Miss Mitchell was "well versed in the manual method" (ABHR, 1879, quoted in Townshend, 1993, p. 40), with Reverend Bradley being fulsome in his praise of her abilities.

It is thought that at about this time, pressure to establish the first school for the deaf in New Zealand came from Bradley, who gained the support of William Rolleston of the Canterbury Provincial Council. By 1878, the New Zealand Government had approved the idea. Given the respect that Bradley had for Miss Mitchell, he offered land for the establishment of a school for the deaf in 1879 and recommended that Miss Mitchell be its first principal. The offer was declined in favor of a site closer to Christchurch in Sumner. Miss Mitchell was not offered the position as principal and disappeared from the scene rather quickly (Stewart, 1982; Townshend, 1993). Instead, Sir Julius Vogel, a former prime minister of New Zealand who at that time was the agent general for New Zealand in London, was asked to find a suitable principal for the school. He set up a committee made up of himself and three other English educators to consider applications. Rollerston, after meeting a deaf tourist who had been taught under the German or oral system, became very keen on that system and is thought to have influenced the final decision about who Vogel appointed.

The principal appointed by Vogel was Gerrit van Asch whose strong advocacy of the oral method of teaching had impressed the government of the day. He was described as a professor of the German system "who teaches his pupils to converse by means of articulate sounds, by lipreading the movement of lips of speakers to the exclusion of all signs except natural ones" (Allen, 1980, p. 11). This description stands in contrast to the approach that Miss Mitchell had been using in her teaching of deaf children in the previous decade.

Van Asch's appointment marked the establishment of the first government-funded residential school in 1880, the Sumner School for the Deaf in Christchurch, serving deaf children from all over New Zealand. The school opened in March 1880 with four students. By the end of the school's first year of operation, the roll had increased to 14 students. At the time van Asch became principal, he was its only qualified teacher of the deaf, and during his tenure, he trained successive generations of teachers in the oral method. When he retired in 1905, 60 students were attending the school (van Asch, 1989).

Moving Into the 20th Century

In 1920, a class for hard of hearing children was established in Wellington, and in 1921, similar classes also were set up in Auckland and Dunedin. Although these classes, including the class at the Myers Park School in Auckland, were considered branches of the school for the deaf in Sumner, their mandate was to serve hard of hearing rather than deaf children.

The speech classes provided a teacher of the deaf who worked with a small class of children identified as requiring specialist help within the regular school. These classes represented an early move toward mainstreaming deaf and hard of hearing children in New Zealand by providing a model for how unit classes for deaf and hard of hearing children in regular schools might be established (Parsons, 2003).

The advent of World War II had a direct effect on the education of deaf children when the school in Sumner was requisitioned for army use in 1942. Because there was not another site large enough to house the entire school, it was split into two branches, with one group remaining in Christchurch temporarily in the Te Kohanga Maternity Hospital in Mona Vale and the other moving to the new Auckland School for the Deaf in Titirangi, housed in a building that was previously a hotel. Children from the Myers Park School were also moved to the Auckland School for the Deaf. In addition to these government-funded schools, a few private schools such as the Epsom Speech School were also operating in Auckland.

St. Dominic's School for the Deaf in Wellington was officially opened in 1944. The impetus for the development of St. Dominic's came from an Australian Father, Dominic Phillips, who was concerned about the lack of Catholic education for deaf children in New Zealand. In the early 1950s, St. Dominic's was relocated to Feilding, close to Palmerston North. (The school closed in 1989 because of the reduced numbers of both residential and day students.)

There were soon problems with overcrowding at the Auckland School for the Deaf in Titirangi, and in 1952, another arm of the school was opened in the Auckland suburb of Mt. Wellington. In 1958, a new school was built in Kelston, and Auckland School for the Deaf became the Kelston School for Deaf Children (Aspden, de Vere, Hunt, Monaghan, & Pivac, 1992).

The development of mainstream initiatives toward the end of the 1950s was to play a very important role in creating a new approach to the education management of deaf children in New Zealand, and to some extent, the developments that occurred were built on the foundations that began with the establishment of speech classes in the 1920s (Parsons, 2003). In 1959, the first class for deaf children was established in the Clifton Terrace Model Infant School in Wellington. The class provided a teacher of the deaf who worked with a small class of children identified as requiring specialist help within the school. This initiative led to the establishment of a number of deaf unit classes throughout New Zealand.

The 1964–65 rubella epidemic in New Zealand led to a significant increase in the number of deaf children (Allen, 1980). By the time these children were of school age, the Kelston school and Sumner School for the Deaf were responsible for 41 deaf education units in early childhood, primary, and secondary schools throughout New Zealand (Parsons, 2003).

At about this time, educators were also developing strategies to achieve full inclusion of deaf children into regular classrooms. It was becoming increasingly common practice in New Zealand for individual deaf students to be placed in a regular classroom with support from a visiting teacher of the deaf and a teacher aide (Parsons, 2003). As those students from the rubella epidemic moved out of the education system and the number of deaf units throughout New Zealand dropped, unit class teachers were retained as visiting or itinerant teachers of the deaf, and their caseloads were expanded to include not only hard of hearing but also deaf students.

Additional specialist positions were established in the late 1950s and early 1960s to more effectively manage the audiological, communication, and education needs of children diagnosed with a hearing loss (Parsons, 2003). These specialists were referred to as advisers on deaf children. The proposal to establish an advisory service was partly driven by the need to tackle the problems posed by New Zealand's demography, typified by a population that was widely dispersed outside its major cities and towns.

The role of these advisers was and remains quite distinct from teachers of the deaf. The purpose of these positions is to provide specialist advice and guidance to families and education professionals on the audiological, communication, and education needs of children with sensorineural or long-term conductive hearing loss. The service is provided from the time children are detected as having a hearing loss until they leave the compulsory education sector.

Establishing Resource Centers

As the Kelston and Sumner Schools for the Deaf developed, they began to designate geographic areas of responsibility, with each school adopting catchment areas of approximately half the population of New Zealand. This setup allowed advisers to be attached to the schools for the deaf and become a part of their outreach services and initiatives to further the inclusion of deaf and hard of hearing children and young people in regular early childhood and school settings (Parsons, 2003).

With both schools for the deaf not only providing services for students at their base schools but also supporting deaf and hard of hearing students in unit class and mainstream settings, there was a growing need to provide specialist services to mainstream classroom teachers, teacher aides, teachers of the deaf, and parents. These services included advice, guidance, and the providing of instructional materials to support programs for deaf and hard of hearing students. During the 1980s, both schools for the deaf increasingly adopted the role as resource centers for their regions, a role that has included creating, adapting, and making available curriculum support materials for personnel working with deaf and hard of hearing children and young people as well as their families. That role has also involved establishing specialist resource teams made up of professionals in deaf education who have specialized skills in speech, language, literacy, visual communication, and later, in NZSL and Deaf Studies.

The auditory-oral method predominated until 1978 when there was pressure from parents, the deaf community, and some educators to implement Total Communication. By 1980, Total Communication had been widely adopted as a communication philosophy in the school system, but it was not widely accepted by the Deaf community because the education focus was on the use of signed forms of English rather than on NZSL. The perspective of most members of the Deaf community was that NZSL was the sign language through which they chose to communicate, and they wanted to see this language represented in the school system.

At the time of the centenary of the Sumner School for the Deaf in 1980, the name of the school was changed to van Asch College in recognition of its founding principal. The 1990s saw further name changes of both schools for the deaf to better reflect the activities and responsibilities of the two organizations. Kelston School for Deaf Children changed its name to Kelston Deaf Education Centre, and van Asch College changed its name to van Asch Deaf Education Centre.

The first deaf teacher of the deaf completed her training in 1983 and was employed at the Kelston center where she taught through the Total Communication approach in 1984. The first bilingual (NZSL/English) pilot class for deaf children was established at the Kelston center in May 1995, working under the premise that NZSL would be developed as the children's first language, with English in its written form as the second language (Nuthall, 1996). A process to introduce Deaf bilingual programs to the van Asch center started in 1995, and Deaf bilingual programs were introduced at both centers in 1997. Deaf cultural practice and Deaf studies were integral aspects of both of these programs.

During this time, there was a move to increase ties to the Deaf community, and in the early to middle part of the 1990s, that move led to an increase in the employment of deaf and hard of hearing adults in education settings. In particular, these deaf employees worked as (a) teachers of the deaf and hard of hearing, (b) language assistants in bilingual classrooms and in deaf studies programs, (c) educational assistants, (d) NZSL tutors, (e) archivists, (f) deaf mentors, (g) Deaf community representatives on boards of trustees and committees, (h) residential managers and staff members of residential facilities, and (i) Maori tutors.

Current State of Education of Deaf and Hard of Hearing Learners

The following sections provide an overview of the current situation as it pertains to the education of deaf and hard of hearing learners in New Zealand and, especially, the effects of recent developments.

Education Programs and Services

Education services for deaf and hard of hearing children and young people throughout New Zealand are made available through a variety of service providers. Using population distribution as the determining factor, Kelston Deaf Education Centre provides services in the northern half of the North Island, and van Asch Deaf Education Centre provides services to the lower North Island and all of the South Island. The Ministry of Education, Special Education, now employs the advisers specializing in deaf children to provide advice and guidance through national district offices. All schools in New Zealand are funded through a special education grant to provide support for those students who are enrolled and who have special needs. Students with significant special education needs, including hearing loss, are verified under the Ongoing and Reviewable Resourcing Schemes. These schemes provide specialist staffing, therapy, and paraprofessional resourcing.

Cochlear Implant Programs

Overall management of cochlear implant programs in New Zealand is facilitated with funding from the Ministries of Education and Health through two trusts. The Northern Cochlear Implant Trust provides devices to those who have had cochlear implants, and it oversees programming and habilitation services in the northern half of the North Island. The Southern Hearing Charitable Trust provides devices for eligible children and young people in the lower half of the North Island and the South Island. Delivery of audiological and habilitation services are provided under contract to each trust. Audiological services in the northern region are provided by the Auckland District Health Board and in the south by the van Asch Deaf Education Centre under contract to the Southern Hearing Charitable Trust. The van Asch center also provides the habilitation service in its region. Habilitation services in the northern region are provided through a joint venture between Kelston Deaf Education Centre and The Hearing House. The Hearing House is a private organization that also offers auditory verbal therapy to preschool children.

School Programs

Both Kelston Deaf Education Centre and van Asch Deaf Education Centre provide early childhood and schooling programs and services for children and young people from the age of identification to the age of 21 years. At the Kelston center, these programs and services are provided at the Kelston school, which includes the base school and satellite units on seven partner school sites. The van Asch center offers a similar range of programs at its base school. Totara Village, the Kelston center's residential facility, accommodates students from Year 7 (age 12) and above, and facilities at the van Asch center accommodate students from Year 6 (age 10) and above. The majority of these residential students at both centers come from families who live outside of metropolitan Auckland or Christchurch but who choose to access the school's educational programs.

Current practice with respect to choice of communication and language to be used in education programs is responsive to individual student needs and is driven by the Individual Education Plan (IEP). Access to communication and language is realized across the full range of modes, including audition, speechreading, print, and sign (both NZSL and English-based sign, particularly within the base and core schools). Most recently, there has been an increase in the number of children accessing language through a multimodal approach, that is, some combination of the modes. This trend is in direct response to the increasing number of children who have cochlear implants and who need access to information by means of both visual and auditory channels.

Preschool Programs

Preschool and early intervention programs at both centers are based on Te Whāriki, the national early childhood curriculum. Children enrolled at the Kelston preschool are deaf, hard of hearing, or hearing. Hearing children who attend the program are the siblings of deaf children or are the children of deaf adults. In this program, children have opportunities to access both NZSL and English.

The Early Intervention Centre at the van Asch facility provides a program of advice and guidance to parents as well as direct service to children and families in the Christchurch area, including a number of siblings of deaf children or the children of deaf adults. Many of these children also attend their local early childhood facilities and from the age of 3 receive support from itinerant teachers of the deaf as part of the center's regional teaching service. Both centers offer residential preschool visits for those families who live outside the cities of Auckland and Christchurch and who have deaf and hard of hearing children. These visits provide families with 3–4-day live-in courses during which they take part in programs of assessment, advice, and guidance that are provided by the center's Specialist Resource Team and Early Intervention staff.

Diversity

The school populations at both centers are culturally diverse. The Kelston center population includes 29% European (Pakeha), 23% Maori, 23% Pasifika, 9% Indian, 8% Asian, and 8% from other countries. One quarter of this population are achieving within an age-appropriate range, 65% have learning factors that significantly affect learning outcomes, and 10% have complex learning needs. At the van Asch center, 52% of students are European (Pakeha), 26%

are Maori, 2% are Pasifika, 10% are Indian, 2% are Asian, and 8% are from other countries. Of the students attending the base school, 40% have disabilities other than hearing loss that have a significant effect on their learning. Some of the issues that account for the delays in learning are late age of diagnosis, lack of access to and development of a first language, language processing difficulties, lack of communication in the home or a language other than English in the home, reduced opportunities for literacy development, late entry into school, and poor school attendance.

Regional Services

Regional teaching services at both the Kelston and van Asch centers provide children and young people in their respective regions with services by itinerant teachers of the deaf. These services continue from early childhood to secondary schooling. Specialist resource staff members at both centers work with library and media staff members to create support materials. These resource professionals also provide specialist advice and guidance through outreach services for personnel working with deaf and hard of hearing children and their families in the areas of speech, language, literacy, visual communication, NZSL, and Deaf Studies. Increasingly, the centers are using video conferencing technology and Web sites to augment these services.

Curriculum Planning

The mandate of the Ministry of Education is to raise achievement and reduce disparity in education for all children, and to this end, three strategic priorities have been identified: effective teaching, engaged families and communities, and quality providers. In addition, within special education, the focus is on presence, participation, and learning that lead to achievement, workforce and community participation, and well-being. These outcomes are closely aligned with the national curricula, which guide learning from early childhood education to the completion of formal schooling.

Teaching and learning programs within the Kelston center's core school and the van Asch center's base school are based on these national curricula across eight essential learning areas: social sciences, arts, technology, science, mathematics and statistics, health and physical education, English, and the learning of languages. A curriculum document for NZSL was published in 2007, which, within the eighth essential learning area, the learning of languages, gives opportunities for students to study NZSL as a first or second language. Three key considerations guide curriculum planning and implementation: (a) understanding the diverse needs of learners, (b) establishing responsive learning pathways, and (c) ensuring that student engagement leads to achievement.

Key considerations to address delays and meet the needs of such a diverse group of learners focus on access and adaptations that include aligning assessment approaches, understanding the process of evaluation, developing quality programs, providing adequate resources, offering targeted professional development, and describing the "big picture." To this end, assessment processes have been aligned with national practice across curriculum areas, with the exception of written English at curriculum levels one and two.

The Kelston and van Asch centers have a close relationship that facilitates the implementation of this national vision and practice and that drives important curriculum developments. Among these was the development of written English benchmarks that reflect the developmental phases of early writing and that more accurately pinpoint the developmental differences between hearing and deaf children in these beginning stages. These exemplars were published in 2005 and have received international attention. The two centers have also collaborated to develop a NZSL lexicon for the teaching and learning of mathematics.

In both centers, a Deaf cultural perspective is integrated into class topics at the primary levels, while older students have opportunities to engage in a Deaf Studies program as part of a senior school timetable. A Deaf Studies curriculum is near completion and will provide a sequential and structured approach to this topic. The NZSL curriculum guidelines, completed in 2006, include social and cultural learning as one of the key strands.

In addition to incorporating a Deaf perspective, there is also a commitment to acknowledging the Maori and Pakeha (European) bicultural nature of New Zealand and to creating authentic and relevant learning opportunities for Maori students and their *whanau* (families). Ruamoko Marae is a unique facility on the Kelston campus.[4] It serves the students and the Deaf community regionally and nationally and realizes the living cultures of Maori people who are deaf in New Zealand.

National Planning for Deaf Education

A National Plan for the Education of Children and Young People who are Deaf or Hearing Impaired in Aotearoa/New Zealand was launched in June 2000 and was revised for the second time in 2005. This plan was devised in response to the development and implementation of the government's policy, Special Education 2000, and has provided an opportunity to advance the interests of children and young people with hearing loss. It was developed collaboratively by the Ministry of Education, the various service providers (e.g., deaf education centers), the national parent group, the New Zealand Federation for Deaf Children, the Deaf Association of New Zealand, and teacher unions. The National Plan outlines a philosophy, describes the nature of the population of deaf and hard of hearing students, and defines a set of education principles and goals.

Deaf Education Aotearoa New Zealand (DEANZ) was established by the Ministry of Education as a charitable trust in partnership to advance the education interests of deaf and hard of hearing learners by monitoring the implementation of the National Plan. DEANZ trustees include four parents, two professionals, and one deaf person; however, there must be at least two deaf trustees on the board at any one time. The DEANZ mandate is to ensure that every child who is deaf or hard of hearing in New Zealand receives an equitable, quality, and effective education.

The Deaf Education Access Forum was founded in 1994 by representative groups within the education sector, including the New Zealand Federation for Deaf Children and the Deaf Association of New Zealand. Meetings are held biannually. Initially, the Deaf Education Access Forum focused on the needs of postsecondary students, but it was soon expanded to encompass issues relating more generally to deaf education. The Deaf Education Access Forum continues to meet biannually, and these meetings are coordinated by DEANZ.

Over time, the Deaf Education Access Forum has adopted the following positions (Deaf Education Aotearoa New Zealand, 2004):

---

4. A Marae is a sacred place where the Maori culture and language is celebrated (e.g., formal welcomes to visitors, weddings, funerals, etc.).

1. The National Plan, in which 18 principles represent the desired strategic outcomes, should be implemented.
2. Principle Three from the National Plan is seen as a primary goal, that is, "an equitable, cohesive, nationally coordinated education service for all deaf and hearing impaired children and young people is provided in a timely manner from birth to the completion of their school years."
3. The vision is for "deaf and hearing impaired children and young people to be educated within a nationally effective, equitable and cohesive service."

DEANZ responded to the Deaf Education Access Forum by developing a proposal to establish the Service Design Group, which includes stakeholders and which will implement the objectives of the National Plan. The terms of reference for the Service Design Group include (a) establishing an effective pathway for service flow based on the child or student, (b) retaining aspects of the sector that are currently working well, (c) acknowledging that differences in deaf education are seen as richness, and (d) developing a framework for healthy reflective practice.

From the pathway for the service flows a working document, the Service Matrix, which details the specific characteristics of children and young people at each stage of their learning as well as the desired characteristics of the education system at each of those stages. The Service Matrix includes four universal aspects: identification, referral, service, and assessment or monitoring. In addition, it outlines the services required and outcomes expected at each of the early childhood, primary, and secondary school levels. The Service Matrix is regarded by the Ministry of Education as a guiding document that is considered along with its own priorities for education and specialist service standards.

Access to Postsecondary Education

The New Zealand Disability Strategy guides government action to promote a more inclusive society for people with disabilities. It is an enduring framework that will ensure that government departments and other government agencies consider disabled people before making decisions. The New Zealand Disability Strategy, along with the National Plan, underpins all education planning considerations and strategizing for deaf children, young people, and adult learners.

Disability support services play a pivotal role in enhancing access for deaf and hard of hearing students engaged in tertiary study. Services include advice on equipment available to assist study, note-taker support, and interpreting access. Although there may be some variation in the ability of universities throughout the country to provide this range of services, deaf tertiary students are entitled to enroll in the institution of choice. As sign language interpreters have become more readily available since 1994, an increasing number of deaf and hearing impaired students are enrolling in polytechnic institutes and universities in a range of programs, including teacher training.

Professionals in the Field

A national training course for teachers of deaf and hard of hearing students (Graduate Diploma in Special Education, Hearing Impairment) was established in Auckland in 2000.

Before this diploma course, teachers of the deaf were trained at Colleges of Education in both Auckland and Christchurch. The Ministry of Education allocates 12 study awards annually for registered teachers to train in this specialized field. This diploma course is generally presented as a 1-year study opportunity on full salary for successful applicants. In response to national need, particularly for those unable to relocate to Auckland for 1 year, this program has also operated as a distance learning opportunity over a 2-year period, with teachers engaged in a combined part-time study and part-time teaching option. The training course provides a broad curriculum within the field of deaf education because trained teachers need to be prepared to teach, across all learning levels, children and young people who have a range of communication preferences and needs.

Subsequent to the training of the first teacher of the deaf in the 1980s, deaf people have engaged in teacher training programs throughout the country. After deaf candidates obtain general teacher training, the usual pathway they take is employment within either the Kelston or van Asch centers before completing the Graduate Diploma in Special Education, Hearing Impairment. Currently, deaf teachers are employed within both special school and itinerant teacher contexts. Some Deaf teachers have also elected to specialize in the area of Deaf Studies and in teaching NZSL.

Typically, advisers on deaf children are trained teachers of the deaf who elect further study to move into more highly specialized positions. Currently, intern advisers combine study and practice toward completing the Masters in Sensory Disability qualification. Three providers have collaboratively developed the curriculum for this course of study: The Ministry of Education, Special Education; The University of Auckland; and Renwick College. The postgraduate degree is awarded through Renwick College by the University of Newcastle, New South Wales, Australia.

Victoria University of Wellington offers a number of Deaf-related study and research opportunities through the School of Linguistics and Applied Language Studies. A Certificate in Deaf Studies: Teaching New Zealand Sign Language, which requires a 1-year qualification or part-time over 2 years, is designed to train Deaf people as teachers or tutors of NZSL. The course focuses on Deaf community and culture, the structure and grammar of NZSL, language and learning processes, and methods for teaching sign language. Deaf people who are employed by either of the two deaf education centers as mentors, resource staff members, or language assistants are strongly encouraged to complete this qualification as part of their professional development program.

The Deaf Studies Research Unit (DSRU) was established at Victoria University in 1995 with the goal of conducting research on topics relating to Deaf people and their language in New Zealand. An initial major project of the DSRU was the production in 1997 of a dictionary of NZSL, the first such book of its kind in New Zealand. Research on NZSL and other topics that are relevant to education contexts for deaf and hard of hearing students is ongoing in the DSRU.

The first professional sign language interpreter training course was established at the Auckland University of Technology (AUT) in 1992. The majority of graduates go on to work in community and tertiary education settings. Interpreters electing to be employed in education can choose from a range within school-based and tertiary education contexts.

The Certificate in New Zealand Sign Language and Deaf Studies is a 1-year course of study that is also offered by AUT. Some teachers complete this qualification either before or after training as teachers of deaf students to enhance their knowledge of NZSL and the Deaf community.

Although the majority of Deaf people are able to access interpreting services within the English-speaking community, the situation for Maori Deaf people seeking to interact within the Maori community is more complex. Maori Deaf people collectively agree that Maori concepts need to be expressed, discussed, and translated into signs that reflect *tikanga Maori* (Maori culture). Tikanga-based signs are being developed both deliberately and naturally by means of growing awareness and discussion of the concepts among Maori Deaf people and interpreters.

Future Issues and Directions

In thinking about current issues and directions for the future of deaf and hard of hearing education in New Zealand, one can identify a number of areas that warrant particular attention. Key among them are Maori and Pasifika communities; national accessibility of resources, monitoring, assessment, and evaluation; early identification and intervention; students with mild to moderate hearing loss; changing trends in education placement and programming; and changing trends in teacher and advisor education programs.

Maori and Pasifika Communities

Given the percentage of Maori peoples in the population as a whole, there is an over-representation of Maori children and young people identified with prelingual hearing loss. Providing education services to Maori and Pasifika learners and their families presents a unique set of challenges. There are concerns with achieving consistent service delivery for the families and with meeting the needs of students attending Te Reo (Maori language) education centers such as Kohanga Reo (preschool) and Kura Kaupapa Maori (primary-secondary school). Although in some areas of the country it is possible for some students to have access to Maori and Pasifika culture through local school programs, it is often the case that many deaf and hard of hearing learners have difficulty accessing Tikanga Maori (Maori culture) because it is traditionally taught through an oral tradition. Providing access to the culture in this traditional way requires trilingual (Maori, NZSL, and English) interpreters, and such individuals are in short supply.

National Accessibility of Resources

Both the Kelston center and the van Asch center employ a range of specialists and resource personnel to work with students, their families, and the staff members who support them in both specialist schools and mainstream settings. It is stated in the National Plan that, irrespective of location, there should be equitable access to all of these resources, even in the more remote regions of the country. The intention is that all deaf and hard of hearing learners should have the opportunity to benefit from education programs such as habilitation services or the NZSL curriculum and have access to the full range of teaching resources, assessment tools, specialist teachers, and resource staff members. Meeting this goal can be a challenging one given the population distribution in the country. Adding to this challenge is the need to be able to provide these resource services across a range of communication modes and languages, including both English and NZSL, and to a population of learners with diverse learning styles and backgrounds. Consequently, more thought must be given to using technology creatively. The use of video conferencing and well-designed Internet sites are two strategies that have potential to enhance the deaf education centers' outreach services.

Interpreters in education are employed at both the Kelston and van Asch centers, and students in the senior schools who are NZSL users have access to a high level of interpreter support. Younger students also have access to interpreters in a range of contexts both inside and outside the classroom. This situation is currently not replicated for students in mainstream contexts where most schools employ education support workers rather than sign language interpreters to provide classroom communication support. Access to quality interpretation services for all students irrespective of school placement is a national intention.

Monitoring, Assessment, and Evaluation

There is a need for more consistency in monitoring and tracking the performance of deaf and hard of hearing students and in evaluating the efficacy of the programs in which they are enrolled. Although there has been progress made toward this end at the local level, agreeing on a national set of assessment tools would go a long way in guiding professionals in the field to determine current ability levels, to identify the most appropriate and effective resources and services, and to track progress against baseline data. The focus in this process would be not only on academic achievement per se but also on the development of language; cognition; visual, perceptual, and motor skills; emotional well-being; and social skills. It is important that tracking and monitoring be conducted by personnel who have not only a knowledge of the particular domain being assessed (e.g., cognition) but also a knowledge of hearing loss and the Deaf community. These personnel also need to be able to interact in a student's preferred language and mode of communication at an appropriate level of competency.

Early Identification and Intervention

Currently in New Zealand, the average age at which children are diagnosed with hearing loss is older than what would be considered ideal, but the country is in the process of introducing a Universal Newborn Hearing Screening program to address this issue. This effort requires a critical interface between service providers in the areas of health and education because early diagnosis and follow-up services must go hand in hand if early identification is to realize maximum benefits. From an education perspective, there is a need to provide training for teachers and advisers to work with this younger population of deaf and hard of hearing infants and preschoolers to provide well-balanced and effective programming as well as support and guidance for families.

In 2006, the Ministry of Education established a project team to consult with the sector about development of services to meet the needs of deaf and hard of hearing children and their families after undergoing a newborn hearing screening. The project team has accomplished the following:

- Established a reference group that is representative of the sector and a "critical friends" group that is made up of both international and New Zealand experts within the sector to provide advice and guidance to the project team
- Reviewed the literature on providing services to children who have been identified as having a hearing loss through newborn hearing screening
- Used the literature review to inform the development of a service model that includes the service matrix developed by the Service Design Group
- Asked the Deaf Association of New Zealand to prepare a proposal for a deaf mentoring service and asked the New Zealand Federation for Deaf Children to prepare a proposal for a parent mentoring service

The feedback provided to the project team from the reference group and the critical friends group has been submitted to the Ministry of Education, Special Education National Management Team. This feedback will inform the next steps in planning the advising services with respect to infants and children, ages 0–3 years, who are identified through newborn hearing screening as having hearing loss.

Students With Mild to Moderate Hearing Loss

Currently, there are between 1,500 and 2,300 children and young people in New Zealand who have been identified with a mild to moderate hearing loss. This group is seen to need less intensive services than their peers with more profound losses, and therefore, they do not generate the same level of funding under the current resourcing framework. Consequently, the resources for this group are stretched very thin in some regions. This situation is especially concerning because there is a growing demand for the mainstream services that support these students. A new framework is needed that would allocate more of the special education resourcing for this population and that would, in particular, fund training for paraprofessionals in this area to enhance their skills to support deaf and hard of hearing learners in accessing the mainstream curriculum.

Changing Trends in Education Placement and Programming

With the advent of Universal Newborn Hearing Screening and the anticipated continued increase in the number of children who receive cochlear implants, it is predicted that there will be fewer students enrolled in the base schools, traditionally seen as the schools for the deaf. Because most students with severe to profound losses will have implants or will be able to make effective use of amplification to meaningfully access the curriculum, it is predicted that there will be increased demand for interventions that make use of some combination of speech and sign as well as interventions that are accomplished solely through audition and spoken language. That future scenario would not exclude the use of NZSL; however, it would be less likely that parents would choose it as a first or only option for their newly identified child. This trend is already becoming evident. Currently, 80% of the Kelston center's student population attend school in satellite units, and less than 10% of the children served by the van Asch center are taught at the base school.

In addition, given the relatively high incidence of additional disabilities identified in conjunction with hearing loss (for an overview, see Jones & Jones, 2003), it is likely that there will be increasing numbers of children with significant additional disabilities in all settings, but especially in congregated settings.

Changing Trends in Teacher and Adviser Education Programs

The amalgamation of the Auckland College of Education (Teachers' College) and the University of Auckland in 2005 has already brought changes to systems and delivery with the development of the Graduate Diploma in Special Education with a hearing impairment pathway. It has been proposed that this diploma be further developed into a postgraduate diploma with a clear link to master's level study.

Content and delivery will need to be considered with respect to future developments within training programs. For example, in terms of content, the advent of Universal Newborn Hearing Screening will require advisers to have expertise in early intervention work with babies and families, including those with multiple disabilities. Ongoing and comprehensive knowledge and understanding of auditory-verbal approaches in working with deaf and hearing impaired children will also be essential as the numbers of children receiving cochlear implants increases. Teachers also will need to learn how to manage increasingly sophisticated technologies. Comparatively, New Zealand has a small population of deaf children. But although teachers may need higher levels of specialization in some areas, the reality in New Zealand, with its comparatively small population of deaf and hard of hearing learners, will be that classes will comprise students with a range of diverse needs. Teachers will need to have flexible knowledge and understanding to best meet the individual learning needs of each student across a range of communication approaches.

CONCLUSION

The Ministry of Education in New Zealand provides a clear direction for education for all students, and there are high expectations that all learners will enjoy a quality of education that enables them to achieve and participate in the community and workforce. To raise student achievement and to ensure that each child is achieving to the best of his or her abilities, the ministry has encouraged service providers to ensure that children have access to quality services that have as their base effective teaching and the engagement of families and communities in children's education (New Zealand Ministry of Education, 2006).

Within deaf education in New Zealand, there has been a strong commitment to these ideals and an acknowledgment that to realize them, the effort needs to include wide consultation with parents, the deaf community, and deaf education professionals. Consequently, over the last 10 years, these communities have been engaged in considerable consultation.

This collaboration has led to substantial points of agreement about the providing of services. The sector is firmly of the view that the achievement of deaf and hard of hearing learners will be raised if learners and their families have access to services that are characterized as being effective, coordinated, equitable, and provided as early as possible. The sector is also in substantial agreement about the services required and the expected outcomes for deaf and hard of hearing learners as they progress through their education.

These points of agreement represent a considerable achievement in an area of special education that is often mired in controversy and disagreement, and they have created a sense of optimism within the sector as it deals with the challenges that it faces in the 21st century.

REFERENCES

Allen, A. B. (1980). *They hear with the eye: A centennial history of the Sumner School for Deaf Children, Christchurch, NZ 1880–1980.* Wellington, NZ: Department of Education.

Aspden, P., de Vere, J., Hunt, J., Monaghan, L., & Pivac, L. (1992). *50 years of deaf schools in Auckland, 1942–1992.* Auckland, NZ: Kelston Deaf Education Centre.

Deaf Education Aotearoa New Zealand (DEANZ). (2005). *The national plan for the education of children and young people who are deaf or hearing impaired in Aotearoa/New Zealand* (2nd rev. ed.). Retrieved July 9, 2008, from http://www.deafed.org.nz/newsletters/NationalPlan2005.pdf

Jones, T., & Jones, J. (2003). Educating young deaf children with multiple disabilities. In B. Bodner-Johnson & M. Sass-Lehrer (Eds.), *The young deaf and hard of hearing child* (pp. 297–327). Baltimore, MD: Paul H. Brookes.

New Zealand Ministry of Education. (2006). *Better outcomes for children: An action plan for GSE 2006–2011.* Wellington, NZ: Ministry of Education.

Nuthall, B. (1996). *Kelston Deaf Education Centre: Pilot bilingual programme, January 1995–December 1996.* Auckland, NZ: Kelston Deaf Education Centre.

Parsons, M. (2003). *Advisors on deaf children: A New Zealand initiative—An overview 1957–2003.* Wellington, NZ: Ministry of Education.

Smiler, K., & McKee, R. (2007). Perceptions of Maori identity in New Zealand. *Journal of Deaf Studies and Deaf Education 12*(1), 93–111.

Stewart, P. (1982). *To turn the key: The history of Deaf education in New Zealand.* Unpublished master's thesis, University of Otago, New Zealand.

Statistics New Zealand. (2006). *QuickStats about New Zealand: Cultural diversity.* Retrieved September 23, 2008, from http://www.stats.govt.nz/census/census-outputs/quickstats/snapshotplace 2htm?id=9999999&tab=CulturalDiversity&type=region&ParentID=

Townshend, S. (1993). *"The hands just have to move": Deaf education in New Zealand—A perspective from the Deaf community.* Unpublished master's thesis, Department of Social Policy and Social Work, Massey University, Palmerston North, New Zealand.

van Asch, C. (1989). *Gerrit van Asch: Pioneer of oral education of the deaf.* Christchurch, NZ: Caxton Press.

The authors wish to acknowledge the following individuals for their input and reading of earlier versions of this chapter: David Foster, Chief Executive Officer, Kelston Deaf Education Centre; Nan Gardner, Senior Lecturer, Deaf Education, University of Auckland; Mark Hutton, Senior Advisor, Ministry of Education; Rachel Noble, Chief Executive Officer, Deaf Association of New Zealand; Rachel McKee, Programme Director of Deaf Studies, Victoria University; Sabine Muller, President, New Zealand Federation of Deaf Children; and Barbara O'Neill, Chairperson, Deaf Education, Aotearoa New Zealand.

Education of Deaf and Hard of Hearing Students in Singapore

Fred R. Mangrubang

THIS CHAPTER presents an overview on the education of Deaf and hard of hearing students in Singapore. Singapore is an island city-state and the smallest country in Southeast Asia. It is located on the southern tip of the Malay Peninsula, south of the Malaysian state of Johor and north of the Indonesian Riau Islands. Singapore is made up of not only one main island but also 63 surrounding islets. The country has a total land area of 424 square miles (Ministry of the Environment and Water Resources, 2005). Today, Singapore has become a prosperous nation that has achieved many world-class accomplishments. It has the biggest shipping port in the world with more than 600 shipping lines and is a leader in ship building. Singapore is also a major supplier of electronic parts and manufacturing. The city is one of the most important financial and high-tech centers in Asia. It is one of the world's major oil refining and distribution centers, and it has one of the world's highest per capita gross domestic products (Ministry of Manpower, 2007). Along with Hong Kong, South Korea, and Taiwan, Singapore's fast-paced industrialization earned it a place as one of the four original "East Asian Tigers" (Ministry of Trade and Industry, 2005).

HISTORY OF SINGAPORE

The first records of Singapore's existence are in Chinese texts from the 3rd century AD, which described Singapore as an island at the end of the peninsula. In the 14th century, Singapore was an outpost of the Sumatran Sri Vijaya empire and originally bore the Javanese name Temasek. During the 14th century, the island earned a new name, Singa Pura, which means "Lion City." According to legend, a visiting Sri Vijayan prince saw an animal whose image he mistook for a head that looked like a lion with a body of a fish, and Singapore's modern day name was born (Ministry of Information, Communications and the Arts, 2004a).

Singapore was a Malay fishing village and had various sea crafts ranging from Indian vessels to Chinese junks to Arab dhows to Portuguese battleships. In the 19th century, Singapore was colonized by the British, and Sir Stamford Raffles, an official with the British East India Company, established Singapore as a trading station. The policy of free trade attracted merchants from all over Asia and from as far as the United States and the Middle East (Ministry of Information, Communication and the Arts, 2004b). Centuries later, the island was the scene of major fighting during World War II. Singapore was considered an impassable fortress, but the Japanese Empire overran the island in 1942 (Taylor, 1997). After World War II, Singapore became a British Crown Colony. Singapore joined the Malaysian Federation in 1963 but separated 2 years later and became independent. In 1965, Singapore became an independent republic (U.S. Library of Congress, 1977). In 1969, Singapore became a self-governing state with Yusof bin Ishak as its first head of state and Lee Kuan Yew from the People's Action Party as its first prime minister. During Lee Kuan Yew's term as prime minister, his administration raised the standard of living, developing the country's economic infrastructure and eliminating the threat of racial tension. Singapore evolved from a developing nation to first-world status toward the end of the 20th century (Lee, 1999). In 1990, Goh Chok Tong succeeded Lee as prime minister. In 2004, Lee Hsien Loong, the eldest son of Lee Kuan Yew, became the third prime minister ("Country Profile," 2006).

Singapore's population of 4.42 million (in July 2005) is racially diverse. The Singaporean Chinese, the majority, account for 76.8% of Singaporeans. Singaporean Malays, who are the indigenous native group of the country, constitute 13.9%. Indian Singaporeans are the third largest ethnic group at 7.9%. The rest of the population is made up of smaller groups such as Arab Singaporeans, Jews, Thais, Japanese, Europeans, and the Eurasian Singaporean community (Singapore Department of Statistics, 2005, Table, p. viii). The people of Singapore came from the southern provinces of China, Indonesia, India, Pakistan, Ceylon, and the Middle East. Though intermarriages have taken place over the years, each racial group within Singapore has kept its own cultural identity while developing as an integral part of Singapore community. There are four official languages in Singapore: Malay, Mandarin, Tamil, and English. English is the language of business and administration since independence, and it is spoken by most of the population. Most Singaporeans are bilingual and speak their native tongue in addition to English. The national language is Malay, for historical reasons, and is used in the national anthem (Promote Mandarin Council, 2007).

History of Deaf Education in Singapore

The education of Deaf and hard of hearing students began in Singapore in 1951. Mr. Peng Tsu Ying, a deaf man born in Shanghai, China, was a pioneer in establishing the first private deaf school at his home in Singapore. His career in education began when he noticed there was no school for deaf children in Singapore. He shared his proposal about setting up a school for the deaf with the Singapore Ministry of Education (MOE). The MOE rejected his proposal because he was deaf and had no teaching certification. Singapore was a British colony, and people with disabilities were not well regarded.

Refusing to give up, Mr. Peng Tsu Ying, with permission of the MOE, advertised in the local newspapers to tutor deaf children at his father's home. Parents with deaf children responded to his advertisement, and he started a small private tutorial class of 12 deaf children. Eventually, in 1951, he set up at his home the first private deaf school for 18 deaf children. He used the teaching method that he learned while attending school as a young child in Shanghai, China. The mode of communication used at his private school in Singapore was the Shanghainese sign language. The mission of the school was to educate deaf Chinese children and thus enable them to become useful citizens. In 1952, while the Chinese deaf children were receiving their education in Shanghainese sign language, the Singapore Red Cross Society set up an oral deaf school. The Red Cross Society conducted classes for deaf children and provided counseling services for parents of deaf children. As classes increased, the Red Cross Society and officials from the Social Welfare Department established the Singapore Association for the Deaf.

In 1954, Mr. Peng's student population grew to 194, and his new school, the Singapore Chinese Sign School for the Deaf, was officially established. He became the first deaf principal in Singapore and received support from the Chinese-educated business leaders (who made up his school advisory committee). In 1963, the Singapore Chinese Sign School for the Deaf was merged with the Oral School for the Deaf, established by the Red Cross Society, into one school at Mountbatten Road. The new school was named The Singapore School for the Deaf. The first principal for the new merged school was Mrs. A. L. Pereira, a hearing person. With the new school in place, Mr. Peng transitioned to the role of head teacher at the Chinese sign section. The mission of the new school was to provide a proper educational curriculum to ensure that deaf children would have equal educational opportunities to that of their hearing peers. The sign section had seven classes, and the oral section had 13 classes. The Singapore School for the Deaf was supported by the Singapore Association for the Deaf.

In 1972, the Minister for Social Affairs, Inche Othman Wok, laid the foundation for the Vocational School for the Handicapped, and in 1975, the Vocational School for the Handicapped was established within the Singapore School for the Deaf. The mission of the Vocational School for the Handicapped was to provide training to deaf students in sewing, cooking, woodworking, and other skills needed to function in the hearing world.

Total Communication philosophy was adopted at the Singapore School for the Deaf in 1976. In 1978, the Signing Exact English II system, developed in the United States, was adopted as the mode of communication and instruction in the school. The goal was to help teach deaf children the English language. The Chinese sign section was phased out in 1981 because of declining enrollment; most parents preferred English to Chinese. In 1986, Mr. Peng retired from the Singapore School for the Deaf and, over the years, has seen many of his former deaf students receive their postsecondary education in the United States.

In 1987, the school moved from Mountbatten Road to Prince Charles Square. The MOE began to provide full funding support for the Singapore School for the Deaf in 1989 and for the Vocational School for the Handicapped in 1991.

Two of Mr. Peng Tsu Ying's former students from the Chinese sign section, Mr. Chin-Heng Lim and Ms. Poh-Pin Lee, went on to become the only other deaf teachers of the deaf in Singapore. Singapore School for the Deaf did not have a secondary education program. At that time, there were no mainstreamed secondary school programs for Deaf and hard of hearing students in Singapore. Most of Mr. Peng's students continued their secondary school years in Taiwan and a few ventured into their families' business enterprises.

Today, parents can opt for their child to attend the Singapore School for the Deaf, the Canossian School, or other mainstreamed primary and secondary schools of their choice. After completing primary education, Deaf and hard of hearing students are allowed to sit for the Primary School Leaving Examination (PSLE) conducted by the MOE. The PSLE is a national examination taken by all primary school students in Singapore before leaving for secondary school. The PSLE is managed by the MOE. The examination assesses students' abilities in the English language, native tongue languages (Chinese, Malay, or Tamil), mathematics, science, and social studies. Each of the examinations tends to be 2 hours long. After successfully completing the PSLE, Deaf and hard of hearing students, move on, based on their scores, to mainstreamed secondary schools or to regular secondary schools with supported services. The students are placed into secondary schools that suit their learning pace and aptitude. There, they attend regular classes and follow the curriculum of mainstream schools. Students who are unable to continue their education in secondary schools move on to one of the training centers or workshops coordinated by Volunteer Welfare Organizations. The training centers help provide them with the necessary skills for employment (Mr. Peng Tsu Ying, personal communication, June 1, 2006).

Singapore Deaf Teachers

Before becoming teachers of the deaf, Mr. Lim and Ms. Lee had neither the opportunity nor the choice to continue their secondary education in Singapore. At that time, there were no secondary residential or mainstreamed schools for the deaf. With the strong encouragement from Mr. Peng Tsu Ying, their former Chinese Sign School principal, and with the financial support from their families, Mr. Lim and Ms. Lee continued their secondary school years at the American School for the Deaf in Hartford, Connecticut.

Mr. Chin-Heng Lim graduated from the American School for the Deaf and entered Gallaudet College (now Gallaudet University) where he majored in mathematics and graduated in 1975 with a bachelor's degree. In 1976, he returned home and was employed by the Singapore Association for the Deaf as general education instructor at the Vocational School for the Handicapped. Eight months later, he was transferred to the Singapore School for the Deaf as a temporary teacher employed by the MOE. He later decided to further his studies in teacher training and earned a master of arts degree in education of the hearing impaired from Gallaudet College in 1981. He returned to Singapore and was hired by the MOE as a resource teacher at Mount Vernon Secondary School until 1991. In the years 1992–2002, he moved on to the Upper Serangoon Secondary School as a math classroom interpreter and resource teacher for Deaf and hard of hearing students. Now, he is at Balestier Hill Secondary School, carrying on the same job responsibilities with Deaf and hard of hearing students in lower and upper secondary level elementary mathematics and in upper secondary level additional mathematics, which is similar to calculus in the United States. As the only deaf resource teacher hired by the MOE, Mr. Lim has been a liaison to several voluntary welfare organizations such as the Singapore Association for the Deaf, Singapore Disability Sports Council, and Sports and Recreation Committee of the Deaf. His commitment with the organizations is to help Deaf and hard of hearing students broaden their experiences by taking part in sports and outdoor activities designed for their needs. In 2004, the MOE recognized and awarded him the Long Service Medal on Singapore National Day (Mr. Chin-Heng Lim, personal communication, May 16, 2006).

Ms. Poh-Pin Lee was one of the first two deaf female primary students in the history of Singapore to pass the PSLE since the MOE allowed Deaf and hard of hearing primary students to sit on the Singapore national examination in 1967. After Ms. Lee completed her secondary school education in the United States at the American School for the Deaf in Hartford, Connecticut, which had granted her a 3-year academic scholarship, she entered Gallaudet College (now Gallaudet University) where she majored in mathematics and graduated in 1978 with a bachelor's degree. In 1978, she returned home to Singapore and was employed by the Singapore School for the Deaf as a primary schoolteacher. She taught science, geography, and math to Deaf and hard of hearing students. After teaching for 1 year, she decided to return to the United States to complete her graduate study in the teacher training program at Western Maryland College (now McDaniel College), Westminster, Maryland. In 1982, she earned a master of education degree in deaf education with a concentration in mathematics. After earning her master's degree, she was hired as a mathematics high school teacher for 1 year at the Alabama School for the Deaf in Talladega, Alabama. She taught algebra I, algebra II, geometry, and general mathematics to Deaf and hard of hearing students. In 1983, she was hired as a high school mathematics teacher at the Model Secondary School for the Deaf (MSSD) on the campus of Gallaudet University, Washington, D.C. She taught all math subjects at MSSD until 1986. Later, she accepted a job offer at Gallaudet University as a mathematics instructor in the math department where she taught algebra and geometry to incoming undergraduates students until 1999. While being an active member of the National Council of Teachers of Mathematics, she held teaching certifications as a high school mathematics teacher for the states of California, New Jersey, and Maryland (Poh-Pin Lee, personal communication, May 31, 2006).

The education experiences that Mr. Lim and Ms. Lee had during their primary school years in Singapore are much different compared with those of Deaf and hard of hearing children in Singapore today. The education system has grown from one that had concerns with economic survival and the need to provide basic education for all to what is now a highly competitive system that prepares students for vocational, polytechnic, and university level education. It is a system in which examination qualifications are stressed and highly valued at all levels, with students being tested regularly, beginning at the age of 7. Primary and secondary education is compulsory in Singapore. The schools are managed by the MOE. The MOE directs the formulation and implementation of educational policies. It has control of the development and administration of public schools and an advisory and supervisory role to private school (Qualifications and Curriculum Authority, 2005).

Because Singapore has few natural resources, there is significant investment in human capital. The Singapore government views education as important to building the nation, mainly in terms of meeting economic needs and securing interethnic harmony (Gopinathan, 2001). Over the years, the education system has continually received international recognition in the International Mathematics and Science Study (Harris & Fernandes, 1997). The rigorous curriculum undergoes regular revision to ensure that education remains relevant for all students ("Singapore Heads School Test Table," 2004).

In recent years, the MOE has revamped the education system from a competition-based system to a broad-based education system with the purpose of providing a holistic education for all students in and out of the classroom. The government looks ahead for its education system to create a labor force that can function in a knowledge-based economy (Yamashita, 2002).

Academic Placement of Deaf and Hard of Hearing Students

Deaf and hard of hearing students today attend special education schools managed by the Voluntary Welfare Organizations, which are funded by the MOE. The English language is the first language learned by children when they arrive at the preschool age and becomes the primary language of instruction in primary school. There are two primary schools in Singapore providing special education for children with hearing loss: the Canossian School and the Singapore School for the Deaf (Ministry of Education, 2006). The Canossian School uses the natural auditory-oral method of instruction in the classrooms, which maximizes the use of residual hearing. In contrast, the students at the Singapore School for the Deaf are taught using a Total Communication approach with Signing Exact English II in the classrooms. The Singapore School for the Deaf, staffed by teachers employed by the Singapore Association for the Deaf, and the Canossian School, staffed by teachers employed by the MOE, both prepare students to be independent and active participants for integration into the mainstream secondary education and into society. Students attend a 4-year foundation stage in Primary 1–4 and a 2-year orientation stage in Primary 5–6. The goal of primary education is to give students a good comprehension of languages, humanities and the arts, mathematics, and science. Students are encouraged to participate in co-curricular activities and in community involvement programs (see Figure 6.1). Students who use their residual hearing continue their education in mainstream secondary schools or in regular secondary schools with special resource teachers. Students who communicate using sign language attend one of two designated secondary schools: Boon Lay Secondary School or Balestier Hill Secondary School.

The Canossian School for the Deaf started as a boarding school for young women in 1956 that was run by the Canossian Sisters, an Italian-based order of Catholic nuns. In 1970, the boarding feature of the school was ended to allow both young men and young women with hearing loss who needed education to be admitted to the school. The Canossian School philosophy is that all children learn language by listening to the world and imitating the sounds

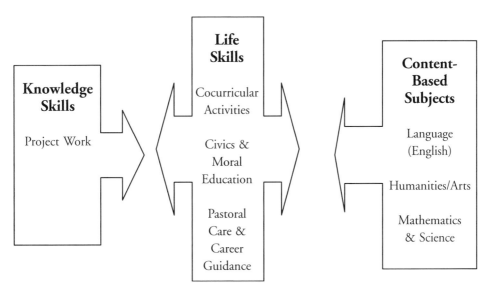

Figure 6.1. Primary school curriculum. The Knowledge Skills area (left box) focuses on developing students' thinking, processing, and communicating skills through project work. The Life Skills area (center box) focuses on preparing students to become responsible adults and active citizens through cocurricular activities, civics and moral education, pastoral care (counseling, social-cultural activities, and values formation), career guidance, national education, physical education, and health education. The Content-Based Subjects area (right box) focuses on preparing students with good foundations across different areas of study, including language, humanities and the arts, mathematics, and science.

around them. The school approach to teaching Deaf and hard of hearing children is oral and mainstream, with strong support for cochlear implants.[1]

The mission of the Canossian School is (a) to reinforce the child's residual hearing and speech capabilities through the auditory-oral program where speech training is developed in preference to signing or fingerspelling, (b) to help the child develop numeracy and literacy skills, and (c) to identify children who are suited for integration to regular school programs. In general, the school offers early intervention, parent guidance, student-teacher individual conversation support, integration with mainstream schools, a cochlear implant program, and audiological services. More specifically, the school offers special education to children with hearing loss from birth to age 16 years through four programs (Ministry of Education, 2006):

1. Nursery Program—provides special education to children from birth to age 4 years. The program focuses on the physical, social, emotional, intellectual, and aesthetic development of children. Emphasis is on spoken language and auditory training.

2. Kindergarten Program—provides special education to children from ages 4 to 6 years. The auditory-oral approach is emphasized. The program focuses on basic numeracy, literacy, and aural skills.

3. Primary Program—provides special education to students from Primary 1 to Primary 6. The program follows the mainstream curriculum. At the end of their primary education, the students take the PSLE.

4. Special Class Program—provides special education, using a modified mainstream curriculum, to students with hearing loss and mild intellectual disabilities. Students are taught using Total Communication in place of the auditory-oral approach. These students are taught life skills and are not required to take the PSLE. At the age of 14 years, the students are placed in the Vocational School for the Handicapped, which is within the Singapore Association for the Deaf, for vocational training to prepare them for open employment.

The mission at the Singapore School for the Deaf is (a) to develop and educate children to their fullest potential to enable them to contribute and be integrated into society and (b) to provide children with opportunities to fully develop their potential in academic, communicative, cognitive, physical, and social skills. The school offers four programs:

1. Nursery/Kindergarten Program—provides special education to children from the age of 2.5 years to 8 years. The program focuses on the social, emotional, and physical needs of the child as an individual.

2. Primary Academic Program—provides special education to students from Primary 1 to Primary 6. The program follows the mainstream curriculum. At the end of their primary education, the students take the PSLE. Students are not required to learn a second language.

3. Primary Special Program—provides special education using a modified mainstream curriculum. The students in this program learn life skills, English, math, social skills, and IT skills. One of the most interesting and enjoyable parts of this curriculum is the program of field trips the pupils go on once a week. The goal of the field trips is to help students become independent travelers.

---

1. The Canossian School Web site provides links on general information about the school (http://www.cshi.com/).

4. Cocurricular Activities Program—provides remedial lessons for each subject area in addition to school activities in drama, swimming, life skills, and song performance. The school offers speech and language therapy, audiological services, social work services, counseling and home visits, a parent education program, multisensory training, and a program that provides emotional and social support to children (REACH).[2]

Primary students at the Canossian School and at the Singapore School for the Deaf are required to take the PSLE. The purpose of PSLE is to assess students' knowledge and skills for secondary education and to place them in one of the appropriate secondary school courses that match their learning styles and ability. Students are placed in different secondary education tracks—Special, Express, Normal (Academic), or Normal (Technical)—according to the results of the PSLE (Ministry of Education, 2006). The different curricular emphases are designed to match the students' learning abilities and interests. The Special and Express tracks are 4-year courses preparing students for the Singapore-Cambridge General Certificate of Education Ordinary level (O-level) examination (see Table 6.1). Students in the Special and Express courses take seven to eight subjects. Students in the Normal course follow either the Normal Academic, or N(A), or the Normal Technical, or N(T), curriculum. The N(A) curriculum is a 4-year course preparing students for the Normal-level (N-level) examination, with the possibility of a fifth year followed by an O-level examination. In the N(T) track, students take five to seven subjects. The curriculum prepares students for the technical-vocational curriculum at the Institute of Technical Education. The N(T) curriculum reinforces the students' skills in mathematics and English (see Table 6.2). In the N(A) track, students take six to eight subjects (see Table 6.3). The secondary education curriculum includes English, mathematics, science, humanities, and the native tongue. Students can move from one course to another based on their performance and on the assessment of their school principal and teachers (see Figure 6.2).

As shown in Table 6.4, Primary 6 Deaf and hard of hearing students completing the PSLE are placed in various Secondary 1 education tracks. It is important to note here that the data collected were from only new Secondary 1 Deaf and hard of hearing students enrolled and mainstreamed at the Upper Serangoon Secondary School for the years 1999–2000 and from the Balestier Hill Secondary School for the years 2003–2006. There was no intake for Secondary 1 new students at the Upper Serangoon Secondary School for the years 2001–2002 because it was closing down and hearing students were being moved to a new school while Deaf and hard of hearing students transferred to Balestier Hill Secondary School. Data for Deaf and hard of hearing students enrolled at Boon Lay Secondary School were not available because their PSLE results were aggregated with those of hearing students. Data for additional hard of hearing students with cochlear implants who are enrolled at other secondary schools were not available because results of their PSLE were aggregated with those of hearing students (Mr. Chin-Heng Lim, personal communication, September 1, 2006).

Examinations function in a gatekeeping capacity with respect to educational opportunities in the Singapore education system. The Singapore education system is ability driven, designed to take full advantages of each student's skills and knowledge (Ministry of Education, 2006). Parents have criticized the Singapore education system as being strict and promoting

---

2. The Singapore School for the Deaf Web site provides general information about the school (http://www.ssd.edu.sg/).

Table 6.1. Special and Express Track Course Curriculum

Knowledge Skills	Life Skills	Content-Based Subjects

Project Work	Cocurricular Activities
	Community Involvement Program
	Civics & Moral Education
	Pastoral Care & Career Guidance
		Language
		  English
		  Mother Tongue
		  Higher Mother Tongue

		Math & Science
		Lower Secondary Subjects
		  Mathematics
		  Science
		  Design & Technology
		  Home Economics

		Upper Secondary Subjects
		  Mathematics
		  Science

		Upper Secondary Electives
		  Additional Mathematics
		  Biology, Chemistry, Physics, Combined
		    Science Options
		  Design & Technology
		  Food & Nutrition
		  Principles of Accounting

		Humanities & the Arts
		Lower Secondary Subjects
		  Geography, History
		  Literature in English
		  Visual Arts, Music

		Upper Secondary Subjects Combined Humanities

		Upper Secondary Electives
		  Geography
		  History
		  Literature in English
		  Malay Literature
		  Tamil Literature
		  Art & Design
		  Music
		  Higher Art, Higher Music

rote learning by using examinations. The Singapore education system today is changing to become more flexible and diverse to provide students more choices to meet their learning styles and interests (Ministry of Education, 2006).

CURRENT DEVELOPMENT AND TRENDS

The current developments and trends occurring in Singapore can be grouped in three categories: the training of special education teachers, support for Deaf and hard of hearing students, and the enrollment of Deaf and hard of hearing students at the two primary schools. The direction of these changes is toward diversity and acceptance.

Before 1984, special education teachers in Singapore were trained overseas. However, untrained individuals wanting to become special education teachers were often recruited by the associations and provided training on the job. In 1984, the Institute of Education, now known as the National Institute of Education, established the special education teacher training

Table 6.2. Normal Technical Course Curriculum

Knowledge Skills	Life Skills	Content-Based Subjects

Project Work	Cocurricular Activities
	Community Involvement Program
	Civics & Moral Education
		Language
		  English
		  Basic Mother Tongue
		
		Math & Science
		Lower Secondary Subjects
		  Mathematics
		  Science
		  Computer Applications
		  Technical Studies
		  Home Economics
		
		Upper Secondary Subjects
		  Mathematics
		  Computer Applications
		
		Upper Secondary Electives
		  Science
		  Technical Studies
		  Food & Nutrition
		
		Humanities & the Arts
		Lower Secondary Subjects
		  Social Studies
		  Visual Arts
		  Music
		
		Upper Secondary Electives
		  Art & Design
		  Elements of Office Administration

Table 6.3. Normal Academic Course Curriculum

Knowledge Skills	Life Skills	Content-Based Subjects

Project Work	Cocurricular Activities
	Community Involvement Program
	Civics & Moral Education
	Pastoral Care & Career Guidance
	National Education
	Physical Education
		Language
		  English
		  Mother Tongue
		  Higher Mother Tongue
		
		Math & Science
		Lower Secondary Subjects
		  Mathematics
		  Science
		  Design & Technology
		  Home Economics
		
		Upper Secondary Subjects
		  Mathematics
		  Science
		
		Upper Secondary Electives
		  Additional Mathematics
		  Combined Science Options
		  Design & Technology
		  Food & Nutrition
		  Computer Applications
		  Principles of Accounting
		
		Humanities & the Arts
		Lower Secondary Subjects
		  Geography
		  History
		  Literature in English
		  Visual Arts
		  Music

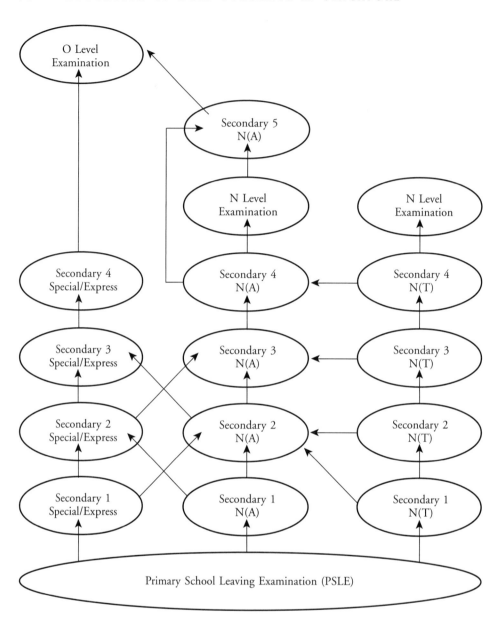

Figure 6.2. Secondary programs' flexibility between courses. Students in the Normal course follow either the Normal Academic N(A) or the Normal Technical N(T) curriculum. A fifth year leading to the O-Level examination is available to N(A) students who perform well in their N-level assessments.

program (Quah, 1990). The program was designed as a basic course for teachers teaching in the schools. Teachers were given a Certificate in Special Education after completing the program (Quah, 1990).

Since 1998, the education of Deaf and hard of hearing students in Singapore has made progress, but there are challenges the education system is confronting in terms of preservice teacher training in special education and support for students with hearing loss. Special Education Inspector Vincent Sim of the MOE noted that the special education teachers undergo

Table 6.4. Placements of Primary 6 Deaf and Hard of Hearing Students to Secondary 1 Education Tracks

Year	Total Deaf and Hard of Hearing Students	Special Track	Express Track	Normal (Academic) Track	Normal (Technical) Track
1999[a]	4	—	2	2	—
2000[a]	8	—	—	2	6
2001[b]	0	—	—	—	—
2002[b]	0	—	—	—	—
2003[c]	10	—	—	3	7
2004[c]	7	—	1	1	5
2005[c]	11	—	1	3	7
2006[c]	14	—	4	1	9

Note. Data furnished by Mr. Chin-Heng Lim, Resource Teacher for both Upper Serangoon Secondary School and Balestier Hill Secondary School, Singapore.
a Upper Serangoon Secondary School
[b] No intake for Secondary 1 students for the years 2001–2002
[c] Balestier Hill Secondary School

a preservice course (Diploma in Special Education) conducted by the National Institute of Education at Nanyang Technological University (Vincent Sim, personal communication, June 30, 2006). The generic course prepares teachers to teach students with disabilities, including intellectual, physical, sensory, and behavioral disabilities. Schools for students with disabilities provide in-service training in the specific disability. Most teachers are employed directly by the schools after completing their in-service training. Schools for students with disabilities are managed by individual associations. Currently, Singapore has no preservice teacher training programs (i.e., bachelor, master, and doctorate degrees) for college or university students in the area of special education and deaf education.

The National Institute of Education in Singapore offers a diploma in special education for candidates who are interested to teach in special education, and it is a 1-year, full-time program. Teachers applying for the diploma program need to have 3 months of teaching experience in a school with disabled students (Chia, n.d.).[3]

Teachers have the choice to earn a bachelor, master, or a doctorate degree in special education in college or universities overseas after completing the diploma program. Many teachers currently teaching in special education have chosen to further their professional development in special education overseas (Chalmers, 1990). Currently, there are no Deaf and hard of hearing teachers employed by the MOE as either a special education teacher or regular classroom teacher in general schools. Mr. Chin-Heng Lim is the only Deaf person hired (in 1981) by the MOE with the title of mathematics resource teacher for Deaf and hard of hearing students in a regular secondary school. At the Canossian School, there are no Deaf and hard of hearing teachers in a teaching position. In contrast, the Singapore School for the Deaf has seen much progress in the last decade in terms of Deaf and hard of hearing teachers teaching at the school. Former students from the Singapore School for the Deaf went on to become classroom teachers at the school, employed by the Singapore Association for the Deaf. Only

3. The National Institute of Education Web site provides links on general information about the diploma in special education program objectives, program structure, and entry requirements for teachers interested in applying into the special education program (http://www.nie.edu.sg/nieweb/programmes/loading.do?id=Foundation&cid=13467651&ppid=14188546).

a few former students who have earned a diploma in special education from the National Institute of Education are teaching at the school. At present, there are six deaf teachers employed as teachers of the deaf at the Singapore School (Mr. Peng Tsu Ying, personal communication, June 1, 2006).

Support for Deaf and hard of hearing students has been an issue the past few years. It is never simple for a Deaf and hard of hearing student to study beside his or her hearing peers in the regular schools. The Singapore Association for the Deaf has always been concerned about the service gaps for students with hearing loss who are mainstreamed into schools and society. In 2004, the Singapore Association for the Deaf established a pilot program for students with hearing loss attending schools in the East Zone. The Itinerant Support Service program was established to provide teachers with appropriate teaching skills to meet Deaf and hard of hearing students' learning styles and to increase teachers' understanding of problems faced by these students. The Itinerant Support Service program will also help Deaf and hard of hearing students learn more effectively and bridge the gap in the long run. Each year, the program will be extended to other school zones (Ho, 2004).

Over the years, parents have stated that the education system is too specialized, strict, and selective. Parents claim that there is too much emphasis placed on learning to excel in examinations and not enough on learning for lifelong skills or creative thinking. Pressure to reform the education system has led to changes implemented by the government and the MOE, particularly, to have students focus more on creative and critical thinking and allow more flexibility for students as they progress across school levels and into postschool environments (Shanmugaratnam, 2005).

Another recent trend is the enrollment of Deaf and hard of hearing students at the Singapore School for the Deaf and the Canossian School. Since 1988, there has been a change in enrollment. Enrollment figures at these two schools for Deaf and hard of hearing primary students in Singapore are shown in Table 6.5, which reveals an increase in enrollment at the Canossian School and a decrease in enrollment at the Singapore School for the Deaf from 1988 to 2005.

One factor related to the enrollment trend is that the shift toward using the natural auditory-oral method of instruction in teaching Deaf and hard of hearing students at the Canossian School has led to a dramatic decrease in enrollments at the Singapore School for the Deaf. According to Mr. Peng Tsu Ying and Ms. Poh-Pin Lee (personal communication, June 1, 2006), the debate over the years has been over what is considered the best communication method of educating Deaf and hard of hearing primary students in Singapore.

Table 6.5. Enrollment of Deaf and Hard of Hearing Students in Two Primary Schools

Schools for Deaf and Hard of Hearing Students	1988	1993	1999	2003	2004	2005
Singapore School for the Deaf	193	165	115	112	90	85
Canossian School	120	142	148	180	172	168
Total Deaf and hard of hearing students	313	307	263	292	262	253

Note. 1988 and 1993 figures quoted by Quah (1993), and 1999, 2003–2005 figures furnished by the National Council of Social Services (1999, 2004, 2005, 2006).

Hearing parents in Singapore want spoken language emphasized for their Deaf and hard of hearing children, even when sign language accompanies it. Some parents may even assume that the speech-language services their children receive at the Canossian School are superior to those provided at the Singapore School for the Deaf.[4]

Another possible factor is the cochlear implant technology that has been advancing rapidly in Singapore since 2001, resulting in the decrease of enrollment at the Singapore School for the Deaf. The Singapore Ministry of Health (MOH) funded a trial service for more than 50 children to receive cochlear implants. The 4-year trial ended in March 2005. The results showed that two-thirds of these children are in mainstream kindergartens, preschools, and primary schools, or will be soon. On August 31, 2005, Singapore General Hospital officially commemorated the 223rd cochlear implantation there and opened the new Centre for Hearing and Cochlear Implants (Osman, 2005). With the positive support for cochlear implantation, according to Dr. Vivian Balakrishnan, Minister for Community Development, "MOH announced that it would resume funding for cochlear implants" (Balakrishnan, 2005). The new facility will provide holistic care to children with hearing loss as well as social and financial support to parents. As a result of the cochlear implant technology in Singapore, enrollment of Deaf and hard of hearing students at the Singapore School for the Deaf dramatically declined in 1999 and again at the end of the 2003 school year (see Table 6.5).

In contrast, enrollment of Deaf and hard of hearing students at the Canossian School increased significantly between 1988 and 2003 and has declined only a small amount in 2004 and 2005. Other factors also contributed to the change in enrollment at the two schools, for example, the small number of Deaf and hard of hearing students from the Singapore School for the Deaf and from the Canossian School who attended general regular primary schools with the support of resource teachers. The contrast in enrollment between the two schools since 1988 is troubling at the Singapore School for the Deaf. For the 2005 school year, Table 6.5 shows that the total enrollment of Deaf and hard of hearing students at the school was at 85.

In reality, efforts to integrate and support children with disabilities within regular schools in Singapore has been limited to those disabled students who have higher intellectual abilities, usually those with physical and sensory disabilities. Students with more severe disabilities do not presently have the supports to be integrated within regular schools (Lim & Nam, 2000).

Relating to the integration of children with disabilities, the 1988 Report of the Advisory Council for the Disabled: Opportunities for the Disabled stated, "Whenever appropriate and feasible, special education should be provided within the regular educational system. A child should only be placed in a special school if he or she cannot be well educated in a regular school" (Lim & Nam, 2000, pp. 37–38).

CHALLENGES AND THE FUTURE

There are several challenges that those in the education system in Singapore are confronting as they face the future. Rao (1998) examined the beliefs and attitudes of preservice

---

4. See letters from Mr. Liem (Letter 1) and from Angela Chee (Letter 2) at http://www.cshi.com/news/news-parents-page2.html.

teachers toward teaching students with disabilities in Singapore and found them to be positive but not optimistic because of the lack of training, expertise, and support available in the regular general schools. There is no special education legislation. Due process is not available to parents who may be concerned about placement of their children. Mainstreaming Deaf and hard of hearing students in Singapore general schools seems to be a solution that is better than inclusion (Rao, 1998). From this perspective, mainstreaming implies that Deaf and hard of hearing students in Singapore receive their education in the regular general schools but not necessarily within the general classroom. In contrast, inclusion implies that Deaf and hard of hearing students receive most or all of their education in the regular general classroom. The major question to be answered is whether accommodations can be made, or are being made, to educate Deaf and hard of hearing students in the regular general classroom. Another major question is whether the Deaf and hard of hearing student is a full-time member in a regular general classroom where the classroom teacher works collaboratively with the special education teacher and adapts the classroom curriculum and environment to the student's needs.

Studies have shown that teachers in Singapore are still referring students with mild to moderate disabilities to attend special schools (Lim & Nam, 2000; Rao & Lim, 1999). Research findings revealed that preservice teachers believed that students with disabilities should not be educated in the same classrooms as their nondisabled peers (Lim & Nam, 2000; Rao & Lim, 1999). Most of the preservice teachers reported that they would rather not teach students with disabilities. The preservice teachers did not view the general education classroom as the setting where the instructional needs of disabled students could be met (Lim & Nam, 2000; Rao & Lim, 1999).

As in the United States, faculty competence, teacher program accreditation by professional organizations and national board standards, and licensure for teaching primary and secondary students are crucial in preparing preservice teachers to become classroom teachers. They are key not only for the quality of instruction and curriculum but also for the total atmosphere of the teacher education program. Teaching teachers is a demanding profession. College and university professors as well as supervising teachers in the classroom must model practices, create positive learning experiences, assess students' progress, and help connect theory and practice. Considering these factors in terms of the current teacher preparation program at the National Institute of Education, Nanyang Technological University in Singapore, major questions need to be answered:

1. Does the teacher preparation program hold a national accreditation, and does a licensure board certify teachers in special education (i.e., teaching Deaf and hard of hearing students and providing early intervention for Deaf and hard of hearing children)?

2. Are faculty members competent in deaf education (i.e., education for Deaf and for hard of hearing students) based on academic preparation, experience, teaching, and scholarly performance? If so, have they been involved with local educational programs for students who are Deaf and hard of hearing?

3. Is a course in special education a required module in the degree programs (i.e., BA-Education, BS-Education, and Postgraduate Diploma-Education) for preparing teachers in the regular general classroom?

4. Are there any Deaf and hard of hearing teachers currently teaching in regular general schools (primary and secondary) in Singapore who graduated from the National Institute of Education? If not, why?

CONCLUSION

The literature on special education in Singapore is limited. As a young country, Singapore can learn to a great extent about educating Deaf and hard of hearing students from other countries that have longer histories of special education and deaf education. Planning and implementing new programs for Deaf and hard of hearing students will not be an immediate solution. Planning, decision making, managing, and implementing new programs for Deaf and hard of hearing students must involve not only hearing people in Singapore but also Deaf and hard of hearing people in Singapore who have the knowledge, experience, and expertise about educating Deaf and hard of hearing students. Short-term and long-term planning must involve an inclusive committee (i.e., hearing as well as Deaf and hard of hearing people) that consists of parents, teachers, schools, college/university professors with expertise in special education and deaf education, community members, society as a whole, and most important, the policymakers in government and the MOE. Policy and organizational change are key elements to consider in determining how well the education system will be able to prepare future teachers and current educators in the field who will, in turn, support their own students toward productive lives and careers.

For Deaf and hard of hearing citizens in Singapore to be valued members of society, their hearing peers must recognize their abilities and talents, despite their hearing loss, and must consider them as equal. An inclusive society must look forward and work together to better the lives for the next young generations. The challenge is to significantly invest in the potential of every disabled individual in Singapore.

Advances in technology have led to more reliable screening tools, better diagnostic equipment, and sophisticated hearing devices. In Singapore, as in the United States, hearing loss is common for children and adults. Issues have to be addressed with respect to cochlear implantation and the well-being of the child. In particular, factors such as parental concerns, educational issues, and psychosocial effects need to be considered. Even the psychological trauma of simply undergoing ear surgery should not be overlooked.

The goal is for every Deaf and hard of hearing child to develop his or her language skills to ensure literacy and academic success. As professionals in the field of education, we need to maximize each child's communication skills whether they involve written, spoken, or signed communication. By moving out of the box and learning from current research, especially in the areas of deaf education, bilingualism, second-language acquisition, and cochlear implants, professionals in the field of education and parents can make informed decisions about how to best educate each Deaf and hard of hearing child.

The education of Deaf and hard of hearing students in Singapore depends on how its people build on the experience of the past, learn from the circumstances of the present, and prepare for the challenges of the future. Full support in shaping Singapore for the next generation will have to come from an inclusive community that actively involves both hearing and Deaf and hard of hearing people in Singapore. Working together, they can make their children's future, and their children can then make the future for Singapore.

In that effort, Singapore must avoid repeating mistakes from the past. What can we learn about the status of Deaf and hard of hearing adults in Singapore? Most of the early Deaf and hard of hearing immigrants who came to Singapore did not speak or write English. They used the Shanghainese sign language that originated from Shanghai, China. Other Deaf and hard of hearing immigrants communicated in home signs—gestures that are not understood outside the family because no standardized grammar system guides their expression. Many of these Deaf and hard of hearing adults were left behind by the government. When the government established English as the nation's official language in the 1960s, it failed to set up measures to help assimilate these Deaf and hard of hearing adults into mainstream society. The government made no effort to help Deaf and hard of hearing people acquire skills that, in time, could lead to industry expertise. The average age of the first generation of Deaf and hard of hearing people in Singapore educated in English is only 35.

Today, sign language used among the Deaf and hard of hearing adults in Singapore is a blend of American, Shanghainese, and locally generated signs. A Deaf and hard of hearing adult signing natively in Shanghainese can learn to sign in American Sign Language or in locally generated signs, but will do so with an "accent" and will be identifiable by native signers as an nonnative signer. Similarly, a Deaf and hard of hearing adult using Signed English II can learn to sign in Shanghainese, American Sign Language, or locally generated signs with an "accent." Singapore is not alone in using a mixture of different sign languages. Each country has its own unique sign system. In the United States, each state has different "accents" unique to its culture. Because language is linked to culture, Deaf and hard of hearing ethnic groups in Singapore have developed their own set of signifiers specific to their culture for communication.

The present-day situation for providing social services to Deaf and hard of hearing adults in Singapore is not much better. In general, social services are lacking for this group, and although sign language interpreting is the most common service provided, it is not being implemented on a professional scale. Because sign language interpreting in Singapore is not a specialized profession, most interpreters are volunteers who are untrained and have little or no certification in the skill. Often, their help is limited, but it is all the Deaf and hard of hearing people have. In addition, there is a lack of government or private agency support for hearing parents of Deaf and hard of hearing children. Almost 90% of Deaf and hard of hearing children are born to hearing parents, few of whom know what needs to be done. Many hearing parents turn to doctors, who recommend implants, speech therapy, attendance at schools that use the natural auditory-oral approach method of instruction in the classrooms, or some combination of these strategies.

Deaf and hard of hearing Singaporeans do not enjoy basic rights of access to information. There is no closed captioning on television movie programs. The only captioning service recently introduced by the government, with support by the Media Development Authority in Singapore, are for the news broadcasts—a response to a request from the general public and the Deaf and hard of hearing community. The captions are scripts for prepared news that appear at the same time the presenter reads the news. The government does not mandate closed captioning on television movie channels. There are few movies with English subtitles on Chinese, Malay, or Tamil movie channels. Many television movie programs aired in Singapore are American programs, supplied from American satellite feeds. In the United States, the Americans With Disabilities Act requires closed captioning, but there is no equivalent of the Americans With Disabilities Act in Singapore. Every day, basic rights are ignored. Deaf and hard of hearing adults often say that when they request those rights, the official government response is that demand has not yet reached a critical mass to justify the allocation of such resources. Is providing basic rights viewed as a waste of resources? Is the government ignorant or does it lack compassion? Unfortunately, Singapore is not alone in its alienation of Deaf and hard of hearing people. There are countless other cases in other countries.

The Singapore Association for the Deaf is administered by hearing people. The Singapore Association for the Deaf is a member of the National Council of Social Services/Community Chest of Singapore. It is also affiliated to the World Federation of the Deaf. The mission of the Singapore Association for the Deaf, stated on the organization's Website home page, is "to assist the Deaf to achieve a better quality of life and to enable them to integrate and contribute to society."[5] At present, there is no Singapore Association *of* the Deaf. Although many Deaf and hard of hearing adults are members of the Singapore Association for the Deaf, many of them are jobless in the hearing workplace, and those who do have jobs do not receive satisfaction through the work they are doing. Those Deaf and hard of hearing adults with the same education and experiences as that of their hearing peers are given neither the same job responsibilities nor equal pay. Some Deaf and hard of hearing adults in Singapore say that they are a by-product of a government that made the sensible, economic decision to cultivate only the hearing mainstream. Would the employment situation for Deaf and hard of hearing adults in the hearing mainstream make any difference if there were a vibrant Deaf culture or an association such as The Singapore Association *of* the Deaf, administered by Deaf and hard of hearing people?

In the United States, a deaf or hard or hearing person's success and integration into the hearing society does not require them to hear. Just because someone cannot hear does not mean that he or she cannot be successful. Deaf and hard of hearing adults in Singapore are asking for their basic rights as citizens of a free country to be recognized, honored, and protected. Until that happens, Deaf and hard of hearing adults in Singapore will be forced to settle for less.

REFERENCES

Balakrishnan, V. (2005, December 3). Disability awareness public education. Speech presented at the Disability Awareness and Public Education Carnival, HDB HUB Mall, Singapore. Retrieved July 14, 2006, from http://app.mcys.gov.sg/WEB/corp_speech_story.asp?szMod=corp&szSubMod=speech&qid=2463

Chalmers, J. B. (1990). Teacher training for special education in Singapore. *Australasian Journal of Special Education, 13*, 46–51.

Chia, L. W. (n.d.). Diploma programs. National Institute of Education Web. Retrieved June 24, 2006, from http://www.nie.edu.sg/nieweb/programmes/loading.do?id=Foundation&cid=13467651

Country profile: Singapore. (2006, April 7). *BBC News.* Retrieved May 7, 2006, from http://news.bbc.co.uk/1/hi/world/asia-pacific/country_profiles/1143240.stm

Gopinathan, S. (2001). Globalisation, the state and education policy in Singapore. In J. Tan, S.

5. See the Singapore Association for the Deaf home page (http://www.sadeaf.org.sg).

Gopinathan, & Ho Wah Kam (Eds.), *Challenges facing the Singapore education system today* (pp. 3–17). Singapore: Prentice Hall.

Harris, K. W., & Fernandes, C. (1997). *Third International Mathematics and Science Study. (TIMSS). Second national report. Part 1.* London: National Foundation for Educational Research.

Ho, J. S. M. (2004, January 8). Help for hearing-impaired students. *Strait Times.* Retrieved June 25, 2006, from http://www.moe.gov.sg/forum/2004/forum_letters/13022004.pdf

Lee, K. Y. (1999). *The Singapore story: Memoirs of Lee Kuan Yew.* Upper Saddle River, NJ: Prentice Hall.

Lim, L., & Nam S. S. (2000). Special education in Singapore. *Journal of Special Education, 34*(2), 104–109.

Ministry of Education. (2006). *Nurturing every child: Flexibility and diversity in Singapore schools.* Singapore: Author. Retrieved May 22, 2006, from http://www.moe.gov.sg

Ministry of Education. (2008). *Secondary school courses.* Retrieved October 13, 2008, from http://www.moe.gov.sg/education/secondary/courses

Ministry of Environment and Water Resources. (2005). *Towards environmental sustainability, state of the environment 2005 report.* Singapore: Author. Retrieved May 5, 2006, from http://www.nea.gov.sg/cms/ccird/soe/soe_cover.pdf

Ministry of Information, Communications and the Arts. (2004a). *Early history.* Singapore: Author. Retrieved May 5, 2006, from http://www.sg/explore/history.htm

Ministry of Information, Communication and the Arts. (2004b). *Founding of modern Singapore.* Singapore: Author. Retrieved May 5, 2006, from http://www.sg/explore/history_founding.htm

Ministry of Manpower. (2007). *Employment situation in fourth quarter 2005.* Retrieved October 13, 2008, from http://www.mom.gov.sg/publish/momportal/en/press_room/press_releases/2006/20060201_Employmentsituationinfourthquarter.html

Ministry of Trade and Industry (2005). *Performance of the Singapore Economy in 2005 Report. Ministry of Trade and Industry.* Retrieved May 5, 2006, from http://app.mti.gov.sg/data/article/1962/doc/ESS_2005Ann_%20PR.pdf

National Council of Social Service. (1999). *National Council of Social Service annual report 1998/1999.* Singapore: Author.

National Council of Social Service. (2004). *National Council of Social Service annual report (2003/2004).* Singapore: Author. Retrieved July 3, 2006, http://www.ncss.org.sg/documents/0304fund_DA.pdf

National Council of Social Service. (2005). *National Council of Social Service annual report (2004/2005).* Singapore: Author. Retrieved July 3, 2006, from http://www.ncss.org.sg/documents/0405fund_D&A.pdf

National Council of Social Service. (2006). *National Council of Social Service annual report (2005/2006).* Singapore: Author. Retrieved July 3, 2006, from http://www.ncss.org.sg/documents/0506fund_D&A.pdf

Osman, M. (2005, August 31). *The Official Opening of the NKF CMF-SGH Centre for Hearing and Cochlear Implants and Commemorating SGH's 223rd Cochlear Implantation.* Speech presented at the Official Opening of The NKF CMF-SGH Centre for Hearing and Cochlear Implants, Singapore General Hospital, ENT Centre, Singapore. Retrieved July 14, 2006, from http://www.moh.gov.sg/mohcorp/speeches.aspx?id-1994

Promote Mandarin Council. (2007). *History & Background: Speak Mandarin Campaign.* Retrieved October 13, 2008, from http://www.mandarin.org.sg/site/about-the-campaign/history-background.html

Quah, M. L. M. (1990). Special education in Singapore. *International Journal of Disability, Development and Education, 37,* 137–148.

Quah, M. L. M. (1993). Special education in Singapore. In M. L. M. Quah, S. Gopinathan, & S. C. Chang (Eds.), *A review of practice and research in education for all in Singapore: Country report submitted to the Southeast Asian Research, Review, and Advisory Group (SEARRAG)* (pp. 89–102). Singapore: National Institute of Education.

Qualifications and Curriculum Authority. (2005, July 18). *Singapore: Organization and control of education system.* Singapore: Author. Retrieved May 8, 2006, from http://www.inca.org.uk/singapore-organisation-mainstream.html

Rao, S. M. (1998). *Beliefs and attitudes of pre-service teachers toward teaching children with disabilities.* Unpublished master's thesis, National Institute of Education, Nanyang Technological University, Singapore.

Rao, S. M., & Lim, L. (1999). *Beliefs and attitudes of pre-service teachers toward teaching children with disabilities.* Paper presented at the annual conference of the American Association of Mental Retardation, New Orleans, LA. (ERIC Document Reproduction Service No. ED433655)

Shanmugaratnam, T. (2005, September 22). *Achieving quality: Bottom up initiative, top down support.* Address presented at the Ministry of Education work plan seminar at Ngee Ann Polytechnic Convention Centre, Singapore. Retrieved June 24, 2006, from http://www.moe.gov.sg/speeches/2005/sp20050922.htm

Singapore Department of Statistics. (2005, July). *Key indicators of resident population by ethnic group* [Table]. In *Census of population 2000: Demographic characteristics* (p. viii). Retrieved May 7, 2006, from http://www.singstat.gov.sg/pubn/popn/c2000sr1/cop2000sr1.pdf

Singapore heads school test table. (2004, December 15). Retrieved May 10, 2006, from *BBC* News Web site: http://news.bbc.co.uk/1/hi/education/4092133.stm

Taylor, R. (1997). *Fall of Malaya and Singapore.* Retrieved May 5, 2006, from http://www.britain-at-war.org.uk/WW2/Malaya_and_Singapore/body_index.htm

U.S. Library of Congress. (1977). *Road to independence.* Retrieved May 6, 2006, from http://countrystudies.us/singapore/10.htm

Yamashita, M. (Ed.). (2002). Singapore education sector analysis: Improvement and challenges in academic performance in our ethnic groups in singapore. Paper presented at the Annual Meeting of the Comparative and International Education Society, Orlando, Florida. (ERIC Document Reproduction Service No. ED473030)

Deaf Education in South Korea

Sung-Kyu Choi

SOUTH KOREA is located in northern East Asia, bounded by North Korea to north, Japan to the east and south, and China to the west. South Korea has indicated remarkable economic growth during the past few decades; however, because of the financial crisis in 1997, its economic growth has slowed. The country has a population of 48.4 million (2007 figure), and approximately 85% of the population lives in urban areas.

South Korea is a democratic country. Its history goes back 5,000 years. The earliest trial country, Ancient Chosen, was founded by Dan Goon. And the Ancient Chosen was replaced by the Three Kingdoms—Silla, Backjae, and Goguryo in approximately 10 BC. The unification of the country was begun by the Silla kingdom in 668 AD. The Silla kingdom was replaced by powerful Koryo dynasty in the 10th century. The next country was the Chosen dynasty, which began in the 14th century. Japan invaded and subsequently controlled the Korea peninsula from 1910 to 1945.

After Japan's defeat in World War II, Korea procured liberty in 1945; however, the country was divided into two zones. The zone north of the 38th parallel was under Soviet domination, and the southern zone was under the Americans. After being divided into two zones, South Korea became the Republic of Korea. The Republic of Korea is a constitutional country comprising 15 administrative units: the metropolis of Seoul, six other metropolitan cities, and nine provinces. The capital of South Korea is Seoul, which held the Olympic Games in 1988 and is home to half of the population of South Korea.

South Korea was traditionally an agrarian society until 1962 when the country initiated a series of 5-year economic development plans. The economy of South Korea is based on industrialization, producing electronics, autos, chemicals, ships, textiles, and clothing. The country has limited natural resources. The GNP in 2005 was US$16,291, which is ranked 10th in the world. The statistics data describing the religious affiliations of the total population (25,176,274) from 1995 to 2005 indicated that 10,726,463 (42.6%) of the population practiced Buddhism, 5,146,146 (20.44%) practiced Catholicism, 8,616,438 (34.2%) practiced other forms of Christianity, and 104,575 (0.4%) practiced Confucianism. Regardless of the religious statistics, however, South Korea is a single-culture society that is rooted in Confucianism. Most Koreans still believe that Confucianism expresses the traditional spiritual identification for Korea (Choi, 1995).

In the traditional education system in Korea, *Taehak*, which means "great school," is the first school founded by Goguryo in 372 AD. The name was later changed to *Kukhak*. The purpose of the school was to teach Confucian ideology and Buddhism to provide moral education to the public. A few private institutes were established to educate members of the succeeding dynasties; however, the private schools flourished during the Goguryo and the Yi dynasties. The private schools, widespread in local areas, still existed after modern schools were introduced in the late 19th century.

When Korea became independent in 1945, after being ruled for 35 years, South Korea replaced the Japanese colonial education system. The Korean government, the Republic of Korea, in 1948 enacted an education law to set the ground for democracy. A linear school system of elementary (6 years), middle (3 years), high (3 years), and university (4 years) was adopted.

Since that time, South Korea's education system has changed and reformed. In the 1960s and 1970s, the education system changed to contribute to national development. In the 1980s, the emphasis of education shifted from "education for economic growth" to "education for the sake of education." The kindergarten school system comprises 1 to 3 years of preparatory education. Because of the new wave of globalization and the open-door trend in world educational politics, the education system in South Korea had to be readjusted again in the 1990s (UNESCO, 1998). The South Korean government began to secure 5% of the GNP for educational financing. In the 2000s, educational policy in South Korea adopted the systems of adequate yearly progress and teacher evaluation that are similar to those in the No Child Left Behind legislation in the United States.

South Korea's types of educational institutions include kindergartens, elementary schools, middle schools, high schools (trade schools, trade high schools, civic schools, and civic high schools), special schools, and colleges and universities. The gross enrollment rate of institutions higher than kindergarten is considerably high: 99% in elementary schools, 99.3% in middle schools, 98.8% in high schools, and 40.9% at the tertiary level. More than 11.6 million students are enrolled in school.

The Presidential Commission on Education Reform was set up in February 1994 to reform the entire system of education in South Korea. The purpose of the education reform commission is to eliminate the weakness of the existing education system, to ensure leadership in the information and globalization era, and to establish the future directions for educational policies. The new education system seeks to create a lifelong and open-learning society. The main tasks of education reform can be summarized in three parts: (a) development of a creative and humanistic personality; (b) harmony between autonomy and competition; and (c) establishment of learner-centered education system (UNESCO, 1998).

Special Education in South Korea

Many references to people with disabilities can be found as early as 930 AD (Kim, 1994). However, Korean special education as an educational service for people with disabilities was founded in 1894 (Ann, 1994; Kim & Yeo, 1976) by Mrs. Rosetta Sherwood Hall, an American protestant missionary and physician. Four years later, she also founded Pyungyang Girls' School for the Blind. The first public special institution to educate blind and deaf children was established in 1913 (Ann, 1994; Daegu University Special Education Research Center, 1981; Kim & Yeo, 1976; Seo, Oakland, Han, & Hu, 1992). "Education for children with disabilities started in the 1960s when the first personnel preparation program for special education professionals was established at Han-Kuk Social Work University (later renamed as Daegu University) with several special schools affiliated to the university" (Park, 2002, p. 29).

Daegu University, a unique academic institution, was the first private school in South Korea that catered specifically to blind and deaf students. Since its foundation, it has expanded to serve students with other disabilities, running five separate schools on its campus.

Because of the influence of mainstreaming, South Korea made great progress in providing special education in the 1980s, effectively increasing the special education classes. Today, special education in South Korea has a pattern similar to that of the United States. The current trend is to emphasize the importance of full inclusion in special education.

It is estimated that there are about 1,449,000 people with disabilities in South Korea, which is about 3% of the population (Park, 2002). However, because of cultural influences, the number of registered people with disabilities is far fewer than the actual number of people with disabilities. Confucianism emphasizes respect for elders and order, and the authority of leaders still affects the attitudes of the families who have children or adults (or both) with disabilities (Choi, 1995; Kwon, 2005). The Korean Ministry of Health and Welfare cautiously estimates the number of the people with disabilities to be about 4.5%. They based their estimate on data from the schools. As of 2006, there were 3,166 classes and 5,911 teachers at 143 special schools in South Korea. Of those 143 schools, 12 (8.4%) are schools for blind students, 18 (12.6%) are schools for deaf students, 88 (61.5%) are schools for developmentally disabled students, 18 (12.6%) are schools for physically disabled students, and 7 (4.9%) are schools for emotionally disturbed students. In addition, 62.2% of the 143 schools are private special schools (Ministry of Education, 2006). Private schools have a major role in the special and general education of the Korean people and contribute significantly to development of special education in South Korea (UNESCO, 1998).

Today, there are 32,506 school-aged students at 5,204 special classes in 4,171 general schools. There are 5,348 special teachers and 3,074 teacher assistants. Also there are 6,741 students with disabilities in full inclusion environments with general teachers and 569 teacher assistants. The numbers of the students with disabilities who are included in general education classrooms in general education schools between 2002 and 2008 are provided in Table 7.1 (Ministry of the Education, 2008).

Table 7.1 suggests some considerations for future direction and efforts on better educational services for students with disabilities in South Korea. More than 65% of the students with disabilities are attending full-inclusion educational settings. Special education has been changing, increasing inclusion of students with disabilities, and it seems that increasing numbers of the students with disabilities will be included in general education classrooms in the future. Table 7.1 also indicates that the trend of special education in South Korea, including education those with multiple disabilities, is toward inclusive education in regular schools (Kim, 2005).

Table 7.1. Numbers of Students With Disabilities in Special Schools and General Education Environments Between 2002 and 2006

Year	Number of disabled students in special schools	Number of disabled students in general schools	Total disabled students
2002	24,276 (44.6%)	30,194 (55.4%)	54,470 (100%)
2003	24,192 (45.3%)	29,212 (54.7%)	53,404 (100%)
2004	23,762 (42.9%)	31,612 (57.1%)	55,374 (100%)
2005	23,449 (40.2%)	34,913 (59.8%)	58,362 (100%)
2006	23,291 (37.2%)	39,247 (62.8%)	62,538 (100%)
2007	22,963 (34.8%)	42,977 (65.2%)	65,940 (100%)
2008	23,400 (32.7%)	48,084 (67.3%)	71,484 (100%)

Legislation for Individuals With Disabilities in South Korea

Education for the people with disabilities in South Korea is ensured by the Education Law, which was mandated in 1949, and by the Special Education Promotion Program Act, first enacted in 1977 and reauthorized and amended as necessary in 1987, 1990, 1994, 1995, 1997, 2000, 2002, and 2005. It emphasizes the free and appropriate education for students with special needs. However, in 2008 the new law, Special Law for People with Disabilities and So Forth, was mandated to upgrade the rights for the people with disabilities. Students with health impairments and autistic impairments are added in the category of the people with disabilities. Also the name of the speech impairment is changed to communication impairment, and the name of the physical disabilities is changed to physical impairments. And if the people with disabilities who are old regardless with ages of the school want to study at the school, it is accepted to give them a chance to be educated in the school environments.

The Rehabilitation Act, also called the Disability Welfare Law, was mandated in 1989 and defines *individual with disabilities*. It also describes the responsibilities of government and local agencies for ensuring the welfare of people with disabilities and specifies disability registration, financial support, and support for development and dissemination of assistive technology devices. Additional relevant legislation includes the following:

- The Employment Promotion Act for the Disabled, enacted in 1990—guarantees vocational rehabilitation and 2% quota system for people with disabilities
- The Disabled, The Aged, and The Pregnant Convenience Promotion Act, mandated in 1997—ensures the accessibility to facilities, equipment and devices, and information in the community
- Child Welfare Act, legislated in 1981—emphasizes healthy pregnancy and delivery, child protection from abuse and neglect, child health and safety, and guardianship
- Mental Health Law of 1995—mandated appropriate treatment and rehabilitative assistance for people with mental health problems and the rights of patients with mental illness who are placed in hospital and institutions (Park, 2002; UNESCO, 1998)

Curriculum for Students With Disabilities

Curricula for students with disabilities have changed since the Education Law, which was mandated in 1949. Today, there are two different systems of curricula for students with disabilities: the curriculum for general education (which is used also for blind, deaf, and physically disabled students) and the special curriculum for students with disabilities (which was developed for students with developmental disabilities). Deaf students are taught by the curriculum for general education for 10 years. After 10 years, the deaf students can select the next level general education curriculum for at least two more years. Most teachers who are working with deaf, blind, and physically disabled students report that the curriculum for general education is not suitable; however, the Ministry of Education mandated the existing education laws.

Certification System for Special Teachers

About 40 universities in South Korea have a department of special education. However most universities, except the Daegu University, do not divide the department according to the different levels such as early childhood, elementary, and secondary but have just one department, either early childhood, elementary special education, or early childhood and elementary special education.

One can get special teacher certification through college-level programs and through graduate-level programs. On the college level, any of the 40 universities mentioned above can award special teacher certification to the students who fulfill the requirements of the program. On the graduate school level, programs in education or special education can award special school teacher certification to students who already have general school teacher certification. However, if a graduate student has certification for general kindergarten, for example, the student can get special teacher certification only for kindergarten, not for the level of the elementary and secondary education.

Before 2001, special teacher certifications were divided into the four types of disabilities: developmentally disabled, blind, deaf, and physically disabled. However, there was no teacher certification for those teaching students with emotional disorders. After 2001, the system for special teacher certification was changed. New special school teacher certification is divided into four education categories—early childhood, elementary, secondary, and therapeutic special teacher—and not the disability groupings. Therefore, the universities changed their curricula for special education. As a result, the broad courses for special education are offered to the students who will work for students with disabilities. This system for special teacher certification may be unique in the world.

In South Korea, all schools for disabilities have changed rapidly and remarkably since 1998. Specifically, three changes have improved the chances that children with disabilities will obtain an education that meets their goals and needs. The first change was that most general schools adopted a philosophy of inclusion to more easily accept children with disabilities. The second was that all special schools for children who are deaf, blind, or physically disabled have to use the same curriculum as schools for nondisabled students. Third, all special school teaching licenses are the same and are no longer divided into specific disability designations. These changes have helped prepare all special teachers and teachers of nondisabled students to enhance the education of children with disabilities.

SOCIAL ATTITUDES TOWARD DEAF PEOPLE

Not all Koreans respond truthfully about the occurrence of deafness within the population. Even though some people have a member of the family with a disability, many of them may deny this fact. This way of thinking is related to Korean culture. The following account illustrates the negative perception of deaf people among South Koreans:

I know many families who have Deaf people. But they want to hide the Deaf family member from others. For example, my friend's father, a bank manager, would introduce all of his children to new acquaintances except for his Deaf child, who had to stay in his room. . . . One day I visited a Deaf friend and communicated with Sign Language. My friend's father called us urgently to come inside the house. The father was worried that other people were watching us sign. (Kang, 1989, p. 25)

Korea is a single-culture society, unlike the United States. Korean attitudes toward people with disabilities may be generated from cultural characteristics or biases. Cho (1985) and Kim (1990) investigated the Korean societal attitudes toward people with disabilities through analysis of Korean novels and written folktales. They concluded that the Korean people view people with disabilities with sympathy, but also perceive them as insufficient, an inconvenience, or generally incompetent. Unfortunately, little, if any direct research has been conducted in Korea with respect to either the cultural effect of disabilities or social attitudes with respect to disabilities. A possible explanation for this lack of research may be that most researchers do not understand the importance of investigating the relationships between social structure and people with special needs because, within a country with a single culture, this group is not perceived as a separate or deviant social group (Choi, 1995).

DEAF EDUCATION IN SOUTH KOREA

In 1947, at the insistence of Beckweon Yoon, the principal of the Seoul National School for the Blind and Deaf, teachers began to use the manual alphabet in educating deaf students. At the same time, Yongmuk Kim taught his deaf children using the oral method (Ann, 1994; Daegu University Special Education Research Center, 1981; Kim & Yeo, 1976; Seo et al., 1992).

Today, there are 20 schools for deaf students in South Korea: 1 is national, 4 are public, and 15 are private. All 20 schools provide instruction for preschool, elementary, and middle students, and 15 provide instruction also at the high school level. Eleven of them are residential schools. In total, there are 2,806 deaf children and 668 teachers. Of the 668 teachers in 2006, 56 taught preschool, 164 taught elementary, 363 taught middle and high school, and 85 functioned as superintendents, audiologists, counselors, and school nurses. Since 2006, two oral schools also have been established in South Korea, but they are not for high school students.

Education Practices

Most deaf children score in the third or fourth degree on standard achievement tests in reading and writing abilities, prompting educators to focus on which methodology is best for deaf students to increase their literacy achievement. During the past few years, the bilingual-bicultural approach (known as 2Bi in South Korea) has emerged as an important educational phenomenon that could lead to a radical restructuring of deaf education in South Korea. However, that approach is not easily accepted because Korea is a single-culture society; thus, what would be the first and second language for the deaf person? Many South Korean educators believe that Korean Sign Language (KSL) merely translates the Korean language into a form of the language that deaf children can see and that the 2Bi approach is a sign language teaching method. In the standard test for hearing students in South Korea, language achievement levels for deaf children of both KSL and Korean are below the third-grade level of hearing children, despite having the same curriculum. However, that test result does not mean that the deaf child's cognitive and thinking processing are limited to the third-grade level.

Many guarantee that the 2Bi approach will help deaf children improve not only their reading and writing abilities but also their quality of life and human identity. Sign language is a visual language that helps deaf people to connect to the larger community. Therefore, sign language is a key factor in success and a valuable tool in the life of deaf children.

The 2Bi approach is important for deaf children for two reasons. To understand the first reason, one must recognize how the differences between KSL and Korean influence the deaf identity. Most Korean teachers who are working with deaf students think that KSL is the wrong language. KSL is different from Korean, but it is not wrong. The Korean 2Bi teaching method, based on a linguistic approach to sign language, helps overcome linguistic and identity confusion for the deaf.

The second reason why the 2Bi approach is important is that linguistic differences increase the speed at which isolation occurs in inclusion environments and hearing society. Insufficient Korean language achievement does not have to translate to a lower quality of life as human beings.

Despite the importance of the 2Bi approach, however, there are three problems obstructing its development for the deaf children in South Korea. First, all children with or without disabilities have to study the same curriculum for 10 years. After 10 years, children can select a curriculum for two years that is divided into academic or vocational high school levels. The ultimate effect is that, in fact, deaf children study a hearing school curriculum for 12 years. Most deaf children cannot study effectively at grade level in a oral-aural environment. In schools for the deaf, however, the gaps are lower and the grades are higher. Many researchers and teachers for the deaf have disagreed whether the hearing curriculum is sufficient for deaf children.

The second problem is that there is a "language" subject in the schools for the deaf in South Korea, but not in the curriculum for the deaf in the hearing schools. Language is an important subject for deaf children. Any mention of a "language" subject in the school curriculum for the deaf creates a discrepancy in the philosophy of inclusion.

The third problem is that Korea is a single-culture society, an environment that produces experiences related to deeply rooted thoughts. Deaf children may have to suffer to overcome the differences they experience between themselves and the hearing society in a single-culture society.

There are many reasons why the 2Bi approach is accepted to develop sign/written language and human identity for deaf children. However, deaf education in South Korea faces difficult obstacles to developing the 2Bi approach for deaf children because of misunderstandings about inclusion, upper-level curriculum for deaf children, and cultural philosophies about sign language as a first language (Choi, 2005).

School-Based Curriculum

Even though many schools for deaf students do not develop an effective curriculum for the deaf students, one deaf school (A school) has attempted to increase the social and educational achievement with a school-based curriculum that contains the various characteristics of the 2Bi approach. The A school was one of the oral schools; however, the A school changed its teaching philosophy for deaf students. The A school for the deaf teaches KSL to the parents of the deaf students beginning at the kindergarten level. The curriculum is similar to 2Bi approach methods. The students of the A school for the deaf indicate that the academic achievement is higher than for those of other schools for the deaf.

The deaf students are divided into three steps: basic, developing, and advanced. The curriculum for each of the three steps varies according to the degree of the hearing loss and language development. Most activities are carried out in large, middle, and small groups as well as individually. In the basic step, teachers apply a team teaching approach for the students. According to the development of the students, open teaching is carried out in more advanced steps. All teachers of the A school participate to develop the school-based curriculum together. The A school demonstrates a successful effort to teach deaf students effectively (S. W. Kwon, 2005).

Postsecondary Education for the Deaf

There are many colleges and universities throughout the country. Priority is given to students with disabilities who want to study at colleges or universities. There are 4,119 students with disabilities enrolling in these colleges and universities; however, the number of deaf students among them is not high. Nevertheless, there is one national college for students with disabilities, including those who are deaf—Korean National College of Rehabilitation and Welfare, unique vocational college for students with disabilities in South Korea. About 40 deaf students are studying at the college. Vocational education and training is offered by technical college and occupational training centers under the Ministry of Labor and by private institutions. The Ministry of Labor mandates that the companies that have employed more than 20 people should give at least 2% of working opportunities to people with disabilities. Many deaf people want to get a professional job, not an unskilled or semiskilled job.

Deaf Community in South Korea

The function of Deaf organizations in South Korea is the same or very similar to Deaf communities in the United States. Deaf society in Korea is made up of many small local organizations.

In 1981, the Korea Association of the Deaf was established in Seoul. Ki-Chang Kim was selected as the president of the association. The organization's objectives are (a) to support a Parents Association for the Deaf that was established by the Korea Association of the Deaf, (b) to publish a journal named *Chung-Eum* (Clear Sounds) for education and social welfare for the Deaf, and (c) to lobby congress for legal support and civil rights (Handbook for Hearing Impaired, 1991).

Since the organization was established, the social rights of Deaf people have been protected. Furthermore, Deaf culture in Korea is perpetuated through the unified power of the association in Korean society. The objectives of the Korea Association of the Deaf, like American Deaf organizations, are strongly related to promoting Deaf culture (Choi, 1995).

Korean Sign Language

KSL was used in the field of deaf education when the first deaf school was established in South Korea in 1909 (Ann, 1994; Daegu University Special Education Research Center, 1981; Kim & Yeo, 1976; Seo et al., 1992). American missionaries might even have used a sign language to teach the deaf students (Handbook for Hearing Impaired, 1991). However, no evidence suggests that KSL was influenced by ASL. For example, terms such as *school, study, desk, chair, teacher,* and *student,* are different in ASL compared with KSL. It is assumed that American missionaries who established the first school for the deaf did not teach ASL. However, KSL has a few connections with other Asian sign languages used in Japan and China. KSL, as well as other sign languages, have dialects, just like all spoken languages, and they are important cultural factors that identify Deaf people.

A committee was established in 2004 to publish the KSL dictionary that contains about 6,800 entries. The committee discussed the terminology related with KSL and regulation for the KSL lexicon. However, the committee did not discuss possibilities for KSL linguistic research.

South Korea actually has two different sign languages. One is the natural sign language of KSL, and the other one is a Korean-based sign language. Deaf education in South Korea went to ruin by the influences of Total Communication. Even though the underlying philosophy of Total Communication is valid, most Korean deaf school teachers and researchers misunderstood that the sign language they used with that method was Korean-based and that the oral method requires more than just a loud voice (Choi, 2004).

FUTURE EFFORTS

To eliminate the weakness of the existing deaf education system and to ensure the quality of the life in the information and globalization era, South Korea will need to consider four challenges (Choi, 2008). First, the families of deaf students face special challenges. Therefore, there should be organizations from which the families can receive support and necessary information. Currently, there are not enough parent support and advocacy groups for families who want information, services, and support. As a result, many hearing parents of deaf children do not know the effect of sign language on the development of thought and cognition. Parents also misunderstand that the oral method is the best approach to develop language for their children.

The second challenge is that deaf educators, the Deaf community, and the government need to conduct linguistic research on KSL. This work may be not easy. However, without it, deaf education and the Deaf community cannot be guaranteed quality education and quality of life. Language is an important factor in passing on the culture from generation to generation. In addition, education reflects the culture. Therefore, South Koreans have to identify, describe, and understand the linguistic characteristics of KSL. Even though the 2Bi approach is one excellent method by which to improve deaf students' literacy, its effectiveness depends on linguistic research being conducted on KSL.

The third challenge is that, for deaf education, the teacher preparation programs, teacher retraining programs, or both should be considered in terms of the various issues described above. In particular, these programs should seriously consider the results that the A school achieved with its curriculum that takes a bilingual-bicultural approach and should modify their teacher training programs to benefit from that school's success. In particular, the programs should consider how to teach language for deaf children in early childhood and how to assess language development for deaf students. Deaf educators and the government need to develop assessment materials that will enable deaf students to demonstrate what they truly know.

Finally, the forth challenge is to carefully consider the movement toward full inclusion, which is a worldwide educational phenomenon. Full inclusion is an educational method, not an educational purpose. Therefore, South Korea should ensure that the knowledge and skills it uses to teach deaf students are effective regardless of the environment. In addition, because of full inclusion, the characteristics of the deaf schools are changing. Many deaf students are moving to the general education environment. As a result, the deaf students who have additional disabilities will tend to increase in the schools for the deaf. To provide appropriate special education services and related services for the deaf students with multiple disabilities in the schools for the deaf, South Korea must consider the use of modified curriculums, connections with educational support centers, and developmental methods for facilitating teaching and learning.

REFERENCES

Ann, B. J. (1994). History of special education in Korea. *Journal of Special Education, 15,* 129–184.

Cho, Y. S. (1985). *A study of the view of the Korean toward the handicapped from the written folktale: On the views toward the blind.* Unpublished master's thesis, Dankook University, Seoul, South Korea.

Choi, S. K. (1995). *Cross-cultural attitudes toward deaf culture in a multi- and singular cultural society: A survey of residential school based teachers for the deaf who are deaf and hearing.* Unpublished doctoral dissertation, Ball State University, Indiana, United States.

Choi, S. K. (2004). *Teaching language for students with disabilities.* Tageu, South Korea: Korean Speech Hearing Language Association.

Choi, S. K. (2005). Longitudinal study on deaf school teachers' attitudes toward deaf culture. *The Journal of Special Education: Theory and Practice, 6*(1), 57–76.

Choi, S. K. (2008). Tasks and prospects on deaf education in South Korea. The 15th International Seminar & 2008 Audiology Seminar (pp. 3–23). Korean Institute for Special Education & Korean Academy of Audiology, Oct. 21, 2008, Seoul, Korea.

Daegu University Special Education Research Center. (1981). *The present situation and issues of special education in Korea.* Daegu, South Korea: Daegu University.

Kang, J. H. (1989). *Deaf: Who are them?* Korea: Chang-Rok Sa.

Kim, B., & Yeo, K. (1976). *Special education in Korea.* Dageu, Korea: Korea Social Work College. (Eric Document Reproduction Service No. ED138026)

Kim, H. J. (2005). Educational supports for children with multiple disability in Korea. *Journal of Special Education in the Asia Pacific 1,* 14–20. Available at http://www.nise.go.jp/PDF/JSEAP-4.pdf

Kim, M. S. (1990). *A view of the handicapped as expressed in Korean novel.* Unpublished master's thesis, Dageu University, Dageu, Korea.

Kim, Y. H. (1994). Today in special education in Korea. *Journal of Special Education, 15,* 191–209.

Kwon, H. (2005). Inclusion in South Korea: The current situation and directions. *International Journal of Disabilities, Development and Education, 52*(1), 59–68.

Kwon, S. W. (2005). *The qualitative case study on the restructuring of a deaf school curriculum.* Unpublished doctoral dissertation, Daegu University, South Korea.

Ministry of Education and Human Resources Development. (2008). Research on special education in 2008. Seoul, South Korea: Author.

Park, J. Y. (2002). Special education in South Korea. *Teaching Exceptional Children, 34,* 28–33.

Seo, G., Oakland, T., Han, H., & Hu, S. (1992). Special education in South Korea. *Exceptional Children, 58,* 213–218.

UNESCO. (1998). Education management profile: Republic of Korea. Bangkok: UNESCO Principal Regional Office for Asia and the Pacific.

Middle East and Africa

Deaf Education in Israel

Tova Most, Amatzia Weisel, and Shay Ezrachi

THE STATE of Israel received its independence 60 years ago, in 1948. Israel is a small country on the eastern shore of the Mediterranean Sea with an area of about 20,000 square kilometers. The population of 7.3 million people includes many Jewish immigrants who moved to Israel from all around the world. New immigrants came to Israel mainly from Eastern Europe before the establishment of the state, from Arab-Muslims countries during the 1950s, from various countries including Western Europe and North and South America in the 1970s, and mainly from the former Soviet Union in the 1990s. There is a large minority of Arab-Palestinians citizens, about 20% of the Israeli population, most of whom are Muslims. Hebrew and Arabic are the two formal languages of the state.

Israel's educational system is characterized by religious, social, and education factors and can be broken down into four principal sectors: general state (secular) education (about 45%), religious state education (14%), Independent/Orthodox education (18%), and Arab education (23%). Despite the fact that the majority of education in Israel is financed from the state's budget, the great divisions in the educational system make it difficult to implement a unified and general educational policy, a situation that also affects the education of the deaf and hard of hearing children (Weisel, 2001).

In spite of the fact that physical distances between the center and periphery of Israel are relatively small compared with such distances in other countries, access to educational and rehabilitation services often can still be problematic. As a result, deaf and hard of hearing students throughout the country and in the different sectors are sometimes unable to receive equivalent levels of educational and rehabilitation services, resulting in students from a certain sector having to study in the system of another sector.

Educational programs for deaf and hard of hearing students have existed in Israel ever since the beginning of the 1930s. In the beginning, there was only one school in which most of the deaf and hard of hearing students were educated. In time, additional educational programs were established, their numbers increasing with the years, and today, there is a complex and varied system that attempts to fulfill the various and different needs of deaf and hard of hearing students.

With time, many significant changes gradually occurred in this system, particularly in two main areas: students' placement in the different educational programs and access to modern medical technologies. In addition, changes took place with respect to the physical conditions within the educational programs, the professional level of the educators, and the communication clinicians as well as with respect to the educational goals and support services provided within the various educational programs for deaf and hard of hearing students. For a long time, the educational programs for deaf and hard of hearing students did not experience many significant changes. A process of significant changes occurred in the perception of special education in Israel, has been taking place only during the past 20 years, gradually moving from normalization to inclusion, a move that has also had an effect on the education for deaf and hard of hearing students.

HISTORY

For hundreds of years, normative society throughout the world has tended to ignore children with special needs. They have been considered to be handicapped, inferior, and unable to be educated. The establishment of educational frameworks for children with special needs resulted from a feeling of social obligation and from the recognition of effective educational and rehabilitation interventions. Earlier special education systems were established on the assumption that students with special needs cannot be integrated into general schools, and therefore, they need special education programs. The first educational programs for such children were established in Israel in the beginning of the 20th century and were based on that assumption. The first special education schools were established by voluntary organizations as separate educational programs for blind, for developmentally disabled, and for deaf children (Al-Yagon & Margalit, 2001).

No organized educational programs for deaf children existed in Israel before 1932. Wealthy families sent their children to the Institution for Deaf and Dumb Jewish children in Berlin (Der Israelitischen Taubstummenanstalt). However, because most of the parents were unable to bear the heavy expense involved in educating their children abroad, this solution was not a realistic one for most of the children, and therefore, most were left with no educational option at all (Meir & Sandler, 2004; Plaut, 2007).

In November 1932, the first Jewish school for the deaf was established in Jerusalem—Kol Yisrael Chaverim. Deaf children of all ages, as young as age 4 years, came to the institution from throughout the country. The students who came from outside of Jerusalem boarded with families in the city. In accordance with educational philosophy prevalent in Germany, where the founders of the school were educated, teachers in the school taught through the use of speech, vehemently objecting to the use of sign language. Approximately 10 years after the establishment of the school in Jerusalem, additional schools for deaf and hard of hearing students began to appear, first in other big cities and, later, in their periphery.

In 1941, the Niv School for the Deaf was opened in Tel Aviv, which is now the largest city in the country. The school gradually grew from one to eight classes, teaching children ranging in age from 6 to 14. The school principal, Ms. Betti Miller, introduced oral communication in the school by developing speech, taking advantage of any residual hearing, and emphasizing the study of basic concepts. In 1952, the first kindergarten for deaf and hard of hearing children was opened, where children ages 3 to 6 could study. A year later (1953), Dr. Ezra Korin, an ear, nose, and throat (ENT) specialist, established a voluntary organization, called MICHA—Educators of Deaf Children, to ensure the education and rehabilitation of preschool children with hearing impairments. The first MICHA center was opened in Tel Aviv, and over the years, eight additional similar centers have been opened in various places in Israel, including two centers in the Arab sector and two in the Orthodox sector. In the beginning, it was decided that the oral approach would be the sole method of communication between staff members and the deaf and hard of hearing children. Since the 1940s and until the early 1980s, the oral method was dominant, partly because of the initial intensive involvement of

ENT physicians in the establishment of various educational and rehabilitation services and partly because of the role of communication clinicians (speech-language pathologists) within the educational system. With the passage of time, changes occurred and the Total Communication approach was adopted in many programs, mainly in the special schools and the special classes for deaf and hard of hearing students (Zweibel, 1999).

The distances between the peripheral regions and the central part of the country created a situation in which many children who had hearing impairments and resided in outlying areas were left without a suitable educational program. This fact compelled decision makers in the Ministry of Education to establish a local educational programs for hearing impaired children. In 1957, a school for deaf children was opened in Beer-Sheba, the main city in the southern part of Israel. In the beginning, the school had only one mixed-aged classroom with 10 children ages 3 to 9 in attendance. In time, the school's enrolment increased; by 1966, there were already four classes. In 1963, the Yodfat School opened in Upper Nazareth, located in the northern part of the country. Quite often, the learning conditions within these educational programs in remote areas were particularly demanding. The schools lacked basic equipment and enrolled only a small number of students, which is why the ages within classes were mixed. The low socioeconomic status of many of the students' families made the teachers' work very difficult. In addition, most of the teachers had not had any previous training in teaching students with hearing impairments.

All of the programs for children with hearing impairments were established by people originating from the European schools of thought, which were greatly influenced by medical pedagogy. Communication was verbal, and great emphasis was placed on the acquisition of a spoken language by speechreading and developing speech. Plaut (2007) claimed that those schools were mainly the work of the people who headed them (the principals). They were responsible for establishing the first schools, and they were the ones who determined not only the emphases and the priorities in the schools but also their prevalent atmosphere. The principals waged an ongoing battle with the various local authorities, who for their part did not show much understanding or compassion for the special needs of the students with hearing impairments. The harsh physical conditions under which the educational institutions operated and their frequent moves from one place to another testify to the low estimation in which the authorities held the education of students with hearing impairments.

In the first 15 years of the State of Israel, deaf and hard of hearing students were segregated in the newly established schools and kindergartens, and there was no connection between them and hearing children studying in the general educational programs. During the early 1960s, a movement took root in the Western world and in Israel to include students with special needs within the regular education frameworks. This direction also found expression in the education of students with hearing impairments. The move from isolation to inclusion brought about the establishment of special classes for deaf and hard of hearing students in general schools and an ongoing increase in the number of deaf and hard of hearing students who were individually integrated into regular classes with hearing peers.

Within the framework of "individual integration," deaf and hard of hearing students studied as individuals in general local kindergartens and schools along with hearing children. Within the framework of "group integration," special classes were established for children with hearing impairments within general schools or kindergartens. The children studied in special classrooms and were included in parallel general classes on an individual basis, based on their capabilities. The objective of these programs was to expose students with hearing impairments to a learning and communication environment with hearing children and to raise their level of academic achievement. From 1961, when the first 12 deaf and hard of hearing students were integrated into a general school, until now, the number of students in integrated groups (special classes within general schools) and especially in individual integration steadily increased (Plaut, 2007).

During the early 1960s, the first inclusive programs for deaf and hard of hearing students integrated only those students possessing high learning, language, and communication abilities. During those first years, the general schools were not truly aware either of the difficulties faced by deaf and hard of hearing students or of their special needs. The principle that guided the inclusion step was based on the concept that a student with a hearing impairment had to adapt him- or herself to the study requirements of the general classrooms. When participating in lessons in the general classrooms, the students with hearing impairments had to deal on their own with what was being said during the lesson, receiving very little support from the classroom teachers during or after the lessons.

Most of the deaf and hard of hearing students were unable to be successfully integrated in art and science subjects. The vast majority of the children and youths who were individually included with hearing students in the kindergartens and the general schools were hard of hearing, able to speechread, and able to speak, and they, too, found the studies difficult and required help. In the beginning, the Ministry of Education did not provide them with any help, and their parents had to pay for remedial tutoring with private teachers. This situation became a financial burden on the parents. Those parents who did not have the money were unable to bear the heavy cost of such support, and their children did not get suitable help (Plaut, 2007). As a result, in 1967, Dr. Mazor, an ENT specialist, and a group of volunteer parents established the SHEMA organization, designed to help students with hearing impairments who are included in elementary and secondary schools with their studies and their rehabilitation. In time, the SHEMA organization provided help for students who were individually included, and today, children with hearing impairments are tutored by trained teachers for the hearing impaired. The tutoring provided takes the form of two possible models: (a) the students receive help within the general education framework from itinerant teachers of students with hearing impairments and (b) tutoring is provided in the afternoons in an educational center that specializes in teaching students with hearing impairments. Over the years, deaf and hard of hearing students with additional problems, including children with learning difficulties, children with ADHD, and those with emotional problems, began to be accepted in the special classes (group integration) and even for individual integration. When the number of such students greatly grew in the late 1980s, the branches of SHEMA, which had been established in some of the major cities, undertook to organize the tutoring and to train teachers to work with students with hearing impairments (Zweibel, 1999).

The Israeli Special Education Law was passed in 1988. The law is very similar to the American Education for All Handicapped Children Act (PL 94-142) from 1975 and to similar legislation in other countries. The law increased the power of the parents in determining the educational program for their children, resulting in an increase in the number of included students. In addition, the shift from oral to Total Communication within the special classes during the 1980s greatly improved the students' level of understanding, helping them move forward by legitimizing the use of signing. Moreover, in the beginning of the 1990s, interpretation services into sign language were introduced for deaf and hard of hearing students in special classes and for students who were individually integrated into general classrooms. These interpretation services were of great help to the students and improved their understanding of the material being studied in the general classrooms, and they were one of the catalysts for the increase in the number of students being included.

Several additional inclusion models were developed. For example, a co-enrollment model was effective in a Beer-Sheba school for several years. According to this model, two teachers taught in the classroom simultaneously—the "regular" teacher and the teacher for hearing impaired students. The deaf and hard of hearing students received additional tutoring as well as speech and language therapy after school hours. Today, a number of inclusion alternatives are available in many regions in the country, ranging from partial and limited inclusion to full inclusion. Plaut (2007) asserts that the present existence of several models of inclusion and the less rigid approach to communication modes help to fulfill the various learning needs of students with hearing impairments.

Another change that should be mentioned is the increase in the number of deaf and hard of hearing students who take the matriculation exams at the end of high school. This change is partially a result of the improved accessibility to academic material that the educational system offers and to the adaptations that were made to reduce the effect of language on the test results. Still, the budgetary difficulties faced by the governmental and local bodies make it difficult to implement the acknowledged policy that requires the educational programs to provide for all of the students' special needs.

It should also be noted that there are patent differences between the various inclusion programs for students with hearing impairments studying in the large cities and those for students studying in the periphery. The disparities are expressed in the composition of the classrooms and the ability of the educational institutions to offer the students a variety of study tracks. For example, the comprehensive high school in Yehud, which is located in the center of the country and contains a large population of students with hearing impairments, offers its students the possibility of studies at different levels and various specialty tracks such as sciences, liberal arts, technology, mechanics, fashion, architectural design, computer science, art, cinema, and theatre. Many of the students take the matriculation exams in those different areas of study. In contrast, the Comprehensive High School in Beer-Sheba, which does not have many students with hearing impairments, offers only a few study tracks that fit the needs and abilities of deaf and hard of hearing students who are unable to be fully integrated. It seems that when a school has a significant number of deaf and hard of hearing students, more than 20 students in each grade level, it can offer more varied and better educational and rehabilitation services.

The strong tendency for inclusion resulted in a decrease in the number of students in special schools for the deaf at the elementary school level. The number of students in these schools was greatly reduced and those who have remained are mainly students who have additional handicapping conditions. The educational and rehabilitation services provided by the special schools at present have broadened, the number of staff members has increased, and the staff now includes experts in different areas of therapy; nevertheless, parents of deaf and hard of hearing students often prefer to send their children to special classes (group integration) in general schools. This preference exists in spite of the fact that the special classes do not always provide a suitable solution for the children's difficult problems (Plaut, 2007). The result is that despite the constant rise in the number of students with more than one handicapping condition, with the passage of time, the total number of special schools for the deaf has decreased and some of these schools have closed.

EDUCATIONAL PROGRAMS

Students ranging from age 3 to 21 study in the educational system for deaf and hard of hearing students, whether in separate or integrative programs, starting with prekindergartens and continuing through completion of high school studies. The deaf and hard of hearing students come from all sectors of the population—secular Jews, religious Jews, Orthodox religious Jews, and Arabs. Their loss of hearing ranges from 25dB to profound deafness. The population of deaf and hard of hearing students is, therefore, heterogeneous and varies greatly in terms of socioeconomic status, intelligence levels, and personalities. It is therefore difficult to determine an unequivocal position with respect to the proper educational program for a child with a hearing deficiency. In adapting a program, factors such as age at onset of deafness, the severity of the disability, the existence of additional handicapping conditions, special needs arising from the disability, and the social-economic status of the family must all be taken into consideration (Weisel & Zandberg, 2002).

There are about 3 deaf and hard of hearing students for every 1,000 students in Israel's educational system. The exact size of the population of students who are deaf or hard of hearing is unknown because parents are not obliged to report hearing impairments to the authorities. It is estimated that this population comprises approximately 5,000 children studying in preschools as well as elementary, junior high, and high schools. Most of the students (approximately 75%) are included on an individual basis. Approximately 20% of children with severe hearing deficiencies who do not communicate effectively in spoken language or who have language gaps or additional learning disabilities usually study in special classes. Approximately 5% of students who are profoundly deaf and have additional disabilities study in schools for the deaf. There are no residential schools in Israel.

It seems that the vast majority of students are studying in general educational programs. It should be noted, however, that a significant number of these students have mild to moderate hearing losses. It should also be noted that the reasons for inclusion vary from one sector to another. In the Jewish secular and religious sectors, inclusion is related to the general tendency to include students with special needs in general education. In the Jewish Orthodox sector and in the Arab sector, inclusion is sometimes the result of lack of adequate special educational and rehabilitation services (especially in preschool years) and lack of certified professionals such as teachers of the deaf and communication clinicians. Because of these shortcomings, students are placed in regular educational programs as a default.

Weisel and Zandberg (2002) described the variety of frameworks that exist in Israel today for children with hearing impairments: kindergartens (preschools), elementary programs, secondary programs, and postsecondary programs. These are summarized in the following sections.

Kindergartens (Preschools)

Whenever babies are identified as having a hearing impairment, they are referred to MICHA centers that specialize in rehabilitating young children with hearing impairments. These centers take care of babies and their families from the moment the hearing impairment is detected. The Special Education Law applies only to children from the age of 3 years; therefore, MICHA, which is an independent organization, finances mostly the rehabilitation of the younger children (up to 3 years) and in some centers provides services (additional to those given by the Ministry of Education) to the preschool children ages 3–6 years. From age 3, the children usually spend two days a week in a special preschool program run by the MICHA center, and for the other four days, they attend general or integrated preschool kindergartens that combine a group of deaf and hard of hearing children and a group of hearing children. There are nine such centers in Israel, located in the large cities. Every center serves a target population in a broad geographic region. Therefore, access to the center might be difficult for many parents and children and often requires lengthy travel (Weisel & Zandberg, 2002). A typical preschool class for deaf and hard of hearing children contains 6–8 children and is attached to a general preschool class. Children who are in small classes are taught by a preschool teacher who has been trained to work with children who have hearing impairments. In addition, the classes are supported by a teacher aide, a speech and language clinician, and when required, an occupational therapist. The curriculum is run in tandem with the general curriculum. In addition, a personal curriculum—an Individual Educational Plan—is prepared for each pupil, as required by the Israeli Special Education Law of 1988. Yet, even when sign language is used, the communication is usually by means of Hebrew signing and not Israeli signed language. In addition, there are programs for individual inclusion in which children with hearing impairments are integrated in a general preschool that is located near their place of residence, and they receive additional tutoring or therapy in the MICHA center or in the preschool itself.

As required by the Special Education Law, a placement committee meeting is held near the end of the child's inclusive preschool education and as the time approaches for the child with hearing impairments to be entering school. The committee must determine the educational program to which the child will be referred—special school, special class (group integration), or individual integration (Weisel & Zandberg, 2002).

Elementary Programs

At the elementary level, deaf and hard of hearing children have options to study in special schools for the deaf, in special classes within general schools, or in regular classes. Families and educators decide on these options at the end of the preschool programs.

SPECIAL SCHOOLS FOR THE DEAF. Children who study in special schools for the deaf have severe and profound hearing losses, and they use sign language for daily communication. In most cases, these students have other problems in addition to the hearing loss, and they belong to families of relatively low socioeconomic status (Weisel, 1995). The classes in these schools are generally small and contain about eight students. Each student has an Individual Educational Plan. The curricula put great significance on learning language, reading, and developing speech. Communication is done through both sign language (mainly Signed Hebrew) and speech. The school staff is assorted and includes certified educators and teachers of deaf and hard of hearing, special education teachers, speech and language clinicians, and counselors. The children's environment is emotionally protected, but the educational level is very low. Later, these students will follow vocational or semivocational tracks.

SPECIAL CLASSES IN GENERAL SCHOOLS (GROUP INTEGRATION). General schools have small classes of approximately eight deaf and hard of hearing students. If the academic achievements of students with a hearing impairment meet the requirements, they are integrated into a general class with hearing students of the same age for part of the school hours. Normally, communication in a classroom consists of speech and Signed Hebrew. The curriculum is adapted to meet the needs and abilities of the students with hearing impairments, emphasizing the teaching of language and reading as well as development of speech. The objective is to follow the regular curriculum as much as possible. The deaf and hard of hearing students have a support system that is separate from that provided by the general school staff: certified teachers of deaf and hard of hearing students, educational counselors, speech and language clinicians, and tutors.

This type of program makes it possible for a student to be part of a group of deaf and hard of hearing children and, at the same time, be exposed to the hearing environment and associate with hearing peers. Most of the students in this type of program also enter vocational tracks that prepare them for low-level employment opportunities.

INDIVIDUAL INTEGRATION IN REGULAR CLASSES. The child with a hearing impairment who is in an individual inclusion program follows the curriculum used in a classroom of hearing children located in the vicinity of his or her residence. Within this type of program, the student is entitled to help from a tutor and to basic therapy from a speech and language clinician. Deaf and hard of hearing students who are studying in regular classes usually have good oral communication skills and few, if any, other problems in addition to the hearing impairment. These students are quite isolated from other hearing impaired children and must cope by themselves with the social environment of hearing peers. In general, the level of academic achievements of the deaf and hard of hearing students in individual integration is similar to those of hearing students. After elementary school, they continue their studies in either academic or vocational programs and schools.

Secondary Programs

Today, most of the students with hearing impairments are placed in inclusion programs in general high schools, either in individual integration or in special classes (group integration). Each of these students is allocated special tutoring hours, regardless of whether she or he is in individual or class inclusion. Some of the students are provided with sign language interpretation during the lesson to help them successfully integrate in a hearing class and succeed in following what is said (Weisel & Zandberg, 2002). Some students with hearing impairments extend their high school tenure by two additional years (13th and 14th Grades), and thus, the study material and matriculation exams can be spread over a longer period. In addition, a student with hearing impairment is entitled to a number of adjustments when taking the matriculation examinations: extra time during the examination (20% more time per exam), explanations provided with respect to the questionnaire, and an additional 10 points added to the grade of each test. At times, when subjects require more language skills, the exam given will be an in-house exam rather than an external one. When taking the English test, students with hearing impairments will not have to do the oral or hearing comprehension sections, will be entitled to an additional 10 points added to the grade of the test, and will be given additional time and explanations about the questionnaire. In addition, they will be allowed to use a computerized dictionary, and spelling errors will not count against them.

Postsecondary Programs

Deaf and hard of hearing adults are offered three types of programs, each intended for a different type of population. The first, training and rehabilitation centers, offer special services for students with hearing impairments: professional and learning evaluation, training in a profession, and job placement. The majority of the people coming to this track are deaf and hard of hearing students who studied in special schools for the deaf or in special education frameworks. Most of the students in these programs failed to find employment or to hold a job, and they get a "second chance." Their education level is low, and they will probably work in nonprofessional or semiprofessional jobs.

In the second type of program, adult evening classes and classes for new immigrants, new immigrants can learn Hebrew through sign language. The classes are run in cooperation with the Israel Deaf Association, the Ministry of Education, and the Ministry of Absorption. They are designed for any deaf and hard of hearing immigrants. In these programs, these adults study Israeli sign language as well as the spoken and written language. Today, these classes take place in two major cities, Tel Aviv and Haifa.

These special class sessions run for approximately 5 months during which most students are anxious about how they will be able to make a living and look for employment. The Association for the Deaf also tries to be of assistance in this domain. The professional team not only consists of teachers but also includes social workers. Therefore, within the learning framework of the special classes, the students receive a series of additional services: help with a "communications basket" (a list of communication and rehabilitation services), assistance in the purchase of hearing aids, employment, counseling with respect to personal and family problems, celebrations during the Israeli and Jewish holidays, and field trips throughout Israel with an emphasis on Jewish heritage.

The third type of program is found in colleges and universities. Some of the deaf and hard of hearing students, particularly those who underwent individual integration, continue to study in postsecondary tracks with a vocational or academic orientation.

Up until the middle 1990s, very few students with hearing impairments studied in the universities and colleges. The few who did had graduated from individual inclusion programs. Deaf people whose communication was based on sign language were almost never able to continue their studies in institutions of higher education. In Israel, no postsecondary studies were adapted for the needs of the deaf and hard of hearing students, not even a pre academic preparatory program that could help prepare deaf and hard of hearing high school graduates for postsecondary studies. In spite of their communication skills, graduates of individual integration programs found it difficult to follow the college-level lectures, and for the most part, depended on hearing students and photocopied summaries of the lessons. Many of them did not attend the lectures and studied through intensive reading. These students' success depended, to a large extent, on their social skills, particularly their ability to ask for, and receive help from, hearing friends (Weisel & Reichstein, 1991).

Over the past 10 years, there has been a significant increase in the number of deaf and hard of hearing students studying in Israeli institutions of higher education. This phenomenon was a result of the financial support and various other support services provided by the National Insurance Institute and the Institute for the Advancement of the Deaf in Israel to support these students during their studies. These support services included financial support, interpretation and transcription (note-taking by typists), acquiring approval for adapting examinations, laptops, amplification equipment, and peer assistance.

The support services center of the Institute for the Advancement of the Deaf (a not-for-profit organization) began operating in 1996. Six students participated in the program during its first year of operation. During 2007–2008, the institute handled requests of more than 300 students. In addition, there is also a large group of deaf and hard of hearing students who receive services directly from the National Insurance Institute. However, some students, especially the hard of hearing ones, continue their studies without assistance from the National Insurance Institute. They manage on their own or use limited and specific solutions provided by the Dean of Students' office in the academic institution in which they study.

The deaf and hard of hearing students study in a variety of institutions throughout the country and learn a great variety of professions, as do hearing students. They can be found studying professions such as engineering, architecture, photography, graphic design, information systems and computers, medicine, dental hygiene, biotechnology, brain sciences, education, social work, psychology, information, law, industrial engineering and management, accounting, literature, and philosophy.

It seems that those majors considered being profitable among hearing students are considered equally profitable among the deaf students; as a result, the number of students turning to, for example, economics, accounting, and industrial engineering and management has recently increased. Moreover, it is possible to see a slight edge to majors such as graphic design, computers, and various engineering majors that are less dependent on communication.

METHODS OF COMMUNICATION IN SCHOOLS

Good communication between children and others in their environment is important for their cognitive, emotional, and social development. Throughout the history of education of pupils with hearing impairments in Israel and in the world, emphasis has been placed on the various manners of communicating with these students and their effect on educational achievements and quality of life. Researchers and professionals in the area of hearing impairment disagree as to the ideal form of communication that should be used with this population. These disagreement stems from different viewpoints with respect to the concept of deafness.

During the first 40 years of Israel's history, the oral approach was the only approach applied in Israel within the various educational frameworks available to pupils with hearing impairments. According to this approach, the student had to develop the skills required for developing a spoken language (exploiting any residual hearing, developing speechreading skills, and producing speech). The main objective of the oral approach was to prepare pupils with hearing impairments to be able to function in the hearing society.

A gradual change took place in the education system during the 1970s, and there was a transition from the oral approach to Total Communication. This change stemmed from a combination of multiple factors. First of all, many students were unable to learn the spoken language. Teachers became disappointed by the low learning achievements of the deaf pupils who had been educated in the oral approach. It was finally recognized that part of the reason for low learning achievements originated from a lack of high-quality and flowing communication between the teachers and the pupils (Meir & Sandler, 2004).

Medical advances in the domain of early detection of hearing impairments in children, operations involving cochlear implants and the great technological advances that have been made in the domain of sensory aids (hearing aids and cochlear implants) have prompted a return to the oral approach recently and, in certain places, even an auditory-verbal approach. As a result, increasing numbers of educators and parents are emphasizing the study of the spoken language solely through hearing, without the support of speechreading.

ORGANIZATIONS OF AND FOR THE DEAF

A number of organizations in Israel provide services to deaf and hard of hearing people. The goals of these organizations are to provide services to which persons with hearing impairments are entitled according to the law and to handle the education and rehabilitation of deaf and hard of hearing students. The main organization for deaf and hard of hearing people is the Israel Organization for the Deaf (ACHA). This voluntary organization was established in 1944. The organization was established by a few young people who were deaf and who found themselves isolated from the hearing society. Today, the organization has 10,000 members[1] and operates 17 branches deployed nationally, two of which are in the Arab sector. The association operates social clubs that serve as a place for deaf people to take a variety of classes, participate in activities, and socialize. Some of the clubs for the deaf hold lectures, sign language classes for the general public, and courses for interpreters who translate into sign language. In addition, the Israel Organization for the Deaf works to promote social legislation for deaf and hard of hearing people and to increase public awareness of their skills and limitations. The association also conducts public campaigns to improve social conditions for the deaf and hard of hearing population, and it provides welfare and support services (such as translations into sign language) for the deaf community (Gorni & Hacohen, 1999–2000). During the 1990s, the intensified immigration from the countries in the former Soviet Union brought an influx of deaf immigrants, and some of them joined the association. Some of the branches in the country offer special activities for new immigrants, and there are classes for teaching Hebrew and Israeli sign language (Meir & Sandler, 2004).

Another organization for adults with hearing impairments is BEKOL. This organization brings together hard of hearing people who are 18 years of age and older who, for the most part, communicate verbally. The organization has branches throughout the country and works to attain equal rights for people with impaired hearing. BEKOL focuses on expanding public awareness about the needs of people with hearing impairments within a hearing population, initiating legislation, and fighting for equal rights. In addition, the organization provides a variety of services for the hearing impaired community, including providing information and training on the use of sensory aids and rehabilitation possibilities, providing professional advice and assistance in finding employment, providing transcription services, and organizing various social activities.

The Institute for the Advancement of the Deaf in Israel was established in 1993 by professionals working in the field of deafness. The institute's goal is to coordinate, develop,

---

1. For more information, see http://www.deaf.org.il/content.php?id=2.

and promote professional, educational, and emotional services for the welfare of the deaf and hard of hearing population in Israel to strengthen and improve their integration into the whole of society. The institute supports applied research in the fields of education, rehabilitation, and communication in the community. It also develops and runs the "success model" project in which deaf and hard of hearing students and adults are integrated as mentors for groups of deaf children. Based on a belief that the mentor can be a powerfully positive figure, the contact between the child and the mentor is intended to bring about a change in the child with the hearing impairment and make the child feel better about him- or herself, thus empowering him or her with the resources necessary to effectively interact with society. The institute's programs include an Empowerment Center, which runs workshops and courses on various subjects intended to teach and empower deaf and hard of hearing people. The institute is also involved in providing support for deaf and hard of hearing students, in producing a computerized dictionary of Israeli sign language, in building a learning kit for teaching the language, and in holding courses where one can actually learn sign language.

In addition to these organizations, which provide mainly welfare and advocacy services, companionship, support, and culture for deaf and hard of hearing people, a number of organizations were established in Israel to provide solutions for the unique needs of hearing impaired children and youth. The MICHA organization provides educational, rehabilitation, and support services for infants and preschool children with hearing impairments as well as counseling for their family. Each center includes a team of professionals: teachers, speech and language therapists, audiologists, social workers, paramedical attendants, psychologists, and medical doctors. It should be pointed out, however, that the MICHA framework in Tel Aviv, which handles a large number of children, is able to provide a greater number of services and activities compared with MICHA frameworks in other locations (Plaut, 2007).

Another organization that provides therapeutic and educational services to school children is SHEMA. The SHEMA branches throughout the country provide a broad variety of services to 4,000 deaf and hard of hearing students who are learning in all of the existing educational programs (individual inclusion, class inclusion, and special schools for the deaf), including support and assistance in studies and didactic evaluations, training for parents and teachers, speech and language rehabilitation, psychological and clinical evaluations, social services for pupils and their families, adaptation of learning material in a variety of subjects for pupils with hearing impairments, a pedagogic library as well as a light and sound library, various enrichment classes, and a lending bank of hearing devices that children can borrow.

Educational programs for the Orthodox population are different from those in the other sectors with respect to their contents, their atmosphere, and the scope of services they provide for the population of students with hearing impairments. They include the whole range of ages and all types of educational programs existing in Israel.

The SHEMAYA organization is a nonprofit organization whose activities are supported by the Ministry of Education (the branch for independent education) and the Ministry of Social Affairs. The organization was established in Bnei Brak in 1980. Today, SHEMAYA provides rehabilitation and support services for 150 boys and girls with hearing impairments in the Ultra-Orthodox and Orthodox sectors, from the time deafness is detected through adolescence, using the services of a professional team that includes speech and language therapists, social workers, and psychologists. Approximately 80% of the children coming to the center from all over the country have cochlear implants. The type of communication used is, for the most part, oral and auditory-verbal. In addition, children who are unable to acquire spoken language through the oral approach receive help in learning sign language through individual therapy. The organization operates two kindergartens, a social club, and a learning center; holds workshops for training interpreters for the hearing impaired; and helps to integrate children into the general education system.

An additional Ultra-Orthodox and Orthodox center is the SHMA KOLENU organization, a voluntary organization established in 1992 in Jerusalem as a rehabilitative-educational center for children with hearing impairments. Today, there is an additional center in the southern region of the country. The SHMA KOLENU center provides rehabilitation, educational, and learning services through a variety of programs: (a) daycare for children between the ages of 1 and 3 years and preschools for children ages 3–6 who have hearing impairments, (b) an afterschool center for the preschool children, (c) and tutoring and enrichment classes for elementary and high school students studying in general education programs (Plaut, 2007). All staff members of SHMA KOLENU use only the oral communication method.

Legislation

The Israeli Special Education Law of 1988 specifically states the rights of children with special needs with respect to special education. A child is entitled to special education when he or she has sensory, physical, cognitive, emotional, or behavioral problems that limit his or her ability to adjust and function. The range of ages for children entitled to special education was expanded and now includes children and youths from the ages of 3 to 21 years. The goal of the Special Education Law is to promote and develop the child's skills as a means to ease his or her integration into normative society.

Two principal sections in the law touch on education of deaf and hard of hearing children. One section mandates placing deaf and hard of hearing pupils in general education programs as much as is possible rather than placing them in a special school for deaf children. This right, to be able to study in general education programs, is part of the right of a person with hearing impairments to live within his or her community and actively participate in its activities on an equal basis. It fits in with the educational concepts that praise the importance of providing handicapped children with normative behavioral habits while also creating a more tolerant society.

Another section of the law gives parents the opportunity to participate in the educational placement process. This partnership is carried out by the parents' presence and participation in committee meetings. Parents receive relevant documents from the committee, and they have the right to appeal the committee's decision before a District Appeals Committee within 21 days of having received the decision. Moreover, in cases where the decision of the appeals committee is not acceptable to the parents, they have the right to transfer the issue to the courts. The parents are greatly empowered to force those making placement decisions to accept their position, particularly where the parents have a clear position, are determined, and have the appropriate economic and intellectual resources (Weisel, 2001).

As a result of this law, the number of staff members taking care of the pupils increased as the scope of treatment was expanded. Teams now include teaching aides; physiotherapists; vocational therapists; speech and language therapists; and art, music, and movement therapists.

The "basket of services" was also expanded to include transport of children to and from their schools, meals, as well as social and psychological services.

In 2002, additional sections were added to the part of the Special Education Law that deals with the inclusion of children with special needs into general education. The section on inclusion states that a pupil with special needs who is included in general education has the right (a) to receive additional teaching, tutoring, and special services to make his or her inclusion a possibility and (b) to access a well-defined process for the determination of such services. From this time on, school committees will determine not only the eligibility of a child to be part of the school's inclusion program but also what special services, out of a list determined in the law, he or she will be entitled to receive: assistance services, psychological services, paramedical services, and any other service specified by the Ministry of Education.

Classrooms must be acoustically adapted to ensure that the classroom is suitable for deaf and hard of hearing pupils by allowing them to hear to the best of their ability. Very often, steps such as precluding outside noise by placing the classroom in a quiet section of the school, using a quiet air system, and padding the underside of the chair legs improve the audibility in the classroom (Most, 2006). Over the past few years, the National Insurance Institute has undertaken to make classrooms used by students with hearing impairments more accessible, and indeed, there have been great improvements in the physical conditions. Many therapy rooms and classrooms have been acoustically soundproofed and have been equipped with instrumentation and equipment suitable for the needs of therapy and instruction. However, most of the general classrooms in which pupils with hearing impairments are included still do not have suitable conditions for them. Continued improvements are necessary to make additional classrooms more accessible by installing acoustic insulation and adapting them to the needs of the students. Such a task involves large expenditures, and the National Insurance Institute is not in a position to cover all expenses involved (Plaut, 2007).

In 1998, Israel passed legislation that was basically founded on the principles of the "Equal Rights for the Handicapped" law. The objective of this law is to protect the dignity and freedom of the handicapped person and to secure his or her right to equal and active participation in society. In addition, the law requires the society to provide a viable solution for his or her special needs so he or she will be able to lead a private and honorable life, taking into full account his or her personal capabilities (Gorni & Hacohen, 1999–2000).

The law accords communication support services to people with hearing impairments, who, by definition, are included in the classification of the handicapped. According to the law, people who are defined as hearing impaired and who are entitled to support services are those who have a hearing loss of 50dB or higher. The speech and language support services provided for hearing impaired people in Israel include, among others, individual translating services into sign language (translating into sign language, from sign language, or both, or to and from any other language that the hearing impaired person uses). Interpretation services are provided by professional translators, graduates of a recognized school for interpreters and translators. This service is provided for health, education, social welfare, and employment services as well as for contact with government offices and for resolution of special problems. Individual transcription services are provided in addition to sign language interpreting services. Transcription means typing a translation that appears on a computer monitor (Gorni & Hacohen, 1999–2000). A person with a hearing impairment is entitled to receive a certain number of translation and interpreting hours per year. From an educational aspect, there is no doubt that this service greatly helps the integrated high school students and students studying in colleges and universities.

EVALUATION, ASSESSMENT, AND REHABILITATION

Detecting hearing loss early is significantly important, as is carrying out audiological, medical, and educational intervention as early as possible (Weisel & Zandberg, 2002). The health system in Israel, which includes maternity hospitals and branches of mother and child clinics, is aware of the need for this early detection and care and is prepared to act on information it receives with respect to babies who are considered high risks (those with genetic factors, illness during the mother's pregnancy, distress during birth). High-risk babies, who constitute approximately 8% of babies born in Israel, are assessed immediately after birth and undergo follow-up examinations and repeated hearing tests to detect any hearing loss. In the past, the various branches of the mother and child clinics carried out screening tests on a regular basis for all babies reaching the age of 7 months. Babies in whom a hearing loss is suspected are referred to the audiology centers in the hospitals for comprehensive hearing evaluation.

Over the years, many advances have occurred in the domain of detecting and diagnosing hearing impairment in children. Over the past few years, several hospitals in the center of the country and in Jerusalem have been implementing the Universal Hearing Screening Test for newborns immediately after birth and before their release from the hospitals. During the first 3 years of operation, this program tested more than 20,000 babies. In other places of the country, where there are no facilities for these tests, the hearing impairment is detected later.

Babies who have been identified as having a hearing impairment are referred to MICHA centers, which specialize in therapy for and rehabilitation of such children. As mentioned above, these centers provide rehabilitation services for babies and their families beginning at the time the hearing loss is detected, sometimes right after birth.

Rehabilitative intervention through the use of cochlear implants has been implemented in Israel for the past 20 years. Today, approximately 200 children and adults with hearing impairments undergo cochlear implants each year. Approximately 75% of these are children younger than the age of 18. Most of the people with implants have them unilaterally. There are three different types of implants available in Israel: Advanced Bionics, Med El, and Nucleus. A cochlear implant costs approximately US$20,000. In Israel, a cochlear implant is fully financed by the Ministry of Health, even for hearing impaired persons who have an additional handicap. Over the past few years, there has been an increase in adults with prelingual deafness who have undergone implantation. Also, a recommendation for binaural implants is growing.

TEACHER TRAINING PROGRAMS

The first principals of schools for the deaf in the large cities brought with them from Europe, mostly from Germany, knowledge and experience in educating pupils with hearing impairments. However, most of the teachers working in those schools did not have any professional training in this field. A few of the teachers had been trained abroad, but most teachers during that period worked without having any professional training and used any knowledge they had garnered from their work in the field of general education, the field of special education, and their own intuition.

After 30 years during which the education frameworks operated without a curriculum for training teachers in teaching and rehabilitating children and youths with hearing impairments, an initial attempt was made in 1964 by the Tel Aviv Bureau of Education to open courses for preparing and authorizing teachers to teach pupils with hearing impairments. These courses included theoretical and pedagogical knowledge (Zweibel, 1999). Although teachers did acquire basic knowledge in these courses, professionals reached the conclusion that it had become necessary to establish a university track for teaching pupils with hearing impairments that would include high standards of professional training at an academic level. In 1978, the teaching track for teaching pupils with hearing impairments, headed by Professor Jerry Reichstein, was opened in the School of Education at the Tel Aviv University. During the first years, some of the lecturers were teachers from the United States and Europe who represented different schools of thoughts for the education of pupils with hearing impairments. The curriculum included theoretical lessons, seminars, workshops, observations, and practical work (Meir & Sandler, 2004). Studies in this track last 3 years after which the students have to study an extra year to receive their teaching certificate. Today, there is also a master's program, and it is also possible to continue one's studies toward a doctoral degree.

In recent years, some teachers' colleges have opened majors or study tracks for training special education teachers. In two of the colleges, special advanced studies were introduced to prepare teachers for pupils with hearing impairments in the Arab sector.

Today, those teachers who are interested in working with students with hearing impairments are required by law to have a degree in special education, and graduates of programs with tracks that provide training in education of hard of hearing children are given preference. Expertise in sign language is also an advantage; teachers who teach special classes and in special schools need to know sign language. Teachers in individual inclusion, where communication is through spoken language, do not necessarily have to know sign language.

Until the 1990s, only a few deaf teachers worked in the educational system. Most of the deaf teachers studied professions such as art and crafts, domestic science, etc. (Zweibel, 1999). Deaf people who wanted to be accepted by teacher training institutions faced strong opposition (Gur, 1997). The early 1990s marked the beginning of a change in this direction when a few young deaf people began studying at the Tel Aviv University, majoring in the track of education of children with hearing impairments. The trend spread to the other teachers' colleges. Today, young deaf people who apply to teacher training institutions still run into difficulties at times, but the main obstacle has already been removed, and considering the precedents that were created, the battle for future acceptance will be less exhausting.

Despite the successful process of training professional teachers for students with hearing impairments, Plaut (2007) points out that there are still some difficulties and challenges that the educational system must overcome, including training suitable preschool teachers. Children with hearing impairments who are in the critical stages of their development need experts trained not only in teaching preschool children but also in educating children with hearing impairments. Another problem is that many students with hearing impairments studying in the individual integrated track receive help from teachers who have been trained only to teach students with hearing impairment; they do not have adequate training in any specific area of study or in the didactics of teaching all of the subjects studied at the school.

Closing Remarks

The educational system for deaf and hard of hearing children in Israel and the various organizations servicing this population have undergone major changes over the last 60 years of Israel's independence. Most of these changes are similar to the trends in many other countries. For example, the trend of inclusion, the trend of using various communication approaches in a more flexible way, the more frequent use of sign language translation both in the educational system and in the society in general, and the sharp increase in the number of children and adults using cochlear implants. In general, the level of the educational and rehabilitation services has improved and the awareness of the special needs of deaf and hard of hearing populations is better than ever before. The legislation in both areas of special education and rights of the handicapped has expedited these developments. Nevertheless, the future of the Deaf community's social status and recognition is unclear. Similar to the situation in other developing countries, the Deaf community in Israel is threatened by the growing use of cochlear implants. As a result of the great number of deaf children who undergo implantation, the number of potential new members to the Deaf community, or in other words to those using sign language for communication, is reduced. The influence of this issue on the nature and the status of sign language in the educational system will become clearer in the future.

References

Al-Yagon, M., & Margalit, M. (2001). Special and inclusive education in Israel. *Mediterranean Journal of Educational Studies, 6*(2), 93–112.

Dromi, A., & Reingold-Frimerman, D. (1996). *Intervention by communication and language with children with hearing impairment, the pre-verbal stag.* Tel Aviv: Ramot Publications.

Gorni, Z., & Hacohen, R. (1999–2000). *Guide of rights and services for the hearing impaired (deaf and hard of hearing) in Israel/Jerusalem.* Jerusalem: The Ministry of Labor and Social Services, Rehabilitation Branch.

Gur, H. (1997). Equal opportunities and repression: The case of the deaf. *Theories in Education, 2,* 205–219.

Meir, E., & Sandler, V. (2004). *Language in open spaces—A place for Israeli signed language.* Haifa, Israel: Haifa University Publications/Zmora Beitan.

Most, T. (2006). *Communication rehabilitation of children with hearing impairment in the educational setting: A guide to the educational staff.* Jerusalem: The Ministry of Education/Maalot Publishing.

Plaut, A. (2007). *What has changed? The history of educational frameworks for students with hearing impairments in Israel 1932–2005.* Tel Aviv: Mofet Institute Publications.

Weisel, A. (1995). Are there angels in heaven who know sign language? In D. Chen (Ed.), *Education towards the 21st century* (pp. 503–515). Tel Aviv: Ramot Publications.

Weisel, A. (2001). Equality, excellence, and parental choice in the education of deaf and hard of hearing children in Israel: Ethics and balancing individual, group and national agendas. In R. Beattie (Ed.), *Ethics in deaf education* (chap. 6). New York: Academic Press.

Weisel, A., & Reichstein, J. (1991). Routes to postsecondary education for hearing impaired students in Israel. In E. G. Wolf-Schein & J. D. Schein (Eds.), *Postsecondary education for deaf students* (pp. 57–65). Edmonton, Alberta: University of Alberta Press.

Weisel, A., & Zandberg, S. (2002). *Issues of special education: Unit 8. Hearing impairment.* Tel Aviv: The Open University.

Zweibel, A. (1999). Education of the deaf in Israel: Past, present, and future. In H. W. Brelje (Ed), *Global perspectives on the education of the deaf* (pp. 191–204). Hillsboro, OR: Butte.

Perspectives and Reviews on Deafness in the State of Kuwait and the United Arab Emirates

Yasser A. Al-Hilawani

THIS CHAPTER provides information, analyses, and insights on deafness in the State of Kuwait and in the United Arab Emirates (UAE). It represents the first time such an approach has been taken in a comprehensive manner. Because of the extreme shortage of documents to prepare this chapter, the author relied on his personal experiences, a few published works on these two countries, anecdotal reports and personal contacts with practitioners in deafness, internal memoranda, all available official documents, and classrooms observations.

Kuwait and UAE are located on the Arabian Gulf east of Saudi Arabia. The two countries have been influenced by Western lifestyle while at the same time observing traditional local tribal lifestyle. One of the influences of tribal lifestyle has been the practice of hiding individuals with disabilities for fear of stigmatizing the families and labeling the children.

Kuwait and UAE are mainly dependent on oil revenues, although UAE has recently started to capitalize on and to emphasize tourism. The economic prosperity in these two countries has not been accompanied with improved and high-quality special educational services. The current services for the deaf population are fragmented with no clear vision for proper teacher-preparation programs, curricula, and future contributions to the community. The available programs and the future outlook for this group of students are disappointing as depicted in the following documentation and analysis of progress.

HISTORY OF EDUCATIONAL SERVICES

Kuwait started serving deaf people about 22 years earlier than UAE. The country established the first school for deaf males in 1959–60, followed in 1960–61 by another school for deaf females. These two schools have been part of a large complex of educational institutions called the Administration of Schools of Special Education, which opened officially in 1970. This complex includes vocational schools that serve deaf students as well as other students with physical, visual, and mental disabilities (Administration of Schools of Special Education, 2003). This educational system provides free services and is overseen by the Ministry of Education. Statistics covering the academic year 2006–07, dated November 30, 2006, and obtained in person from the system's administration office, revealed that 249 deaf students were being served at that time, representing 13.7% of all the cases with special needs enrolled in this system. This total number consisted of 149 Kuwaitis, representing 9.8% of all Kuwaitis with disabilities in the system, and 100 non-Kuwaitis, representing 33.8% of all non-Kuwaitis with disabilities, being served in the system. These are extremely conservative numbers because deaf Kuwaitis and non-Kuwaitis as well as students with other disabilities are also being

119

served largely in a flourishing but disorganized private sector. An accurate and precise number of Kuwaitis and non-Kuwaitis who are being educated in the private sector to accommodate their disabling condition, including deafness, is not available, nor is it feasible to estimate. At the same time, paradoxically, compiled statistics based on the type of disability are also not readily available in the Higher Council for the Disabled, a government establishment that cares for Kuwaitis with disabilities and that not only issues them identification cards based on the disabling condition but also finances their education in private schools. Surveying each individual school to find the number of students in each category in special education is not feasible because schools consider this information private, and it is not released without permission from the Higher Council for the Disabled.

UAE started to provide services to deaf students in 1981 by establishing special education centers that serve the deaf students and others with visual, mental, and multiple disabilities. These centers have been under the authority of the Ministry of Social Affairs, previously known as the Ministry of Labour and Social Affairs. The number of special education centers increased from 11 government-run centers in 1998 to an additional 21 private centers by the year 2004–05. Statistics published in 1995 by the UAE Ministry of Labour and Social Affairs revealed 398 cases of deaf students who were being educated in UAE. This number represented 19.4% of all students with disabilities. Recent statistics by the Department of Programs for Individuals with Special Needs (2004/2005) in UAE Ministry of Education—Educational Administration revealed that 201 deaf children are being served in the 11 government-run centers, representing 18.1% of all the cases with special needs. In the private sector, 211 deaf children are being served in private centers, representing 10.4% of all cases served in these centers. The percentage of deaf students served in both private and government-run centers is 14.6%. UAE deaf children are served in government-run centers at no cost to parents whereas expatriate deaf children are served in private centers at their parents' expense.

Although perception of today's society about deafness has witnessed improvements in Kuwait and in UAE compared with the past and with other disabling conditions such as mental and severe physical disabilities, the overall status of deaf people is still tainted with social stigma and myths about their abilities and has not advanced much (see Sartawi, Al-Hilawani, & Easterbrooks, 1998, for a brief review on deafness in UAE).

CURRICULUM AND CURRENT EDUCATIONAL PLACEMENT

Deaf students in Kuwait and UAE study the regular curriculum. However, the curriculum of one regular grade level is stretched to cover almost 2 years of study. The regular curricula in Kuwait for Grades 1, 2, 3, and 4 are used to teach deaf students up to Grade 6, and the regular curricula for Grades 5, 6, 7, and 8 are used to teach deaf students during the next 6 years of study. Even with this stretching, regular curricula from first to eighth grades are not comprehensively or completely covered even though contents are being distributed over 12 years of schooling. During the second 6 years of schooling, deaf students are trained in skills needed for jobs related to offset copying, typing, secretarial functions, computer-related areas, advertising, woodworking, and decorating. Students are offered a vocational diploma by the time they are finished the 12 years of schooling (Administration of Schools of Special Education, 2003).

Some students with very mild hearing losses (27 dB to 40 dB levels) are enrolled in public schools with hearing counterparts and study the regular curriculum. However, it is not unusual to find cases of students with mild losses (41 db to 55 dB levels) and moderate losses (56 db to 70 dB levels) being educated in special education centers and school for the deaf side by side students with severe losses (71 db to 90 dB levels) and profound losses (levels of 90 db and above) (Administration of Schools of Special Education, 2003). Many of these students have low verbal abilities and, often, the regular classroom teachers are unable or unwilling to accommodate and modify their instructions, assessment methods, and classroom arrangements to meet the needs of these students and enhance their success in regular education settings. Regular classroom teachers are most likely unfamiliar with children with special needs. Teacher preparation programs do not require that future teachers study the introductory course to exceptional learners, which covers history and types of disabilities, definitions, characteristics, prevalence, teaching methods, and issues related to the disability being studied. This situation has changed in UAE starting from 2000 onward but has not yet changed in Kuwait (see the section on Teacher Preparation Programs).

COMMUNICATION MODES

In the late 1990s, a group of people from Arab countries that provide services to deaf people met to agree on a unified form of Arabic sign language for communication and instruction purposes. Officials and practitioners from Kuwait and UAE participated in these meetings the outcome of which was the introduction of a dictionary containing several hundreds of the so-called unified Arabic signs to be taught and used by deaf students in these countries. Sentences formed using the unified signs are in a form of iconic speech where a sign is used to represent a word, contrary to the deaf native sign language, which is rule-governed to represent meanings and concepts.

Anecdotal reports revealed that the Deaf community rejected the unified Arabic signs because they were alien, had not grown naturally from their local culture, were confusing, created unnecessary obstacles to learning, and did not fit into the linguistic system of the sign language that deaf people naturally use when communicating with one another. Deaf students have to use the unified signs, however, when signs are required in school educational settings. Among themselves, deaf people have and continue to integrate willingly into their native sign language some signs from other countries, especially when those signs are useful for traveling abroad and interacting with other deaf individuals. The new imported signs are modified to fit into the linguistic system of the deaf native sign language.

Deaf people in Kuwait and UAE are also trained in educational settings on signing exact Arabic. Some of them receive speech and speechreading training to facilitate communication with others who are hearing. They are taught the fingerspelling of 28 Arabic letters to represent the written format of spoken words (e.g., names) that have no matching signs.

Generally speaking, sign language is visual in nature and is viewed as the manipulation and movements of hands in relation to the body to communicate messages and meaning. The movements and shapes of hands along with the total body language are substitutes for the spoken words. The sign language and spoken Arabic in Kuwait and UAE share the common ground of using the written Arabic symbols, but they differ in structure. That is, sign language in Kuwait and UAE is independent of spoken Arabic and has not originated from it. Instead, it has originated from the interaction of Deaf people with one another and with the environment. Apart from the so-called unified Arabic sign language, the native deaf sign language in each of the two countries is viewed as a separate language that has evolved naturally within the social and cultural values of its community. Nevertheless, the two languages have similarities because of the frequent visitations between the two populations of Deaf people and because of the resemblances in social and cultural values, types of living, and oral language. Another reason for the similarities relates to the influence that sign language used in Kuwait had on UAE deaf students who used to come to Kuwait some years ago to study in the school for the deaf. Interestingly, dialect differences in sign language exist among deaf male and female Kuwaitis because they are educated in segregated school settings, unlike UAE deaf males and females who are educated in the same setting.

Sign language in Kuwait and UAE can be analyzed in terms of specific components that must be recognized and performed simultaneously to give the intended meaning. In an interview about sign language used in Kuwait, Bader Al-Dookhi (personal communication, May 2, 2007) stated that extracting meaning in social and educational settings depends, first, on the principle of symmetry, which includes coordination in using hands in terms of location on forehead, chest, or in the air; movements in the up, down, forward, or circular directions; shape of palms to be open-close, extended-straight, or half-closed; and orientation where the palms of hands are upward or outward. Second, meaning depends on the principle of dominance where one hand makes one of seven fixed formations and the other hand moves to make other shapes. Third, meaning also depends on body movement accompanied by facial expressions that are loaded with grammatical rules. Al-Dookhi added that the principles of symmetry and dominance along with body movements and facial expressions are all performed simultaneously during communications with other signers. Given this analysis, one can clearly understand why an oversimplified matching of sign to Arabic word (as in the unified Arabic signs or any form of signing exact Arabic) can provide only the most basic forms of meaning.

Sign language in Kuwait and UAE is still in its infancy. It is limited in scope and has not been developing and advancing in sophistication to express knowledge available on all aspects of life. A barrier to the development of a complex sign language is the rudimentary and limited educational opportunities available to deaf students. Current educational practices and procedural limitations hinder developing a complex sign language that is suitable for presenting, introducing, and expressing current knowledge and experiences and for accommodating future ones. This issue is one of the many issues to be addressed in deaf education in Kuwait and UAE.

TEACHING METHODS

Classroom observations of teachers in Kuwait and UAE revealed striking similarities in the way arithmetic and reading comprehension skills are taught to deaf students. Although teachers know of the problems they face when teaching these skills, no practical actions have been taken to address these difficulties. Individualized Education Plans (IEPs) are either inaccurate or nonexistent, and teachers concentrate on teaching rote memorization of low-level arithmetic skills in spite of the fact that deaf students could show significant improvements in learning higher level skills. A study conducted in UAE reported that students using the cognitive behavior modification technique (Meichenbaum & Burland, 1979) as a mediated learning strategy showed significant improvements in learning math skills compared with those who did not (Al-Hilawani, 2000a).

In the area of reading comprehension, both literature (Al-Hilawani, 2003a; Sartawi et al., 1998) and classroom observations revealed that teachers in Kuwait and UAE followed similar teaching steps. Teachers in both countries implemented five general steps in a single class period. First, teachers discuss the content of the reading passage and help students recall past related experiences. Teachers use pictures linked to the content of the reading passage. Sometimes an out-of-school activity precedes presentation of the reading lesson. Second, teachers introduce the reading passage on a plastic board or hard piece of cardboard, reading it orally and signing at the same time. Third, teachers request students to take turns reading orally and signing the reading passage. Fourth, teachers use speaking and signs to explain new concrete vocabularies. Fifth, teachers ask students questions about the content of the reading passage.

These five steps are insufficient and are ineffective in teaching reading comprehension and in developing and enhancing the vocabulary repertoire of deaf students. There is no training on answering various types of questions, and the vocabularies that are not represented by pictures are likely to be overlooked during the lesson because of difficulties involved in communicating their meanings to students. During one of the visits to a school for the deaf to collect data for this chapter, a teacher mentioned that a small number of teachers occasionally use acting and dramatization to communicate meanings to students. The teacher added that this practice is unusual and rarely happens. The overall picture of teaching reading comprehension to deaf students is shallow and scrappy, with disappointing outcomes.

Teacher Preparation Programs

Teacher preparation programs in deaf education are far below expectations in Kuwait and UAE. Higher education institutions in both countries do not prepare qualified teachers in deaf education, and many expatriates from other Arab countries who teach the deaf are also inadequately trained. The majority of teachers of the deaf either have bachelor degrees in general education or in noncategorical special education or have two-year diplomas after high school and use different signing symbols. The following is a chronological documentation of the past and current teacher preparation programs in Kuwait and UAE. The discussion starts with United Arab Emirate University (UAE-U) because it is known in the gulf region as one of the few leading institutions to have started a teacher preparation program in special education.

In 1987, the UAE-U administration initiated the special education program to provide educational services to the citizens of UAE who have disabilities. One of the goals of the program at that time was to prepare teachers not only in deaf education but also in areas of learning problems and mental disabilities. A little after the mid-1990s, the categorical teacher preparation program was replaced with a noncategorical one as part of an overall restructuring of academic programs in the college of education. This noncategorical program was basically a collection of courses in special education. Preservice student teachers studied general information about deaf students at the introductory level and received neither specialized training in assessment and teaching methods nor training in sign language. The student teachers learned sign language from deaf students and from in-service teaching experiences during practicum training. Field supervisors at that time could not conduct proper evaluations of student teachers because either they lacked sign language skills or they used signs not used by the deaf students or teachers of the deaf. The special education program at UAE-U was understaffed not only in the area of deaf education but also in areas of learning problems and mental disabilities.

During the 1998–99 academic year, the college of education started another restructuring endeavor in pursuit of academic accreditation from an international organization, the National Council for Accreditation of Teacher Education (NCATE), a U.S.-based educational organization. In addition to implementing NCATE standards, the college of education also applied the principles of the Interstate New Teacher Assessment and Support Consortium (INTASC), which required, among other things, preparing teachers to teach diverse learners. Every department in the college of education applied the relevant standards and learning outcomes as specified by specialty organizations. The department of special education implemented the Council for Exceptional Children (CEC) learning outcomes in knowledge, skills, and aptitude areas.

To meet the needs of UAE citizens and NCATE standards, the department also conducted interviews with officials in the Ministry of Education (which oversees schools), the Ministry of Labour (which oversees special education centers), in-service teachers, and graduates of the special education department. The outcome of these interviews led to the conclusion that the field of special education lacked skillful and professional personnel with broad and up-to-date research-based knowledge necessary to teach children with exceptional learning needs. Surveying the field of special education at that time yielded a list of recommendations to be taken into consideration when designing the new teacher preparation program. These recommendations included the need for educators to have in-depth knowledge in the characteristics of individuals with exceptional learning needs, their identification, and their legal rights; to master professional skills related to administering, developing, and preparing assessment tools and individualized education programs; to possess a large repertoire of instructional, technical, and behavior management skills; and to receive in-depth professional training in the intended area of exceptionality.

In fall 2000, all students admitted into the college of education to major in special education followed the new study program that had been based on NCATE, INTASC, and CEC standards. This new program consisted of four tracks: mild/moderate disabilities, sensory impairments (visual and hearing), gifted and talented learners, and students with severe disabilities. Visual and hearing impairments were grouped into one track because of the small number of school-age students with these two disabilities that were served in special education centers. The department accepted student teachers in the mild/moderate disabilities track but *froze* indefinitely admission to the other three tracks because of lack of faculty members. On May 18, 2005, Arthur E. Wise, president of NCATE, stated in his speech in UAE that the college of education has been judged by the Center for Quality Assurance in International Education to have met NCATE standards and had received international recognition for such achievement (Wise, 2005).

This latest restructuring of the teacher preparation program has improved teaching services to students with mild/moderate disabilities but not to deaf students or those with other special needs. The college of education overseeing the department of special education at UAE-U has no intention to activate in the near future the deaf education program in the sensory impairments track. The period from 1987 to 2007 reveals that preparation of qualified teachers in deaf education has not improved. Current teachers of deaf students are either graduates of the mild/moderate track or are expatriates from other Arab countries, with little or no experience in deaf education. Deaf students in UAE are improperly served, and the fact that they have the ability as a group to reach the highest education levels has not been a convincing enough reason to supply them with qualified teachers.

In Kuwait, the teacher preparation program in deaf education was opened officially in 2001–02 as part of an ambitious endeavor in the College of Basic Education at the Public Authority for Applied Education and Training Institution, an autonomous higher education establishment, to prepare the teaching staff in various areas of education and special education. Preservice teachers enrolled in the College of Basic Education can major in math, science, social studies, Islamic studies, or Arabic and have the option to choose to supplement their major with a specialty area in giftedness and creativity (27 credit hours), mental disabilities (42 credit hours), hearing disabilities (36 credit hours), or visual disabilities (36 credit hours). Before 2001–02, those who taught students with special needs were regular teachers graduating from Kuwait University, the first higher education institution in the State of Kuwait, or were expatriates from other Arab countries. Many of those regular education teachers have little or no simple practical knowledge of deaf students or of other students with special needs because studying the introductory course Teaching Exceptional Learners is not compulsory (except at Kuwait University for those majoring in kindergarten education, also known as childhood education).

By 2004, the department of special education in the college of basic education stopped admitting new student teachers, and it closed the deaf education and other special education programs indefinitely, citing the reason of limited available vacancies for the new graduates in special education. The 2004 statistics published by the department of special education showed 113 preservice teachers enrolled in the deaf education program alone (Department of Special Education, 2004). This number of preservice teachers exceeded the available vacancies in the area of deaf education, which meant that a large number of those 113 preservice teachers would be looking for jobs outside the field of deaf education. The admission policy that had been based on the yearly needs for teachers in deaf education as well as other specialty areas was not strictly followed.

Reviewing the program of teachers in deaf education revealed that they studied the following compulsory courses: Introduction to Hearing Impairment, Language Development and Articulation Training (focusing on articulations and converting articulated sounds into signs), Sign Language 1 and Sign Language 2, Issues and Applications in Hearing Impairments, Communication Disorders, Measurement and Evaluation in Special Education, Physiological Aspects of Human Behavior, Methods of Teaching and Training the Deaf, and Classroom Management in Schools of Special Education. Students also had to choose two optional courses from a list that includes Special Topics in Special Education, Counseling in Special Education, Play for Individuals With Special Needs, Learning Disabilities, Physical Disabilities and Health Impairments, Rehabilitation, and Inclusion of Students With Disabilities in Regular Schools. The overall program was ill-structured and lacked prerequisites, and course contents were not covered comprehensively; for example, students were allowed to enroll in the teaching methodology course before taking the sign language courses. A critical issue in the program is the lack of specialists in deaf education. Among the six full-time faculty members who were teaching in the college of basic education, not one had a PhD in the field of deaf education. The department of special education operated its programs by assigning courses to available faculty members and by using part-time instructors with BA or MA degrees.

SOCIAL AND PSYCHOLOGICAL PERSONNEL

Theoretically speaking, social and psychological personnel are available in educational settings to help the deaf and their families deal with aspects related to deafness. This support supposedly includes conducting educational assessments as well as assisting families in accepting their children and overcoming stigmas associated with the disability. The social specialist within a setting has a BA degree in sociology or social work and cooperates with and provides consultations to schools or special education center administrators to assist deaf people in overcoming obstacles that hinder their learning and the implementation of their rehabilitation programs. Other duties include fostering cooperation and interaction between home, school, and community and helping address issues related to achievement, absenteeism, and behavior problems.

The main duty of the psychology personnel is to uncover students' potential and special abilities, determine levels of performance, and use the collected data for admission purposes. They conduct observations and interviews, carry out case studies, implement remedial and preventive measures, perform testing, and counsel students and their families. During family counseling sessions, the focus is on mental, physical, psychological, and social characteristics of deaf students to help parents accept their deaf children.

In practice, the social and psychological services are less than satisfactory. The social worker usually does nothing more than go through the paperwork, producing little or no tangible outcomes. The work of the psychology personnel has more drastic negative effect on the lives of the deaf students than that of the social worker. It is not unusual to have deaf students assessed by a person with a BA degree in psychology, educational psychology, sociology, or even social work, depending on what is available in the educational institutions. Having the deaf student assessed by a person with an MA degree in psychology is the exception. The school psychology personnel have little or no training in proper psychological assessments, and they view their role not as clinical diagnosticians but as data collectors or test givers for sorting, classifying, and placement purposes. They administer tests such as the Point Scale of Performance Tests—Revised Form II (Arthur, 1947), Raven's Standard Progressive Matrices Test (Raven, Court, & Raven, 1996), and Draw-a-Person Test (Machover, 1951), which have not been properly normed for deaf populations. The psychology personnel have little or no proficiency in the preferred mode of communication with the deaf population and have poor skills with respect to interpreting tests results and writing proper psychological evaluation reports. It is not uncommon to find deaf students misdiagnosed with low mental ability and be viewed erroneously as concrete learners.

This outcome of improper psychological assessment is not surprising considering the absence of accredited school psychology programs, not to mention qualified faculty members in school psychology, to prepare qualified school psychologists. The flawed information about the ability of deaf students has shaped the kind, quality, and method of presenting knowledge and skills to them and has restricted their future prospects in all aspects of life.

SPECIAL EDUCATION LAW

The State of Kuwait and UAE have both passed special education laws to protect the rights of individuals with disabilities. Kuwait passed the Care for the Handicapped law number 49 (Higher Council for the Disabled, 1996) on August 31, 1996, making it a proactive leader in the region in terms of addressing issues related to individuals with disabling conditions. The law uses the term *handicapped*, which is not differentiated in Arabic from the term *disabled*, and defines it as individuals who are partially or completely unable to guarantee for themselves normal life necessities. The law mandates implementing the following:

1. Free rehabilitation, medical, educational, social, housing, transportation, and employment assistance to all handicapped individuals. This list of services could be modified to meet the needs of those with specific handicaps.
2. An extra 50% pay raise in addition to the regular child support pay to families who have children with disabilities. The extra pay is given for each disabled child with disabilities in a given family.
3. Full-pay maternity leave for pregnant women with disabilities, in addition to other leave if recommended by a medical committee; those who cannot work get a pension.
4. Application of international standards for disabled access to buildings, roads, government support housing, entrances to shopping and entertainment areas, parking, and all public facilities.
5. Tax-exemptions and supported prices for all equipment and augmentative devices and tools.
6. Employment for all qualified individuals with disabilities in the public sector and in private establishments with 50 or more employees, based on 2% quota, and imposed fines for refusing to hire individuals with disabilities without providing acceptable justifications.
7. Formation of a government body, the Higher Council for the Disabled, to specify the needs of the disabled, approve public policies on disabilities, determine proper procedures for the care of the disabled, and propose rules and regulations to grantee the rights of the disabled.
8. Imposed 2-year imprisonments, fines of up to 2,000 KD (about US$6,000), or both on those who are sentenced with negligence and who cause harm to those who are handicapped. If the negligence causes death, the punishment would be up to 3 years in prison, a fine of 3,000 KD (about US$9,000), or both.

This law does not address issues related to educational assessment and placement options. Daily practices indicate that the law is not strictly enforced, although public or governmental institutions are more likely to be in compliance than private institutions. Even though this law has helped promote and protect some of the rights of disabled Kuwaitis, it has not clearly stated the legal procedures for its implementation and has not brought about the necessary changes to improve the quality of life of children with disabilities. This law lacks the mechanisms to guarantee judicial procedures. Consequently, employers can refuse to hire any individual with a disability without being forced to provide appropriate justifications. Also, employers hiring fewer than 50 people do not have to adhere to the law and do not have to make necessary adjustments and modifications suitable to the type of disability that the individual has.

With reference to the special education law in UAE, the president of that country signed on August 13, 2006, the Rights of Individuals With Special Needs, federal law number 29 (Ministry of Social Affairs, 2006). The purpose of this law is to protect the rights of individuals with disabilities; to provide all the services they need; and to prevent discrimination in social, economic, health, learning, cultural, and recreational care and welfare areas. The law defines the individual with a special need as any person who has a total or a partial disability on a temporary or permanent basis in his or her physical, sensory, mental, communicative, learning, and psychological abilities to a degree that it reduces possibilities to meet his or her regular needs without assistance. The law also defines discrimination as any action taken to set apart, to exclude, or to limit access based on a disability, and it requires that a disability identification card be issued to guarantee rights to services.

This law calls for the proper authority, which is the Ministry of Social Affairs, to inform individuals with special needs and their families of their rights to have the following:

1. Equal learning opportunities similar to nondisabled children
2. An appropriate curriculum presented in a suitable mode of communication (e.g., sign language)
3. Free legal assistance and medical, health, diagnostic, remedial, and rehabilitation services provided in specialized centers and institutions
4. Education with nondisabled children
5. Family training on effective methods of inter- and intrapersonal interactions
6. Early intervention programs and qualified health and academic personnel in all areas of special needs including, social, educational, psychological, medical, and vocational rehabilitation
7. Nondiscriminatory treatment to access educational institutions, private or public, or to apply, hold, and be selected for a job
8. Employment opportunities available in private and public sectors based on a quota
9. Accessibility to all public facilities
10. Court fees waived in case of litigation and any need to file lawsuits
11. Free government-supported housing facility, the right to acquire a driver's license, eligibility to receive tax-exemption when purchasing a new vehicle, and entitlement to free postal and parking services

The UAE special education law is comprehensive in that it covers daily life aspects related to individuals with special needs starting from early intervention and including access to all needed specialists. This law echoed many critical aspects covered in other laws such as the one in Kuwait and the federal laws in the United States, including (a) Section 504 of the Vocational Rehabilitation Act of 1973, which is a civil rights act prohibiting discrimination by any federally financed programs against qualified individuals solely on the basis of disabilities; (b) Individuals With Disabilities Education Act of 1990, which is the new name given to the historic and landmark Education for All Handicapped Children Act, also known as Public Law 94-142 passed in 1975 to protect rights and guarantee free and appropriate public education and individualized assessments; and (c) the Americans With Disabilities Act of 1990, which bars discrimination in federally and nonfederally funded aspects of life, including employment, public accommodations, telecommunications, and transportation.

CURRENT DEVELOPMENTS AND TRENDS

Officially, there are no major developments or new trends in deafness in Kuwait and UAE with the exception of research efforts at the individual level to examine the concept of metacognition in real-life situations as a way of measuring mental ability. Forms of objective tests of metacognition that can be used by teachers and school psychology personnel alike have been explored as a way to assess higher order thinking processes and activities. Metacognition is considered for this purpose as a process that enables the individual to perform mental recognition, discrimination, judgment, reflection-on-action, reflection-in-action, and cognitive restructuring of events. It has also been viewed as a mental ability that is associated with how one perceives, explains, performs, and stays connected to activities in various everyday situations for obtaining continuous evaluations and feedback (Al-Hilawani, 2000b, 2003b, 2006). This view of metacognition includes abilities to monitor ones' own as well as others' mental processes and activities. It has expanded the traditional approach of metacognition from being associated with study skills (Al-Hilawani, 1999) and achievement (e.g., reading comprehension, spelling, and mathematics) to currently being associated with understanding and responding to real-life situations.

The first work in metacognition has focused on visual analyses of real-life situations using colored pictures in which four verbal or signed options are presented (Al-Hilawani, 2000b). These options have provided possible explanations of what the pictures reveal or represent. Participants have to choose the correct answer from the four options. Although this measure could be administered objectively with little training, there is still a need for a person to administer it by means of sign language because of difficulties that deaf people might have in reading and understanding written language. Searching for a different procedure that does not heavily depend on options that must be signed to the deaf person has led to a second approach that capitalizes primarily on visual analyses and discriminations where all options are real-life pictures (Al-Hilawani, 2003b). Research using the two approaches showed that deaf and hard of hearing students were as competent as their hearing counterparts in metacognitive performance (Al-Hilawani, 2000b, 2001, 2003b). This research contradicted widespread, erroneous conceptions that deaf people are concrete learners and have low mental ability.

Further research (Al-Hilawani, 2005) analyzing performances on these two forms of measurement (i.e., the visual-verbal measures) indicated (a) that the performance of males in the hearing and deaf groups did not differ significantly on the visual-verbal measure from their performance on the visual-visual measure and (b) that hearing and deaf females performed significantly higher on the visual-verbal measure than on the visual-visual measure. This study pointed out that hearing and deaf participants are not qualitatively different from each other in the way they process verbal and visual stimuli and that they are more similar than different in the cognitive processing activities of daily life, which may indicate having similar conceptual systems. Further support for this conclusion comes from recent research (Al-Hilawani, Dashti, & Abdullah, 2008) at Kuwait University, which examines the relationship between metacognition in real-life situations and reaction time by using a computerized metacognitive instrument that can be administered objectively and accurately by teachers and school psychology personnel without the need for intensive training. Traditionally, reaction time has been studied with reference to students' IQ. Studies (e.g., Bates & Stough, 1998; Jensen, 1998) reported positive correlation between reaction time and IQ; individuals who have high abilities processed information faster than those who have low abilities. The research of Al-Hilawani et al. (2008) reported no significant differences between the performance of hearing and deaf and hard of hearing students on the test scores of metacognition, on reaction time to test items, and on the test scores obtained based on the mean of reaction time to each test item. This result reveals that hearing and deaf and hard of hearing students are more alike than different with reference to performance on the tests of metacognition and with reference to the duration of time they took to respond correctly to the presented stimuli. This result indicates that deaf and hard of hearing students have the ability to manage, to manipulate, and to reason about stimuli in a timely manner and in a fashion similar to that of hearing students.

Research conducted in Kuwait and UAE contradicts the de facto status quo of peoples' judgments with respect to the ability of deaf students compared with hearing peers. Although this research reports important new developments in deafness, the outcome of this research by itself is not enough to change perceptions and craft the positive attitudes and intentions necessary to create appropriate and vital teacher preparation programs to meet the needs of deaf students, to prepare qualified professionals who can use test results to determine performance outcomes, and to facilitate access to higher education institutions.

Conclusion

Fair practices, appropriate services, and equal opportunities for deaf individuals in Kuwait and UAE have not yet been realized. Good intentions at the administrative level to improve students' learning outcomes are hindered by the lack of qualified teachers, proper college programs, and the glass-ceiling effect that limits the education of deaf students.

Personal experiences as well as anecdotes and written documents collected for this chapter revealed inconsistencies that favored exaggerating the quality of services being provided to deaf students. In fact, these services perpetuate low-level education, divert attention from pursuing advanced levels, and pacify problems, all of which will not lead to prosperous, independent lives for deaf people that allow them to reach their potential and gain full citizenship status.

The kind of education provided in Kuwait and UAE to deaf students is based on the fallacy that deaf people are incapable of learning and mastering abstract information. Although increasing numbers of practitioners know that deaf people are as capable and competent as hearing individuals when served properly, the current education system in both countries is impotent and cannot accommodate the needs of deaf students because their knowledge of deafness is distorted and their vision for deaf education is fuzzy at best.

Knowing the curriculum that deaf students are currently studying and the qualifications of teachers who teach those deaf students helps to explain why deaf students suffer linguistic and learning deprivations in educational settings and why accessing higher education institutions is unattainable goal for them at this time. Deaf native language is not developing and expanding to address all areas of knowledge because it is being ignored in schools and centers, giving the impression that such language is not important and unacceptable.

Government agencies and funded educational institutions are being blamed for setbacks and lack of progress in deaf education. This blame occurs because people expect these services to be offered on a humanitarian basis and with good intentions. The vision of parents joining forces with professionals and advocates in legal battles for appropriate education is not foreseeable anytime soon.

Special education laws in Kuwait and UAE are tangible ways of protecting the rights of individuals with disabilities. However, the law in Kuwait has not been fully implemented as intended in all walks of life, and it remains to be seen whether the new special education law in UAE will face the same destiny. Is the UAE special education law going to be enforced in all aspects of life? Sartawi et al. (1998) mentioned that job opportunities in UAE have been very limited for people with disabilities. Will the 2006 special education law make a difference in employing more individuals with disabilities and improving the quality of their lives? We will not know for some years down the road.

Compared with hearing counterparts, deaf people in Kuwait and UAE face more difficulties related to independence and marriage. Deaf females, in particular, suffer the most. They do not have the luxury of free movement without being with the family or accompanied by a family member. It is not easy for them to get married, which is the primary way that females achieve independence by starting their own autonomous living arrangements. Anecdotal reports revealed that it is not uncommon for deaf females to suffer from psychological difficulties more often than deaf males who have more freedom to move and interact with other deaf individuals.

Finally, two points are informative to mention. First, although this chapter has shed some light on deaf individuals, other individuals with disabling conditions suffer the same, if not worse, in terms of social, psychological, and educational services and future outlooks. Second, the overall conditions of students with disabilities, including deafness, are neither prosperous nor improving in other Arab countries in the region. There will be many years to go before quality improvements occur in all services offered to all students with disabilities.

References

Administration of Schools of Special Education. (2003). *Special education in Kuwait.* Hawally, State of Kuwait: Ministry of Education.

Al-Hilawani, Y. (1999). A comparison among average-achieving, underachieving, and deaf/hard-of-hearing students on effective study skills and habits. *International Journal of Special Education, 14*(1), 12–24.

Al-Hilawani, Y. (2000a). Cognitive behavior modification: A technique for teaching subtraction skills to hearing and deaf/hard-of-hearing elementary students. *International Journal of Rehabilitation Research, 23,* 217–225.

Al-Hilawani, Y. (2000b). A new approach to evaluating metacognition in hearing average-achieving, hearing underachieving, and deaf/hard-of-hearing elementary school students. *British Journal of Special Education, 27*(1), 41–47.

Al-Hilawani, Y. (2001). Examining metacognition in hearing and deaf/hard-of-hearing students: A comparative study. *American Annals of the Deaf, 146,* 45–50.

Al-Hilawani, Y. (2003a). Clinical examination of three methods of teaching reading comprehension to deaf and hard-of-hearing students: From research to classroom applications. *Journal of Deaf Studies and Deaf Education, 8*(2), 146–156.

Al-Hilawani, Y. (2003b). Measuring students' metacognition in real-life situations. *American Annals of the Deaf, 148,* 233–242.

Al-Hilawani, Y. (2005, October). *Metacognitive performances of hearing and deaf and hard-of-hearing students on two types of measures: Visual-verbal VS. Visual-visual stimuli.* Paper presented at the annual meeting of the Mid-Western Educational Research Association, Columbus, OH.

Al-Hilawani, Y. (2006). Visual analyses and discriminations: One approach to measuring students' metacognition. *American Annals of the Deaf, 151,* 16–24.

Al-Hilawani, Y., Dashti, F., & Abdullah, A. (2008). *Measuring metacognition: A prospect for objective assessment*. Manuscript submitted for publication.

Arthur, G. (1947). *Point scale of performance tests—Revised form II*. New York: Psychological Corporation.

Bates, T., & Stough, C. (1998). Improved reaction time method, information processing speed, and intelligence. *Intelligence, 26*(1), 53–62.

Department of Programs for Individuals with Special Needs. (2004/2005). [Statistical data]. Dubai, United Arab Emirates: Ministry of Education—Educational Administration.

Department of Special Education. (2004). *Statistics on the number of students enrolled in the department of special education according to their majors and minors up to 2004-03-17*. Internal memo signed by the department chairperson on September 20, 2004. Kuwait City, State of Kuwait: Public Authority for Applied Education and Training—College of Basic Education.

Higher Council for the Disabled. (1996). *Law number 49 for the year 1996: Care for the handicapped*. Kuwait City: State of Kuwait.

Jensen, A. R. (1998). The suppressed relationship between IQ and the reaction time slope parameter of the Hick function. *Intelligence, 26*(1), 43–52.

Machover, K. (1951). *Personality projection in the drawing of the human figure*. Springfield, IL: Thomas.

Meichenbaum, D., & Burland, S. (1979). Cognitive behavior modification with children. *School Psychology Digest, 8*, 426–433.

Ministry of Labour and Social Affairs (1995). [Census and statistics]. Abu-Dhabi: United Arab Emirates.

Ministry of Social Affairs (2006). *The federal law number 29 for the year 2006: The rights of individuals with special needs*. Abu-Dhabi, United Arab Emirates: Author.

Raven, J. C., Court, J. H., & Raven, J. (1996). *Manual for Raven's standard progressive matrices*. Oxford, England: Oxford Psychologists Press.

Sartawi, A., Al-Hilawani, Y., & Easterbrooks, S. R. (1998). A pilot study of reading comprehension strategies of students who are deaf/hard-of-hearing in a non-English-speaking country. *Journal of Children's Communication Development, 20*(1), 27–32.

Wise, A. E. (2005). Speech of Arthur E. Wise in United Arab Emirates on May 8, 2005. Retrieved May 18, 2007, from http://www.ncate.org/documents/NCATENews/UAESpeechMay2005.pdf

Education of the Deaf in South Africa

Claudine Storbeck, Lucas Magongwa, and Ingrid Parkin

OFTEN REFERRED to as the "rainbow nation" (Tutu, quoted in Allen, 2006, p. 391), South Africa has a complex history of colonial immigration and rule; local turmoil for power; apartheid; and most recently, democracy for all. The history of Deaf people in South Africa closely mirrors that of the country, where segregation based on race and culture affected both the language development and access to education for Deaf learners.[1] In this chapter, we discuss Deaf education in South Africa and the effects and challenges this unique history has created. We end by sharing our hopes and dreams for the future of the South African Deaf community and offer possible solutions to challenges that are often seen as insurmountable.

SOUTH AFRICA: THE COUNTRY AND ITS HISTORY

The Republic of South Africa, situated at the southern tip of Africa, currently has an estimated population of 47.9 million people (Statistics South Africa, 2007). Africans make up the majority (almost 80% of the population), with the White and colored populations estimated at approximately 9% each and the Indian/Asian population at 2.5% (see Figure 10.1).[2]

The government of South Africa recognizes 11 official languages, a testament to the country's diverse population (see Figure 10.2). Section 6 of the Constitution of South Africa 1996 ensures that all languages enjoy parity of esteem and are treated equitably. Of the 11 official languages, 9 are African, reflecting a variety of ethnic groupings, which nonetheless have a great deal in common in terms of background, culture, and descent.[3] South African Sign Language (SASL) is not yet accorded official status, but it is officially recognized in the Constitution and other legislation such as the South African School Act of 1996 as the language that needs to be developed and should be used as the learning and teaching medium in schools for the deaf because of the fact that SASL is a necessary language for the purposes of learning at a public school (Department of Education, 1997a).

Historically, South Africa was invaded by Dutch settlers (1652) and later colonized by the British (1806), events that led to many skirmishes for power and control of land between all

---

1. The term Deaf is used in this chapter to reflect a cultural and linguistic perspective; the term deaf is used to represent a clininal view.

2. The term *African* refers to the indigenous people of the African continent and reflects a variety of ethnic groupings that nonetheless have a great deal in common in terms of background, culture, and descent. The terms *Black* and *African* differ in the present political climate. Black people include Africans, Indians, and colored people whereas Africans refer only to the indigenous people of the African continent. The term *colored* is the contentious term for people of mixed race, usually the offspring of one Black and one White parent.

3. The African languages include those of the Nguni people (comprising the Zulu, Xhosa, Ndebele, and Swazi), the Sotho-Tswana people (comprising the Southern, Northern, and Western Sotho/Tswana), the Tsonga people, and the Venda people.

133

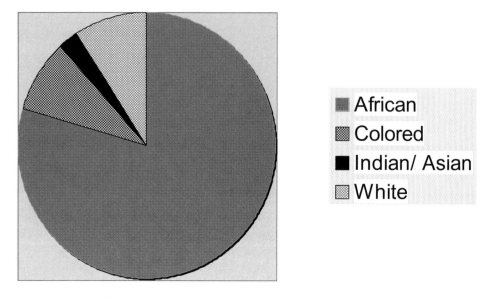

Figure 10.1. The South African population.

inhabitants. In 1910, South Africa became a union, with apartheid being formally instituted in 1948 (although segregation and discriminatory laws limiting Black people to menial labor, minimal land ownership, and no fundamental right to vote existed as far back as the early 1900s). In 1961, the union became a republic, and South Africa formally left the commonwealth. Inequality abounded, and after many turbulent years a new constitution was drafted. In April 1994, the first democratic elections were held in South Africa. The African National Congress gained the overwhelming majority, and on May 10, 1994, Nelson Mandela was inaugurated as the first Black African president of democratic South Africa.

Geographically, South Africa is divided into nine provinces and is formally noted as one of the Southern African development countries that include Namibia, Botswana, Zimbabwe, Angola, Lesotho, Swaziland, and Mozambique. South Africa takes a strong leadership role in the African Union.

HISTORICAL BACKGROUND ON DEAF EDUCATION

Because of the political upheavals of the apartheid era, many missionaries were sent to South Africa, and this missionary-minded approach also reached the South African Deaf community in the 1860s in the form of the Irish Dominican nuns and, later, the Dutch Reformed Church. The first school for the deaf in South Africa was established in Cape Town in 1863 by the Irish Dominican Order under the leadership of Bishop Grimley and was known as the Dominican Grimley Institute for the Deaf. This school enrolled all races (which was probably tolerated because of its being the first service for deaf learners and primarily a missionary endeavor). It used Sign Language as a medium of instruction. Irish Dominican sisters used Irish signs and the Irish one-handed alphabet to organize interpreted church services for deaf members of their congregations in the second half of the 19th century. The German

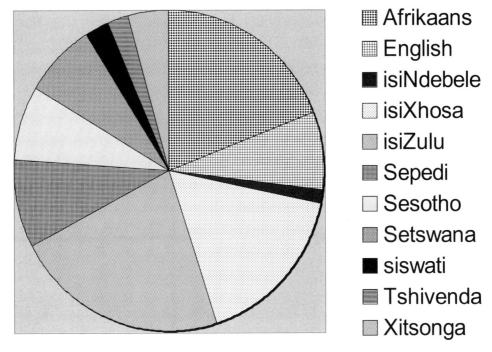

Figure 10.2. Language distribution of the South African population.

Dominican sisters followed, bringing with them German signs and the two-handed European alphabet. Additionally, the German Sisters brought with them an oral approach to educating deaf learners, thus introducing South Africa to the modality debate.

Internationally, the year 1880 was a watershed year in deaf education when oralism became the formally adopted system of education (after the Milan Congress decision). These decisions affected South African schools a few years later. More and more teachers were trained using oral methods, and Sign Language became marginalized in terms of its use as a language of communication and education. Within the teaching community, conflict arose as the modality debate heightened, and within the broader Deaf communities (including parents and extended families), there were splits on the basis of their acceptance or rejection of sign language and the oral method.

In answer to this international declaration, The Worcester School for the Deaf and Blind was established in 1881 (by the Dutch Reformed Church in the Western Cape) and combined oral and manual methods. In 1884, German Dominican nuns established a school at King Williams Town in the Eastern Cape, which followed a policy of strict oralism. Both these schools were for "European deaf children" only. In 1933, the Dutch Reformed Church set up another school in the Cape, this time for "colored deaf" children known as Nuwe Hoop, and it, too, combined oral and manual methods. The first school for Black deaf children, Kutlwanong, was opened in 1941 in Gauteng. That school used a system of signs invented in Britain known as the Paget-Gorman System, a sign system that is a manually coded form of English using 37 basic hand signs and 21 distinct hand postures. Although it did not correspond to the natural signs of the Deaf community, it did allow for the development of a strong visually based communication code that facilitated rather than repressed a strong Deaf culture.

When the Nationalist Party government came into power in 1948, there was greater fragmentation of Deaf communities along racial lines, and as a result of the homelands policy, a number of additional schools for African deaf children were established in the rest of the country, divided according to the spoken language of the ethnic groups, and in line with the Bantustan separate development policy. For example, the Kutlwanong School moved to Rustenburg and served the Setswana, Sesotho, and Sepedi "users"; Efata School in the Transkei was for isiXhosa "speakers"; Bartimea School at Thaba'nchu catered to Setswana and Sesotho users; Vuleka School at Nkandla served isiZulu users; St. Thomas in King Williams Town was for isiXhosa users; Tshilidzini School at Shayadima served Tshivenda and Xitsonga users; Thiboloa at Witsieshoek served Southern Sothos; Dominican School in Hammanskraal was for Sothos; and two schools in Soweto and Katlehong catered to urban Black deaf children (Ross, 2004).

This segregation led to the further entrenchment of oralist policies in White schools (which was seen as the more educated elitist approach) and a manual system of instruction (assumed to be the more basic approach) in Black, colored, and Indian schools. Thus, ironically, because these schools used visually based communication that enhanced the development of their sign language and strengthened their identity as part of a Deaf culture, they reaped some benefits from apartheid and were in some ways superior in their education offerings to those offering education to "privileged" White deaf learners. Additionally, the relative poverty of Black institutions and communities meant that highly developed acoustic technology aids were not available to Black deaf children, so little or no pressure was exercised to enforce the implementation of the oral approach to education.

The establishment of access to schools for Deaf learners in South Africa has continued to this day, and now currently totals 47 schools, units, and classes that accommodate deaf learners (see Table 10.1).

Despite the abolition of apartheid (and thus segregated education), schools for the deaf are currently still geographically (and, thus, often racially) focused and quite disparate in terms of their facilities and what they offer the learners. The majority of teachers are untrained in the specialized pedagogy of deaf learners and in their language (SASL) and are thus unable to effectively meet the specific needs of the deaf and hard of hearing learners in a modality or language that is accessible to the learner.

SOUTH AFRICAN SIGN LANGUAGE

SASL has been around as long as there have been South African Deaf people to communicate with one another. Very little has been formally researched about SASL in particular by Deaf or hearing linguists who are native signers; however, we know that through the development of deaf education (with the help of the Irish and German Dominican orders as well as through the Paget-Gorman system), SASL has had influences from Irish, German, and British Sign Languages. More recently, with teachers of the deaf studying deaf education (such as the groups of teachers sent by the V. N. Naik School to study at Gallaudet University years ago) and Deaf adults traveling and studying in the United States, ASL has also had an effect

Table 10.1. An Historical Overview of Deaf Education in South Africa

Year Established	Name of School	Location
1863	Dominican Grimley School for the Deaf (In 1960s, moved to Houtbay and became oral)	Western Cape
1881	Worcester Skool vir Dowes	Worcester, Western Cape
1881	Pioneer School for the Deaf-Blind	Worcester, Cape Town
1884	German Dominican School for the Deaf (later moved to JHB and was renamed St Vincent School)	King Williams Town, Eastern Cape
1933	Nuwe Hoop School for the Deaf	Worcester, Western Cape
1933	Mary Kihn School for partially hearing pupils	Observatory, Cape Town
1934	St Vincent School for the Deaf	Johannesburg
1937	Wittebome Dominican School for the Deaf	Wittebome
1941	Kutlwanong School for the Deaf	Roodepoort, then moved to Rustenburg, NW
1954	TransOranje Skool vir Dowes	Pretoria
1957	Bosele School for the Deaf	Nebo, Limpopo
1958	Efata School for the Deaf	Umtata, Eastern Cape
1959	Fulton School for the Deaf	Gillits, KZN
1962	Dominican School for the Deaf	Hammanskraal
1962	St. Thomas School for the Deaf	King Williams Town, Eastern Cape
1962	Bartimea School for the Deaf	Thaba'nchu, Free State
1962	Vuleka School for the Deaf	Nkandla, KZN
1969	Durban School for the hearing impaired	Durban, KZN
1971	Tshilidzini School for the Deaf	Shyandima, Limpopo
1971	Reubin Birin School for the Deaf	P E, Eastern Cape
1972	Thiboloha School for the Deaf	Witsieshoek, Free State
1973	Sonitus School for the hard-of-hearing	Pretoria
1973	Carel du Toit Centre	Cape Town
1974	Centre for Language & Hearing Impaired children	Johannesburg
1978	Sizwile School for the Deaf	Soweto, Gauteng
1979	KwaVulindlebe School for the Deaf	Umlazi, KZN
1980	MCKharbai School for the Deaf	Lenasia, GT
1983	KwaThintwa School for the Deaf	Inchanga, KZN
1984	V. N. Naik School for the Deaf	Newlands, KZN
1985	Filadelfia School for the Deaf	Soshanguve
1986	Indaleni School for the Deaf	Richmond, KZN
1988	Noluthando School for the Deaf	Western Cape
1989	Yingisani School for the Deaf	Tzaneen, Limpopo
1991	St. Martin de Porres Comprehensive School	Port Shepstone, KZN
1993	Sidibeng Combined School	Ellisras
1993	Retlameleng School for Children with Disabilities	Kimberley, NC
1993	Setotolwane LSEN Secondary School	Polokwane, Limpopo
1994	North West Secondary School for the Deaf	Rustenburg, NW
1994	Sive School for the Deaf	Cedarville, Eastern Cape
1994	Osizweni Special School (regular school established in 1987, but opened its doors for deaf learners only in 1994)	Leslie
1996	Ka Magugu Primary School for the deaf and blind	Nelspruit
1996	Carel du Toit Centre	Pretoria
1998	Deaf Child Centre preschool	Observatory, Cape Town
1999	NW Secondary School, moved to Leeudoringstad	Leeudoringstad, North West
2001	Katlehong school for the deaf and blind renamed as Sinethemba and then renamed again in 2007 as Ekurhuleni School for the Deaf	Kathlehong, Gauteng
2004	St. Vincenzo School for the Deaf (registered, but not functioning yet)	Welkom, Freestate
2005	Silindokuhle School for Specialised education Inkazimulo Kankulunkulu (class for deaf learners)	Kwalugedlane, Mpumalanga Standerton

Note: Adapted from Ross, Storbeck, and Wemmer (2004).

on SASL. However, as with all natural languages that grow, develop, borrow, and expand based on communicative need and outside influences, the language remains intact.

Historically, as was discussed previously, segregation kept the various communities separate, thus affecting the variation of signs used locally. The differences were seen to be substantial (Simmons, 1994, referred to them as different sign languages). In fact, at meetings held by the National Organization of the Deaf (South African National Council for the Deaf, as it was known previously), a variety of Sign Language interpreters were provided to ensure that all Deaf people of all races and ethnicities could access the meetings. However, with the abolition of apartheid and the frequent mixing of all Deaf people, the variations that seemed apparent have either diminished or have been shown to be less substantial than initially assumed (perhaps limited only to differences in vocabulary). The limited research available has found that despite diversity in vocabulary, there is one South African Sign Language—SASL—evident by, among other things, its mutual intelligibility (Aarons & Akach, 2002). This finding is functionally verified because, currently, national meetings of the Deaf Federation of South Africa (DeafSA) have only one SASL interpreter interpreting at a time and all delegates (of all races, languages, and cultures) understand and participate equally. The unity of SASL is also verified by Penn and Reagan (1994) who refer to the syntactic unity evident in SASL despite the lexical diversity and by Aarons and Morgan (1998) who found that the uniform classifier system as well as syntactic and morphological structures were evidence enough of SASL being one language.

Although it is clear that SASL is indeed a language within its own right, it is a language that needs to grow sufficiently to allow the Deaf community to access greater opportunities. The vocabulary within SASL will improve as Deaf people gain better access to education and career opportunities and develop the need to start discussing a wider variety of topics at deeper levels of learning.

STATUS OF DEAF ADULTS IN DEAF EDUCATION IN SOUTH AFRICA

Locating the Deaf community within the South African population requires an understanding of the disability population in South Africa. The latest data we have recorded for this group are from Census 2001 (Statistics South Africa, 2001). The census revealed that 2,255,982 people identified themselves as having disabilities, including deaf people who constituted 5% of the total population at the time. The number of people identified with a "hearing disability" totaled 20.1% of the disability population, with the prevalence among African, Colored and Asian/Indian being almost equal (19.7%, 18.2%, and 16.2%, respectively), and the prevalence among the White community with disabilities being 26.1% (Statistics South Africa, 2001).

Although Deaf people in South Africa do not see themselves as a disability group (rather, as a linguistic and cultural minority group), they do affiliate with various lobbying groups on disability to ensure they are "heard" during policy development and implementation at various levels of government and civic society.

Additionally, Deaf and hard of hearing people in South Africa have worked hard at representing themselves at various decision-making bodies locally and nationally. To this end, the South African National Council for the Deaf, which was founded (by hearing people) in 1929, was transformed in 1995 (by Deaf people) into the DeafSA, and subsequently, South Africa became a member of the World Federation of the Deaf. This national organization representing the rights of Deaf and hard of hearing people has lobbied vigorously at various forums and national departments such as the Departments of Education, Arts and Culture, and Social Welfare as well as at South African Qualifications Authority and various other decision-making bodies.

Some key achievements have been the official recognition of the linguistic rights of Deaf South Africans and the subsequent inclusion of SASL as language for promotion in the constitution (Constitutional Assembly of the Republic of South Africa, 1996); the acknowledgment of SASL as the official language of the Deaf for educational purposes (Republic of South Africa, 1996); and recognition or noting of the specific needs of Deaf learners in a variety of policies and legal documents. These achievements will be discussed in the following section.

Special Laws, Legislation, and Policies as They Relate to Deaf Education and South African Sign Language

DeafSA, through its provincial offices and affiliates, has fought and lobbied successfully at various levels of South African decision making to ensure that the Deaf plight remains on the national and provincial agenda. South Africa is advanced in terms of the laws and legislation that relate to deaf education and SASL. A selection of the main laws and pieces of legislation are detailed as follows.

South African Constitution (Constitutional Assembly of the Republic of South Africa, 1996)

The Constitution of South Africa has enshrined equality for all, and in particular, it recognizes SASL as the language of Deaf South Africans. This acknowledgment, we believe, is the "basis for the recognition of [South African] Sign Language as the first language of choice for Deaf learners" and thus for the official status of SASL that we hope for (Department of Education, 1997a, p. 42).

Because of the focus on language rights in Section 6 in the Constitution, Parliament established the Pan South African Language Board (PanSALB) to promote multilingualism and develop the 11 official languages, including Khoe, San, and SASL. A SASL unit has been established within PanSALB to ensure that SASL remains a focus in all their activities.

The South African Schools Act (Republic of South Africa, 1996)

This act confirms the right of equal access to basic and quality education for all learners and recognizes SASL as an official language for the purposes of learning at a public school. This instance is the first time any particular method of teaching deaf learners has been legislatively recognized in South African law books.

An Integrated National Disability Strategy (Department of Education, 1997b)

The Integrated National Disability Strategy (INDS) is a groundbreaking document that was commissioned by the president's office. This document and the disability office within the presidency focus on the rights, rehabilitation, welfare, education, employment, and the role of people with disabilities. It underscores government's commitment to end any form of discrimination against people with disabilities.

In particular, one of the recommendations in the INDS speaks to the education of Deaf learners. Recommendation 9B (Education) suggests that the Department of Education, in consultation with the Department of Arts and Culture, DeafSA, and other stakeholders, facilitate a process for the development of a comprehensive education policy to "promote and protect equal education opportunities for children with communication disabilities and to protect their language medium" (Department of Education, 1997b, p. 68).

This recommendation is vital because it brings together all the relevant stakeholders that will make an important contribution toward the development and awareness of SASL in all sectors of South Africa and, in particular, the education of deaf children. Unfortunately, however, this recommendation has not yet been implemented

Inclusive Education Policy

In an attempt to prevent segregation and discrimination from ever occurring again, particularly within the educational context, the Department of Education began exploring inclusion in the late 1990s (Department of Education, 1997a), and in 2001, White Paper No. 6 (Department of Education, 2001) was finalized and released. Both of these documents will be briefly discussed as key components in the launch of Inclusive Education, a government priority for education.

Quality Education for All (National Commission on Education Support Services/ National Commission on Special Needs in Education and Training Report) (Department of Education, 1997a)

The National Commission on Education Support Services and the National Commission on Special Needs in Education and Training were appointed in 1996 to work toward researching collaboratively the needs of learners and the concomitant services required to meet their needs within the school environment. The efforts of these two groups focused on identifying various barriers to learning (both intrinsic and extrinsic to the learner) rather than on disabilities, and their report became the foundation document on which inclusion was built.

For deaf education, the report highlighted the dilemma of accessing equal education by identifying language and communication as one of the key barriers for Deaf learners and acknowledging SASL as the language of teaching and learning. It also stressed the issue involving the need for trained and qualified Deaf educators. Although this report was written more than 10 years ago, most of the items in the report remain relevant to this day, and many are still inadequately addressed.

Education White Paper No. 6: Special Needs Education (Department of Education, 2001)

Education White Paper No. 6 was then published to spell out the government's support of inclusive education and how it would be implemented in South Africa. In contrast to the goal of mainstream education, the goal of inclusive education is to remove the barriers to education that children with special needs face (whether they are disabled or not) by means of adjusting the school environment around the needs of these learners.

Of the barriers discussed in the report, the following barriers to learning have particular importance to Deaf learners:

- Inappropriate languages or language of learning and teaching
- Inappropriate communication
- Inappropriate and inadequate support services
- Inadequately and inappropriately trained education managers and educators

In response to the key recommendations in White Paper No. 6, the Ministry of Education recommended undertaking the following objectives:

- To improve participation in special schools (p. 32) and to develop "funding strategies that ensure redress for historically disadvantaged communities" (p. 6)
- To continue its "discussions with all national community-based organisations, NGOs, organisations of the disabled, . . ." (p. 50)
- To provide educators with access to both preservice and in-service training (p. 29) as well as to support the requirement for continual education
- To ensure that "all curriculum development, assessment and instructional development programmes . . . address barriers to learning that arise from language and the medium of learning and instruction; teaching (p. 49)

In response to White Paper No. 6 and the drive for inclusion, DeafSA published a position paper (DeafSA, 2006) that clearly outlined the history and current situation of deaf education in the country, giving specific recommendations with respect to the inclusion of deaf learners and paying particular attention to teacher training in deaf pedagogy, SASL, and the use of Deaf assistants and educational interpreters. One major concern is that the department has no deaf education specialist in its ranks, and the implementation of inclusion in this regard remains unclear as is evident from a recent meeting during which the inclusive needs directorate of the Department of Education recognized the following assistive devices as necessary to help a deaf child cope in an inclusive setting: hearing aids, FM systems, technology-aided text-magnifying computers, and augmentative and alternative communication devices. It is proposed that before implementing inclusion for Deaf learners, further research and consultation needs to be done with respect to the needs of the Deaf learners (Peel, 2005; Storbeck, 2005).

Although South Africa seems to have some impressive laws and legislation pertaining to deaf education, there is still a lot of work to be done. Policies need to be explored in terms of specific needs related to deafness and then effectively implemented; teachers of the Deaf need to be required to have specialist training and skills; and schools for the deaf need more guidelines, leadership, and support (from specialists) as they plan to meet the needs of their unique learners.

The Curriculum and the Extent to Which It Matches Regular Education

After apartheid was abolished, the government of national unity introduced a system called outcomes-based education, which focused on achieving desired outcomes rather than prescribing fixed content. The curriculum used was called Curriculum 2005, which was later revised and polished to become the Revised National Curriculum Statement (Department of Education, 2002). The central goal was to unify education across race and class and ensure that learners understood that the process of learning was more important than merely getting the answers.

To date, education at schools for the deaf has not been consistent. Teachers leave out certain topics or areas of studies based on individual biases and opinions about what Deaf students can and cannot learn. It is believed that the lack of sufficient signing skills has also been a determining factor in what individual teachers teach or do not teach. Assessing the standards and comparative outcomes at schools for the deaf has been very difficult, not because Deaf children are difficult to assess or because their curriculum does not allow for it, but because each school covers different content. Many teachers of the deaf in South Africa believe that Deaf children should have their own specific curriculum and that outcomes-based education cannot work for Deaf children; however, it is only through a shared curriculum that equity can be achieved.

Recently, the Department of Education supported the idea that *all* learners in South Africa must write a National Senior Certificate (Grade 12) examination. Learners could be exempted from this examination only with special motivation, psychological examinations, or both (Department of Education, 2008). A number of deaf schools responded negatively to this idea, coming up with a wide range of reasons why Deaf children cannot be expected to write the National Senior Certificate. DeafSA maintains the position that Deaf learners must be expected to write the National Senior Certificate, except in extenuating circumstances that would also prevent hearing children from taking the exam.

PREPARATION OF SPECIAL PERSONNEL—TEACHER TRAINING

Teachers of the deaf are not required to have any specialized qualification or skill to teach in a school for the deaf, nor do they receive recognition or financial incentives if they do. The teachers who do study, do it part-time during their vacations and do it at their own cost, showing great commitment to improve their roles as educators of the deaf. One university offers such specialization at a postgraduate level. The Centre for Deaf Studies at The University of the Witwatersrand (Wits) offers two postgraduate options for teachers to specialize as teachers of the deaf: An ACE (Advanced Certificate in Deaf Education) or a BEd honors degree. Both options require teachers to have foundational training as teachers before they specialize as teachers of the deaf. Both hearing and Deaf teachers are encouraged to specialize, but particular focus is placed on those teachers currently in schools for the deaf who have no training or skills. Those untrained teachers, for the most part, had never met a Deaf person before beginning to teach Deaf students and learn SASL from the Deaf students as they go along. In some cases, outside service providers are recruited to train teachers in SASL for a few days.

The two biggest problems with acquisition of SASL and training of teachers is, first, that teachers often enter schools not being able to sign at all and consequently learn on the job and, second, that although they get short-term training, they are not exposed to the academic level of SASL required to deliver the curriculum. Therefore, they attempt to deliver the curriculum with only a basic social competency in SASL. This limitation greatly affects curriculum delivery, particularly because it has been often observed that teachers leave out parts of the curriculum that they cannot sign. The issue SASL in education is not about learning SASL per se but more about becoming competent in the level of SASL required for academic content.

The large majority of teachers of the deaf are hearing; however, there is a handful of Deaf teachers and assistants at some schools for the deaf. Some of these educators were deafened while in the profession, some have been trained in mainstream institutions of higher learning (such as Wits, that provides support for Deaf students through its disability unit), and some were given specialized undergraduate training at Springfield College of Education that has since closed down because of restructuring of the higher education institutions in Kwazulu-Natal. Some schools have employed Deaf assistants who also have a crucial role to play in the education of Deaf learners as cultural models and first-language mentors. In terms of leadership in deaf education, Deaf adults have not yet played a significant role; only one Deaf principal and one Deaf vice principal are listed to date among those working in the 47 schools for the deaf. Additionally, Wits has two Deaf lecturers who train teachers of the deaf, thus ensuring that, through training, teachers of the deaf are exposed to Deaf cultural and linguistic models.

CURRENT DEVELOPMENTS AND TRENDS

The education system in South Africa is moving from one of segregation and discrimination on a racial basis to a unified, centralized national education system that is designed to meet the needs of all learners equally (Department of Education, 2001). The benefit for deaf education, despite the obvious, is that change is already in motion and that the role of the greater deaf education community would be to ensure that the "voice" of the Deaf community is heard and acknowledged in the current process to strategize and implement policy.

The strong national Deaf association (DeafSA) and local Deaf community make South Africa a country of great possibilities for deaf and hard of hearing children. In addition, key legislation is already in place as a foundation for the work that lies ahead. To ensure effective implementation, we propose seven key areas for development:

- Lobbying for SASL to be recognized as the 12th official language
- Requiring all teachers of the deaf to have specialized training in deaf education and SASL before they enter schools
- Cultivating more Deaf teachers of the deaf, leading to more Deaf heads of departments and principals, thus ensuring that schools for the deaf are run by and for Deaf educators
- Initiating a Deaf culture curriculum in schools for the deaf (Storbeck & Magongwa, 2006) and implementing the SASL curriculum as a first language
- Implementing research into SASL by native signers (preferably Deaf)
- Improving the skills of and access to SASL educational interpreters
- Initiating sufficient research on what inclusion should look like for the Deaf learner and what concomitant support services would be required

These recommendations along with the tenacity of a rainbow people who have proven to be respectful of others and their unique needs is, we believe, a recipe for success for the South African Deaf community.

REFERENCES

Aarons, D., & Akach, P. (1998). *One language or many? A sociolinguistic question.* In *Stellenbosch papers in linguistics* (Vol. 31, pp. 1–28). Stellenbosch, South Africa: University of Stellenbosch.

Aarons, D., & Akach, P. (2002). South African Sign Language: One language or many? In R. Mesthrie (Ed.), *Language and social history: Studies in South African sociolinguistics* (2nd ed., pp. 127–147). Cambridge: Cambridge University Press.

Aarons, D., & Morgan, R. (1998). How many South African Sign Languages are there? In *Proceedings of the13th World Congress of the World Federation of the Deaf.* Sydney, Australia: Australian Association of the Deaf.

Allen, J. (2006). *Rabble rouser for peace: The authorized biography of Desmond Tutu.* London: Random House.

Constitutional Assembly of the Republic of South Africa. (1996). The Constitution of the Republic of South Africa, Act No. 108 of 1996. Pretoria: Government Printers.

Deaf Federation of South Africa (DeafSA). (2006). *Education position paper* (Draft No. 17). Unpublished manuscript.

Department of Education. 1997a. *Quality education for all: Report of the National Commission for Special Needs in Education and Training (NCSNET) and the National Commission on Education Support Services (NCESS).* Pretoria: Government Printers.

Department of Education. 1997b. *White paper on an integrated national disability strategy (INDS).* Pretoria: Government Printer.

Department of Education. (2001). *Special needs education: Building an inclusive education and training system* (Education White Paper No. 6). Pretoria: Government Printer.

Department of Education. (2002). *Revised national curriculum statement.* Pretoria: Government Printers.

Department of Education. (2008). *National strategy on screening, identification, assessment and support.* Pretoria: Inclusive Education Directorate.

Peel, E. (2005). *Inclusive practice in South Africa: A deaf education perspective.* Unpublished master's dissertation, University of the Witwatersrand, South Africa.

Penn, C., & Reagan, T. (1994). The properties of South African Sign Language: Lexical diversity and syntactic unity. *Sign Language Studies, 85,* 319–327.

Republic of South Africa. (1996). South African Schools Act, No. 84 of 1996. Pretoria: Government Printers.

Ross, E. (2004). [History of deaf schools in South Africa]. Unpublished manuscript.

Ross, E., Storbeck, C., & Wemmer, K. (2004). Pre-lingual deafness. In E. Ross & A. Deverell (Eds.), *Psychosocial approaches to health, illness and disability: A reader for health care professionals* (pp. 141–176). Johannesburg: Van Schaik.

Simmons, R. (1994). The role of educational systems and deaf culture in the development of sign language in South Africa. In C. Erting, R. Johnson, D. Smith, & B. Snider (Eds.), *International Conference on Deaf Culture* (pp. 78–84). Washington, DC: Gallaudet University Press.

Statistics South Africa. (2001). *Census 2001: Prevalence of disability in South Africa.* Pretoria: Government Printers.

Statistics South Africa. (2007). *Mid-year population estimates 2007.* Pretoria: Government Printers.

Storbeck, C. (2005). Educating the deaf and hard-of-hearing learner. In E. Landsberg, D. Kruger, & N. Nel (Eds.), *Addressing barriers to learning: A South African perspective* (pp. 348–362). Johannesburg: Van Schaik.

Storbeck, C., & Magongwa, L. (2006). Teaching about deaf culture. In D. F. Moores, & D. S. Martin (Eds.), *Deaf learners: New developments in curriculum and instruction* (pp. 113–126). Washington, DC: Gallaudet University Press.

Deafness in Sub-Saharan Africa

Nassozi B. Kiyaga and Donald F. Moores

DEAF EDUCATION in sub-Saharan Africa originated in the 19th century, primarily through efforts by hearing European missionaries who typically followed their homelands' oral-only practices. But education became available to only a fraction of the deaf population. In the 20th century, Andrew Foster, a deaf African American missionary and Gallaudet University's first African American graduate, had an unparalleled effect on deaf education in the region, establishing 31 schools for the deaf, training a generation of deaf leaders, and introducing his version of Total Communication, which embraced both American and indigenous signs. Nigeria, Kenya, Uganda, and South Africa have provided leadership in deaf education, but throughout the region, there is growing acceptance of sign language use in school, and secondary and postsecondary education for the deaf is increasingly available. Some national constitutions safeguard the rights of citizens with disabilities and even recognize indigenous sign languages. International disability organizations, particularly the World Federation of the Deaf, have helped change attitudes and train leaders. Despite some grim present realities, prospects for continued progress are good.

Sub-Saharan Africa is an enormous area geographically, with rich human and material resources. It occupies the bulk of the African continent and consists of 54 countries. The populations of the area represent wide ethnic, linguistic, religious, and cultural diversity. Despite unlimited potential, progress has been uneven in the region; indeed, sub-Saharan Africa includes some of the poorest countries in the world. Violence, disease, and hunger are endemic in many areas. The current plight of the continent is too complex and too great to treat in detail in this chapter, but some comments are in order to provide background on the condition of deaf individuals in the region.

As did many other parts of the world such as the Middle East, the Indian subcontinent, North Africa, and China, sub-Saharan Africa came under the influence of European imperialism for a period of several centuries. The dynamic nature of African cultures, history, and local traditions were completely ignored, repressed, and misused. Colonial systems were established for the benefit of the imperial countries at the expense of indigenous peoples. At the Berlin Conference of 1884–85, the major colonial powers agreed on the partition of Africa. With a few notable exceptions such as Liberia and Ethiopia (the latter of which was invaded and annexed by Italy before World War II), all of sub-Saharan Africa came under colonial rule. Great Britain and France were the major powers, but Germany, Portugal, and Belgium also had significant colonies. After World War I, Germany lost its colonial empire, mostly to British interests.

The colonial powers, with limited knowledge of the lands they had taken and without the consent of the Africans, carved sub-Saharan Africa into administrative units that served the colonizers' economic purposes but did not recognize boundaries between different ethnic, cultural, and linguistic groups. In some cases, rival kingdoms with historical hostilities were included within the same administrative units, leading to outbreaks of civil unrest after the dissolution of colonial rule that, in some nations, continue to the present. Europeans administered the area, and education for Africans was limited to a select few Africans who became civil servants under the control of European administrators and who constituted a small, elite middle class.

The impetus for the breakup of the colonial systems in sub-Saharan Africa was supplied by India's struggle for independence from Great Britain, which finally came to fruition in 1947 under the leadership of Mahatma Gandhi. In 1956, Sudan became the first sub-Saharan African country to achieve independence, beginning a process that extended over two generations and eventually led to the independence of all former colonies in the region. But the transition from colonization to independence was not easy. The states that emerged were based on political systems that had been established by the former colonial powers with the understanding that the new nations would maintain the borders drawn up in the 1880s. As in other parts of the world such as the Balkans, this decision, while arguably logical, set the stage for continuing ethnic and civil strife.

Although the new nations were nominally independent, they continued to be influenced by their former colonizers. For example, France retained a military presence in much of francophone Africa, as it does to this day. Much of the industry that had been developed by the Europeans was extractive—involving commodities such as gold, diamonds, and oil— and continued to be controlled by outside forces. The elements of self-sufficiency were lacking. There was no infrastructure to run a modern state. The European powers had never trained African administrators to manage a democracy and had never provided universal education.

Progress toward the creation of a sustainable state has been significant in some nations, for example, Nigeria, Kenya, and South Africa. On the whole, however, the situation is dire. A chief reason is the poor state of public health. For instance, an acute lack of access to safe drinking water, which is vital to the eradication of poverty, is both the direct and the indirect cause of water-related diseases and innumerable deaths. The HIV/AIDS pandemic is devastating parts of the region, and the response of the various nations has been uneven. At issue here is the difficulty of access to affordable generic drugs and the resistance of major American and European pharmaceutical companies to the providing of such drugs. Drought, hunger, and even starvation are constant presences in parts of sub-Saharan Africa. Unsustainable debt tied to unrealistic demands by the World Bank and International Monetary Fund have compounded the problem. Finally, political corruption and violence have condemned large parts of the area to underdevelopment.

Although civil war, religious conflict, ethnic strife, drought, and poverty persist, there is some reason for hope. For instance, the newly organized African Union is designed to play a role in ensuring that African nations themselves will take control of their destinies by strengthening inter-African cooperation, overcoming the prevalence of poverty, promoting peace, and combating the scourge of HIV/AIDS. Accommodations are being made to provide medicine to those in need and to improve water supplies and sanitation. Education is becoming available to growing numbers of the population, and there is a commitment to universal primary and secondary education throughout the region.

EDUCATION OF DEAF STUDENTS IN COLONIAL TIMES

Education of deaf children in sub-Saharan Africa began as a component of the European missionary movement in the 19th century. Roman Catholics and members of various Protestant denominations established schools for the deaf as part of conversion efforts in many countries. In other countries, royalty, wealthy philanthropists, charitable institutions, and teachers of the deaf established schools. As a whole, these schools reached only a small proportion of the deaf population of the region. They tended to serve children from relatively affluent African families in urban areas, even though most deaf Africans lived in poor rural environments. The majority of schools, following the examples of schools for the deaf in Great Britain and France, were strictly oral-aural and did not allow the use of any kind of manual communication, either signed or fingerspelled. There were some exceptions. Fay (1999) notes that missionaries from the United States and Scandinavia started schools for the deaf children in Ethiopia. These missionaries taught using the sign languages and manual alphabets of their own countries, even though the primary language of Ethiopia, Amharic, has a different alphabet. Burton (2002) also comments on how foreign sign languages were introduced without regard to indigenous signs. He claims that European and American educators left the African education system like a shattered playground, and that the enforced use of foreign sign language was disrespectful.

The linguistic diversity of sub-Saharan Africa was a reality that many American and European missionaries, coming from monolingual or bilingual backgrounds, did not grasp (Fay, 1999). Heine and Nurse (2000) cite Grimes as estimating that more than 2,000 languages are indigenous to the region. Most countries are multilingual, with additional creole or pidgin languages to facilitate communication across tribal groups. To establish standard educational, commercial, and business communications, countries of the region use either a common indigenous language such as Swahili in East Africa or the ex-colonial language (or both) while many other languages may be used in the same region by various tribal and ethnic groups. For example, Gabon has 44 spoken languages in addition to French, Uganda has 41 languages in addition to English and Ugandan Sign Language, Angola has 42 languages in addition to Portuguese, and Chad has 132 languages in addition to French and Arabic (SIL International, 2003). Nigeria, the most populous nation with one quarter of Africa's population, has an estimated 370 ethnic groups with more than 200 languages spoken.

Typically, hearing children in sub-Saharan Africa learn the mother tongue, that is, the family language, and perhaps one or more other regional languages. They then enter school to learn the national language. Day-to-day communication often is conducted in the indigenous language.

Those deaf children fortunate enough to attend school are taught in the national language. Problems of communication between deaf child and hearing parent impede or prevent acquisition of the family language, thus closing off enculturation and the benefits of incidental learning enjoyed by hearing siblings. It is commonly agreed that there are numerous sign languages, but there is no accurate measure. Discussing his efforts to develop a comprehensive South African sign dictionary, Alan Jones (1994) wrote, "When you realize that this dictionary will have to encompass no less than seven completely different languages, you will know why I refer to the task as gigantic" (p. 699).

Andrew Foster (1927–1987), a pioneering deaf African American missionary, provided the single most important contribution to the education of deaf Africans in the colonial and postcolonial periods. Widely acclaimed as the father of deaf education in Africa, Foster was the first African American to graduate from Gallaudet College, now Gallaudet University. A deeply religious and charismatic individual, Foster established the Christian Mission for Deaf Africans in the United States in 1956. He traveled to Accra, Ghana, in 1957, the year Ghana gained its independence. He found that in all of Africa there were only 12 schools serving deaf children and that "unknown numbers of deaf children were illiterate, languageless, and isolated" (Moore & Panara, 1996, p. 216). Ghana itself had no programs, no schools, and no teachers for deaf people. Foster established a school for the deaf in Ghana that was the first in the region to use any form of manual communication. He introduced American Sign Language and English-based signs. Functioning as a teacher, evangelist, administrator, and public-relations specialist, he established an amazing total of 31 schools (9 in Ghana alone) for deaf children in 17 different African countries (Carroll & Mather, 1997). In addition to Ghana, he established training centers in Nigeria and Kenya by 1975. Throughout his travels, he expanded deaf education by identifying deaf individuals to be sent to his school in Ghana for training and completion of a certificate course (Ojile, 1994). Foster has been compared with Laurent Clerc, a deaf man who was the first teacher of the deaf in the United States and who trained teachers of the deaf to return to their own states and set up schools (Moores, 2001).

Gabriel Adepoju, who pioneered the first government-owned and funded school for the deaf in Nigeria, is quoted by Moore and Panara (1996) as comparing Foster with Thomas Hopkins Gallaudet, the first superintendent of a school for the deaf in the United States. In reality, however, Foster surpassed both of these leaders. In the sheer numbers of schools he established by himself, Foster is unrivaled by anyone, hearing or deaf, in the history of education of the deaf. He not only left behind educated deaf Africans trained to teach their own people but also demonstrated to thousands of hearing Africans that deaf people had unlimited potential (Carroll & Mather, 1997).

Foster (1975) stressed that deaf children should be served immediately, even when adequate resources and trained personnel are not available. He argued that although schools are expensive to build, schools and classes could start in rented houses and storefronts as well as under thatched roofs. Personnel could tutor untrained teachers in rural areas. Governments could be shown the benefits that educated deaf individuals contribute to the national welfare through taxes and social activities. He also argued that only a few children could succeed through the predominant oral method. African languages are highly tonal, as Foster pointed out. If its tone is altered, one utterance can have three or four different meanings, which cannot be detected by speechreading.

Foster's greatest influence was in Nigeria, where the federal government has established schools of the deaf throughout the country. These schools follow Foster's Total Communication philosophy, which embraces the use of natural sign languages (Foster, 1975). This approach is not the case in most sub-Saharan countries. For example, the lead author of this chapter, a Ugandan citizen, visited the only school for the deaf in Rwanda in 1997, le Centre des Jeunes Sourds-Muets (Center for Young Deaf-Mutes), an institution established by a congregation of French and Belgian Catholic priests. There, attempts to communicate manually with the students were discouraged by the instructors. The children were totally forbidden to sign despite their apparent desire to do so. The condition of these children, however, was far superior to that of the large majority of deaf children in sub-Saharan Africa who have no access to any kind of education at all.

PRESENT-DAY EDUCATION

The challenges facing educators of deaf children in sub-Saharan Africa are similar to those identified by Mazurek and Winzer (1994) in all developing countries trying to establish appropriate services for children identified as disabled. In the face of widespread poverty, socio-econoimic crises, a scarcity of funding and other resources, and a lack of trained professional personnel, most societies give priority to general education, which serves the large majority of children. The emphasis, by necessity, is on basic education for these children; consequently, children classified as disabled are often neglected. Major challenges to the providing of services to children with disabilities include problems of early identification and intervention, a lack of enabling legislation, and limited teacher training.

Abang (1994) reported that preventable diseases accounted for significant proportions of African populations being disabled. There is a close link between poverty, disease, and disability. For example, poliomyelitis is a major cause of physical disability. Trachoma, malnutrition, and onchocerciasis can lead to blindness. Onchocerciasis is caused by the nematode worm and is sometimes treated by herbalists by applying drops to the eye, a treatment that can cause blindness. Abang reported that there were 20 million cases worldwide, 95% of them in Africa. She cited a survey in Mali, Ghana, and Burkina Faso in which 498,000 people in a population slightly greater than 4 million were reported to be infected with onchocerciasis, of whom 21,860 were blind. Abang also reported that otitis media was a major cause of hearing loss in Nigeria.

There are neither reliable data nor reliable estimates of the number of school-age children in sub-Saharan Africa. No country in the region has ever counted its deaf population in a census. Deaf people tend to live in isolation, making it difficult to build viable Deaf communities. Wilson (2001) has commented on the lack of documentation of education in developing countries and calls for research to establish procedures for reaching and serving children and adults in rural areas who are deaf.

We assume that, because of higher rates of malnutrition, chronic otitis media, meningitis, and other diseases that may affect hearing, along with limited access to medical treatment and hearing aids, the incidence of deafness is higher in the region than in the United States and Europe. It is clear that the majority of deaf children in sub-Saharan Africa lack access to education. The situation is especially serious in the rural areas of most countries, where poverty is widespread and services are limited or nonexistent.

An additional complicating factor is the fact that there are many hard of hearing children who would be able to process speech with the help of a hearing aid, children who would not be enrolled in programs for deaf children in more affluent countries. However, the cost of hearing aids is prohibitively high for the great majority of families, most of whom live below the poverty line. According to Ashoka (2001), the average cost of a hearing aid is US$971. In many countries of the region, family income may be less than US$2 a day, and food is a much higher priority than hearing aids.

In general, teachers of the deaf in Africa, most of whom are hearing, lack appropriate training and certification to equip them with the knowledge and skills necessary to work effectively with deaf children. Many cannot sign and do not view sign language as a complete language. Expectations are low and standards are inferior. Textbooks and other materials are in short supply. In most countries, this meager education ends at the primary level, with no incentive or opportunity to continue into secondary or higher education, except for a fortunate few.

With the exception of a few nations, in particular Nigeria, South Africa, and Kenya, most sub-Saharan African countries have left the education of deaf children to private missionary, charitable, or other nongovernmental organizations, most of which work independently, with no government support or regulation. This laissez-faire attitude has resulted in inconsistent standards and a tendency to provide instruction only at the elementary level. Instead of secondary or higher education, the only opportunities available to most deaf children who complete primary school are in a small number of trades such as carpentry, masonry, crafts, and brick making. The situation in Uganda provides an example. The country has very few primary schools for deaf children and one secondary school. Some may go to Kenya for vocational training, but only if they have the financial resources. Most do not have such resources.

CULTURAL ATTITUDES

Given the diversity of sub-Saharan Africa, there are exceptions to any generalizations. Attitudes toward deafness in African societies range from acceptance and protection to rejection, including considerations of infanticide. Many traditional beliefs characterize deafness as a manifestation of a mysterious fate, perhaps God's will. Some societies pity children who are deaf and see them as burdens, dependent on their families and lacking the ability to be independent. This type of belief in the lack of capability of deaf children may by itself impede access to education. In African tradition family ties extend beyond the family to include members of the community; the child is the community's responsibility. Unfortunately, the majority of deaf children suffer abuse, isolation, discrimination, rejection, and neglect at the hands of their parents and family members. Fear of social ridicule may result in the child being hidden away inside the house. However, even the most well-meaning parents are overwhelmed by having a deaf child.

In the absence of government programs to foster knowledge of deafness and the capabilities of deaf citizens, there is the threat and reality of social, political, economic, and educational discrimination. Federal legislation is needed to mitigate the prejudice and discrimination that exists in many countries.

One example of the effect of discrimination occurs in Gitarama, a small town in Rwanda familiar to the lead author of this chapter. There, deaf people live in abject poverty. Deaf adults cannot find gainful employment, and deaf children have no access to schooling. When the children venture outside their community, they always do so in groups, for self-protection. Stones are thrown at them when they sign to each other and they are labeled *ibiragi*, a derogatory Kinyarwanda word for deaf people meaning "foolishness." In Uganda, the lead author's native country, the word used in Luganda (one indigenous language) identify deaf people is *kasiru*, a term meaning one who is subhuman and incomplete. In Ethiopia, a common identifier is *denkoro*, which means "those who cannot be enlightened." Some people in Ethiopia believe that deaf people are possessed by the devil and must be cured by witchcraft or purifying waters. The application of derogatory labels to deaf people is, of course, not limited to African languages; the implications of English terms such as *deaf mute* and *deaf and dumb* are similarly offensive.

In some African societies, it is common for families to replace a deaf child's given name with a generic name, "the deaf one." Naniwe (1994) reported that in Burundi, harmful stereotypes portray deaf individuals as dependent, sick, or tragic victims who are often subjected to family exclusion and social isolation, with the result that they generally are described by family members as quick-tempered and aggressive. Naniwe quoted from an interview with a mother of a deaf child:

When people see a deaf person on the street they have the impression that he is a well person, someone like everyone else. But . . . he is a brainless person, because you have to feed him, nourish him, dress him. In fact, you have to do everything for him. (Naniwe, 1994, p. 575)

QUALITY OF LIFE

Although there is great diversity across nations, the quality of life for a large segment of the sub-Saharan African population is depressed; conditions common to developing nations in other parts of the world, including poverty, malnutrition, lack of access to education, and inadequate medical care, are widespread. Generally, the situation is worse in rural areas, where services are substandard and access to medical care is often not possible. A paradoxical situation exists: Although most of sub-Saharan Africa is rural, organizations of and for deaf people are concentrated in large cities, leaving most deaf individuals marginalized and isolated from society. Although no data are available, it is probable that rural deaf Africans, especially women and children, suffer even more from disease and malnutrition than the general population. For example, because deaf individuals in sub-Saharan Africa lack access to even the relatively limited mass communication that is available to hearing people and must endure the absence of communication within family units, the majority lack knowledge about the existence of HIV/AIDS or its cause, prevention, and treatment. Traditional misconceptions that deaf people are sexually inactive and therefore not at risk for HIV/AIDs prevail in most African societies. Many deaf people have died of AIDS-related illnesses and yet remain largely excluded from accessing preventative treatment, care, and rehabilitation services. In Uganda, a country that leads Africa with its anti-retroviral therapy programs, the majority of deaf people continue to be marginalized in both national and international AIDS programs. The vulnerability of deaf people (especially women) is highlighted by personal stories of sexual violence, exploitation, coercion, and powerlessness. In addition, deaf children orphaned due to HIV/ AIDS face innumerable difficulties.

GENDER CONSIDERATIONS

We stress that deaf women in the region often face triple discrimination because of deafness, gender, and poverty; this situation increases their vulnerability and exclusion and often results in physical, psychological, and sexual abuse. Gender disparities are a critical issue in the education of African girls in general because of patriarchal, male-dominated societies, most of which still define women solely as wives and mothers and are often treated as property and denied their human rights. Boys get first priority in access to education, and it is common, especially in rural areas, for girls to be forcefully confined at home and tend to household chores. On the basis of a finding that 24 million African girls were not receiving a primary education, the United Nations Children's Fund launched the Girls' Education Movement (Bellamy, 2001), noting that in countries besieged by HIV/AIDS, a lack of schooling can be life threatening. Deafness compounds the situation. Deaf girls are also exposed to relatively greater exploitation, sexual violence, and abuse. Many deaf women, their freedom curtailed, are denied the right to marry or to lead independent and fulfilling lives. Naniwe (1994) quoted the mother of a 33-year-old deaf woman:

Do you think I consider my daughter to be like other children? Other daughters of her age already have three, four, or even five children. And her, what is she? Always dragging next to me, she never married: She will never be able to. (p. 88)

Naniwe learned from another source that this mother had forced her daughter to have an abortion.

POSITIVE DEVELOPMENTS

Despite the grim realities that hamper the lives of deaf individuals in sub-Saharan Africa, positive developments are occurring. One of the most significant developments in recent years has been the inception of a Deaf HIV/AIDS awareness campaign in Kenya. Liverpool VCT, Care & Treatment (an NGO) created an intervention program known as the Liverpool Deaf VCT (http://www.liverpoolvct.org) targeting Deaf communities in Kenya. The organization trains deaf people to become professional counselors to provide testing and support services to deaf clients. In addition, there are more than 100 Deaf mobile VCT services to serve deaf people in rural communities. Deaf people who test HIV+ are given free treatment, care, and support. Zimbabwe, Botswana, Uganda, and South Africa have prohibited discrimination against people with disabilities, and Uganda is one of the few countries in the world to recognize a national sign language (in this case, Ugandan Sign Language) as an official language in its constitution (Yeo, 1999). Togo, Burkina Faso, and Benin have followed the lead of Uganda (Michailakis, 1997). The Ghanaian constitution commits Ghana to promote the welfare of its citizens with disabilities, foster equality of opportunity, and create environments that lead to social integration of these individuals. In Ethiopia, there is a weekly television news program for the Deaf community that is presented in Ethiopian Sign Language.

The World Federation of the Deaf recently established the Eastern and Southern Africa Regional Secretariat, which is concentrating on human rights, interpreting issues, and promotion of African sign languages. At Deaf Way II, an international festival held in Washington, DC, which was hosted by Gallaudet University, deaf representatives from 24 African countries participated.

In Nigeria, several of Andrew Foster's students have carried on his work, and Total Communication has become the dominant mode of instruction in schools for the deaf (Adepoju, 1999). Along with Kenya and South Africa, Nigeria is one of the leading countries in sub-Saharan Africa in the providing of high school educational opportunities to large numbers of deaf students. Nigeria's Ibadan University was the first institution of higher education in Africa to establish a department of special education. A highly regarded teacher training program for teachers of the deaf has been established at Jos University, another Nigerian postsecondary institution. The Nigerian Educational Research Council has been working on Ibo, Hausa, and Yoruba sign language vocabularies. The progress of education of the deaf in Nigeria is illustrated by the fact that Nigeria trails only Canada and China in the number of deaf students enrolled at Gallaudet University.

A recent development has been for the creation of the *African Annals of the Deaf,* whose first issue is scheduled to go to press in the near future. This journal is projected to be a mechanism for development and dissemination of information of benefit to people who are deaf or hard of hearing throughout sub-Saharan Africa and will follow the *African Journal of Special Education* as only the second scholarly journal on the continent focusing on people with disabilities.

SUMMARY

Sub-Saharan Africa is an enormous region of more than 50 nations, with a rich mosaic of peoples displaying complex racial, ethnic, linguistic, cultural, and religious diversity. It is continuing to struggle to throw off the effects of colonial rule and the attendant plagues of poverty, disease, civil strife, and illiteracy. The overall condition of deaf people in sub-Saharan Africa remains dire. Challenges range from socioeconomic deprivation (poverty among deaf Africans is escalated by lack of employment, lack of skills/qualifications, social exclusion, and discrimination at all levels of society due to intense cultural prejudices, superstitions and misconceptions about deafness). Cases of despicable human rights violation against the deaf are many and deaf people's plight is further escalated by systems of terrible governance (despotic, tyrannical, and corrupt regimes that don't care about the welfare of their citizens). So if the ordinary citizen suffers, can you imagine what the deaf, disabled, and other vulnerable people go through? It is fair to say that there have been developments—but we still have a very long way to go. When people become listless, their attitudes are greatly affected—there is less tolerance of people who are different, such as the Deaf community. I feel that in striving to search for solutions to Africa's problems, we need to urgently look within Africa's cultures, economics, and political institutions. It is a great continent and a great people. But the exclusion and abuse of deaf people is detrimental to national and global development. If their potentials are undermined and exploited, we destroy our own communal and social abilities. Issues such as the relative importance of indigenous sign languages and the use of American Sign Language as the lingua franca have not been resolved. Multilingual countries, the most obvious example being South Africa, which not only have several spoken languages but also several signed languages, provide intriguing challenges and opportunities. Clearly, there is an overall critical need for specialized programs to train a wide range of professional personnel to work with people in the region who are deaf.

Although detailed treatment of the subject is beyond the scope of the present article, the special situation in South Africa as it moves toward a multiracial democracy from the vestiges of apartheid deserves a mention. Apartheid imposed a system of rigid segregation. Whites, who made up about 13% of the population, controlled the economy and most of the land. Nine separate homelands were established for the major Black groups, each with its own language. Race registration laws were in effect and all non-Whites were required to carry passports at all times. It was not until the early 1990s that the apartheid laws were rescinded; free elections did not occur until 1994, when Nelson Mandela, who had spent 27 years in prison, was elected to head the government. In its present form, the country is less than 10 years old. It has 11 languages, including Afrikaans and English, and segregation is outlawed, although change occurs slowly. Until recently, education for children who are deaf was limited mostly to Whites, with some children of Indian heritage and some children classified as "colored" (or mixed-race) attending racially segregated schools. The situation has changed dramatically in a short period, with educational opportunities from elementary to postsecondary schools becoming available for all deaf students.

REFERENCES

Abang, T. (1994). Nigeria. In K. Mazurek & M. Winzer (Eds.), *Comparative studies in special education* (pp. 77–87). Washington, DC: Gallaudet University Press.

Adepoju, G. A. (1999). *Trends in the development of education of the deaf in Nigeria between 1950 and 1985: An interview and historical study.* Unpublished doctoral dissertation, University of Maryland, College Park.

Ashoka. (2001). David Green (Profile). Retrieved July 31, 2008, from http://www.ashoka.org/fellow/3146

Bellamy, C. (2001, August). *On the launch of the Girls' Education Movement (GEM).* Retrieved July 31, 2008, from http://www.unicef.org/media/media_10450.html

Burton, T. (2002, June). *A deaf person's perspective on third world deaf children's education.* Paper presented at "What Does the South Really Want From the North?" a seminar co-organized by the Deaf Africa Fund and the Enabling Education Network, Birmingham, England.

Carroll, C., & Mather, S. M. (1997). *Movers and shakers: Deaf people who have changed the world.* San Diego, CA: DawnSign Press.

Fay, M. (1999). *Deaf people around the world: Their lives and organizations.* Unpublished manuscript.

Foster, A. (1975, July). *The social aspects of deafness: School years.* Keynote address to the Seventh World Congress of the Deaf, Washington, DC.

Heine, B., & Nurse, D. (2000). *African languages: An introduction.* Cambridge, England: Cambridge University Press.

Jones, A. (1994). Deaf awareness programs in South Africa. In C. Erting, R. Johnson, D. Smith, & B. Snider (Eds.), *The deaf way: Perspectives from the International Conference on Deaf Culture* (pp. 698–701). Washington, DC: Gallaudet University Press.

Mazurek, K., & Winzer, M. (1994). *Comparative studies in special education.* Washington, DC: Gallaudet University Press.

Michailakis, D. (1997). Government implementation of the Standard Rules as seen by member organizations of the World Federation of the Deaf-WFD. Retrieved July 31, 2008, from http://www.independentliving.org/standardrules/WFD_Answers/WFD.pdf

Moore, M. S., & Panara, R. F. (1996). *Great deaf Americans* (2nd ed.). Rochester, NY: Deaf Life Press.

Moores, D. F. (2001). *Educating the deaf: Psychology, principles, and practices* (5th ed.). Boston: Houghton Mifflin.

Naniwe, A. (1994). The deaf child in Burundi society. In C. Erting, R. Johnson, D. Smith, & B. Snider (Eds.), *The deaf way: Perspectives from the International Conference on Deaf Culture* (pp. 574–580). Washington, DC. Gallaudet University Press.

Ojile, E. (1994). Education of the deaf in Nigeria: A historical perspective. In C. Erting, R. Johnson, D. Smith, & B. Snider (Eds.), *The deaf way: Perspectives from the International Conference on Deaf Culture* (pp. 268–274). Washington, DC: Gallaudet University Press.

SIL International. (2003). Ethnologue country index: Languages of Africa. Retrieved July 31, 2008, from http://www.ethnologue.com/country_index.asp?place=Africa

Wilson, A. T. (2001). *Development assistance from American organizations to deaf communities in the developing world. A qualitative study in Jamaica.* Unpublished doctoral dissertation, Gallaudet University, Washington, DC.

Yeo, R. (1999, June). *A community-based sign language program in Uganda.* Paper presented at "Inclusion and Deafness," a seminar organized by the Enabling Education Network, Manchester, England. Retrieved July 31, 2008, from http://www.eenet.org.uk/key_issues/deaf/incdeafrep/ugandasl.shtml.

Europe

The Flemish Deaf Community and the Challenge of Breaking Through Barriers in the Educational System

Goedele De Clerck

FLANDERS HAS known a strong oral tradition. It has been only been 10 years since the first and still only deaf school established a bilingual-bicultural program. The establishment of the program is illustrative for the emancipation process and activism of the Flemish deaf community, leading to the recognition of Flemish Sign Language (Vlaamse Gebarentaal, VGT) in 2006. Although more opportunities and access for Flemish deaf people can be expected in the next decade, the recent empowerment of the Flemish deaf community is challenged by changes in the deaf landscape: the numbers of individuals receiving cochlear implants and being educated in mainstream settings are increasing fast, and statistics foresee that in the next 10 years, 70% of deaf children will be mainstreamed and 80% of all deaf children will have a cochlear implant (De Raeve & Loots, 2007).

Against this backdrop, this chapter will focus on the question of how the Flemish deaf community will be able to face these challenges and meet the (changing) needs of deaf children. Therefore, the current training provided for professionals working with deaf children and students will be examined, as well as the opportunities available for deaf children to learn VGT and to come into contact with deaf persons and deaf role models.

Flanders is the northern area of Belgium; since 1993, it has been one of the two states of a federalized monarchy. The second state is formed by the southern part of Belgium and is called Wallonia. In Flanders, the official spoken language is Dutch (Flemish); in Wallonia, the official spoken language is French. The spoken languages of Flemish and Dutch are similar, with only minor differences that can be compared with differences between American English and British English. Additionally, Belgium has a small German-speaking jurisdiction in the east, with German as the official spoken language (Van Herreweghe, 2002). Almost 6 million people live in Flanders, and there is a Flemish parliament and a Flemish government. Brussels is the capital of both Flanders and Belgium.

In the Flemish deaf community, there are about 4,500 Flemish Sign Language users (Loots et al., 2003). Flemish Sign Language or Vlaamse Gebarentaal (VGT) is different from Nederlandse Gebarentaal (Sign Language of the Netherlands). In Wallonia, deaf people use Belgian-French Sign Language (Langue des Signes de Belgique Francophone, or LSFB), which differs from Langue des Signes Françaises (French Sign Language). In April 2007, VGT was recognized as the "first or preferred language of the Deaf community in Flanders" (Heyerick, n.d.). In Wallonia, LSFB received official recognition in 2003 (Timmermans, 2005).

Before the 1970s, the Belgian deaf community was represented by one national deaf federation: Navekados. After that time, Fevlado (Federatie van Vlaamse Dovenorganisaties, or Federation of Deaf Organizations) represented the Flemish deaf community, and Fédération Francophone des Sourds de Belgique (French Federation of Belgian Deaf) advocated for the Walloon deaf community. Before the two federations separated, Flemish and Walloon deaf leaders often met and interacted. Because the organizations now receive their own funding and have their own planning of events, deaf people from the north and the south have less contact with one another, and VGT and LSFB continue to "develop separately and deviate further from each other" (Van Mulders, 2005, p. 51).

DEAF EDUCATION IN FLANDERS: A STRONG ORAL TRADITION AND THE EMERGENCE OF THE FIRST BILINGUAL-BICULTURAL PROGRAM

In 1820, the first deaf school in Ghent opened its doors, and that event was the start of deaf education in Flanders. Most of the seven current deaf schools in the north of Belgium would open between 1820 and 1883 (Kasterlinden in Sint-Agatha Berchem, Brussels, was the last deaf school that was established). The school of Abbé de l'Epée in Paris was known in Belgium, and a few deaf people left Belgium to study in Paris. Deaf education benefited from their knowledge and experience (Boonen, Van Herreweghe, & Vermeerbergen, 2004; Buyens, 2005; Gerday & Thomas, 2001; Le Maire, 1996, 1997). The Milan Conference of 1880 that influenced deaf education all over the world also had huge consequences for deaf education in Belgium. Deaf teachers and signs were banned from deaf schools (Gerday & Thomas, 2001; Van Herreweghe, 2002). Deaf children were not allowed to use signs or fingerspelling in the classroom and were stimulated to use speech, speechreading, and hearing aids. Boonen et al. (2004) put this period in perspective, stating that although deaf schools would keep this strict theoretical stance until 1980, 100% oralism was rarely practiced in everyday school life: "The children signed among each other and it seems that even many teachers and educators used signs and/or sign language in the past. Especially many people older than 40 claim to be educated in sign (language)" (2004, p. 11, translated from Dutch by G. De Clerck).

In the 1970s, special education specialists in Flanders (and The Netherlands) realized that deaf children in oral education did not achieve the expected results in oral language competence as well as in reading and writing competence. As a result, they developed a "differentiating communication"(DC) vision: "The goal of this vision is to educate deaf pupils to a choice between the hearing and/or the deaf world when they are grown-ups, however they choose for a monolingual approach. The priority is on acquiring Dutch as good as possible. Also mainstreaming is encouraged as much as possible" (Boonen et al., 2004, p. 12, translated from Dutch by G. De Clerck). When the Total Communication [TC] method became an international trend, Flanders followed, and in 1979, the method was implemented in one school. Classes were taught in "Signed Dutch," a system of signs accompanying the grammatical structure of the spoken language (Van Herreweghe, 2002). Boonen et al. (2004) noticed the use of Signed Dutch in DC visions, sometimes only for children with multiple disabilities, remarking that "the difference between those two [DC and TC] is slowly but definitely diminishing anno 2003" (p. 11, translated from Dutch by G. De Clerck).

Looking back on the history of deaf education in Flanders, Van Herreweghe (2002) concludes, "Consequently, all the adults in Flanders, including deaf and Deaf adults, were educated orally, either in a special education setting or in a mainstream setting (although a small minority of young adults in this group were educated in Total Communication programs using what is called 'Nederlands met Gebaren,' or 'Signed Dutch')" (p. 75).

When international trends in the 1990s were moving in the direction of bilingual-bicultural education for deaf children, Flanders followed, but slowly: "In Flanders in the midst of the 1990s, any form of bilingual education of Dutch and Flemish Sign Language was still out of the question. Yet some deaf schools set up experiments with the use of sign language (e.g., a deaf adult doing storytelling a couple of hours a week)" (Boonen et al., 2004, p. 20, translated from Dutch by G. De Clerck). In 1997–98, Kasterlinden in Brussels established the first bilingual program in elementary education (De Weerdt, Vanhecke, Van Herreweghe, & Vermeerbergen, 2002), and in the academic year of 2000–01, bilingualism was implemented in secondary education (I. Kestemont, personal communication, March 8, 2007).

Yet it is important to look at the practical realization of the program to gain a better understanding of the notion "bilingual-bicultural" as it has been used in Flanders. In 1997, the elementary school hired two deaf teaching assistants (at that time there were no certified teachers in Flanders), and in 1998–99, visits to learn from the expertise of those in bilingual programs abroad were organized. In 2003–04, VGT was implemented in the curriculum as an official course ("Evolutie tweetalig onderwijs in Kasterlinden," 2007). Currently, VGT is used as an instructional language for all children whose first language is VGT. Deaf culture is taught for 2 hours a week ("Bevragingsproject onderwijs," 2007). In 2000–01 when the bilingual-bicultural program started in secondary education, Deaf culture was taught for 1 hour a week, there were contrastive exercises on the grammatical differences between Dutch and VGT, and texts on deaf issues were discussed in Dutch classes. These classes were taught by a hearing teacher who developed her teaching materials in collaboration with Fevlado. Two years later, a deaf teaching assistant joined the effort. The teach of VGT as a course in the curriculum started only in Spring 2007 (I. Kestemont, personal communication, March 8, 2007). The following overview of the Flemish educational system (mainstream and special education) will provide important context for the later discussions of deaf education, the deaf school-age population, and training programs in Flanders.

VGT (Flemish Sign Language): Up to the Status It Deserves?

Because VGT has only recently been used in deaf education and recognized as an official language, one can say that it "has only recently developed from a language that existed mostly 'underground' in the Deaf community to one with a more general role in mainstream (hearing) society" (Van Herreweghe & Vermeerbergen, 2004, p. 111). VGT has developed in and around the deaf schools in the different towns, and currently still consists of five regional sign language variants (Van Herreweghe, 2002). Most deaf schools were established by Catholic clergy (De Clerck, 2005a). Education for boys and girls was separate, and some towns even had two deaf schools. Consequently, deaf men and women signed differently. Because deaf education has since mixed boys and girls and because people from different regions interact more, "an ongoing process of spontaneous standardization is occurring" (Van Herreweghe, 2002, p. 75).

In 1980, Fevlado established a "sign committee" to develop and promote "Signed Dutch." This effort led to the publication of a series of small books starting from 1981, a first dictionary of Sign Dutch in 1983, and a large Signed Dutch dictionary in 1995. Because Signed Dutch has been used in deaf education and in the sign language interpreter training, there has been influence on the lexical elements of VGT (De Weerdt et al., 2002; Van Herreweghe & Vermeerbergen, 2004, 2006).

Until the beginning of the 1990s, research on VGT was fragmented and scarce (De Weerdt et al., 2002). Then, hearing researchers set up two research projects on VGT. These projects focused on the grammar of VGT (Van Herreweghe, 1995; Vermeerbergen, 1996). In 1999, research findings about VGT grammar were made available to the deaf community in VGT through a "signing book" (Vermeerbergen, 1999). VGT research has continued to develop since then.

Following international trends in favor of natural sign languages, Fevlado officially decided in 1997 to promote and teach VGT instead of Signed Dutch (Van Herreweghe & Vermeerbergen, 2004). The first VGT dictionary was published in 2004 and is currently available online[1] (Van Mulders, 2004). Because VGT was never used as an instructional language in education, in the media, and in other areas of mainstream society, researchers noticed lexical gaps, and a project was set up to develop signs for concepts that did not have a VGT equivalent, especially concepts used in education (Van Herreweghe & Vermeerbergen, 2004).

The research on VGT also influenced interpreting training. The VGT interpreter training programs that had been established in the early 1980s started by teaching Signed Dutch. After the first VGT results had been published, the programs changed to teaching VGT by the end of the 1990s (Van Herreweghe & Vermeerbergen, 2006).

Currently, VGT is not used on Flemish television. There are no television programs for deaf people, and it is not used to interpret the news or other programs. However, in 1998, a Flemish TV station broadcast "At Home in a World of Signs" ("Thuishoren in een wereld van gebaren"), an informational television series predominantly for hearing people about VGT and the Flemish deaf community.

THE EMPOWERMENT AND EMANCIPATION OF THE DEAF COMMUNITY

The empowerment and emancipation movement in the Flemish deaf community started only in the early 1990s. For this discussion, the author draws on De Clerck's (2005a, 2007) study of deaf empowerment in Flemish deaf role models. The oral education system provided deaf students with neither deaf teachers (or role models) nor information about sign language and deaf culture. The low educational level in deaf schools resulted in limited knowledge of the world and limited reading skills, which were barriers to information acquisition (e.g., about emancipation trends of other minority groups), and the television news was not accessible until the early 1990s. In the Flemish deaf association and in many deaf clubs, deaf people were confronted with authoritarianism and paternalism of hearing clergy. Typically, deaf cultural rhetoric was not passed on in the deaf community, but in 1990, Fevlado set up a deaf awareness course so deaf people could acquire knowledge about deaf issues and come into contact with deaf cultural rhetoric. Before that time, only a small number of deaf people had gained some awareness through traveling abroad, mostly for deaf sporting events (e.g., Deaflymics). Visits to international deaf centers (Gallaudet University Center for Deaf Studies

---

1. See http://gebaren.ugent.be.

in Bristol and Center for Total Communication in Denmark) and international deaf role models who came to Belgium were necessary for Flemish deaf consciousness raising, empowerment, and activism. Only after coming into contact with bilingual-bicultural educational programs abroad did Flemish deaf people start to advocate for bilingual and bicultural instruction methods in Flemish deaf schools. This movement was supported by the VGT research in the 1990s that provided the Flemish deaf community with the necessary scientific arguments for community advocacy.

In the meantime, a first generation of deaf role models has been able to transfer deaf cultural rhetoric to the deaf community and empower young deaf people. Yet more than 10 years after the first deaf awareness course, young deaf people still find their empowerment abroad rather than in Flanders, and the first generation of deaf leaders brings up the lack of opportunities to develop further and expand their knowledge in Flanders (De Clerck, 2007).

Through semi-structured interviews of 30 deaf people in the West-Flemish deaf community, Van Herreweghe and Verhelst (2004) find changes in attitudes in the deaf community toward a better acceptance of VGT and cultural deafness. Yet the researchers notice that the active knowledge of aspects of deaf culture and VGT is still very limited. Deaf education could be a source of deaf cultural information and a support for the emancipation process in the deaf community. The following sections will describe the organization of the mainstream and special system in Flanders and will provide an outline of the organization of education for deaf children in Flanders.

THE FLEMISH EDUCATIONAL SYSTEM

Educational matters in Flanders are managed by the Education Department of the Ministry of the Flemish Community, represented by the Flemish minister of education and training. Flanders has its own educational system, yet there are federal principles that apply for the three communities in Belgium. Education in Belgium is compulsory, starting from September 1 in the year of a child's sixth birthday and continuing until the child turns 18: "The Belgian Constitution provides that everyone has a right to education, thus respecting the fundamental rights and freedom. In order to guarantee this right for all children, there is compulsory education" (Ministry of the Flemish Community, 2005, p. 8).

The Belgian education structure can be perceived as consisting of three clusters: (a) nursery and primary education, (b) secondary education, and (c) tertiary education (or advanced education). Children between the ages of 2.5 and 6 years can attend nursery education; then there are 6 years of primary education for children between the ages of 6 and 12. Students between the ages of 12 and 18 years attend secondary schools. For nursery, primary, and secondary education, there is both mainstream and special education. The special education system distinguishes between eight different groups, or "types," of students that are based on the students' special needs. Type 7 includes education for students who are deaf.

Apart from special education, the Flemish educational system also offers integrated education (Geïntegreerd Onderwijs) from nursery until tertiary education (in tertiary education, it is called "Pedagogical Support," or "Pedagogische Begeleiding"). This effort is "the result of co-operation initiatives between mainstream . . . education and special education. This education is aimed at making disabled children or children with learning or educational difficulties attend classes or activities in a school for mainstream education, with assistance from special education" (Ministry of the Flemish Community, 2005, p. 15).

The Flemish educational system has standards for mainstream education. For mainstream nursery and primary education, there are developmental objectives. For special nursery education, developmental objectives do not yet apply, but there are developmental objectives for special primary education that apply for deaf education (see further in this text). At the end of primary education, all children who obtained the developmental objectives receive a certificate. In some cases, special education can award a diploma that is equal to that for regular education.

Secondary education is organized in four education forms: general secondary education, technical secondary education, secondary education in the arts, and vocational secondary education. After 6 years in the first three education forms and 7 years of vocational secondary education, students receive a certificate of secondary education that "gives unrestricted access to tertiary education" (Ministry of the Flemish Community, 2005, p. 17).

The goal of special secondary education is "to integrate the pupil as far as possible in the educational environment and in society, by means of an individual educational and teaching provision" (Ministry of the Flemish Community, p. 17). Consequently, special secondary education is highly individualized: "The years in special secondary education (BuSO), rarely coincide with the school years in mainstream secondary education. Indeed, a pupil only passes on to the next 'learning stage' when he/she is ready for this" (Ministry of the Flemish Community, p. 17). Special secondary education, like regular secondary education, is organized in four educational forms (*Opleidingsvormen*, or OV). The first and second educational forms (OV1 and OV2) are for students with multiple disabilities and have as their goal to educate students toward a protected life environment and a protected work environment (Het curriculum in BUSO OV1-OV2: Een terreinverkenning, n.d.). Educational Form 3 (OV3) "aims to provide students with a general, social and vocational education in order to prepare their integration in a regular work and life environment." Educational Form 3, for deaf children without additional disabilities, consists of a general part with developmental objectives (25%) and a specific, vocational part (75%) (Curriculum: Wat heb je vandaag op school geleerd?, n.d.f; DEAFVOC, n.d.). The curriculum in Educational Form 4 (OV4) is parallel with mainstream education but is tailored to the special needs of the students (DEAFVOC, n.d.).

DEAF EDUCATION IN FLANDERS

Currently, seven school groups in Flanders provide elementary deaf education, secondary deaf education, or both: Antwerp (Jongelinckshof and Emmaüs, Siblo 7), Bruges (Spermalie), Brussels (Koninklijk Instituut Woluwe, Kasterlinden), Ghent (Sint-Lievenspoort–Sint-Gregorius), and Hasselt (Koninklijk Instituut voor Doven en Spraakgestoorden) (De Meulder, 2005). There is a strong trend toward mainstreaming in Flemish education, and those children who do attend deaf schools often have multiple disabilities (Loots, Maes, Van Herreweghe, & Vermeerbergen, 2002). In addition, there is a new growing population of immigrant children (Lichtert, 2007). The overview of current visions in deaf schools in De Meulder (2005) indicates that most schools (Jongelinckshof Antwerp, Spermalie Bruges, Koninklijk Instituut, Woluwe Brussels, Sint-Lievenspoort Ghent, and Koninklijk Instituut voor Doven en Spraakgestoorden Hasselt) still provide a DC vision approach with both an oral-aural and a manual stream. Jongelinckshof in Antwerp is reconsidering its vision. Koninklijk Instituut voor Doven en Spraakgestoorden Hasselt and Sint-Gregorius Bruges work toward a bilingual and bicultural environment for deaf children, yet it is not clear how this goal is realized in everyday class situations. At the time of this writing, Kasterlinden is still the only deaf school in Flanders that officially offers bilingual and bicultural education.

In Flanders, curricula in special education are highly individualized and tailored to the needs and possibilities of each student. There is no standard curriculum. Deaf schools are free to select developmental objectives for regular elementary or secondary education, developmental objectives for a specific type in special education, and developmental objectives for other educational types (Curriculum: Wat heb je vandaag op school geleerd?, n.d.a).

Primary Deaf Education

In achieving the goal of inclusive education, the final and developmental objectives for deaf elementary education are designed to match with the curriculum for mainstream elementary education as much as possible. The population in schools for the deaf is diverse in terms of hearing loss, onset of hearing loss, linguistic background, and additional disabilities, and schools are able to select developmental objectives that match the educational needs of each child. Curricula in physical education, mathematics, and learning to learn are parallel with mainstream education. For curricula in world orientation and music, additional developmental objectives have been developed that focus on deaf culture and music for deaf people. The curriculum for teaching Dutch is replaced by one of language and communication that is divided into VGT and Dutch. The curriculum for social skills is replaced by one that teaches social-emotional development. For students with additional disabilities, the special education school can choose from the developmental objectives for children with other disabilities (Curriculum: Wat heb je vandaag op school geleerd?, n.d.b).

Four groups of developmental goals can be distinguished for deaf culture: (a) human (e.g., personal reflection, feelings, and experiences concerning deafness; problem-solving skills and strategies in conflict situations concerning deafness); (b) sociocultural (e.g., the difference between medical and cultural perspectives on deafness, knowledge of associations and federations for deaf people, knowing how to use interpreters and communicate with hearing people, use of basic deaf cultural rules and awareness of differences with hearing culture); (c) political and judicial phenomena (knowledge of national and international deaf federations); and (d) historical time (knowledge of important stages in deaf history and technological and social developments with positive influence for the deaf community) (Curriculum: Wat heb je vandaag op school geleerd?, n.d.d).

For VGT, the following eight goals can be distinguished: (a) reading (understanding video books and reading sign writing); (b) writing (making texts in VGT that are videotaped, writing texts in sign writing); (c) linguistics (knowing that VGT consists of regional variants, knowing that there are different spoken and sign languages, knowing whether language use is proper for a situation); (d) attitude (e.g., enjoying visual listening, signing, reading, and writing; reflecting on own visual listening, signing, reading, and writing behavior); (e) morphology and syntax (e.g., understanding, recognizing, and using classifiers and turn-taking; knowing how VGT expresses plurality); (f) VGT lexicon (e.g., comprehending the meaning of signs; understanding basic knowledge of name signs, sign parameters, oral components in sign language, creation of new signs); (g) fingerspelling (e.g., using and understanding finger-spelling fluently, knowing when to use fingerspelling); and (h) aids (e.g., being familiar with aids and media for deaf and hard of hearing people) (Curriculum: Wat heb je vandaag op school geleerd?, n.d.c).

Secondary Deaf Education

Deaf schools can offer OV1, OV2, OV3, and OV4. In Flanders, the majors that are offered for OV3 in deaf schools are limited to the following:

- Koninklijk Instituut voor Doven en Spraakgestoorden Hasselt—baker's assistant, butcher's assistant, painter-decorator, shop assistant (O. De Raeve, personal communication, June 4, 2007)
- Kasterlinden—trade, management, account assistant, mechanic, electrician, welder, kitchen assistant (K. Aerden, personal communication, March 9, 2007)
- Sint-Gregorius—worker in market garden, kitchen assistant, baker's assistant, carpenter, storage assistant (G. Geysels, personal communication, June 21, 2007)
- Jongelinckshof and Emmaüs —welder, kitchen assistant, maintenance assistant (wood-working, painting, market gardening) (P. Boutsen, personal communication, September 17, 2007)
- Spermalie Bruges—module of industrial techniques: woodworking, welding, painting-decorating, electricity, technical drawing; module of logistic assistant–organization assistant: cooking meals, domestic work, taking care of people ("Informatiebrochure Secundaire School Spermalie," 2007)

In 2004, DEAFVOC, a language competency project funded by the European Union, did a survey on vocational training for deaf people in the EU and found that in Belgium, "the teach-ers usually develop their own material or they work with instructional material used in regu-lar schools. Since there are only about 100 deaf children at vocational training level in the Flemish speaking (signing) part of Belgium, the interest in producing material for such a small group is rather low" (DEAFVOC, n.d., p. 15).

Because there are no uniform curricular programs for special secondary education and edu-cation is organized according to individual action plans, students in OV3 receive a qualifica-tion certificate that can be equated with a study certificate that students in regular education receive after the fourth year of vocational secondary education (M. Van de Casteele, Educa-tion Department of the Ministry of the Flemish Government, personal communication, May 21, 2007). As a result, deaf students who graduate from OV3 in secondary deaf schools and plan to continue to advanced education have to start in the fifth year of vocational second-ary education in regular schools and receive a certificate after the seventh year. Within OV3, deaf schools have the option to implement developmental objectives of regular vocational secondary education. Some deaf schools offer students the opportunity to study at the regu-lar education level and then take the exams of the Flemish Exam Commission and gain a (partial) certificate of mainstream vocational secondary education. Deaf schools (e.g., Koninklijk Instituut voor Doven en Spraakgestoorden Hasselt) can organize an OV3+ stream that spreads the first and secondary year of vocational secondary education over 3 years. After the exam for the Flemish Exam Commission, deaf students attend regular vocational secondary education schools with itinerant services, a VGT interpreter, a note taker, or some combination (O. De Raeve, personal communication, June 4, 2007). Emmaüs also offers a program for deaf students to receive a certificate of the first and second year regular education through the Flemish Exam Commission (P. Boutsen, personal communication, September 17, 2007). Spermalie Bruges organizes OV4 for the first and second year of secondary education: students follow the same program as in regular secondary education and receive the same certificate. They can attend regular education after the first or second year, either vocational secondary education, technical secondary education, or even general secondary education ("Informatiebrochure Secundaire School Spermalie," 2007).

Some deaf schools also organize alternating vocational training (*Alternerende Beroepsopleiding*). Students with an OV3 qualification certificate can attend a 1-year additional training that consists of two parts: internship in a company and classes at school. The goal of this training is to improve employment opportunities for deaf students (Curriculum: Wat heb je vandaag op school geleerd?, n.d.e).

VGT, Deaf Culture, and Deaf Personnel in Flemish Deaf Schools

Considering the DC or TC vision in Flemish deaf schools, it is not clear to what extent they provide VGT as a course, namely, the extent to which they follow the VGT objectives and the teaching of VGT as a language of instruction (De Meulder, 2005; "Bevragingproject onderwijs," 2007). Because the government approved developmental and final objectives for VGT for elementary education, Kasterlinden, the only bilingual-bicultural deaf school in Flanders, is developing a VGT curriculum for elementary education, a project for developmental objectives for VGT, and a VGT curriculum in secondary education (K. Aerden, special education specialist, Kasterlinden, personal communication, March 9, 2007). At the secondary level, the curriculum contains 1 hour of VGT a week. The students are also provided with information and exercises that contrast the grammar of Dutch and VGT (K. Aerden, personal communication, March 8, 2007).

The (lack of) teaching of VGT and its use as an instructional language correspond with the absence of deaf staff members in deaf schools. De Meulder (2005) provides an overview of deaf personnel working in an educational function in deaf schools. There are only a few deaf people working in deaf schools (not yet in all deaf schools), and they often have "dual roles" of house parent in the dorms and instructor of VGT or deaf culture (or both).

However, it seems there is more openness toward the implementation of deaf culture classes in the curriculum than toward the implementation of VGT. In June 2004, the Commission of Development and Research for People With an Auditive Disability (CORA)—a group of people consisting of deaf school representatives—established a "deaf culture" working group. CORA represents all the Flemish medical pedagogical institutions connected to deaf schools; Siblo 7 is the only deaf school that is not part of CORA. The deaf culture working group produced (basic) educational material for teaching deaf culture in elementary and secondary deaf education. In 2006, a deaf culture day was organized for all Flemish deaf schools. In the future, this event will be organized every year. Currently, all secondary deaf schools teach deaf culture courses for 1 hour a week; in elementary schools, the teaching of deafness-related content ranges from teaching with no real organization in one-time attempts to teaching 2 hours a week (Bevragingsproject onderwijs, May 25, 2007).

The rather marginal place of VGT and deaf culture in the curricula in deaf schools can be explained by the attitudes toward the use of sign language in the field of Flemish deaf education. Rymen, Maes, and Ghesquière (2001) did exploratory research on the place of sign language and deaf culture in special education in which they interviewed both providers of deaf education (teachers, directors, and special education specialists) and users of deaf education (parents, teachers, and deaf and hard of hearing adults). The researchers found that many respondents, especially parents and teachers, are not familiar with, or well-informed about, the new trends in deaf education, which leads to wrong representations of bilingual-bicultural education. The researchers found an openness toward VGT and deaf culture, but also noticed that deaf schools preferred not to give up the knowledge they have acquired.

The rather marginal initiatives in the direction of deaf-centered education should be placed against the strong oral background of Flemish deaf education and the development of cochlear implants and mainstreaming. The next part of this chapter will illustrate this contrast.

What Schools Do Deaf Children Attend?

Lichtert (2007), De Raeve (2006a), and De Raeve and Loots (2007) provide information on the numbers of deaf and hard of hearing children in mainstream and deaf education. In 2006, CORA counted 211 deaf children in primary education (120 in deaf schools, 91 mainstreamed), 367 deaf children in elementary education (195 in deaf schools, 172 mainstreamed), and 376 deaf children in secondary education (147 in deaf schools, 229 mainstreamed)—a total of 954 deaf and hard of hearing children in nursery, primary, and secondary education.

Lichtert (2007) is the first quantitative study that has been published about deaf children in primary and elementary education in Flanders from1990 to 2006. As Lichtert (2007) noted, the Education Department of the Flemish Government does not provide detailed statistics of deaf school-age children in Flanders. The department provides statistics of Type 7 children who attend special education, but Type 7 includes not only children who are deaf and hard of hearing but also children with language disorders and autism.

Lichtert (2007) found that the total number of deaf and hard of hearing children has not decreased in the last 16 years. His study draws on information collected by CORA on the numbers of deaf and hard of hearing children. Consequently, his population includes all deaf and hard of hearing students who receive service from a Flemish deaf school and Medical Pedagogical Institution. Comparing the total number of deaf students in primary, elementary, and secondary deaf education from 1990–91 ($n = 590$) to 2005–06 ($n = 462$), however, Lichtert (2007) found a significant decrease in the numbers of deaf students in secondary education—from 227 deaf students in deaf schools in 1990 to 147 deaf students in deaf schools in 2006. For primary and elementary education, the statistics indicate a less dramatic decrease from 363 deaf students in deaf schools in 1990 to 227 deaf students in deaf schools in 2006.

In the academic year of 2005 and 2006, for the first time, the number of deaf students mainstreamed with itinerant services ($n = 492$) was higher than the number of deaf students in deaf schools ($n = 462$). Moreover, Lichtert (2007) remarked that hard of hearing children do not receive itinerant services every year and that the actual number of deaf and hard of hearing children in mainstream education is probably even higher. In the last 5 years, 26%

more deaf and hard of hearing children received itinerant services than before 5 years ago; the number of hard of hearing and deaf toddlers who are mainstreamed even increased by 32%. Lichtert (2007) mentioned two factors that can mask the lack of a significant decrease of toddlers in deaf education: the new group of immigrant toddlers in deaf education and the small total number that can hide any statistical trend. Lichtert (2007) asked for data collection and data analysis to get further insight into migrations of the deaf school-age population in Flanders and expressed hope that the Education Department would follow up with the CORA statistics. Qualitative research should be done to tailor care, education, and therapy to the needs of deaf children.

This situation brings up the question of the factors contributing to this strong mainstream trend: the marriage of mainstreaming and cochlear implantation. First is the other trend toward increasing cochlear implantations. Since 1998–99, a public agency screens babies on hearing loss at birth. Most parents agree to the screenings, and as a result, 95% of all babies are tested. If hearing loss is found, it is confirmed before the babies are the age of 1 month (De Raeve, 2006b). De Raeve (2006b) noticed that in 1998, Flanders was the first European region to screen deaf babies before they reached the age of 6 weeks, and this development seriously advanced the age of cochlear implantation. Deaf babies receive cochlear implants mostly at the average age of 12 months (De Raeve, 2006a) and sometimes even earlier (7–8 months) (De Raeve, 2006b. Since 1991, the government has financially supported cochlear implantation for deaf children. In 2003, the government even supported a second implant in children who had already received one; however, this practice was not continued (Clays, 2005). In 1998, 25% of deaf toddlers received cochlear implants, and that number has increased to 80% in 2005 (De Raeve, 2006a).

Currently, 55% of all deaf children in elementary school and high school have cochlear implants. The numbers differ according to the level of education: 80% of the deaf children in kindergarten have been implanted compared with 60% of the children in elementary education and 30% of the deaf children in secondary education (De Raeve, 2006b). From 1999 to 2006, the percentage of deaf children with cochlear implants attending mainstream schools increased from 17% to 40% (De Raeve & Loots, 2007). De Raeve and Loots (2007) foresee that in the next 10 years, 80% of all deaf children will have a cochlear implant and that 70% of all deaf children will attend regular schools.

A second factor that stimulates mainstreaming is the government support of integration and inclusion: "The legal principle of inclusion . . . was included in the 1970 law on special and inclusive education. The law of February 1997 on primary education incorporates mainstream and special primary education in the same legal framework, respecting the specific characteristics of special education" (DEAFVOC, n.d.). In 2002, the government passed the "Decree concerning equal education opportunities" ("Decreet betreffende gelijke onderwijskansen-I," September 14, 2002) that should create more opportunities for inclusion. Recognizing accessibility for students with disabilities, the government made support services available. Since 1994, students with a severe hearing loss of at least 90 dB in both ears and no more than 40% phoneme discrimination in vocal audio tests can receive 4 hours a week of itinerant service during each school year. Students with an average hearing loss can receive only 2 years of itinerant service at each educational level (primary and secondary) ("Omzendbrief geïntegreerd onderwijs," 2006). The government also provides sign language interpreting and note taking.

Until the middle of the 1990s, mainstreaming was possible only for deaf children with good oral skills and for hard of hearing children (Broekaert, Bogaerts, & Clement, 1994), but now, mainstreaming is accessible for a larger group of deaf children. In the academic year of 1996–97, the Education Department initiated an experiment with sign language interpreters in advanced education for one student (De Weerdt, 2003). The experiment was so successful that in the year 2000, 29 deaf students received VGT interpreting, increasing to 50 students in 2003. In the academic year 2006–07, 58 deaf students used VGT interpreters (D. De Witte, personal communication, July 6, 2007). Currently, deaf students with a hearing loss of 90 dB or more in both ears can receive interpreting support when they are mainstreamed in secondary and postsecondary education. The support can be provided by either a qualified VGT interpreter or a note taker. The note taker can be any person who has a bachelor's degree. Per week, students can receive a maximum of 12 hours interpreting in VGT and 6 hours of note taking. If students apply for both VGT interpreting and note taking, the maximum is still 12 hours a week (Omzendbrief Doventolken in het voltijds gewoon onderwijs, 2007).

Yet there are restraints. Each year, the government makes a limited package of interpreting hours available ("Het tolken VGT," 2006). Because of the limited amount of interpreting hours that has to be divided among all the students, deaf students in secondary education received an average of 5 hours a week (vocational secondary education), 6 hours a week (technical secondary education), and 8 hours a week (general secondary education) of VGT interpreting ("Informatiebrochure Secundaire School Spermalie," 2007) in the academic year 2006–07. Students in advanced education received an average of 5 hours VGT interpreting a week (D. De Witte, personal communication, July 6, 2007). Apart from the limited hours of interpreting available, deaf students who are being mainstreamed also experience other barriers (De Weerdt, 2003; Vermeerbergen, 2003). Because there is no special training for interpreters to interpret in educational settings, there is often a lack of professionalism. The latter is the case for both VGT interpreters and note takers (De Weerdt, 2003; Van de Walle & Rijckaert, 2007). The number of active interpreters is also limited (De Weerdt, 2003).

Other factors that influence the trend of mainstreaming are the limitations of deaf education. In a survey of 10 deaf and hard of hearing students, De Weerdt (2003) found that the students, although they preferred deaf schools for communication and deaf peers, often chose mainstream education for three reasons: higher level of education, wider choice of majors, and an accredited diploma. Secondary education students of Kasterlinden also discussed this situation in their documentary movie WORLD DEAF (De Clerck, 2005b). De Weerdt (2003) also mentions the social isolation of deaf students in a mainstreamed environment.

Nevertheless, deaf students who are mainstreamed still experience a lot of barriers. The Education Department does not provide enough interpreting hours; there are not enough active VGT interpreters; and consequently, students cannot reach the maximum of 12 hours a week (De Weerdt, 2003; Vermeerbergen, Fevlado visietekst). Because there is no special training for interpreters to interpret in educational situations, there is often a lack of professionalism (De Weerdt, 2003, Van de Walle & Rijckaert, 2007). De Weerdt (2003) also mentions social isolation.

Opportunities for mainstreamed deaf children to have contact with deaf peers and deaf role models are still scarce and often are not systematically part of the curriculum. In an e-mail survey, the author of this chapter asked deaf schools about "grouping" of deaf students and about activities for mainstream deaf students. Some deaf schools (Sint-Lievenspoort,

Sint-Gregorius) "group" deaf children in the same classrooms. This practice provides peer support and increases the amount of interpreting hours that can be used (the total sum of each child's allotment of interpreting hours). Last April, Sint-Lievenspoort organized an afternoon for deaf and hard of hearing children, starting from the oldest class in kindergarten (B. Ranschaert, director, personal communication, June 21, 2007). At Sint-Gregorius, all deaf children have the opportunity to meet other deaf children or deaf staff members through the medical-pedagogical institution connected to the deaf school, including students who didn't attend the school before mainstreaming. Students can meet for study coaching at night or on Wednesday afternoon. They are also able to stay over in the dorms (G. Geysels, special educational specialist, personal communication, June 21, 2007). Koninklijk Instituut voor Doven Spraakgestoorden Hasselt organizes "Saturday-KIDS," a once-a-month program on Saturdays in which all deaf children who are mainstreamed gather for activities led by the itinerant teachers. Because the age varies from 13 to 20 years, the older students are role models for younger members of the group, and the meetings are very successful (O. De Raeve, director, personal communication, June 4, 2007). Jongelinckshof and Emmaüs organize some activities on Wednesday afternoons or on weekends. Deaf students and their families and friends are invited to get to know one another and exchange experiences (P. Boutsen, personal communication, September 17, 2007). Spermalie Bruges organized "G.On.-trefdag," a meeting day for all mainstreamed deaf children to get in touch and join in activities. This tradition already existed for deaf children mainstreamed in elementary education (A. Adriaens, personal communication, July 5, 2007). Kasterlinden does not mention any activities except that in March 2008, all Flemish deaf children who are mainstreamed were invited for a "G'ontmoetingsdag," a daytime program for deaf children of different age groups and parents. Deaf teachers and class assistants were involved, and deaf culture was part of the program (K. Aerden, special education specialist, personal communication, May 25, 2007).

Smessaert (2005) describes the experiences of four deaf students who were mainstreamed successfully in the fifth year of vocational secondary education. Because the students were mainstreamed in the same classroom, they could use a larger number of interpreting hours. The mainstream school environment supported the students and even gave them opportunities to promote deaf culture in a positive way in activities at school. The students experienced mainstreaming as empowering and as contributing to their deaf consciousness. Yet the author remarks that this kind of success can be the case only when the itinerant teacher has deaf cultural knowledge, is able to transfer this knowledge to the mainstream school, and is able to empower the students.

Deaf Students in Advanced Education

For advanced education, the Education Department of the Flemish Government provided the author with statistics of the last 10 years (academic year 1996–97 until academic year 2005–06) (P. Willems, Education Department, personal communication, June 6, 2007). These statistics identify students in Type 7 as deaf and hard of hearing students, distinguishing between moderate and severe hearing loss. In 1996–97, the Education Department registered two students with an average hearing loss and one student with a severe hearing loss. In 2002–03, it registered 13 students with severe hearing loss and 5 students with an average hearing loss, and in 2005–06 the statistical count included 28 students with a severe hearing loss and 26 students with an average hearing loss.

For the academic years of 2006 and 2007, the Education Department was able to provide the author with the results of a recent survey (P. Willems, personal communication, June 6, 2007). This survey found 71 deaf and hard of hearing students in tertiary education: 23 students who attend university and 48 students who attend schools for advanced education. This survey has not yet been completed, and it is an estimation rather than an exact number. Universities and institutions for advanced education do not always register the number of students with disability in the central administration of the institution; institutions also differ in their registration codes. The evaluation in the Department of Education should be interpreted with care, and systematic statistical data collection and analysis is called for. Because sufficient educational access is lacking in Flemish advanced education for deaf and hard of hearing students, and because there are no majors in VGT and deaf studies, deaf students in advanced education sometimes prefer to study abroad (Scandinavia, the United Kingdom, or the United States). However, only those in a small "elite" group of deaf students have the educational background, linguistic background (knowledge of English), financial resources, and deaf awareness required to pursue advanced education abroad. Most students who study abroad have already graduated from a bachelor or master degree program in Flanders and specialize in "deaf"-related majors such as sign language linguistics and deaf studies (panel "Studeren in het buitenland"). De Meulder and Van Mulders (2007) even call this trend a "deaf brain drain" that is "immediately linked to the lack of research opportunities in Flanders and thus to the lack of researchers to work and/or establish connections with," which is also the perspective of this author. In addition, other reasons also influence deaf graduates in their decision to return to Flanders or stay overseas, including personal life choices, limited accessibility of mainstream society (Loots et al., 2003), the monolingual orientation in deaf schools and changes in deaf education, limited opportunities for equal employment in general and employment in the field of deaf studies in particular, and an intrinsic motivation to return to Flanders or contribute to the Flemish deaf community.

The clash between this rather small group of deaf students who are members of the deaf community and the large group of deaf and hard of hearing students who probably join mainstream society challenges the deaf community to promote itself and its sign language positively and to attract new members who can pass on knowledge (also see Broeckaert et al., 1994).

PREPARATION OF SPECIAL PERSONNEL

The current new developments in the Flemish deaf landscape require professional programs specializing in working with deaf people. The information in this section was obtained through personal correspondence with professionals who are working in the field (deaf school directors, university professors, lecturers in advanced education, special education specialists in deaf schools). Because Flemish scientific research in deaf issues is still relatively young, and because the Flemish population is small, it can be expected that the lack of professional programs is serious.

The information provided at Flemish universities is rather scarce. Currently, there are no majors in VGT, deaf studies, and deaf education. In addition, specialization programs for psychologists, counselors, social workers, etc., are not available. Consequently, it is not possible for psychology, counseling, social work, special education students, and students in other fields to specialize in working with deaf people at Flemish Universities. Because these majors are oriented toward mainstream society and include all minority groups and people with disabilities in general, the amount of information that is provided about deafness, sign language, and deaf culture differs among the institutions and depends on the students' personal interests. Often, the information is limited to single courses or even chapters in courses.

For example, for special education students at Leuven University, there is an introduction on deaf children in the course on children with special needs in the first year of the bachelor's degree program; in the third year, part of the course "Pedagogical Assistance to People With Disabilities" discusses deaf people; and in the master's program, students may choose the course "Descriptive and Therapeutic Aspects Concerning Hearing Impairments," which offers audiological information (15 hours) as well as information about "bilingual and bicultural education" and "the socio-emotional well-being of children, youngsters, and adults with a hearing impairment" (15 hours) (B. Maes, personal communication, July 13, 2007). The master's program in special education at Ghent University offers a course about deaf culture and sign language under the program of Disability Studies. Some students choose to write their thesis about deaf issues or do an internship in the deafness field and expand their knowledge of deafness in this way (G. Van Hove, personal communication, June 14, 2007). Although these master's programs train special education specialists, the programs provide some background information but do not include specialized content related to deaf education. Consequently, there is no one with a degree in deaf education in Flanders. Currently, VGT and Introduction to VGT are taught as a three-credit course at two Flemish universities (M. Van Herreweghe, personal communication, April 18 and August 23, 2007).

Programs for teachers in elementary education do not really enable discussion of deaf issues in their curricula. Yet all students are required to do an internship in special education, and some students choose to do their internship in deaf education. Often, these students are enrolled in a VGT-interpreter training program or in a VGT course or are familiar with, or interested in, working with deaf people. Consequently, competence in working with deaf children is learned by doing rather than acquired by receiving training through advanced education programs (P. Veevaete, personal communication, May 30, 2007). Teachers in special education do have the opportunity to receive additional training by enrolling in programs for teachers in special education (a bachelor program for special education that can be achieved after a bachelor degree in primary/elementary education). The information about teaching deaf children in this program differs from institution to institution. For example, one program provides about eight 3-hour classes focused on deaf issues (e.g., bilingual education, psychology, deaf culture, cochlear implants, testimony of deaf adults) whereas another program focuses instead on developing teachers' general competence and assumes that teachers should receive their specific training in the deaf schools for which they are working (B. Wuyts, personal communication, June 1, 2007).

The recruitment policy in deaf schools is indeed another way of providing teachers with information about deafness and knowledge about VGT. Koninklijk Instituut voor Doven en Spraakgestoorden Hasselt requires that teachers of deaf children enroll in the training program for teachers in special education and provides required intern training once a month for people who are working with deaf children. This training can include information about cochlear implants and hearing aids, audiology, sign language and deaf culture, language acquisition and deaf children, as well as pedagogy and reflective language methods. Koninklijk Instituut voor Doven en Spraakgestoorden Hasselt also requires and provides basic training in sign language and mentions that teachers often enroll in the VGT interpreter training program (O. De Raeve, personal communication, June 5, 2007). Similarly, Kasterlinden encourages teachers to enroll in at least 2 years of a VGT interpreter training. The itinerant teachers at Kasterlinden all graduated from the VGT interpreter training program (K. Aerden, personal communication, May 30, 2007). Sint-Lievenspoort recruits new teachers through announcing opportunities on the Web sites of Fevlado or the VGT interpreter training program. The school notices that only a few teachers are available who already have competencies in VGT, deaf culture, and the Flemish deaf community before employment and brings up the problem of interim teachers who are expected to start working at the school in a very short period of time. Teachers also take sign language courses at Fevlado or through the interpreter program. When the teacher does not have enough knowledge of VGT, the deaf class assistant will compensate (B. Ranschaert, personal communication, June 14, 2007). Jongelinckshof and Emmaüs prefer to recruit personnel with experience in working with deaf children; most of the teachers are either VGT interpreters or VGT interpreter students. An internship working with deaf and hard of hearing children and students is mandatory. The schools also offer a 2-year training program for teachers, parents, and house parents (P. Boutsen, personal communication, September 17, 2007). Spermalie Bruges provides for all the personnel a required course in Signed Dutch on deaf culture, deaf awareness, technical aids, etc. The deaf culture section of the curriculum for deaf students is taught in VGT by two deaf class assistants (A. Adriaens, personal communication, July 5, 2007).

Currently, there are six certified deaf teachers in Flanders (one primary education teacher and five secondary education teachers). Two deaf teachers are currently living abroad. A few deaf adults are currently working as teacher assistants in deaf schools, and one Gallaudet alumni is teaching deaf culture in two deaf schools. Two deaf students are currently enrolled in teacher training programs.

CONCLUSION

Flemish deaf education has known a strong oral tradition. As a result, most Flemish people still understand the concept of "disability" from a medical-functional point of view that focuses on deficits and on a state of being "not able to function" rather than on a cultural or social perspective on disability (Van Hove, Lenoir, & Vanpeperstraete, 2003). Yet parallel to the developments of cochlear implantation and mainstreaming that have occurred, a recent emancipation process has taken place in the Flemish deaf community, leading to the recognition of VGT. For the Flemish deaf community and larger society to be able to face the challenges of these recent developments, Fevlado will need to take advantage of the current (political) openness after the recognition of VGT, manifest itself as a strong and equal partner, and open the discussion on how to meet the needs of deaf students.

Fevlado and the Flemish government need to play a crucial role to positively promote VGT and create opportunities in the educational system to study and learn VGT. At the time of this writing, the Department of Culture in the Flemish government is working toward the establishment of a center to provide information and knowledge about VGT in support of research, teaching materials, etc. In August 2008, for the first time, a VGT camp will be organized for children between the ages of 6 and 12 with (and without) cochlear implants. This language immersion camp will be designed as 10 monthly gatherings on Saturdays. Fevlado is also organizing a symposium on the social-emotional development of children with a cochlear implant, which will take place in November 2008 (M. De Meulder, personal communication, September 26, 2007).

Researchers from different universities and Fevlado are advocating for more courses in VGT in advanced education and have developed proposals for the following degree programs: Master of Flemish Sign Language, Master of Deaf Studies, and Master of VGT-Interpreting ("Hoger Onderwijs van (en omtrent) Vlaamse Gebarentaal (VGT)," 2005).

In 2008, Flemish universities that make an effort to support students with disabilities will receive more support from the government ("Fundamentele hervorming financiering hoger onderwijs," 2007). Currently, deaf students at Flemish universities and institutions for advanced education are taking action to address their needs and remove the barriers they are experiencing. The providing of full-time sign language interpretation, real-time captioning services, note taking, or some combination, which is necessary to improve education access and equal opportunities for deaf and hard of hearing students in advanced education, will be requested. In 2008, the Flemish government will also make (limited) interpreting services available for deaf adults enrolled in adult education programs ("Tolken in volwassen-enonderwijs vanaf januari 2008," 2007).

The Flemish deaf community needs to claim an active role in the discussion on deaf education. The Flemish deaf community and its partners will need to continue its advocacy for deaf children to have the opportunity to learn VGT and have contacts with deaf role models, deaf peers, and the Flemish deaf community. Basic knowledge in deaf studies should be provided by itinerant teachers, and interpreters need to be trained to interpret in the classroom setting. Hearing classmates and teachers should be supported with adequate background knowledge. The broader questions of (a) how to improve academic achievement, (b) how to meet the needs of deaf children, and (c) how to arrange deaf education so questions a and b can be achieved should receive proper attention. These questions relate to both education for deaf children who attend deaf schools and education for deaf children who are mainstreamed. Because programs for teachers of deaf children refer their teachers in training to deaf schools to receive further competencies and skills and deaf schools refer their personnel to training programs to get the necessary competencies and skills, the system is in a vicious circle that results in a lack of appropriate training. What is needed is a special program for teachers of deaf children and specialized training for itinerant teachers working with deaf children.

Because these new trends ask for knowledge and expertise, the Flemish ministry of education needs to put deaf education on the agenda and make the necessary resources available for Flanders to acquire the expertise needed. This effort also includes a strong need for more deaf-centered and deaf-led research at Flemish universities as well as a need for collaboration and exchange of information with foreign universities.

References

Bevragingsproject onderwijs [Inquiry project "education"]. (2007). In *Bevragingsproject "Dovengemeenschap in Vlaanderen"* [Inquiry project "Deaf community in Flanders"]. Manuscript submitted for publication.

Boonen, D., Van Herreweghe, M., & Vermeerbergen, M. (2004). De evolutie van Gebarentaal in Vlaanderen [The evolution of sign language in Flanders]. M. Van Herreweghe & M. Vermeerbergen (Eds.), *Gent in Oktober* (pp. 7–23). Ghent, Belgium: Academia Press.

Broekaert, E., Bogaerts, J., & Clement, J. P. (1994). *Wat doven zeggen. Onderzoek naar de socio-economische leefsituatie van volwassen doven en slechthorenden uit het Buitengewoon Onderwijs in Vlaanderen* [What deaf people say: Research on the socioeconomical life situation of deaf and hard of hearing adults of Special Education in Flanders]. Leuven, Belgium: Garant.

Buyens, M. (2005). *De dove persoon, zijn gebarentaal en het dovenonderwijs* [The deaf person, his sign language, and deaf education]. Antwerpen, Belgium: Garant.

Clays, F. (2005). *CI en/of (een) gebaren(taal). Onderzoek naar het gebruik van (een) gebaren(taal) bij peuters, kleuters en kinderen uit het lagere onderwijs met cochleaire implantaten* [CI and/or sign (language). Research on the use of sign (language) by toddlers, kindergarters, and children in elementary education with CI]. Unpublished master's thesis, Ghent University, Belgium.

Curriculum: Wat heb je vandaag op school geleerd? [Curriculum. What have you learned at school today?] (n.d.a). *Buitengewoon onderwijs* [Special education]. Retrieved May 20, 2007, from http://www.ond.vlaanderen.be/dvo/buitengewoon/index.htm

Curriculum: Wat heb je vandaag op school geleerd? [Curriculum. What have you learned at school today?] (n.d.b). *Buitengewoon basisonderwijs—Type 7: Algemene uitgangspunten* [Special elementary education—Type 7: General basic principles]. Retrieved May 20, 2007, from http://www.ond.vlaanderen.be/dvo/buitengewoon/buitengewoon_basis/type7/uitgangspunten/t7algemeen.htm

Curriculum: Wat heb je vandaag op school geleerd? [Curriculum. What have you learned at school today?] (n.d.c). *Buitengewoon basisonderwijs—Type 7: Ontwikkelingsdoelen communicatie en taal: Nederlands/2 Ontwikkelingsdoelen communicatie en taal: Vlaamse Gebarentaal* [Special elementary education—Type 7: Developmental objectives communication and language: Dutch/2 Developmental objectives communication and language: Flemish Sign Language]. Retrieved May 20, 2007, from http://www.ond.vlaanderen.be/dvo/buitengewoon/buitengewoon_basis/type7/ontwikkelingsdoelen/taal.htm

Curriculum: Wat heb je vandaag op school geleerd? [Curriculum. What have you learned at school today?] (n.d.d). *Buitengewoon basisonderwijs—Type 7: Ontwikkelingsdoelen wereldoriëntatie: Dovencultuur* [Special elementary education—Type 7: Developmental objectives world orientation: Deaf culture]. Retrieved May 20, 2007, from http://www.ond.vlaanderen.be/dvo/buitengewoon/buitengewoon_basis/type7/ontwikkelingsdoelen/wereldorientatie.htm

Curriculum: Wat heb je vandaag op school geleerd? [Curriculum. What have you learned at school today?] (2006, August 28). *Buitengewoon secundair onderwijs, opleidingsvorm 3: Richtlijnen: I.V.M. alternerende beroepsopleiding (Omzendbrief 28/08/2006)* [Special secondary education—Educational form 3: Guidelines concerning alternating vocational training (Circulation letter 08/28/2006)]. Retrieved on May 20, 2007, from http://www.ond.vlaanderen.be/edulex/database/document/document.asp?docid=13496.

Curriculum: Wat heb je vandaag op school geleerd? [Curriculum. What have you learned at school today?] (n.d.f). *Buitengewoon secundair onderwijs OV3. Algemene uitgangspunten* [Special secondary education OV3. General basic principles]. Retrieved May 20, 2007, from http://www.ond.vlaanderen.be/dvo/buitengewoon/buitengewoon_secundair/ov3/uitgangspunten/OV3algemeen.htm

DEAFVOC. (n.d.). *DEAFVOC Sign Languages and European written languages in the virtual vocational training of the deaf* (Survey of the current situation of the vocational training of the deaf in the countries of the European Union). Belgium (Flemish). Retrieved May 30, 2007, from http://www.deafvoc.fi

De Clerck, G. (2005a). *Wake Up Wake Up. Stories of growth, strength and fire. Meet Meet, Visit Visit: Nomadic deaf identities, deaf dream worlds, and the imagination leading to translocal deaf activism.* Ghent, Belgium: Ghent University, Department of Special Education.

De Clerck, G. (Director). (2005b). WORLD DEAF [Movie]. Ghent, Belgium: Fevlado-Diversus.

De Clerck, G. (2007). Meeting global deaf peers and visiting ideal deal places: Deaf ways of education leading to empowerment. An exploratory case study. *American Annals of the Deaf, 152*(4), 5–15.

Decreet betreffende gelijke onderwijskansen-I. [Decree concerning equal educational opportunities]. (2002, September 14). Retrieved September 26, 2007, from http://www.ond.vlaanderen.be/edulex/database/document.asap?docid-13298

De Meulder, M. (2005). *Macht en onmacht op school. De invloed van een onderwijssysteem op dove kinderen en volwassenen: een etnografisch onderzoek.* Unpublished master's thesis, Ghent University, Belgium.

De Meulder, M., & Van Mulders, K. (2007). *Deaf studies in Flanders: To be or not to be?* Manuscript submitted for publication.

De Raeve, L. (2006a, April). *Inventarisatie gehoorgestoorde kinderen in Vlaanderen door CORA-01.04.06.* [Inventarisation of hearing impaired children in Flanders by CORA-04/01/06]. Poster session presented at the CORA meeting, Belgium.

De Raeve, L. (2006b). Invloed van de vroege gehoorscreening op de resultaten na cochleaire implantatie [Influence of early screening on the results after cochler implantation]. *Tijdschrift voor Geneeskunde, 62,* 245–252.

De Raeve, L., & Loots, G. (2007). Cochleaire implantatie [Cochlear implantation]. In *Bevragingsproject "Dovengemeenschap in Vlaanderen"* [Inquiry project "Deaf community in Flanders."]. Unpublished manuscript.

De Weerdt, D. (2003). *Buitengewoon onderwijs of gewoon/geïntegreerd onderwijs? Waar horen d/Doven?* [Special education or regular/mainstream education? Where do d/Deaf people belong?]. Unpublished bachelor's thesis, Katholieke Hogeschool Zuid-West-Vlaanderen.

De Weerdt, K., Vanhecke, E., Van Herreweghe, M., & Vermeerbergen, M. (2002*). De dovengemeenschap in Vlaanderen: Doorlichting, sensibilisering, en standaardisering van de Vlaamse Gebarentaal. Luik 2: Lexicografisch onderzoek. Eindrapport* [The deaf community in Flanders: Investigation, sensitization, and standardization of Flemish Sign Language. Part 2: Lexicographic research. Final report]. Ghent, Belgium: Ghent University.

————. (2007). Evolutie tweetalig onderwijs in Kasterlinden [The evolution of bilingual education in Kasterlinden]. In *Bevragingsproject "Dovengemeenschap in Vlaanderen"* [Inquiry project "Deaf community in Flanders"]. Manuscript submitted for publication.

Fundamentele hervorming financiering hoger underwijs goedge keurd. (2007). Retrieved May 16, 2007, from http://www.ond.vlaanderen.be

Gerday, C., & Thomas, V. (2001). *L'histoire des sourds* [History of the deaf]. Liège, Belgium: Centre Robert Dresse.

Het curriculum in BUSO OV1-OV2: Een terreinverkenning [The curriculum in special secondary education, educational forms 1–2: An exploration]. (n.d.). Retrieved May 20, 2007, from http://www.ond.vlaanderen.be/dvo/buitengewoon/buitengewoon_secundair/ov1ov2/terreinverkenning.htm

Het tolken VGT in Vlaanderen in een oogopslag [Interpreting Flemish Sign Language in Flanders in a nutshell]. (2006, December). Retrieved May 20, 2007, from http://www.cabvlaanderen.be/f_documenten.aspx

Heyerick, I. (n.d.). *Flemish Sign Language (VGT) unanimously recognized.* Retrieved October 31, 2006, from the Fevlado Web site: http://www.fevlado.be/themas/gebarentaal/overzicht.aspx.

Informatiebrochure Secundaire School Spermalie. Opleidingstrajecten voor dove en slechthorende leerlingen [Information brochure Spermalie Secondary School. Educational paths for deaf and hard of hearing students]. (2007). Unpublished manuscript.

Le Maire, B. (1996). *Joseph Henrion. Premier professeur sourd de Belgique* [Joseph Henrion, first deaf teacher in Belgium]. Liège, Belgium: Centre Robert Dresse.

Le Maire, B. (1997). *Histoire des sourds en Belgique, en France: Et dans les autres pays, Deuxième partie* [Deaf history in Belgium, and France: and in other countries. Second part]. Liège, Belguim: Centre Robert Dresse.

Lichtert, G. (2007). Het dove en slechthorende schoolkind in Vlaanderen van 1990 tot 2006. Een kwantitatieve analyse. [The deaf and heard of hearing school child in Flanders from 1990 until 2006. A quantitative analysis.] *Logopedie, 20*(2), 41–47.

Loots, G., Devise, I., Lichtert, G., Hoebrechts, N., Van De Ginste, C., & De Bruyne, I. (2003). *De Gemeenschap van doven en slechthorenden in Vlaanderen: Communicatie, taal en verwachtingen omtrent maatschappelijke toegankelijkheid* [The community of deaf and hard of hearing people in Flanders: Communication, language, and expectations of access to society]. Ghent, Belgium: Cultuur voor Doven.

Loots, G., Maes, B., Van Herreweghe, M., & Vermeerbergen, M. (2002). De Dovengemeenschap in Vlaanderen: Samenvatting en beleidsaanbevelingen.

Ministry of the Flemish Community. (2005). *Education in Flanders. The Flemish educational landscape in a nutshell.* Brussels: Author.

Omzendbrief Doventolken in het voltijds gewoon onderwijs Circular: Interpreters for deaf people in full-time mainstream education]. (2007). Retrieved August 18, 2007, from http://www.cabvlaanderen.be/f_documenten.aspx.

Omzendbrief geïntegreerd onderwijs [Circular: Integrated education]. (2006). Retrieved April 12, 2007, from http://www.ond.vlaanderen.be/edulex/database/document/document.asp?docid=13422

Rymen, L., Maes, B., & Ghesquière, P. (2001, October). Visies over de plaats van gebarentaal en dovencultuur in het buitengewoon onderwijs. Een exploratief onderzoek bij onderwijsverstrekkers en gebruikers [Visions on the place of sign language and deaf culture in special education. An exploratory study of education providers and users]. In M. Van Herreweghe & M. Vermeerbergen (Chairs), *Gebarentaal in Vlaanderen: Lexicografische, onderwijs-pedagogische, en socio-culturele aspecten* [Sign Language in Flanders: Lexicographic, educational-pedagogical and socio-cultural aspect]. Proceedings of the Congress at Ghent University, Belgium. Ghent: Fevlado-Diversus.

Smessaert, I. (2005). *Dovencultuur en empowerment bij dove jongeren in het geïntegreerd onderwijs* [Deaf culture and empowerment in deaf teenagers in integrated education]. Unpublished manuscript, Vormingsleergang voor Sociaal en Pedagogisch Werk, Ghent, Belgium.

Timmermans, N. (2005). *The status of sign language in Europe.* London: Council of Europe Publishing.

Tolken in het volwassenenonderwijs vanaf. (2008). Retrieved February 26, 2009, from http://www.fevlado.be/nieuws/nieuwsDetail.aspx?item=472

Van de Walle, Y., & Rijckaert, J. (2007). De dove/slechthorende studenten van BSH Gent stellen voor: 'schrijftolkencrisis' [The deaf/hard of hearing students of BSH Ghent presents: Crisis of note takers].

Van Herreweghe, M. (1995). *De Vlaams-Belgische gebarentaal: Een eerste verkenning* [Flemish-Belgian Sign Language: A first exploration]. Ghent, Belgium: Academia Press.

Van Herreweghe, M. (2002). Turn-taking mechanisms and active participation in meetings with deaf and hearing participants in Flanders. In C. Lucas (Ed.), *Turn-taking, fingerspelling, and contact signed languages* (pp. 73–103). Washington, DC: Gallaudet University Press.

Van Herreweghe, M., & Vermeerbergen, M. (2004). Flemish Sign Language and some risks of codification. In M. Van Herreweghe & M. Vermeerbergen (Eds.), *To the lexicon and beyond: Sociolinguistics in European deaf communities* (pp. 111–135). Washington, DC: Gallaudet University Press.

Van Herreweghe, M., & Vermeerbergen, M. (2006). Deaf signers in Flanders and 25 years of community interpreting. *Lingüística Antverpiensia, 293–308.*

Van Hove, G., Lenoir, S., & Vanpeperstraete, L. (2003). Beeldvorming over personen met een handicap. Een onderzoek in opdracht van het Ministerie van de Vlaamse Gemeenschap Gelijke Kansen in Vlaanderen. Eindrapport maart 2003.

Van Mulders, K. (2004, March). *Informatie* [Information]. Retrieved November 5, 2005, from http:// gebaren.ugent.be/informatie.php

Van Mulders, K. (2005). Name signs in Flemish Sign Language. *Deaf Worlds*, *21*, 49–78.

Vermeerbergen, M. (1996). ROOD KOOL TIEN PERSOON IN. Morfo-syntactische aspecten van gebarentaal. [RED CABBAGE TEN PERSONS IN. Morphosyntactic aspects of sign language]. Unpublished doctoral dissertation, Vrije Universiteit Brussels, Belgium.

Vermeerbergen, M. (1999). *Grammaticale aspecten van de Vlaams-Belgische Gebarentaal: Videoboek.* [Grammatical aspects of the Flemish-Belgian Sign Language: Signing book]. Affligem, Belgium: Vlaams Gebarentaalcentrum.

Vermeerbergen, M. (2003). *Het inschakelen van tolen bij de integratie van dove in slechthorende leerlingen en studenten in het "gewone" onderwijs.* [Calling in interpreters for deaf and hard of hearing students mainstreamed in "regular" education]. Unpublished manuscript.

Trends and Developments in Deaf Education in Germany

Klaus B. Günther, Johannes Hennies, and Manfred Hintermair

THE EDUCATION of deaf people in Germany is widely associated with the oral, or so-called "German method," which focuses primarily on the use of spoken language, excluding the use of sign language and marginalizing written language as means of communication in education. The term *German method* came into use during the 19th century in reference to the views of Samuel Heinicke (1727–1790), who founded the first German institute for deaf-mute children in Leipzig in 1778,[1] which was the first government-funded school of its kind worldwide. Heinicke and the founder of the institute for deaf students in Paris, Abbé Charles-Michel de l'Epée (1712–1789), became engaged in a historical controversy about the right method of teaching deaf-mute students, which they debated through a series of letters (Schumann & Schumann, 1912). Epée claimed that deaf education should use all means of communication such as (methodical) sign language, spoken language, and written language. Heinicke dismissed written language and sign language and argued that education should be built on spoken language.[2]

The perception of this controversy has led to the misleading impression that from these early days on, only the oral method was practiced at German institutions for deaf-mute students. However, probably not even Heinicke himself taught his students purely orally (Schumann & Schumann, 1912); especially his successors in the first half of the 19th century did not solely apply oral teaching methods but, rather, what was later called a "combined method." Most important, for methodical ideas and conceptions, the founder of the influential Royal Deaf-Mute Institute at Berlin, Ernst Adolf Eschke (1766–1811), turned to the works of Epée's successor Abbé Roch-Ambroise Sicard (1742–1822) rather than to the approach of his own father-in-law Heinicke. As a result of this tendency, there were a considerable number of deaf-mute teachers at German schools for the deaf-mute who realized and justified the use of sign language in the classroom.[3] Two of the best-known deaf teachers were Otto Friedrich Kruse (1801–1880) and Karl Heinrich Wilke (1800–1876), who for more than

---

1. *Deaf-mute* (*Taubstumm*) was the usual term used in German-speaking countries up to the 1960s. Therefore, it will be used throughout this paper in that historical context.

2. Both Heinicke and Epée saw their achievement in aspects of their work that did not become their historical legacy: Epée considered his main contribution to be the establishment of "methodical signs," but became known for accepting and integrating deaf people and their language. Heinicke is seen as one of the founders of the oral method, but considered himself as having invented a method that would teach deaf-mute children the sounds of language using different flavors, as put down in his post-mortem published "Arcanum" (Schumann & Schumann, 1912).

3. Based on Vogel (1999) and Kruse (1832), 12 deaf teachers worked in German schools in the 19th century.

50 years not only taught deaf students in various northern German institutions but also contributed fundamentally to the educational and methodical foundation of deaf-mute teaching concepts (Dröge, 1999; Vogel, 1999). The list of deaf-mute teachers in the 19th century also includes a female teacher, Margaretha Hüttmann (1789–1854), and a deaf-mute school founder and director, Hugo von Schütz (1780–1847).

During the 19th century, voices advocating a purely oral method became increasingly influential not only in German states but also internationally—resulting at least partly from the rise of nationalism in Europe, which was founded on the idea of cultural and linguistic unity. Friedrich Moritz Hill (1805–1874), who became internationally recognized, claimed that "everything should include language instruction," meaning that all educational efforts for deaf-mute children should be linked to the use of spoken language (Schumann, 1940, p. 315). There was a series of conferences with teachers for deaf-mute students, which led to the Milan Congress in 1880 where the purely oral method was finalized, excluding sign language or signing. One of the few German teachers who argued strongly against this development was the deaf Otto Friedrich Kruse, who 10 years before the Milan Congress had pointed to the necessity of an education including sign language and had presented his ideas in a little book, also translated into English[4] and French, titled "Negotiating the extremes of the German and French methods in the teaching of the deaf-mutes—An attempt to connect both," which with its combined method presents the precursor of today's bilingual concept (Kruse, 1869).

The decision made by the conference in Milan to focus on spoken language and exclude sign language in deaf education was strongly welcomed in the newly founded "German Reich" and was enforced in the following years, even though sources allow the assumption that Germans, in particular Prussians, were not invited to Milan for political reasons, but were present only as observers. One of them was Edmund Treibel, who wrote the only known German documentation of the conference (Treibel, 1881).

The Milan Congress falls into a period between 1876 and 1893 in which the last German deaf-mute teachers of their time died: Karl Heinrich Wilke, Otto Friedrich Kruse, Ferdinand Rasch (1831–1885), and Karl Max Löwe (1834–1893). Their deaths marked the symbolic end of employing deaf-mute teachers and of using sign language at institutions for deaf-mute students in Germany.

After these events, alternative concepts to the predominantly oral method rarely appear. A group of teachers for deaf-mute students in Leipzig constituted an exception when they were looking for ways to compensate for the problems connected to articulation and speech practice by promoting early written language in a fairly successful way before 1918 (Günther, 1985), but could not gain support of other teachers for their ideas.

In November of 1918, after the defeat of the German Reich and the resignation of the German Emperor, there was a short "revolutionary" period not only in general German politics but also in educational politics that reached all the way into the education of deaf-mute students and, after almost 40 years, put the results and the consequences of the Milan Congress to the test.[5]

---

4. According to Schumann (1940, p. 349), it was published in the *American Annals of the Deaf and Dumb* in October 1872.

5. Events, data, and quotations for the time period between 1919 and 1921 are found in Schumann (1940, pp. 419).

As early as 1919, a state conference with delegates from German deaf associations took place, which resulted in a unanimously decided resolution for the Ministry of Cultural Affairs; in it, several demands were outlined, for instance, that the most suited deaf-mutes should be employed to teach and that sign language should be used. The result was a "meeting for a reform of the school of the deaf-mutes" at the beginning of 1921, initiated by the "Deaf Reich-Association" and the "Deaf Party-Association" in Berlin where next to deaf-mute people themselves, representatives of teachers of deaf-mute students as well as parents of deaf-mute children participated. Out of this reform meeting emerged a study group of representatives of deaf-mutes and teachers, which stated more precise and distinctive claims.

At the meeting of the "Association of German Teachers of the Deaf-Mutes" (Bund Deutscher Taubstummenlehrer, or BDT), these claims were described on the daily schedule as "claims and our position thereto raised by the circle of deaf-mute adults concerning the organization and methodology of deaf-mute education" (Schumann, 1940, p. 420). At the BDT meeting, some of the claims were supported but only in a reduced form. Especially the claims to the employment of deaf-mute teachers and social workers as well as the far-reaching use of sign language in the classroom were rejected.

Only a minority of teachers for deaf-mute students actively promoted the use of sign language in the classroom. Notable are the efforts of Markus Reich (1844–1911), the founder and first director of the "Israelite Institute of Deaf-Mutes" in Berlin-Weißensee and his son and successor Felix Reich (1885–1964), who both used sign language and signing primarily in the first classes. Felix Reich became an influential and active figure in German deaf education, serving many years as secretary and member of the administrative committee of the BDT. He promoted the realization of equal educational opportunities for deaf-mute children in the 1920s particularly by playing a lead role in the setup of a middle school program for deaf-mutes in Berlin-Neukölln and by supporting Wladislaus Zeitlin (1907–ca.1940),[6] the first deaf-mute to graduate from a university, whom he described in a little book (Reich, 1927). Gustav Wende (1915), school inspector in Berlin, called Reich's school the "best equipped institution of its kind in the German Reich" (p. 40), although it was financed solely through donations by private Jewish funds. After the rise of the National Socialists, Felix Reich was suspended from his public function because of his Jewish heritage (Sonke, 1993) and was later sent to a concentration camp for most of 1938. After his release, he managed to immigrate to England with 10 of the Jewish deaf-mute children from his school. There, he prepared to rescue the rest of the children and staff members, but was not able to do so because of the outbreak of World War II.

After gaining power in 1933, the National Socialists almost immediately introduced the law to "prevent genetically diseased offspring" ("Gesetz zur Verhütung erbkranken Nachwuchses," or GzVeN). German teachers of the deaf-mutes played a negative roll in enforcing this law (Biesold, 1999): In many documented cases, teachers and directors reported their own students to the public health department, and leading teachers of deaf-mute students publicly promoted the concept of eugenics. Although teachers of the deaf-mutes defined their profession, in part, in terms of the concept of eugenics and the cooperation of the institutions for

---

6. Zeitlin was murdered by the Gestapo during World War II in Paris, but the exact date of his death is unknown (Sonke, 1993).

deaf-mute students to carry out the GzVeN, it took the Professional Association of German Teachers of the Hearing-impaired (formerly BDT) 50 years to apologize to the deaf-mute community (Hartmann-Börner, 1997).

After World War II, the education of deaf-mute students remained purely oral. In West Germany, the main method from the 1950s on was based on the idea of a "Systematical Language Construction," designed to build up the language skills for deaf-mute students "systematically" through a gradual increase of difficulty. As additional visual support to the spoken language, the Phoneme Transmitting Manual System (Schulte, 1985) was introduced in West Germany whereas, in East Germany, teachers of deaf-mute students relied on the manual alphabet to support the buildup of spoken German under the influence of the Soviet Union.[7]

In the 1970s, the problems connected to oral education were more and more apparent, the discrepancy being the expectation on the one hand and the actual success of the education on the other. These problems developed into an open crisis concerning the oral teaching methods not only in Germany but also worldwide.

In 1982, the German Deaf Association and the Association of German Teachers of Deaf-Mute students together drew up a conceptual outline—the so-called Signing Paper of Munich—for the use of "Sign-Supported Language" (Lautsprachbegleitendende Gebärden, or LBG) with deaf students (Braun, Donath, Keller, Rammel, & Tigges, 1982). This 22-page paper is remarkable for the fact that it presents the first written outline for education and social work for deaf children prepared by both deaf people and teachers of the deaf since the failed reform of 1921–22. Moreover, it is significant that with the integration of LBG, signs were officially allowed again in Germany for the first time after 1880, even though they had never fully disappeared from the informal communication of deaf students. However, only a small number of schools for the deaf consequently introduced and developed LBG. Nevertheless, the consistent continuation of the LBG concept led to the first trial bilingual class with deaf students at the Hamburg School for the Deaf in 1992, which was fiercely disputed at first. With the successful progression of this first trial bilingual class, as documented in scientific surveys (Bizer & Karl, 2002; Günther, 1999; Günther & Schäfke, 2004; Hennies, 2006b; Schäfke, 2005), and the establishment of a second trial bilingual class in Berlin in 2001 (Günther & Hennies, in press), bilingual methods have become more accepted but are still in the minority.

From the very beginning of the education of deaf-mute students until the current education of deaf and severely hard of hearing students, these children have been taught almost exclusively in special schools in Germany. The idea of integrating them into mainstream schools has been discussed since the days of the first schools for the deaf because the schools for the deaf were not geographically accessible to all deaf children. Especially in the 19th century, these mainstreaming ideas were promoted by internationally recognized educators such as Johann Baptist Graser (1766–1841), who intended to increase the number of deaf-mute children in mainstream schools but eventually failed (Leonhardt, 2001). Despite this long tradition of discussing integration for deaf and hard of hearing students, the percentage of integrated children is still low compared with other countries such as the United States (Karchmer & Mitchell, 2003).

---

7. This effort was known as "Dactylology," comparable to the Rochester Method (Quigley, 1969).

CURRENT ACADEMIC PLACEMENT

During their lives, deaf children and adolescents in Germany will be placed in various educational settings. After the first diagnosis, parents and children can get assistance through an early intervention program until the children enter preschool or school. After completing primary schools, these students will go on to secondary school opportunities and vocational establishments.

Early Childhood Intervention

Similar to other countries, Germany is establishing newborn hearing screening throughout the country to identify hearing loss in a child as early as possible (Lenarz, 2007). According to the most recent survey on early childhood intervention in 1996, there are 71 institutions that support 2,300 deaf and hard of hearing children (Diller, Graser, & Schmalbrock, 2000). More than 70% of these institutions work with an aural approach and thereby exclude sign language and deaf culture.[8] Achievement surveys have suggested that 50% of the aurally taught deaf children show delays in language development when they enter school (Diller et al., 2000). This situation also seems to be the case for about 40 to 50% of children with a cochlear implant (Diller et al., 2000; Szagun, 2001) and for about 30% of children with a less-than-severe hearing loss (Kiese-Himmel, 2006; Kiese-Himmel & Ohlwein, 2002, 2004).

Primary and Secondary Schools

After reaching the proper age for schooling, these children can attend either a special school or a mainstream school with a pedagogical assistant. Official census data from the school term 2005–06 show that there are about 11,000 students in special schools for the deaf and hard of hearing, and about 2,600 students with a hearing loss are taught in a mainstream school with special assistance (Statistisches Bundesamt, 2006). Thus, according to official census data, only 20% of the children who are getting special support because of their hearing loss are integrated in mainstream schools. Although other sources estimate the number of deaf and hard of hearing children who get special support in mainstream schools to be up to 4,500 (Günther, 2002), surveys indicate that more than 90% of these children are hard of hearing and not deaf (Große, 2003). It is likely that the vast majority of children with a severe and profound hearing loss are educated in a special school. Neither aural nor sign-inclusive methods of integration have been developed on a greater scale; the main method remains a single integration of hard of hearing children on an individual basis. Programs such as co-enrollment classes (Leonhardt, 2001) or integration with a sign language interpreter for a group of students (Latuske, 2004) are provided only for a minority of the deaf and hard of hearing students who are integrated in regular schools. However, it has been estimated that there is a much higher number of hard of hearing children in regular schools without any special assistance, and therefore, they do not appear in any statistics (Günther, 2002).

---

8. For about 14% of these institutions, there are no data about their methodical orientation, and about 13% have a "different approach," but it is not clear whether this approach includes signing (Diller et al., 2000).

Currently, there are about 70 schools for the deaf and hard of hearing in Germany (Große, 2003). Because of the federal structure of Germany, each of the 16 federal states has its own educational system. As a result, the institutional structure of schools varies, so in some places, there are separated schools for deaf and hard of hearing students and, in others, combined institutions for these two groups. The latter form of organization has become more and more common over the last years (Große, 2003). Besides these forms of institutions, there are regular schools with separated classes for deaf and hard of hearing students and special schools for hearing impaired students who have additional handicaps. The total number of students in schools for the deaf and hard of hearing has increased over the last decade (Statistisches Bundesamt, 1999–2006). Concurrently, there has been a shift from a majority of deaf students to a majority of hard of hearing students. In addition, a new group of children with a central hearing loss has come to the schools recently, so the number of students for whom the need of signing or sign language has gained general acceptance is now decreasing. At the same time, it has become more difficult over the last years to effectively teach these students because deaf students, hard of hearing students, and students with a central hearing loss are often instructed together within one class.

Communication Modes in Schools

Although the communication method has been in the limelight of emotional debates over the last 20 years, little is known about how deaf and hard of hearing children are taught outside of trial classes. The only survey evaluating this issue includes 1,019 classes in 2000 (Große, 2003) and, thereby, 73% of the classes according to official census data (Statistisches Bundesamt, 2000). In that study, school directors had to label the communication mode in their classes according to five given categories: (a) a focus on "aural acquisition of spoken language" (43.1% of the classes); (b) emphasis on an "aural acquisition of spoken language" but including "manual means of communication" (24.7% of classes); (c) a method described as "acquisition of spoken language plus manual means of communication" (22.4% of classes); (d) a "total communication" approach (7.9% of classes); and (e) a "bilingual method" (1.9% of classes). This result can be interpreted in two ways. On the one hand, a majority of about 90% of classes in Germany still concentrate on the instruction of spoken language as the primary goal, and on the other hand, in about 60% of the classes, "manual means of communication" are included to a certain extent, from the use of the Phoneme Transmitting Manual System, use of the manual alphabet, occasional use of signed German, and German Sign Language to a full, bilingual approach. Compared with the distribution of the hearing loss in the same survey (Große, 2003), it is likely that, on a certain scale, hard of hearing students, too, are exposed to signing in their education.

Achievements

There are no regular achievement tests in German schools for the deaf and hard of hearing; there are only a few studies on writing (Günther, 1999; Günther & Schäfke, 2004; Günther & Schulte, 1988; Schäfke, 2005) and reading (Hennies, 2006a, 2006b). These studies indicate that a majority of students with a severe or profound hearing loss who attend a school for the deaf and hard of hearing do not reach a sufficient literacy level, with the exception of students brought up in a bilingual setting that includes the use of sign language. It would be interesting to verify these findings with larger groups and to include a number of additional factors that are important for an extensive evaluation of these relations.

Secondary Opportunities

The majority of deaf and hard of hearing students in Germany receive either a lower general school-leaving certificate ("Hauptschulabschluss") after the completion of Grade 9 or a higher general school-leaving certificate ("Realschulabschluss") after the completion of Grade 10. Most of these students are in a special school, and only a minority of them are integrated in regular schools. All of the 70 special schools for deaf and hard of hearing students offer the lower general school-leaving certificate. The higher general school-leaving certificate can be obtained only at a limited numbers of institutions, which means that some students have to board at the school because it is too far away from their home.

To achieve a general higher education entrance qualification ("Abitur," which enables entrance to university) after 12 or 13 years, deaf students have two choices: either they can enroll in a special school offering a secondary school program (Rheinisch-Westfälisches Berufskolleg in Essen, Bildungs- und Beratungszentrum für Hörgeschädigte in Stegen near Freiburg, Samuel-Heinicke-Schule in Munich) or they can be educated in a regular school near their home.

Vocational Education

The main goal of postsecondary education of deaf and hard of hearing students in Germany is still the certificate of vocational competence ("Facharbeiterbrief"), which is procured in a "dual" vocational education program ("Duales System"): students receive actual job training in a working environment, and they learn specific and general knowledge in a secondary education establishment. Deaf and hard of hearing students have the option to enroll in special preparation classes before they enter the actual vocational education.

The vocational education for deaf and hard of hearing students can be either "dual" or "integrated-dual." In the first case, the training of the actual technical skills and the teaching of specific and general knowledge are in the hands of different institutions and take place in different locations and times. In the second case, both sections are provided by the same secondary education establishment, often as part of a special institution for students with handicaps. Very often, these establishments provide for additional service for deaf and hard of hearing students, for example, psychological and social counseling and sign language interpreters. In Germany, there are 19 secondary education establishments for the vocational education for deaf and hard of hearing students, some of which provide the opportunity to get a vocational education regardless of the economic situation, which influences the number of places that are available in the regular vocational education system in Germany. Currently, there is a growing number of privately funded establishments that are entering into competition with the traditional publicly funded establishments, a situation that leads to a more diverse but also less concise system in which the students' ability to gather information and weigh their options becomes more important.

Higher Education

Deaf and hard of hearing people generally have the opportunity to apply for any German university if they have a general higher education entrance qualification. People with handicaps who fulfill this criterion can more easily gain access to places in universities as part of a quota regulation that varies among the institutions. Students have the option to use the service of counselors in the Public Employment Office ("Agentur für Arbeit") before they decide on a subject and university. Some of the universities have more experience with deaf and hard of hearing students than others. There are special adjustments in the admittance process and the examinations during the studies, for example, the use of sign language interpreters in oral exams and more time for examinations, which are especially important in the final exams (Bündnis Barrierefreies Studium, 2007). Assistance while studying for a degree can be provided in the form of note takers, sign language interpreters, oral interpreters, use of FM systems, special tutors, etc., but that assistance has to be organized by the deaf and hard of hearing students themselves through the university's particular counselor for the handicapped, with whom the (sometimes quite complicated) way to receive financial aid for these services has to be worked out (Gattermann-Kasper, 2006). The "self-help organization of hearing impaired students and alumni" (Bundesarbeitsgemeinschaft Hörbehinderte Studenten und Absolventen) is of significant importance because it is where deaf and hard of hearing academics and alumni give their support and advice to students with a hearing loss.[9]

Further Education

In the days of globalization and individualization, there is a demand for lifelong continuing education in Germany as in all Western societies. For deaf and hard of hearing people, there are various opportunities to receive further education either together with a group of hearing participants (with the assistance of a sign language interpreter) or in a special class with other students affected by a hearing loss. Classes are offered by a lot of different institutions such as adult education establishments, self-help organizations, and vocational education establishments, and they cover areas like general knowledge, special skills, and life-coping strategies.

Curriculum and the Extent to Which It Matches Regular Education

Because of Germany's federal structure, an independent legal framework for schools for deaf and hard of hearing students is established in every state. But there are national guidelines in which the states agree on common goals (such as an orientation with respect to the regular curriculum) for the education of deaf and hard of hearing children but in which states also emphasize the need for special speech training and the inclusion of signing, if necessary (KMK, 1996). Only a few states have a special curriculum for deaf and hard of hearing students (Große, 2003), and most of them have not been improved over the last decades. The standards of regular education become increasingly important because in a growing number of states, a student can receive a school-leaving certificate only if he or she performed accept-

---

9. For more information, see http://www.bhsa.de/html.

ably well on central exams. In these examinations, some adjustments can be made for the deaf or hard of hearing students, but the students have to be assessed on the same content as students in regular schools.

STATUS OF DEAF ADULTS

The extent to which deaf and hard of hearing adults are included in the pedagogical service is closely related to the historical development in the German education of the deaf, as shown above. Until the second half of the 19th century, it was quite common for deaf-mute adults to teach deaf-mute children, not unlike other countries (Vogel, 1999). The decisions made by the Milan Congress in 1880 had a massive effect on the German educational system, and as a result, deaf-mute teachers almost completely disappeared. These decisions promoted a deficit perspective with respect to people with a hearing loss that had devastating consequences for the social status of this group. After the Milan Congress, a very intense phase of almost pure oralism began in Germany, which led to the enduring exclusion of signs and, consequently, of deaf teachers, whose employment was only occasionally demanded, namely, by Johann Heidsiek (1891).

The deficit perspective began to change when Siegmund Prillwitz, a linguist, not a pedagogue, started to conduct research on German Sign Language in the mid-1970s and included deaf coworkers as important team members (Prillwitz, 1985). Although this work was initially rejected by teachers and scholars in the field of deaf education, it has led to a changing perspective with respect to deaf individuals within the pedagogical system. As a result, the deficit perspective became less vivid and was partly replaced by an empowerment perspective—comparable with the development after the Deaf President Now movement in the United States in 1988, only a few years later. In this process, changes in law, the culture, and the educational system evolved over the years, and especially the aspect of social and cultural participation has gained significance with the explicit recognition of German Sign Language in social laws and in antidiscrimination ("handicapped equalization") laws (Sozialgesetzbuch IX of 2001; Behindertengleichstellungsgesetz of 2002). Also, the German public currently sees the culture of deaf people in a positive light. Deaf and hard of hearing individuals have contributed to all these changes, they are present in public and scientific discussions, and in many cases, they are well accepted.

In the field of education, however, one can get the impression that these social developments are just slowly unfolding. In the early intervention programs, there is almost no one involved who is deaf or hard of hearing, especially because of the increasing importance of the cochlear implant. Only one private initiative offers counseling with the participation of deaf *and* hearing professionals. Limited feedback about this counseling comes from the small number of families who accepted this offer, but their feedback has been very positive (Hintermair & Lehmann-Tremmel, 2003). Since the first trial class for bilingual education started in Hamburg in 1992, in which deaf teachers play an important role in the central concept of "two teachers representing two languages" (Günther & Schäfke, 2004, p. 7), bilingual education that includes deaf teachers has been established in different schools throughout the country (e.g., Berlin, Frankfurt, Munich).

In 2000, there were 16 deaf and 12 hard of hearing teachers in schools for hearing impaired children, representing just about 1% of the teachers in these schools (Große, 2003).

This percentage may seem small, but it is nevertheless comparably high when considered in terms of the historical background: There have never been so many deaf and hard of hearing professionals in German deaf education. Their number is likely to grow over the next years because there are more deaf and hard of hearing students in German universities studying to become teachers. There is an increasing need for them even outside of bilingual classes because new topics such as identity work and deaf studies are being implemented in the schools and programs are placing a stronger focus on the social and emotional development of the children, all of which cannot be provided for without the substantial integration of deaf and hard of hearing adults into the educational process.

PREPARATION OF SPECIAL PERSONNEL

Deaf and hard of hearing students are taught both by teachers with special training for this occupation and by teachers without such qualifications (Berufsverband Deutscher Hörgeschädigtenpädagogen, 2004). The latter usually teach in elementary schools, especially subjects such as physical training and crafts, but there are also teachers without special training in secondary and postsecondary education who are teaching main subjects such as English, mathematics, physics, or chemistry.

Teachers for the deaf and hard of hearing can study at five universities in Germany; their course of studies usually takes 4 years. Besides the special skills for educating deaf or hard of hearing children, teachers in training have to study only one or two subjects (usually German or mathematics and at some universities an additional subject such as English, biology, physics, etc.). Most universities also require one additional qualification in special needs education (very often for children with learning difficulties) and educational science, none of which include knowledge about the situation in schools for deaf and hard of hearing children. This situation has led to the result that many teachers educating deaf or hard of hearing students "lack content training in the courses they teach, so there is no reason to believe that they will offer deaf students much more than a content-knowledgeable public school teacher who has no experience with deaf students" (Marschark, Convertino, & LaRock, 2006, p. 191).

At the five universities, there is no common curriculum for the training of teachers for the deaf and hard of hearing because every university has its own structure and profile. In only some of these universities is sign language a part of the curriculum and exams (especially in Berlin and Cologne); it is still possible to become a teacher for the deaf without attending a sign language or signing course at some universities. Sometimes, there is a gap between a technological vision at the universities about the success of the cochlear implant and aural training and the reality at the schools for the deaf and hard of hearing, where sign language skills are needed for a significant part of the population.

Pedagogical professionals and counselors outside of classrooms very often work in residential schools, which are decreasing because of greater efforts to integrate children with a hearing loss into mainstream classes. These social pedagogues and care workers have no special training and, at best, may have the opportunity to undergo advanced training while learning on the job. The extent and the quality of the training depend on where in Germany they work. Some of these professionals stay a long time in their job, with the result that the once-acquired competencies make a productive contribution for many years.

Professionals in the field of psychological counseling face the same circumstances: There is no special training for psychologists who work with deaf and hard of hearing children or adolescents. Although all professionals who work in this area have a psychological degree and advanced training, they have to develop specific abilities during their working experiences with deaf and hard of hearing clients. For about 25 years, there has been an annual meeting of psychologists working in this field, where an exchange of experiences is possible.

The state of psychological and social care for deaf and hard of hearing children in Germany can be described only as desolate. The number of problematic cases in schools for the deaf and hard of hearing is increasing, but there is nowhere near the needed number of professionals who are capable of dealing with these children.

SPECIAL LAWS

There are special laws that include the possibilities of financial aid and social services for deaf and hard of hearing citizens in Germany. Remarkable special laws to improve the situation of this group were passed in the last years. In particular, a milestone was reached when sign language gained legal acceptance at a national level in the Social law (Sozialgesetzbuch IX of 2001) and the National Handicapped Equalization Law (Behindertengleichstellungsgesetz of 2002), making it easier for deaf and hard of hearing people to receive financing for the service of a sign language interpreter. This acceptance of sign language was preceded by regulations of the State Handicapped Equalization Law of Berlin (Berliner Landesgleichberechtigungsgesetz of 1999), which also included the obligation for teachers of the deaf to learn sign language by the end of 2007, but its success depends on teachers to meet this obligation voluntarily. Almost all other federal states of Germany have passed handicapped equalization laws; however, none of them makes as decisive a claim for the field of deaf education as the bill in Berlin does.

SIGN LANGUAGE

The term *German Sign Language* (Deutsche Gebärdensprache) came into use in the 1980s following the example of the United States. Before this date, sign language was often labeled as "chatting" ("Plaudern"), without any awareness of the status of a regular language (Heßmann, 2001). This perspective changed with an emerging empowerment movement among deaf people as well as a developing linguistic acceptance of sign language. German Sign Language consists of different regional variations, especially in vocabulary, but shows a general structure in grammar and discourse. Although sign language plays a bigger role in university programs, schools, and the adult education sector for hearing people, linguistic knowledge about German Sign Language and the way to teach it still needs to be developed (Heßmann, 2001). Only in recent years have attempts been made to write a concise description of its grammatical structure (Happ & Vorköper, 2006).

CURRENT DEVELOPMENTS AND TRENDS

Currently, there are two developments that greatly influence the field of deaf and hard of hearing education: (a) the development of early childhood intervention and the massive implementation of cochlear implants in deaf and hard of hearing children and (b) the social and scientific acceptance of sign language and deaf culture as important contributions to a deaf child's development. A hearing loss is identified much earlier than in former times, particularly because of the spread of newborn hearing screening systems, and as a result, hearing aids and cochlear implants are available for children at a very young age. This development has received praise by medical professionals, although the social and psychological effect on parents and families remains unclear and needs much more research and attention in practical work (Fiebig & Hintermair, 2007). Hence, early education counselors face new challenges without having proper training for these developments. Very often, early identification of hearing loss and an early cochlear implantation are regarded as a basis for the guaranteed success in an aural, sign-excluding education program. Despite this expectation, the number of children who fail in an aural program still remains high, leading to the assumption that some of these children learn the pragmatic aspects of spoken German without acquiring an adequate central representation of the language.

Although signing, sign language, and deaf culture play a more important role in the education of deaf and hard of hearing children, their possible benefits have not been sufficiently acknowledged by teachers and scholars. The focus is still put on the question of which child might *need* sign language rather than on the question of which child *could benefit from* the use of sign language or a bilingual approach. National and international research data that suggest that deaf and hard of hearing children achieve more by the inclusion of sign language are only slowly being accepted in schools.

The current situation in education of deaf and hard of hearing students in Germany reflects a new orientation between the traditional perspective focusing on spoken language and the present openness to sign language and deaf culture. Part of this new orientation is an awareness of the increasing number of studies from all over the world that show how important it is to discuss developmental processes of deaf and hard of hearing children within the context of their cognitive, social, and emotional functioning (Hintermair, 2006; Marschark et al., 2006) to find the best way for each child to be deaf in his own way (Ohna, 2003). It is still undecided whether an integration of all of these aspects, including a general acceptance of the benefits of a bilingual setting, will be achieved in the future.

REFERENCES

Berufsverband Deutscher Hörgeschädigtenpädagogen (Hg.). (2004). *Wer? Wo? Was? in der deutschen Hörgeschädigtenpädagogik. Bildungseinrichtungen für Hörgeschädigte in Deutschland, Luxemburg, den Niederlanden, Österreich und der* Schweiz [Who? Where? What? in German education for the hearing impaired. Institutions for the education of the hearing impaired in Germany, Luxemburg, the Netherlands, Austria, and Switzerland]. Heidelberg: Median-Verlag.

Biesold, H. (1999). *Crying hands: Eugenics and deaf people in Nazi Germany.* Washington, DC: Gallaudet University Press.

Bizer, S., & Karl, A.-K. (2002). *Entwicklung eines Wortschatztests für gehörlose Kinder im Grundschulalter in Laut-, Schrift- und Gebärdensprache* [The development of a vocabulary test in spoken, written, and sign language for deaf children in primary schools]. Unpublished doctoral diss., Universität Hamburg. Retrieved May 6, 2006, from http://www.sub.uni-hamburg.de/opus/frontdoor.php?source_opus=881

Braun, A., Donath, P., Keller, R., Rammel, G., & Tigges, J. (1982). *Kommunikation mit Gehörlosen in*

Lautsprache und Gebärde [Communication with the deaf in spoken language and signing]. München: Bundesverband der Elternvertreter und Förderer Deutscher Gehörlosenschulen.

Bündnis Barrierefreies Studium. (2007). Chancengleichheit im Bologna-Prozess für behinderte und chronisch kranke Studierende sowie Studienplatzbewerberinnen und -bewerber [Equal chances in the Bologna process for handicapped and chronically diseased students and student applicants]. Retrieved April 2, 2007, from http://www.dobus.uni-dortmund.de/equal/tandem/Bologna.rtf

Diller, G., Graser, P., & Schmalbrock, C. (2000). *Hörgerichtete Frühförderung hochgradig hörgeschädigter Kleinkinder* [Aural early education with severely hearing impaired children]. Heidelberg: Edition Schindele.

Dröge, K. (1999). *Wilke's bunte Bilderwelt: Carl Wilke—Bilder für den Taubstummen- und Elementarunterricht im 19. Jahrhundert* [Wilke's colorful world of pictures: Carl Wilke—pictures for the education of deaf-mutes and the elementary education in the 19th century]. Westoverledingen: Ostfriesisches Schulmuseum Folmhusen.

Fiebig, S., & Hintermair, M. (2007). *Psychosoziale Implikationen des Neugeborenen-Hör-Screenings (NHS) für die Früherfassung und Frühförderung hörgeschädigter Kinder* [Psychosocial implications of the newborn hearing screening (NHS) for the early identification and early intervention of hearing impaired children]. *Frühförderung interdisziplinär 26,* 107–120.

Gattermann-Kasper, M. (2006). Studium und Hörschädigung [University study and hearing impairment]. *Hörgeschädigte Kinder—Erwachsene Hörgeschädigte, 43,* 18–25.

Große, K.-D. (2003). *Das Bildungswesen für Hörbehinderte in der Bundesrepublik Deutschland. Daten und Fakten zu Realitäten und Erfordernissen* [The educational system for hearing handicapped in the Federal Republic of Germany. Data and facts about realities and necessities]. Heidelberg: Edition Schindele.

Günther, K.-B. (1985). *Schriftsprache bei hör- und sprachgeschädigten Kindern. Bedeutung und Funktion für Sprachaufbau und Entwicklung; dargestellt am Beispiel gehörloser Kinder* [Written language of hearing and speech-impaired children. Role and function for the buildup of language and development, demonstrated by the example of deaf children] (2nd rev. ed.). Heidelberg: Groos.

Günther, K.-B. (1999). *Bilingualer Unterricht mit gehörlosen Grundschülern: Zwischenbericht zum Hamburger Bilingualen Schulversuch* [Bilingual education for deaf primary school students: First report on the bilingual trial class of Hamburg]. Hamburg: Verlag hörgeschädigte kinder.

Günther, K.-B. (2002). Förderschwerpunkt Hören—Perspektiven für die Hörgeschädigtenschule [Educational support 'hearing'—perspectives for the schools of hearing impaired]. *DFGS-Forum, 10,* 5–19.

Günther, K.-B., & Hennies, J. (Eds.). (in press). *Bilingualer Unterricht in Gebärden-, Laut- und Schriftsprache mit gehörlosen SchülerInnen in der Primarstufe: Zwischenbericht zum Berliner Bilingualen Schulversuch* [Bilingual education in sign language, spoken language, and written language for deaf primary school students: First report on the trial bilingual class of Berlin]. Berlin: Druckerei der Humboldt-Universität.

Günther, K.-B., & Schäfke, I. (Eds.). (2004). *Bilinguale Erziehung als Förderkonzept für gehörlose SchülerInnen. Abschlußbericht zum Hamburger Bilingualen Schulversuch* [Bilingual education as an educational concept for deaf students: Final report on the trial bilingual class of Hamburg]. Hamburg: Signum.

Günther, K.-B., & Schulte, K. (1988). Berufssprachbezogene Kurzuntersuchung (BSK)—Konjunktionale Verbindungen und Prädikatskonstruktionen als Indikatoren für berufssprachlich geforderte Kompetenz [Short assessment of language used in vocational settings—Conjunctions and predicate constructions as indicators for language needed in vocational settings]. In K. Schulte, C. Schlenker-Schulte, & K.-B. Günther (Eds.), *Fortentwicklung berufssprachlicher Fähigkeiten Hörgeschädigter: Forschungsergebnisse* [Further developments of hearing impaired's vocational language abilities: Empirical data] (pp. 246–329). Bonn: Der Bundesminister für Arbeit und Sozialordnung.

Happ, D., & Vorköper, M.-O. (2006). *Deutsche Gebärdensprache: Ein Lehr- und Arbeitsbuch* [German Sign Language: Textbook, and exercise book]. Frankfurt am Main: Fachhochschulverlag.

Hartmann-Börner, C. (1997). Heidelberger Erklärung [Declaration of Heidelberg]. Retrieved May 1, 2007, from http://www.taubenschlag.de/kolumnen/erklaer.htm

Heidsiek, J. (1891). *Ein Notschrei der Taubstummen* [A cry of distress by the deaf-mutes]. Breslau: Woywod.

Hennies, J. (2006a). Lesekompetenz an der Ernst-Adolf-Eschke Schule [Reading literacy in the Ernst-Adolf-Eschke-School]. Retrieved July 20, 2006, from www.johannes.hennies.org/bilder/LesekompetenzEAE.pdf

Hennies, J. (2006b). Lesekompetenz und Schulleistungstests: Eine PISA-bezogene Lesestudie mit gehörlosen SchülerInnen des Hamburger Bilingualen Schulversuchs und schwerhörigen SchülerInnen zweier Vergleichsklassen [Reading literacy and achievement tests: A reading study based on PISA with deaf students of the trial bilingual class of Hamburg and hard of hearing students of two comparison classes]. *Das Zeichen, 72,* 82–95.

Heßmann, J. (2001). *Gehörlos so!: Materialien zur Gebärdensprache* [That's deaf!: Material on sign language]. Hamburg: Signum.

Hintermair, M. (2006). Parental resources, parental stress, and socio-emotional development of deaf and hard of hearing children. *Journal of Deaf Studies and Deaf Education, 11,* 493–513.

Hintermair, M., & Lehmann-Tremmel, G. (2003). *Wider die Sprachlosigkeit. Beratung und Förderung von Familien mit gehörlosen Kindern unter Einbeziehung von Gebärdensprache und gehörlosen Fachkräften* [Against being without language: Counseling and support of families with deaf children integrating sign language and deaf professionals]. Hamburg: Signum.

Karchmer, M., & Mitchell, R. (2003). Demographic and achievement: Characteristics of deaf and hard-of-hearing students. In M. Marschark & P. E. Spencer (Eds.), *Oxford handbook of deaf studies, language, and education* (pp. 21–37). New York: Oxford University Press.

Kiese-Himmel, C. (2006). *Eine Dekade Göttinger Hörsprachregister: Persistierende periphere Hörstörung und Sprachentwicklung im Kindesalter* [A decade of the register of hearing and speaking in Göttingen: Persistent hearing impairment and language development in the early years]. Heidelberg: Median.

Kiese-Himmel, C., & Ohlwein, S. (2002). Die frühe Sprachentwicklung permanent hörgeschädigter Kinder im Verlauf [Early language development of permanently hearing impaired children over time]. *Sprache—Stimme—Gehör, 26,* 84–91.

Kiese-Himmel, C., & Ohlwein, S. (2004). Entwicklungsverlauf des rezeptiven und expressiven Wortschatzumfangs bei sensorineural schwerhörigen Kindern [Development of receptive and expressive vocabulary in hard of hearing children with a sensorineural hearing loss]. *Heilpädagogische Forschung, 30,* 188–197.

KMK—Secretariat of the Standing Conference of the Ministers of Education and Cultural Affairs of the Länder. (1996). *Empfehlungen zum Förderschwerpunkt Hören: Beschluss der Kultusministerkonferenz vom 10.05.1996* [Advice on the educational support 'hearing' for the schools: Decision by the Conference of the Ministers of Education and Cultural Affairs from May 10, 1996]. Retrieved January 1, 2006, from http://www.kmk.org/doc/beschl/hoeren.pdf

Kruse, O. F. (1832). *Der Taubstumme im uncultivierten Zustande, nebst Blicken in das Leben merkwürdiger Taubstummen* [The deaf-mute in a noncultivated situation, with insights in the life of notable deaf-mutes]. Bremen: Wilhelm Kaiser.

Kruse, O. F. (1869). *Zur Vermittelung der Extreme in der sogenannten deutschen und französischen Taubstummen-Unterrichts-Methode: Ein Versuch zur Vereinigung beider* [Negotiating the extremes of the German and French methods in the teaching of the deaf-mutes: An attempt to connect both]. Schleswig: Verlag der Schulbuchhandlung.

Latuske, M. (2004). Modellprojekt: Gehörlose Kinder an der Regelschule mit Gebärdensprachdolmetscherinnen [Trial project: Deaf children in mainstream schools with sign language interpreters]. Retrieved May 1, 2006, from http://gehoerlosekinder.de/Ebene02/infos_zub_02/projekt_regelschule/Projekt_Lat_komplett.pdf?nach_id=480

Lenarz, T. (Ed.). (2007). *Neugeborenen-Hörscreening 2007: Workshop und Symposium: Tagungsprogramm und Abstractband* [Newborn hearing screening 2007: Workshop and symposium: Program and abstracts]. Retrieved May 24, 2007, from http://www.mhh-hno.de/download/NHS2007_Abstractband.pdf

Leonhardt, A. (2001). Gemeinsames Lernen von hörenden und hörgeschädigten Schülern: Historische Aspekte und aktuelle Sichtweisen [Hearing and hearing impaired students learning together: Historical aspects and current perspectives]. In A. Leonhardt (Ed.), *Gemeinsames Lernen von hörenden und hörgeschädigten Schülern: Ziele—Wege—Möglichkeiten* [Hearing and hearing impaired students learning together: Goals—ways—possibilities] (pp. 11–21). Hamburg: Verlag hörgeschädigte kinder.

Marschark, M., Convertino, C., & LaRock, D. (2006). Optimizing academic performance of deaf students: Access, opportunities and outcomes. In D. F. Moores & D. S. Martin (Eds.), *Deaf learners: Developments in curriculum and instruction* (pp. 179–200). Washington, DC: Gallaudet University Press.

Ohna, E. S. (2003). Education of deaf children and the politics of recognition. *Journal of Deaf Studies and Deaf Education, 8,* 5–10.

Prillwitz, S. (1985). *Skizzen zu einer Grammatik der Deutschen Gebärdensprache* [Outline for a grammar of German Sign Language]. Hamburg: Forschungsstelle DGS.

Quigley, S. (1969). *The influence of fingerspelling on the development of language, communication, and educational achievement in deaf children.* Illinois: University of Illinois.

Reich, F. (1927). *Wladislaus Zeitlin, der taubstumme Student* [Wladislaus Zeitlin, the deaf-mute university student]. Leipzig: Taubstummen-Verlag Hugo Dude.

Schäfke, I. (2005). *Untersuchungen zum Erwerb der Textproduktionskompetenz bei hörgeschädigten Schülern* [Research on hearing impaired students' acquisition of text production competencies]. Hamburg: Signum.

Schulte, K. (1985). *Research projects in applied phonetics.* Heidelberg: Pädagogische Hochschule.

Schumann, P. (1940). *Geschichte des Taubstummenwesens vom deutschen Standpunkt aus dargestellt* [History of the institutions for the deaf-mutes described from a German point of view]. Frankfurt am Main: Moritz Diesterweg.

Schumann, P., & Schumann, G. (Eds.). (1912). *Samuel Heinickes gesammelte Schriften* [The complete writings of Samuel Heinicke]. Leipzig: Ernst Wiegandt Verlagsbuchhandlung.

Sonke, M. (1993). Die Israelitische Taubstummenanstalt in Berlin-Weißensee—Von der Gründung 1873 bis zur Vernichtung 1942 [The Israelite Institute of Deaf-mutes in Berlin-Weißensee—From its founding in 1873 to its destruction in 1942]. In V. Bendt & N. Galliner (Eds.), *Öffne deine Hand für die Stummen—Die Geschichte der Taubstummen-Anstalt Berlin-Weißensee 1873–1942* [Open your hands for the mutes—The history of the Israelite Institute of Deaf-mutes in Berlin-Weißensee] (pp. 43–99). Berlin: Transit.

Statistisches Bundesamt (Federal Office of Statistics). (1999–2006). *Fachserie 11—Reihe 1: Bildung und Kultur: Allgemeinbildende Schulen* [Field Series 11—Part 1: Education and culture: General schools]. Published annually. Wiesbaden, Germany (FRG): Author.

Szagun, G. (2001). *Wie Sprache entsteht: Spracherwerb bei Kindern mit beeinträchtigtem und normalem Hören* [How language is developed: Language acquisition of children with and without hearing loss]. Weinheim, Basel: Beltz.

Treibel, E. (1881). *Der 2. Internationale Taubstummenlehrerkongress in Mailand* [The 2nd international congress of teachers of the deaf-mutes in Milan]. Berlin: Wilhelm Issleib.

Vogel, H. (1999). *Gebärdensprache und Lautsprache in der deutschen Taubstummenpädagogik im 19. Jahrhundert: Historische Darstellung der kombinierten Methode* [Sign language and spoken language in the German education of the deaf-mutes in the 19th century: Historical description of the combined method]. Unpublished masters thesis, Universität Hamburg.

Wende, G. (Ed.). (1915). *Deutsche Taubstummenanstalten, -schulen und -heime in Wort und Bild* [German institutions, schools, and asylums for the deaf-mutes in words and pirctures]. Halle/Saale: Marhold.

The Education of Deaf Children in Greece

Venetta Lampropoulou

IN THE works of Greek philosophers, one can find useful information about the society's attitudes toward the disabled and about the status of deaf people during ancient times. Herodotus' works on the Muses are considered to be some of the oldest sources written about deaf people. His description of the attitude of King Kroisos of Lydia when he found out that he could not make his deaf son speak, is indicative of the society's attitude toward deaf people at that time. Kroisos, according to Herodotus, considered his deaf son useless, hopeless, and nonexistent.

Two well-known philosophers, Socrates and Aristotle, considered deafness and deaf people. In his work *Problems,* Aristotle believed that the sense of hearing was the most important of all of the senses because, as he stated, it contributed to the mental development of man. He thought that hearing was the major organ of instruction and that deafness was organically connected with being speechless. In his work *The Senses,* Aristotle also claimed that blind people were in a more advanced position mentally compared with deaf people because blind people could communicate with their environment.

In Plato's *Dialogues,* Socrates, Hermogenus, and Cratylus talk about word-object correspondence and the arbitrary relationship of the two elements. Socrates here is talking about the deaf people who use signs to communicate. He suggests that signs are spontaneous tools that hearing people will use if they suddenly lose their speech. In another of Plato's dialogues, Socrates proposes the idea that thought is expressed by people through speech, except if someone is deaf or speechless. This claim indicates the fact that the philosopher is aware that deaf people do not speak. He also makes a distinction between deafness and speechlessness.

From the works of Plato, we can assume that deaf people and sign language were very much accepted by Athenian Society. That assumption might not be true for Sparta. In Sparta, according to Plutarch (in *Lycurgus*), all babies were inspected soon after birth, and the disabled ones were thrown into a gully of the mountain Tavgetus, known as Kiadas or Apothetas. Some writers have doubted Plutarch's statements, but given the militaristic ideology of Lycurgus's Sparta, the position of people with disabilities could not have been as good as in other Greek cities of the same period. In Athens, for example, according to some reports, the disabled people who were not slaves received an allowance (Lazanas, 1984).

During the Byzantine time, asylums and orphanages were established and children in need were protected and cared for. Some deaf children benefited from those social and welfare programs, but education was not yet provided for them (Lazanas, 1984).

THE FIRST SCHOOLS

The first schools for children with disabilities, including deaf children, were developed in Greece during the beginning of the 20th century. This development took place in three distinct phases included the provision of services, societal attitudes, and government involvement: the periods of 1907–1960, 1960–1980, and 1980–present.

1907–1960: Establishment of the First Schools

Special schools for children with different disabilities began to develop in Greece early in the 1930s. During this period and up to the 1960s, the general incentive was to protect the "pitied" and "weak" children. Charity organizations, rich people, and people with special interests took the initiative to establish asylums, special institutes, and schools. Government involvement was minimal up until 1960. The majority of the special schools operated outside of the Ministry of Education. Most of them were under the auspices of the Ministry of Health and Welfare. The protection model of disability was the dominant ideological model for the providing of services and for special education.

During this period, the only school for deaf children was the school of the National Institute for the Deaf (NID) based in Athens. This institution is the oldest residential school for deaf children in Greece. It was formally established in 1937 by the Ministry of Health and Welfare under the name of National Institute for the Protection of Deaf-Mutes (Greek Government, 1937). However, the first attempts to establish this school began much earlier.

In 1907, an initiative was taken by a rich man named Charalampos Spiliopoulos to establish a school for deaf children in Athens. In May 1907, he established a philanthropic asylum for the deaf (Greek Government, 1907), but for some reason, he did not see his wish materialize. On his death in 1922, he left a substantial financial endowment and property for the establishment of the school (Fillipidis, 1950).

In the meantime, in 1922, after the defeat of the Greek army by Turkey and the destruction of the Greek civilization on the east coast of Turkey and in Constantinople (Instanbul), a ship carrying Greek refugee orphans from Turkey approached Pireas, the port of Athens. Among the orphans were 10 deaf children. The American philanthropic organization, Near East Relief, which during this period was helping Greek refugees from the east coast of Turkey, established an orphanage for the refugee children, first in Athens and, later, on the island of Syros. That organization also took the responsibility to establish a school for the 10 deaf orphans. To accomplish this goal, the Near East Relief organization hired a teacher named Helen Palatidou. She was a Greek refugee from Turkey and a former teacher for deaf children in Constantinople. She was sent by the Near East Relief organization to the Clarke School for the Deaf in the United States, a school with an oral-aural approach to education, to receive training as a teacher of the deaf. On her return to Greece in 1923, she began teaching the deaf orphans. The results of her teaching became well known in Greece, and the number of deaf students in her class soon increased. More teachers were also recruited to teach in this boarding school. Some of those who were recruited were also sent to the Clarke School for the Deaf for training.

In 1932, the Near East Relief organization met with the Ministry of Welfare to discuss the future of the school. At this meeting, it was decided that the school would come under the auspices and support of the Ministry of Welfare. Later in 1937, the property of Spiliopoulos was transferred over to this school that was named The National Institute for the Protection of Deaf-Mutes. The school finally moved into a large new building and extended its services to include additional deaf children.

In addition to Palatidou, other teachers have played a leading role in the development of the NID. One of the most important figures, according to the deaf people of Greece and NID records, was Helen Varitimidou. She went to the United States in 1945–46 to receive her training as a teacher of the deaf. On her return to Greece, she taught deaf students for a number of years through the use of the oral method and trained new teachers of the deaf. She soon became the director of the NID. In 1948, she helped deaf graduates from her school to establish the first association of deaf people in Greece. Helen Varitimidou was dedicated to her job and to her students.

Although the oral method of communication was used at the NID and the emphasis of the school was on the articulation of sounds and the development of speech, some of the teachers knew how to sign and, according to deaf graduates of the school, used signs unofficially in the classrooms. In the residence halls and schoolyard, the deaf students communicated among themselves through the use of sign language.

Another influential figure at the NID was Vasilis Lazanas. He was not a teacher but a scholar with a great interest in deaf people. He was the administrative director of the NID from 1955 to 1979. Lazanas wrote many articles about the education of deaf children and the position of deaf people in different societies. Most of his works have been included in a volume titled *The Problems of the Deaf.* Vasilis Lazanas had been influenced by the oral method of teaching the deaf used at the NID and tried to convince his readers that deaf people could learn to talk (Lazanas, 1984).

During World War II, the NID building was made into a hospital. The school was forced to move to a small building near the Acropolis. This period of time was as difficult for the NID and the deaf as it was for all Greek people in general. Finally, in 1960, the NID took back its original building and began to thrive again.

1960–1980: Legislative Actions and Private Schools

Although the period of 1960–1980 could be characterized as a period of legislative actions, the majority of the special schools during this period operated outside of the Ministry of Education (see Table 14.1). Most of them were under the auspices of the Ministry of Health and Welfare. Between the years 1956 and 1970, the NID established residential schools in five more cities. These schools are in operation today, under the Ministry of Education, but the number of students has decreased during the last two decades. NID currently provides a free education, residential facilities, as well as diagnostic and related services for deaf children from infancy to the age of 14 or 16. It is supervised by the Ministry of Health and Welfare, through a board of directors that is appointed by that ministry.

During this period of 1960–1980, the medical model of disability was replaced or became an extension of the protection model of the previous period. Meanwhile, another development took place in Greece that influenced the education of deaf children. Andreas Kokkevis, a member of the Greek Parliament, had a deaf daughter and became very interested in the education of deaf children. From his position in Parliament and, later, as Minister of Health and Welfare (1964, 1974), he helped initiate legislative action and other measures favorable to the welfare of deaf children in Greece.

In September of 1956, Iro Kokkevis, the wife of Andreas Kokkevis, established a private oral school for deaf children in Glyfada, near Athens (Greek Government, 1956). In 1966, a junior high school program was added to that school. This school was recognized by law as equal in accreditation to all public schools for hearing children (Greek Government, 1956). Amalia Martinou, a teacher at the NID, was recruited to teach at this private school. She became the director for life and owned the school until 1986. This school was transferred to the state in the 1980s and is now a public school, which is named Public School for Deaf and Hard of Hearing of Argyroupolis. Argyroupolis is a southeastern suburb of Athens.

Another private, nonprofit school was established in 1973 by an organization called the Institution for the Welfare and Education of Deaf and Hard of Hearing Children (Greek Government, 1973). The president of this organization, Sofia Starogianni, was the mother of two deaf sons. This oral residential school included preschool, elementary, and high school departments. The director of the school was Victoria Daousi, a Greek language teacher who was very skillful and dedicated to the education of deaf children. In 1982, the control of this school was given over to the state.

All NID schools and the two private schools for the deaf that were developed during the 1960s in Athens were oral schools. During this period, the disabled people's movement, which included parents, was organized and became very visible. In 1968, the Greek Federation of the Deaf was established in Athens. Today, this organization is known as the National Organization of Deaf People of Greece and has a membership of 2,500 people. It is an umbrella organization comprising 19 different organizations and Deaf clubs that are based in 15 cities throughout Greece.

Deaf education in Greece began relatively late compared with other European countries. The early efforts were initiated either by philanthropic organizations or by individuals such as parents of deaf children who had a direct interest in the field. The government had little involvement in the early development of the education of the deaf in Greece and in special education in general (Lampropoulou & Padeliadou, 1995). From 1975 on, however, parents of disabled children and people with disabilities themselves began to lobby and pressure the government to address the problems of children with disabilities (including deaf children) and to take responsibility for the education of all children with disabilities. As a result of this pressure, in 1975, a 2-year in-service training program in special education was established at one of the Teachers' Academies (Greek Government, 1975). In 1976, an office for special education was developed at the Ministry of Education. This office undertook the responsibility to supervise special education.

1980–Present: Ministry of Education Involvement

During the decade of 1980–1990, a movement of parents, professionals, and people with disabilities demanded the integration of special needs students in general education. At the same time, the Ministry of Education began to take over the responsibility of the education of children with disabilities. As a result, legislative actions took place and special day schools and classes were developed in general schools throughout Greece (Lampropoulou & Padeliadou, 1995). Day schools of different levels (preschool, elementary, high school) and special classrooms for deaf children in regular education were also established by this ministry in Athens and in other cities of Greece during this period. All these schools were oral schools (see Table 14.1).

Table 14.1. The Education of Deaf Students in Greece

PERIODS	EDUCATIONAL SYSTEMS	MAJOR IDEAS
Ancient Times Socrates, Plato,		The Sign Language is a language, Deaf use it
Aristotle		Hearing: The organ of learning
1907	First Attempts to establish a school for the Deaf	Private-Philanthropic "to protect the deaf"
1923	Establishment of the first school (Helen Palatidou)	Oralism
		Protection Model of Disability
1937	N.I.D.- Residential Schools (Ministry of Health and Welfare)	Oralism
1948	Establishment of Deaf and Parents' Associations (The Union of Deaf-Mutes)	Philanthropic Attitudes
1956-1973	Private Schools for the Deaf by Parents (Kokkevi-Martinou)—Expansion of N.I.D. in 5 cities	Medical Model of Disability; Parent and Deaf Organizations are militant and demand quality education—Oralism
1968	Greek Federation of the Deaf Newspaper "The World of Silence"	The Movement of the Deaf
1984 (Law 1566/85)	Ministry of Education Involvement	Free Public Education
	Establishment of Public Day Schools and Integration Units	Acceptance of Signs by NID (Total Communication)
	Schools of N.I.D.—Ministry of Health, Establishment of Early Parent Intervention Programs (N.I.D.)	The education of deaf children must start early and families must be helped.

1990	1. University of Patras, Department of Primary Education, Deaf Studies Unit
	  a. Teachers Training graduate level
	  b. Research in G.S.L.
	
	2. Local Authority of Argyroupolis
	  a. Vocational Training Programs for the Deaf
	  b. Sign Language Courses
	
	3. Greek Federation of the Deaf
	  a. Sign Language Courses
	  b. Deaf Tutors Organization
	  c. Greek Sign Language Interpreters
		Teachers and those working with the Deaf must have training and should know G.S.L.
		  —G.S.L. is the primary language of the Deaf and should be taught in school.
		  —Deaf children should be taught with a bilingual approach and in a bilingual environment.
		  —Deaf people should have good and ongoing vocational training.
		  —Residential Schools for the Deaf are considered to be a part of the Deaf Community and should fulfill their role of preserving the Deaf identity.
		  —Deaf people need qualified Sign Language Interpreters.
		  —Movement for the recognition of the Greek Deaf Community and Greek Sign Language.

2000 (Law 2817)	Mainstreaming—Diagnosis, Evaluation and Support Centers (KDAY), special Schools for the Deaf—Integration Units Technical Schools (TEE- EEEEK) Cochlear Implantation	Official Recognition of Greek Sign Language Teachers should know G.S.L. Increase Population of deaf children with cochlear implants Deaf Community gains support from the State

The first comprehensive law for the education and vocational training of "handicapped" children was passed in 1981. This law was replaced in 1985 by Public Law No. 1566/85 (Greek Government, 1981, 1985), which was a main education law for all children. Special education was included in it. During that period, the parents and disabled people's movement was very visible and active, demanding a better education for all children with disabilities. The medical model of disability was attacked by these organizations and professionals.

The Greek Federation of the Deaf, representing the Deaf people in Greece, was also very active during this period. The major demands they made were for acceptance of Greek Sign Language (GSL) by the schools and quality public education for all deaf children. Participation of Deaf people in the decision-making bodies for deaf education was a major issue. As a result, in 1986, a representative of the Greek Federation of the Deaf became the first Deaf member of the board of directors of the NID ("A Deaf Member on the Board," 1986).

In 1984, a new program director with a U.S. education and experience in the field of deafness was placed in NID, and soon, the institute's oral philosophy changed to one of Total Communication. Sign language classes began to be offered to NID teachers, students, and parents as well as to the public. Deaf teachers also were hired in the schools. The NID established, for the first time in Greece, early intervention programs in three major cities: Athens, Thessaloniki, and Patras. The Greek Federation of the Deaf and the parents' organization of NID, in cooperation with NID itself, organized several conferences at which the rights of Deaf people were made public. In these conferences, GSL interpreters were provided for the first time. The National Theater of the Deaf was established at this time, too, and began to give performances to the public.

During the 1990s, more special units in regular schools and some small mainstreaming programs were developed by the Ministry of Education. At the same time, the social model of disability gained momentum among the people involved. The European Community's directives and programs for the integration and inclusion of disabled students into mainstream education had a direct influence on the policies and attitudes related to the kinds of services to be provided for children with disabilities in Greece, including those that affected deaf education. At the same time, the social model of disability gained momentum among the people involved.

In 1992, the Department of Primary Education of the University of Patras, which is located at the northern part of Peloponnesus, established the Deaf Studies Unit and began to train teachers of deaf students. Since then, University of Patras is the only university in Greece that provides research and training in the area of deafness. The Deaf Studies Unit of the University of Patras also organizes courses for deaf tutors teaching GSL, for teachers working with deaf students, for interpreters of GSL, and for the public who want to learn sign language.

In addition, in 1992, the Local Authority (Mayoralty) of Argyroupolis in the Athens area, the NID, and the Greek Federation of the Deaf began to offer vocational programs for deaf people and sign language courses to the public. With the help of the European Community, the Deaf Studies Unit of the University of Patras, in collaboration with the Greek Federation of the Deaf, the Local Authority of Argyroupolis, and other European Centers of Deaf Studies, began to offer training programs for the first time in Greece for GSL interpreters and Deaf tutors of GSL. As a result, the first trained GSL interpreters established an organization and began to offer their services. Today, some of these interpreters work at general and special TV programs interpreting the news and the programs for Deaf citizens. In addition, the first trained GSL Deaf tutors also began to offer their services to people who wanted to learn GSL. Later, in 2004, as more Deaf people were trained by the Deaf Studies Unit of the University of Patras, an organization of Deaf GSL tutors was also established. Today, the major organizations involved with specialized programs for deaf children and adults are the three major bodies: the Deaf Studies Unit of University of Patras, the Greek Federation of the Deaf, and the Local Authority of Argyroupolis.

In March of 2000, the government passed a new educational law for children with disabilities, known as Law 2817/2000. This law was replaced in 2008 by the 3699/2008 Law. According to that law, GSL is recognized as the formal language of Deaf people in Greece. All teachers and specialists working with deaf pupils are required to have fluency in GSL, which is a new development for deaf people in Greece. Teachers working in schools and programs with deaf pupils have to take courses in GSL to fulfill the law's requirements (Greek Government, 2000).

CURRENT ACADEMIC PLACEMENT OF DEAF STUDENTS

Demographic data concerning the number of deaf people in Greece are not readily available. According to figures provided by the president of the Greek Federation of the Deaf (K. Gargalis, President, Greek Federation of the Deaf, personal communication, September 6, 2008), the estimated number of Deaf people in Greece is about 10,000 to 11,000. Of these people, 1,200 are likely of school age.

Figures provided by the Ministry of Education show that during the 2002–03 academic year, there were 1,519,000 students from the ages of 3 to 18 attending school programs (preschool through high school) throughout Greece (Skartis, 2003). If we assume that one school-age child per thousand is deaf, then the estimated number of deaf school-age children in Greece would be about 1,500. Data provided in 2005 by the office of special education showed that the number of deaf students attending all different special programs for the deaf (special schools, integrations units, etc.) was 529 (Sotiropoulos, 2005). In a comprehensive study done in 2004, it was found that a total of 15,850 students were attending special programs and schools for students with disabilities. Of these students, 672 were attending different programs for the deaf students (Padeliadou & Lampropoulou, 2004). A more recent study that was carried out for the purpose of this paper showed that only 425 deaf students were attending programs for the deaf during the academic year 2006–07 (see Table 14.2). Thus, one can easily conclude that there has been a rapid decline of the population of deaf students in special programs in recent years.

Table 14.2. Programs for Deaf Students in Greece, 2006–2007

Programs	Residential Schools (NID)[1]			Day Schools (ME)[2]			Integration Units in Regular Schools (ME)		
	N.Pr[3]	N.S.[4]	N.T.[5]	N.Pr	N.S.	N.T.	N.Pr	N.S.	N.T.
Infant Programs	3	24	3	—	—	—	—	—	—
Preschool Programs	—	—	—	4	11	5	4	9	3
Elem. Programs	4	61	24	9	99	39	6	18	7
Junior High Schools	—	—	—	3	117	46	3	13	25
High Schools	—	—	—	3	24	21	2	7	7
Technical Schools	—	—	—	4	42	38	—	—	—
Total	7	85	27	23	293	149	15	47	42

[1]National Institute for the Deaf
[2] ME = Ministry of Education schools
[3] N.Pr = number of programs
[4] N.S. = number of students
[5] N.T. = number of teachers

One of the main reasons for the decline of deaf students in special schools and programs is probably the cochlear implantations that have been performed on large numbers of young deaf children the last few years in Greece. These children, usually after the implantation, are placed in mainstream schools and classes often with minimal or no help. Another reason for the declining numbers of deaf students in special schools and programs is the inclusion movement that has affected parents, who most of the time choose to place their children in public regular schools in their neighborhoods, even if no special help is provided in these schools.

Finally, comparing the estimated total number of deaf school-age children (1,500) to the actual number of deaf students currently attending the different special programs for the deaf in Greece (425), one can conclude that a relatively large number of deaf school-age children are not presently receiving any special education services. These children, according to some reports from teachers, are placed in mainstream classes, usually without special help.

Current Placement Choices

As seen in Table 14.2, there are three types of schools for deaf children in Greece: residential schools, day schools, and integrations units or classes in schools for hearing students.

All of the above schools provide free education and services to deaf and hearing impaired students from the age of 3 to 24. According to the law, special education is the responsibility of the state and should be provided for free to all children who need it. Private schools for children with disabilities are not allowed to be established in Greece (Pub. L. No. 1566/1985, Pub. L. No. 2817/2000, and Pub. L. No. 3699/2008).

The Residential Schools of the National Institute for the Deaf

The schools of the NID are the oldest educational establishments for deaf children in Greece. The same curriculum is used by the NID schools as well as the day schools and the integration units.

Although the schools of the NID are all residential, they also accept day pupils. As seen in Table 14.2, NID at the present time has four special elementary schools and three infant programs. The largest schools are located in Athens and Thessaloniki while the remaining two smaller schools are located in the cities of Serres in northern Greece and in Patras in the southern part of Greece. In the past, NID had more elementary schools in three other cities of Greece, but because of the decline of the number of students attending special schools, those schools have been closed. The age level of children attending the elementary schools of the NID ranges from 6 to 16. The corresponding age level for hearing students at the elementary school level ranges from 6 to 12. Attached to the schools of the NID are preschool and nursery school programs as well as junior high and high schools. These additional programs use the facilities and services of the NID.

On graduation from one of the elementary schools of the NID, the students continue their education in public junior high schools for the deaf, controlled by the Ministry of Education. Compulsory education for all children in Greece, except for some groups of children with special needs, extends through the junior high school level. After junior high school, the students who want to follow academic careers continue through high school and the university. The ones who want to follow technical careers continue in technical schools.

The NID also provides infant programs for deaf children younger than the age of 3 and their families. There are three such programs in Athens, Thessaloniki, and Patras. The largest program is the one that operates in Thessaloniki.

Ministry of Education Public Schools

The public schools for the deaf are all governed by the Ministry of Education. All of these schools were developed after 1982 (Special Education Office, 1994). The public school system of the Ministry of Education includes day schools or programs and integration units within regular schools. Residential facilities are not provided by the Ministry of Education school system. However, deaf students attending these schools who need a place to reside can use the facilities of the NID or some other welfare residential homes at no cost.

The Ministry of Education school system includes preschool, elementary, junior high, and high school programs for deaf children from the age of 3 to 25. Table 14.3 shows the location and kind of schools for the deaf in Greece. The large day school programs are located in Athens and Thessaloniki. Smaller programs or classes are located in smaller cities and towns throughout the country. The day schools and programs are independent schools where deaf students do not mix with hearing students during school hours.

The deaf students in the integration units usually spend part of the school day in classes with hearing students and part of the day in separate classes. As seen in Table 14.3, during the academic year 2006–07, there were two large elementary schools for deaf children in Athens and six smaller programs in the cities of Volos, Ioannina, Thessaloniki, and Chalkis and on the islands of Crete (Heraklion) and Rhodes. Special preschool programs are located mainly in the large cities and are usually attached to the above elementary schools. Since the passage of the new special education legislation in 2000, integration units were developed in regular hearing schools. As seen in Table 14.3, there are three such units at the preschool level, six at the elementary school level, and five in junior high and high schools. Most of these units have been developed in small cities where there are not special schools for the deaf.

The age groupings of children in programs for the deaf is as follows: preschool, ages birth to 7 years; elementary, 4 to 17; junior high and high school, 13 to 23 (see Table 14.3). The age range for the technical schools is between 16 and 28 years. Deaf children remain in school programs much longer than do hearing students, most likely because normally, deaf children do not enter the special school at a very early age; the program of the special school is more flexible; and the pedagogy used follows a slower and more repetitive pace.

According to the law, the special schools and schools for the deaf must follow the same curriculum that is used in the regular schools. Some of the teachers have tried to modify the regular school curriculum to make it more accessible to their deaf students' needs. These curricular modifications are done on an individual basis and cannot be considered as an organized effort at designing a curriculum appropriate for deaf children.

In 1986, a curriculum for the development of literacy skills was developed and is used by teachers working with deaf pupils. This curriculum consists of six books for the teacher and six for the student (Lampropoulou et al., 1992). In 2002, a major project was undertaken by the Department of Special Education of the Pedagogical Institute (Ministry of Education) to develop curricula guidelines and adaptations for all different groups of students with disabilities, including deaf students. As a result, curricula, including GSL

Table 14.3. Schools and Programs, Students and Methods of Communication 2006–2007

Schools	Number of Students	Age	Sex		Resident	Methods of Communication
			Boys	Girls		
Infant Programs NID	24	0–4	15	9	—	Total\bilingual
Elem NID* Athens	20	6–15	12	8	3	Total
Elem NID Thessaloniki	25	6–15	18	7	13	Total
Elem. NID Patras	11	11–15	9	2	4	Total
Elem. NID Serres	5	6–14	5	—	3	Total
Pre-SC Argyroupolis—Athens M.E.**	4	4–6	3	1	—	Total
Pre-SC Philothei—Athens M.E.	3	4–7	3	—	—	Total
Pre-SC Thessaloniki M.E. (Int.Unit)	5	4–6	3	2	—	Oral
Pre-SC Volos M.E.	2	4–7	2	—	—	Oral
Pre-SC Chalkis M.E.	2	4–6	—	2	—	Oral
Pre-SC Katerini M.E. (Int.Unit)	1	5	—	1	—	Oral
Pre-SC Patras M.E. (Int.Unjt)	3	4–6	2	1	—	Total
Elem. Argiroupolis—Athens M.E.	48	4–14	31	17	—	Total\bilingual
Elem. Philothei—Athens M.E.	23	7–15	14	9	2	Total
Elem. Chalkis M.E.	3	8–10	2	1	—	Oral
Elem. Thessaloniki M.E.	7	6–13	3	4	—	Oral
Elem. Ioannina M.E.	2	13–17	1	1	—	Total
Elem. Volos M.E.	2	9–11	1	1	—	Total
Elem. Rhodes M.E.	4	7–12	3	1	—	Total
Elem. Heraklion M.E.	7	6–16	2	5	—	Total
Elem. Chania M.E.	3	8–12	1	2	—	Oral
Elem. Int.Unit*** Kalamata.	3	7–12	3	—	—	Total
Elem. Int.Unit Thessaloniki	2	9–10	1	1	—	Total
Elem. Int.Unit Patra	6	7–13	3	3	—	Total
Elem. Int.Unit Karditsa	2	11-12	2	—	—	Total
Elem. Int.Unit Katerini	1	9	—	1	—	Total
Elem. Int.Unit Mykonos	2	6–11	1	1	—	Oral
JH-HS Ag. Paraskevi—Athens M.E.	53	13–23	30	23	9	Total\bilingual
JH-HS Argiroupolis—Athens M.E.	54	13–23	32	22	-	Total
JH-HS Thessaloniki M.E.	34	13–20	18	16	15	Total
JH-HS Patras M.E. (Int.Unit)	2	17–19	1	1	—	Oral
JH-HS Kalamatas M.E. (Jnt.Unit)	6	14–18	1	5	—	Ora1\Total
JH-HS Thessaloniki M.E. (Int.Unlt)	2	15–16	1	1	—	Oral
JH-HS Heraklion M.E. (Int.Unit)	8	13–18	2	6	—	Total
JH-HS Chania M.E. (Int.Unit)	4	16–17	3	1	—	Oral
Technical School- TEE Athens M.E.	16	16–28	10	6	—	Total
Technical School- TEE Thess/ki M.E.(2)	9	19–24	6	3	—	Total
Tech. School-EEEEK- Thess/ki M.E.	17	17–25	11	6	10	Total
TOTAL	425		255	170	59	

* NID = National Institute for the Deaf (Ministry of Health)
** M.E. = Ministry of Education Schools
*** Int. Unit = Integration Unit in Regular School

curricula, for deaf and hearing impaired students of all school levels were developed (Lampropoulou, 2004a, 2004b).

Finally, appropriate tools to measure the academic achievement of deaf or hearing children have not been developed. Therefore, it is rather difficult to make any valid evaluation with respect to the achievement level of deaf children in Greece. However, reports from parents, deaf adults, and teachers suggest that the overall achievement level of deaf students graduating from high school is much lower than that of hearing students. As one would expect, the most problematic academic area is that of literacy (Lampropoulou, 1993).

Communication Modes in Schools

The history of deaf education in any country is very much connected to the history of the communication ideology of professionals working in the schools for the deaf. The first school for the deaf (NID), which was established in Athens in the 1930s (Lampropoulou, 1994), was in close cooperation with oral schools of the United States. As mentioned earlier, the teachers who worked in this school were sent to the Clarke School for the Deaf in the United States to receive training before their work in Greece and were very much influenced by that school's oral methodology. On their return to Athens, they established the basis for the oral tradition in their school, and spread their method to other schools that developed later on in Greece. In 1960, two additional private schools were established in Athens by parents. These schools also use a strictly oral approach and were very much influenced by the oral schools for the deaf in England with which they developed relationships.

Up until 1984, oralism was the only communication methodology used with deaf children in Greece. In their clubs, Deaf people often tell stories about the rigidity of the oral method and the oppression they felt, especially in the two private schools that exercised the oral approach in a very strict way. According to their accounts, articulation was one of the major subjects of the school's curriculum. Deaf adults were often forbidden to enter these schools, and deaf children of Deaf parents were not easily enrolled in them. Deaf people were not hired in these schools either.

In contrast, the oral policy of the NID within its residential schools was more liberal compared with the policy of the private schools. Sign language was allowed in the dormitories and during the after-school programs of NID. Deaf adults usually visited these schools, sometimes standing outside of the schoolyards, and signed to children during the weekends. During the 1970s, Deaf people, through their organizations, often criticized the strict oral method used in schools and demanded that sign language be included in the schools' communication methodology. However, the directors of the schools, the teachers, and the parents were not willing to accept the use of sign language in schools up until 1984.

Things began to change in 1984. For the first time in Greece, NID organized a series of seminars on sign language. This event, together with the results of the poor academic achievement of deaf pupils, led the teachers and the board of directors of the NID to change the policy and to adopt the Total Communication philosophy. The teachers began taking courses in GSL and using signs together with speech when communicating with the students in their classrooms. This change was welcomed by the Deaf community and occurred at a time when a newly elected socialist government promised more democratic and radical changes in the educational system of Greece. As a result of these democratic changes that began to take place, Deaf representatives of the Greek Federation of the Deaf (the National Organization of Deaf People) participated for the first time as members of the NID board of directors. Representatives of parents also participated on this board. The participation of Deaf people in the decision-making policy of NID had a direct influence in the education and the communication choices of NID. This influence also spread to other schools. As a result of all these events, a number of teachers of NID presently use signed Greek, which is a form of sign language that follows the syntax and grammar of the spoken Greek language. This sign system is not coded by the teachers and is generally used in a loose sense. The Greek manual alphabet is also used to supplement signed Greek.

Research in GSL and training courses for teachers of deaf students began to be offered for the first time in 1992 by the Deaf Studies Unit of the University of Patras. Materials to be used in teaching GSL were also developed by the same center, and, on request, Deaf teachers and interpreters began to serve the Deaf community, the schools, and the public. All these developments had a direct influence on the education of deaf children.

Today, GSL, the native language of Greek Deaf people, is used by Deaf teachers in their classrooms as well as in the schoolyards and the dormitories of NID. The NID, the Deaf clubs, and the University of Patras offer sign language courses to the personnel working at the schools as well as to parents and other groups. One of the early intervention centers of NID (Thessaloniki) recently began using the bilingual approach with deaf infants.

As is mentioned above, the current special education laws (Pub. L. No. 2817/2000 and Pub. L. No. 3699/2008) has recognized GSL as the prime language of Deaf people. According to this law, teachers, regardless of the method they choose to communicate with their deaf pupils in their class, should be fluent in GSL.

As seen in Table 14.3, teachers in most schools for the deaf use Total Communication. However, the Deaf teachers within these schools use GSL. Since the implementation of the law in 2000, the majority of teachers in schools for the deaf are required to take sign language courses to fulfill the law's fluency requirement. However a large number of teachers working in schools with deaf students are hearing teachers who have limited exposure to Deaf culture and sign language. Most of them have been trained to be oral teachers, and this change is a long process for them. As seen in Table 14.4, out of a total of 218 teachers working in schools and programs for deaf children, 31 are Deaf teachers. This number of Deaf teachers has been increased rapidly over the last few years, mainly after passage of Pub. L. No. 2817/2000.

DIAGNOSIS OF DEAFNESS AND EARLY INTERVENTION

At the present time, newborn infants and young children are not routinely screened. Parents or pediatricians who suspect that an infant or a young child may have a hearing loss refer the

Table 14.4. Professionals working Schools for the Deaf in Greece 2006–2007

Schools	No. of Programs	No. of Students	No. of Teachers	Deaf Teachers	Sex of Teachers Men	Women	Other Specialists
A) NID Schools (M.H.)*							
Infant Programs	3	24	3	—	—	3	4
Elem. Sch. Programs	4	61	24	2	5	19	19
B) M.E.** Schools							
Preschool Int. Units	4	9	3	1	—	3	—
Special Preschools	4	11	5	—	—	5	4
Special Elementary Schools	9	99	39	13	18	21	21
Elem. Schools Int. Units	6	16	7	—	2	5	—
Special Junior HS/High School	3	141	67	12	16	51	10
Junior HS/High School Int. Units	5	22	32	1	10	22	—
Technical Schools TEE/EEEEK	4	42	38	2	15	23	5
TOTAL	42	425	218	31	66	152	63

*M.H. = Ministry of Health Schools
*M.E. = Ministry of Education Schools

child to an audiological clinic located at a children's hospital or to the Medical-Pedagogical Center of the National Institute for the Deaf in Athens. According to the present law of special education, children entering a school program must be diagnosed and evaluated by the Centers of Diagnosis, Evaluation and Support, which are based in every district of Greece throughout the country. In these centers, specialists such as psychiatrists, psychologists, social workers, speech therapists, physiotherapists, special teachers, sign language teachers offer early identification, diagnosis, assessment, evaluation, and support services to educators, parents, and students in both special and regular schools. Assessment and evaluation in these centers is connected with the planning of the Individualized Educational Program in which parents participate. Placement is also proposed and supported by these centers.

The Medical-Pedagogical Center of the NID has been providing diagnostic services for deaf children of all ages for more than 20 years. This center is composed of a team of specialists that includes an eye and ear specialist, an audiologist, a hearing aid specialist, a pediatrician, a psychologist, a social worker, a speech therapist, and a teacher of the deaf. Children referred to the Medical-Pedagogical Center of NID complete a comprehensive audiological, psychological, and academic assessment. Hearing aid selection, evaluation, and fitting are also provided by this center.

A few audiological clinics that are usually attached to ear, nose and throat clinics of children's hospitals in major cities of Greece also provide for young children an audiological assessment and guidance for in the selection of a proper hearing aid. According to the law, hearing aids should be provided free of charge for all hearing impaired school children who attend a special school program.

Nursery classes and preschool programs are often attached to elementary schools for the deaf. Children can be admitted to a nursery class, preschool program, or residential school at the age of 3. Services for children younger than the age of 3 are limited in Greece. Parent-infant programs are provided by the NID and are found only in three large cities: Athens, Thessaloniki, and Patras. The infant programs of the NID, which were developed in 1986, provide guidance and educational services to families and their deaf infants.

Parents and their deaf infants visit these centers weekly. Usually, the visits are on an individual basis, but periodically the parents of deaf infants meet as a group. A teacher of the deaf, with the assistance of the psychologist and social worker, provides guidance and information as needed. Advice on education, communication, and technical matters as well as on the general problems of coping with a deaf child at home are some of the areas covered by this guidance program.

However, a large number of deaf infants and their parents are not benefiting from these services. Limitations in space, program availability, and comprehensive state policy concerning early infant screening, diagnosis, and intervention are major shortcomings that have to be overcome in the future if parents are to be adequately served. In addition, according to our research data (Lampropoulou & Mavrogianni, 2000), parents of deaf children are very critical about the present condition of audiological clinics based in the hospitals. The existing audiological clinics are not providing the needed guidance and services that parents require. They do not work cooperatively with the schools for the deaf, and often, doctors refer parents of deaf infants only to speech therapists for private sessions at a high cost (Lampropoulou & Mavrogianni, 2000).

Lately, according to K. Gargalis, president of the Greek Federation of the Deaf (Personal communication, September 6, 2008), doctors in Greece have become very interested in cochlear implantations and are increasingly performing these operations on a growing number of deaf children. However, many problems exist in this area because the ear, nose, and throat clinics lack the experience and the support personnel for training after the operation. Deaf people and teachers have expressed their firm disagreement with the present policy of cochlear implants, but parents are not clear about this issue and an increasing number of them choose the high-priced cochlear implants (usually covered by their health insurance) for their children.

LEGISLATION

Legislative action in Greece has been influenced both by the politics of the European Community and by Greek realities and priorities.

The European Context

Historically in Greece, as in other European countries, special education has been the subject of separate legislation and has been developed in small pieces as the needs of specific groups of children came to attention and legislation was deemed necessary for them. A reason for this development might be that special education was provided outside of general education, often involving Ministries of Health and Social Welfare. This situation has changed a great deal in the last two decades, not only in Europe but also in Greece—however, not completely. For example, in some European countries such as Sweden, preschool education is still under the responsibility of the Ministry of Social Welfare (Hegarty, 1995). Infant programs for deaf children in Greece are provided by the Ministry of Health and Welfare. In some countries such as Ireland, psychological assessment is under the Ministry of Health (Hegarty, 1995), which was also true for Greece until 2000.

During the 1970s, the movement away from the medical model of disability and the reaction against categorization of children with disabilities had a direct effect on legislation in many European countries. During this period, integration laws were developed within the framework of general education legislation, and in some countries such as the United Kingdom, Denmark, Finland, Iceland, Ireland, and Norway, the use of categories of children with disabilities was replaced by the more general concept of special educational needs. The only categories that are still used even in the countries that have abandoned the categories, are deaf, blind, and multiply disabled. This exception was made because of the highly specialized services required by those three categories of students. However, categorization has not been abandoned in Greece by the professionals or by the legislation.

The Greek Context

The first legislative actions in Greece concerning special education took place in the 1930s with the establishment of the special schools. In 1937, when the first school for the Deaf was formally established, the Ministry of Health and Welfare issued the regulations for its function (Greek Government, 1937).

In August 1956, a Greek parliament member, Andreas Kokkevis, who was a parent of a deaf daughter, proposed an addition to a law that was under discussion in the Parliament. This law was passed and became the first law supporting the education of deaf children in Greece. According to this law, public insurance organizations were required to pay the tuition of deaf students attending special schools (Parliament Records, 1956).

However, it was not until 1981 that the first comprehensive special education law of the Ministry of Education was passed in Greece (Pub. L. No. 1143/81). This law favored separate special education, and therefore, special schools, classes, and institutes for different categories of children with disabilities (including deaf children) were increased during this period (Lampropoulou & Padeliadou, 1995).

A few years later, the new socialist government of the Panhellenic Socialist Movement prepared a new draft of an education law in which special education was included as an integral part of the general education system. This law (Pub. L. No. 1566/85) was passed in 1985 and is known as the integration law because it encourages school integration and recognizes the right of students with disabilities to integrate in school and society. As a result of this new legislation, "special units or classrooms," also known as "resource rooms," were developed mostly in primary schools throughout the (public) schools of the country. Students would attend these classes or resource rooms on a part-time basis and according to their specific needs. The rest of the time they would attend their regular class. Special schools were also established, but usually within the grounds of regular schools. Special classrooms with deaf students also were developed in regular schools during this time.

According to Pub. L. No. 1566/85, the Ministry of Education is responsible for special education, including the development, organization, and curricula of special schools. The Office of Special Education of the Ministry of Education and regional counselors of special education undertook the responsibility to supervise the schools, the integration units, and the teachers of special education in Greece. All these schools and programs covered students ages 3 to 18 years. This law made no provision for early intervention, while vocational training was limited to some special technical schools. The Mainstream National Curriculum was to be implemented by all special schools and programs, and individualized instruction could be offered to students who needed it. No provision was offered for special adaptation or development of Individualized Educational Programs. Diagnosis and evaluation was carried out by the medical-pedagogical centers of the Ministry of Health and Welfare.

During the 1980s and 1990s and with the support of the European programs Helios I and II, full-time integration (inclusion) was implemented mostly in Athens and in some other big cities of Greece for students with disabilities, including deaf children. As a result of these activities, a special committee was established in April 1994 (Polychronopoulou, 1995) by the Ministry of Education to draft new legislation for special education. This new bill, Pub. L. No. 2817/2000, was passed in 2000. According to this legislation, integration and inclusion should be offered as a first choice to students with mild or moderate disabilities. If the needs of these students cannot be satisfied in a regular unit, then the second choice for them would be a part-time placement in an integrated class (or resource room) within the regular school. Special schools, institutes, clinics, or home instruction can also be available to children as a third choice and as needed.

As a result of this new legislation, integration units were developed not only in regular primary schools but also for the first time in secondary schools. In addition, such units were developed in mainstream technical schools. Vocational Special Schools were also developed throughout the country, providing vocational training for students who could not follow academic programs and careers. According to Pub. L. No. 2817/2000, the age range of students attending all schools and units is from below 3 to 24 years. Under this law, the Centers of Diagnosis, Evaluation, and Support were developed by the Ministry of Education in each district of Greece. Free hearing aids are provided to hearing impaired students by the Ministry of Education.

Another innovation of the new law was the establishment of the Special Education Department in the Ministry's of Education Pedagogical Institute. The responsibility of this department is to develop and supervise the special education program in the country, including the development of research in the area of special education, curricula and materials, assessment, techniques and tools, and proposals of new programs and services. The author was the first appointed president to this department from 2000 to 2003. During this time, the new Pedagogical Institute developed the Centers of Diagnosis, Evaluation, and Support, vocational programs, integration units, and curricula for special education.

Finally, Pub. L. No. 2817/2000 has special significance for the education of deaf students because it recognizes GSL as the formal language of Deaf people in Greece. Teachers working with deaf students, regardless of the methodology used in their schools, are required by law to be fluent in GSL. As a result of this regulation, for the last 5 to 6 years, teachers and professionals working in programs for deaf students as well as those in teacher training programs have been required to take courses in GSL. In the fall of 2008 the Greek parliament passed a new set of legislation related to special eduction. However, this new legislation does not seem to affect the field of deaf education (Pub. L. No. 3699/2008).

TEACHER PREPARATION PROGRAMS

During the 2006–07 academic year, there were a total of 218 teachers of the deaf working in schools and classes for deaf students. Of these teachers, 66 were men and 152 were women (see Table 14.4), perpetuating the common notion that teaching the deaf is a woman's job. In addition, among the 218 teachers working in schools for the deaf, 31 teachers are Deaf (see Table. 14.4). The teaching profession, especially in the area of elementary education, is presently a growing profession for Deaf people in Greece. According to reports from the Greek Federation of the Deaf, approximately 10 deaf students are presently studying to become teachers at the different universities in Greece.

Nevertheless, teacher training for teaching deaf students is still an area of concern for Greece. Only at the School of Humanities in the Department of Education at the University of Patras are courses offered in the area of the education of the deaf for students enrolled in an elementary education program. Since 2000, graduate studies leading to a masters degree in deaf education have also been offered to students by this university. This new development has been received with much enthusiasm by the Deaf community and by the parents of deaf children in Greece. However, most of the teachers presently working in the schools for the deaf have not received any formal training. Table 14.5 shows the amount of education received by teachers at different levels.

To overcome the shortage of teacher training opportunities in the past, the NID offered a 1-year, in-service course of study to prepare new teachers of the deaf. This program has been discontinued since the Ministry of Education undertook the responsibility of special education. A 2-year, in-service training program is now being offered by the Universities of Greece (Departments of Education) that focuses on special education for those who wish to work with children with disabilities. This course is general in nature and does not provide the specific training to work successfully with deaf students. However, in keeping with present legislation, the degree received from these programs is recognized for a position in a school for the deaf.

Table 14.5 indicates that very few of the teachers now working in schools for the deaf hold an MA or a PhD degree in education of the deaf. However, the majority of these teachers have attended an in-service training related to the area of deaf education run by the Deaf Studies Unit of the University of Patras. All of these teachers hold a bachelor's degree in general education.

VOCATIONAL EDUCATION AND POSTSECONDARY OPPORTUNITIES

According to the present legislation, the state is responsible for the vocational education of students with special needs. Special vocational schools have been established to meet the individual needs of such students (Pub. L. No. 1566/85, Pub. L. No. 2817/2000, and Pub. L. No. 3699/2008). As a result, technical school programs have been developed by the Ministry of Education, mainly in the Athens and Thessaloniki area, serving 42 students (see Table 14.3). These recently developed technical school programs fall into two categories: the technical special schools for students who can pursue a technical career (one in Athens and two in Thessaloniki) and the Special Workshops for Vocational Training for students with additional problems, usually mental disabilities (the remaining technical schools in Thessaloniki).

Table 14.5. Teacher Training

Schools	Ph.D.	MA	In Service	Spec. Educ.	Greek Sign Lang.	Non Training	Number of Teachers
A) NID Schools (M.H.)*							
Infant Programs		1	3		3		3
Elem. Sch. Programs		1	24		24		24
B) M.E.** Schools							
Preschool Int. Units		1		3	1		3
Special Preschools		1	5		5		5
Special Elementary Schools	1	1	27	7	39		39
Elem. Schools Int. Units			4	4	5	3	7
Special Junior HS/High School	1	2	62		56	5	67
Junior HS/High School Int. Units			17		12	15	32
Technical Schools TEE/EEEEK			17		27	7	38
TOTAL	2	7	132	14	172	30	218

* M.H. Ministry of Health
** M.E. Ministry of Education Schools

Some local authorities have also developed vocational training programs for deaf students that are partially funded by the European Community programs. The local authority of Argyroupolis, at a southeastern suburb of Athens, is very active in this area. This authority has developed programs in computer operation and in graphic arts. These programs are considered by deaf people to be good, but they are offered for only a limited number of deaf students.

Despite the shortcomings of the Greek special educational system, a number of deaf students manage to continue their education in the universities. According to reports from the Greek Federation of the Deaf, more than 50 students are presently attending university programs. More than 40 Deaf people in Greece hold university degrees and work in a variety of professions. The universities, however, do not offer any support services (such as interpreters, note takers, etc.) for deaf students (K. Gargalis, President, Greek Federation of the Deaf, personal communication, September 6, 2008).

CURRENT ISSUES AND FUTURE TRENDS

Education services for deaf children in Greece are developing at a slow pace. Problems and shortcomings in existing services for deaf students are common. Some of the problems appear to be of a critical nature. One of the most pressing problems is the need to extend education services to children who are not currently being served. In particular, programs have to be developed in early intervention and in supporting deaf students in inclusive settings, especially students with cochlear implants. Programs for deaf students with additional disabilities should also be established.

In addition, there is a need to develop comprehensive vocational training programs for deaf students. Such programs help deaf people advance their general occupational and financial status. Another high priority is the need to develop more teacher training programs at the university level that can produce teachers who can provide quality instruction to deaf students.

Parents of deaf students and the Deaf people of Greece themselves are becoming more militant and are demanding a better education for deaf children. These groups have recently organized meetings and conferences and have drawn up policies covering all of the issues that have been mentioned above. These groups are emphatic about the need for quality services.

The inclusion of deaf people into the larger society and in education are important issues in Greece. Deaf people, the majority of the teachers of the deaf, and many of the parents are skeptical about the value of inclusive education. They feel that the regular schools are not equipped to serve deaf students. They seem to prefer day schools or special classes in which deaf children are taught in separate groups (Lampropoulou, 1995).

During the past two decades, the government of Greece seems to have become more sensitive to the needs of children with disabilities. This recent sensitivity could be the result of renewed benevolence and moral responsibility for the citizenry of the country, or it could be a result of pressure applied to the government by organizations consisting of parents of deaf children and Deaf adults. This organized pressure, coupled with the activities of the European Community and their advances in medicine and technology, has significantly influenced the development of deaf education in Greece in the last decade and has set the basis for its further development.

REFERENCES

Fillipidis, L. (1950). *Epetiris.* Athens: National Institute for the Deaf.

Greek Government. (1907). *Official Journal,* FEK 96/17-5-1907. Athens: Ethniko Typographeio.

Greek Government. (1937). *Official Journal,* FEK 228/15-6-1937. Athens: Ethniko Typographeio.

Greek Government. (1956). *Official Journal,* FEK 281/16-11-1956. Athens: Ethniko Typographeio.

Greek Government. (1973). *Official Journal,* FEK a53/19-1-1973. Athens: Ethniko Typographeio.

Greek Government. (1975). *Official Journal,* FEK 273/4-12-1975. Athens: Ethniko Typographeio.

Greek Government. (1981). *Official Journal,* FEK 80/31-3-1981. Athens: Ethniko Typographeio.

Greek Government. (1985). *Official Journal,* No. 1566/1985, FEK 167/30-9-1985. Athens: Ethniko Typographeio.

Greek Government. (2000). *Official Journal,* No. 2817/2000, FEK 78/14-3-2000. Athens: Ethniko Typographeio.

Greek Government. (2008). *Official Journal,* L. 3699/2008, FEK 199/02/2008. Athens: Ethniko Typographeio.

Hegarty, S. (1995, December). *Changes in legislation in the field of education.* Paper presented at the HELIOS European Seminar, Athens.

Lampropoulou, V. (1993). An evaluation of the written language of deaf students in Greece. *Glossa, 30*(12), 40–50.

Lampropoulou, V. (1994). The history of deaf education in Greece. In C. J. Erting, R. C. Johnson, D. L. Smith, & B. D. Snider (Eds.), *The deaf way.* Washington, DC: Gallaudet University Press.

Lampropoulou, V. (1995, July). *The integration of deaf people in Greece: Results of a needs assessment study.* Paper presented at the 18th International Congress on Education of the Deaf, Tel Aviv, Israel.

Lampropoulou, V. (2004a). *Curricula for hearing impaired students in elementary education.* Athens: Pedagogical Institute, Ministry of Education.

Lampropoulou, V. (2004b). *Curricula for hearing impaired students in secondary education.* Athens: Pedagogical Institute, Ministry of Education.

Lampropoulou, V., Alevizos, G., Balafouti, K., Samara, M., Filianou, A., Fitsiou, A., et al. (1992). *Let's write.* Athens: Publication Company of School Books (O.E.D.B.).

Lampropoulou, V., & Mavrogianni, T. (2000). The needs of parents of deaf children: An evaluation through the systems theory. In A. Kypriotakis (Ed.), *Proceedings of Special Education* (pp. 637–657). Rethymno, Greece: Department of Primary Education, University of Crete.

Lampropoulou, V., & Padeliadou, S. (1995). Inclusive education: The Greek experience. In C. O'Hanlon (Ed.), *Inclusive education in Europe* (pp. 49–60). London: David Fulton.

Lazanas, V. (1984). *The problems of the deaf.* Athens, Greece.

Padeliadou, S., & Lampropoulou, V. (2004). *Mapping Special Education.* Athens: Pedagogical Institute, Ministry of Education.

Parliament Records. (1956, August). *The discussion of the act to support schools for the deaf.* Athens, Greece.

Polychronopoulou, S. (1995, December). *Legislative trends in the field of special education in Greece.* Paper presented at the HELIOS European Seminar, Athens.

Skartis, P. (2003). *Greek education system: Facts and figures.* Athens: Center of Educational Research.

Special Education Office, Ministry of Education. (1994). *Booklet of information.* Athens: Author.

Sotiropoulos, P. (2005). *Special education report 2004–2007.* Retrieved October 14, 2008, from http://www.ypepth.gr/docs/site_eid_agwgn.doc

A deaf member on the board of the National Institute for the Protection of Deaf-Mutes. (1986, February). *The World of Silence* (Newspaper of the Greek Federation of the Deaf), *1*(Special ed.), 1.

The Deaf Community in Spain: Historical Perspectives, Educational Opportunities, and the Consolidation of Sign Language

Aníbal Puente, Jesús M. Alvarado, and Marian Valmaseda

THE HISTORY of education of the deaf in Spain is one of extremes. On the one hand, it has been seen as a model for educational innovation (during the 16th and 17th centuries), and on the other hand, it has been seen as lacking in educational initiative (18th and 19th centuries and part of the 20th century). Today's situation represents an intermediate point, one increasingly characterized by a move toward modernity.

The origins of education of the deaf are attributed to the Benedictine monk Pedro Ponce de León (1506–1584), who proposed educating the deaf children of a rich, bureaucratic family from Madrid's royal court despite the general belief of the time that the "deaf and the mute" were unable to learn how to speak, read, or write. Ponce de León kept his methods secret. Nevertheless, later writings have revealed that he used speechreading, fingerspelling, and the use of signs and of a manual alphabet (the origin of today's International Alphabetic System), which was published by Melchor de Yebra in 1593 (Oviedo, 2006). Later, in 1620, Juan Pablo Bonet (1573–1633) published his book *Reducción de las Letras y Arte para Enseñar a Hablar a los Mudos* (The Reduction of Letters and the Arts for Teaching the Mute to Speak), the educational effect of which was very influential.

Historical sources reveal, therefore, that it was during the 16th century in Spain that the education of the deaf began (Plann, 1997), although the clumsiness and secretiveness surrounding these first efforts (Gunther, 1996) resulted in their being forgotten and wrongly attributed to the Abbé de l'Epée and his 18th-century school for the deaf in Paris. Bonet's book, inspired by Ponce de Leon's methods, was translated and published in English, French, and German in the 19th century, and it had significant influence on John Bulwer (1614–1684), William de Holder (1616–1698), and John Wallis (1616–1703). Bonet's book introduces modern concepts of phonetics and speech therapy to the teaching of the deaf. Although it defends the practice of oral training for older students, it argues, nevertheless, that the first pedagogic task consists of teaching the letters of the manual alphabet in their written form. After this task, the teacher should begin teaching how to pronounce the sound of each letter, later moving on to syllables, then to concrete and abstract words and, finally, to grammatical structures (Marchesi, 1987).

Manuel Ramírez de Carrión (1579–1652) and Jacobo Rodríguez Pereira (1715–1780) directed their efforts toward reinforcing the work begun by Ponce and Bonet. Pereira was born in Extremadura but left, first for Portugal and then for France, in the face of religious persecution. He taught deaf students in France before Epée and used the Spanish manual alphabet. His work clearly influenced Epée, and legend has it that he introduced the alphabet to Epée and gave him a copy of Bonet's book (see Moores, 2001).

After a long gap of more than a century, Lorenzo Hervás y Panduro (1735–1809) published *Escuela Española de Sordos* (The Spanish School for the Deaf) in 1795 (Hervás, 1795a, 1795b), thus prompting the creation of the first school for the deaf, an effort that emulated what had already been achieved in France, Italy, and other countries 30 years earlier. As a professor of the deaf, Hervás promoted the simultaneous teaching of words and gestures, thus predating what has been termed "simultaneous communication." Nevertheless, Hervás never considered sign language as a complex language, one capable of expressing not only emotions but also propositions. Additional relevant contributions made by Hervás include his description of "barriers to communication," whose objective of social integration was several centuries ahead of its time; the introduction of advanced linguistic concepts such as "grammatical ideas"; and his rejection of the prejudice that identified deaf people as "idiots" (Gascón-Ricao & Storch, 2004). The 18th and 19th centuries witnessed a vacuum in Spain as educational initiatives disappeared almost completely, despite the fact that deaf education elsewhere in Europe was advancing and becoming more consolidated. Despite the adverse conditions of the times, the figure of Roberto Prádez Gautier (1772–1836) stands out for his pedagogic efforts. In 1805, Prádez became the first Deaf teacher at the Real Escuela de Sordomudo (Royal School for the Deaf and Mute) where he taught reading, writing, and drawing.[1]

The painter Francisco de Goya is known as the "Enlightened Deaf Man." At the age of 46, he contracted a strange illness that left him profoundly deaf. Once this deafness had set in, Goya had serious difficulties communicating orally, so he tended to communicate through writing. Nevertheless, at some point in his life, Goya began to use signed speech and a manual alphabet to communicate. Proof that Goya had a command of the manual alphabet is a painting titled "Las Cifras de la Mano" ("The Codes of the Hand") (see Figure 15.1), which reproduces the current alphabet with only the minimal variations that one would expect to find. It is not a painting that is typical for Goya; it is small and drawn on a simple piece of paper, which leads one to conclude that it was a drawing made for pedagogic purposes.

The 19th century began with a failed attempt to implement deaf education when, between 1800 and 1802, Juan Albert Martín founded the first Municipal School for the Deaf in Barcelona (Llombart, 1991). His teaching methods constituted an application of the writings of Ponce, Hervás, and Epée. He used the Spanish Manual Alphabet at first, followed by Bonet's oral and phonetic method and Epée's "methodical signs." The school lasted 3 years, until it was forced to close because of lack of funds and administrative support. In 1806, the school was reopened under the direction of Salvador Vieta, but a few years later, it closed down again in the face of similar problems. Nevertheless, modern education of the deaf began in Spain, particularly Madrid, in 1805 with the founding of a school created by the Crown, financed by the state, and run and directed by the Sociedad Matritense de Amigos del País (The Madrid Society of Friends of the Country). Before the creation of the Real Colegio de Sordos (Royal School for the Deaf) by King Charles IV in Madrid, and excepting precedents in the Colegio de San Fernando de Lavapiés (San Fernando School of Lavapiés) in Madrid and the

---

1. Prádez owes the vindication of his work to the admirable research carried out by Susan Plann (1992).

Figure 15.1. The Codes of the Hand (Francisco de Goya). This etching, catalogued by Sánchez Cantón in 1923 as one of Goya's works, was done in pen and sepia ink on a 24 x 40 cm piece of ochre paper, signed and dated in the bottom right-hand corner with the words: "Goya en Piedrahita/ año de 1812" ("*Goya in Piedrahita/ year 1812*"). It consists of 20 drawings on a striped background depicting the configurations of a right hand representing 21 letters of the Spanish alphabet (*k, x,* and *z* excluded) and the digraphs *ch* and *ll*, ordered in the following manner: (first line), *a, b, c, d, e*; (second line), *f, g, ch, i, l, m*; (third line), *n, o, p, q, r, s*; and (fourth line), *t, u, y* (commentary, Gascón-Ricao, 2004).

Escuela Municipal del Ayuntamiento de Barcelona (The Barcelona Municipal School), there had never been any specific public, general, or universal education program for deaf children and teenagers in Spain.

From the mid-19th century until well into the 20th, changes took place in Spain that reflected the disorientation of policies with respect to deaf education. Changes were made back and forth, and these swings represent the best and the worst of educational policies and methods (Alcina, 2005).

After 1975 and the arrival of democracy in Spain, Spanish society began to become aware of the problem of educating deaf students, and policies promoting their integration in society were implemented. In this sense, the intervention of the Ministry for Education, the National Confederation of Spanish Deaf People (Confederación Estatal de Personas Sordas, or CNSE), and parents' movements have played a key role in promoting a more modern system of education for deaf students in Spain. The resulting integration practices were initiated in 1985 (see specifics in the following section). In addition, a more recent series of important changes with respect to educational opportunities for deaf students were initiated in the mid-1990s. Those changes were brought about by the following factors:

- The experience accumulated over 10 years of educational integration
- The active role played by associations of Deaf people, which championed the use of Spanish Sign Language (Lengua de Signos Española, or LSE) as a vehicle for learning and called for the incorporation of Deaf professionals in schools

- The information gathered from experiences in bilingual education using sign language in northern European countries
- The educational trends that called for more inclusive schools and the elimination of barriers to participation
- Technological advances such as improved hearing aids and, especially, cochlear implants, which have allowed young deaf students to connect aurally with the world around them in a qualitatively different way than they were previously able to do

CURRENT EDUCATIONAL OPPORTUNITIES

To better understand the educational opportunities for deaf students that currently exist in Spain, the reader needs to keep in mind that the education measures adopted by the Spanish Ministry for Education refer only to general legislation, which is later adapted and put into effect in very different ways in each of the country's 17 Autonomous Communities. Some of these Autonomous Communities have an official language in addition to Spanish, which creates a situation of oral and written bilingualism for deaf children and their families. The communities' autonomy is likewise reflected in their health and social services systems, leading to differences among the communities in terms of the existence of early detection programs for deafness, access to technical aids or cochlear implants, availability of sign language interpreters, etc. The following pages represent an attempt to reflect the wide range of existing opportunities in the most complete manner possible. The reader should be aware, however, that some of these opportunities are, in fact, quite singular examples that are being developed in only a few schools in all of the country.

School Age

As can be seen in Table 15.1, education in Spain is compulsory between the ages of 6 and 16. Nevertheless, the majority of hearing children begin their formal education at the age of 3 in preschool, and a significant proportion of children younger than the age of 3 (especially in urban areas) attend children's schools especially designed for this age group.

In the case of deaf children, school attendance before the age of 6 depends largely on the age at which their deafness is first diagnosed. Some communities' hospital services have early detection protocols in place that not only allow a diagnosis to be made in the first months of life but also enable the child to begin receiving early stimulation and attend a children's school before the age of 1 year. In other cases, the diagnosis comes later, between the ages of 2 and

Table 15.1. Educational Levels in the Spanish School System

Age	Educational Level	Status of Attendance
0–6 years	Preschool	Noncompulsory
6–12 years	Primary school	Compulsory
12–16 years	Secondary school	Compulsory
16 years and older	Baccalaureate	Noncompulsory
	Basic level professional education	Noncompulsory
18 years and older	University studies	Noncompulsory
	Advanced level professional education	Noncompulsory

3, when the child's lack of oral language use and lack of response to aural stimuli set off alarm bells in the family environment. In these cases, school attendance typically begins between the ages of 3 and 6.

Models of School Organization

The topic of currently available models of school organization can be approached from several different perspectives. If we limit ourselves to an examination of the educational context in which deaf children receive schooling, we find two different organizational models of service: integration and special education. If we approach the topic from a communication perspective, we find ourselves faced with a question of monolingual versus bilingual education. However, the reality of schooling opportunities is much more complex because within each of these organizational models for service there is a continuum of possibilities (see Table 15.2). Decisions with respect to models of school organization are based on a process of psychopedagogic evaluation that are conducted under the direction of the corresponding educational services and according to the opinions and wishes of the child's family.

Education Integration

Ever since legislation with respect to education integration came into effect in 1985, more and more deaf students have been enrolled in regular schools with hearing classmates. Some of these deaf students are enrolled in the school closest to their home. This type of integration could be classified as individual integration in the sense that there is generally only one deaf student in each class and, in many cases, in the entire school.

Nevertheless, a sizeable portion of Autonomous Communities have *Centros de Integración Preferentes de Sordos* (Deaf Preferred Integration Schools). These are ordinary schools in which deaf students have preference for the school's "special needs students" enrollments (two per class). These schools were created with several objectives in mind (Marchesi, 1987): they provide deaf students with opportunities to interact and establish relationships with both their hearing peers and other deaf children, thus avoiding situations of social and personal isolation; they attempt to make the most of specific resources, both personnel-related (specialist teachers, speech therapists, interpreters, etc.) and materials-related (technical aids, modulated frequency kits, etc.); and they facilitate professional training programs for teachers, especially those programs related to the use of signed communication systems.

The curriculum offered to deaf students in these schools is the ordinary curriculum, adapted to the particular needs of each student. These adaptations (modifications) tend to be either "slightly significant" (for example, the adaptation of school texts or of certain testing procedures) or very significant (those that affect the contents of educational subjects themselves).

Table 15.2. Different Schooling Organization in Terms of Students' Placement

Integrated Schooling			Special Education		
Integration in the school nearest the student's home	Integration in a Deaf Preferred School	Joint or Combined education (groups of 4–6 deaf students per class)	Special classes for deaf students in ordinary schools	Special schools for the deaf	Special classes for deaf students in generalized special education schools

All adaptations must be detailed in writing and students' families must be adequately informed.

Education integration in these schools can be considered to be a positive step for the majority of hard of hearing children. A greater controversy exists, however, in the case of profoundly deaf students, who access information primarily through sight. Although the educational perspectives and the intentions of many teachers reflect the necessity of using signed communication systems, this idea has not had significant repercussions in educational practices at the majority of integrated schools. Teachers have not incorporated visual communication systems into their classrooms in a systematic way, and when these systems have been included, it has been only at certain times and fundamentally by support teachers during individual or small group work.

In the opinion of the authors, the reasons why these systems have not been completely incorporated are practical ones because providing deaf children with opportunities for a normalized education through the use of visual communication systems, though possible, nevertheless requires a series of conditions that are difficult to create in ordinary classrooms. The learning and especially the use of signed communication systems requires a great effort, and the presence of one or two deaf students per classroom does not provide sufficient motivation for their use by ordinary teachers. Even in the case of those teachers who are willing to use these systems, their systematic and continued use in classes composed of, say, 23 hearing students and 2 deaf students does not seem viable (Díaz-Estébanez & Valmaseda, 1995). In the case of secondary education, this problem is mitigated to a certain extent by the presence of sign language interpreters in the classroom. However, this resource is not one that is available in primary schools, which leads to a gap between some students' need to use a signed communication system (whether Signed Spanish or LSE) and the difficulty ordinary schools have in providing that resource.

It is obvious that the above-mentioned difficulties are not shared by schools that follow an oral approach. In that approach, emphasis is placed on the notion that deaf students will have greater possibilities for interacting with their hearing peers—and, therefore, for undergoing a process of acquisition or learning of a more functional form of oral speech—if they are in an oral context.

Recent years have seen the emergence of new educational services in the context of education integration: the *Escuelas de Educación Combinada o Conjunta* (Combined or Joint Education Schools). These schools are designed to guarantee all students' access to information and, therefore, to education, be they hearing students or deaf students; to increase the opportunities for interpersonal interaction between deaf children and their deaf and hearing peers; and to provide all students within a particular classroom with the same curriculum.

Combined education involves the grouping of several deaf students in the same classroom, with a total of 4–6 deaf students and 16–20 hearing students. These combined groups of deaf and hearing children generally have two teachers in the classroom. The two teachers plan the classwork together. The hearing or deaf status or the linguistic profile of each teacher (oral language or sign language use) differs from one school to the next. In general, one teacher assumes more of the responsibilities related to the teaching of the deaf students in the class and can take on several roles: teaching through LSE, carrying out small group activities, reinforcing certain contents, encouraging the use of oral and written language, etc. Students also receive LSE classes (under the tutelage of LSE specialists) and individual speech therapy sessions.

This type of educational experience is based on two pillars of thought. The first of these is a clear trend toward inclusive education, *inclusive* referring to the identification and elimination of barriers to participation and learning for all students and with a heightened focus on those students whose risk of exclusion or academic failure is greatest. The second is a bilingual and bicultural conception of Deaf students, which understands that an educational setting that includes both deaf and hearing children must necessarily incorporate different students' languages and cultures in a manner that gives equal status to all (Alonso & Echeita, 2006).

It is interesting to note that some of these experiences involving inclusive, bilingual processes have taken place in integrated schools. However, the majority of these initiatives have been based in special schools for the deaf (González de Ibarra & Molins, 1998; Escuela Infantil Piruetas, 2002; Las Heras, 1999; Sanjuán & Pérez-Garcia, 2005).

Special Education

Currently, two types of students are given preference for enrollment in special education programs for the deaf: (a) those students who have additional handicaps on top of profound deafness and who require very specific educational measures and attention and (b) deaf students with a serious educational gap, generally as a consequence of poor educational opportunities in their past, and the majority of whom come from immigrant families who have only recently arrived in Spain. Students may be enrolled in these schools until the age of 21 to complete the compulsory stage of their basic education (normally completed between the ages of 6 and 16) and to have access to a basic professional education (at 16 or older). The curricula offered by these schools are special curricula with significant modifications and adaptations designed to give priority to the development of communication skills and to the functional learning required for students' future autonomy in adult life. Some special schools have organized bilingual education models (based on sign language and oral language) with a marked presence of Deaf teachers in the classroom (Ardanuy, 1998; Rodríguez, 1998, 2006).

Communication Approaches

As has already been mentioned, the education of the deaf in the 20th century was marked by a strong oralist trend. It is therefore not surprising that the communication system most often used in classes with deaf students nowadays continues to be a system of oral and written language. Strangely, the initiation of the integrated schooling program was accompanied by a heated debate with respect to the necessity of incorporating sign language and augmentative systems of communication in deaf students' education. It is surprising that, in contrast to the then "traditional" special schools (which rejected the use of signs as a tool for teaching or learning), it was in the context of integrated schooling that sign language (especially by means of interpreters) and other augmentative systems of communication (such as simultaneous communication or signed speech, cued speech, and fingerspelling) began to be incorporated into the classroom. The role of these systems will be reviewed briefly here, and sign language will be discussed in further detail in the following section.

Simultaneous Communication or Signed Speech

The accompaniment of speech by signs is, in all likelihood, the communication strategy most often used in the education of deaf students. Unlike signed speech systems in other countries where quite formal strategies have been developed (SEE I and SEE II in the United States, for example), signed speech in Spain is used more as an open, flexible communication strategy whose goal is both to foster communication between deaf and hearing students and to facilitate the learning of lesson contents, which are usually presented in oral form, written form, or both. In the case of younger children's education, the use of signs to complement and reinforce spoken communication is quite common even in more oralist contexts and especially during the first stages of oral language teaching.

Cued Speech

From the mid-1980s to the present day, the diffusion of the research carried out by Jesús Alegría and his team in Brussels has had a great effect. Their research, focused on the processes of written word recognition, gives great importance to the use of phonological codes in the accessing of the lexicon and to the role of cued speech in the creation of these phonological representations (Alegría, 1999, 2003; Leybaert & Alegría, 2002). The influence of these studies has led some Spanish schools to use cued speech as a tool to aid the acquisition of oral language skills. This use of cued speech is found not only in oralist settings (Santana, Torres, & Garcia, 2003; Torres, Moreno-Torres, & Santana, 2006) but also in the context of bilingual (sign language and oral language) education, where cued speech is used as an augmentative system for oral language (Alonso, Domínguez, Rodríguez, & Saint-Patrice, 2001; Domínguez, Alonso, & Rodríguez, 2003; Rodríguez, Domínguez, & Alonso, in preparation).

Fingerspelling

The presence of the fingerspelling alphabet is also quite normal in Spanish classrooms, although its pedagogic uses are diverse. It tends to be used in signing contexts as a quick strategy for spelling proper nouns or oral terms whose signed equivalent is unknown, but in Spain, fingerspelling has never been considered a communication strategy in itself (in the style of the Rochester Method). In some schools, it is used as a support strategy in reading and writing activities, especially in the early stages of learning (Bellés, 1998). Recent investigations have analyzed the role of sign language and fingerspelling in the development of the reading, writing, and phonological representations (Puente, Alvarado, & Herrera, 2006).

Sign Language

The last two decades have seen many very positive changes made in terms of the linguistic and social status of LSE. These changes have largely been prompted by linguistic research (Martínez, 2000; Minguet, 2001; Muñoz, 1999; Rodríguez, 1992; VVAA, 2001) and psycholinguistic investigations on LSE (Álvarez et al., 2002; Caamaño, Juncos, Justo, López, & Vilar, 1999; Justo, Juncos, Caamaño, Vilar, & López, 1999), but above all, they are a result of (a) the intense activity carried out by Deaf people's associations in support of the teaching and diffusion of LSE as well as of the creation of interpretation services and (b) the continued calls by Deaf people's associations for the official recognition of this language (see Table 15.3).

Nowadays, sign language is more present in Spanish society. Numerous courses are available for learning LSE; materials have been created to aid its teaching; and the presence of interpreters during political debates in the Houses of Congress is quite common, as is their presence in public service and other institutional announcements broadcast on television.

Sign language is ever more present in the educational field, too. This presence is a result of LSE interpreters in the classroom (in secondary schools) and of the creation of bilingual education experiences (sign language and oral language) that, as has already been mentioned, can be carried out with groups made up of solely deaf students (in special education schools) or in mixed groups with deaf and hearing children (in combination or joint settings). In general, these programs offer a simultaneous form of bilingualism; that is, students begin to learn LSE and oral language in the same school year, although members of the teaching staff often work on each language separately in clearly differentiated and defined times and spaces.

The majority of these bilingual experiences are characterized by the emphasis they place on what could be considered more linguistic factors or elements. In other words, sign language is seen as a tool for facilitating deaf students' learning of school materials, but its related cultural aspects are not explored in any more depth. Along these lines, a recent investigation into the implicit ideas and beliefs held by hearing teachers in bilingual settings in Spain reveals that teachers combine different concepts and beliefs ("deaf students as handicapped students," "deaf students as students who experience language difficulties," "deaf students as normal students," and "Deaf students as Deaf people") in complex and often contradictory ways (Gascón-Ramos, 2005).

Meanwhile, the Deaf community is calling for a form of bilingual education where sign language, in addition to being used as a tool for communication and learning, is treated as a

Table 15.3. Important Developments in Spain, Many of Which Can Be Attributed to the Work of the Deaf People's Movement

Date	Development
1987	Creation of the first interpretation service and the organization of training for interpreters (carried out by the CNSE)
1990	The first linguistics research paper on LSE presented and published by the CNSE (Rodríguez, 1992), which constitutes a fundamental reference for later linguistic investigations
1992	The first of several congresses organized by the Deaf people's movement, titled "Our Identity," offering a linguistic and cultural perspective of the Deaf community
1993	Signing of a charter of collaboration between the CNSE and the Ministry for Education to incorporate Deaf Advisors and LSE interpreters in schools
1995	Creation of the title of Advanced Expert in Sign Language Interpretation, including the corresponding minimum educational requirements for the job definition
1995 to the present	Parliamentary debates with respect to Sign Language held by several Autonomous Communities; in some Autonomous Communities, start of television stations broadcasting programs in which Deaf people's level of involvement is significant
1998 to the present	Creation and publication of a large amount of LSE teaching materials (curricula, dictionaries, etc.) by the CNSE
2003	Publication of the "Libro Blanco de la Lengua de Signos en el Sistema Educativo Español" (The White Paper of Sign Language in the Spanish School System)
2006	LSE curricula proposed for preschools and for the primary and secondary school levels of compulsory education
2007	Approval of the Bill 27/2007, October 23rd for the recognition of Spanish Sign Language and regulate the resources for oral communication aids for Deaf, Hearing Impaired, and Deaf and Blind People

vehicle for the transmission of the cultural heritage of this minority group and as a guarantee for the recognition of the rights of Deaf people (CNSE, 2002, 2004; Ladd, 2003). From this point of view, a new way of looking at Deaf students and a better understanding of their learning processes become necessary (some authors allude to a "pedagogy of Deafness" or a "pedagogy of the Other" (Ladd & West, 2004; Skliar, 2003). Hence, calls have been made for a more extensive incorporation of Deaf people in teaching environments as well as for the application of training mechanisms that would shine light on hearing teachers' implicit ideas and beliefs. Some authors go still further and suggest it may be necessary for hearing teachers to undergo a process of resocialization in the Deaf community. This new socialization, which focuses on hearing teachers' interacting and establishing some sort of connection with the Other (in this case, Deaf people), would be vital for learning about and grasping, or interiorizing, the ways in which Deaf people behave, think, and feel. It is only with this sort of deep understanding that a real adjustment to the needs of Deaf children and young people can be achieved.

One of the most recent developments in the context of bilingual education, the product of a collaboration agreement between the Ministry for Education and the CNSE, is the "Propuesta Curricular de la Lengua de Signos Española para las Etapas Educativas de Infantil, Primaria y Secundaria Obligatoria" (Curricula Proposals for Spanish Sign Language at the Preschool, Primary and Secondary Levels of Compulsory Education) (CNSE, 2006). Incorporating sign language in the education of Deaf students implies that, in addition to its being used as a tool for communication and learning in the classroom, it will be considered as an object of study and analysis, a situation that will require its being granted academic and curricular status similar to those of other languages. That is, it will be necessary to consider sign language as a curricular subject. Objectives, content, and assessment criteria have been defined for each educational level (preschool, primary, and secondary) and have a structure similar to the rest of the subjects in the national curriculum. The proposal is a guide that will allow teachers to organize teaching and learning processes and activities, thus becoming a foremost instrument for the linguistic normalization of LSE.

STATUS OF DEAF ADULTS

The number of people with hearing loss in Spain is nearing 1 million, which is 2.3% of the total population. About 90,000 of those people (10%) have early, profound deafness, and approximately 30% of the hearing impaired population are of working age (see Table 15.4). In 1999, the employment and unemployment rates of the hearing impaired were better than those for handicapped people in general; however, their employment levels are still far behind those of the general population (see Table 15.5).

One of the CNSE's main objectives is to try to reduce these differences in employment and unemployment rates by promoting deaf people's equal access to jobs, and they have developed policies as well as effective training and employment measures to this end. Between 2000 and 2003, the CNSE, through the *Servicio de Intermediación Laboral para Personas Sordas* (SILPES, or Job Services for Deaf People), carried out a study that allows for a better understanding of the labor situation of deaf adults. SILPES has provided services to 17,000 people— 52% men and 48% women—and has secured work contracts for more than 4,000 of these, the majority in small and medium-sized enterprises.

Table 15.4. The Hearing Impaired Population by Gender and Age Group

	6-24 years	25-64 years	64 and older	Total by Gender
Men	18,706	133,440	268,678	420,824
Women	14,696	129,027	396,944	540,667
Total by Age Group	33,402	262,467	665,622	961,491

Source: INE, Encuesta de Discapacidades, Deficiencias y Estado de Salud (Survey of Handicaps, Impairments and Health Status), 1999.

The people who used SILPES's job services were between the ages of 25 and 45. This fact indicates that, generally, deaf people join the job market at a later age; only 28% of SILPES clients were younger than the age of 25 years. This late incorporation is mainly the result of educational difficulties this group faces when they are of school age, difficulties that imply their having less competitive curricula vitae on entering the job market. The study also found that 51% of the people who used SILPES's services did so to receive additional, complementary training that would make it possible for them to improve their performance in their current posts, while 41% did so to look for a new job.

The situation cannot be considered very positive when one observes, for example, that of the 17,000 deaf people in the study, 25% had no work experience at all and 37% had less than 2 years of experience. Nevertheless, the majority of people under the age of 25 who participated in training workshops ended up finding work in a relatively short amount of time. At the other extreme is the deaf group of those who are 45 and older, who participated the least in training programs and of whom only 12% were later hired.

SECONDARY AND POSTSECONDARY OPPORTUNITIES

One of the main reasons for the Deaf community's lower insertion rate in the job market and for their being predominantly employed in unskilled labor posts is the scant training available to them as a group: of the total 290,647 Deaf people between the ages of 10 and 64 in Spain, 28.51% have no studies, 41.78% have completed primary school, 20.14% have completed secondary school, 5.50% have vocational training, and 4.06% have university studies.

The group's lower level of education means that approximately two-thirds of all Deaf applicants hold only a scholastic certificate (primary level) or a general education or elemen-

Table 15.5. Employment and Unemployment Rates in the Deaf Population, the Handicapped Population, and the General Population for People of Legal Age for Working

Population Category	Employment Rate			Unemployment Rate		
	Men	Women	Total	Men	Women	Total
Deaf	57.2	32.8	45.4	15.0	28.7	19.8
Handicapped	40.6	23.7	32.3	22.1	33.1	26.1
General Population	65.9	40.7	52.9	10.7	22.5	15.3

Note: The term *deaf* refers here to any degree of auditory loss; the term *handicapped* refers to all disabilities except deafness.

tary baccalaureate degree (secondary level). The CNSE, the Confederación Española de Padres y Amigos de Sordos (FIAPAS, or Spanish Confederation of Parents and Friends of the Deaf), and other associations recognize that the typical Deaf person's level of educational achievement is generally low. One of several causes that determine this low level of achievement is the small and indeed insufficient number of specialists to be found in schools.

The majority of training activities are developed by the Ministry for Education and other associations. The CNSE, for example, has developed 500-hour courses to train Deaf people as LSE teachers within the framework of European agreements. It likewise offers 400-hour courses for the training of Deaf Advisors in collaboration with the National Employment Institute. Currently, a number of public universities have identified the training of deaf people older than the age of 25 as a priority. One example that could be cited is that of the Universidad Autónoma de Madrid, which offers a course designed to develop the skills necessary for deaf students to successfully complete their university entrance exams. Signed agreements also exist between the Universidad Complutense de Madrid and the Universidad de Sevilla to train LSE teachers and to promote and improve the image of LSE. There is likewise a masters degree in Audiovisual Translation, Captions for the Hearing Impaired, and Self Description from the Universidad Las Palmas de Gran Canarias, which is designed to provide university-level training to deaf people.

Despite the above-mentioned efforts, Deaf people's integration in the Spanish university system is clearly insufficient. Only one in four hearing impaired people have university studies (the percentage among the profoundly deaf is 1%). The majority of these studies are in the Universidad Nacional de Educación a Distancia (National University for Distance Learning). Associations and others involved affirm that distance learning should not be the only alternative available to students because it limits their integration. The most important problems facing deaf university students are mobility, access to information, and tutoring. The nearly 1,000 deaf students enrolled this year in Spanish universities have made demands for more interpreters and more resources such as recorded class lessons and other support materials.

It is difficult to establish the exact number of hearing impaired people in Spanish universities because many of them (with the exception of the profoundly deaf) prefer not to make their audiological condition known, despite the fact that doing so can entitle them to the waiving of their tuition fees and open access to other types of public scholarships and aid. In any case, the openings set aside for handicapped students in universities (3% of total openings) are almost never completely filled.

PREPARATION OF SPECIAL PERSONNEL

The teaching of the deaf requires the presence of qualified professionals, but training for such personnel is seriously lacking in Spain. Some decades ago, there existed the post of "teacher of the deaf"—generally a teacher who received specific training to teach deaf students at a primary school level (at the time, these students were usually enrolled in special education schools). Currently, preschool and primary school teachers are trained in an Educational Studies program with a specialization in auditory studies and language (there are no specific programs in place to train teachers who wish to work with Deaf students. Training in auditory studies and language for teachers at the university level is generalized and not specific to the education of Deaf students). Professional teachers therefore find themselves faced with the need for supplementary, self-organized training, which is not regulated in any way. With respect to secondary education, no formal training for the specialized teaching of the deaf exists.

The participation of deaf education specialists in the classroom depends on school organization and academic level. At the preschool and primary school levels, the main specialists are the special education teachers and the auditory and language teachers. When working in integrated schools, the latter should be skilled in alternative systems of communication, in signing, and in intervention and rehabilitation methods for hearing and language impairments.

At the secondary school level, the teacher of each particular subject is in the lead teaching role, and he or she is assisted by an interpreter and a teacher's aide. The LSE interpreter is a qualified, two-way interpreter of LSE and oral speech. Under no circumstances does the interpreter take on a teaching role, although he or she does participate in school meetings (such as faculty meetings, tutoring sessions, departmental orientation sessions, and departmental didactic meetings).

The specialists present in classes in special schools for the Deaf are the special education teacher and the auditory and language teacher previously mentioned. The presence of two staff members, who share the responsibility for the education of their Deaf students, is required for combined or joint bilingual programs. For this method of teaching to function satisfactorily, the two staff members, each of whom has equal professional status, must put forth a significant cooperative effort.

Recent years have witnessed a slow but steady increase in the number of Deaf people carrying out educational work in schools. Some work as teachers, others as what are called "Deaf Advisers." The advisers act as adult "educational models" for Deaf students as well as for their families and the hearing teachers in charge of their education. Another important function of the advisers consists of promoting and supporting the use of LSE, both by teaching students directly and by training their families and teachers. The bilingual education model requires the inclusion of posts that have not yet been incorporated in the Spanish school system, for example, LSE teachers—specialists who teach students about the linguistic aspects of LSE (lexicon, phonology, morphology, syntax, semantics, and pragmatics) in a manner similar to that in which oral language is taught to the hearing students. Knowledge of the structures by which LSE is organized and of the laws that govern such structures is the focus of a new discipline called signolinguistics—a discipline that is poorly developed in Spain.

SPECIAL LAWS

In Spain, as in many European countries, legislative initiatives exist that recognize the need to offer deaf children the opportunity to learn sign language. One such initiative can be found in the text of the Real Decreto (Royal Decree) 696/1995 of April 28, by which the Educational Administration supported the recognition and study of LSE and its use in schools. The same year saw the establishment of the Advanced Degree for Spanish Sign Language Interpretation Experts by the Real Decreto 2060/1995, the passing of which represented the formal recognition of a professional figure whose role has already become consecrated at the levels in the educational system to which it corresponds.

Another relevant event was the publication of a report by the Ministry for Education and Culture in the Boletín Oficial de las Cortes Generales del Senado (Official Bulletin of the

General Courts of the Senate) on September 24, 1999. This report included, among others, measures for the elaboration of LSE curricula and the development of specific didactic material. Complementing this report, the Ministry of Education signed a collaboration agreement with the CNSE in 1994 to improve the education of Deaf students. A product of this collaborative framework was the publication of "The White Paper of Spanish Sign Language in the Educational System," a document that describes basic approaches for the elaboration of Spanish Sign Language curricula, namely, guidelines for objectives and contents, methodology, and evaluation approaches. It also includes the first proposed curriculum for the teaching of the Deaf, which has provided the groundwork for ideas currently being introduced.

In any case, the most relevant initiative of recent times came with the announcement from the Council of Ministers of the approval—in a meeting held on September 16, 2005—of the *Proposed Bill for the Recognition of Spanish Sign Language and the Regulation of the Right to Learn, Know and Use It, and for the Establishment and Guaranteeing of Resources for Oral Communication Aids for Deaf, Hearing Impaired and Deaf and Blind People.* This law, whose parliamentary processing is nearing completion, has been well received by the most important groups representing this minority group and their families, specifically the Comité Español de Representantes de Personas con Discapacidad (Spanish Committee of Representatives of Handicapped People), whose members include the CNSE and FIAPAS. The calls that these organizations made in the past to fill the normative gaps with respect to the Deaf appear to have been "heard" by the competent authorities. Note the reaction of Luis Cañón (2006), president of the CNSE, when he heard about the law: "This new law represents the greatest accomplishment ever achieved by Deaf people in our country, and it will place us in the vanguard of Europe."

This initiative is the cornerstone on which the first Spanish law related to LSE and resources for oral communication aids in the Deaf community will be built. It is an anxiously awaited step that the Deaf movement has long been demanding. Indeed, it is quite an ambitious bill whose dispositions will be applied to all areas of Deaf people's lives. It will contribute to a more complete integration of Deaf people in society (a) by promoting measures that will adequately provide for their incorporation in the job market; (b) by strengthening their participation in cultural and political life; (c) by facilitating their access to a university education, to judicial protection, to the health care system, to means of social communication, and to the new technologies that form part of the Knowledge-Based Society (the Internet, mobile phones, and land-based digital television services); and (d) by facilitating their interaction with the Public Administration (Romero, 2006).

CURRENT DEVELOPMENTS AND TRENDS

In Spain, various debates, both long-standing and recent, with respect to the Deaf community exist and remain unresolved. The majority of these are related to the concept of deafness itself (medical-pathological versus sociolinguistic perspectives). The oldest and most dominant is the medical-pathological perspective, which understands deafness to be an abnormality requiring correction and curing through oral rehabilitation. In recent decades, the sociolinguistic perspective has gained force, placing "the Deaf issue" in an intercultural or multicultural context rather than a context of handicap. Both trends can be found in Spain at the present time.

The social status of LSE in Spain has still not achieved the level of social recognition it has in some other European countries. Nevertheless, changes have taken place in the last decade that have resulted in a wider use of LSE among those who are Deaf and those who are hearing in different environments. These changes are also reflected in a heightened awareness in Spanish society of the needs and demands of the Deaf community. As a result, one of the most urgent challenges is that of linguistic planning to obtain not only legal and social status for LSE but also its application in educational and, especially, family environments.

The use of cochlear implants and other technologies beginning at an early age is a strategy that has gained strong support as an alternative to bilingual solutions. The principle of the "period of sensitivity" to language (applied indiscriminately at times) has led many families to opt for cochlear implants as an ideal means of immersion in one's dominant oral language and of connection to the hearing environment. Despite the advantages of these new technologies, two words of caution with respect to cochlear implants should be mentioned. The first relates to the effectiveness of such devices and the difficulties that may arise from their prolonged and indiscriminate use (as of yet there are no data to prove the absence of serious long-term side effects). The second is that although these technical resources are helpful for many deaf people, they do not reestablish hearing.

It is the opinion of the authors that, with respect to the communication and education of Deaf people, it is necessary to advance toward a nonrestrictive philosophy—toward models in which technological advances can coexist with the "solutions" that Deaf people have created over time (namely, their language and their culture). It is impossible to deny that an underlying conflict of cultural values exists and that, for some, the search for a "balanced" position may seem ingenuous, if not superficial. Nevertheless, today's Deaf children, as future citizens of an ever more multicultural and open society, need to have diverse strategies at their disposal that will allow them to participate actively and creatively in the construction of society. And it is the responsibility of all, of Deaf and hearing alike, to help turn this need into reality.

Spain finds itself poised on the brink of an historic moment. A new horizon is unfolding that, ideally, will allow those involved to overcome sterile controversies and to consider both technical solutions and a respect for the use, learning, and diffusion of LSE. Once the future law is passed, regulatory mechanisms and mechanisms of application should be established in all Autonomous Communities. It is necessary to create specialized bilingual schools, to train personnel, to provide infrastructures, to create a plan for adequate financing, and to carry out other measures such as the creation of a Center for the Normalization of Sign Language and a Spanish Center for Subtitling.

REFERENCES

Alcina, A. (2005, January 10). 200 años de enseñanza para alumnos sordos en Madrid [200 years of teaching deaf students in Madrid]. *El País.*

Alegria, J. (1999). La lectura en el niño sordo: Elementos para una discusión [Reading in deaf children: Elements for a discussion]. In A. B. Domínguez & C. Velasco (Eds.), *Lenguaje escrito y sordera. Enfoques teóricos y derivaciones prácticas* (pp. 59–76). Salamanca: Publicaciones de la Universidad Pontificia de Salamanca.

Alegria, J. (2003). Deafness and reading. In T. Nunes & P. Bryant (Eds.), *Handbook of children's literacy* (pp.459–489). Dordrecht: Kluwer Academic.

Alonso, P., Domínguez, A. B., Rodríguez, P., & Saint-Patrice, J. (2001). El acceso al código alfabético en los niños sordos: Papel de la palabra complementada en un modelo educativo bilingüe [The accessing of the alphabetic code in deaf children: The role of cued speech in bilingual educational models]. *Revista de Logopedia, Foniatría y Audiología, 21*(4), 181–187.

Alonso, P., & Echeita, G. (2006). Barreras para el aprendizaje y la participación de los alumnos sordos [Barriers to learning and participation for deaf students]. In V. Acosta (Ed.), *La sordera desde la diversidad cultural y lingüística.* Barcelona: Masson.

Álvarez, M., Juncos, O., Caamaño, A., Justo, M. J., Costa, M. J., Fernández, C., & Quintans, M. (2002). Adquisición temprana de la sintaxis en lengua de signos española (LSE) [Early acquisition of syntax in Spanish Sign Language (LSE)]. *Revista de Logopedia, Foniatría y Audiología, 22*(3), 157–162.

Ardanuy, M. (1998). Escuela Josep Pla, Barcelona [Josep Pla School, Barcelona]. In A.P.A.N.S.C.E. *Experiencias bilingües en la educación del niño sordo.* Barcelona: Ediciones Mayo.

Bellés, R. (1998). Dactilología y escritura en niños y niñas sordos pequeños [Fingerspelling and writing in young deaf boys and girls]. Lecture presented at the II International Encounter on the Acquisition of State Languages, Barcelona.

Bonet, J. P. (1620). *Reducción de las Letras y Arte para Enseñar a Hablar a los Mudos* [The reduction of letters and the arts for teaching the mute to read]. Madrid: n.p.

Caamaño, A., Juncos, O., Justo, M. J., López, E., & Vilar, A. (1999). Gestos y signos en la transición a los enunciados de dos elementos en lengua de signos española [Gestures and signs in the transition to two-element enunciations in Spanish Sign Language]. *Revista de Logopedia, Foniatría y Audiología, 29*(4), 184–189.

Cañón, L. J. (2006, April 26). Speech in the Spanish Congress. *Sessions log.*

CNSE. (2002). *Guía para la educación bilingüe para niños y niñas sordos* [Guide for the bilingual education of deaf boys and girls]. Madrid: Author.

CNSE. (2004). *Libro Blanco de la Lengua de Signos Española en el sistema educativo* [The White Paper of Spanish Sign Language in the school system]. Madrid: Author.

CNSE. (2006). *Propuestas curriculares orientativas de la Lengua de Signos Española para las etapas educativas de infantil, primaria y secundaria obligatoria* [Orientational curricula proposals for Spanish Sign Language at the preschool, primary and secondary levels of compulsory education]. Madrid: Author.

Díaz-Estébanez, E., & Valmaseda, M. (1995). En el camino hacia una educación de calidad para los alumnos y alumnas sordos [On the path to quality education for deaf students]. *Infancia y Aprendizaje, 69–70,* 45–61.

Domínguez, A. B., Alonso, P., & Rodríguez, P. (2003). "¿Se puede enseñar conocimiento fonológico a los niños sordos? [Can phonological knowledge be taught to deaf children?]. *Infancia y Aprendizaje, 26,* 485–501.

Escuela Infantil Piruetas. (2002). Escuela Infantil Piruetas: Niños sordos y oyentes compartiendo la vida [Piruetas Preschool: Deaf and hearing children sharing life]. *Aula de Educación Infantil, 5,* 42–45.

Gascón-Ramos, M. (2005). *Laying the foundations for well-being in deaf children: Exploring professional roles in the delivery of deaf bilingual-bicultural education.* Unpublished doctoral diss., University of Bristol, United Kingdom.

Gascón-Ricao, A. (2004). Las cifras de la mano de Francisco de Goya. *Separata del Boletín del Museo e Instituto "Camón Aznar," 82,* 273–284.

Gascón Ricao, A., & Storch, J. G. (2004). *Historia de la educación de los sordos en España* [The History of deaf education in Spain]. Madrid: Editorial Universitaria Ramón Areces.

González de Ibarra, J., & Molins, E. (1998). CEIPM TresPins, Barcelona. In A.P.A.N.S.C.E. *Experiencias bilingües en la educación del niño sordo* [Bilingual experiences in the education of a deaf child]. Barcelona: Ediciones Mayo.

Gunther, K. B. (1996). The role of the manual alphabet in deaf education in the 16th/17th century.

In R. Fisher & T. Vollhaber (Eds.), *Colalle: Works on international deaf history* (pp. 107–116). Hamburg: Signum.

Hervás, L. (1795a). *Escuela española de sordos o arte para enseñar a escribir y hablar el idioma español* [The Spanish School for the Deaf or art for the teaching of writing and speaking Spanish]. Vol. 1. Madrid: Imprenta Real.

Hervás, L. (1795b). *Escuela española de sordos o arte para enseñar a escribir y hablar el idioma español* [The Spanish School for the Deaf or art for the teaching of writing and speaking Spanish]. Vol. 2. Madrid: Fermín de Villalpando.

Instituto Nacional de Estadística (INE; National Institute of Statistics). (2005). Encuesta sobre discapacidad, deficiencias y estado de salud [Survey on handicaps, impairments and health status], 1999. Madrid: Author.

Justo, M., Juncos, O. Caamaño, A., Vilar, A., & López, E. (1999). Características del "input" que reciben los niños pequeños de sus padres sordos [Characteristics of the input small children receive from deaf parents]. *Revista de Logopedia, Foniatría y Audiología, 19,* 11–18.

Ladd, P. (2003). *Understanding deaf culture. In search of deafhood.* Clevedon: Multilingual Matters.

Ladd, P., & West, D. (2004). Seeing through new eyes. Bristol, United Kingdom: University of Bristol. Retrieved August 7, 2008, from http://www.bris.ac.uk/deaf/downloads/summary03.pdf.

Las Heras, T. (1999). La educación de las alumnas y alumnos sordos [The education of deaf students]. *Aula de Innovación Educativa, 83–84,* 13–14.

Leybaert, J., & Alegría, J. (2002). The role of cued speech in the language development of deaf children. In M. Marschark & P. E. Spencer (Eds.), *Handbook of deaf studies, language and education* (pp. 261–275). New York: Oxford University Press.

Llombart, C. (1991). *De 1800 al CREDAC "Pere Barnils": Biografía de dos segles d'atentió educativa a l'alumne sord* [From 1800 to CREDA "Pere Barnils": A biography of two centuries of the educational treatment of deaf students]. Barcelona: Generalitat de Catalunya-Ajuntament de Barcelona.

Marchesi, A. (1987). *El desarrollo cognitivo y lingüístico de los niños sordos* [Cognitive and linguistic development in deaf children]. Madrid: Alianza.

Martínez, F. (Ed.). (2000). *Apuntes de lingüística de la Lengua de Signos Española* [Linguistics notes for Spanish Sign Language]. Madrid: CNSE.

Minguet, A. (Ed.). (2001). *Signolingüística. Introducción a la lingüística de la LSE* [Signo-Linguistics. An introduction to LSE linguistics]. Valencia: FESORD.

Moores, D. (2001). *Educating the deaf: Psychology, principles, and practices.* Boston: Houghton Mifflin.

Muñoz, I. (1999). *¿Cómo se articula la Lengua de Signos Española?* [How is Spanish Sign Language articulated?]. Madrid: CNSE.

Oviedo, A. (2006). *España y los inicios de la educación de los sordos* [Spain and the beginnings of deaf education]. Retrieved August 7, 2007, from http://www.cultura-sorda.eu.

Plann, S. (1992). Roberto Prádez: Sordo, primer profesor de sordos [Roberto Prádez: Deaf man, first professor of the deaf]. *Revista Complutense de Educación, 3*(1–2), 238–262.

Plann. S. (1997). *A silent minority: Deaf education in Spain, 1550–1835.* Los Angeles, CA: University of California Press.

Puente, A., Alvarado, J., & Herrera, V. (2006). Fingerspelling and sign language as alternative codes for reading and writing words for Chilean deaf signers. *American Annals of the Deaf, 151*(3), 299–310.

Rodríguez, M. A. (1992). *Lenguaje de Signos* [Sign Language]. Madrid: CNSE-ONCE.

Rodríguez, P. (1998). Instituto Hispano-Americano de la Palabra Madrid [Hispano-American Institute of Words, Madrid]. In A.P.A.N.S.C.E. (Coord.), *Experiencias bilingües en la educación del niño sordo* [Bilingual experiences in the education of a deaf child] (pp. 39–56). Barcelona: Ediciones Mayo.

Rodríguez, P. (2006). El bilingüismo en la educación de los alumnos sordos [Bilingualism in the education of deaf students]. In V. Acosta (Ed.), *La sordera desde la diversidad cultural y lingüística.* Barcelona: Masson.

Rodríguez, P., Domínguez, A. B., & Alonso, P. (in preparation). Conocimiento fonológico y lectura: un estudio longitudinal con alumnos sordos en un centro educativo bilingüe [Phonological knowledge and reading: A longitudinal study of deaf students in a bilingual school].

Romero G. A. (2006). Breve comentario sobre el Anteproyecto de Ley de la Lengua de Signos Española y de apoyo a la comunicación oral para las personas sordas o con discapacidad auditiva y sordociegas [Brief commentary on the proposed bill regarding Spanish Sign Language and oral support for the deaf, hearing impaired and the deaf and blind]. *Boletín jurídico.* Retrieved on December 16, 2008, from http://www.derecho.com/articulos/2006/01/01/breve-comentario-sobre-el-anteproyecto-de-ley-de-la-lengua-de-signos-espa-ola-y-de-apoyo/.

Sanjuán, M., & Pérez-García, M. (2005). Proyecto de integración "inclusiva" de niños sordos en educación infantil ["Inclusive" integration project for deaf children in preschools]. *Monografías para el debate, 1,* 47–57.

Santana, R. Torres, S., & García, J. (2003). The role of cued speech in the development of Spanish prepositions. *American Annals of the Deaf, 148*(4), 323–332.

Skliar, C. (2003). ¿Y si el otro no estuviera ahí? Notas para una pedagogía (improbable) de la diferencia [What if the other weren't there? Notes for an (improbable) pedagogy of difference]. Buenos Aires: Miño y Dávila.

Torres, S., Moreno-Torres, I., & Santana, R. (2006). Qualitative and quantitative evaluation of linguistic input support to a prelingually deaf child with cued speech: A case study. *Journal of Deaf Study and Deaf Education, 11*(4), 438–448.

VVAA. (2001). *Actas del I Congreso Nacional de la LSE . Estudios sobre la Lengua de Signos Española* [Acts of the I National LSE Congress. Studies on Spanish Sign Language]. Alicante, Spain: CNSE.

The Situation for the Deaf in Sweden

Gunilla Preisler

ONE OF the human rights, stated by the United Nations, is to have access to a language. The Convention on the Rights of the Child declares that the child's right to a language is to be especially attended to (United Nations, 1989). In December 1993, the United Nations General Assembly approved standard rules to ensure full participation and equality for people with functional disabilities. These rules specifically state that, in relation to deaf children, the use of sign language in education, within the family, and in the society ought to be considered. It is also stated that sign language interpreters ought to be accessible to facilitate communication between hearing and deaf people. Children who are deaf and deaf-blind are considered to have special needs in communication, and therefore, their education can be better provided in special schools or special classes or in special units in the ordinary school. The right to have a language is also stated in the Swedish constitution dated 1974.

In 1981, the Swedish Parliament acknowledged sign language as the official language of deaf people in a new law that became a turning point in the history of the deaf in Sweden. It had been preceded by intensive studies of sign language (Bergman, 1978), language development in deaf children (Ahlgren, 1978), learning processes and personality development in deaf children (Nordén, Preisler, Heiling, Hülphers, & Tvingstedt, 1981), and early patterns of communication in deaf children (Preisler, 1983). The different studies showed that

- sign language possessed all the properties characteristic of a true language, however expressed and processed in modalities different from speech; and
- children with early sign language experience showed more positive development in language learning, in personality development, and in social development than children who experienced sign language later, often after having failed in accomplishing comprehensible speech production and speech perception.

Representatives from sign language users—The Swedish National Association of the Deaf; the National Association of the Hard of Hearing; and the National Association of Parents of Deaf, Hard of Hearing, and Speech Impaired Children played a very important role in launching the new law. Years of oral/aural training of deaf children had shown little progress. But the resistance toward sign language had been intense among pediatricians, technicians, and educators. Sign language was considered a hindrance to learning to talk and hear. But finally, after years of struggle, sign language was finally acknowledged as the language of deaf people (Mahshie, 1995).

Ten years later, in 1991, the first cochlear implantation in a deaf child was made in Sweden. In 2007, approximately 90% of deaf children in Sweden received an implant, many of them bilaterally. Sign language is recommended for these children, but the main focus in habilitation is once again on speech perception and speech production as well as auditory perception and stimulation.

Thus, the situation for deaf children has changed in a very short period of time because of this new technical device. To understand more about the present and the future situation for deaf people, we might learn from the past. The following section will present a brief history of the situation for deaf people in Sweden during the last 200 years, which might be helpful in understanding and explaining the situation they are facing today.

THE HISTORY OF DEAF EDUCATION IN SWEDEN

The First School for the Deaf

In the beginning of the 19th century, Pär Aron Borg, a clerk in need of new employment, started to teach blind and deaf pupils. He had been inspired by the teaching methods of Abbé Charles-Michel de l'Epée in France. Borg started the first school for the deaf in Sweden, the Manilla School, situated just outside Stockholm, the capital of Sweden. This school represented the first effort to provide deaf children any formal education in the country. (Compulsory school education for hearing children did not start until 1840.) Borg and his teachers, some of whom were deaf, used sign language with their deaf pupils, but also reading, writing, and speech. He constructed a Swedish manual alphabet for the deaf students that was inspired by the Epée's manual alphabet. Borg's idea was to give deaf students opportunities to learn different work-related skills so they could earn their own living. The vocational training was primarily related to manufacturing and included tailoring, shoe making, sewing, and weaving. It was not considered possible to educate the deaf students in any theoretical subject. A second school for the deaf was founded in 1875 in Örebro, a city in the southern middle part of the country. This city has since become a central place for education of the deaf.

Teachers from these schools for the deaf traveled to other schools in Europe to learn more about educating deaf students. Many of them were influenced by the German method, (i.e., the oral method). This method of teaching the deaf was gradually introduced in the two existing schools for the deaf at the time. The rationale for using this strictly oral method of teaching was to make the deaf children "normal."

Teacher Training

Borg remained headmaster of the Manilla school until his death in 1839. He was succeeded by his son Ossian. Ossian Borg saw the need for qualified teachers of the deaf and started a teacher training program in 1874 at the Manilla school. But this education was not accessible to deaf students. Disabled people were not considered to have the necessary abilities to educate deaf pupils. Ironically, however, there were deaf teachers instructing the pupils in different handicrafts. It was not until the end of the 1970s that deaf people were admitted to formal teacher training at the Stockholm Institute of Education.

The teacher training program emphasized morals and character building of the deaf pupils. The instructors took a patriarchal view of leadership; the unquestioned nature of power and the hierarchical structure of society were key themes in the texts from this education program (Domfors, 2000).

After the Milan Congress in 1880, the oral method of educating deaf students was introduced all over Europe. Many of the Swedish and the American delegates opposed the oral method, but it became the accepted method in teaching deaf pupils in most schools from that time until well into the 20th century.

School Education Becomes Compulsory for the "Deaf and Dumb"

In 1889, a new law called "The Education of the Deaf and Dumb" was introduced. The law made education compulsory for deaf children. Regional schools had to provide an 8-year school education. This education could be provided through speech only, by speech and writing in combination, or in special cases, by the sign method. The children were sorted in groups, A, B, and C, depending on their auditory and intellectual capacities. However, because there were no objective instruments to measure auditory perception or intelligence at this time, the differentiation was highly subjective. Sign language was used for the children with the poorest auditory capacity, those who were also considered the least intelligent. The method of communication, however, varied between the different schools for the deaf (Nyström, 1990).

The law from 1889 also included statutes for education of the teachers of the deaf. Domfors (2000) writes that

with regard to communication modes, the law was diplomatic, making both competing modes mandatory.

Education imparted at the college, which is mainly theoretical includes the following subjects and exercises: . . .

   d) of manual communication, its origins, development and use in education;
   e) of the speech tools including manners and orders of bringing forth the speech sounds.
      (p. 245)

Thus, Swedish sign language never disappeared completely from education of the deaf. It has always been used to teach low-performing pupils.

Until the beginning of the 20th century, deaf people had been able to work in municipalities, the county councils, and the state government. But at the beginning of the 20th century, they were no longer allowed to do so. As a result, deaf people who had worked as teachers in the special schools for the deaf had to leave their jobs.

The Idea of Bilingualism Emerges

During the period before the World War I, the school for the deaf in Stockholm received a new director, Johan Prawitz. He was married to a deaf woman. He knew sign language, and he understood that deaf people reacted, both cognitively and emotionally, the same way as a hearing person, although the language was different. Therefore, he became an important person for the education of deaf children for many years. His idea was that the children should be educated in signs and in speech to become bilingual. However, it took half a century until his ideas were fully acknowledged.

The Use of the Oral Method Becomes Intensified

In 1938, the Swedish National Board of Education began to administer centrally the education of deaf children. The value of vocational training was again recognized, and two national vocational schools for the deaf were established (Heiling, 1999). The use of the oral method now became intensified. From the 1930s to the 1960s, a shift occurred in teacher education that stressed the importance of technical devices for improving pupils' achievement (Domfors, 2000). Small-scale research essays and papers, especially related to topics of developmental and differential psychology, appeared for the first time in the Manilla College syllabi. In addition, medical science subjects and expertise became part of the college programs.

Spoken Swedish was the official language at the schools for the deaf, although sign language in combination with written Swedish existed side by side. In the early 1950s, new technical hearing devices and new instruments to measure auditory capacity were constructed. The hope was to improve the situation for deaf people by these refined hearing aids in combination with more intensive oral-aural training. The thought was that speech and hearing would in this way be accessible for them.

During the 1960s, all of the deaf pupils in their eighth year at the special school for the deaf were presented a large test battery consisting of tests in the Swedish language and tests of mathematical and numerical abilities. The results were generally low on most tests, but there were also large individual differences (Nordén, 1975).

In 1968, the Manilla College was closed down. Instead, the education of teachers of the deaf was provided at the Stockholm Institute of Education. Swedish sign language became included in the education of the teachers for the deaf. A new communication rationality started to emerge (Domfors, 2000).

The Importance of Sign Language Reemerges

During the 1970s, parents of deaf children along with psychologists, linguists, and not the least, the organizations of the deaf started to react to the oral-aural approach to teaching deaf children. The children's academic achievements were too poor in comparison with all the efforts made in oral teaching. Instead, the importance of using signs in communication with the children was emphasized. At first, signed Swedish was introduced, later followed by Swedish Sign Language. International and Swedish studies of sign languages had shown that sign language had all the properties of a language. It was no longer considered to be gestures and movements conveying only information about the here and now but was also recognized as a language for communicating abstract thoughts and ideas. Parents of deaf and hard of hearing children now had a growing influence in the planning of education for their children—which had never been the case before.

In the mid-1970s, sign language became popular among hearing children because of a television series for children called *Hands Up*. Sign language was introduced as a "secret" language that children could use among themselves without the knowledge of adults. Thus, many factors cooperated in making sign language accepted as a language: the poor academic achievements of deaf children, studies of sign language, pressure from the parents' organizations for the deaf, and new information and raised awareness among people in the hearing society.

A follow-up study of deaf pupils' academic achievement at the deaf schools 20 years after the Nordén study, showed that the subjects now were superior to their deaf age-mates from the 1960s to the early 1970s in all tests measuring ability to understand and use written Swedish (Heiling, 1995). The students also performed significantly better on tests of mathematical and numerical ability, but the difference was more pronounced in the tests measuring language proficiency.

During the 1980s and 1990s, a medical view on functional disabilities gradually changed to a more political question of inclusion and participation in the society. That change took place not only in Sweden but also in the other Scandinavian countries. The question of care, treatment, and training was transformed into questions of similar rights to participate in public life (SOU: 1982, 19).

Organizations for Deaf and Hard of Hearing People

Different organizations of the deaf and hard of hearing started early and they have played an important role in creating better living conditions for the deaf and hard of hearing population from childhood and onward. In 1868, Ossian Borg started an organization called the Deaf and Dumb Organization, together with two deaf people. From its beginning, that organization was a local assembly for the deaf community in Stockholm. One of their goals was to function as a bank for deaf people who were sick or had to pay for a funeral. From having been a local institution, it became a national organization in 1922. The goal now was primarily to promote the interests of the deaf community, to give advice and information to the deaf community about their rights, to give information to others about the situation for deaf people in the hearing society, and to promote higher education for deaf people. Members changed the organization's name in 1950 to the Swedish National Association of the Deaf (Sveriges Dövas Riksförbund, or SDR).

In 1921, a new organization for the hard of hearing was started. It was first called the Association for the Well-Being of the Deaf. Members have changed names several times since then and now call the organization The National Association of the Hard of Hearing (Hörselskadades Riksförbund). One of the main goals of this organization has been to promote the use of hearing aids among hard of hearing people. Members have also been active in initiating the establishment of preschools and schools with a high technological standard for children who are hearing impaired. In 1970, the first organization for parents of hard of hearing children and adolescents was started. During the 1970s, the parents also became very active in advocating the use of sign language in education.

In 1995, another parents' organization was started. Members are primarily parents of children with cochlear implants. Those parents found it important to form a new organization. One of their main issues concerns the school education of their children. Many of them believe that the special schools for the deaf are not giving these children an appropriate education in spoken Swedish.

CURRENT ACADEMIC PLACEMENT

Population Data

Approximately 100,000 children are born in Sweden each year. According to official statistics, approximately 200 children are born deaf or with such a severe hearing impairment that they are in need of hearing devices; the need for habilitation is considered if the hearing status in the best ear is less than 40 dB within the frequency area of 0.5–4 kHz. Between 70 and 75 children of these children are born deaf. The total population of people born deaf or severely hearing impaired is estimated to be 9,000, and another 4,000 have become deaf as adults; at the end of 2006, the Swedish population consisted of a little more than 9 million people. As in most other western countries, 95% of deaf children have hearing parents. Neonatal screening using oto-acoustic emission, has been introduced in most maternal hospitals. As a result, diagnosis is made at a very early age, 1–2 months.

Preschool and School Education

There are on average two deaf pupils in each of the 290 municipalities in the country. Thus, it is not possible for a single municipality to keep up a high academic competence in educating deaf children. Instead, there are several special preschools or special groups for deaf and hard of hearing children that are placed throughout the country. Sign language and spoken Swedish are used as means to communicate.

For school children, there is a Special School Authority consisting of the six state-run comprehensive schools for the deaf and hearing impaired in the country. Five of them are regional schools and offer an education equivalent to the schools for hearing pupils run by the municipalities. One school offers education for deaf and hard of hearing pupils from all over the country and is directed at pupils who are deaf or severely hard of hearing with a mental developmental disorder and at pupils who are deaf and blind. This education is highly individualized.

In most parts of the country, deaf pupils attending special schools are now able to live at home and commute to school daily by taxi. But it was not long ago that the special schools mainly were boarding schools. In the northern part of the country, a sparsely populated area, many children live too far away from any special school. Instead, they live during the weeks in small groups in villas or flats in residential areas close to the school. Some of them live with private families who often have experience and knowledge of deaf children. All pupils can go home for weekends and school holidays.

In October 2005, there were 549 pupils enrolled in the special schools for the deaf and hard of hearing. That number represents a decrease since the years before, especially for those in the first three school years. There was little decline in numbers of pupils in their fourth year and on. One explanation for this decrease may be that the total number of children born each year has decreased during the end of the 20th century. Another reason may be that there are now at least six other schools or programs for deaf and hard of hearing pupils that are run privately or by municipalities. More than 1,000 pupils are enrolled in these schools or programs, which are adapted to suit the needs of pupils with hearing impairments. A third possible explanation has to do with the increased number of pupils with cochlear implants. Because the implantation is done early, as many of the children start to speak, many parents choose a preschool placement in the municipalities for their child and, later, a school in the neighborhood.

The cost for one pupil in a special school (in 2006) was estimated to be 71,000 Swedish crowns (approximately US$10,000) per year if the pupil lives in the community where the school is located; otherwise, the cost was 207,400 Swedish crowns (approximately US$30,000) per year.

Communication Modes Used in the Schools

The Swedish National Curriculum from the early 1980s states that deaf children should be educated bilingually with Swedish Sign Language as their first language and Swedish in its written form as their second. In this national curriculum for education, it is stated that sign language and Swedish are two separate languages. It is further stated that bilingualism does not emerge spontaneously. Although sign language is learned in a signing environment, Swedish has to be taught. The two languages are said to fulfill different functions. Sign language is the primary instrument for acquiring knowledge and for communicating with other signing people, but Swedish is learned by reading and writing. Some years later, a supplement to the national curriculum was published, which stated that deaf children are dependent on sign language communication and need to get access to sign language from an early age to avoid being seriously language delayed.

Because 9 of 10 deaf children are born in families where all the other members of the family are hearing, parents and siblings are urged to attend sign language courses. A special 240-hour course of sign language is offered to parents free of charge. During the period 2002–2006, on average, almost 800 parents per year attended these courses. Courses for siblings are also arranged by several organizations for the deaf, by the special schools, and by the county councils.

Curriculum

Since 1994, there has been a National Curriculum for *all* children attending school in Sweden. It is the first time that all schools have a common curriculum with the same goals, the same common value system, and the same responsibilities. A certain adaptation of educational goals has been made to provide for the special needs of deaf children.

The differences between the regional schools for the deaf and hard of hearing and the schools for hearing children can be summarized as follows:

- Education is in sign language, speech in a sign language environment, or both.
- Education is offered in a special additional subject: sign language.
- Education continues for 10 years instead of 9.
- Education is offered in rhythm and drama instead of in music.
- Education in language, except sign language, is directed at providing the majority of pupils command in language in its written form.

Learning outcomes are the same for deaf children as hearing children for most of the subjects. The exceptions are for sign language, Swedish, English, modern languages, and rhythm-drama. These exceptions have been designed to be used by all the pupils in the special schools.

Secondary and Postsecondary Opportunities

Deaf pupils graduating from the schools for the deaf can proceed to the National Secondary School for the Deaf. This school is situated in Örebro. There, they can choose to study a large number of different subjects with either a theoretical or a vocational orientation. Pupils in the special secondary school attend an extra school year compared with the hearing children.

The teachers are trained as teachers of the deaf and are considered to have a good command of sign language.

Deaf children can also attend separate classes in secondary schools or attend classes with hearing children in the regular school. The pupils are required to follow the same curriculum as the hearing children. Sign language interpreters can be used for some of the children in classes with hearing children.

In the special schools, the number of hard of hearing adolescents is growing as they begin to recognize the importance of sign language to acquire knowledge. When they proceed to higher education, at university level, they choose to have the lessons and seminars interpreted in sign language, if possible.

Studies at the University Level

In 2006, 5,174 students with functional disabilities (those known to the coordinators for students with functional disabilities) were registered at the universities in Sweden. Table 16.1 describes the distribution of students with deafness or with hearing impairments from 1994 to 2006. As the table shows, the number of deaf students who use interpreters increased three times during the period, and the number of hearing impaired students without need of interpreters increased approximately five times during the period.

Table 16.2 describes statistics for male and female students at the universities from 2001 to 2006. Women are in majority in all three groups (deaf with an interpreter, deaf with signing teacher, hard of hearing without an interpreter). Women are also in majority among hearing university students, but the gap between hearing men and women is not as wide as that for deaf students. According to official statistics, there were 58% women and 42% men beginning their university studies in 2003–04.

In the group "Deaf (teachers sign)," hearing signing students are also included. The courses that typically provide a teacher who can sign are in Swedish Sign Language, Swedish as a Second Language, and Sign Language Interpretation. At Stockholm University, there are two professorships in linguistics with a focus on language of the deaf: one in Swedish Sign Language (Professor Brita Bergman) and one in Swedish as a Second Language for the Deaf (Professor Kristina Svartholm). The deaf students attend courses in languages and in natural, technical, and social sciences. At two of the Swedish Universities, there are special courses for deaf and hearing students in Swedish Sign Language and Sign Language Interpretation, where the classes are conducted in sign language.

At the universities, the students can receive sign language interpretation. A law from 2002 concerns similar treatment for all students at university level. The law includes issues such as preventing harassment as well as eliminating direct and indirect discrimination of deaf, hear-

Table 16.1. Number of Undergraduate and Graduate Students at Swedish Universities, 1994–2006

	1994	1995	1996	1997	1998	1999	2000	2001	2002	2003	2004	2005	2006
Deaf with interp.	48	53	87	55	57	68	78	116	109	149	145	134	143
Deaf (teachers sign)	—	—	—	75	60	20	50	8	19	15	15	14	24
Hard of hearing (without interp.)	30	64	92	92	63	81	100	95	119	140	153	168	167

Table 16.2. Number of Female and Male Students With Deafness and Hearing Impairments at Swedish Universities, 2001–2006

	2001		2002		2003		2004		2005		2006	
	F	M	F	M	F	M	F	M	F	M	F	M
Deaf with interp.	84	32	79	30	101	48	93	52	89	45	95	48
Deaf (teachers sign)	7	1	12	7	11	4	10	5	14	0	17	7
Hard of hearing (without interp.)	64	31	83	36	95	45	100	53	108	60	115	52

ing impaired, and deaf-blind students. At Stockholm University, for example, the overall goal is that the university shall fulfill the demands that the law of similar treatment for students prescribes. There is a special unit working with these questions. The objectives of this special unit are

- to ensure that students with functional disabilities such as deafness, hearing impairment and deaf-blindness have access to complete, relevant interpretation services in all situations concerning studies or related situations;
- to offer interpretation services in the teaching of Swedish, English, and Sign Language;
- to offer interpretation services for other languages, if possible;
- to continuously improve the quality of interpretation services to the students in need of such services;
- to assist other seats of learning within the region with relevant interpretation services, at cost, for students enrolled at Stockholm university; and
- to assist employees at Stockholm University with interpretation services when needed.

Similar documents are formulated at other universities in the country. The interpreters can be asked to interpret during lessons and seminars as well as during other formal or informal activities at the university where hearing and deaf students and teachers meet. At present, there are 18 sign language interpreters employed by Stockholm University and 8 employed by the Stockholm Institute of Education.

Since the late 1970s, deaf and hard of hearing students have enrolled in various courses and programs at the Department of Education at Örebro University. Three sign language interpreters are employed by this university.

At Gothenburg University, situated in the second largest city in the country, there are 10 sign language interpreters employed, and Lund University has 7. Lund is situated in a densely populated area in the southern part of the country. Thus, four of the universities situated in areas with a large population have employed interpreters. In areas with sparser populations, there are fewer interpreters available, and the students are required to report their needs before they start their studies.

An increased demand of interpretation and too few interpreters makes it difficult for many deaf students to follow the curriculum at the university level. The general knowledge among university teachers about circumstances for sign language interpretation is low; for example, they are typically unaware (a) of the need to send prepared lessons in advance to the interpreters, (b) of how various technical equipment is used, (c) of how to use a microphone in a classroom setting, (d) of the importance of special seating arrangements for the student to be able to speechread, etc.

There is also a Folk High School for deaf people at Västanvik in Dalekarlia, a small village in the very middle part of the country. This school is owned and run by the Swedish Association for the Deaf. The school could be compared with a college, and it offers theoretical courses of various length and content for deaf adults. The school also offers a large number of sign language courses as well as training programs for interpreters and sign language teachers. The school gives intensive courses in sign language for parents, relatives, or other people working with or for deaf people. They produce video programs in sign language, and the school is a center for the study of deaf history and culture.

There are now plans to start an art school for deaf students. That school will be situated in Örebro. It will be the first sign language art school in Europe.

EMPLOYMENT

It was not long ago when most deaf people were limited to manual work such as that of carpenters, bookbinders, shoemakers, and dressmakers. Today, most deaf pupils find employment after graduation in a wider array of jobs. Approximately 80% of the deaf adult population belong to the work force. They are professionals such as psychologists, social workers, and dentists. Many of them work as teachers for deaf pupils.

CURRENT DEVELOPMENTS AND TRENDS

In our modern society, there has been a radical increase in the use of a wide selection of technological devices such as mobile telephones, video recorders, DVD players, and the World Wide Web, to name just a few. For many deaf people, this technology has enabled them to receive and send information and to acquire knowledge not only in face-to-face interaction but also in other circumstances.

In 2004, the Board of Post and Telecommunication on assignment for the Swedish Government started a project focusing on mobile video communication for people who are deaf. The goal of the project was to investigate how deaf people could benefit from video calls by means of 3G video phones, how well the technology supports sign language communication, and which of various mobile services might be useful to people who are deaf. More than 50 deaf people with sign language skills participated in the project, which was lead by the SDR. Equipped with ordinary 3G telephones and subscriptions, the participants have tested three different services: mobile video communication between people who are deaf; mobile video messages; and a distance interpretation and communications service. The conclusions drawn are that people who are deaf have great use of 3G and mobile video communications. Comments from the participants claimed that the technology was "a revolution for deaf people" and "the biggest thing that has happened in the last hundred years." The primary net gain consisted of being able to use one's first language—sign language—in direct communication by means of a mobile telephone with other sign language users, with hearing people, or with both.

The use of 3G is extensive among people who are deaf. According to the SDR, an estimated 4,000 to 6,000 deaf people use a 3G telephone. However, there are still inadequacies with the new technology. For example, practical tests conducted by SDR as part of the project showed that there is only one 3G telephone considered to have sufficient image succession frequency for acceptable sign language communication. Another limitation of this new technical device is that it is still expensive to download video messages.

In 2001, the Swedish government stated that at least half of the Swedish programs in the two public service channels run by the Swedish Television Company should be subtitled at the latest by 2005. Half of the programs broadcast by that company are imported from abroad, and those programs are always subtitled. All imported programs in the commercial channels are also subtitled. Because many of the Swedish programs are broadcast at least twice, the second broadcasting is usually subtitled. There is a news program each week in sign language, which is produced by Västanvik Folk High School, and 60% of the deaf population are watching this program. Some short news programs are also interpreted in sign language or subtitled. Since 1979, news information is given in text television, accessible all day and night.

During the twentieth century, four sign language dictionaries were published in Sweden. Pär Aron Borg started this work, and it continues today. In 1916, the first dictionary was published. The next one was published in 1960, followed by another one in 1971. Some of the pictures of different signs in this dictionary were taken from a Danish dictionary. But it soon turned out that many of the signs used in Denmark were unknown to Swedish signers. Three years later, in 1974, a fourth dictionary was published.

With new technical possibilities, there is now a digital dictionary available on the Internet. It has been constructed at the Department of Linguistics, Studies of Sign Language, Stockholm University. The dictionary is an interactive database that contains the information written in Swedish and short video clips illustrating how the sign is performed.[1] The sign is shown in isolation and in a sign language sentence. There are all together 11,500 signs documented in this database, with 1,056 signs for different sport activities, 370 for the game of bridge, and 469 signs for mathematical concepts. All these resources have enabled deaf people to communicate through sign language.

At the same time, new technologies such as cochlear implants have enabled many deaf people to perceive sounds and even speech sounds to an extent that has not been possible with other technical devices. Thus, sign language is not considered as important as before for many deaf children. For people who have lost their hearing as adults, a cochlear implant has allowed them to hear to such an extent that they more or less can live a life much the same as before their hearing loss. For the deaf child who has not heard environmental or speech sounds, the situation has been shown to be somewhat more complicated. Results from a Swedish longitudinal study, and from several international studies, show that if communication and education is based on speech only, then the children with cochlear implants have difficulty taking part in more advanced reasoning and social interaction with hearing parents, teachers, and peers, even after many years of use of the implant (see Preisler, Ahlström, & Tvingstedt, 1997; Preisler, Tvingstedt, & Ahlström, 2002; Spencer & Marschark, 2003). Parents, teachers, the children themselves are of the same opinion in this matter (Preisler, Tvingstedt, & Ahlström, 2005). A cochlear implant cannot replace the importance of using sign language, but it can facilitate everyday life in hearing families.

----

1. For more information, see www.ling.su.se/tsp.

With the introduction of cochlear implants, a more medical view on deafness has returned. Habilitation has changed focus from sign language communication to vocal communication. Many parents begin sign language courses at a later point in time than before. They hope that their child can develop oral skills with intensive training to such an extent that sign language is not needed. Gradually, many of them realize that they cannot rely totally on speech and start to learn some sign language. But learning signs later means that there is an obvious risk that sign language competence in both parents and children will be of a very basic level and that they will not be able to use the language in more advanced discourses.

CONCLUDING REMARKS

Our knowledge of sign language structure and language learning in deaf children have improved because of intensive studies in the field (see Ahlgren, 1990, 1994; Bergman & Wallin, 1990, 2003; Svartholm, 1994). When sign language was accepted as the first language of deaf children and the goal of education was bilingualism, deaf children were given opportunities to acquire language spontaneously. The effect turned out to be very positive on the children's communication, language, social, and cognitive development (Heiling, 1995; Nordén et al., 1981; Preisler, 1983; Preisler & Ahlström, 1997). These results are in accordance with the latest findings in developmental psychology, which say that the roots of language are to be found in the early preverbal communication between child and parent, where parent and child share focus of attention in a joyful and meaningful interaction.

Vocal language has for a long time been regarded as a communication system apart from gestures and other nonverbal means of communication. However, recent research in linguistics and psycholinguistics regard the vocal and gesture system as part of the same language system (Armstrong, Stokoe, & Wilcox, 1995; Corballis, 2002; McNeill, 2000). The use of signs has for a long time been considered a hindrance to developing speech. But studies now give clear evidence that the use of gestures for hearing children is a transitional device in the process of developing two-word speech (Capirci, Iverson, Pizzuto, & Volterra, 1996; Iverson, Capirci, & Caselli, 1994).

For the young deaf child, the use of gestures is the most natural means of communication, as it is for any child. One important finding in the psychosocial study of preschool children with a cochlear implant was that the children with well-functioning speech also had good command of sign language (Preisler, Tvingstedt, & Ahlström, 2002). Thus, the use of signs can promote speech development.

Studies of bilingual (hearing) children have shown that these children perform better on both episodic and semantic memory tests compared with monolingual children (Moniri, 2006). The bilingual children performed even better on episodic memory tasks if they were allowed to use an action memory paradigm. The results indicate that information will be more integrated if both the action and the verbal memory systems are involved. If we are allowed to use speech as well as sign language and gestures, then our memory system potential will probably increase and thereby increase our learning capacity.

It is obvious that the cochlear implant gives a child with a hearing impairment a possibility to hear sounds and speech to an extent that other hearing devices up to now have not been able to achieve. But as the children grow older, greater demands on language and communication skills will be put on them. Will these children manage to pass exams and to take part in higher education and in cultural and social activities where language has a crucial part? These and many other questions still remain to be answered.

REFERENCES

Ahlgren, I. (1978): Early linguistic cognitive development in the deaf and severely hard of hearing. Forskning om teckenspråk II [*Sign Language Studies II*]. Stockholm: Department of Linguistics, Stockholm University.

Ahlgren, I. (1990). Swedish Conditions: Sign language in deaf education. In S. Prillwitz & T. Vollhaber (Eds.), *Sign language research and application. Proceedings of the International Congress on Sign Language Research and Application: Vol. 13. International studies on sign language and communication of the deaf.* Hamburg: Signum.

Ahlgren, I. (1994). Sign language as the first language. In I. Ahlgren & K. Hyltenstam (Eds.), *Bilingualism in deaf education: Vol. 27. International studies on sign language and communication of the deaf.* Hamburg: Signum.

Armstrong, D. F., Stokoe, W. C., & Wilcox, S. E. (1995). *Gesture and the nature of language.* Cambridge, MA: Cambridge University Press.

Bergman, B. (1978). Current developments in sign language research in Sweden. Forskning om teckenspråk IV. *Sign Language Studies IV.* Stockholm: Department of Linguistics, Stockholm University.

Bergman, B., & Wallin, L. (1990). Sign language research and the deaf community. In S. Prillwitz & T. Vollhaber (Eds.), *Sign language research and application. Proceedings of the International Congress on Sign Language Research and Application: Vol. 13. International Studies on Sign Language and Communication of the Deaf.* Hamburg: Signum.

Bergman, B., & Wallin, L. (2003). Noun and verbal classifiers in Swedish Sign Language. In K. Emmorey (Ed.), *Perspectives on classifier construction in sign language.* Mahwah, NJ: Lawrence Erlbaum.

Capirci, O., Iverson, J. M., Pizzuto, E., & Volterra, V. (1996). Gestures and words during the transition to two-word speech. *Journal of Child Language, 23,* 645–673.

Corballis, M. (2002). *From hand to mouth. The origins of language.* Princeton, NJ: Princeton University Press.

Domfors, L-Å. (2000). Döfstumlärare—specialpedagog—lärare för döva och hörselskadade. [Deaf and Dumb Teachers—special education teachers—teachers for the deaf and hard of hearing.] (Doctoral dissertation, Örebro University, 2000). *Örebro Studies in Education 1.*

Heiling, K. (1995). *The development of deaf children: Academic achievement levels and social processes.* Hamburg: Signum.

Heiling, K. (1999). Education of the deaf in Sweden. In W. Brelje (Ed.), *Global perspective of the education of the deaf in selected countries.* Hillsboro, CO: Butte Publications.

Iverson, J. M., Capirci, O., & Caselli, M. C. (1994). From communication to language in two modalities. *Cognitive Development, 9,* 23–43.

Mahshie, S. N. (1995). *Educating deaf children bilingually. With insights and applications from Sweden and Denmark.* Washington, DC: Gallaudet University Press.

McNeill, D. (2000). *Language and gesture.* Cambridge: Cambridge University Press.

Moniri, S. (2006). *Bilingual memory: A lifespan approach.* Unpublished doctoral diss., Department of Psychology, Stockholm University.

Nordén, K. (1975). *Psychological studies of deaf adolescents.* Lund, Sweden: Gleerup.

Nordén, K., Preisler, G., Heiling, K., Hülphers, E., & Tvingstedt, A-L. (1981). Learning processes and personality development in deaf children. *International Journal of Rehabilitation Research, 4*(3), 393–395.

Nyström, A. F. (1990). *Foundations of the education for the deaf and dumb in Sweden.* Örebro, Sweden: 1900–1908 (in Swedish).

Preisler, G. (1983). *Deaf children in communication.* Unpublished doctoral diss., Department of Psychology, Stockholm University.

Preisler, G., & Ahlström, M. (1997). Sign language for hard of hearing children: A hindrance or a benefit for their development? *European Journal of Psychology of Education, 12*(4), 465–477.

Preisler, G., Ahlström, M., & Tvingstedt, A-L. (1997). The development of communication and language in deaf preschool children with cochlear implants. *International Journal of Pediatric Otorhinolaryngology, 41,* 263–272.

Preisler, G., Tvingstedt, A-L., & Ahlström, M. (2002). A psycho-social follow-up study of deaf preschool children using cochlear implants. *Child: Care, Health and Development, 28*(5), 403–418.

Preisler, G., Tvingstedt, A-L., & Ahlström, M. (2005). Interviews with children with cochlear implants. *American Annals of the Deaf, 150*(3), 260–267.

Spencer, P. E., & Marschark, M. (2003). Cochlear implants: Issues and implications. In P. E. Spencer & M. Marschark (Eds.), *Oxford handbook of deaf studies, language and education.* Oxford: Oxford University Press.

Svartholm, K. (1994). Second language learning in the deaf. In I. Ahlgren & K. Hyltenstam (Eds.), *Bilingualism in deaf education: Vol. 27. International Studies on Sign Language and Communication of the Deaf.* Hamburg: Signum.

United Nations. (1989). *Convention on the Rights of the Child.* Retrieved August 8, 2008, from http://www2.ohchr.org/english/law/crc.htm.

Deaf Education and the Status of Deaf People in the United Kingdom

Jim Kyle and Paddy Ladd

THE ADVANCES in understanding and the real progress in social terms for the Deaf community over the last 30 years offer a range of possible themes for a chapter on the topic of Deaf people in the United Kingdom (UK). We could celebrate the research on British Sign Language (BSL) beginning in the mid-1970s, coming to fruition at last in 2003 when sign language was formally recognized by a government department, and further illustrated in 2008 with the formal invitation to delegates of the Deaf community to meet with the Prime Minister at Downing Street to discuss the providing of services and development for the BSL-using community. We could highlight the sociopolitical activities of community members that have drawn in the grassroots membership to political rallies and marches in London and elsewhere. In addition, we could discuss cultural growth. There are numerous festivals and displays of Deaf Arts and Culture as well as exhibitions and presentations in sign language. There has been enormous growth in the providing of sign language interpreting services—the emergence of a new respected profession. It is now commonplace for Deaf young people to aspire to university studies and for them to progress through undergraduate into graduate study and even to doctoral level success. There has been an enormous shift in employment of Deaf people—from factories and closed-ended occupations to creative industries, offices, and even entrepreneurship. Successive Broadcasting Acts (1996, 2003—laws in the UK) have led to increased providing of sign language on public television, reaching 5% of all programs with the majority of all programs also subtitled. That development, in turn, is about to lead to the creation of a BSL television authority to exploit the opportunities for Deaf program making. Contributions by Deaf people to all parts of community life have increased enormously as public awareness of sign language has expanded.

Any one of these achievements might occupy the whole of this chapter. However, at the heart of these developments has been an opening up of Deaf education, prompted by Conrad's (1979) questioning of the performance of the deaf education system. Research interest and publications brought trials in educational methodology and produced a gradual movement from Total Communication toward what is now Sign Bilingualism—the understanding that Deaf children can achieve in two languages and that sign language has a crucial role in establishing this pathway to growth. As part of that story, the engagement of Deaf people in schools has been central, even though as we will later discover, they have little status in the formal education system. To understand the successes of Deaf adult life, we need to recognize the struggles of Deaf people to gain entry to the educational process and to be able to offer their knowledge base and skills through which new generations of Deaf children can acquire Deaf identity.

For these reasons, we have chosen to focus on deaf education in this chapter, not only to provide a snapshot of Deaf UK life but also to offer an analysis of the status accorded to Deaf people and, ultimately, to be able understand their position in society as a whole. At the heart of the issue is the status of Deaf people as a community, and at the heart of the community is their natural language, sign language. Sign language is accepted in UK society—being apparent in the media and in the thousands of people registering to study it each year.

However, at the same time as there has been progress for the Deaf community, there have also been contrary forces at work, which have produced changes within the Deaf community itself. Alexander Graham Bell's recipes have begun to be applied almost faultlessly; by keeping deaf people apart as children, removing the intergenerational contacts, and offering the "obvious" advantages of normality, their adult association patterns have been grossly altered in the UK. Deaf clubs are poorly attended because Deaf young people meet in locations without heritage; young people may have to struggle for knowledge of culture, of values, and even of the language itself; this struggle can place the young person in a state of exclusion-wishing-for-inclusion—on hearing people's terms. Medical intervention also has increased its effect and from a younger age. The result is a stronger but smaller Deaf community. The problem is that, although the case for sign language may have been won and Deaf culture has been promoted successfully, many hearing educators argue quite simply that a *Deaf child is born into hearing society and has the right to a hearing-led education*. The use of capital *D* in application to children is therefore disputed implicitly. Deaf sign-using children are presented as a small minority of the hearing impaired population. Without an established power base or presence in deaf education, members of the Deaf community are simply absent from the decisions on these policy implementations.

There is a fundamental dissonance even among policy makers. Deaf community, Deaf culture, and sign language are all seen as positive, yet the promotion of mainstreaming, the active cochlear implantation program, as well as genetic research and counseling all promise a different normality to the parents of the Deaf child. In this chapter, we consider this complex situation in deaf education and analyze its implications.

FROM THE BEGINNING

As a starting point, we need to describe the fundamental shifts that have taken place in UK education over the last 30 years, shifts that have seen huge reductions in the population of special schools and a centralizing of curricula and government management. To set that shift in context, we need to know something about preschool services and the ground that has been claimed by the medical professions. These services are set out in policy documents issued by the UK Government Departments of Health and of Education. Two major programs have come into play in recent times: the Every Child Matters Initiative (Department for Education and Science, 2003b) and the Early Support Program (Department of Health, 2003). Arising from these programs designed specifically to deal with children who have a hearing loss, there is an official guide (supplied by an organization for deaf people, RNID, or Royal National Institute for Deaf People) for dealing with Deaf children and their families (Department for Education and Science, 2003a).

These proposed services are built around procedures and guidance in the health and education sectors. A guiding system for early years is the National Service Framework for Children, Young People, and Maternity Services (Department of Health, 2004). Not surprisingly, the emphasis in the policy framework is on accessible care and the achievement of normality, even though there is occasional mention of sign language—usually as a means to provide information to Deaf parents but often referred to in terms of nonspeech: "Professionals should . . . consider the needs of children who use non-verbal communication such as sign language" (Department of Health, 2004, para. 5.10). The central guiding principle of the approach is Core Standard 8:

Children and young people who are disabled or who have complex health needs receive coordinated, high-quality child and family-centered services which are based on assessed needs, which promote social inclusion and, where possible, which enable them and their families to live ordinary lives. (Department of Health, 2004, p. 7)

This principle derives from the Framework of Assessment of Needs (Department of Health, 2000), which considers a child to be "in need" if he or she is disabled. This definition applies also to Deaf parents who may need to communicate through BSL (Department of Health, 2000, para. 1.45). Although the framework is couched in terms of support and action in favor of families, it is relatively clear that the approach draws on the images of normal development (which are good) and differences (which are deviant). However, the framework also states the following:

When assessing a child's needs and circumstances, care has to be taken to ensure that issues which fundamentally shape children's identity and wellbeing, their progress and outcomes are fully understood and incorporated into the framework for assessment. . . .

   In assessing the needs of children, practitioners have to take account of diversity in children, understand its origins and pay careful attention to its impact on a child's development and the interaction with parental responses and wider family and environmental factors.

   To achieve sensitive and inclusive practice, staff should avoid:
   • using one set of cultural assumptions and stereotypes to understand the child and family's circumstances;
(Department of Health, 2000, paras. 2.27–2.29)

However, such recognition of diversity tends to be related to race or ethnicity and not to Deaf people. Much emphasis is placed on interprofessional agency collaboration, and speech therapy is mentioned with respect to assessing communication needs and even in facilitating communication. There is of course, no profession of "Deaf expert." Even though there are Deaf communication support workers in preschool education services, none have penetrated the health services; there are a small number of Deaf workers in social services departments, but there appears to be no specific acknowledgment of their specialist skills.

   If we return to the Core Standard, we find the following statement:

This standard locates the experience of disabled children and young people, and their families, within the wider community. It promotes their inclusion and their ability to live as ordinary a life as possible through effective partnerships with them, joint working between agencies, and a commitment to extending and improving services to meet their needs collectively and individually. (Department of Health, 2004, para. 2.6)

From a societal perspective, this statement seems plausible and is claimed (in the official documents) to be in line with young people's expression of their own wishes for participation.

However, there appears to be no move toward the acceptance of the difference in experience of these young people. The rationale for this logic can be seen in the earlier initiative of Early Support (Department of Health, 2003; Department for Education and Science, 2003a).

In the specific guidance for Deaf children, the suggestion is that median discovery of hearing loss in children will move from age 20 months to 3 months (because of universal neonatal screening). This advance implies significant expansion of services to parents of infants—something that has not been attempted previously, except in theory. However, the guidance still contextualizes the development in a hearing-centric way:

Deafness in young children interrupts the developmental process for acquiring language, normally observed in hearing infants. (Department for Education and Science, 2003a, para. 9)

Earlier identification of deafness, when combined with effective service provision in the preschool years, will dramatically improve the chances of successful inclusion of deaf children into mainstream schools and into society. It therefore has the potential to significantly reduce the long term costs to society of providing support services. (Department for Education and Science, 2003a, para. 11)

Although there is later indication that sign language is an option and that development of positive Deaf identity is a goal, the guidance promotes teachers of the Deaf (who are all hearing) as the key workers in the Early Support Framework.[1] The general theme is that language equates to speech and normality whereas sign language is a parental add-on, "where this is part of the communication approach they have chosen" (Department for Education and Science, 2003a, para. 36).

The appended description of skills and knowledge required for professionals in the early support teams includes "basic sign language" and an undefined "ability to communicate with deaf adults." It appears neither to promote cultural models of Deaf experience nor to require the access to Deaf adult models, which we have found to be particularly valuable in preschool programs (Sutherland & Kyle, 1993).

A recent review of progress (Department of Health, 2007) presents a wholly positive view of services for children (without reference to any of the above issues on culture and language) and, in the paragraph it devotes to deafness, reminds us of the introduction of universal screening for hearing loss in newborns from 2006 and refers to the planned integration of hearing services with other mainstream services to children and their families.

Despite the major shift in focus over the last 40 years, from handicap to needs to inclusion, the Deaf child is still measured against hearing-speaking expectations as if the child would "wish to be hearing" if he or she could. Parental aspirations are cited as the basis for this assumption: Parents wish to have a normal child. The way in which this assumption is then reflected back to parents is that *the child is really a hearing child who does not hear well enough.* This characterization then leads naturally to intervention and, in particular, to invasive therapies. At present, the most prominent of these is cochlear implantation, which is routinely offered to parents of even very young children. It plays to parental aspirations and to social perceptions of normality. And it is claimed to work.

---

1. *Key worker* here has a specific meaning as the contact and advisory point for parents with respect to all services for their children.

O'Donoghue (1999) in an editorial in the *British Medical Journal*, states and answers the question as follows: "Do cochlear implants work in children? *Yes, so long as they are given to the right children early enough.*" He goes on to set out his principles:

The vast majority of candidates for implants, however, are congenitally deaf; over 90% of them have normally hearing parents who want their children to hear and speak. Parents who think that deafness is a way of life and not a disability are unlikely to consider implantation. The evaluation process should encompass a child's social, domestic, psychological, and educational needs. No child should be considered too young or too disabled to be evaluated for cochlear implantation. The delivery of a high quality service for children thus requires well founded multidisciplinary teams, capable of making the complex assessments demanded. . . .

A longitudinal study comparing speech perception in cochlear implanted children with matched controls who used conventional hearing aids showed significantly better performance in the implanted group.[6] An uncontrolled longitudinal study of 61 implanted children showed that more than two years of implant use was needed before intelligible speech emerged: an average speech intelligibility score of 40% was achieved after 3.5 years of implant use.[7] An educational setting that encourages oral rather than signed communication is probably more conducive to developing spoken language skills, but this remains to be confirmed. Emerging evidence suggests that implantation will result in a shift in educational placement in favor of mainstream schooling.[8]

6. Geers A, Moog J. Effectiveness of cochlear implants and tactile aids for deaf children: the Sensory Aids Study at the Central Institute for the Deaf. In: *Volta Review*. Washington: AG Bell Association for the Deaf, 1994:232-235.
7. McConkey RA, Kirk KI, Osberger MJ, Ertmer D. Speech intelligibility of implanted children. *Ann Otol* 1995; 104 (suppl 166): 399-401.
8. Nevins ME, Chute PM. Success of children with cochlear implants in mainstream educational settings. *Ann Otol* 1995; 104 (suppl 166): 100-102. (pp. 72–73)

These changes in medical services have enormous implications for the future Deaf community. The general expectation now is that implanted children are to be placed in mainstream schools, even though a significant number of implanted children continue to be in signing Deaf schools.

O'Donoghue's editorial provoked a challenge from Hindley and Parkes (1999) on the lines that the perspective ignores the advances in understanding of sign language:

Thus substantial evidence indicates that there are effective, non-invasive means of ensuring that deaf children achieve their full linguistic, social, and academic potential, yet O'Donoghue chooses to ignore this. The beliefs suggested by this editorial—that deaf children are disabled and that sign language is a wholly inadequate means of communication— are shared by many doctors across Britain. These doctors wield enormous power and influence with parents, and yet the consequences are frequently perceived only in later years by mental health practitioners such as ourselves. (Hindley & Parkes, 1999, p. 73)

The statement by Hindley and Parkes more or less summarizes the whole situation across the UK. The medical view of normality still holds sway, and parents, and then teachers, are obliged to exist within that framework. The incidence of mental health problems in the Deaf community remains high (on average five times more common than in the population at large, ages 18 to 44 years) and this high incidence is typically associated with nonrecognition of the child's natural signed language (Kyle, 1999).

The general impression one forms in the area of preschool and family services is of a huge infrastructure of medical professionalization pursuing a goal of normality and inclusion for all. Deaf children occupy a tiny space in this landscape. Deaf adults are not considered to be a resource at all.

EDUCATION

Responsibility for education is devolved to each of Scotland, Wales, Northern Ireland, and England—who then manage the consistency of educational standards. The educational implementation is managed by local authorities through the school system, which has the day-to-day responsibility. Education is compulsory for all children ages 5 to 16 years (4 to 16 years in Northern Ireland), which in most areas means the child begins regular school at the age of 4 years. Education is provided free (although 7% of parents opt to pay for education), and all students who go on to take courses in Further Education Colleges up to the age of 19 years have free education.

There are a total of 9.3 million children in the school system and approximately 103,000 in more than 1,200 special schools.[2] The official policy is that, wherever possible, taking parents' wishes into account, children are to be educated in ordinary schools. All children who have special educational needs are assessed and normally provided with a *statement,* which is a contract between the parents and the local authority to provide a certain level of special education. In 2003–04, 209,000 students in the UK school population (2.5%) had statements; of these, 64% were educated in mainstream schools.

All schools and preschools in England are required to follow a national curriculum. There is also a Foundation Stage that applies to children ages 3 to 5 years. Centralized national curricula also exist in Wales and Northern Ireland with some variations. In Scotland, the curriculum is not prescribed by statute and is the responsibility of local authorities and individual head teachers. The national curriculum mandates English and Mathematics as core subjects with foundation subjects such as design and technology as well as information and communication technology and traditional subjects such as history and geography. A modern foreign language is taught. Children are assessed nationally at the ages of 7, 11, 14, and 16 years.

All teachers must be qualified from recognized teacher training institutions, and those teaching Deaf children additionally have to obtain a specialist qualification for that purpose. Numbers of disabled teachers in schools are very low (in Scotland, only 0.79%; Denholm, 2007), and there are relatively few Deaf teachers of the deaf.

Students applying to university are required to reach certain levels in national examinations, and this requirement applies equally to those with special needs. However, on being accepted to college or university, disabled students can receive up to £20,000 (almost US$40,000 per annum [at the time of this writing] in additional funding according to their

---

2. The Every Child Matters Web site (see http://www.everychildmatters.gov.uk/ete/agencies/specialschool/) reports for 2004 that more than half the pupils at special schools have either a moderate learning difficulty (31.5%) or a severe learning difficulty (24%). A further 13.7% have behavioral, emotional, and social difficulties. Nearly 1 in 10 pupils has an autistic spectrum disorder, while 7% have a profound and multiple-component learning difficulty, and 6% a physical disability. A small proportion of children at special schools have speech, language, and communication needs (3.4%), a hearing impairment (2%), or a visual impairment (1%).

needs). Deaf students typically use that money for their interpreting and note-taking services. Students attending university now pay approximately £3,000 ($6,000) each year for fees.

There are extensive career guidance procedures, support in job interviews, and support in maintaining a place in the workforce (i.e., financial support for services to maintain a disabled person in work, which can be as much as £12,000 per annum). In the case of Deaf people, there is little difficulty in obtaining the funding to pay for interpreters in further education, in training, or in the workplace itself.

Unlike most systems in the world, the UK education system places peer group progress above academic achievement. It is therefore relatively rare for children to be held back if they have not passed the achievement tasks for that year. Children move on in school according to age, not according to grades passed. Teachers are therefore typically faced with mixed ability groups throughout schooling. Low-achieving Deaf children often do not stand out in mainstream schools because low achievement is not considered a barrier to progress through school.

PRINCIPLES AND STRUCTURES OF DEAF EDUCATION IN THE UK

The British Association of Teachers of the Deaf Survey 2000 (British Association of Teachers of the Deaf, 2003) of the education of hearing impaired children in England (there are separate figures for Northern Ireland and Scotland) offers the most useful statistics at this time. The survey claims that 25,020 people with a diagnosis of hearing loss are in the education system. Of those, 11% are "profoundly deaf." At the time of their census, there were 28 schools for the deaf and 376 units for Deaf children attached to mainstream schools. There are said to be 1,766 teachers of the deaf, of whom 9% were unqualified. The vast majority of children with a hearing loss attend mainstream schools, and the most common communication used across all groups is reported as monolingual (i.e., English)—nearly 80%. However, among schools for the deaf, approximately one third of children are said to be in sign bilingual programs.

Deaf education in the UK has to follow the national guidelines and expectations. According to the Code of Practice,[3] Deaf children have special educational needs, and those needs, in turn, are defined as meaning the presence of a learning difficulty. However, all children are expected to be educated in ordinary schools. The detailed guidance in this code is informed by the following general principles, and it should be read with these principles clearly in mind:

- A child with special educational needs should have their needs met.
- The special educational needs of children will normally be met in mainstream schools or settings.
- The views of the child should be sought and taken into account.
- Parents have a vital role to play in supporting their child's education.
- Children with special educational needs should be offered full access to a broad, balanced and relevant education, including an appropriate curriculum for the foundation stage and the National Curriculum. (Department for Education and Science, 2001, p. 7, para. 1.5)

---

3. The Code of Practice is the guidance issued by the UK Government in relation to special educational needs. It is binding on all schools and is detailed in its provisions for assessment and special educational support for all children whether in mainstream or special schools.

The implication is that *the child* has the needs—not the education system nor the school nor the family. The procedure focuses on assessment of the child, defining his or her competencies but setting goals mainly with respect to the UK National Curriculum and its specified levels of achievement. Virtually all assessment, from the time the child is born until he or she leaves school, is carried out by hearing people with no firsthand experience of Deafness and, usually, with limited sign language competence. The assessment and treatment of the child is English-centric and based on a definition of need that assumes the normality of mainstream education.

Another factor is that Deaf children's achievements still lag behind their hearing peers. Conrad (1979) remains a benchmark, but Powers, Gregory, and Thoutenhoofd (1998) have analyzed much of the literature since Conrad. They concluded that there was "no evidence to demonstrate an overall significant improvement in the education of deaf children since Conrad's study" (p. 8). Likewise, Webster (1999), in an analysis (not confined to UK studies) specifically focusing on literacy, found "some of the reading problems of deaf children as secondary to their hearing impairment and co-created by the difficulties some hearing parents and teachers have in communicating with deaf children" (p. 14). He considered that the style of interaction and the lack of use of sign language affected the literacy development of the deaf children.

More recent studies tend to confirm the lack of progress in curriculum areas. Tymms, Tate, Walker, and Fitz-Gibbon (2003) report on a national survey to monitor school achievement that has included Deaf children. On entry to school (average age 4 years 7 months), their figures for vocabulary, early reading, and early mathematics for severely and profoundly hearing impaired pupils suggest a delay of some 15 months at that age. By age 7, when the sample is smaller, the severely hearing impaired group has caught up somewhat, showing a 10-month delay whereas the profoundly hearing impaired group remain at a 15-month delay. These assessments can also be equated to being at the 25th and 16th percentiles, respectively (using Cohen's standard, 1988). The Achievements of Deaf Pupils in Scotland study similarly found a lack of school achievement and poor literacy at age 12, even though most children are mainstreamed. Thoutenhoofd's (2006) analysis of the same database but considering those with cochlear implants still finds problems:

Most deaf pupils, including most deaf pupils with cochlear implants, attain below the national cumulative average. And . . . as the expected level of attainment increases across year groups, increasing numbers of deaf pupils, including increasing numbers of those with cochlear implants, fall behind the national average. (Thoutenhoofd, 2006, p. 183)

In a report for the guidance of educators, the Inspectors of Schools in Scotland set the context:

The national survey, *The Achievements of Deaf Pupils in Scotland* has tracked the progress of deaf pupils over four years. The last survey of 5–14 national assessments in 2004 showed that the percentage of P7 deaf pupils in primary schools who had achieved in line with national expectations in mathematics, reading and writing was approximately half that of the pupil population as a whole. (Her Majesty's Inspectorate of Education, 2007, p. 6)

Although we consider there to have been progress in our thinking and in the sophistication of our services, we are not as yet able to see in research analysis any major national improvements in Deaf children's performance as measured against the national standards.

BRITISH SIGN LANGUAGE PRESENCE

Deaf children sign in school—true since the beginnings of deaf education more than 240 years ago. No matter what approach is taken by teachers, parents, and others, Deaf children have learned to sign and continue to interact with one another wherever it is possible. The philosophies and methodologies applied to deaf education have nearly always ignored the reality that Deaf people choose to associate with one another. By now, we can describe this pattern as a characteristic of Deafhood (Ladd, 2003), and it pervades all societies throughout the world: "Other Deaf people of all colors, races and ages . . . know that if they met any of those people they could, despite their very different sign languages fall into conversation and learn about each others' cultures and ways of life as viewed from the inside outwards" (Ladd, 2003, p. 29). There is a shared experience and usually a shared life in adversity and marginalization. Ladd identifies how some modern societies, including the UK, have embraced sign language as culturally "hip" but also how the Deaf community has been unable to turn this phenomenon into legislation or even into formal educational change.

Part of the power of the status quo has been built around the claim that all hearing loss equals being deaf. The education system is then able to focus attention on the success of those who have little hearing loss, who speak well, and who are, most of the time, indistinguishable from hearing people. By widening this claim even further and in effect hijacking the definition of *Deaf,* the sign-using community (i.e., Deaf people) is viewed as unrepresentative of the whole (i.e., the population of those who have hearing losses). The fact that the Deaf community does not want to be "people who have hearing losses" is conveniently sidestepped in claims for prominence of this or that approach.

A good example is the Royal National Institute for the Deaf, which claims to represent one in seven of the UK population—about 8.5 million. Because the Deaf community is probably about 25,000 in the UK, they are only 0.29% of the supposed "deaf in the UK." Why should the other 99.71% of nonsigners give pride of place to the Deaf community? The tactic works very well, sadly, and allows hearing people to dominate the largest most profitable organization for the Deaf. Similar arguments apply in "deaf education" (see Department of Health, 2007; Teachernet, 2007)—arguments that bury Deaf children in the general hearing loss group and re-assert the hearing-centric approach.

Sign language, though well researched and reported, is almost invisible in education sources online. The newly created (as of 2007) Government Department for Schools, Children, and Families[4] ought to provide guidance on BSL. In fact, there is a distinct lack of information, and certainly, there is no reference to acceptance of sign language or of its use in school. On the basis that the decisions about methodology rest with local education authorities, we can examine the information available for Birmingham, the largest authority. As with the UK Government department, there is virtually no mention of BSL and certainly nothing that looks like an obvious policy. Although there is information on other languages on the Internet, there is nothing on BSL. Education principles are written in global terms and focus primarily on systems for delivery and not on community or language. Although there exists a "comprehensive" grid describing the resourcing of children with special needs, there is no mention of

---

4. For more information, see http://www.dcsf.gov.uk.

BSL. The section on language focuses on supporting English, and signing appears to be provided as one of the forms of augmentative communication.

This lack of BSL information prevails in spite of the significant campaigns mounted in 2001–02 by the British Deaf Association and by the Federation of Deaf People, an organization created by Deaf people for engagement with the political process. The Federation of Deaf People accomplished the following during the campaign for recognition of BSL:

- Drafted the Rationale for BSL Recognition
- Organized four national conferences
- Organized three national BSL marches in London
- Collected more than 50,000 names in petitions
- Sent questionnaires to all councils in the UK to find out whether or not they recognize BSL as a community language
- Worked with some local councils on incorporating BSL into their policies to show that it does not cost as much as feared

This pressure at least created an effect in a smaller local authority like Bristol, where there is now a clearly stated policy of acceptance of BSL as well as explanations and translations on its Web site.[5] The policy is presented in strong terms:

Bristol City Council calls for
1. Official recognition of British Sign Language as a minority language under the European Charter for Regional or Minority Languages.
   Bristol City Council is committed to
   1. The equal status of English and British Sign Language and recognizes the right of all Deaf and hearing impaired children to learn through their first language, whichever that may be.
   2. The right to a bicultural education for Deaf children and young people, ensuring that Deaf children are able to access this culture, socialize with other Deaf children and to have Deaf adult role models.

However, the local authority area devoted to sensory impaired (Deaf) children talks about hearing needs and not about BSL, nor does it explain about BSL to parents, for whom the Web site is created. It does mention Deaf workers in the Service for Sensory-Impaired Children but offers no explanation to parents about the local authority's policy of use of BSL. It appears that there is no mechanism within the council whereby these policies are actively applied to those in charge of Deaf children's education.

TEACHER TRAINING

There has been mandatory teacher training for teachers of the deaf for more than 100 years. There is also a long tradition of oralist emphasis in this training because it was established in Manchester within a medical framework. Only in the last 25 years has there been the encouragement to learn sign language as part of that training. Those taking the route to teacher of the deaf status must proceed through generic teaching (i.e., requiring graduate status, a recognized teaching qualification, and experience of working in hearing schools) before being considered

---

5. See http://www.bristol.gov.uk/ccm/content/Community-Living/Equality-Diversity/bsl-equality.en.

for a teacher of the deaf course. Not surprisingly, this route forms a major barrier to Deaf candidates, and relatively few have ever made it through this system.

An information leaflet prepared by the teaching organization and two national deaf organizations (but not the British Deaf Association) provides the detail on current preliminary characteristics (British Association of Teachers of the Deaf, 2005). A trainee teacher of the deaf should be a clear-spoken language communicator and should have "a positive attitude towards deaf people and a commitment to acquire basic sign language skills to at least CACDP stage I or equivalent." This level of sign competence is minimal, and the curriculum is unrelated to children's signing. There are seven part-time (distance learning) courses and one full-time course in the UK. The majority of teachers now qualify by distance learning while continuing to teach in their Deaf school. The content of the Birmingham course titled "Hearing Impairment" is not untypical. The program content includes the following modules:

- Language Acquisition in Deaf Children
- Educational Audiology
- Working with Families Who Have a Deaf Child
- Multi-Professional Work
- Approaches to the Education of Deaf Children and Young People

Practical work is given particular emphasis and includes two periods of assessed teaching, an extensive program of visits to schools, and workshops in audiology and language assessment. In most of the course prospectuses, it is hard to determine the extent of attention given to sign language or, indeed, to ensuring that teachers have communicative competence in signing. This ambiguity is in keeping with the view expressed by the British Association of Teachers of the Deaf (2005) that severely and profoundly Deaf children need skilled teaching to acquire language and communication skills and that most children are in mainstream schools. The word *Deaf* is taken to mean all those with a hearing loss of whom signing Deaf people are a small minority.

ANALYSIS OF THE STATE OF DEAF EDUCATION FROM THE INSIDE

All schools in the UK are subject to regular inspection. In England, these inspections occur every 3 to 4 years. The inspection reports are published and can be examined online. The number of functioning schools for the deaf has dropped significantly in the last 30 years; we have lost probably 60% of the dedicated school services. The children are likely to be in mainstream schools. In many cases, there are dedicated units, and in some of these units, there are bilingual policies. Nevertheless, it is in the schools for the deaf that the roots of language and culture should be apparent. We have analyzed the most recent reports published for the 21 schools that are still active (reduced from 28 in 2000); nineteen reports are within the last 4 years, and two are from 2001. The total number of pupils in these schools is 1,619. The format of the reporting changed in 2005, and these new reports lend themselves to better comparison across school sectors and nationally (in England). Eleven schools have been inspected since 2005, and these are termed Section 5 inspections.

Inspectors report on overall effectiveness of the school, achievement and standards, quality of services, leadership and management, and other factors related to the well-being of the learners. Inspection teams are made up of professional members of the inspectorate—

experienced teachers who have progressed into the inspection role and additional inspectors who are recruited by independent agencies and go through a training program. A list of these additional inspectors is published; however, there is no indication of how many of the members of these inspections teams are Deaf (the suspicion is very few and they would certainly never be in the majority in an inspection team even for a Deaf School; it also remains unspecified as to how many members of the inspection team are fluent in BSL; again, the suspicion is very few). The reports of the inspection are extremely important to the school, which is obliged to display the details and required by law to deal with any queries arising from the inspection. In cases of concern, staff members may be replaced and even emergency senior management individuals may be inserted in the school.

The Statistics

Taking the simple ratings for the schools' overall performance, deaf schools seem to be considered to be much better than the average; the difference is statistically significant compared with all schools (see Table 17.1). The ratings for Deaf schools in these Section 5 reports are very high, except when it comes to the achievement of the pupils. In that area, the average ratings are Grade 3.45 (Grade 3 = broadly average to below average; Grade 4 = exceptionally low), implying that Deaf children's achievement in academic areas is well below average.

A more extensive comparison is shown in Table 17.2, this time separating out the primary schools (ages 5 to 11) and secondary schools (ages 11 to 18). Again, in almost every measure, Deaf schools are rated more highly than any other group of schools. There are several ways one can interpret these figures. First, we might congratulate all the Deaf schools for being better than all the other school groups. At the same time, we need to consider how it is that achievement can be left out of the equation when it is also acknowledged that Deaf children are equally intelligent to all the other children. The possible answer is in the qualifying question about how well the schools manage with students who have *learning difficulties*. In effect, a value judgment is being made by inspectors: Given the difficulties that Deaf schools face with the nature of their pupils, they are considered to be doing a better job than any other type of school.

Second, we might be concerned. If Deaf schools are so much better than hearing schools, why are Deaf children being moved out and placed in these other schools that are rated poorer by the inspectors? That is, the principles of mainstreaming are placing Deaf children in less strong educational environments—except, of course, if we consider the overall academic achievement (of hearing peers) as the only criterion. Mainstream schools are rated higher in

Table 17.1. Inspection Grades for the Question How Effective, Efficient, and Inclusive Is the Providing of Education, Integrated Care and Any Extended Services in Meeting the Needs of Learners? (average performance)

	All Schools Inspected Autumn–Spring 2006–07 (*n* = 5,647)	Special Schools (*n* = 268)	Deaf Schools Since 2005 (*n* = 11)
Inspection Grade	2.33	2.04	1.73

Note: Inspection grade of 1 = outstanding; 2 = good; 3 = satisfactory; 4 = inadequate

Table 17.2. Comparison of Ratings for Selected Questions in the Inspection Report (average value) by Type of School

Item in the Inspection	Type of School and Inspection Grade			
	Deaf (n = 11)	Special (n = 268)	Primary (n = 4,276)	Secondary (n = 923)
How effective, efficient, and inclusive is the providing of education, integrated care, and any extended services in meeting the needs of learners?	1.73	2.04	2.33	2.48
How well do learners achieve?	1.73	2.06	2.33	2.50
How well to learners reach the standards?	3.45	3.85	2.48	2.61
How well do learners with learning difficulties and disabilities make progress?	1.64	2.07	2.22	2.39
How good is the overall personal development and well-being of the learners?	1.73	1.68	1.80	2.11
How high is the extent of learners' spiritual, moral, social, and cultural development?	1.73	1.71	1.82	2.11
How effective are teaching and learning in meeting the full range of the learners' needs?	1.73	2.06	2.31	2.48
How well do the curriculum and other activities meet the range of needs and interests of learners?	1.73	2.01	2.2	2.17
How well are learners cared for, guided, and supported?	1.64	1.71	2.00	2.04
How effective are leadership and management in raising achievement and supporting all learners?	1.55	2.01	2.25	2.25
How well is equality of opportunity promoted and discrimination tackled so all learners achieve as well as they can?	1.60	1.94	2.21	2.25

Note: Inspection grade of 1 = outstanding (exceptionally and consistently high); grade of 2 = good (generally above average with none significantly below average); grade of 3 = satisfactory (broadly average); and grade of 4 = inadequate (exceptionally low).

terms of (hearing) pupil achievement (we do not have figures for Deaf pupils) but poorer in terms of education quality.

The Evaluation

We have also examined the qualitative aspects of the inspection reports for all 21 schools for Deaf children. We considered the way in which the assessment was made, looking for clues as to the values manifested by the inspectors as well as considering the nature of the language and achievement issues that are themes in this text. The inspections are designed to determine the performance of the school, and we started by looking for the concept of *outstanding performance* and the references to *achievement*.

Outstanding Performance

Nine out of 21 schools for Deaf children were rated outstanding in some respect. The following comments describe some of these ratings:

- This is an outstanding school. The school knows itself well but is far too unassuming about its successes. BS
- This is a school that works extremely hard to achieve its best. It is an outstanding school which has gone from strength to strength since its last inspection. HL
- XX is an exceptional school. There is an outstanding commitment to pupils on the part of all those who work in the school. OL
- The curriculum keeps pupils closely in line with their mainstream peers whilst also including outstanding innovative aspects such as Deaf Studies. FB

The first three judgments appear to be subjective and based on impressions. There are implications of commitment and hard work. The fourth criterion seems to be an implicit comparison with mainstream schools.

Achievement

Twenty (out of 21) school reports mention achievement—with very frequent references in most cases. Achievement appears to be a central concept. The difficult part is determining what achievement should be judged. For most of the time, the children's rating against the inbuilt measures in the UK National Curriculum and the annual test scores are presented. However, there are also more qualitative aspects. There is a general belief that achievement is related to the quality of the teaching:

Standards are rising throughout the school and pupils' achievements are very good because teaching, learning and the curriculum are very good. BW

The intertwined set of concepts is clearly expressed here:

The main reasons for pupils' very good achievement are very good teaching which is enshrined in high expectations for learning, good subject knowledge and the development of pupils literacy and communication skills. Very good teamwork between communicators, therapists and support staff promotes pupils' learning and their high achievement. Another major factor in high achievement is the highly relevant and very well planned curriculum, which ensures that basic skills are very well promoted and provide very good opportunities for pupils to follow examination courses with extensive opportunities for learning within the mainstream school. BW

This description is the classic view of a good school. However, it is hard to operationalize this view when we think of Deaf children's experiences with hearing teachers. The perceived relationship to mainstreaming and its positive value appear again:

Further opportunities to raise pupils' achievements are materializing, due to the very good inclusion of deaf pupils in the mainstream school. This is a significant development since the last inspection and the school through shared initiatives with mainstream staff, is now uniquely placed to raise standards further. BW

Organization and leadership are considered important, and value-for-money judgments can be made:

Teamwork among all staff is very strong. Very good leadership and management have resulted in very good teaching and learning and a very good curriculum. As a result, pupils' achievements are very good. The school provides very good value for money. BS

In another case, the praise is so extensive that one wonders at there being special needs:

Achievement and standards measured against a very low starting point are outstanding. Pupils make rapid gains in speaking and listening because of the effective method used to promote their communication skills. Progress in reading is excellent. By age 16 the vast majority of pupils are confident readers and well equipped to become life-long learners. BS

Despite this glowing report, the actual quantitative rating of the pupils' achievement in that school is "exceptionally low." It seems likely that relative judgments are being made. The same claims are made in schools that promote the use of speech, but the statements can be somewhat confusing:

All pupils, whatever their needs or backgrounds, make impressive gains throughout their time in school and their progress and achievement are outstanding. The range of attainment within any of the small groups is very wide but data on pupils' improvement put KF school in the top few per cent of schools in England. The pupils' most significant achievement is in their ability to use the hearing they have and to communicate with peers and adults. This has a really positive effect on their work in other areas. As a result, they make significant progress in their academic work with a few reaching the standards expected of hearing pupils. KF

By the time they leave, pupils reach standards that are below the national average but this represents very good achievement in their language development. MH

It is also clear that judgments of low performance are being centered on the children's English performance because many of the children in this last school come from Deaf families where their BSL development is (and has been) at least age appropriate. BSL achievement is occasionally considered in relation to a national vocational qualification, which is designed for hearing people and not likely to be appropriate to Deaf learners.

Mainstreaming

One of the issues that appears frequently is the need either to compare with or to engage with policies and practices for mainstreaming. Often, the school is pressured to ensure that its pupils spend time in a mainstream school. In two cases, schools have been relocated inside a mainstream school, one of which is described here:

The school relocated to new premises on a mainstream secondary school site in . . . 2003, to promote greater inclusion, as part of the Local Education Authority's inclusion initiative. . . . Very strong links with the mainstream school and highly effective teamwork among staff contribute effectively to pupils' achievements. . . . Since moving to the new building on the mainstream school site, further opportunities to raise pupils' achievements are materializing, due to the very good inclusion of deaf pupils in the mainstream school. BW

The implication is that educational opportunity arises *because of* mainstream contact. There is also a reverse implication that teachers in mainstream situations can enrich the Deaf school.

There are sufficient teachers and good numbers of support staff with experience and qualifications to meet the demands of the curriculum. Many teachers are new to the education of deaf pupils. A high number have recently arrived from mainstream schools. As such, they contribute strongly to an understanding of the requirements of the National Curriculum and of the levels pupils should attain. BF

The clear aspiration is for the children to be part of the mainstream. In some cases, there is a suggestion that Deaf instructors should provide joint sessions for Deaf and hearing children. It is not obvious how the Deaf instructors will function without personal support for their own communication if the hearing teachers are nonsigners, but it is a common model to place Deaf assistants in mainstream settings.

Methodologies

Some of the old priorities are no longer expressed. None of the reports mention oralism, and speech is mentioned only in relation to speech and language therapists. There is almost no mention of cochlear implants, despite the fact that they are quite prominent in deaf schools. Perhaps it is now accepted ideology that oralism is mainstreaming and the attendance of children with cochlear implants at a deaf school represents failure. Sign bilingualism does appear in three reports as a policy, one of which is related here:

The school has a sign bilingual approach; the school values the development of British Sign Language (BSL) alongside English and uses BSL as the main mode of communication. BF

However, perhaps the major concern from our perspective is the way in which the features that are natural to Deaf people are treated. With respect to this concern, we have considered Deaf Studies, the role of Deaf teachers, BSL–signing, and Deaf culture.

DEAF STUDIES. Six of the reports mentioned Deaf Studies. Those reports tend to be couched in positive terms, and the references imply an acceptance of this topic for study:

In addition to the direct teaching of BSL, deaf staff also teach Deaf studies, which contributes to the development of pupils' deaf identity and the promotion of positive images of deaf people. . . . Leadership and management in BSL and Deaf studies are good and the senior deaf instructor is an effective key member of the leadership team. There is a framework for the teaching of BSL and Deaf studies and a broad curriculum outline, which support the goals of the sign bilingualism policy. BF

Pupils were achieving certificated levels in BSL, and the school was currently developing a 5-14 BSL curriculum. The very good Deaf Studies course developed by the school covered a range of aspects including identity, British deaf culture, social issues and history. DS

There is as yet no national curriculum in Deaf Studies for schools, but some schools have made considerable progress.

THE ROLE OF THE DEAF TEACHER. Deaf teachers are mentioned only three times in the 21 reports; these may not be regular teachers who are Deaf but rather Deaf instructors of BSL. However, their value is acknowledged. Two of these quotes are provided here:

Staff, including a large number of deaf teachers, provide very good role models which does much to raise pupils' ambitions and expectations. OL

Pupils achieve very well in this subject because they are very well taught by deaf teachers who are natural users of BSL. These deaf adults have very good relationships with the pupils and provide them with very positive role models. They are supported very well by many education assistants, who are extremely proficient signers and work extremely well with teachers. Teachers are very skilled at ensuring all pupils are involved in lessons and use many opportunities to evaluate pupils' learning. However, there is one feature of some lessons that needs to be addressed. Deaf studies lessons are silent, with all communication being carried out using BSL, but, quite properly, teachers do try to support learning by using text, such as writing on the whiteboard pupils' suggestions of different methods of communicating. Unfortunately, on a few occasions words are not spelt correctly and this problem is further compounded when pupils copy these misspellings into their exercise books. DY

The final negative point is interesting for the fact that it again prioritizes English even in after having praised the Deaf Studies lessons. One might consider whether the signing of hearing staff in other lessons "are spelt correctly" and expressed correctly in terms of the grammar of BSL.

BSL—SIGNING.   Fourteen reports mention British Sign Language or BSL. Three schools we believe, have expressly non-BSL oralist policies. However, there is often an acknowledgment of BSL in the opening statement about the school—something that we would not have seen in the past. For example, consider the following two statements:

The majority of pupils have British Sign language (BSL) as their first language. LW

Around half the staff are also profoundly deaf and use BSL as their first language. FB

Sometimes the school's philosophy is more apparent:

The school considers that two thirds of its pupils do not have English as their first language; their first language is British Sign Language (BSL). This is reflected in the school's philosophy and practice. It describes itself as a signing and speaking community where the languages and cultures of both deaf and hearing people are valued and pupils' skills in BSL and English are taught and assessed formally. DS

Although the weight of duty to English is still felt in other cases, this school appears to more closely reflect the knowledge that we now have about the Deaf community:

BSL is very well established as the primary mode of communication in the school in all subjects. It is also a subject in its own right and is taught throughout the school from the Nursery to Post 16. This is firmly in line with the school's policy on sign bilingualism and the social and cultural model of deafness adopted. The school promotes the development of BSL as a linguistic foundation for learning and the acquisition of skills in English. However, in some classes there is a lack of clarity about the relationship between BSL and English, with inconsistent attention to English. In these classes, there is not enough use of the spoken English, particularly where there are pupils who might make good use of residual hearing in the development of their speaking and listening. BF

BSL here is not considered as part of a bilingual program but as more of a support to the English goals for hearing pupils. The request for more English would be typical of a hearing person feeling isolated in a group using a foreign language. Although most of the schools in our analysis consider BSL as a part of everyday life, official observers continue to relate what they see as the need for English speech.

DEAF CULTURE. Eight of the reports mentioned Deaf culture and set it in a positive, identity-forming context, as in this example:

The school has a particularly strong approach to deaf culture. A very effective communications tutor ensures that issues relating to deaf identity and rights are explored fully but in a balanced way. She provides a range of opportunities for pupils to discuss and form their own opinion about where they themselves feel happiest and how they best relate to both the hearing and deaf communities. Every effort is made to encourage deaf role models into the school and this works well in further increasing pupils' independence and confidence. MG

Such views might serve as a basis for the next step to analyze and to alter the curriculum from a Deaf culture perspective, bringing with it a much stronger role for Deaf staff. There is as yet no indication that this step is happening.

This analysis of inspection reports on the schools for the deaf is both heartening and disappointing. There is rather more attention to Deaf identity and culture as well as sign language than would have been expected only 20 years ago. There are some Deaf instructors in the schools. Yet at the same time, there are few Deaf teachers, there is no real move toward a Deaf-centered curriculum, and significantly, the inspectors continuously set English and mainstreaming as the main goals. There may be some alternatives if we look beyond the schools to current thinking and research.

DEAF PEDAGOGY

Those who have no prior knowledge of what has transpired in the 250+ years of deaf education would be shocked to learn that all things Deaf were removed from the education system under oralism. On hearing that to some extent BSL and Deaf educators had been restored to the system, they might think that all was beginning to change for the better (Senghas & Monaghan, 2002; Storbeck, 2005). But they would be disappointed to learn that the idea that one might teach from Deaf-child-centered pedagogies, first connecting with the children through their inner "Deaf selves," and then leading them outward from there to full bicultural citizenship, are pedagogies still virtually unheard of in Deaf education. For, although hearing teachers have the potential to learn to use these pedagogies effectively, the BSL–Deaf culture "turn" is still so recent that most teachers are unaware of its fullest implications, and almost none have received adequate training in these subjects, let alone gained qualifications for their use with Deaf children.

Recent ethnographic studies of Deaf educators at work (Goncalves, in process, in Brazil; Ladd & West, in press, in the UK; West, 2001), together with studies of Deaf children's own statements about Deaf and hearing teachers (West, 2001) offer us a unique insight into the full implications of this turn of events. These findings reveal that those Deaf people who have become educators in the past 20 years (the vast majority being officially powerless and unrecognized teaching assistants), experience huge frustrations in being compelled to implement systems that are far removed from what they consider to be necessary to ensure maximal development of the Deaf children's abilities (compare Young, Ackerman, & Kyle, 1998; Santini, 2001). Their minimal opportunities to express their views are dwarfed by the huge, overarching system of educational administration (augmented by the lobbying forces of the medical and technological industries, most of which are newly arrived in deaf education), which we have described in this chapter. This huge system is not, as it were, even "facing their direction," just as it has not faced the direction of the Deaf child.

As many describe it, the system (and its hearing teachers) are not even aware of the extent to which the children's abilities could be stretched and brought nearer to majority society standards if the insights of Deaf adults were systematically heeded. Deaf assistant teachers have expressed grief at the thousands of small opportunities to teach more "efficiently" that pass unnoticed on a daily basis in deaf education. This lack of recognition of what deaf education in its most efficient form might become is thus naturally reflected in the hearing educators' limited awareness of all the unseen work that Deaf educators are actually carrying out. Because hearing teachers cannot perceive the full implications of Deaf-child-centered pedagogies, they are unable to recognize the range and depth of the praxis that is taking place in the Deaf classrooms of their own schools.

Ladd and West (in press) identify the sheer extent of this praxis as amounting to "The Unrecognized Curriculum," which they identify as taking place in six stages over a Deaf child's educational life and being underpinned by (at least) 37 different cultural strategies. These stages derive from, and are deemed to form a part of, the wider concept of "Deafhood epistemologies." This curriculum is described therefore as being taught through "Deafhood pedagogies." It is a telling comment on the real "agenda" of deaf education that only a few recent articles and dissertations exist that describe what deaf educators actually do, and why. These books will therefore be the first of their kind, 250 years after the first Deaf person taught in a classroom.

The importance of these observations is that once they are absorbed and digested, they turn the deaf education system on its head, from the medical and disability model to the cultural-linguistic model. For, with respect to minority education generally, no one would expect the minority in question to occupy anything other than a controlling role in the education of their own children, and yet as we have seen, this expectation is the last thing on the minds of those who control deaf education. Once the sophistication and efficiency of Deafhood pedagogies is realized, the present emphasis—that if Deaf persons wish to become teachers, they must emulate hearing standards for deaf education—is turned on its head. The questions become instead,

- What must hearing teachers learn from Deaf educators?
- How must that knowledge then be incorporated into hearing teacher training?
- How must the term *qualified teacher of the Deaf* thus be reworked to ensure that the training satisfies Deaf educators' own high standards?

The extent to which this position is presently unthinkable reveals how far deaf education remains from where Deaf communities believe it should be and thereby gives a powerful indication of just why educational outcomes are no better, 30 years after the Conrad Report. Indeed, one day we all may come to realize that Deafhood pedagogies were the missing factor in the past 130+ years of Deaf underdevelopment.

Deaf Steps From Deaf Studies to Deafhood Studies

The gradual changes in school with respect to incorporation of sign language and Deaf participation can be linked to a much greater Deaf community awareness, self-confidence, and assertiveness. These elements of empowerment have been built on a general realization of the existence of sign language, the research on Deaf community views, and the increasing prominence of sign language on television and in all aspects of life.

Advances in education can lead to a coherent curriculum and educational approach that promotes the Deaf perspective, and that curriculum would go a long way to bridging the gap between the acceptable presence of Deaf people in society and the need to embrace that presence as normality. An understanding of the importance of Deafhood to quality of life and a recognition that Deaf is not purely a medical concept would create a real acceptance of Deaf as difference in a vibrant way.

Brennan (2000) proposes that Deaf Studies in the school curriculum can

- provide Deaf children and young people with a positive sense of individual and group identity;
- enable Deaf pupils to become aware of historical and social influences on the lives of Deaf people;
- encourage Deaf pupils to become aware of the different types of linguistic expression, including signed language and spoken language;
- help young Deaf people to prepare themselves for the realities of post-school life; and
- help young Deaf people to develop their own perspectives on political and policy issues that directly affect their lives.

To a large extent, this potential is viewed sympathetically by educators, but there is still a need for a Deaf-sourced model. Taylor and Darby (2004) have collected a range of stories to illustrate what they feel is the *range* of Deaf identities; their stories represent narratives of a community in transition to an outward facing public image. However, it does not go far enough in analyzing the common threads of the core identity.

Ladd (2003), starting from accounts of Deaf people's schooldays, has laid the foundation for a real understanding of this complex identity forming process. His accounts cover the period up to the early 1970s in terms of recollections and views. From these accounts, we can see the importance of Deaf interaction and of the development of meaningful communication. However, the primary finding is a process that Ladd has defined as Deafhood—the development of a collectivist identity and culture based on shared experiences. Deaf community advocates have been able to use this research and the effects can be seen on a national scale.

With respect to education policy, Ladd (2003) concludes that the changes in approach that have occurred since the 1970s, including those indicated earlier in the inspection reports, do not go far enough in understanding Deaf perspectives. He argues that to make realistic change, there is a need for education to

- recognize the essential difference of Deaf minds (from hearing minds),
- realize that this "mind" is a valid basis for Deaf education itself,
- understand that the vitality of Deaf education is crucial to the later health of the Deaf community, and
- be aware that the Deaf community has a primary role in influencing and developing the education itself.

In short, there is a need for a wholesale revision of education goals and practices with respect to Deaf people. Ladd's (2003) proposals on Deafhood go much further than the Brennan (2000) Deaf Studies initiative (above) and, in doing so, offer a proposal for the decolonization of the deaf education system. He views the above proposals as only a partial change leading to a partial improvement. Significant advances can be made only when the schools themselves become Deaf-centered, that is, when schools acknowledge that Deaf children and adults have their own epistemologies and their own ways of thinking about and constructing the world (Ladd, 2003).

Such a view is entirely in keeping with work on the development of bilingual education in the spoken language field that focuses on the heritage language (Baker, 2006). Given the extent of interest in the concept of Deafhood (Google returns more than 14,000 hits on this word, which did not exist more than 5 years ago) and the awareness of sign language, there are some grounds for optimism that Deafhood Studies and sign bilingualism have a significant future.

LEGAL ACTIONS

Society also provides the means for Deaf people to challenge the system. A range of relevant legislation now appears to protect the benefits of Deaf members of society and mandates their treatment. The Disability Discrimination Act (Office of Public Sector Information, 1995) sets out the arrangements for public treatment of disabled people—and thereby the treatment of Deaf people—in employment and in every aspect of life. The law was amended in 2005 to promote the Disability Equality Duty, a requirement to involve disabled people in achieving that equality. There are also clear guidelines for the way in which the police must deal with Deaf people (Police and Criminal Evidence Act, 1984, especially chapter F).

Unfortunately, the Deaf community presence in the professional legal system is minimal. Although the legal profession closely matches the national working population in terms of gender and ethnicity (Office of Public Sector Information, 2005), fewer than 10 Deaf people (out of 100,000 professionals) are working in the legal system,[6] with even fewer of these at fully practicing status levels. Deaf people are not allowed to be jury members, and there is very limited awareness in the profession as a whole about how to deal with legal cases involving Deaf people.

Nevertheless, there has been some progress in the application of the legislation. A legal precedent has been established that now requires not only reasonable adjustment in the workplace and in working practices for Deaf people but also adjustments to require that hearing people take courses to become aware of Deaf issues in employment (*Simpson v. West Lothian Council*, 2004; *Osborne-Clark v. Inland Revenue*, 2005).

However, legal attempts to claim negligence in the light of failure in education have not been successful. In the negligence case brought to court in 2003, Calvin Medall sued his local education authority for negligence on the basis of the (undisputed) failure of his oralist education, which left him with serious linguistic and cognitive problems. The case was strong given the demonstrable extent of deprivation. However, the case foundered on the Bolam defense (*Bolam v. Friern Hospital Management Committee*, 1957) that a doctor is not liable in negligence if he or she has acted in accordance with the practice accepted as proper by a responsible body of medical opinion. In this case, although it was a medical precedent, the education authority was able to claim that the strict oralist policies being applied (even in the face of a failing child) were also being used by a substantial group of other education authorities.

---

6. For more information, see http://www.deaflawyers.org.uk.

Strange though it seems, the case hinged on the testimony of an expert witness who was asked by the defense counsel whether the strict oral approach was used in other parts of the UK at the time of Calvin's education. The response, "Yes it was, but . . .", was immediately seized on by the judge who more or less terminated the case at that point. An appeal was considered and then dropped on independent legal advice, and a plan to approach the European court was determined to be inadmissible because of the failure in the national court. Further litigation with respect to failing Deaf children now seems unlikely because of the diverse range of policies in place in schools and the lack of consensus among professionals.

IN THE FINAL ANALYSIS

The situation of Deaf people in the UK has seen enormous advances in the last 30 years. Their situation, once an ignored and excluded handicapped group, has experienced significant progress in terms of sign language acceptance, Deaf people's advanced education, and the study of sign language. In terms of community prominence and entrepreneurship, there has probably never been such dynamic Deaf community engagement. Sign language is present in everyday life and is understood as linguistic communication by hearing people.

Yet at the same time, the government places deafness inside a disability wrapper. This wrapper brings some advantages—mainly in disability benefits (reduced travel costs, direct government benefit payments, special allowances for advanced study, interpreter services). Not surprisingly, members of the Deaf community may buy into these benefits and so cloud the issue for a strategic approach to minority language recognition.

We can be sure that the core of Deaf people's self-belief comes from education and childhood experiences, and when that core continues to be affected by lack of acceptance of difference, the lifetime effects are disastrous not only for the Deaf community but, actually, also for the hearing educators. The Deaf community is changing, becoming more self-assured and aware. It is more able to present its views, and the outward pressure is forcing hearing people to accord more rights and to accept sign language. It remains to be seen whether the higher levels of social achievement by Deaf people will be accompanied by greater power over educational change and the real acceptance of Deafhood, which will be necessary to create a successful Deaf-centered education.

REFERENCES

Baker, C. (2006). *Foundations of bilingual education and bilingualism* (4th ed.). Clevedon, U.K.: Multilingual Matters.

Bolam v. Friern Hospital Management Committee 2 All ER 118, 26 February 1957. Retrieved August 11, 2008, from http://oxcheps.new.ox.ac.uk/casebook/Resources/BOLAMV_1%20DOC.pdf

Brennan, M. (2000, November). Deaf studies in the curriculum. *BATOD Magazine,* 7–13.

British Association of Teachers of the Deaf. (2003, June 3). BATOD survey 2000. *BATOD Magazine,* 29–30.

British Association of Teachers of the Deaf. National Deaf Children's Society, & Royal National Institute for Deaf People. (2005). *Teaching deaf children* [Television broadcast]. High Wycombe, UK: British Association of Teachers of the Deaf.

Cohen, J. (1988). *Statistical power analysis for the behavioral sciences* (2nd ed.). Hillsdale, NJ: Lawrence Erlbaum.

Conrad, R. (1979). *The deaf school child.* London: Harper and Row.

Denholm, A. (2007, April 17). Call to encourage more disabled into teaching. *The Herald.* Retrieved August 11, 2008, from http://www.theherald.co.uk/news/news/display.var.1332543.0.0.php

Department for Education and Science. (2003a). *Developing early intervention/support services for deaf children and their families* (LEA/0068/2003). London: Author.

Department for Education and Science. (2003b). *Every child matters* (No. CM5860). London: The Stationery Office.

Department of Health. (2000). *Framework for the assessment of children in need and their families.* London: The Stationery Office.

Department of Health. (2003). Together from the start: Practical guidance for professionals working with disabled children (birth to third birthday) and their families. London: Author.

Department of Health. (2004). *Disabled children and young people and those with complex health needs: National service framework for children, young people and maternity services.* London: Author.

Department of Health. (2007). *Children's health, our future A review of progress against the national service framework for children, young people and maternity services 2004.* London: Author.

Goncalves, J. (in process). *Brazilian deaf educators and the 'pedagogy of difference.'* Unpublished doctoral diss., Deaf Studies, University of Bristol, United Kingdom.

Her Majesty's Inspectorate of Education. (2007). *Count us in: Achieving success for deaf pupils.* Edinburgh: Author.

Hindley, P., & Parkes, R. (1999). Speaking sign language from birth can make deaf children confident. *British Medical Journal, 318,* 1491.

Kyle, J. G. (1999). Deafness, well-being and mental health. In A. Weisel (Ed.), *Insights into deaf education: Current theory and practice* (pp. 36–45. Tel Aviv: Academic Press of the School of Education.

Ladd, P. (2003). *Understanding deaf culture: In search of deafhood.* Clevedon, U.K.: Multilingual Matters.

Ladd, P., & West, D. (in press). *"Seeing through new eyes": Deafhood pedagogies and the unrecognised curriculum.* New York: Oxford University Press.

O'Donoghue, G. M. (1999). Hearing without ears: Do cochlear implants work in children? *British Medical Journal, 318,* 72–73.

Office of Public Sector Information. (1995). *Disability Discrimination Act 1995.* Retrieved August 11, 2008, from http://www.opsi.gov.uk/acts/acts1995/ukpga_19950050_en_1.htm

Office of Public Sector Information. (2005). *Disability Discrimination Act 2005.* Retrieved August 11, 2008, from http://www.opsi.gov.uk/acts/acts2005/ukpga_20050013_en_1.htm

Osborne-Clark v. Inland Revenue (2005). Retrieved August 11, 2008, from http://www.handsonaccess.com/xhtml/article.asp?PageName=123

Police and Criminal Evidence (PACE) Act. (1984). Code of Practice F. Retrieved August 11, 2008, from http://police.homeoffice.gov.uk/news-and-publications/publication/operational-policing/PACE_Chapter_F.pdf?version=1

Powers, S., Gregory, S., & Thoutenhoofd, E. (1998). *The educational achievements of deaf children.* (Research Report No. 65). London: Department for Children, Schools, and Families.

Santini, J. (2001). *Multicultural politics at bilingual deaf schools in Britain.* Unpublished master of science diss., University of Bristol, United Kingdom.

Senghas, R. J., & Monaghan, L. (2002). Signs of their times: Deaf communities and the culture of language. *Annual Review of Anthropology, 31,* 69–97.

Simpson v. West Lothian Council (19 October 2004), BAILII case number: [2004] UKEAT 0049_04_1910 Appeal No. UKEAT/0049/04. Retrieved August 11, 2008, from http://www.bailii.org/cgi-bin/markup.cgi?doc=/uk/cases/UKEAT/2004/0049_04_1910.html&query=Simpson+v.+West+Lothian+Council&method=all

Storbeck, C. (2005). Respecting diversity: In search of a deaf pedagogy. In *Proceedings of Inclusive and Supportive Education Congress/International Special Education Conference, Inclusion: Celebrating*

Diversity? Retrieved August 11, 2008, from http://www.isec2005.org.uk/isec/abstracts/papers_s/storbeck%20_c.shtml

Sutherland, H., & Kyle, J. G. (1993). *Deaf children at home.* Bristol: Deaf Studies Trust.

Taylor, G., & Darby, A. (2004). *Deaf identities.* Coleford, U.K.: Douglas Mclean.

Teachernet. (2007). *British Sign Language—Signed, sealed and delivered.* Retrieved August 11, 2008, from http://www.teachernet.gov.uk/teachingandlearning/library/signedsealedanddelivered/

Thoutenhoofd, E. (2006). Cochlear implanted pupils in Scottish schools: 4-Year school attainment data (2000–2004). *Journal of Deaf Studies and Deaf Education, 11,* 171–188.

Tymms, P., Tate, G., Walker, A., & Fitz-Gibbon, C. T. (2003). *The education of deaf and hearing-impaired children in the UK* (Final Report to the Nuffield Foundation, Grant No. HQ/338 EDU). Durham, U.K.: CEM Centre, University of Durham.

Webster, A. (1999). *Literacy interventions and pupils with hearing impairments, DfEE commissioned review.* Bristol, U.K.: Graduate School of Education, with National Foundation for Educational Research.

West, D. (2001). *"Here forever"—The importance of ethnographic research in the search for an understanding of deaf children's identity development.* Unpublished master of science diss., University of Bristol.

Young, A., Ackerman, J., & Kyle, J. G. (1998). *Looking on: Deaf people and the organisation of services.* Bristol, U.K.: Policy Press and Rowntree.

North and South America

Deafness: Educational-Historical Aspects in the Brazilian Context

Ana Cristina Guarinello, Ana Paula Santana,
Ana Paula Berberian, and Giselle de Athayde Massi

BRAZIL IS one of the largest and most extensively populated countries in the world. Its cities of São Paulo and Rio de Janeiro have larger populations than New York City. Among the main determinants that characterize Brazilian society are the diversity and heterogeneous environmental and cultural conditions that affect a growing population approaching 200,000,000 in a geographic area equivalent to the 48 contiguous states of the United States.

Brazil's continental dimensions and the vast diversity of the population, the geography, and the climate influence the types and degrees of economic development. Even though Brazil is the largest economy in Latin America, and ranks as 10th within the world economy, the challenge remains for the Brazilian nation to effectively attain a fairer and more evenly balanced income as well as the democratization of education, at all modes and levels, in a truly balanced form throughout the country.[1]

To address these challenges, especially concerning the development of an educational system that may effectively achieve the goal of the Brazilian Constitution of 1988 (Brasil, 1988)—that education is everyone's due right—we must face not only the differences in the educational profile of the Brazilian population but also the linguistic diversities historically present in our country. Concerning the first challenge, it is worth mentioning that according to the National Institute for Functional Literacy, in research done in 2001 (Ribeiro, 2004), 9% of the Brazilian population between the ages of 15 and 64 years are considered completely illiterate, 31% have poor literacy, 34% have medium literacy, and 26% have a high level of education.

In relation to the linguistic diversity that characterizes the different manners of speech in the country, it is important to make a few comments about Brazilian history. The Portuguese language, brought to Brazil during the Portuguese colonization around 1500, was

---

Much of the material for this chapter has grown out of collaboration that began in 2003 with a group of researchers who participate in the "Language, Deafness, and Education" work group, linked to the Speech Language Therapy and Audiology Graduate Course and to the Master and Doctor in Communication Disorders Program at the Universidade Tuiuti do Paraná. The scope of this work ranges from theoretical to applied research in education, family dynamics, therapy, and the lives of deaf individuals across the age range.

1. In Brazil, the educational system is represented by public and private schools at the following levels: *Educação Infantil* (preschool), *Ensino Fundamental* (grammar and middle school), *Ensino Médio* (high school) and *Universitário* (university). The private schools are generally used by the privileged upper classes, and the public schools by the less privileged social classes. This relationship tends to be reversed when it comes to the university level.

declared the official language in 1759. However, this language became the one predominantly spoken by Brazilians only at the beginning of the 20th century. In 1937, the standard of Portuguese elected to be representative of the national language in Brazil was a form of Portuguese spoken in Rio de Janeiro, the nation's capital at that time, a decision that was to the detriment of the other Portuguese dialects. The Portuguese spoken in Rio was considered the standard much as London, Paris, and Madrid were the standards for English, French, and Spanish, respectively, even though there was significant dialectical variation within each country. Languages from Brazilian natives, from Africa, from Europe, and from Japan are largely used throughout Brazil—evidence of the diversity that constitutes the formation of the Brazilian people.

Until the middle of the 20th century, the linguistic diversity represented an obstruction to the growing national trends and the industrialization of Brazil. In that period, even in urban centers, Portuguese was not the main language spoken by the population. In fact, studies that analyzed Brazilian demographics in that period point out the following facts about that time: foreign schools were predominant in Brazil; children from different ethnic groups in national schools used more than 20 spoken languages; and newspapers were written in many languages, including Italian, French, German, Polish, Japanese, English, and Ukrainian (Bagno, 2000; Berberian, 1995). In light of this diversity, some initiatives were adopted to expand the use of the Portuguese language to the whole Brazilian population. Those initiatives led to laws that mandated written and spoken Portuguese in the press, schools, and public organizations.

Despite the significant reduction of foreign schools, the linguistic diversity is still apparent among the descendants of immigrants who try to preserve their languages and habits, thus producing linguistic communities that are mostly bilingual, using Portuguese and their ancestors' native languages. Also important to mention is the fact that the Portuguese used as the official language in Brazil, apart from being partially different from the language spoken in Portugal and other Portuguese-speaking countries, is presently used by only a portion of the Brazilian people.[2] Others speak nonstandard Portuguese dialects that are less socially acceptable.

It is in this context that initiatives are being presently adopted to legitimate Brazilian Sign Language (Língua Brasileira de Sinais, or LIBRAS),[3] which has not yet reached the same level of acceptance as the standard variety of Brazilian Portuguese. Among the misconceptions that many have is the mistaken belief that LIBRAS is less complex and expressive than spoken language.

---

2. Portuguese in Brazil varies from that in Portugal, much as the English spoken in Australia and the United States varies from that spoken in England or the French spoken in Quebec varies from that spoken in France.

3. LIBRAS, considered the official Brazilian sign language, is used in most parts of the Brazilian territory. Note that, apart from this language, the Urubu Kaapor sign language is also considered to be a Brazilian sign language. The sign language of the Urubus-Kaapors Indians, who live in the state of Maranhão and who use as a spoken language the Tupi-guarani, was initially studied by Kakumasu (1968). This population's sign language was developed because a significant part of the tribe's population was born deaf (7 deaf people per 500 inhabitants). Therefore, the tribe developed a sign language used in villages where there are or were deaf people. This language, called Brazilian Kaapor Sign Language (Lingua de Sinais Kaapor Brasileira, or LSKB), has been used by many generations in that region of the Amazon and is a language that is totally Brazilian. The language is different from that of the American Indians because it is intratribal and not intertribal (Brito, 1993).

Table 18.1. Enrollment in Special and Regular Schools of the Private and Public Brazilian System

	Number of Students	Total Enrollment in Public Schools	Percentage	Enrollment in Private Schools	Percentage
Hard of Hearing	19,646	15,895	81.0%	3,751	19.0%
Deaf	46,668	36,671	78.5%	9,997	21.5%
Deaf and blind	1,127	796	70.6%	331	29.4%

Note: From Ministério da Educação (2005).

However the official recognition of LIBRAS, in April 2002 (Law No. 10436; Brasil, 2002), is a significant step toward the inclusion of deaf children in the regular educational system.[4] It is important to emphasize the fact that this law does not foresee the substitution of LIBRAS for the teaching and learning of the written Portuguese language. Concern with respect to the access of deaf people to standard Portuguese is clearly stressed, and Portuguese is taught.

Another factor that stresses the relevance of these concerns is the incidence of deaf people in our country. According to the Instituto Brasileiro de Geografia e Estatística (The Brazilian Institute of Geography and Statistics), in 2002, the Brazilian society had 5.7 million deaf people, including hearing impaired people with losses from mild to profound (Instituto Brasileiro de Geografia e Estatística, 2002). The Schooling Census reported by the Ministry of Education and Culture in 2005 (Ministério da Educação, 2005) showed that in Brazil there are 19,646 hard of hearing people, 46,668 deaf people, and 1,127 deaf and blind people registered in special and regular schools of the public and private Brazilian system. The majority of students attend public schools, as can be seen in Table 18.1.

Apart from those numbers, there are 617 public and private special schools registered in the Federação Nacional de Educação e Integração dos Surdos (FENEIS),[5] which provide some kind of support for deaf people, even though they do not specialize only in deafness.

EDUCATION FOR THE DEAF IN BRAZIL

The history of education of deaf individuals in Brazil is, to a large extent, similar to that of Europe and America. In early years, deaf children were frequently abandoned by their families or confined to their homes (Monteiro, 2006). This situation was a result of a very common

---

4. It is important to clarify that the official recognition of LIBRAS in Brazil began first at municipal and state levels during the 1990s and then at the federal level only in 2002 through Law No. 10436, which also legally makes provisions that municipal, state, and federal educational systems must guarantee the inclusion of LIBRAS in the university-level courses of Special Education, Teaching and Speech Language Therapy and Audiology and as an integral part of the National Curricular Parameters.

5. The founding in 1987 of the Federação Nacional de Educação e Integração dos Surdos (FENEIS; National Federation for Education and Integration of the Deaf), directed by deaf people, also contributed to the recognition of LIBRAS and, consequently, to the strengthening of the deaf people's rights. Linked to the World Federation of the Deaf, FENEIS has the mission of guaranteeing the social, cultural, and linguistic rights of that community. To promote sign language, FENEIS founded 140 associations throughout Brazil. In addition, it is responsible for certifying and inspecting the sign language interpreters.

view at the time in which children who were "different" were considered abnormal and, therefore, should be excluded from social interaction and from the regular school system.

The education of deaf people in Brazil, apart from being influenced by those common views of deaf people and by European methodologies formulated during the 16th and 18th centuries, was also influenced by studies of hearing and deafness that were conducted in Europe and in the United States, usually by medical professionals, through the 19th century until the middle of the 20th century. Strobel (2006) notes that these studies followed a logic in which deaf people were considered "sick or deficient," and, thus, were seen as people who needed specialized healing procedures. The classification as to the degrees of deafness also established the distance between those deaf people and the socially established norm.

The education of the deaf began to show a change in paradigms between the end of the 19th century and the beginning of the 20th century as a result of the economic and social necessities stemming from industrialization. Within this context, the idea was that a deaf person should take on a productive role and that the overall objectives of the educational system for this population should involve training deaf people to become productive workers (Strobel, 2006). Specific initiatives toward schooling of deaf students on a systematic basis started from the end of the 19th century up to the middle of the 20th century, which resulted in the founding of special institutions that had teachers who specialized in deafness. During this period, groups of deaf people went to regular schools, but had no access to differentiated learning methods. Therefore, the prevailing logic was that deaf students in the regular school system had the responsibility to adapt to the characteristics of this educational system and to correspond to its demands and expectations. After the 1990s, proposals to include deaf students in the regular school system began to be reformulated, and institutions became more aware of the need to recognize, respect, and consider the educationally relevant characteristics of deaf students when presenting their pedagogic proposals.

Deaf Students in the Special Schools

Notable among the initiatives for deaf students that marked the trajectory of their schooling in Brazil is the founding of the first special institution, the Imperial Instituto de Surdos-Mudos (Imperial Institute of Deaf and Dumb), presently known as the Instituto Nacional de Educação de Surdos (National Institution of Education of Deaf, INES). This institution was founded in 1857 by Ernest Huet, a Frenchman who became deaf at the age of 12 and later graduated from a program in France as a teacher. Huet immigrated to Brazil with a letter of recommendation issued by the French Minister for Public Education to work in the education of the deaf. Up to 1931, this institute educated only male students from ages 7 to 14. Throughout its history, the INES has been considered as one of the main educational pillars for deaf people in Brazil because it not only has been a center for dissemination of educational proposals but also has accepted students from all over Brazil. For this reason, it deserves our attention. It is, still, the only federal school for deaf students.

During the 19th century and practically up to the end of the 20th century, the INES prioritized initiatives that focused on the correction of speech and the rehabilitation of hearing, although the students were allowed to use sign language when out of their classrooms. In 1911, the INES determined that the pure oral method would be adopted in all the disciplines. However, because many of the students showed minimal progress with the use of this method, it was recommended only for young children (maximum age, 10 years) who could benefit from speech; meanwhile, the other children were taught by means of the written language. The use of sign language continued up to 1957 when the INES officially forbade the use of this method in the classrooms.

In 1929, more than 70 years after the founding of the INES in the state of Rio de Janeiro, the Instituto Santa Terezinha (Saint Terezinha Institute) was founded in the state of São Paulo, through the initiative of the Catholic Church, as a special school for deaf girls.[6] Since its beginning and up to the 1990s, the Santa Terezinha Institute, following the oral perspective predominant at the time, had as its main objective the integration of deaf students into the world of the hearing.

The clinical focus on speech rehabilitation had a predominant position in the educational history of deaf people. As a result of that focus, concentration on academic achievement in math, science, and literacy took second place. The oral approach that was used, which had the intention of normalizing the deaf child, that is, turning them into "speakers," resulted in a series of objective and subjective factors that restricted their overall development. Among those factors were the difficulty in accepting and dealing with the differences resulting from deafness; the reduced learning expectations for deaf students, particularly through non-pedagogical models; and the resistance to accepting sign language as a language (Santana, 2003).

The oral approach, based on the idea that the written language functions as a transcription of speech, presupposes that learning to speak is a prerequisite to learning the Portuguese language in the written mode. By emphasizing the speechreading mechanism, the expectation is that deaf students, through speechreading what they cannot hear and submitting to speech-training activities, learn how to write Portuguese. Studies have insistently pointed out the restriction of this approach and have demonstrated that deaf people generally receive only fragments of the spoken language through speechreading (Botelho, 2002; Guarinello, 2007). Similarly, being limited to educational experiences that have been reduced to simple repetition activities, deaf students are unable to effectively elaborate and interpret texts in a significant manner (Botelho, 2002).

Guarinello (2004, 2005), Santana (2003), and Skliar (1997), among others, emphasize that the oral approach, still present in clinical and educational facilities for deaf people in our country, are depriving deaf children socially, emotionally, cognitively, and psychologically. Those studies indicate the pedagogical failure of this approach because they show that under those learning conditions deaf students, even after a number of years, have difficulty acquiring overall knowledge and the use of the written language, both of which contribute to a process of social marginalization. Also noteworthy is that, even though gestures and sign language have been restricted and even prohibited, a result of the predominant oral perspective, groups of deaf people have faithfully continued to use sign language, which clearly indicates not only its power of expression but also the fundamental role that it plays in establishing their social relationships.

---

6. The Catholic Church played a key role in founding and maintaining institutions focused on educating and rehabilitating deaf people in many parts of Brazil, including the Domingos Sávio Institute, in Recife, in 1952; the Epheta Special School, in Curitiba, in 1956; and the Ludovico Pavoni Center of Hearing and Language, in Brasília, in 1973.

Worthy of note is the fact that only at the end of the 1970s did teachers begin to use signs in educating deaf students. At that time and continuing into the 1990s, studies of LIBRAS had begun to be developed in a more systematic way (Karnopp, 1994; Quadros, 1995). The contact between Brazilian teachers and Gallaudet University added to the discontent with the use of oral methods and fostered the recognition that sign language played an important role in deaf students' development. At the end of the 1970s, these changing perspectives culminated with the adoption of a philosophy called Total Communication by the Brazilian special schools. That approach was based on the idea that oral and sign systems should be used simultaneously. Therefore, signs should be used as a support to the teaching of Portuguese.

The Total Communication approach does not exclude resources and techniques that stimulate hearing, the adaptation of individual hearing aids, speechreading, speaking, reading, and writing. Programs derived from this philosophy are focused on allowing people to communicate and, thus, encourage use of any linguistic-communicative resource. All in all, priority is given to interaction between deaf and hearing people and not to the learning of a language (Ciccone, 1990).

Toward that goal, Total Communication uses the manual alphabet (a manual representation of the alphabet),[7] cued-speech (manual signals that represent the sounds of the Portuguese language), a system of signed Portuguese (an artificial system that combines signs from LIBRAS with spoken Portuguese syntactic structure and some invented signs to represent the grammatical structures nonexistent in sign language), and pidgin (the simplification of two languages coming into contact—in this case, Portuguese and sign language). It is important to stress that discussions about the use of this philosophy are quite recent and polemic in linguistic and in educational spheres.

Some specialists further recommend the simultaneous use of oral language and manual codes, which is called Simultaneous Communication (Goldfeld, 1997). The objective of Simultaneous Communication is to teach a deaf person the oral language's grammar through an artificial language. This emphasis ends up inhibiting important language functions and characteristics that could be the basis of language development and of cognition. The correlation between the grammar of one language and the respective signs in another, although justified for educational purposes, in this case, ends up decharacterizing both the Portuguese language, in its oral and written modes, as well as the actual sign language used among deaf people (Santana, 2003).

Simultaneous Communication prevails in many classrooms for the deaf in Brazil, more than other techniques suggested in Total Communication. The simultaneous use of spoken Portuguese and some kind of signed Portuguese system that borrows much of its vocabulary, but not syntax, from LIBRAS is used in deaf schools to facilitate the learning of the written Portuguese language. Thus, the main focus of this approach is the development of the oral language and its written form (Moura, 2000)—not development of knowledge related to actual sign language and its linguistic, social, political and educational implications.

Presently in Brazil, the Simultaneous Communication practice either is being treated as a synonym for bilingualism or is offered as part of proposals that are labeled as being bilingual.

---

7. The Brazilian manual alphabet is based on the French manual alphabet and, as such, is almost identical to the American manual alphabet.

Although some schools support the proposal of a bilingual education, studies show that the linguistic know-how teachers have about the subject is rudimentary because the great majority have only just begun learning sign language (Fernandes, 2003). According to Fernandes (2003), the bilingualism adopted in Brazil is, to a great degree, pseudo-bilingualism because the teachers are not proficient in sign language and use Simultaneous Communication. The following insights help to explain this situation: (a) bilingual education began to be discussed in Brazil only in the 1990s; (b) a bilingual approach involves a series of variables that involve a lot more in the educational process than the simple use of two languages and that are complicated by specific, historical, political, regional, and cultural mechanisms; (c) a bilingual approach requires, first and foremost, the recognition of LIBRAS as the language of the Brazilian deaf community and, second, the understanding that deaf people are a part of a minor linguistic community whose characteristics are the sharing of a sign language, cultural values, habits, and socializing modes of their own (Fernandes, 2003; Skliar, 1997).

Bilingualism inaugurates a debate in the deafness area concerning the importance of having a language. This approach defends, in the Brazilian case, the priority of sign language over the Portuguese language.

Quadros and Skliar (2004) declare that bilingual education for deaf students can be defined as a complex phenomenon because it reflects social-political issues and not simply the presence of two languages (LIBRAS and the Portuguese language). Although bilingual education is an academic project, it is also intimately associated with linguistic policies, identities, and peculiarities that hinder deaf people's lives. In addition, educational proposals based on true bilingualism presume that the deaf child should be in a bilingual school until becoming an adult and that deaf adults must take part in this bilingual education. This reasoning means that the language used in bilingual schools must be the actual sign language and that the teachers in those schools must be either (preferably) deaf or hearing and proficient in that sign language.

Therefore, according to the bilingual proposal, the school represents the privileged space in which one may acquire sign language, an opportunity presented by the interaction with deaf companions and bilingual teachers. Deaf children should be exposed to sign language at the earliest possible moment. This proposal also suggests (a) that the deaf person be taught the Portuguese language in the oral or written mode and (b) that Portuguese will be taught based on the knowledge acquired through sign language (Lacerda, 2000).

The bilingual approach advocates separating from the clinical model that emphasizes oral methodologies and invites the teacher to assume the role of an educator and to relinquish the role of a "speech rehabilitator." As an educator, he or she has to teach, considering the singularity that constitutes deaf students and taking on LIBRAS as the instruction language. Deaf educators are necessary to enable "ownership" of sign language by deaf children and to disseminate this language to the children's families (Nascimento, 2002).

Even though these discussions and proposals based on the bilingual approach have made headway, there are actually very few deaf teachers working in special schools. Moreover, the majority of the hearing teachers are not proficient in sign language. The effectuation and the broadening of bilingual education for deaf students depends on the commitment and concrete initiatives from the different social agents involved in the process, including interpreters, public agents, public and private universities, deaf and nondeaf teachers, deaf people's organizations, and researchers.

However, as evidence of measures that are more democratic in teaching deaf students, some government strategies are already being implemented as far as special education is concerned, especially related to curricular structure, school evaluation, as well as material and human resources focused on deafness. There is no significant difference between the curricular structure proposed by the Ministry of Education for special schools and the structure adopted in the regular schools[8] except with respect to aspects that involve the teaching of Portuguese and sign language; special consideration is given to the idea that deaf students need more study time to learn the Portuguese language in the written mode than do non-deaf students (Ministério da Educação, 1997). In terms of pedagogy, deaf students in these schools have a right to differentiated teaching strategies such as deaf instructors and teachers who are completely at home with sign language,[9] and as an overall rule, their families are offered courses in sign language.

In the future, child education goals include the following: a curricular complementation focusing on learning of the Portuguese language in the oral mode, with teachers specialized in hearing training, reading facial expressions, speech development, and linguistics; acquisition of LIBRAS through talking to another deaf person or through a teacher proficient in LIBRAS; services from an itinerant interpreter; psycho-pedagogical services; services in the health area; resource classrooms with specific physical features and materials for the students (e.g., electronic resources such as hearing aids and cochlear implants,[10] speech trainers, educational software, computers, slides, etc.).

Despite the policy that special schools should follow the same national curriculum adopted by regular schools, most Brazilian special schools for the deaf still concentrate on oral language development. Not much attention is given to academic achievement.

Deaf students who are already enrolled in the special education system have the option of simultaneously enrolling in regular schools. According to the Ministry of Education–Brazil (Ministério da Educação, 1997), preschooling for children from birth to age 6 years can take place either in a regular school or in special institutions, depending on the family's choice. The *Ensino Fundamental*, for children ages 7 to 14 years, can also be undertaken in either

---

8. It is important to clarify that the Brazilian Ministry of Education is responsible for all national policies related to education and plays a major role in education. There is a national curriculum based on the Lei de Diretrizes e Bases (Directives and Basis Law), and each state should adapt the national curriculum to its reality and peculiarities.

9. Deaf instructors go through preparation courses that take place all over the country. The intention is that, in the near future, as in other countries, universities will be founded to graduate deaf teachers in the teaching of LIBRAS. FENEIS has battled for the recognition of the LIBRAS instructor as a professional and has already undertaken 31 courses to prepare deaf instructors. In turn, FENEIS trained deaf people throughout Brazil, who went back to their 27 states as instructors, and those instructors were able to train an average of 20 new LIBRAS instructors in each one of the states.

10. It is important to mention that cochlear implant surgeries began in Brazil in the 1990s. The first surgery was made at Hospital Universitário de Reabilitação de Anomalias Crânio-Faciais HRAC (University Hospital of Rehabilitation of Skull and Face Anomalies), part of the Centro de Pesquisa Audiológicas (Center of Audiologic Research). In addition, there are six other public hospitals and some particular services located in Brazilian regions that are scientific and economically more developed that also perform the surgery. Since the 1990s, Brazilian deaf people, from all social groups, can register in federal programs to have the cochlear implant surgery and the accompanying therapy. Also noteworthy is that not many people have participated in this program, in part, because of the lack of human and material resources available in health public institutions and the lack of awareness about this device. To overcome this situation, the Brazilian government is now implementing public policies to assist deaf people in relation to this program.

one of the institutions; the recommendation is that the child study in both schools but in different time periods (mornings and afternoons). The *Ensino Médio*, for young people between the ages of 15 and 18, and the *Universitário* studies are generally undertaken only in regular institutions[11] because, in Brazil, special learning institutions for the *Ensino Médio* are extremely rare, and special institutions for deaf university students are nonexistent. We also would like to emphasize that there are no residential schools for the deaf in Brazil. Some states operate day schools for deaf children, but the preferred choice is simultaneous study at regular and special schools.

However, there is a shortage of special schools in the country, and these numbers are decreasing each year. According to the Ministry of Education (Ministério da Educação, 2005), in 1998, 87% of the special schools that had been operating in Brazil previously were still providing services; in 2005, that percentage decreased to 59%. The support being given to inclusive proposals is helping teachers from regular schools to be prepared to work with the diverse students. In 1998, only 13% of special children studied at regular schools; this number increased to 41% in 2005.

Most of the Brazilian special schools are located in privileged economic regions such as the South and Southeast. In these regions, deaf people from all social levels have more access to education; access for deaf children from distant rural communities is more restricted. In other Brazilian regions (North, Northeast, and Central), cities far away from the capital do not have special schools. Thus, deaf children from those regions have only the option to study at regular schools that are not prepared to work with this population.

Deaf Students in Regular Schools

At the very beginning of the 20th century, deaf children went to regular schools; however, at the time, there were very few specific supportive measures for their education. The greater part of the deaf students who attended regular schools had to adapt to the same pedagogical methods used for the hearing students. It was only from 1990 that inclusive proposals for students with special needs began to be discussed in the national education policies.

In the Brazilian Constitution of 1988, article 208 defines that attendance of disabled students should be, preferentially, in the regular schooling system. In addition, the 1996 *Lei de Diretrizes e Bases* (Directives and Basis Law; Brasil, 1996) states that education should be as integrated as possible and proposed that students with special needs be included in the regular school system. This integration, however, presumed that it was up to the student to keep up with what the school taught.

The change to this situation came about only after the Salamanca Declaration (UNESCO, 1994), as a result of a conference in Salamanca (Spain), which declared that it is the school's responsibility to adapt to each student's needs. This declaration gave support to the discussions that confront and counter the earlier inclusive approach (Lacerda, 2000).

---

11. The *Universitário* (University studies) in Brazil is undertaken through a selection process, therefore, the Circular Edict 277/96 of the *Ministério de Estado da Educação e do Desporto* (State Ministry for Education and Sports) suggests that, when evaluating a deaf candidate in the selection process, the semantic aspects of knowledge are to be taken into more consideration than the formal aspects of the Portuguese language.

Later, after those discussions, curricular proposals for regular schools became a part of the *Projeto Escola Viva—Brasil* (Live School Project—Brazil) (Ministério da Educação, 2000), prepared by the Ministry of Education. Those proposals are divided into the following:

- Large Adaptations—Actions to be undertaken by the institution to accommodate the student with special needs, for example, hiring interpreters, providing sign language tuition for teachers, etc.
- Small Adaptations—Actions to be undertaken by the teacher, for example, promoting access with respect to the curriculum and teaching objectives, teaching methods, and evaluation process.[12]

In relation to the specific inclusion of deaf students in regular schooling, the Ministry of Education—Brazil (Ministério da Educação, 2002) proposes that regular schools should offer the following within their organizations:

- Activities in regular classrooms—with teachers qualified to meet the special educational needs of their students, supported by a special education teacher and a LIBRAS-Portuguese language interpreter, according to the institution's pedagogical program[13]
- Specialized support services provided in resource classes, in special classes, in home attendance, or in other situations as defined by the teaching system

The resource classes are to be found in regular schools and should be taught by a teacher prepared to educate students with special needs. The students should partake in these classes concomitantly with their regular schooling. The resource class teacher reinforces the subjects taught in the regular classes, using LIBRAS to supplement information on the subject and emphasizing the written Portuguese language.

Special classes in regular schools are recommended to students who do not attend regular classes. These special classrooms are made up of approximately 10 deaf students, who should be taught, preferably, by a teacher who has specialized in teaching of deaf students and has knowledge of both the Portuguese language and Brazilian sign language. This teacher should be responsible for the pedagogical support of the deaf students, acting as a facilitator for their learning process and their integration into the hearing world.

Special classes or resource classes for deaf students are not yet available in all of the Brazilian towns because financial and human resources for their implementation are lacking. Therefore, the federal government launched the *Programa Nacional de Apoio a Educação dos Surdos* (The National Program to Support the Education of the Deaf), focused on implementing *Centros de Capacitação de Profissionais da Educação e de Atendimento às Pessoas com Surdez* (Training Centers for Professionals in Education and Support of Deaf People) throughout the country. These centers, to be found in the capital cities, have the objective of qualifying

---

12. As to the evaluation of the deaf student learning process, The Ministry of Education—Brazil (Ministério da Educação, 1997) suggests that it is not a good idea to permit a student's linguistic performance to interfere with his or her academic performance; therefore, the regular school teacher has to be aware of the pedagogical difficulties of many deaf students concerning the Portuguese language.

13. The educational legislation, through Law No. 10.098 of 2000, guarantees to the deaf community that the federal government will provide for the elimination of communication barriers, will ensure that deaf people have access to information and to education, and therewith will ensure the training of sign language interpreters to facilitate any kind of direct communication with a deaf person.

teachers from smaller towns, preparing didactic material specific for bilingual education, as well as providing guidance to family members and professionals dealing with deaf students.

It is important to note that, even though the Ministry of Education proposed the participation of interpreters in regular classes, this profession has as of yet to be regulated throughout Brazil and is present only in a few of the Brazilian states. Technically, sign language interpreters may work in the *Educação Infantil*, in the *Educação Fundamental*, in the *Ensino Médio*, at the university, and in postgraduate courses. Unfortunately, there are very few places in Brazil that have experience with in-class interpreters, especially in the *Ensino Fundamental*. Interpreters who are skilled in LIBRAS is a recent advance, and only those in large urban cities have access to them. Only a limited number of people are capable of taking on this function at this time. Moreover, it is clear that most of the teachers who work in regular schools are not ready to handle deaf students because the communication difficulty between teacher and deaf student restricts the learning possibilities of those students.

It is also important to mention that according to the Brazilian Ministry of Education, in 2003, there were 665 hearing impaired people registered in institutions of higher education; in 2004, this number increased to 974, comprising 95 in public institutions and 879 in private. As mentioned earlier, in general, it is more difficult for deaf students to get into a public university because the selection process is more rigorous in these institutions and there are fewer higher education public institutions.

Raymann (2001) collected data from 34 deaf university students attending a university located in Porto Alegre (South Brazil). Those students were studying the following: education, art, computer sciences, biology, computer technology, geography, industrial design, physiotherapy, architecture and urbanism, history, languages, mathematics, mechanical engineering, physical education, and social service. According to Raymann, the highest concentration of deaf students was found in education, which may be related to the possibility that students perceive a good chance of future employment in deaf education.

Despite the fact that the number of jobs for deaf people is increasing, Brazil still has a huge unemployment problem not only for deaf people but also for the population in general. To address this situation, some institutions such as deaf associations, deaf schools, and especially FENEIS are helping deaf people to get jobs and to improve their professional qualifications by creating partnerships with private and public companies. These institutions provide social and psychological assistance to deaf people and adapt jobs, thus guaranteeing the partnership success.

FINAL CONSIDERATIONS

Presently, Brazil is encountering educational, linguistic, political, and social difficulties in the education of Brazilian deaf people. Among the challenges to be overcome are insufficient training of bilingual teachers and lack of trained deaf teachers; insufficient sign language courses; lack of knowledge among families with respect to sign language; use of bimodal practices (such as Simultaneous Communication) by most of the teachers in special schools; insufficient number of people who are proficient in LIBRAS; lack of support from the universities and teaching institutions; the size of the country; and social and educational differences in the many regions.

Improvement in the education of deaf people depends on changing the way in which those in power perceive deaf people and deafness. It also depends on linguistic and social acceptance of sign language, particularly LIBRAS, as a legitimate language to be used in schools as well as in the Brazilian society. In addition, Brazil must take practical actions to establish an educational project for deaf people that includes historical and cultural heritage of the deaf communities in the curriculum, cultivates new educational technologies based essentially on visual resources, invites the participation of the deaf community in education management, and more.

Another necessary practical action has to do with allocating financial resources for preparing special classes and for training bilingual teachers and deaf instructors as well as interpreters who will function not only in the educational context but also in public institutions such as airports, hospitals, bus terminals, banks, etc. Finally, Brazil needs to take steps and provide financial resources that guarantee the continuous graduation of teachers, both in special schools and regular schools, who will emphasize not only the learning of LIBRAS and written Portuguese but also the cognitive, linguistic, and social aspects involved in the overall development of deaf people.

REFERENCES

Bagno, M. (2000). *Preconceito lingüístico no Brasil* [Linguistic prejudice in Brazil]. São Paulo: Edições Loyola.

Berberian, A. P. (1995). *Fonoaudiologia e educação: Um encontro histórico* [Speech language therapy and education: A historic meeting]. São Paulo: Plexus.

Botelho, P. (2002). *Linguagem e letramento na educação dos surdos: Ideologias e práticas pedagógicas* [Language and literacy in deaf education: Ideologies and pedagogic practices]. Belo Horizonte: Autêntica.

Brasil. (1988). Constituição Federal [Federal Constitution].

Brasil. (1996). Lei de Diretrizes e Bases da Educação Nacional [Directives and Basis Law]. Lei No. 9394/96. Brasília: Ministério da Educação.

Brasil. (2000). Lei No. 10 098, de 19 de dezembro de 2000. Acessibilidade das pessoas com deficiências (Law No. 10 098. Access for disabled people).

Brasil. (2002). Lei No. 10 436, de 24 de abril de 2002. Língua brasileira de sinais—LIBRAS [Law No. 10 436. Brazilian sign language].

Brito, L. F. (1993). *Integração social e educação de surdos* [Social integration and deaf education]. Rio de Janeiro: Babel Editora.

Ciccone, M. M. C., (1990). *Comunicação Total. Introdução. Estratégia. A pessoa surda* [Total Communication. Introduction. Strategy. Deaf individual]. Rio de Janeiro: Cultura Médica.

Fernandes, S. (2003). *Educação bilíngüe para surdos: Identidades, diferenças, contradições e mistérios* [Bilingual education for the deaf: Identity, differences, contradictions and mysteries]. Unpublished doctoral diss., Universidade Federal do Paraná, Curitiba, Brasil.

Goldfeld, M. (1997). *A criança surda* [The deaf child]. São Paulo: Plexus.

Guarinello, A. C. (2004). *O papel do outro no processo de construção de produções escritas por sujeitos surdos* [The role of the other in the written language constructions of deaf individuals]. Unpublished doctoral diss., Universidade Federal do Paraná, Curitiba, Brasil.

Guarinello, A. C. (2005). O papel do outro na produção da escrita de sujeitos surdos [The role of the other in written productions of deaf people]. *Distúrbios da Comunicação, 17*(2), 245–254.

Guarinello, A. C. (2007). O papel do iutro na escrita de sujeitos surdos [The role of the other in deaf people's written language]. São Paulo: Plexus.

Kakumasu, J. (1968). Urubu Sign Language. *International Journal of American Linguistics, 34*(4), 275–281.

Karnopp, L. B. (1994). *Aquisição do parâmetro configuração de mão dos sinais da língua de sinais brasileira: Estudo sobre quatro crianças surdas filhas de pais surdos* [Acquisition of hand configuration in Brazilian sign language: Study of four deaf children with deaf parents]. Unpublished masters thesis, Pontifícia Universidade Católica do Rio Grande do Sul, Porto Alegre, Brasil.

Lacerda, C. B. F. (2000). A prática pedagógica mediada (também) pela língua de sinais: Trabalhando com sujeitos surdos [Pedagogical practice through sign language: Working with deaf individuals]. *Cadernos CEDES, 20*(50), 70–83.

Ministério da Educação. (1997). *Parâmetros Curriculares Nacionais: Introdução aos parâmetros curriculares nacionais* [National Curriculum]. Brasília: Secretaria de Educação Fundamental, Ministério da Educação.

Ministério da Educação. (2000). *Projeto Escola Viva: 5 e 6: Garantindo o acesso e permanência de todos os alunos na escola—alunos com necessidades educacionais especiais* [Live School Project]. Brasília: Secretaria de Educação Especial, Ministério da Educação.

Ministério da Educação, Secretaria de Educação Especial. (2002). *Ensino de língua Portuguesa para surdos: Caminhos para a prática pedagógica* [Teaching Portuguese language for deaf students: Paths to pedagogical practice]. Brasília: Author.

Ministério da Educação, Secretaria de Educação Especial. (2005). *Conceitos da educação especial—Censo escolar* [Special education school census]. Retrieved October 17, 2008, from http://portal.mec.gov.br/seesp/index.php?option=content&task=view&id=114

Monteiro, M. S. (2006). História dos movimentos dos surdos e o reconhecimento da LIBRAS no Brasil [Deaf motion history and LIBRAS recognition in Brazil]. *Educação Temática Digital, 7*(2), 279–289.

Moura, M. C. (2000). *O surdo: Caminhos para uma nova identidade* [The deaf: Path for a new identity]. Rio de Janeiro: Revinter.

Nascimento, L. C. R. (2002). *Fonoaudiologia e surdez: Uma análise dos percursos discursivos da prática fonoaudiológica no Brasil* [Speech language therapy and deafness: A discursive analysis of speech language therapy Brazilian practice]. Unpublished doctoral diss., Universidade Estadual de Campinas, Campinas, Brasil.

Quadros, R. M. (1995). *As categorias vazias pronominais: Uma análise com base na LIBRAS e reflexos no processo de aquisição* [Pronominal empty categories: An analysis based on LIBRAS and its acquisition process]. Porto Alegre: Pontifícia Universidade Católica, Porto Alegre.

Quadros, R. M., & Skliar, C. (2004). Bilingual deaf education in the South of Brazil. *Bilingual Education and Bilingualism, 7*(5), 368–380.

Raymann, B. C. W. (2001). *Family factors as predictors for academic development and progress: A self-report by hearing parents of deaf university students and by deaf university students.* Unpublished doctoral diss., Wisconsin International University, Wisconsin, USA.

Ribeiro, V. M. (Ed.). (2004). *Letramento no Brasil* [Literacy in Brazil]. São Paulo: Global.

Santana, A. P. (2003). *Reflexões neurolingüísticas sobre a surdez* [Neurolinguistic reflections about deafness]. Unpublished doctoral diss., Universidade Estadual de Campinas, Campinas, Brasil.

Skliar, C. (Ed.) (1997). *Educação & exclusão: Abordagens sócio-antropológicas em educação especial* [Education & exclusion: Social anthropologic approaches in special education]. Porto Alegre, Brasil: Mediação.

Strobel, K. L. (2006). A visão histórica da in(ex)clusão dos surdos nas escolas [A historic perception about ex(in)clusion of deaf people at schools]. *Educação temática digital, 7*(2), 244–252. Retrieved August 24, 2006, from http://143.106.58.55/revista/viewissue.php?id=8

UNESCO. (1994). *Declaração de Salamanca: Sobre principios, politia e práticas n área das necessidades educativas especiais* [Salamanca Declaration]. Retrieved September 12, 2008, from http://portal.mec.gov.br/seesp/arquivos/pdf/salamanca.pdf

Education of Deaf and Hard of Hearing Learners in Canada

Connie Mayer, C. Tane Akamatsu, Mary Ann Bibby,
Janet R. Jamieson, and Raymond LeBlanc

CANADA IS the second largest country in the world, spanning six time zones from the Atlantic to the Pacific and stretching 4,800 kilometers from north to south. The southern portion consists of 10 provinces, and the northern region is divided into three territories. For such a large country, the population is small, slightly less than 34 million people, with most living in areas of urban concentration in the south, close to the border with the United States. Rural areas are spread out and sparsely populated, particularly in the north. It has been estimated that there are more than 200,000 profoundly deaf people in Canada and an additional 1.5 million with milder hearing loss (Rodda & Hiron, 1989). However, the Canadian Association of the Deaf argues that there are problems with the way in which this information is collected and recommends using one-tenth of the United States numbers as a guideline, which would produce a more accurate calculation of 310,000 deaf and deafened people and about 2.8 million hard of hearing Canadians (Canadian Association of the Deaf, 2007).

Although Canada has only two official languages, French and English, Canadians pride themselves on the multicultural nature of their citizenry as well as the linguistic and ethnic diversity of their population. Minority rights and linguistic cultural freedom are seen as central and are enshrined in the Canadian Charter of Rights and Freedoms (Department of Justice, Canada, 1982). All minority groups can demand, and expect to receive under the law, recognition and equality in every area, including that of education. Deaf and hard of hearing people share these linguistic and cultural rights. Signing deaf Canadians who come from Anglophone families use American Sign Language (ASL) as it is used in the United States, with a few lexical or regional differences. These differences are described in *The Canadian Dictionary of ASL* (Bailey & Dolby, 2002), a volume that was developed in conjunction with the Canadian Cultural Society of the Deaf and lists more than 8,700 signs, many unique to Canada and capturing regional differences across the country. Signing deaf Canadians who come from Francophone families (usually in Québec or northern and central New Brunswick) use La Langue des Signes de Québecois (LSQ). The two sign languages have many cognates, but are considered to be two different languages. Although ASL and LSQ have not yet achieved official language status nationally or provincially, they are recognized as languages of instruction in three provinces—Manitoba, Alberta, and Ontario. There are no known standard signed languages used by the aboriginal, First Nations peoples of Canada, although there is some evidence that an indigenous form of sign language may exist among deaf Inuit people in Nunavut Territory (MacDougall, 2001).

In Canada, responsibility for education is a provincial rather than a federal responsibility, resulting in significant diversity among provincial services. On the positive side, this diversity contributes to the growth of innovative and creative solutions to meet the varying needs found in different areas of the country. However, this decentralized administrative control has contributed to a lack of continuity and cohesive development across the country as a whole. Moreover, although provincial governments directly control a few schools, including some provincial schools for deaf students, most educational facilities are run by local school boards. The positive and negative conditions created by this diversity affect all of special education in a very direct way, and these effects become evident in a closer examination of the education of deaf and hard of hearing students. Indeed, this diversity presented challenges in the writing of this chapter because it was often difficult, given the limitations of space, to provide a comprehensive account of each region of the country.

LOOKING BACK: HISTORICAL FRAMEWORKS

The history of the education of deaf and hard of hearing individuals in Canada parallels the history of the country more broadly in that it had its roots in eastern Canada and moved west over time as the country opened up with the building of the railroad (Clarke & Winzer, 1983).[1] The first school for the deaf was opened in 1831 in Champlain, Quebec, under the direction of Ronald McDonald. McDonald had been sent to visit schools for the deaf in New York and Philadelphia and had been trained and supervised by Thomas Hopkins Gallaudet and Laurent Clerc. This out-of-country preparation set the stage for a practice that continued for close to 130 years, that is, the formal training of teachers outside the boundaries of the country—in the United States (because of its close proximity) and in Britain (because of its cultural, historical, and Commonwealth links to Canada). In this way, both of these countries were instrumental in influencing early trends and policies in Canada through this teacher education connection (Bibby, 1999).

This early Quebec school closed after 5 years because it lacked funds, typifying what happened with many schools and classes that opened throughout the 19th century in Prince Edward Island, New Brunswick, and Quebec. Operating costs were a critical factor in survival, and many of these new endeavors were entirely dependent on the goodwill and financial assistance of private benefactors, although by the 1860s, some provincial governments were providing support through grants.

After the closure of the early school in Champlain, two Francophone schools for the deaf were established by the Catholic church in Montreal, Quebec—the Institution Catholique des Sourds-Muets (for boys) in 1848 and the Institution Catholique des Sourdes-Muettes (for girls) in 1851. In the same city in 1870, a deaf Englishman, Thomas Widd, opened the Protestant Institution for Deaf-Mutes that later became known as the Mackay Centre.

Outside of Quebec, the first facility to be opened was the School for the Deaf in Halifax, Nova Scotia, in 1856, co-founded by two deaf Scotsmen, William Gray and George Tait. Three schools in New Brunswick were opened (and subsequently closed) in the late 19th and

---

1. See Carbin (1996), whose volume on the history of the Deaf community in Canada is the most comprehensive in the field.

early 20th centuries—the New Brunswick Institution for the Deaf and Dumb (1874–1890), which was founded by a deaf man named Alfred Abell; the Fredericton Institution for the Education of the Deaf and Dumb (1882–1902); and the New Brunswick School for the Deaf (1903–1918).

The first school for deaf children in Ontario was established in 1858 as the Upper Canada Institution for the Instruction of the Deaf and Dumb in Toronto. This school moved to Hamilton in 1864 and was renamed the Hamilton Institution for the Instruction of the Deaf and Dumb. In 1870, the Ontario Institution for the Education and Instruction of the Deaf and Dumb opened in Belleville. It became known as the Ontario School for the Deaf in 1913 and was renamed the Sir James Whitney School for the Deaf in 1974 after a former premier of the province.

In the west, the Manitoba Institution for the Deaf and Dumb, now known as the Manitoba School for the Deaf, was opened in 1888, with a temporary closure during World War II that ended up lasting for 25 years from 1940 to 1965. The first school for the deaf in Saskatchewan, the Saskatchewan School for the Deaf, was opened in 1915 but closed after 1 year. The next school was not opened until 1931 when Rupert Williams, a deaf man, founded the Saskatchewan School for the Deaf in Saskatoon. In 1982, that school was renamed the R. J. Williams School for the Deaf after its founder, becoming the only Canadian school for the deaf to date that is named after a deaf individual. Two early schools opened in Victoria, British Columbia—the British Columbia School for Deaf-Mutes (1888–1889) and the Victoria School for the Deaf and Dumb (1899–1900)—but each lasted only 1 year. The British Columbia School for the Deaf was founded in Vancouver in 1922, in great part because of the measures of a deaf woman named Lucy Jane Gosse. In 1955, it was renamed the Jericho Hill School for the Deaf. It was subsequently moved to Burnaby, a suburb of Vancouver, where it operates as a "congregated model" and is known as the British Columbia Provincial School for the Deaf.

As is evident from this brief overview, deaf people were instrumental in establishing these early schools, and in most cases, manual communication was used by the teachers. However, after the meeting of the International Congress on Education of the Deaf held in Milan in 1880, oral instructional methods began to predominate, and there was much less use of signed language in the classrooms.

During the second half of the 20th century, a number of additional schools for the deaf opened across the country. In eastern Canada, three schools were opened—the Newfoundland School for the Deaf in 1964 (which was relocated to a new building in 1987) and, in Ontario, the Ernest C. Drury School for the Deaf in 1963 and the Robarts School in 1972. In western Canada, the Alberta School for the Deaf was opened in 1955.

In Atlantic Canada,[2] the School for the Deaf in Halifax was moved to Amherst, Nova Scotia, in 1961 and was renamed the Interprovincial School for the Deaf; there were two subsequent name changes, first, to the Atlantic Provinces Resource Centre for the Hearing Handicapped and, second, to the Atlantic Provinces Special Education Authority Resource Centre for the Hearing Impaired. In January 1975, the four Atlantic provinces signed an interprovincial agreement that brought into being the Atlantic Provincial Schools Education

---

2. Atlantic Canada comprises the provinces of Newfoundland and Labrador, Nova Scotia, Prince Edward Island, and New Brunswick.

Authority (APSEA). It was enacted into legislation later that year in New Brunswick as the Education of Aurally or Visually Handicapped Persons Act and as regulations in Section 20 of the Handicapped Persons Education Act in Nova Scotia. In 1995, the resource center was relocated to Halifax as the Atlantic Provinces Special Education Authority (also known as APSEA), a facility that serves the four Atlantic provinces with on-campus and outreach programs.

All of these schools for the deaf provided some kind of residential facility, an arrangement that assisted in solving the rather serious transportation problems that exist in a country the size of Canada. Students in the Atlantic provinces traveled many kilometers to the Halifax Institution and even went as far as the schools in Ontario and Quebec. For many years, students from the West coast traveled 1,500 miles to the Saskatchewan and Manitoba schools, and students from Alberta traveled even further to Montreal. Today, deaf and hard of hearing students generally have access to educational services much closer to home and in their own province. However, this convenience still does not apply to students from the North— the Yukon, the Northwest Territories, and Nunavut. If students in those territories wish to receive their education in a specialized school, they must leave their homes and travel to live at the schools or in foster homes in one of the provinces to the south.

In addition to residential schools, the Canadian provinces also started day classes for deaf students. The first province to make a deliberate and systematic attempt was Ontario, with classes opening in Toronto in 1924, in Ottawa in 1928, and in Hamilton in 1944. Eventually, in 1964, the Metropolitan Toronto Public School Board established the largest Canadian day school for children with hearing loss, the Metropolitan Toronto Public School for the Deaf. During the 1960s, increased parental pressure demanded that locally accountable school boards take more responsibility for educating children with special needs and, as a result, programs for deaf and hard of hearing learners sprang up all across Canada. These programs typically included three approaches:

- Special classes for hard of hearing children, which were predominantly auditory-oral, at the elementary level, and often organized on the basis of partial or gradual integration;
- Special classes for deaf children, which used either an auditory-oral or combined approach and typically functioned as alternative placements to the schools for the deaf; and
- Special services such as speechreading, auditory training, speech teaching, tutoring, remediation, counseling, and interpreting, which were provided to students on an individual basis by itinerant teachers (Clarke & Winzer, 1983).

In Quebec, the Montreal Oral School for the Deaf was founded in 1950 by a small group of English-speaking parents, and in British Columbia, the Vancouver Oral Centre for Deaf Children was established in 1960, receiving the Alexander Graham Bell Award for excellence in auditory-oral programming in 1981. Many other Canadian cities operated smaller oral day classes and programs, including the Quebec Catholic school boards, which offered French oral options to large numbers of deaf and hard of hearing students.

By the early 1970s, a variety of educational options were available to Canadian deaf and hard of hearing children. Students could be educated in manual or in oral settings, and they could be integrated into regular classes or attend a school for the deaf. The re-introduction of sign language in schools during the 1970s was largely done through the use of signing systems such as Signed English or Signing Exact English, under the umbrella of a Total

Communication philosophy. This approach was used for the most part at the provincial schools for the deaf and in a few congregated classes in school districts. Hard of hearing and oral deaf students, whether in congregated or integrated settings, continued to be educated primarily through auditory-oral approaches.

The latter two decades of the 20th century marked a time of significant change and development. Arguably the most significant of these changes were the push for the recognition of ASL as a language of instruction and the move to bilingual-bicultural models of education for deaf and hard of hearing students. There was particularly strong support for this position among members of the Deaf community, and by the early 1990s, most provincial schools for the deaf across the country had adopted a bilingual-bicultural philosophy. In practice, this instruction consisted largely of ASL for face-to-face communication and the development of English through text. In three provinces (Manitoba, Alberta, and Ontario), ASL was recognized officially as a language of instruction. Across the country, the same time period also saw the introduction of legislation requiring students to be educated within the least restrictive environment, the development of ever more sophisticated communication technologies, and advances in cochlear implant technology, with increasing number of students receiving implants during the 1990s.

TAKING STOCK: THE CURRENT STATE OF EDUCATION IN CANADA FOR DEAF AND HARD OF HEARING STUDENTS

Educational Programs and Services

Across the country, there has generally been a move from congregated settings such as schools for the deaf and designated classes for learners with hearing loss in public schools to settings that are integrated with hearing students. Overall, the student population in schools for the deaf is declining, and currently, there are only seven schools for the deaf in Canada, three being located in the most populous province of Ontario. The language of instruction at these schools is ASL, although some students may use contact sign for educational purposes. Although exact numbers are not available, it would be fair to say that, on school entry, students who rely on spoken language for communication and/or have cochlear implants tend to be educated in integrated settings whereas ASL users tend to be at the schools for the deaf, although there are some signing students who are educated in mainstream settings with interpreters. It is also the case that significant numbers of students in all settings, but especially in congregated classes and schools for the deaf, have additional disabilities.

Most provinces offer educational options in all communication philosophies, covering the range from auditory-verbal therapy to bilingual-bicultural programs. However, not every deaf and hard of hearing student in Canada has equal access to all of these options. As is the case with so many educational issues in Canada, those who live in the more populated regions are more likely to have access to the full range of language and communication options. For example, access to auditory-verbal therapy, teachers who sign fluently, and interpreters who are highly skilled can be quite varied and tends to be concentrated in the urban areas.

All provinces have adopted inclusive education as a prevailing practice guideline, and this approach has had an effect nationally on the way in which deaf and hard of hearing students are educated. It would be fair to say that the prevailing ethos is that students should be allowed access to educational services in their home communities unless their needs are so complex that it is necessary to provide a more specialized level of support. Against this backdrop, the range of available educational placement options for any deaf and hard of hearing students depends to a large extent on geography. Some provinces are able to provide a fuller array of choices than others, and within provinces, students in rural areas or in the northern areas tend to have more limited choices than those in urban regions.

Each province has not only a process for the identification and educational placement of deaf and hard of hearing students but also a process whereby this placement is regularly reviewed. Although there are some differences in the specifics of these processes in each region, the overall practice is similar. Identification, which typically occurs in a hospital or clinic, triggers services from the school board, school for the deaf, or an early intervention program. These services may include the involvement of a specialist teacher of the deaf and hard of hearing, an educational audiologist, a speech-language pathologist, an auditory-verbal therapist, an interpreter, an intervener, or an educational assistant, depending on the child's level of need. Providing appropriate audiological and technological support is also part of this process.

Because of great distances and the geopolitical diversity of Canada, more region-specific services have been developed to enable efficient delivery of educational services to deaf and hard of hearing learners. What follows are descriptions of current services organized geographically, beginning with the Atlantic provinces and moving westward to British Columbia.

Atlantic Provinces

In the move from a traditional, residential service to an inclusionary model (following the policies of the provincial departments of education), the current trend has been to place the majority of deaf and hard of hearing students in their local schools with support services such as itinerant teachers and interpreters. In fact, there is now only one school for the deaf remaining in Atlantic Canada, the Newfoundland School for the Deaf, and it has been facing the challenge of declining enrollment in recent years.

Education of deaf and hard of hearing students in Atlantic Canada is managed under the auspices of APSEA, which is governed by a board of directors consisting of three people from each of the four Atlantic provinces. The deputy minister of education from each province is a permanent member of the board, and two other members from each province are appointed by the lieutenant governor-in-council for a term of 2 years. The board of directors has responsibility for planning and policy development.

Children and youth from birth to age 21 years who are deaf, deaf-blind, or hard of hearing and are residents of Nova Scotia and New Brunswick are served directly by APSEA. Since 1987, the New Brunswick Department of Education–Francophone Division assumed responsibility for the education of all Francophone children throughout New Brunswick. Newfoundland and Labrador provide services for children from birth to age 21 years within that province. Prince Edward Island provides itinerant teacher service and accesses support services from the APSEA Centre.

The APSEA Centre is situated in Halifax, Nova Scotia, and provides a wide range of support services, including direct itinerant service, consultation, student and family counseling, educational interpreting, tutoring, assessment, technological assistance, short-term intervention programs in a residential setting, and transition services. These supports are provided to school personnel and students in inclusive settings and in public, private, and First Nations schools under the direction of the itinerant teacher. APSEA directly employs itinerant teachers of deaf and hard of hearing students in Nova Scotia and New Brunswick. These services are also offered through APSEA to Prince Edward Island where itinerant teachers are employed by the provincial Department of Education. Itinerant teachers in Newfoundland and Labrador are employed by school boards, and the Department of Education of Newfoundland and Labrador operates the Newfoundland School for the Deaf.

Inclusionary policies of the individual provinces apply to all students. The school is ultimately responsible for the implementation and delivery of curriculum. The itinerant teacher participates as part of the school team and advises on individualization, modification, and adaptation within the educational environment. School districts are supported by programs and services offered by APSEA, with itinerant teachers designing an individualized plan, based on assessments, in the following areas: language and communication, audition and speech, cognition, critical thinking, academic skill-building strategies, and social-emotional development. These teachers work with classroom teachers to adapt the curriculum, and they participate in school-based individual planning teams.

Consultation is also a critical component of the itinerant service. School personnel are provided with information about program modifications, the acoustic environment of their classrooms, and teaching techniques to use with deaf and hard of hearing students. In collaboration with the school-based team, the itinerant teacher monitors student progress and recommends assessments, tutorial support, or short-term programs at the APSEA Centre. Itinerant teachers also ensure that amplification equipment is well maintained and used appropriately, and they attend case conferences when appropriate. In addition, they provide direct, hands-on instruction with students as needed. This consultative model is designed to ensure that students receive the necessary support at the appropriate time to prevent the need for more intensive intervention at a later date.

On referral, itinerant teachers provide services for preschool children with diagnosed hearing loss in New Brunswick and Nova Scotia. Newborn hearing screening is done in the major hospitals in both provinces, although only New Brunswick has implemented a universal program for infant hearing screening. Prince Edward Island also has a universal newborn hearing screening program, with infant and preschool services provided by Hearing Education Auditory Resources or by itinerant teachers employed by the Department of Education. In Newfoundland and Labrador, itinerant teachers employed by school boards provide preschool services for children who are deaf and hard of hearing or deaf-blind.

At the preschool level, services are provided in the home or preschool settings. The itinerant teacher designs an individualized education plan, based on assessment, to address and serve the needs of the child and family. Itinerant teachers model appropriate teaching strategies in the areas of speech, language, audition, and appropriate use of amplification to guide parents and preschool staff members in creating the optimal learning environment for each child.

Quebec

Historically, education in Quebec was organized by religious denominations (Catholic and Protestant), but as a result of reforms brought about by the Education Act in July 1998, the public school system was reorganized along linguistic lines, with 60 of 72 school boards designated as Francophone, 9 as Anglophone, and 3 as special status (some combination of French, English, or a First Nations language).

One of the other major reforms to come out of this reorganization was to give more autonomy to schools. The Ministère de l'Education continues to set the general orientation of the school system through the development of policy and regulations concerning preschool, elementary, secondary, and postsecondary education as well as by distributing learning resources, providing funding, and monitoring activities. However, individual schools have been given a set of powers and functions previously held by school boards to enable the schools to make the most appropriate choices for all students to be successful. Schools must develop an annual success plan that mobilizes all the resources of the educational community, including partners in health, social services, early childhood, and justice sectors to accomplish the objectives outlined in the educational project. The Education Act provides for the creation of a governing board for each school, made up of parents, members of the school staff, members of the community, and secondary school students, where applicable.

The Education Act also reaffirms the right of students with special needs to receive educational services. For students with disabilities such as vision and hearing loss, this right extends to the age of 21. A new Special Education Policy, launched in 2000, places particular emphasis on the providing of support and services for school personnel working to meet the needs of students with a range of disabilities. The mandate of these services is to (a) support school boards and schools, (b) offer professional development for educators and paraprofessionals, (c) aid research and development activities, and (d) develop provincial expertise.

Regional support services for deaf and hard of hearing students are not direct services to students. Rather, consultants train and equip school personnel to adapt their teaching methods to the particular needs of students with hearing loss. The consultants may advise school personnel on special equipment required by the student, train them in its use in the educational setting, and make referrals to professionals as needed. Resource personnel may, at the request of the school administration, attend planning meetings to offer their expertise; however, resource personnel do not administer tests or conduct assessments.

The school boards provide direct intervention for students and have the responsibility of organizing services for students with special needs as evaluated by the board and documented in the Individual Education Plan (IEP). Some boards have the resources and the availability of qualified personnel to hire itinerant teachers who provide either consultative and assessment support a few times per year or more frequent direct services. However, in cases where school boards do not have the expertise or human resources to provide these services, the boards may contract for these services with other school boards. A recent evaluation of these regional and supraregional services indicated that a high priority is the development of local expertise in the providing of services for students with vision impairments or hearing loss.

Given this provincial structure, the majority of deaf and hard of hearing students are integrated into regular classrooms in local schools. That said, there are also a number of schools in Quebec that serve only deaf and hard of hearing students. From 1997 to 2004, one of these schools piloted a bilingual LSQ/French approach, which is now used in two schools. This bilingual-bicultural service delivery model requires the presence of a Deaf educator in the class. The Mackay Centre now provides services to both deaf and hard of hearing students and students with motor and language impairments, with the latter group forming the majority of the school population.

The Montreal Oral School for the Deaf (MOSD) offers services to deaf and hard of hearing children who have been referred from the Montreal Children's Hospital Audiology Department; l'Hôpital Sainte Justine; pediatricians; ear, nose, and throat specialists; and school personnel in the Montreal area. MOSD provides a wide range of services, including parent-infant programs (home or center-based); preschool programs for 3- to 5-year-olds; academic programs at the school; and itinerant services, professional development workshops, and audiological management in local nursery schools or kindergartens as well as elementary and secondary schools in the Montreal area. The focus of all MOSD programs is to develop spoken language through listening and speaking.

Ontario

The Ontario Ministry of Education provides educational opportunities for students up to age 21, and local authorities are given the responsibility for identifying and placing deaf and hard of hearing students in appropriate programs through the processes mandated in the Ontario Education Act. The majority of students are served through their local school boards through itinerant or resource services. The students may be placed in a regular class with indirect support, where the regular classroom teacher receives consultative services, or they may receive direct support either within the regular classroom or through withdrawal assistance, where the student leaves the regular classroom for one-on-one assistance with a specialized itinerant teacher. Students in these settings tend to be those with lesser hearing losses or those who communicate well orally, although increasing numbers with severe to profound losses and those with cochlear implants are now being served in their local schools.

Students with more significant hearing losses, those who communicate primarily through a signed language, or those with additional disabilities are more likely to be placed in congregated classes housed within public schools where there are possibilities for partial integration as deemed appropriate on an individual basis. The availability of these classes is determined to a large extent by population, with more options being available in populated, urban areas than in rural areas or the North, where there are not enough students living close enough together to form a viable class.

Ontario also has three schools for the deaf, which are managed directly by the provincial Ministry of Education: the Sir James Whitney School in Belleville, the Ernest C. Drury School in Milton, and the Robarts School in London. All of these schools follow a bilingual-bicultural philosophy, with both ASL and English as languages of instruction. In addition, there is a day school in Toronto, Davisville Public School/Metropolitan Toronto School for the Deaf, which is "twinned" to the public elementary school next door. ASL is taught as a heritage language at this school to all students, both deaf and hearing. Since 1986, Francophone deaf and hard of hearing students have received educational services from Centre Jules-Léger located in Ottawa and under the governance of the Ministry of Education.

Throughout Ontario, there are also children with varying levels of deafness who are served in other specialized settings. The W. Ross Macdonald Provincial School in Brantford serves children who are both deaf and blind. In addition, there are several specialized schools or facilities around the province designed to meet the needs of children who have multiple disabilities, including those with hearing loss.

Preschool services for children in larger urban areas such as Toronto and the surrounding regions are provided through the local school board. Services for children living outside such jurisdictions are provided through one of the three provincial schools for the deaf, based on geographic location. There are also a number of private or hospital-based services that provide speech-language or auditory-verbal therapy to preschool-aged children.

Western Canada

The range of educational opportunities available to deaf and hard of hearing students in the western region of Canada varies significantly among the provinces. In Manitoba, the level of service provided is determined by the 36 local school boards, with some boards providing clustered services and others providing only a mainstreamed classroom option. Inclusive education is the prevailing policy, but a full range of options continues to be available, including the Manitoba School for the Deaf in Winnipeg. In Saskatchewan, all deaf and hard of hearing students are served in inclusive settings. There are no congregated classes. The province provides consultative supports, educational assistants, and interpreters as needed, and there is one outreach teacher of the deaf for the province. Students who want to attend a school for the deaf typically go to schools in the neighboring provinces of Alberta or Manitoba.

The two most populous provinces of Alberta and British Columbia provide a full range of options and services for deaf and hard of hearing students and their families, including a school for the deaf, clustered services (i.e., provincial resource programs), and itinerant teachers (who provide direct or consultative services in inclusive, mainstreamed settings). For the purposes of service delivery, the province of Alberta is divided into two major areas (north and south), with centers in Calgary and Edmonton serving as the hubs. Support for children in the early years (from birth to 36 months) is provided through the Ministry of Health, and the school system takes over until the age of 18. In British Columbia, educational support for children from birth through age 5 is provided through the Ministry of Children and Family Development and for children from ages 5 to 18 in the school system through the Ministry of Education.

The three schools for the deaf in western Canada are located in British Columbia, Alberta, and Manitoba. Through the increasing use of technology (e.g., videoconferencing) they are able to provide outreach services in their respective provinces. These outreach services include support in the areas of academic and psychological assessments, audiology, ASL development, speech and language development, and interpreting services. In British Columbia, there is also a provincial outreach consultant for deaf and hard of hearing students who travels extensively throughout the province and provides support to itinerant teachers and integrated students. All three schools have a significant number of deaf and hard of hearing individuals on staff and employ at least one full-time interpreter.

All four western provinces have opportunities for family support and intervention for children in the preschool years. Options include services from trained interventionists in hospital settings (e.g., teachers of the deaf, speech-language pathologists) and are usually home-based up to approximately age 36 months. Although specialists often travel to provide services to families in their homes, there are also opportunities for the families to come into specialized centers for support and information. All communication options are offered by the provinces, but as stated previously, they are more easily accessed in or near urban centers.

In Saskatchewan, there are early childhood intervention (Early Entrance) programs, but a specialist in deaf education is not necessarily part of this early intervention team. Transition to a school setting takes place at age 3 when the Early Childhood Education for Children

With Disabilities program provides intervention support services. The Society for Manitobans with Disabilities provides services for preschool deaf and hard of hearing children and outreach for families, although it is harder for families in rural areas to access these specialized services.

Alberta provides a range of early intervention options that include family/home-based interventions, support centers in cities that provide direct services and weekly classes, and telehealth conferencing for parents in rural areas. The Ministry of Education provides early intervention funding for children from ages 2.5 to 6 years with severe-profound losses and for children from ages 3.5 to 6 years with mild-moderate losses.

British Columbia has four specialized early intervention programs—three in the Lower Mainland (i.e., Vancouver area) and one in Victoria. All provide services to children and their families from birth to age 5 years, and among the four programs, all communication options are available. There is also a provincial outreach program that provides consultation to families and professionals in outlying areas of the province where no specialized early intervention programs are available. British Columbia recently established a universal newborn hearing screening and provincial early intervention program, with the goal of identifying all infants with hearing loss and providing early intervention to them and their families by the time the child is 6 months.

Curriculum

The trend for deaf and hard of hearing students educated in all settings is that the standard provincial curricula be followed as much as possible. These provincial curricula vary slightly among provinces but typically specify learning objectives in the subject areas of language (both English and French), math, social studies, the sciences, physical education, technology, media, and the arts. Although it is the goal that these curricula are followed for most deaf and hard of hearing students, it is also the case that, regardless of placement, an IEP is developed for all identified students. This plan, which is based on a thorough assessment and evaluation and includes parental input, outlines a student's strengths and needs, specifying the level at which the student is working, immediate learning goals, and expected outcomes. The IEP also identifies (a) any accommodations and modifications to be made to the standard curriculum, (b) whether the student achieved the outcomes and how this progress was assessed, and (c) the teaching strategies and approaches that would be used in meeting the identified goals.

Typical accommodations, which allow students access to the curriculum but do not change the substance of the curriculum itself, include changes such as the use of FM systems, the use of an interpreter, additional test time, preferential seating, and the preteaching of vocabulary. Modifications are changes made to the curriculum itself such that similar content may be addressed but at a different grade level (typically lower) or at a different depth (typically less) from what is typically addressed in the standard classroom. Deaf and hard of hearing students in congregated classes are often exempted from French (if they are in English-based programs) and music instruction and, instead, work on a modified curriculum. In certain circumstances, an alternative curriculum may be provided if it is deemed that a particular deaf and hard of hearing student has learning needs so complex that the standard curriculum is not relevant (e.g., students with significant cognitive delays). During the secondary school years, transition planning is an integral part of the curriculum. Many high schools provide cooperative education experiences in which students hold part-time jobs and receive credit for that work experience.

Issues of accommodation and modifications also have an effect in the area of assessment, particularly with respect to high-stakes testing. For example, the Ontario Ministry of Education requires that all secondary students pass a literacy test, usually administered in Grade 10, to receive the Ontario Secondary School Diploma. Deaf and hard of hearing students are at a decided disadvantage on this test, as are other new English language learners and some students with disabilities. Although the test may be re-taken several times, significant numbers of deaf and hard of hearing students do not pass the reading and writing tests successfully by the time they finish their other course requirements for Grade 12. There is ongoing discussion about alternative ways for students to meet this requirement, including offering coursework and building portfolios of their work to document progress in literacy.

Postsecondary Education

Just as is the case with elementary and secondary school education, postsecondary education in Canada is managed at the provincial level with a system of colleges and universities. Colleges are distinguished from universities in that they are nondegree granting institutions that offer vocational, technical, and academic learning opportunities, typically awarding certificates or diplomas in career areas. In recent years, partnerships have been established between colleges and universities, and some cooperative programs have emerged (e.g., Seneca College and York University in Toronto).

There are no specialized institutions at the postsecondary level for deaf and hard of hearing students in Canada, although there are institutions that have made particular efforts to accommodate the needs of students with hearing loss through their Offices for Persons with Disabilities. Typically, deaf and hard of hearing students who stay in Canada for their postsecondary education attend regular colleges and universities and are eligible for support services such as interpreting, note-taking, and captioning. Some deaf and hard of hearing students go to the United States to attend Gallaudet University or the National Technical Institute for the Deaf as international students, although the numbers in recent years have declined as funding for students to pursue this option has dwindled.

A number of colleges across the country (e.g., Vancouver Community College Program for Deaf and Hard of Hearing Adults in British Columbia) offer academic upgrading[3] for postsecondary students and adult immigrants who are deaf and hard of hearing. There are also colleges in several provinces that offer Deaf Studies programs (e.g., Red River College in Manitoba and Grant MacEwan College in Alberta, which also offers an International Deaf Studies Initiative). At the university level, the University of British Columbia and the University of Alberta recognize ASL as meeting the second-language requirement for an undergraduate bachelor of arts degree. ASL is offered as a credit course at the undergraduate level at York University in Toronto, and at the University of Alberta, ASL is one of many languages offered for study in the humanities.

---

3. Academic upgrading could include earning a high school diploma, improving literacy skills, or upgrading academic qualifications to pursue postsecondary study.

Programs for Teacher Education and Educational Interpreting

At present in Canada, there are only three teacher preparation programs in the education of deaf and hard of hearing students that either meet or are working to meet the national certification standards of the Canadian Association of Educators of the Deaf and Hard of Hearing (CAEDHH), a national organization formed in 1973 to bring together educators of deaf and hard of hearing students across the country.[4] The three programs are located at the University of British Columbia in Vancouver, at York University in Toronto, and at Mount St. Vincent University in Halifax. All three programs are university based, are a minimum of 1 year in length, provide rigorous course work in a comprehensive model, and include supervised practica. On completion, students are awarded a masters degree (British Columbia and Nova Scotia) or a postbaccalaureate diploma (Ontario).

Applicants to these teacher preparation programs must already hold basic teacher certification, typically a Bachelor of Education degree from an accredited university. This certification is mandatory for all teachers in all provinces. To be certified as a teacher of deaf and hard of hearing students by CAEDHH, applicants must then complete a course of study in deaf and hard of hearing education that includes supervised practicum placements in settings with deaf and hard of hearing students. In Ontario, legislation requires that all teachers of deaf and hard of hearing children be certified by the Ontario College of Teachers.

Unfortunately, not all teachers working with deaf and hard of hearing learners have a background in the education of deaf and hard of hearing students. Although holding certification is considered the ideal situation and in the best interests of deaf and hard of hearing students, there is a chronic shortage of qualified teachers of deaf and hard of hearing students across the country, with the most profound effect on rural and remote communities. In such circumstances, it is often the case that there is little or limited choice with respect to finding qualified staff members, and it becomes a question of doing the best that is possible under the circumstances. In some provinces such as Alberta, Manitoba, and Saskatchewan, there is not even a specific requirement for a teacher of the deaf and hard of hearing to be employed to work with deaf and hard of hearing students, let alone any requirement for CAEDHH certification eligibility.

There are many deaf and hard of hearing individuals who hold certification in Canada, and by and large, they tend to work in congregated settings, often with children who use a signed language. That said, there are also deaf and hard of hearing individuals who work as itinerant teachers with students who are hard of hearing, who use oral communication, or both. In addition, a number of deaf and hard of hearing individuals work as educational assistants. In this role, they work under the guidance of the teacher, assisting in the implementation of the classroom program.

There are currently interpreter education and training programs in six provinces (Nova Scotia, Ontario, Manitoba, Saskatchewan, Alberta, and British Columbia) and in the Northwest Territories. These are typically 3-year programs housed at colleges. Graduates of these programs can apply for membership in the Association of Visual Language Interpreters of Canada.[5]

---

4. When formed in 1973, this organization was known as the Association of Canadian Educators of the Hearing Impaired. The name was changed to CAEDHH in 1995.

5. For more information, see www.avlic.ca.

Looking Forward: Issues, Challenges, and Questions

As we look forward to the future challenges of educating deaf and hard of hearing learners in Canada, we must consider several issues: (a) the rapidly changing nature of the student population, (b) the task of developing and providing appropriate education options for current and future students, (c) universal newborn infant hearing screening and early intervention, (d) the providing of services in remote and underserved communities, and (e) professional development to serve the "new" deaf and hard of hearing population.

The Changing Nature of the Deaf and Hard of Hearing Student Population

Although the numbers of children identified with hearing loss across the country have remained relatively stable, the nature of this population has changed significantly. This change is the result of increased numbers in three areas: deaf and hard of hearing students identified with additional disabilities; deaf and hard of hearing students from families in which English, French, ASL, or LSQ are not the first language; and deaf and hard of hearing students with better access to audition through cochlear implants or improved amplification technologies than were conventionally available in the past.

The increasing numbers of deaf and hard of hearing children identified with additional disabilities create challenges for the education system in several ways. The anticipated academic, social, and emotional outcomes for these students will likely differ from the expectations for typical deaf and hard of hearing learners of the past (Christensen, 2000). These students will often require a significantly modified or alternative curriculum, and teachers will need to be able to assess and program to effectively meet these needs. Issues for these learners go far beyond the traditional questions of identifying the most effective communication approach. Furthermore, large numbers of students with complex needs who are congregated in one setting can fundamentally change the nature of that setting. In the case of the schools for the deaf, such a shift can raise questions as to the nature of these schools in the future and their traditional role as hubs for the Deaf community and Deaf culture.

Also reflected in the population of students with hearing loss are the high levels of immigration in the general population in Canada. In certain parts of the country, there are significant numbers of deaf and hard of hearing students whose families do not claim English, French, ASL, or LSQ as the language of the home and who face the challenge of acquiring one of these languages, often without benefit of having a solid foundation in their native signed or spoken language. This situation is particularly evident in large urban centers such as Vancouver, Toronto, and Montreal. For example, the Vancouver Oral Centre for Deaf Children has an English as a Second Language (ESL) student population of approximately 50%, and in a recent study involving deaf and hard of hearing adolescents in Toronto, interpretation and translations needed to be provided in nine languages (Akamatsu, Mayer, & Farrelly, 2006).

This diversity brings with it a new set of challenges and the need for cultural "brokering" among professionals who work with ESL children with hearing loss and their families. The issues is no longer one of considering only Deaf culture and experiences in the hearing majority, but one that involves thinking about the ways in which other cultures and their attitudes toward hearing loss come into play. This ethnic and cultural diversity also raises questions with respect to language, specifically with respect to maintaining a first language other than English. Although first-language maintenance has been shown to be a viable and desirable option for hearing learners (Cummins, 2000), there is little research evidence to date to indicate whether the same holds true for all students with hearing loss, given the challenges these students have typically faced with language learning.

It is also the case that ever increasing numbers of students in the education system have cochlear implants. In Canada, cochlear implants are fully funded through the public health system and are available at selected hospitals in British Columbia, Alberta, Ontario, and Nova Scotia. Children who are deemed not to be suitable candidates for a government-funded implant but whose families nevertheless select this option must either go without or go elsewhere (often the United States) to have the implant surgery. In these cases, the families must pay for the implant and surgery. These children generally return to Canada and enter the education system for follow-up services.

Because children with cochlear implants tend to be educated in mainstream settings, the proportion of children in congregated settings and schools for the deaf is dwindling. At the same time, the education system faces challenges in adequately addressing the needs of these newly implanted children and in providing the appropriate intervention after implantation that is critical for success.

Providing Appropriate Educational Options

Given the diversity of the deaf and hard of hearing student population, it would seem reasonable to suggest that there will continue to be a need for a wide range of services and programs as well as communication and language options. It is also true that the current population of deaf and hard of hearing students poses very different educational needs than in the past, necessitating changes in educational practice.

Nationwide, there are fewer students in sign bilingual programs than in previous years, particularly in the preschool and primary years. For example, of the approximately 1,000 students who receive services from APSEA in eastern Canada, 8% have cochlear implants whereas just less than 5% use sign language as their primary mode of communication. Earlier identification by means of newborn hearing screening has meant that there are increasing numbers of younger children receiving cochlear implants, and for children without implants, improved amplification technologies have meant that greater numbers can access language meaningfully by means of audition. Although a form of signed communication (e.g., sign supported speech) may play a role in educational programming for some of these students, it is not typically the case that they are enrolled in sign bilingual programs. In addition, because these learners have enhanced auditory potential, more attention is being paid to the teaching of speech, oral language development, and the use of amplification. These features were not typically seen as central in most bilingual-bicultural programs in the past, and the challenge becomes one of rethinking this approach to accommodate the needs of students with cochlear implants who would benefit from a bilingual educational setting.

In general, there has also been a move away from congregated settings of any type as the trend is toward models of inclusive education for all students with disabilities (Dworet & Bennett, 2002; Hutchinson, 2002). This shift has created a challenge in terms of identifying and providing adequate and appropriate supports for deaf and hard of hearing learners in integrated settings to be successful. For example, it is not always easy to find an oral interpreter for a student with a cochlear implant or an ASL or LSQ interpreter for a student who signs.

Newborn Hearing Screening and Early Intervention

Only four provincial governments (Ontario, New Brunswick, Prince Edward Island, and British Columbia) and one territory (the Yukon) have funded and implemented a universal program for infant hearing screening. Screening in other provinces usually occurs only for high-risk infants (i.e., those admitted to a neonatal intensive care unit or those with familial hearing loss) or through a hospital's local initiative. Consequently, only about 41% of newborns in Canada are screened for hearing loss, meaning Canada lags behind Europe and the United States, where more than 86% of newborns are screened (Canadian Academy of Audiology, 2002; The Hearing Foundation of Canada, 2007).

Postidentification intervention models also vary across the country. In British Columbia, the British Columbia Early Hearing Program (BCEHP) provides a provincial early intervention program that is family-centered, equitable, and accessible to infants diagnosed through the BCEHP and their families. The intervention is based on currently existing services and includes parent choice for communication approach. In Ontario, under the auspices of the Ontario Ministry of Child and Youth Services, infants identified through the Infant Hearing Program are eligible to receive early intervention in oral, visual, or dual approaches.

Because all of these programs are relatively new, it is unclear to what extent they are effective (a) in aiding parents as they make choices for their infants and (b) in supporting them throughout the process. Careful tracking is needed to ensure that the approaches being taken are optimal. The coordination of services after identification is also an area that needs to be studied because it is often the case that several individuals may be involved in a child's follow-up (e.g., speech language pathologist, teacher of the deaf and hard of hearing, social worker, auditory verbal therapist). This situation becomes even more complicated when a child has complex needs that involve even more professionals (e.g., occupational and physical therapists). Although early intervention programs do exist in all provinces, the initiation of newborn hearing screening is providing a focus for the need to rethink cooperative services and enhance seamless transitions from identification and diagnosis to intervention.

Rural, Northern, and Aboriginal Communities

In a country the size of Canada, providing equitable access to programming and resources is a chronic problem and one that is not easily solved. The absence of information on northern and aboriginal communities would be apparent to any reader of this chapter, and what has been said about rural communities is usually a reference to the fact that there is a lack of services in these areas. Overall, it would be fair to say that there is generally poorer or much more limited access to support of any kind (e.g., educational, audiological, health-related, etc.) in rural, northern, and aboriginal communities. In addition, it is often difficult either to find qualified teachers and other professionals who are willing to work in these communities on a permanent basis or even to access staff members for a shorter term. These problems are compounded for aboriginal communities who live on reserves because they are outside provincial jurisdictions. Creative uses of technology such as teleconferencing appear to hold the most potential for developing outreach services to better meet the needs of these populations.

Ongoing Challenges in Teacher and Professional Education

Although teaching deaf and hard of hearing students has always presented particular challenges, especially with respect to language and literacy development, the job has become increasingly complex in the past decade. Teachers must now have the knowledge and skills to work with

- learners who have multiple needs for whom the development of any language or communication can be particularly challenging;
- infants, preschoolers, and their families;
- children and young people with cochlear implants;
- students who have immigrated from other countries, often without a fully established first language; and
- students from homes in which English, French, ASL, or LSQ are not the first language.

For many experienced teachers, these issues were not addressed during their initial teacher education program, and there is usually not adequate access to professional development in these content areas. With respect to initial certification, teacher education programs are struggling to find ways to address these issues in their curriculum and courses, given the constraints of time, resources, and funding. Collaboration and sharing of expertise among the teacher education programs (nationally and internationally) and with other professionals in the field, through strategies such as on-line courses, videoconferencing, and distance education, will be central in meeting this challenge.

In some regions of the country and in some program areas, there continues to be a dearth of qualified professionals—teachers, interpreters, auditory-verbal therapists, psychologists, etc. This shortage results in an inequity of support wherein some deaf and hard of hearing students are being served by occasional support from a consultant or by a resource teacher who may not be a teacher of the deaf. In some situations, professionals are asked to assume roles for which they do not have the requisite certification (e.g., teachers functioning as interpreters, educational assistants working as teachers). This situation is exacerbated by the fact that, across the country, there are not consistent, national standards for certification in a number of areas (e.g., educational interpreters).

SUMMARY

Pulling together a coherent picture of the past, present, and future of the education of deaf and hard of hearing learners, especially in a country as large and diverse as Canada, is no easy task. Yet there is value in looking back and taking stock of where we have been and where we are headed to assist us as we plan for the decades ahead. We live in times of great possibility for many deaf and hard of hearing children. But realizing these possibilities rests on being able to work collaboratively as a national community of educators and researchers, along with parents, their deaf and hard of hearing children, and deaf and hard of hearing adults, to develop the most efficacious models of intervention and education. In the end, that collaborative effort may prove to be the greatest challenge of all.

REFERENCES

Akamatsu, C. T., Mayer, C., & Farrelly, S. (2006). An investigation of two-way text messaging use with deaf students at the secondary level. *Journal of Deaf Studies and Deaf Education,11*(1), 120–131.

Bailey, C. S., & Dolby, K. (2002). *Canadian dictionary of ASL*. Edmonton: University of Alberta Press.

Bibby, M. A. (1999). Canadian education of deaf and hard of hearing students in the 1990s. In H. W. Brelje (Ed.), *Global perspectives on the education of the deaf in selected countries* (pp. 31–46). Hillsboro, OR: Butte Publications.

Canadian Academy of Audiology. (2002). *May is hearing awareness month*. Retrieved September 23, 2008, from http://www.canadianaudiology.ca/consumers/may

Canadian Association of the Deaf. (2007). *Statistics of deaf Canadians*. Retrieved August 14, 2008, from http://www.cad.ca/en/issues/statistics_on_deaf_Canadians.asp

Carbin, C. (1996). *Deaf heritage in Canada: A distinctive, diverse and enduring culture*. Toronto: McGraw-Hill Ryerson.

Christensen, K. (Ed.). (2000). *Deaf plus: A multicultural perspective*. San Diego: DawnSignPress.

Clarke, B., & Winzer, M. (1983). A concise history of the education of the deaf in Canada. *ACEHI Journal, 9*(1), 36–51.

Cummins, J. (2000). *Language, power and pedagogy: Bilingual children in the crossfire*. Clevedon, United Kingdom: Multilingual Matters.

Department of Justice, Canada. (1982). *Constitution Act, 1982*. Retrieved September 23, 2008, from http://laws.justice.gc.ca/en/charter/

Dworet, D., & Bennett, S. (2002). A view from the north: Canadian policies and issues in special education. *Teaching Exceptional Children, 34*(5), 22–27.

The Hearing Foundation of Canada. (2007). *Newborn hearing screening*. Retrieved September 23, 2008, from http://www.thfc.ca/cms/en/ChildrenYouth/NewbornHearingScreening.aspx?menuid=106

Hutchinson, N. (2002). *Inclusion of exceptional learners in Canadian schools: A practical handbook for teachers*. Scarborough, ON: Pearson Education Canada.

MacDougall, J. C. (2001). Access to justice for deaf persons in Nunavut: The role of "Inuit sign language." *Canadian Psychology/Psychologie Canadienne, 42*, 61–73.

Rodda, M., & Hiron, C. (1989). Postsecondary educational services for deaf and hard of hearing students in Canada: A survey of need. *ACEHI Journal, 15*(2), 44–56.

The Situation of Deaf Education in Chile

Valeria Herrera, Aníbal Puente,
and Jesús M. Alvarado

THE HISTORY of deaf education in Chile goes back over 150 years (see Caiceo, 1988). Chile was the first Latin American country to open a residential school for deaf children: the *Escuela de Sordo-Mudos* (School for the Deaf and Mute), founded in the city of Santiago on October 27, 1852, during the presidency of Manuel Montt. Eliseo Schieroni, a former teacher of the Deaf in Milan, was the school's first director. The first subjects taught in this school were reading, writing, Spanish grammar, arithmetic, religion, and book binding. The school continues its work today under the name *Escuela Anne Sullivan* (*Anne Sullivan School*) and is still teaching with the traditional oral method.

In 1854, a second residential school for the deaf was founded in Santiago, this one a school for girls. The students studied reading, writing, Spanish grammar, arithmetic, religion, sewing, and embroidery. This girls' residential school was closed in 1877 and reopened in 1885 under the tutelage of the religious congregation of *El Buen Pastor* (The Good Shepherd).

The *Instituto de Sordo-Mudos* (Institute for the Deaf and Mute) was created in 1889 with the goal of educating deaf children in Chile and preparing teachers to work in special schools. The school's philosophy dictated that "spoken language and lip reading methods shall be adopted exclusively. The signed communication system is prohibited and exercise of the auditory organ shall be applied whenever possible" (Caiceo, 1988, p. 48). This philosophy reflected the Congress of Milan agreements of 1880, which were put into effect across the country, strictly regulating the education of the Deaf population.

The Educational Reform of 1927 marked the beginning of a second stage in the history of deaf education, which lasted from 1927 to 1964. This reform obliged the Chilean state, for the first time ever, to maintain "live-in schools for poor children, weak children, children with organic inferiorities, and abnormal or mentally retarded children" (Caiceo, 1988, p. 48). With the passing of Decree Number 653 in 1929, special education became part of the Chilean Educational System.

In 1932, one of the 20th century's most emblematic schools for the deaf was created in Santiago, the *Escuela de Sordos La Purísima* deaf school directed by the Franciscan nuns of the Immaculate Conception. The nuns imported the oral education method developed in Spain and applied it in Chile in its entirety, its advantages along with its disadvantages. One of the system's most pernicious aspects that should be mentioned is its systematic rejection of the use of signs as a means of communication among deaf students, a rejection based on the argument that this form of communication is more appropriate for monkeys than for humans (Demartini & Letelier, 2006). Despite this stance, the school was highly prestigious in the community and also offered professional training for students. The school finally closed in 1998 because of serious economic problems.

In 1958, Dr. Jorge Otte Gabler created the *Instituto de la Sordera* (Institute of Deafness), offering professional training to young deaf people. Workshops that were taught included carpentry, clothes-making, cooking, and much later in the mid-1990s, computer typing. In 1974, the Department of Special Education at the University of Chile (now the *Universidad Metropolitana de Ciencias de la Educación,* or Metropolitan University of Education Sciences) created the *Centro de Educación, Experimentación e Investigación Dr. Jorge Otte Gabler* (The Dr. Jorge Otte Gabler Center for Education, Experimentation and Investigation), offering special education for deaf children from preschool through the sixth year of primary education. The two institutions merged in 1998, and the new administration decided to close the professional workshops and, instead, provide education from preschool through the eighth year of primary education. Currently, the *Escuela Especial Dr. Jorge Otte Gabler* (Dr. Jorge Otte Gabler School) acts as an internship site for future teachers of the deaf trained at the Metropolitan University of Education Sciences and is a leader in the implementation of bilingual-bicultural educational models at a national level. Nevertheless, this pioneering experience was not the norm during the 1960s, when special schools for the deaf based on the Congress of Milan agreements of 1880, that is, based on the exclusive teaching of oral language, were opened across the country.

The creation of the Specialist Teacher in Special Education degree at the University of Chile in 1964 marked the beginning of a third stage in the history of Deaf education that continues to the present day. In 1965, the government of Eduardo Frei Montalva passed an Educational Reform that proposed a series of changes. An advisory commission was formed whose mission was to formulate measures to solve problems relating to special education. The Department of Special Education was created within the Ministry of Education (MINEDUC), giving greater administrative power and institutional legitimacy to this educational subsystem. In 1966, the University of Chile began to offer specialized studies in auditory and language disorders with the goal of training specialist teachers for deaf students.

In 1974, during the military dictatorship of Augusto Pinochet, the MINEDUC formed Commission Number 18, presided over by Dr. Luis Bravo Valdivieso. The commission's task was to analyze the problems surrounding special education in the country. The commission's work resulted in the elaboration of study plans and programs, the creation of separate groups in regular primary schools, the presence of technical cabinets in special schools, and the creation of psychopedagogic bodies. The commission also proposed offering incentives for the creation of private special schools (Godoy, Meza, & Salazar, 2004).

The systematic incorporation of the first deaf students in the regular education system began in the early part of the 1980s. Separate evaluation methods and exemptions from certain subjects in the study plan (generally English language) were implemented to facilitate deaf students' access to education. In 1981, the Supreme Exempt Decree Number 15 approved the first *Planes y Programas de Estudio para la Educación Especial en Trastornos Auditivos* (Study Plans and Programs for the Special Education of Auditive Disorders), which had a marked clinical focus.

New study plans and programs were created in 1990, maintaining a focus on treatment and rehabilitation of hearing loss, to the detriment of the teaching of normal coursework. These programs are still in effect today. With the return of democracy to Chile in 1990, the state is involved in legislation involving the disabled population and has passed a series of laws and decrees. Law Number 19.284 on the Full Social Integration of Disabled Persons was passed in 1994. This law created the *Fondo Nacional de la Discapacidad* (FONADIS; National Disability Fund), an autonomous public service related to the state through the Ministry of National Planning. Its mission is to contribute to the social integration of and equality of opportunity for people with disabilities through the efficient administration of financial resources allotted to it for that purpose. These legislative advances have not materialized in practice, however, because the curricular reform initiated in 1996, which implemented new curricular frameworks at the preschool, primary, and secondary levels, did not take special education into account. Educational integration policies were developed between 1998 and 2003 and included teacher training, increased subsidies, educational integration projects, etc.

A decisive moment in the history of the Deaf community in Chile was the creation of the *Confederación Nacional de Sordos en Chile* (National Confederation of the Deaf in Chile) in 2002. After 50 years of division and long periods of struggle in Chile, this confederation has unified the country's Deaf community in one single, national institution.

In 2005, the MINEDUC presented the *Nueva Política Nacional de Educación Especial* (New National Policy for Special Education; MINEDUC, 2005b), whose strategic principles for the period from 2006 to 2010 are to

- increase access to education,
- improve curricula and educational administration,
- improve educational integration and diversity,
- strengthen the capacity of special schools,
- promote family participation,
- improve teachers' and teaching professionals' training in special education,
- increase financing,
- reinforce the MINEDUC's technical teams, and
- increase awareness of and dialogue on disabilities.

CURRENT EDUCATIONAL OPPORTUNITIES

Since 1990, the Chilean Educational System has been regulated by the *Ley Orgánica Constitucional de Educación* (Organic Constitutional Law on Education), which applies the logic of free markets to education, thus regulating educational opportunities through the laws of supply and demand. On the one hand, private education is stimulated by the transfer of public funds as well as financial, administrative, and pedagogic functions to autonomous, private bodies and, on the other hand, the administration of primary and secondary schools is transferred from MINEDUC to the country's municipalities (Maldonado, 2003). The result of this law is an increase in social inequality and a deterioration of the quality of public education as reflected in both national and international evaluations (*Sistema de Medición de la Calidad de la Educación* [System for Measuring the Quality of Education], Program for International Student Assessment, Third International Mathematics and Science Study, & *Organizacion para la Cooperación y el Desarrollo Económico* [Organization for Cooperation and Economic Development], 2004). More particularly, this law, developed during the years of military dictatorship, does not include information on the role that special education should play in the overall national educational system; it proposes neither the strategies nor the educational resources necessary to serve disabled students within either the regular or the special education systems (Blanco, 2005). The law is

Table 20.1. Number of Deaf and Hard of Hearing Individuals by Gender and Age Group

	0–5 years	6–14 years	15–29 years	30–44 years	45–64 years	> 65 years	Total
Male	1,402	4,810	10,554	13,848	46,393	65,466	142,473
Female	1,470	2,679	7,281	19,816	43,344	75,656	150,246
Total	2,872	7,489	17,835	33,664	89,737	141,122	292,719

Note: From Fondo Nacional de la Discapacidad (2004).

currently being revised by an education commission formed by President Bachelet after protests by the student movement in May of 2006.

It is difficult to establish the exact number of individual with disabilities in Chile. No reliable statistical data yet exist in Chile, and the various studies that have been carried out differ in their assessments. The national socioeconomic survey (MIDEPLAN, 2000) registered 5.3% of the total population as having a disability, the national population Census for 2002 registered 2.2%, and a FONADIS survey (Fondo Nacional de la Discapacidad, 2004) registered 12.9% (this last percentage is nearest to international figures). The explanation for this disparity could be the use of measuring instruments that are inadequate for the evaluation of disabilities. Taking the limitation of the data into account, the FONADIS survey found 292,720 deaf and hard of hearing people in Chile, a figure that represents 1.8% of the national population. Half of these are people older than age 65 (see Table 20.1). People who are deaf or hard of hearing make up 8.7% of the total disabled population in the country.

Less than half of the deaf and hard of hearing population has completed their primary education. Approximately 11% have no approved studies, and a very significant number have extremely low academic performance at the various levels of the educational system. The data provided by MINEDUC's statistics unit (2005a) indicate that, in the whole country, 1,210 deaf students are enrolled in special education and an estimated 1,200 are integrated in the regular education system with additional and specific reinforcement. These figures are a poor approximation, however, given the fact that it does not take into account the 7,489 deaf children between the ages of 6 and 14 who should be enrolled in both special education and regular primary schools. In other words, nearly 70% of deaf children and teenagers are enrolled in regular schools but do not receive adequate attention.

In contrast to this desolate view, the Chilean Ministry of Education defines special education as a transversal and interdisciplinary program within the school system.[1] The program is charged with strengthening the principle of equality of opportunity and ensuring that this principle is met for all children and young people with special educational needs, whether or not those needs derive from a disability, across all levels and teaching modes of the educational system.

The deaf population has, in theory, three educational options. The first and most widely used of these are special schools and centers for professional training. There are currently 13 schools for the deaf in the whole country and 20 special schools that accept deaf students, among other disabled students. These schools use study plans and programs designed specifically for deaf and hard hearing students (Decree 86/90 [Decreto Supremo de Educación

---

1. Administrative policies and measures are general and do not differentiate between students of different ages and profiles. For more information, see the Chilean Ministry of Education Web site at http://www.mineduc.cl.

No. 86 de 1990]). According to a report by the Commission of Experts on Special Education (2004), 100% of special schools have implemented projects for educational improvement, 53% have computers and Internet connections, and 27% are on a full-day school schedule.

The second educational option is regular schools with integration projects, separate groups made up of deaf and hard hearing students, or both. To apply this educational mode, regular schools must present a *Proyecto de Integración Escolar* (Project for Educational Integration) to MINEDUC. The conditions for acceptance of these projects relate to the hiring of professional aides, the acquiring of appropriate didactic resources and material, the perfection of teaching methods, and the adaptation of infrastructures when necessary. This option also includes the incorporation of separate groups in regular schools. However, no statistical data are available on how many Deaf students are taught in this way.

The third option is hospital schools and classrooms, which give pedagogic aid to hospitalized students. However, the deaf population does not require this educational option to the same degree as other populations.

Study Plans and Programs

Study plans and programs for the education of Deaf students in Chile are regulated by Supreme Educational Decree Number 86, 1990, which addresses special schools and specific classes inserted in regular schools. According to current legislation, two types of study plans exist (common and complementary), with three levels (prebasic, basic, and professional), six cycles (preschool, first prebasic cycle, second prebasic cycle, first basic cycle, second basic cycle, and professional cycle) and five areas of development (psychomotor, cognitive, social, artistic, and vocational). The preschool cycle is for deaf children between birth and 2, the prebasic and basic levels are for children between the ages of 2 and 15, and the professional level is for young people between the ages of 15 and 24.

The Common Plan for study plans establishes the general goal of deaf students' social, academic and professional integration by means of the training and rehabilitation of their communicational abilities, which is achieved by stimulation in the five different areas of development. Meanwhile, the general goal of the Complementary Plan is corrective: to capacitate, compensate, and rehabilitate students' handicapped areas through specialized attention.

With respect to the five areas of development, the study plan identifies the following aspects. Psychomotor abilities are fostered through physical, sports-related, and recreational activities. The cognitive area develops cognitive processes by means of sensory perception and communication processes that involve efficient command of basic instrumental techniques (reading, writing, and calculating). The social area stresses the general goal of deaf students' bio-psycho-social development to enable them to interact well with their surroundings. The artistic area is focused on the stimulation of students' creative capacity, which allows them to express their feelings and emotions and, thus, favors their overall development. Finally, the goal of the professional area is to develop the abilities and skills that will allow students' vocational interests to be identified for their later improvement.

Currently, because of the clinical focus that characterizes these study plans and programs, some schools for the deaf have carried out curricular modifications and have adhered instead to regular education plans and programs.

The curriculum used at the Dr. Jorge Otte Gabler School is a special case worth highlighting because of the extent to which curricular modifications have been proposed there, modifications based on the bilingual-bicultural model of education that adhere to regular curricula and are adapted for deaf students where necessary. This school's study plans and programs are based on Decree Number 40, 1996, of the Chilean Educational Reform and were approved by MINEDUC in 1999 for students in the first cycle of primary education (Grades 1 through 4) and in 2001 for students in the second primary education cycle (Grades 5 through 8). These modifications allow the school to offer curricular proposals that are equivalent to those offered in regular primary schools. The school's plans and programs argue that it is a basic necessity for "students to develop both languages fully, CHSL [Chilean Sign Language] as a vehicular tool of communication and as a means of access to the curriculum, Spanish language as a basic tool for being able to meet academic requirements and for their future integration in both the educational system and the labor market" (MINEDUC, 1999, p. 20). The main curricular modifications are found in the area of language and communication, which is divided into two parts: CHSL as a first language (with 6 pedagogic hours for students in the first cycle and 4 for students in the second cycle), and Spanish as a second language (with 8 pedagogic hours for students in the first cycle and 7 for students in the second cycle).[2] In the social area, contents related to the history and culture of the Deaf community at both the national and international level have been added to the proposed goals and contents to strengthen students' sense of identity, culture, and pride in their community. In the artistic area, goals related to students' auditory capacity for music appreciation have been substituted for goals related to the technological area. The application of this curricular plan has allowed students to develop academic abilities congruent with academic contents in regular schools.

Communication Modes in Schools

Chile has not avoided the worldwide controversy having to do with which communication mode is most effective, oral or signed, for deaf education. As was pointed out earlier, Chile accepted the Congress of Milan of 1880 conclusions in their entirety and has applied the oral method as the communication option for deaf students. The oral method adopted in Chile is characterized by a clinical conception of deafness that substitutes pedagogic objectives for therapeutic ones, which results in the deaf student being treated as a patient and the teacher acting as a therapist. This view of deafness is present in educational policies that focus on students' disabilities, with corrective and reparative practices being put to use in the classroom as a consequence.

This conception of deafness views deaf students as people outside the norm, people lacking language and intelligence. It likewise maintains that oral language and cognitive development are unequivocally interdependent, and it assumes that sign languages are incomplete linguistic systems whose use impedes the learning of oral language. This tendency is supported by pedagogic behaviorism, which is focused on the memorization of grammatical rules and the decoding of isolated words. Its main objective is the social integration of the deaf student

---

2. In Chile, a 1-hour lesson is equivalent to 45 minutes.

through the teaching of speech as the only means of access to knowledge and culture. This oralist mode was the accepted mode of communication in the education of deaf students for a century. Fortunately, the International Congress on Education of the Deaf in Hamburg in 1980 questioned the oral method and had a profound effect on the Chile's Deaf community, on teachers of the deaf, and on institutions formed by teachers of the deaf. The recognition at that Congress of the right of deaf people (a) to be educated in a language such as sign language that is accessible to them without any learning restrictions and (b) to use the oral language common to the community in which they live constituted a turning point after which changes began to take shape.

Beginning in the 1980s, Chile became familiar with the educational strategies developed at Gallaudet University (in the United States), which had a great effect on the Deaf community and on the universities that trained teachers of the deaf and motivated processes of pedagogic experimentation. This process was led by the Metropolitan University of Educational Sciences, through the D. Jorge Otte Gabler Center for Education, Experimentation and Investigation, which was a proponent of the Total Communication philosophy. The adoption of this perspective requires the use of all available means to give deaf students the opportunity to develop communication strategies that will allow them to develop their linguistic abilities, including auditory stimulation, speech, sign language, fingerspelling, gestures, and speechreading. It is at this point that CHSL first appeared in the country's deaf classrooms, thus initiating a process of methodological experimentation in the classroom, with teachers learning CHSL and using it to communicate with their students.

More recently, a debate has arisen with respect to the adoption of the Simultaneous Communication Mode, also known as Signed Speech, because it involves the use of both speech and signs. This method is characterized by the simultaneous translation of speech into signs, using words from spoken language and CHSL signs simultaneously, and following the structure of spoken language. The goal of this communication strategy is both to foster communication between deaf and hearing students and to facilitate the learning of lesson contents, which are usually presented in oral or written form (or both). In the case of younger children's education, the use of signs to complement and reinforce spoken communication is quite common even in more oralist contexts and especially during the first stages of oral language teaching. This strategy, whose development has been more or less formal and whose results have been quite good in countries such as the United States, France, Spain, etc., has not had the same positive record in Chile, and the Chilean Deaf community has rejected its use because of the communicational incoherence resulting from the simultaneous use of two different languages.

The International Congress on Bilingualism held in Stockholm in 1992 gave a new twist to the process of transforming deaf education by supporting a bilingual mode of communication. In 1998, the Dr. Jorge Otte Gabler School inaugurated the first ever bilingual-bicultural program in deaf education in the country, recognizing CHSL as the primary language in the education of deaf students, a language that allows deaf children to acquire all the cognitive and linguistic skills necessary for symbolizing their experiences and broadening their knowledge. Oral language is taught as a second language and principally in its written form. The adoption of this model involves adherence to a sociolinguistic view of deafness with all the accompanying educational consequences, ranging from adherence to regular academic curricula to the hiring of deaf and hearing personnel who are fluent in CHSL (teachers, psychologists, aides, secretaries, etc.).

It must be noted that, although some bilingual-bicultural educational experiences do exist in Chile, the clinical view of deafness, and its pedagogic practices focused on the development of students' speech, are more common. Schools for the deaf generally encourage the development of oral language skills and, as has already been mentioned, the FONADIS study (Fondo Nacional de la Discapacidad, 2004) points out that the use of CHSL is not generalized among deaf people. We also observe that the majority of the deaf population does not use hearing aids, and the conclusion is that a large number of deaf people do not have at their disposal effective means of communication, learning, or social integration.

The first historical precedents with respect to the presence and use of sign language in Chile date back to the beginning of the 20th century. In 1913, a small group of Deaf people began to meet in the Plaza de Armas in the city of Santiago to organize recreational activities. The first formal Deaf group in the country was created on October 24, 1926, and was called *Asociación de Sordomudos de Chile,* or Deaf and Mute Association of Chile (Demartini & Letelier, 2006). For more than 40 years, participation was exclusively male; women did not begin to participate until the 1970s. Currently, this association is called *Asociación de Sordos de Chile* (The Deaf Association of Chile) and is affiliated with the World Federation of the Deaf. Its goals are to promote mutual aid and cooperation between members, to improve members' well-being and morale, to promote education, and to promote the diffusion of their culture and the popularization of CHSL. There are currently 16 Deaf groups across the country affiliated with the National Confederation of the Deaf in Chile, and all have the same common objective: to popularize CHSL and to promote its official recognition. Nevertheless, despite the Deaf organizations' intense efforts, CHSL is still not recognized as an official language in Chile.

The first investigations into CHSL took place at the University of Chile in the 1980s, led by linguist Franklin Sentis. The first research team directed by Sentis to include a Deaf person was formed in 1985. Since then, several studies on CHSL have been carried out by a CHSL linguistics research group from the Metropolitan University of Educational Sciences. The Chilean manual alphabet is very similar to the French, Brazilian, and American alphabets, as well as to the Spanish one.

In recent years a project has been carried out in the Dr. Jorge Otte Gabler School to evaluate the effect of implementing CHSL and fingerspelling in teaching deaf students to read and write, and it has demonstrated great success (Alvarado, Puente, & Herrera, 2008; Puente, Alvarado, & Herrera, 2006). According to the results obtained by the project, both CHSL and fingerspelling significantly enable deaf children's and adolescents' internal representation of words as mechanisms, which facilitates the reading and spelling of words.

Secondary and Postsecondary Education

Data on auditory disabled students' access to higher education and retention and on subsequent graduation rates show higher education to be the most exclusionary level of education (see Moreno, 2006). The FONADIS report (Fondo Nacional de la Discapacidad, 2004) warns that only 1 in 20 disabled people have access to higher education. Among the deaf population,

13.2% complete secondary studies, 1% complete some form of technical or professional education, and 2.1% complete a university education (see Table 20.2). According to the data from the First National Study on Disabilities (Fondo Nacional de la Discapacidad, 2004), 175,282 disabled people are currently studying. If we assume that 8.7% of these are deaf, we would estimate that there are approximately 15,249 deaf people currently studying. However, official registries cite a much lower number of deaf students who are currently studying (MINEDUC, 2005a), a fact that demonstrates the inequality of access to the educational system for the deaf population.

In 2006, the FONADIS responded to the situation in which people with deaf and hard of hearing find themselves, and to promote their access to, retention in, and egress from the higher education system, the organization implemented a technical assistance program for disabled students integrated in the higher education system. It was designed specifically for young people in unfavorable economic circumstances who have a disability and are enrolled in public or private postsecondary centers. This program includes the payment of students' annual tuition fees; the total or partial financing of their educational materials, transportation, computer equipment and software; appropriately adapted living quarters; architectural modifications; and professional aides. Sixty-six candidates in 30 higher education institutions across the country applied for the program. Students with disabilities enrolled mainly in course topic areas such as archeology, law, special education, pedagogy, journalism, programming and information technology, social work, clerical skills, and graphic design as well as in various bachelor degree programs. Of the total number of candidates, 15% were students who were deaf and hard of hearing. Among the types of higher education institutions were universities (60%), professional institutions (20%), and technical or vocational training centers (13%).

Higher education institutions are beginning to become more open to the integration of disabled people. Of the 50 universities in the country, 8 have specific mechanisms in place for the integration of disabled people, 5 of which have institutionalized support programs for disabled students (González & Araneda, 2005). However, despite public opinion being in favor of the acceptance of students with disabilities, only 10% of Chilean universities have

Table 20.2. Level of Education Completed by People Who Are Deaf and Hard of Hearing

Level of Education	Number of People	Percentage
None	34,339	11.7%
Some primary school	126,109	43.1%
Primary school	25,033	8.6%
Some secondary school	42,441	14.5%
Secondary school	38,574	13.2%
Some technical school	1,640	0.6%
Technical school	47	0.0%
Some professional school	1,580	0.5%
Professional school	2,541	0.9%
Some university studies	6,498	2.2%
University studies	6,041	2.1%
Special education	3,133	1.1%
Unknown	4,743	1.6%
Total	292,719	100.0%

Note: From Fondo Nacional de la Discapacidad (2004).

specific openings for such students. Although regulatory and promotional entities working for the integration of students with disabilities in the higher education system do exist, it is the academic institutions themselves that decide whether to allow these students to enter, whether to make efforts to retain them, and whether to enact compensatory measures to prevent their egress (González & Araneda, 2005). In conclusion, although the higher education system in Chile does show some minimal signs of change, it is far from offering a complete acceptance of people who are deaf and hard of hearing.

STATUS OF DEAF ADULTS

Traditionally, deaf adults in Chile have been socially outcast and marginalized when it comes to decisions about the issues that affect them such as education, health, social organization, etc. This invisibility has not only affected deaf people's daily lives but also has made the Deaf community's linguistic and cultural peculiarities go unnoticed.

Before the passing of the Law on Social Integration of 1994, there existed no means of communication that would allow Deaf people to become more informed about current national and international events. Since the law came into effect, television stations must now broadcast at least one daily news programs with CHSL interpretation. This measure has allowed the Deaf community's language to be shared with the rest of the country and has sensitized the hearing majority to deafness. Another significant advance that has been made is related to civil rights. Before the law's passing, deaf adults could not contract marriage without consenting orally to the presiding judge's questions. Until that law's passing, the job of CHSL interpreter did not exist.

Recently, deaf teachers with university degrees have begun to be incorporated into the educational system in a manner that has allowed them to participate in the process of educating deaf students. Until now, their participation had been as recess monitors, aides, assistants, and co-educators. Nevertheless, a vicious circle exists in the sense that only 3% of the deaf population completes postsecondary studies (see Table 20.2) and consequently face limited possibilities of finding a professional post. Academic opportunities are limited, and access to them is insufficient.

The educational experience accumulated over the years, together with the new paradigms in deaf education, evidence the need to incorporate deaf adults in society. Unfortunately, the education of deaf people in Chile is sorely lacking in this sense. One relevant piece of data is the fact that nearly half the deaf and hard hearing population has not completed their primary school studies, 11.7% have no formal education, and slightly more than half of those deaf students who do enroll in higher education never finish their university studies (see Table 20.2).

As has already been pointed out, specialist teachers of deaf and hard hearing children have existed in Chile since 1964. They receive 4.5 years of university-level training in specific aspects related to deafness and generally teach classes at the primary school level and in special schools. Nevertheless, there are no teachers of the deaf in secondary schools. Currently, with the sudden popularity of integration, many specialist teachers have widened their work to include regular primary and secondary schools that integrate deaf students and young people. This development has led educational professionals to seek training in the various disciplines of knowledge necessary for the secondary-level teaching-learning process.

At the secondary level, the specialist teacher supports the regular class teacher's work, suggesting, where necessary, adaptations to the curriculum, methodologies, evaluation methods, or some combination. Nevertheless, in practice, this support teacher is not enough, and in the end, the integrated deaf student can rely only on his or her own resources and his or her teachers' and classmates' will to help the deaf student to integrate in the regular classroom. There are no CHSL interpreters to mediate communication between hearing teachers and deaf students in integrated classrooms in Chile.

SPECIAL LEGISLATION

In the 1990s, at the end of the dictatorship, Chile joined several international initiatives to improve living conditions for disabled people. In 1989, the country joined the World Convention on the Rights of the Child; in 1990, the World Conference on Education for All; in 1993, the Uniform Norms about Equal Opportunities for People With Disabilities; in 1994, the Salamanca Declaration on Special Education Needs: Access and Quality; and in 1998, the Inter-American Convention on the Elimination of All Forms of Discrimination Against Persons With Disabilities, among many others.

With the Supreme Education Decree Number 490 of 1990, norms for the integration of disabled students in regular schools were established for the first time, highlighting the state's focus on disabled students' academic integration. In the same year, Supreme Education Decree Number 86 approved new study plans and programs for students who are deaf and hard of hearing. As was mentioned earlier, Law Number 19.284 on the Full Social Integration of Disabled Persons was passed in 1994, leading MINEDUC to regulate and ensure the integration of disabled students in the regular education system.

Beginning in 1998, special education programs began receiving additional economic resources with which to institute changes necessary for the process of academic integration.[3] In that same year, Supreme Education Decree Number 1/98 replaced Decree Number 490. Education Law Number 19.598 was likewise modified in 1998 to include (a) the granting of a special, additional subsidy for disabled students integrated in any level of the regular education system and (b) an increase in subsidies for students with auditory, visual, and multisensory disabilities who must be taught in classes of no more than eight students.

In 1999, Supreme Education Decree Number 291 regulated the manner in which separate groups for disabled students in regular schools function, (a) establishing that the program for pedagogic support must conform to the regular course plan and study programs currently in force and (b) encouraging joint efforts between the regular class teacher and the special education teacher.

The Commission of Experts on Special Education report (2004) indicates that one of the main problems affecting the quality of educational processes in special education programs is the way in which special education is defined in the various legal frameworks on education that, in themselves, are confusing and even contradictory. The commission cites as examples the Organic Constitutional Law on Education, which does not even mention special educa-

---

3. The subsidies for special education have increased 330%, in real terms, since 1990 (Blanco, 2005).

tion in the framework of the country's general education system, and Article Number 26 of the Law on Disabilities Number 19.284 of 1994, which defines special education as a

different mode within the general education system, characterized by being a flexible, dynamic system preferably carried out within the regular system. This definition contradicts that established by the Law on Subsidies of 1998, in which Special Education is considered more restrictively as a different mode within regular education. (p. 23)

Professional Opportunities

Among the main problems facing the disabled population in Chile, particular note must be made of unemployment and marginalization in the workplace. Approximately 70% of disabled people older than age 15 do not have a paying job (Fondo Nacional de la Discapacidad, 2004; MIDEPLAN, 2000). If we compare the percentages of people with paying jobs in the disabled and nondisabled populations, we find a difference of more than 20%.

The national socioeconomic characterization survey (MIDEPLAN, 2000) notes that the rate of employment in the disabled population is less than half that of the nondisabled population: 25.1% and 51.6%, respectively. More disabled women are unemployed (81%) than disabled men (59.5%), and 40% of all disabled workers receive only minimum wage[4] and have less job security than nondisabled workers. The majority of disabled workers (33%) are unskilled laborers, 12.5% are operators and artisans, 12% are agricultural workers and skilled workers, and 13.9% work in sales and business. The areas of economic activity that provide the greatest amount of work to the disabled population are agriculture (20.1%) and manufacturing (11.4%).

The high unemployment rates of deaf workers are generally attributed to lack of training and to communication difficulties. Within the working-age deaf population, 29.6% have a paying job, which though low, nevertheless makes the deaf employment rate the highest of all disabled workers (Fondo Nacional de la Discapacidad, 2004).

To examine the vocational interests of deaf people, Briones (2002) carried out a study in the city of Santiago with young deaf students enrolled in secondary school. The sample included 30 deaf and 35 hearing teenagers between the ages of 16 and 18. *Kuder's Vocational Interest Inventory* was applied. The results show that, according to areas of vocational preference and without making any distinction for age, deaf students are more interested in artistic endeavors than are hearing students. Their second most preferred vocational area is literature, and their third is marketing, although these results may be a result of the use of instruments designed to study the preference of hearing subjects. The author argues that a relationship exists between deaf students' preferred area of vocational interest and their oral language skills. She likewise argues that there is a relationship between the number of years a deaf student has been enrolled in the regular education system and his or her level of interest in vocational areas requiring a greater command of oral language. Briones (2002) concludes that deaf students' vocational interests are determined by factors such as their experience in integrated classrooms, their command of communicational skills in oral language, and their cognitive development.

---

4. Minimum wage equals 120,000 pesos (US$230) a month.

CURRENT DEVELOPMENTS AND TRENDS

A clinical perspective of deafness continues to dominate in Chile and, despite the enactment of educational policies designed to foster the academic integration of deaf students in the regular school system, a "hearifying" focus on deafness persists. That is, there is still the expectation that deaf students will "manage" to have a similar type of development as hearing students, that they will learn by the same methods, that they will act in the same way, etc. Fortunately, as has been mentioned throughout this chapter, some change is beginning to occur, reflected in the advancement of sociolinguistic perspectives on deafness and the strength of the country's Deaf communities.

Since 2002, Chile's Deaf communities have been associated in the *Confederación Nacional de Sordos en Chile* (National Confederation of the Deaf in Chile), whose main objective is to act as a consulting body for both the public and the private sectors in matters relating to the national Deaf community. The confederation calls for, among other things, (a) the recognition of the right to a bilingual education and to the use and recognition of CHSL, (b) the regularization of Deaf CHSL teachers, and (c) equality of opportunity as regards access to higher education.

Although the Law on the Social Integration of Disabled Persons has made some advances in terms of civil rights, important challenges still exist. Among these challenges, one of the most pressing is without a doubt the recognition of CHSL as a real language, a recognition that would have a direct effect on the deaf population's quality of life.

An additional priority is to arrive at a more precise understanding of the situation of the deaf population through the development of studies that would offer a clearer view of this group's specific needs and that would enable more effective political efforts. Of vital importance to achieving this goal is availability of reliable statistical data on the disabled population in general and on the deaf population in particular. To this end, national population censuses should include specific forms on disabilities. It is also crucial that census forms collect information not only on health, employment, and assistance but also on education.

With respect to improvements still to be made in the education of the deaf, extending access to early attention and aural stimulation is fundamental; although detection of hearing loss takes place at earlier and earlier ages, there are no public bodies that monitor deaf infants' initial stages of development. Likewise, it is urgent that access to primary and secondary education be increased, that the scope of special education programs be widened, and that special education study plans and programs be revised to include scientific and social advances relevant to the education of the deaf. The Chilean Ministry of Education has the duty to protect the right of all Chileans across the country to receive an equal, quality education, and to this end, it is vital that teachers of the deaf be provided with clear, flexible, and updated guidelines.

Finally, it is necessary that policies designed to increase disabled students' access to higher education be strengthened so disabled students who have managed to successfully complete their primary and secondary educations have a better chance of being able to enroll in universities that are prepared to accept them.

REFERENCES

Alvarado, J., Puente, A., & Herrera, V. (2008). Visual and phonological coding in working memory and reading skills in deaf subjects using Chilean Sign Language. *American Annals of the Deaf, 152*(5), 467–79.

Blanco, R. (2005). *Avances y desafíos de la Educación Especial* [Advances and challenges in special education]. Retrieved August 18, 2008, from http://www.mineduc.cl/biblio/documento/Doc_avances_y_desafios_de_la_educacion_especial.pdf

Briones, J. (2002). *Los intereses vocacionales de los alumnos con pérdida auditiva, integrados en educación secundaria y su relación con los alumnos oyentes* [The vocational interest of students with hearing loss integrated in secondary schools and their relationship with hearing students]. Unpublished humanities master's thesis, Universidad Metropolitana de Ciencias de la Educación, Santiago.

Caiceo, J. (1988). La educación especial en Chile: un esbozo de su historia [Special education in Chile: An outline of its history]. *Revista de Pedagogía, 306,* 47–50.

Commission of Experts on Special Education. (2004). *Nueva perspectiva y visión de la Educación Especial* [A new perspective on and a new vision of special education]. Santiago: Ministerio de Educación.

Decreto Supremo de Educación No. 1 regula la integración escolar de alumnos con discapacidad [Supreme Decree of Education No. 1 regulates the integration school students with disabilities]. (1998, January 4). *Diario Oficial de la República de Chile* [Official Journal of the Republic of Chile], January 5, 1990.

Decreto Supremo de Educación No. 15 aprueba planes y programas de estudio para atender niños con trastornos auditivos [Supreme Decree of Education No. 15 approves plans and programs of study for children with hearing disorders]. (1981, January 10). *Diario Oficial de la República de Chile* [Official Journal of the Republic of Chile], March 11, 1990.

Decreto Supremo de Educación No. 51 aprueba planes y programas propios para segundo ciclo básico, escuela especial de sorgos Dr. Jorge Otte Gabler [Supreme Decree of Educaton No. 51 approves plans and programs to second basic cycle, special school of the deaf Dr. Jorge Otte Gabler] (2001, January 23). *Diario Oficial de la República de Chile* [Official Journal of the Republic of Chile], January 24, 2001.

Decreto Supremo de Educación No. 86 aprueba planes y programas de estudio para atender niños con trastornos auditivos [Supreme Decree of Education No. 86 approves plans and programs of study for children with disorders of hearing] (1990, January 25). *Diario Oficial de la República de Chile* [Official Journal of the Republic of Chile], March 11, 1990.

Decreto Supremo de Educación No. 291 regula el funcionamiento de grupos diferenciales en los establecimientos educacionales del país [Supreme Decree of Education No. 291 regulates the functioning of groups differential in the schools of the country] (1999, July 13). *Diario Oficial de la República de Chile* [Official Journal of the Republic of Chile], July 14, 1999.

Demartini, G., & Letelier, K. (2006). *Historia de la comunidad sorda: elaboración de un texto escrito para niños y jóvenes Sordos en edad escolar* [History of the deaf community: Development of a written text for deaf, school-aged children and young people]. Unpublished manuscript, Universidad Metropolitana de Ciencias de la Educación, Santiago.

Fondo Nacional de la Discapacidad. (2004). *Primer estudio Nacional de la discapacidad en Chile* [First national study on disabilities in Chile]. Santiago: Fondo Nacional de la Discapacidad And Instituto Nacional de Estadísticas (National Institute of Statistics).

Godoy, P., Meza, M., & Salazar, A. (2004). *Antecedentes históricos, presente y futuro de la educación especial en Chile* [The historical antecedents, present and future of special education in Chile]. Santiago: Ministerio de Educación.

González, F., & Araneda, P. (2005). *Integración de las personas con discapacidad en la educación superior en Chile* [The integration of persons with disabilities in the higher education system in Chile]. Santiago: Instituto Internacional Para la Educatión Superior en America Latina y El Caribe and UNESCO.

Law 18.962/1990. *Ley Orgánica Constitucional de Educación* [Organic Constitutional Law on Education], LOCE. March 10, 1990.

Law 19.284/1994. *Ley Sobre la Plena Integración Social de las Personas con Discapacidad* [Law on the Full Social Integration of Deaf Persons]. January 4, 1994.

Law 19.598/1998. *Ley de Educación* [Law on Education]. December 28, 1998.

Maldonado, M. (2003). La privatización de la educación en Chile [The privatization of education in Chile]. *Internacional de la Educación. Oficina regional para América Latina.* Retrieved October 1, 2008, from http://odiseo.com.mx/marcatexto/2005/05/La-privatizacion-de-la-educacion-en-chile

Ministerio de Educación de Chile (MINEDUC). (1999). Resolución Decreto Exento 434 Aprueba Planes y Programas Propios para primer ciclo básico, Escuela Especial de Sordos Dr. Jorge Otte Gabler [Exempt Decree Resolution 434 to approve separate plans and programs for the first basic cycle, Dr. Jorge Otte Gabler Special School for the Deaf]. December 27, 1999, Santiago, Chile.

Ministerio de Educación de Chile (MINEDUC). (2005a). *Estadísticas de la Educación* [Statistics on education]. Santiago: Author.

Ministerio de Educación de Chile (MINEDUC). (2005b). *Nueva Política Nacional de Educación Especial. Nuestro Compromiso con la diversidad* [National policy on special education: Our commitment to diversity]. Santiago: Author.

Ministerio de Planificación Nacional de Chile (MIDEPLAN). (2000). *Encuesta de Caracterización Socioeconómica Nacional. Situación de las personas con discapacidad en Chile* [National socio-economic characterization survey. The situation of disabled persons in Chile]. Santiago: Author.

Moreno, T. (2006). Integración/inclusión de las personas con discapacidad en la educación superior [The integration/inclusion of disabled persons in higher education]. In UNESCO, *Informe sobre la Educación Superior en América Latina y el Caribe* [Report on higher education in Latin America and the Caribbean] (pp. 144–155). Santiago: UNESCO.

Puente, A., Alvarado, J., & Herrera, V. (2006). Fingerspelling and sign language as alternative codes for reading and writing words for Chilean deaf signers. *American Annals of the Deaf, 151*(3), 229–310

Sistema de Medición de la Calidad de la Educación [System for Measuring the Quality of Education], Program for International Student Assessment, Third International Mathematics and Science Study, & Organizacion para la Cooperación y el Desarrollo Económico [Organization for Cooperation and Economic Development]. (2004). *Revisión de políticas nacionales en educación: Chile.* París: Organizacion para la Cooperación y el Desarrollo Económico [Organization for Cooperation and Economic Development].

Deafness in Jamaica

Ownali N. Mohamedali

JAMAICA IS an island nation with a population somewhat smaller than 3,000,000 located in the Caribbean Sea south of Cuba, west of Hispaniola (Haiti and the Dominican Republic), and northeast of Central America. The original Arawak people became extinct in the years that followed Columbus's landing in 1494 and Spain's subsequent claim to and settlement of the island. England took control in 1655, and Jamaica remained a British colony until 1958, when it gained independence as part of the British West Indies Federation. Full independence was achieved in 1962 when Jamaica established itself as an independent country.

The official language of Jamaica is English with Jamaican Patois also recognized. It is a parliamentary democracy and a constitutional monarchy, with Queen Elizabeth II as the monarch. The population is approximately 91% West African; 7% mixed race; and 2% East Indian, White, and Chinese. Approximately 7,070 people (2,985 males and 4,085 females) have a hearing loss, forming 0.271% of the population (Statistical Institute of Jamaica, 2004).

JAMAICAN GOVERNMENT POLICIES ON DISABLED PEOPLE

The Jamaican government has long recognized that the human rights, education, and productivity of disabled people are valuable elements in the development of the people and economy of the country.[1] The former Prime Minister of Jamaica, The Most Hon. P. J. Patterson, assured disabled people of the government's commitment to their educational, social, and economic empowerment (Prime Minister's Speeches, 2003). Similarly, the current Prime Minister of Jamaica, The Hon. Portia Simpson Miller, in her contribution to the 2006–07 budget debate in the House of Representatives, emphasized the fact that the well-being of any society depends on the well-being of all its people and that the measure of a good society is how it treats the poor, the aged, those with disabilities, women, and children (Prime Minister's Speeches, 2006). Moreover, the *Jamaica Five Year Development Plan 1990–1995* (Planning Institute of Jamaica, 1991) ensured equal opportunity for all children in Grades 1–9 and improved access to special education at the primary and secondary levels. The *Green*

The author wishes to express his gratitude to the University of the West Indies, Mona Campus, for the award of the Mona Research Fellowship to undertake research necessary for this article.

1. Not much information is published directly under the terms *hearing impaired* or *deaf* in Jamaica. To obtain the information relevant to this paper, I conducted searches using terms such as *physically handicapped, disabled, disability,* as well as *hearing impaired* and *deaf* in Jamaica. Any discussions in the paper under the general terms *disabled* and *disability* would, therefore, include Jamaicans who are deaf. In Jamaica, the terms *deaf* and *hearing impaired* are used interchangeably to signify people with varying degrees of hearing disability ranging from mild to moderate to severe to profound deafness. For purposes of this chapter, the term *deaf* is used.

Paper (Ministry of Education, 1999) of the Ministry of Education of Jamaica affirmed the providing of lifelong learning opportunities to all Jamaicans.

It is encouraging to note that the International Disability Rights Monitor surveyed 24 countries in the Americas in 2003 and found Jamaica to be the fifth most inclusive country in dealing with its disabled population (Edwards, 2004). Its judgment was based on the answers that International Disability Rights Monitor received to questions on seven issues: support for the United Nations treaty, legal protection for disabled people, education and employment opportunities, accessibility, health services, housing, and communications. The countries that rated better than Jamaica were the United States, Brazil, Canada, and Costa Rica. Jamaica is not complacent about its present ranking and progress and, hence, continues to work diligently to improve the quality of life, education, and standard of living of its disabled population (International Disability Rights Monitor, 2004).

CULTURAL BELIEFS

Wilson (2001) referring to a survey done by Thornburn in 1995 to determine the Jamaicans' general attitudes toward disability, categorized common responses: (a) 18% of the families interviewed believed the disability was the result of an evil spirit, punishment for a sin, or the product of the mother's having seen a disabled person when she was pregnant; (b) 40% believed a disabled child was sent by God; (c) 50% recognized the rights of people with disabilities in terms of employment; and (d) 90% said they would be willing to help out neighbors who had someone in their home who had a disability. The lowest level of supernatural beliefs was found in the professional and teacher groups, and the most superstitious groups were housewives, unemployed people, and agricultural workers.

Referring to yet another survey by Thornburn in 1998, Wilson (2001) highlighted the most frequently reported misconceptions about disabled people in Jamaica:

- Seventy-two percent believed "disabled children can go to school but they will not be able to work or get married."
- Sixty percent agreed that "disabled persons will always be a burden."
- Seventy-two percent believed that "the best place for a handicapped child is a special institution."
- Fifty-three percent agreed that "handicapped children should attend only special schools," while 18% said "sometimes."
- In contrast, 80% agreed that disabled children should play with nondisabled children.
- Seventy-four percent disagreed with the statement "my child should not go too close to a disabled child."
- Sixty-nine percent reported that they "don't really like to look at or listen to disabled children."

The Jamaica Association for the Deaf (JAD), describing the situation in the Caribbean, particularly in Jamaica, expressed the view that people who are deaf are often shunned, ridiculed, and denied access to vocational and educational opportunities (Jamaica Association for the Deaf, n.d.). The association attributed this situation to parental neglect, society's ignorance, and superstitions with respect to deafness that isolated the deaf and inhibited their emotional, economic, and educational progress. JAD observed that deaf people are often considered helpless and dependent burdens, enigmas, or curiosities and that they are not considered as individuals capable of achieving as much as hearing people, even if given the necessary support system. The association lamented the fact that such an attitude on the part of the Caribbean society affected the self-concepts of deaf people and their integration into all segments of society. JAD, in its 60th year in 1998, acknowledged that although there had been some achievement in educating and integrating deaf people in society, there was still need for a renewed thrust to increase parental cooperation and support (Ortega, 1998).

PARENTAL COOPERATION AND SUPPORT FOR DEAF PEOPLE

A Jamaican mother whose deaf child was successfully integrated into mainstream society suggested that parental cooperation could best be achieved through the establishment of an effective communication between the parents and the deaf children (Ustanny, 2004a). JAD attempted to bring about such communication by providing sign language classes for parents. However, not many parents attended these classes. Sharon Andrews, a teacher at one of the preschools, reported that less than 10% of parents with deaf children made an effort to learn sign language. She bemoaned the fact that when her school organized sign language classes, only two parents turned up. She observed that some parents neglected their deaf child because they felt that if they spent time and money on their deaf child, they would not get the same returns that they would on a nondeaf child. Moreover, she explained that the parents grumbled about the costs attached to the care and education of their deaf child. They complained that it cost them between J$17, 000 to J$90, 000 to provide hearing aids and that the education for their hearing impaired children was expensive (Ustanny, 2004b).

NATIONAL POLICY FOR DISABLED PEOPLE

A group of self-advocates of disabled people in Jamaica had long found that the conditions for disabled people were intolerable. The group asserted that the country needed a government policy to support, strengthen, and sustain its efforts to help disabled people. The commemoration of the International Year of Disabled Persons in 1981 strengthened their resolve to have a policy that would remove some societal barriers, foster greater self-determination within the population of people with disabilities, and very importantly, contribute to the norm of inclusion rather than marginalization (Ministry of Labour and Social Security, 2000).

In 1993, this group had a meeting with the Ministry of Labour and Social Security, which had responsibility for people with disabilities. The meeting resulted in the establishment of a committee delegated with the responsibility to prepare a national policy for the disabled community. The membership of this committee included representatives from the already existing organizations, associations, and societies such as the Jamaica Association for Children with Learning Disabilities, the JAD, the Jamaica Association for Children with Mental Retardation, Abilities Foundation, Private Voluntary Organizations Limited, 3D Projects (dedicated to the development of the disabled community), Jamaica Society for the Blind, Combined Disabilities Association, and the Jamaica Council for Persons with Disabilities (JCPD).

The joint efforts of the committee members resulted in the establishment and publication of a government policy for disabled people called the *National Policy for Persons with Disabilities* (Ministry of Labour and Social Security, 2000). When formulating this policy, the committee was guided in its endeavors by the 1993 United Nations Standard Rules for an Equalization of Opportunities for Persons With Disabilities, which provided them with a framework for cooperation between the government and civil society to equalize opportunities for people with disabilities. This policy was intended not only to strengthen the government's ability to address disability issues but also to assist agencies for the disabled to improve their capacity to address disability issues in areas such as education, employment, health, housing, and transportation. These objectives have served, and do still serve, as a guide to all those involved with work related to disabled people in Jamaica.

One of the drawbacks of the policy, however, was that it had no legal sanctions and thus was not enforceable. Although the policy provided guidelines for a concerted national action to improve the lives of the disabled, these guidelines could be implemented more effectively only through the enactment of government legislation that would ensure sustained financial resources, practical support, and opportunities for the disabled community. It is heartening to note that such legislation in the form of the draft National Disability Act is currently being prepared for submission to Parliament. The visually impaired senator, the Hon. Floyd Morris, the State Minister of Labor and Social Security, confirms that when this act becomes law, it will assist in giving teeth to the National Disability Policy (Ustanny, 2003).

Meanwhile, parents of deaf children had come together and formed a lobby group in 2004 dubbed The National Parent Action Group (Ministry of Labour and Social Security, 2005). The group's mission is to make every hearing impaired child a fully participating citizen of Jamaica. It advocates integrated education system (elaborated below), better social services, and greater access to sign language classes by the public to enable people in government offices and business places to communicate effectively with those who are hearing impaired. It also campaigns for insurance coverage of hearing aids for hearing impaired children.

EDUCATION FOR DEAF PEOPLE

Two methods are used to educate people with disabilities in Jamaica: (a) education within separate special education schools and (b) an integrative method in which students with disabilities are educated in the mainstream schools. The trend in Jamaica has been to encourage acceptance of children with disabilities within the mainstream schools to ensure equity in education for all. This trend is in keeping with the Jamaica Ministry of Education and Culture objective of education for all. A similar approach has been adopted in the United States where technological advances in hearing aids have encouraged mainstreaming of hearing impaired students in elementary and high schools. The idea is that such an approach encourages interaction of disabled students with peers and helps to motivate a greater number of disabled students to attend a college and a university, a step that they at one time thought was not possible (Norton, 1992).

Jamaica has special schools for children who are deaf, blind, or mentally challenged as well as enrollment in combined (integrated) schools. All these special schools are either government owned or government aided. They cater mainly to children from preschool through to the secondary level. More than 3,400 students are enrolled in these schools with 300 teachers (Ministry of Education, Youth & Culture, n.d.). There are 12 schools serving deaf students in Jamaica. They have a total enrollment of 1,055 and an academic staff of 95 (*Ministry of Education*, n.d.). There are also private, community-based facilities some of which are partially funded by the government. Their goal is to train people to work with special children in their homes. The Ministry of Education and Youth supervises them all.

The Special Education Unit in the Ministry of Education and Youth was established in January 1989 to facilitate improvement in education for people with disabilities. The ministry has seven special education units attached to government-run all-age and primary schools that cater to children with a wide range of learning disabilities. These units were built to facilitate the concept of mainstreaming and to provide support and curriculum supervision as well as to monitor services and facilitate training, net-working, assessment, and program planning. They are a resource base for expertise, advice, and hands-on information across all levels of the education system. They collaborate with one another and with other agencies that offer services to people with special needs.

Sign Language Training

Earlier, we saw the attempts being made by the JAD to facilitate effective communication between parents and hearing impaired children by teaching parents sign language (Ustanny, 2004a). Similar attempts are also being made by the JAD to facilitate communication between deaf and hearing members of the society. The Ministry of Justice Training Institute, for example, with the assistance of the JAD, offered for 3 years, a 1-month course in sign language competence to approximately 40 people drawn from the island's special constabulary force, courts' offices, and the Department of Correctional Services. The participants found the course helpful in that it enabled them to develop a better appreciation for people who are deaf. They also felt that their ability to communicate with deaf people would help them to get vital information from those who are hearing impaired that, in turn, could lead to the arrest of criminals. Chief Justice of Jamaica, Lensley Wolfe, praised the initiative undertaken by the Justice Training Institute as useful in preparing people to interpret and communicate in courts with people who are deaf (*Improving access to justice for the deaf and mute community*, 2005).

The Ministry of Labour and Social Security also conducted a basic sign language course for its employees with assistance from the JCPD, which is an agency under the Ministry of Labour. The course was designed to facilitate better communication between the ministry's staff members and deaf people and to enable deaf people to transact business with the ministry. JCPD has in mind to extend basic sign language training to other ministries to ensure that those in the public sector are well equipped to communicate with people who are deaf (*Labour Ministry staff benefit from sign language training*, 2005).

Jamaica could become a enticing destination for deaf tourists in addition to its already known reputation as the all-inclusive destination. With this goal in mind, Sandals, a chain of all-inclusive hotels in Jamaica, has conducted training for its staff members in sign language with instructors from the Caribbean Centre for the Deaf. The Sandals chain has also equipped all its properties with closed-caption decoders for use by deaf guests (*Sandals responds to the hearing impaired*, 2001).

Vocational Training for the Hearing Impaired

Vocational training for young adults with disabilities is provided by a number of private voluntary organizations and nongovernmental organizations such as the JAD, Woodside

Clarendon School for the Deaf, School of Hope, Abilities Foundation, 3D Projects Private Voluntary Organization Limited, and the McCam Child Care and Development Centre. The Lister-Mair-Gilby Comprehensive High School (School for the Deaf), the JAD, and the School of Hope provide vocational training for students with disabilities in the formal school system (*EFA 2000 assessment*, 2000).

Informal training is provided through the 3D Project, which provides community-based training in horticulture and papermaking. This effort is based in four parishes: St. Catherine, Manchester, St. Thomas, and St. Mary. The private voluntary organizations provide community and home-based training in the remaining parishes. Another organization providing a home-based training program with a parent education component is the Clarendon Group for the Disabled.

The Abilities Foundation, a vocational training center for people with disabilities, was established in 1991. It offers a comprehensive skills training program to meet the needs of the entire spectrum of young disabled adults. Each year, an average of 30 people graduate from the institution, but only a small number have been successful in finding jobs (Bartley, 2001). The employment prospects for deaf people are discussed later in this chapter.

TEACHER TRAINING IN SPECIAL EDUCATION

Teachers for special education schools are trained at the Mico Teachers' College; Sam Sharpe Teachers' College; and the University of the West Indies (UWI), Mona Campus, Kingston, Jamaica. At the UWI, students may read for degrees with one of three majors in the Bachelor of Education (BEd) program (University of the West Indies, Faculty of Humanities and Education, 2007):

- Special Education (Administration)
- Special Education (Clinical)
- Special Education (Multiple Handicapped)

The Mico Teachers' College formal Special Education Program includes the following (Anderson, 2007):

- Diploma programs in Primary and Special Education
- Training of teachers in Special Education
- Degree in Guidance and Counseling
- Bachelor Degree in Special Education (BEd) offered in collaboration with the UWI

The BEd program offered by the UWI includes an option for students to specialize in school librarianship whereby the Department of Library and Information Studies at the UWI offers selected courses to interested BEd students to enable them to pursue an interdisciplinary program leading to the BEd degree with specialization in school librarianship (University of the West Indies, Department of Library and Information Studies, 2007). This program was started in 1998 in direct response to the government of Jamaica's initiative to place teacher-librarians in primary schools. Moreover, the Public Library Service courses offered by the Department of Library and Information Studies to students at undergraduate and graduate levels include modules designed specifically to meet the information service requirements of hearing and visually impaired individuals.

The Ministry of Education organizes sensitization seminars and workshops across the island to enlighten teachers to the problems of children with learning difficulties and to identify and cater to children with various learning characteristics. The ultimate goal of these seminars and workshops is to make available at least one special educator in every school. However, it seems unlikely that this goal can be achieved in the short run because an exodus of a large percentage of teachers trained to deal with students with mental and physical disabilities has resulted in a staff shortage. Mary Dixon, head of the Special Education Department at the Mico University College, revealed that about half of those trained by the college are foreigners who eventually go back home, and approximately 40% of those who remain end up leaving the country for employment overseas (Editor's forum, 2006). There are presently some 390 teachers and 6,500 students in special education facilities in the island, and only about 100 out of 390 teachers have been trained in special education. The teacher-pupil ratio varies from 1:5 to 1:16, depending on the type and severity of learning problems (Ministry of Education, Youth & Culture, n.d.). It is envisaged that those responsible for the formulation of the Disability Act would include in the act the provision for the expansion of training of special education teachers (McDonald, 2002).

Adult Education for Hearing Impaired People

Presently, the deaf community on the island does not have access to decentralized adult education like its hearing counterparts in the rest of the country. Representatives from the Kingston Deaf Community in their 2005–2009 strategic plans have requested that the island-wide deaf communities be provided with access to decentralized adult education. A survey is being undertaken by members of the Kingston Deaf community who have been employed by the JAD to identify the potential adult education needs in eight sample parishes of Jamaica (Runnels, 2005).

Training for disabled people in information and communications technology (ICT) is facilitated by the government's ICT Training for Persons with Disabilities Program conducted by the National Youth Service. Since its inception in November 2001, this program has trained some 300 disabled people. Currently, 50 disabled people are enrolled in the program, which is conducted at four sites: the Social Development Commission's office complex in Spanish Town; the Jamaica Society for the Blind in Kingston; the Lister Mair Gilby Senior School for the Deaf; and the Waterford High School in Portmore, St. Catherine. The curriculum of the program includes topics such as occupational health and safety procedures, working effectively in a technology environment, communicating in the workplace, interacting with clients, operating a personal computer, accessing the Internet, introduction to the computer peripherals, and operating a presentation package. Mr. Michael Thorney, project coordinator for the program, sees the need for future expansion of this program both geographically and in content (Tomlinson, 2006).

Professor Fay Durrant, in her analysis of the survey undertaken in 2004 by Darrell West on Global E-government, reported that only 14% of the government Web sites out of the 1,197 from 198 different nations (including Jamaica) offered some form of disability access (Durrant, 2005). The access rate for Jamaica was only 6%. Such a low percentage of accessibility obviously dictates the need for enhancing Web access to disabled people in Jamaica.

However, it is one thing to enhance Web access and quite another to ensure that disabled people in Jamaica take full advantage of such access. Technology needs of Jamaicans who have full use of hands, eyes, and ears are evidently different from those who are unable to use their hands, eyes, or ears. There is, of course, also the problem of affordability by those disabled people who wish to make use of the Internet but are unable to afford the expenses involved. Costs for the purchase of necessary computer hardware and software, training of trainers and users, fees for Internet access, and amplification devices such as hearing aids must be taken into account to ensure that all disabled citizens can access and make use of the available Internet resources and services. Indeed, it has been reported that teachers and disabled students alike are experiencing difficulties because of costs of training materials such as multimedia programs, data projectors, textbooks, and proper Internet access (Brett, 2004).

These concerns no doubt suggest a greater need for support services whether in the form of individual assistance or special equipment to facilitate learning. A suggestion has been made that the government of Jamaica should keep these concerns in mind in any plans to provide support services to enhance Internet access to the disabled (Thomson, 2005). Some support in the form of equipment and free access to the Internet in schools has been forthcoming from the private Internet providers such as the Cable and Wireless Jamaica Limited and Digicel, but their contributions need to be supplemented by the government on a continuing basis.

EMPLOYMENT FOR THE DISABLED

It was mentioned earlier that only a small number of disabled people trained were successful in securing jobs (Bartley, 2001). Employment thus remains a major area of concern for people with disabilities. Lola Wright, principal of the Caribbean Christian Centre School for the Deaf, acknowledged that she had deaf people working as school teachers, assistant librarians, housekeeper, and teacher aides. However, she was not able to satisfy the demands made by many parents who wanted their children to be employed after they graduated from school. She therefore appealed to employers in the country to employ deaf graduates who she said had acquired the necessary vocational skills through school's curriculum consisting of vocational training subjects and through Caribbean Examination Council and Human Employment and Resource Training subjects. She emphasized the fact that her school's curriculum was not different from that used by the Human Employment and Resource Training Academies across the island (Hines, 2004).

In a letter to the *Jamaica Gleaner* newspaper of April 21, 2003, a hearing impaired person implored the ministers, prominent business places, and the general public to provide employment opportunities to deaf people. He pleaded that without employment, hearing impaired people were a burden to their families (Stewart, 2003).

When asked by the Jamaica Information Service about the employment prospects for those who were trained, Mr. Thorney (coordinator for the government's ICT Training for Persons with Disabilities Program) replied that not all who were trained found jobs, but he was trying to get assistance from the Jamaica Employers Federation to organize internship programs to enable disabled people to get some practical on-the-job experience to improve their employment prospects. He added that some of those who were trained were given the opportunity to go for advanced training to the Caribbean Institute of Technology, and others who were interested in starting up their own businesses were given the necessary encouragement and support (Tomlinson, 2006).

HEALTH SERVICES FOR THE DEAF

Dr. Nicholas Dorah from the Child Health Section of the UWI carried out a study between 1998 and 2000 in which she performed screening tests on a random sample of children chosen by the Statistical Institute of Jamaica from a national survey (Sixteen per cent of children, 2002). The study found that about 16.2% of Jamaican children, ages 4 to 10 years, had a hearing loss. She warned that significant hearing loss was one of the most common major abnormalities present at birth, and if undetected, it would impede speech, language, and cognitive development. The JAD recognized the importance of screening and assessment in the identification of children with disabilities and for early intervention. It undertook the responsibility to create public awareness and to strengthen its capacity to support these services (*Hearing awareness and assessment project*, 2006). It started its awareness program in March 2006 by organizing a health fair in Morant Bay, St. Thomas. The goal of the fair was to provide free medical consultation for members of the community and to increase their awareness on the care of the body and maintenance of healthy lifestyles. During the fair, 140 people from the community and surrounding areas were provided services such as hearing screening; vision testing; blood, sugar, and blood pressure checks; hemoglobin tests; foot care; and ear, nose, and throat consultations (*JAD health fair*, 2006).

The Thelma Tweedle Clinic operated by the JAD offers a screening program designed to identify infants who may have hearing loss at birth. Its goal is to initiate early detection, intervention, and prevention because children who are born with hearing loss may be deprived of the speech and language stimulation that is required to help them maximize their speech and language skills (Safeguarding the sense of hearing, 2006). The Mico College Child Assessment and Research in Education Centre established in 1981 also provides services such as diagnoses of the hearing, speech, and language problems of children referred to the center (Mico College Child Assessment and Research in Education, n.d.). It coordinates referrals to medical specialists where necessary.

A study carried out by the JCPD revealed that deaf women and girls were exposed to high levels of rape, incest, and sexual abuse and were consequently vulnerable to contracting HIV/ AIDS (Hearing-impaired women speak out about sexual abuse, 2006). JCPD thus began spearheading the HIV/AIDS prevention program for deaf women in 2006. This program, which is jointly funded by the Government of Jamaica and the United Nations Program on HIV/AIDS (UNAIDS), is designed to empower deaf women as well as girls and their guardians with survival and defense strategies that could help protect them from violence associated with sexual abuse. Commenting on the program, Senator Floyd Morris, the minister in the Ministry of Labour and Social Security, pointed out that the move by the JCPD should not suggest that HIV/AIDS is rampant among disabled people. He expressed the view that HIV/AIDS prevention program should sensitize both the abled and disabled equally. He suggested that the advertisements designed for television must incorporate sign language or closed captioning to enable the deaf population to get the required message (Kelly, 2006).

Senator Floyd Morris has been active in helping to implement the Program for Advancement Through Health and Education (PATH), which is a social security initiative introduced in March 2002 that is designed to deliver benefits by way of cash grants to the most needy persons in the society. The program is administered by the Ministry of Labour and Social Security and replaces three major social assistance programs—Food Stamps, Public Assistance, and Outdoor Poor Relief programs. Among the major objectives of the program are the following: to provide assistance for vulnerable groups in the society; to increase educational attainment and improve health outcomes; to serve as a safety net for the poor; and to reduce poverty by increasing the value of benefits to the poor. All beneficiaries of the program are expected to adhere to certain conditions; for example, school-age children between the ages of 6 and 17 years are required to maintain an 85% attendance record in school, and the elderly, poor adults, pregnant women, and people with disabilities are required to maintain a schedule of visits to health centers. In his contribution to the 2006–07 sectoral debate in the House of Representatives, Minister of Labour and Social Security Derrick Kellier stated that PATH had become a model program for other countries. The World Bank and the United Nations Children's Fund had sent delegations from South Africa, Belize, Suriname, Bahamas, and Kenya to study the program (PATH Streamlined for greater efficiency, 2006).

LIBRARY AND INFORMATION SERVICES FOR HEARING IMPAIRED PEOPLE

Although attempts are being made to establish communication through sign language between employees in the government ministries and hearing impaired people (see, for example, *Improving access to justice for the deaf and mute community*, 2005; *Labour Ministry staff benefit*, 2005), there has been no such effort to promote communication between hearing impaired people and librarians employed in the various types of libraries in Jamaica. In fact, no efforts have been made in spite of the fact that the public libraries have been mandated by the IFLA (International Federation of Library Associations and Institutions)/UNESCO (United Nations Educational, Scientific and Cultural Organization) Public Library Manifesto, to provide specific services and materials for their disabled clients (IFLA & UNESCO, 1994).

Observation shows that librarians employed in the Jamaican libraries have very little knowledge of how to serve their deaf users effectively. One of the reasons for this deficit could be that the regional (Caribbean) library school at the UWI, Mona Campus, where most librarians receive their library education, does not have sign language instruction in its curriculum. Although the library school offers courses on public library services that include modules on library service to hearing and visually impaired clients, these modules do not contain sign language classes (University of the West Indies, Department of Library and Information Studies, 2007). Either these modules need to be upgraded to include the study of sign language or else a new course in its own right called The Library and Information Service for the Disabled needs to be developed. A new course, in addition to having a component of sign language instruction, would also need to include modules such as Management of Information Units for Disabled Clients, Acquisition, Organization, Information Retrieval, Reference Services, and Application of New Information Technology for Disabled Clients. Such a course would help librarians provide hearing impaired and other disabled people with expected effective and efficient library and information services.

TRANSPORTATION FOR THE DEAF

Transportation is a major problem for Jamaica's disabled citizens, especially those living in the rural areas. They are usually assisted by caregivers and relatives. Concessionary bus fares were introduced by the government, but the buses are not always accessible or available (Bartley, 2001). Some deaf people would very much like to drive their own vehicles but are unable to do so because of the country's outdated 1938 Road Traffic Act, which prohibits them from obtaining licenses to drive. Ironically, deaf people who had obtained driving licenses from countries overseas such as the United States are free to drive in Jamaica. However, efforts are underway to correct this anomaly. Senator Floyd Morris is working with the Ministry of Transport and Works to have the outdated Road Traffic Act amended to enable deaf citizens to obtain licenses to drive (Lim, 2004).

CONCLUSION AND SUGGESTIONS

Today, deaf people in Jamaica are no longer ignored and taken for granted as in the past. The perception that they are unable to make a worthwhile contribution to society because of their handicap is changing. This trend is evident in reassuring statements by the former and current prime ministers of Jamaica with respect to the well-being of deaf people and the importance of their contribution to the development of people and economy of the country (see Prime Minister's Speeches, 2003; Prime Minister's Speeches, 2006).

Various societies and organizations for disabled people are working to achieve equality, nondiscrimination, and the inclusion of all persons with disabilities in all aspects of the country's economic and social life (Ministry of Labour and Social Security, 2000). There is no letup in such efforts, as is evident from the discussion in a recent debate in Parliament on occupational health and safety, where Senator Professor Trevor Munroe pleaded that discrimination against people with disabilities be made unconstitutional (Campbell, 2007). The suggestions that follow are therefore made to strengthen the existing efforts made by the government and various associations, organizations, and societies to improve the quality of life and to enhance the opportunities for independence and self-reliance of disabled people, including those who are deaf in Jamaica.

Legislation for Disabled People

The government's sincere desire to improve the prospects for a better future of disabled people is seen in the process now underway to formulate and adopt comprehensive legislation in the form of a National Disability Act (Brown, 2004). It is suggested that before its enactment into law, the act must identify and reduce to a minimum all obstacles to integration of people with disabilities into the mainstream of society. The act not only must ensure that the policies concerning the welfare of disabled people are effectively enforced but also should ensure participation of all disabled people as equal partners in all spheres of political, economic, social, and cultural life.

Education for Disabled People

There has been expansion and extension in educational opportunities for disabled children and adults in infant, primary, and secondary schools as well as in tertiary educational institutions since the International Year of the Disabled Persons was declared in 1981. Progress in this area is exemplified by the initiative recently undertaken by the UWI to construct on the Mona campus the Lions Resource Centre for Students With Disabilities. The two-story, 438-square meter facility will be equipped with a state-of-the-art computer lab and library as well as lecture, exam, and meeting rooms. The construction of the facility was expected to be completed in 2007 (construction began in 2006). Endeavors of this type are welcomed; however, they should not be confined to urban areas but should also extend to rural areas (Runnels, 2005).

Health Services for Disabled People

Progress in the providing of health care for disabled people has included the successful implementation of the Program of Advancement Through Health and Education (PATH), mentioned earlier. However, more needs to be done if the country is to realize Prime Minister Portia Simpson Miller's vision of Jamaica as a country where all people will have access to first-class health care (Prime Minister's Speeches, 2006). Thus, it is perhaps useful to heed and acknowledge what Director Ransford Wright of the Jamaica Council for Persons with Disabilities said about collaborative efforts of the ministries of education, labor, and social security and health being pivotal in achieving best practices for those who are physically challenged (Edwards, 2004).

Employment for the Deaf

Existing efforts to enhance employment opportunities for disabled people must continue. Vocational and skills training programs leading to self-employment must be encouraged. Cooperation between educational and vocational institutions and employers in government, industries, and businesses must be strengthened. Employment agencies interested in learning sign language should be given the opportunity to do so. Public awareness programs to sensitize the public about the employment problems of disabled people must be improved through the creation of a Web site that will allow those who are disabled not only to share ideas, skills, and abilities but also to make these known to actual and potential employers.

Library and Information Services for Disabled People

The UNESCO/IFLA Public Library Manifesto has proclaimed that both abled and disabled people should enjoy equal rights of access to information (IFLA & UNESCO, 1994). Any information gap that may exist can therefore be bridged by having well-trained library and information personnel capable of providing effective and efficient library and information service to all library patrons. Two ways in which this goal can be accomplished is by incorporating sign language instruction into the existing library school curriculum or by establishing an entirely new course on Library Services for the Disabled, with the study of sign language constituting an essential component.

Transport for Hearing Impaired People

Finally, the desire of hearing impaired people to possess driving licenses must be heeded. Legal processes to amend the existing outdated 1938 Road Traffic Act, which prohibits hearing impaired people from obtaining a driver's license must be given immediate attention. Such an act on the part of the government will facilitate the empowerment of deaf Jamaicans so they can enjoy the same human rights and fundamental freedoms as other people. Jamaica must catch up with other Caribbean countries such as Barbados, St. Lucia, and Trinidad and Tobago who grant driver's licenses to their disabled citizens (Spence, 2003).

References

Anderson, H. (2007, January 14). Mico launches BEd in Language and Literacy. *Jamaica Observer*. Retrieved October 11, 2006, from http://www.jamaicaobserver.com/news/html/20070113T190000-0500_117850_OBS_MICO_LAUNCHES_BED_IN_LANGUAGE_AND_LITERACY_.asp

Bartley, M. (2001, December). *United Nations expert group meeting on disability-sensitive policy and programme monitoring and evaluation: Caribbean region.* Paper presented at the 2001 Observance of the International Day of Disabled Persons, United Nations Headquarters, New York. Retrieved August 18, 2006, from http://www.un.org/esa/socdev/enable/disid2001f.htm#top

Brett, P. (2004, March 30). IT specialist set to fill gap. *The Gleaner*, p. A6.

Brown, J. (2004, December 7). *Government targets the disabled with far reaching laws.* Retrieved September 10, 2006, from http://www.jis.gov.jm/labour/html/20041206T090000-0500_4387_JIS_GOVT__TARGETS_THE_DISABLED_WITH_FAR_REACHING_LAWS.asp

Campbell, E. (2007, January 29). Munroe lobbies for the disabled. *Jamaica Gleaner*. Retrieved June 6, 2007, from http://www.jamaica-gleaner.com/gleaner/20070129/lead/lead5.html

Construction begins on UWI Lions Resource Centre for students with disabilities. (2006). *UWI Development and Endowment Fund Newsletter, 2,* 7. Retrieved December 11, 2006, from http://www.uwifundmona.org.jm/thefund.pdf

Durrant, Fay. (2005, August). *The World Wide Web enhancing e-government in the Caribbean.* Paper presented at the World Library and Information Congress, 71st IFLA General Conference and Council, Oslo, Norway. Retrieved December 5, 2006, from http://www.ifla.org/IV/ifla71/papers/167-e_Durrant.pdf

Editor's forum: Special education exodus a threat. (2006, November 9). *Jamaica Gleaner*. Retrieved June 11, 2007, from http://www.jamaica-gleaner.com/gleaner/20061109/news/news2.html

Edwards, C. (2004, December 12). Jamaica's disabled count their blessings. *Daily Observer*, p. 10–11.

EFA 2000 Assessment: Country reports, Jamaica. (2000). Retrieved February 6, 2007, from http://www2.unesco.org/wef/countryreports/jamaica/rapport_1.html

Hearing awareness and assessment project—June 2005—Nov 2006. (April 21, 2006). Retrieved November 1, 2006, from http://www.jamdeaf.org.jm/articles/hearing-awareness-and-assessment-project-june-2005-nov-2006

Hearing-impaired women speak out about sexual abuse. (2006, October 2). *Daily Observer*, p. 3.

Hines, H. (2004, June 8). Making its voice heard: Caribbean Christian Centre for the Deaf. *Jamaica Observer.* Retrieved December 11, 2008, from http://www.deaftoday.com/news/archives/2004/06/making_its_voic.html

IFLA & UNESCO. (1994). *IFLA/UNESCO public library manifesto.* Retrieved December 11, 2006, from http://www.ifla.org/VII/s8/unesco/eng.htm

Improving access to justice for the deaf and mute community. (2005, April 5). Retrieved May 23, 2007, from http://www.jis.gov.jm/justice/html/20050405t120000-0500_5307_jis_improving_access_to_justice_for_the_deaf_and_mute_community.asp

International Disability Rights Monitor (IDRM). (2004). *Jamaica.* Retrieved December 27, 2006, from http://www.cirnetwork.org/idrm/reports/americas/countries/jamaica.html

JAD health fair 2006. (April 1, 2006). Retrieved November 1, 2006, from http://www.jamdeaf.org.jm/articles/jad-health-fair-2006

Jamaica Association for the Deaf. (n.d.). *General information.* Retrieved August 30, 2006, from http://www.jamaica-kidz.com/jad/

Kelly, P. (2006, September 11). *Government implements HIV/AIDS prevention program for deaf women.* Retrieved December 17, 2008, from http://www.jis.gov.jm/health/html/20060910T1000000500_9964_JIS_GOVT__IMPLEMENTS__HIV_AIDS_PREVENTION__PROGRAMME_FOR_DEAF_WOMEN.asp

Labour Ministry staff benefit from sign language training. (2005, February 22). Retrieved October 11, 2006, from http://www.jis.gov.jm/labour/html/20050219t090000-0500_4922_jis_labour_ministry_staff_benefit_from_sign_language_training.asp

Lim, A-M. (2004, January 25). Why shouldn't the deaf drive? *Daily Observer,* pp. 4–5.

McDonald, S. (2002, December). A profile of selected government and non-government agencies providing services for persons with disabilities. *JA People 18,* 3–15.

Mico College Child Assessment and Research in Education (CARE). (n.d.). [Brochure]. Retrieved November 10, 2006, from http://www.micocarecentre.org/referral_docs/brochure_new.doc

Ministry of Education. (n.d) Retrieved May 23, 2007, from http://www.jis.gov.jm/education/index.asp

Ministry of Education. (1999). *Green paper.* Kingston, Jamaica: Author.

Ministry of Education, Youth & Culture. (n.d.). *Overview of special education.* Retrieved November 9, 2006, from http://www.moec.gov.jm/divisions/ed/specialeducation/index.htm

Ministry of Labour and Social Security. (2000). National policy for persons with disabilities. Kingston, Jamaica: Author.

Ministry of Labour and Social Security. (2005, September 16). *Parents of hearing impaired children form a lobby group.* Retrieved May 23, 2007, from http://www.jis.gov.jm/labour/html/20050915t080000-0500_6803_jis_parents_of_hearing_impaired_children_form_lobby_group.asp

Norton, M. J. (1992). Effective bibliographic instruction for deaf and hearing impaired college students. *Library Trends, 41*(1), 118–150.

Ortega, D. (1998, May 18). A new thrust for the deaf. *Jamaica Gleaner,* p. A2.

PATH streamlined for greater efficiency—Senator Morris. (2006, July 14). Retrieved January 1, 2007, from http://www.jis.gov.jm/labour/html/20060713t120000-0500_9396_jis_path_streamlined_for_greater_efficiency__senator_morris.asp

Planning Institute of Jamaica. (1991). *Jamaica five year development plan 1990–1995: Education and training.* Kingston, Jamaica: Author.

Prime Minister's Speeches. (2003, September 24). The passing out exercise and prize giving ceremony of the early stimulation program. Retrieved May 23, 2007, from http://www.jis.gov.jm/pmspeeches/html/20030924t100000-0500_588_jis_the_passing_out_exercise_and_prize_giving_ceremony_of_the_early_stimulation_program.asp

Prime Minister's Speeches. (2006, May 09). *Contributions by the Hon. Portia Simpson Miller, Prime*

Minister to the 2006/2007 Budget Debate in the House of Representatives on Tuesday May 9, 2006. Retrieved May 23, 2007 from www.jis.gov.jm/special_sections/BudgetDebate2006/PMBudget 2006.pdf

Runnels, J. (2005, November 25). *Island-wide adult education survey.* Retrieved September 5, 2006, from http://www.jamdeaf.org.jm/modules.php?op=modload&name=News&file=article&sid= 40&mode= thread&order=0&thold=0

Safeguarding the sense of hearing. (2006, October 23). *Jamaica Gleaner.* Retrieved October 23, 2006, from http://www.jamaica-gleaner.com/gleaner/20061023/flair/flair5.html

Sandals responds to the hearing impaired. (2001, January 13). *Daily Observer*, p. 16.

Sixteen per cent of children have hearing impairment—study. (2002, October 23). *Daily Observer,* p. 4.

Statistical Institute of Jamaica. (2004). *Population census 2001: Jamaica, disability*, 11. Kingston, Jamaica: Author.

Stewart, M. (2003, April 21). Job plea for the deaf. *The Gleaner*, p. A5.

Spence, V. (2003, March 29). Enable the disabled. *The Gleaner*, p. A4.

Thomson, L. (2005, December 4). Education of persons with disability. *The Gleaner,* p. A9.

Tomlinson, O. (June 13, 2006). ICT training available for persons with disabilities. Retrieved October 10, 2006, from http://www.jis.gov.jm/commerce_science/html/20060612t100000-0500_9081_ jis_ict_training_available_for_persons_with_disabilities.asp

University of the West Indies, Faculty of Humanities and Education. (2007). *Academic programs.* Retrieved January 1, 2007, from http://www.mona.uwi.edu/admissions/programs/mona_hedu.htm

University of the West Indies, Department of Library and Information Studies. (2007). *Bachelor of arts in Library and Information Studies.* Retrieved January 1, 2007, from http://www.mona.uwi.edu/dlis/ program/ba.htm

Ustanny, A. (2003, September 21). Senator Floyd Morris, 21st century man. *Sunday Gleaner, Outlook Sunday Magazine*, pp. 14–15.

Ustanny, A. (2004a, May 30). It's all about love—'God gave me a special gift, my daughter.' *Sunday Gleaner, Outlook Sunday Magazine,* pp. 2–3.

Ustanny, A. (2004b, May 30). Parenting the deaf child. Retrieved August 30, 2006, from http:// www.jamaica-gleaner.com/gleaner/20040530/out/out3.html

Wilson, A. T. (2001). *Development assistance from American organizations to deaf communities in the developing world: A qualitative study in Jamaica.* Unpublished doctoral dissertation, Gallaudet University, Washington, DC.

The United States:
Deaf People in a Pluralistic Society

Donald F. Moores, Margery S. Miller, and Edward Corbett

THE UNITED STATES is a federated republic of 50 states, the District of Columbia, the Commonwealth of Puerto Rico, and several territories. The 48 contiguous states and District of Columbia stretch across North America from the Atlantic Ocean to the Pacific Ocean. Geographically, it is the third largest country in the world, after Russia and Canada. With more than 300,000,000 inhabitants, it is also the third most populous country in the world, after China and India. Because of natural population increase and immigration, the United States has had a higher population growth than other developed countries, increasing from approximately 180,000,000 people in 1960 to 300,000,000 in 2005. The annual rate of growth currently is approximately 3,000,000 people.

The population is clustered in heavily urban and suburban areas, with 4 of the 50 states—California, Texas, New York, and Florida in that order—containing close to 100 million inhabitants, or roughly one-third of the total population. Texas more than doubled and Florida more than tripled its population from 1960 to 2005.

The United States is a multicultural, multiethnic, and multiracial nation. As such, its demographic composition is complex, and reporting by the U.S. Census Bureau takes several forms. The Census Bureau's *Population Profile of the United States: 2005* (Census Bureau, 2005) estimated that, in 2004, 80% of the population was White, 13% was Black or African American, 4% was Asian, 1.5% was American Indian and Alaska Native, and 0.3% was Native Hawaiian or Other Pacific Islander. The Hispanic population, which is multiracial, is estimated to be 14% of the U.S. population. A small percentage of people self-identified with two or more races. It should be noted that all data are self-reported.

AMERICAN EDUCATION

There are approximately 50,000,000 children ages 5 to 18 enrolled in public schools and 5,000,000 in private schools. Although there is some variation, usually there are three quite distinct school settings and levels: elementary school (kindergarten through Grades 5 or 6), middle school or junior high school (Grade 6 or 7 through Grade 8 or 9), and high school (Grade 9 or 10 through Grade 12).

Because education is not mentioned explicitly in the American Constitution, primary responsibility rests with the individual states. The federal government has been involved in education almost from the beginning of the union, and its involvement has increased substantially in recent years, but education still is primarily a state responsibility. Unlike many countries that have uniform, nationwide curricula, there is wide variation in curricula in the

332

United States from one state to another. Federal law requires that each state have rigorous standards of learning for each grade and that there be testing at different points, but the standards of learning and the testing vary from one state to another. The states allow each school district—which may consist of a town, city, or county—to develop its own curriculum consistent with the standards of learning, but testing is the same within each state.

The goals of American education have changed over the centuries, reflecting developments in technology, immigration, demography, and evolving societal values. As in many countries, there has been disagreement over whether education should be child centered or content centered. The prevailing philosophy in the 20th century was known as progressive education, which promoted a child-centered curriculum based on problem solving and the needs and motivation of the child. Teachers acted as guides to learning, evidencing flexibility and acceptance. The counter philosophy favored the traditional, highly structured, teacher-controlled, content-centered curriculum, which emphasized rote learning, memorization, and a defined sequence of instruction.

Progressive education was never without critics; critics argued that educational standards were lax and achievement was low. Concern peaked temporarily before 1960, when the Soviet Union launched the Sputnik satellite, and some elements of American education were restructured in response, but the changes were not dramatic or long-lasting. Significant efforts to fundamentally change American education did not begin until the 1980s. Spurred by reports of declining academic achievement over a period of more than 20 years, several reports were disseminated, with *A Nation at Risk: The Imperative for Educational Reform* (National Commission for Excellence in Education, 1983) having the greatest effect. The commission stated that "the educational foundations of our society are being eroded by a rising tide of mediocrity that threatens our very future as a Nation and as a people.... If an unfriendly foreign power had attempted to impose on America the mediocre educational performance that exists today, we might well have viewed it as an act of war" (National Commission for Excellence in Education, 1983, p. 5).

The report led to a widespread reconsideration of public education and educational reform at state and national levels. Results indicated that poor students, minority students, and students from southern states lagged in academic achievement. Led by William Clinton, then governor of Arkansas, the Governors' Educational Summit established six national goals for the year 2000. The federal government cooperated in 1991 and 1992 to establish voluntary national standards. In 1994, President Clinton signed the Educate America Act of 1994, or Goals 2000. The legislation set specific goals in seven areas:

- All children will start school ready to learn.
- School achievement will improve.
- Good citizenship will be fostered.
- Teacher education will be upgraded.
- The United States will be number one in the world in math and science achievement.
- Adult literacy and lifelong learning will be emphasized.
- Schools will be safe, disciplined, and alcohol and drug free.

Annual progress reports were made. By 2000, not one goal of the seven had been attained. The National Assessment of Educational Progress reported that minority students, poor students, and students from southern states continued to lag. Several reasons were advanced for the failure. First, there was not enough support in the form of either money or leadership from the U.S. Department of Education. Second, participation was voluntary and there was no external motivation for change. Other reasons included low expectations, poorly qualified teachers, progressive education, and social promotion, echoing the criticisms of *A Nation at Risk*.

In view of the results, the federal government established criteria for new initiatives under the No Child Left Behind (NCLB) Act of 2001, signed into law by President Bush in 2002. The Act was a revision and a broad expansion of the Elementary and Secondary Education Act, first enacted in 1965. Different timetables were set for various goals, but NCLB states that, by 2014, all third-grade children will read on grade level and all children will be proficient in academic subjects, as verified by rigorous statewide assessments aligned with each state's standards of learning approved by the federal government. Each state must set minimum performance standards for various categories of students based on race, family income, and English language proficiency, with the standards increasing annually until 100% of all children in all categories test at the proficient level. Schools must make adequate yearly progress toward the goals or face consequences, including a restructuring of the school. NCLB applies to all children, including deaf children.

HISTORICAL OVERVIEW OF EDUCATION OF DEAF PEOPLE IN THE UNITED STATES

The first permanent school for the deaf in the United States was established through the efforts of Mason Fitch Cogswell, a surgeon in Hartford, Connecticut, and the father of a deaf girl, Alice Cogswell. Dr. Cogswell raised the money to send Thomas Hopkins Gallaudet to Europe to study education of deaf people. At the Royal Institute for the Deaf in Paris, Gallaudet recruited a deaf teacher, Laurent Clerc, to return with him to the United States. On April 15, 1817, the school now known as the American School for the Deaf opened in Hartford. Clerc communicated with the students using a combination of Old French Sign Language and the methodical sign system, which approximated English grammar, and he also trained teachers in its use. The permanence of the school was secured in 1819 when the United States Congress provided that school a land grant of 23,000 acres in what now constitutes the city of Mobile, Alabama. The school sold the land for more than $300,000 (Moores, 2001) and established a fund that supported the school's operation in Connecticut.

For a period of about 50 years, education of deaf students was carried on completely through signing, either Methodical Signs, based on English, or Natural Signs, which constituted a different language. The situation was somewhat analogous to the present-day distinction between signed English systems and American Sign Language (ASL). Proponents of Natural Signs argued that they constituted a real language, with its own structure and vocabulary, that was used every day by deaf people. Proponents of Methodical Signs argued that they represented the most effective way to model English. Some schools stayed with one or the other approach consistently while others switched back and forth depending on the positions of their leaders (Stedt & Moores, 1990).

Laurent Clerc remained active in deaf education for its first 40 years. He trained many of the teachers and most of the first school leaders. Clearly, he was the most influential educator of deaf people during a period in which there were significant numbers of deaf teachers and other deaf leaders, perhaps more so than at any time since, including the present. In fact, many of the 19th-century schools for the deaf were established by deaf professionals (Gannon, 1981).

In 1864, the United States Congress authorized the Columbia Institution for the Instruction of the Deaf and Dumb in Washington, D.C. (now the Laurent Clerc National Deaf Education Center), to establish a college department, which grew into Gallaudet University. Gallaudet remains the only liberal arts college for the deaf in the world. Because of its unique nature, Gallaudet University became the central training ground for generations of deaf leaders.

Oral-only education of the deaf children began in the United States in 1867 with the founding of the Lexington School for the Deaf in New York City and the Clarke School for the Deaf in Northampton, Massachusetts. Although the American School for the Deaf had hired a full-time speech teacher in 1957, classroom instruction was conducted through signs, unlike the Lexington and Clarke schools, which relied solely on speech and speechreading. In the ensuing years, a conflict developed between supporters of oral-only education and those of manual education, a conflict that often became bitter and, in the case of the leading proponent of oral education and inventor of the telephone, Alexander Graham Bell, and the leading proponent of manual education, the president of Gallaudet College, Edward Miner Gallaudet, deeply personal.

In 1871, Bell, a native of Scotland, introduced to the United States a method of teaching articulation, Visible Speech, developed by his father, Alexander Melville Bell (Moores, 2001). A eugenicist, A. G. Bell opposed the establishment of residential schools for the deaf, which brought deaf people together and encouraged the use of sign language. In 1883, he published *Memoir Upon the Formation of a Deaf Variety of the Human Race* to discourage deaf people from marrying one another. He followed that work with an article in 1884 titled, "Fallacies Concerning the Deaf." Bell recommended the elimination of separate schools for deaf students, the prohibition of "gesture language," and a cease to the hiring of deaf teachers, noting that in 1883 they constituted almost one-third of teachers of the deaf in the United States.

Bell's position was supported by the triumph of oral-only education in Europe and the proclamation of the 1880 International Congress of teachers of the deaf in Milan in favor of the "pure oral method." In the United States, this influence resulted in the slow erosion of the use of Methodical and Natural Signs in education of deaf students, the growth of oral-only education, and a steady decline in the number of deaf teachers.

By the last quarter of the 19th century, three separate systems of educating deaf students had been established. The largest consisted of residential schools, mostly supported by the individual states or territories. In the southern and some midwestern states, these schools served only White children. After the American Civil War, which ended in 1865, a second system of segregated residential schools for African American deaf students were established in those states that previously had served only White children. The schools were located adjacent to the White schools, in different parts of the same town, or in different towns. They supposedly functioned under a "separate but equal" doctrine, but, in reality, they were not equal. Facilities were poorly maintained, textbooks often were nonexistent, and the schools were administered by White men. In 1954, the United States Supreme Court declared the separate but equal doctrine to be unconstitutional and ordered an end to segregated education. Some states resisted, arguing that education was not mentioned in the Constitution and therefore the Supreme Court did not have the authority to dictate to the individual states.

The conflict continued for nearly two decades, but eventually, all states complied. During this period, state residential schools were desegregated.

The third major system consisted of public day schools for deaf children. The Boston Day School, the first such school, opened in 1869. Within a few years, most large cities such as New York, Chicago, Detroit, and St. Louis had opened day schools. These schools served a predominantly immigrant population and almost exclusively followed an oral-only philosophy.

From the late 19th century until after World War II, the growing influence of oral-only education suppressed the use of sign language in most classes for deaf students. As a result, the Deaf community faced more overt oppression. The National Association of the Deaf (NAD) formed in 1880 to serve as an advocacy group for deaf people. At this time, the influence of deaf professionals was declining; White hearing men controlled the residential schools, and White hearing women ran the day schools. No deaf individuals held leadership positions within the schools, and none of the day schools hired deaf teachers. Although there was great variation, most of the residential schools used the oral-only method with students through the age of 12. Some continued in this manner through graduation. Other schools sent the "oral-failures" to the manual or combined oral-manual departments. In the manual departments and vocational training classes of residential schools, as well as in dormitories with deaf supervisors, deaf students came under the aegis of deaf adults and were acculturated into the deaf world. Ironically, the Deaf community perpetuated itself in these residential schools that were dominated by hearing educators who were opposed to the use of sign language.

This continuation of a sense of Deaf community was unique to the United States and parts of Canada. After the conference in Milan, the oral method was adopted as the exclusive method in all countries except the United States, which still used the "silent" mode to some extent (Bender, 1970, p. 168). That different stance was largely the result of the influence of the NAD and of Gallaudet College graduates, many of whom were also members of NAD. Although Gallaudet College began a graduate teacher training program in 1892, it did not allow deaf students into the program until 1964. Still, it was common for a deaf man from one state to meet a deaf woman from another state at Gallaudet, marry, and then both go to a state residential school in a third state to work as vocational teachers, high school teachers, or dormitory supervisors. In this way, deaf students were exposed to deaf role models, and Gallaudet sign language became a national standard. This phenomenon did not happen in the public day schools or in the state residential schools for deaf African American children, which developed their own variations of sign language. Gallaudet College did not accept African American children until 1954.

TRENDS FROM WORLD WAR II TO THE PRESENT

Change and development in deaf education has been steady from World War II to today. The trends in this area can be grouped in five areas: school attendance, mode of instruction, early identification and intervention, curriculum, and postsecondary education.

School Attendance

Although it was little recognized at the time, fundamental changes began to occur shortly after the end of World War II in 1945. The "Baby Boom" from 1946 until after 1964 produced an unprecedented number of deaf children, but state legislatures did not move to build new residential schools. As a result, increasing numbers of deaf children began attending public school programs after 1950, and by 1970, fewer than half of deaf children attended residential schools. The trend was intensified by the effect of the worldwide rubella epidemic in the mid-1960s in which the numbers of deaf children born in a 2-year period doubled. The passage by the U.S. Congress of Public Law 94-142, the Education for All Handicapped Children Act of 1975, provided further impetus for change. Among other things, the law stipulated that handicapped children be provided a free appropriate public education in the least restrictive environment.

In ensuing years, Public Law 94-142 has been modified several times and is now known as the Individuals with Disabilities Education Act (IDEA). It has been expanded to include children from birth through age 21. The law has been interpreted to mean that the preferred placement is within an educational setting with nondisabled children whenever possible, a philosophy now known as *inclusion*. The most recent data available indicate that 42% of deaf children are in regular classrooms with hearing students, 20% are in self-contained classrooms in regular education settings, and 12% spend time both in classes for deaf students and classes for hearing students (Gallaudet Research Institute, 2007). Separate data are no longer reported for residential and day school attendance. A combined 26% attend a special or center school, either residential or day.

Residential schools in some of the smaller states have closed, and several others are nearing a point where there may not be a critical mass of students to justify keeping the school open. Many residential schools currently serve a large day population sometimes with more than half the students commuting from home. In many states, the residential school population tends to be concentrated at the middle school and high school levels because children attend either regular classes or self-contained classes in public elementary schools and then transfer to a residential setting at later ages.

Mode of Instruction

As previously noted, oral-only instruction was predominant through the first two thirds of the 20th century. The situation began to change with the publication of research indicating that oral-only preschool programs were relatively ineffective and with research reporting that the academic achievement and English proficiency of deaf children of deaf parents were superior to those of deaf children of hearing parents, leading to the conclusion that the use of manual communication would be beneficial academically (Moores, 2001). Within a short period of time, more than half of the deaf students in the United States were being taught with some kind of manual communication system, but typically not ASL. Roy Holcomb, the first deaf director of a public school program for deaf students, promulgated the concept of Total Communication in which all forms of communication would be used—ASL, English-based signs, fingerspelling, speech, writing, gestures—depending on individual needs and situational requirements. However, most programs used only a combination of speech and English-based signs, or what is known as Simultaneous Communication. Other manual systems, including Seeing Essential English, Signing Exact English, and Signed English were created to represent English on the hands, much like the Methodical Sign system developed by Clerc in the 19th century (Stedt & Moores, 1990).

Around 1990, a movement began to establish bilingual-bicultural programs distinct from oral-only and Total Communication instruction. These programs use ASL as the language of instruction and do not use invented systems or speech in the classroom, although auditory training and speech training may occur separately. ASL is used to develop literary skills, and the bilingual component is written English.

According to the most recent data available for 2006–07, 52% of children are taught through speech only, 36% through sign with speech, and 11% through sign only (Gallaudet Research Institute, 2007). This information represents an increase in speech-only instruction and may be at least partially explained by the growing use of cochlear implants and the effect of neonatal screening and accompanying services.

Early Identification and Intervention

Although some preschool services for deaf children date as far back as the 19th century, pre-school education really began in the 1960s for children younger than the age of 6, mostly in large cities and metropolitan areas. The lowering of the ages by IDEA for providing services to disabled children, combined with legislation concerning neonatal hearing screening, means that services theoretically are available from birth through age 21. As is the situation in other areas, the quality of services varies across the states. Early identification may be universal for all intents and purposes, but the providing of effective family plans, as mandated by IDEA, and implementation of plans for the benefit of children and their families is problematic in many states. Frequently, first contacts with parents are with medical personnel, who may be unfamiliar with or reject the concept of deafness as a social construct. They may have a mind-set that cochlear implantation will "solve" what is seen as the problem of deafness, a naive assumption at best. This scenario is not the situation in all states but it is all too common, especially because relatively few deaf professionals are involved in the providing of services to parents and their children from birth to age 4. As a result, children have little or no exposure to deaf role models, and hearing parents do not have the benefit of the perspectives of deaf adults.

Curriculum

Traditionally, the curriculum for deaf students has been different from that for hearing students. Much of the school day was devoted to the development of English skills, speech skills, and auditory training—essentially, skills that a hearing child brought to school from the beginning. For deaf students, there was little time for instruction in content areas such as math, science, social studies, literature, or foreign languages. Growth of the mainstream-integration-inclusion movement started to bring the curriculum for deaf students in line with regular education. By definition, deaf children in classrooms with hearing children follow the regular curriculum of the particular school district, and children who divide their day between a resource room and regular classrooms for subjects such as mathematics and science also are exposed to at least part of the regular curriculum.

As growing numbers of older children transfer into the residential schools from regular education programs, there is a need to align the curriculum with the public schools. Most residential schools now have curricula based on local public schools or that address a state's standards of learning. The requirements of No Child Left Behind have finalized the move to the general curriculum. Deaf children are expected to pass rigorous content-area state tests at grade level. The percentage of children passing must increase each year until 2014, when there is an expected 100% level of success. This goal, of course, is not possible, but it has influenced educators of deaf students, among others, to concentrate on academic achievement.

Postsecondary Education

Perhaps the greatest success in education of deaf people has occurred at the postsecondary level since the 1960s. For 100 years, Gallaudet University was the only postsecondary program specifically for deaf students. In 1965, Congress authorized the establishment of the National Technical Institute for the Deaf (NTID) at the Rochester Institute of Technology in New York State. NTID has become the technical counterpart of Gallaudet, that is, a national program serving highly qualified deaf individuals. In 1968 and 1969, Congress established three regional vocational-technical training programs within existing facilities in St. Paul, Minnesota; New Orleans, Louisiana; and Seattle, Washington. The federal government also specified that states were obligated to spend significant amounts of money to provide vocational training for disabled individuals, and several states decided to invest in vocational education of deaf individuals. The federal government also provides support for programs for deaf students at California State University, Northridge (CSUN). Postsecondary education is one area in which deaf professionals play a leadership role. The academic heads of Gallaudet, NTID, and CSUN are all deaf.

The Americans with Disabilities Act (ADA) of 1990 deserves mention here because of its mandate to make postsecondary education accessible to qualified disabled students, including deaf students. The law requires that higher education institutions provide reasonable accommodations, which for deaf students may include interpreters, note-takers, test accommodations, counseling, and tutoring. The ADA has provided deaf students with educational options in addition to Gallaudet, NTID, CSUN and other programs specifically established for deaf students.

The ADA also applies to areas outside of education, especially in its prohibition of any discrimination against qualified individuals in employment and its mandate for reasonable on-the-job accommodations. The effect in employment and in education has been significant. ADA also mandates public accommodations to ensure full and equal enjoyment of lodging, recreation, social services, transportation, and communication. Title IV of the law stipulates that all telecommunication companies in the United States must provide functionally equivalent telecommunications services to deaf customers. Originally, the companies provided the accommodations through publicly available services using teletypewriters and telecommunication devices for the deaf and have now included telecommunication relay services and video relay services. ADA also specifically recognized the importance of Communication Access Realtime Translation (CART), which has special importance for deaf individuals. CART involves instant translation of speech into English text by means of a stenotype machine, computer, and realtime software and displays it on a computer monitor. NTID was a pioneer in developing classroom applications of CART, and it is spreading to elementary and secondary schools as well as to other postsecondary institutions.

THE DEAF COMMUNITY

Cohesive Deaf communities have existed in the United States since the establishment of schools for the deaf two centuries ago, and probably before. Deaf communities have resisted attempts by the larger society at marginalization and have fought the stereotype of deafness as pathology, insisting instead that it is a normal part of the human condition. The support of ASL is a key component of the deaf community, going back to the 19th century and including films made at the beginning of the 20th century under the auspices of the NAD to preserve sign languages. As is the case with other ethnic groups, deaf people tend to marry other deaf people; tend to belong to clubs, social organizations, and religious congregations consisting of deaf members; and often, are members of larger organizations. In general, federal legislation as well as increased acceptance and opportunities have led to dramatic increases in the numbers of deaf lawyers, professors, physicians, entrepreneurs, accountants, etc. More and more administrators of residential schools for the deaf are deaf themselves.

However, the medical-pathological view of deafness still prevails to a large extent. Alexander Graham Bell's argument more than 100 years ago—that deaf students should be educated only with hearing students—is reflected in today's inclusion movement in many school districts. Cochlear implants are being advertised as "cures" for deafness. There are relatively few deaf teachers and administrators in the public schools, where most deaf children in the United States are now being educated, and there are certainly no deaf policymakers in the United States Senate and House of Representatives. In an unpublished paper in 1975, Tom Humphries coined the term "Audism," which he defined as the notion that one is superior based on one's ability to hear or behave in the manner of one who hears. The term has been subjected to a large amount of discussion and interpretation in the ensuing years, but it still encapsulates the prejudices faced by deaf individuals on a daily basis. After more than 125 years, the NAD and other organizations of and for the deaf still face significant challenges.

There are literally hundreds of organizations of the deaf in the United States. In other chapters in this book, Roslyn Rosen discusses the World Federation of the Deaf, and Donalda Ammons describes the International Committee of Sports for the Deaf. There are organizations in the United States with similar missions at local, state, and regional levels as well as organizations based on any number of factors, including racial-ethnic identity, career orientation, and leisure interests. We list some of them below, with the knowledge that many more could be included. Any oversight is inadvertent.

- National Association of the Deaf (NAD)—www.nad.org—Established in 1880, has the mission to preserve, protect, and promote the civil, human, and linguistic rights of the deaf. During its existence, it has played a leadership role in championing the use of ASL, removing barriers to employment of deaf workers in the federal government, supporting the establishment of NTID, and administering the federal Captioned Media Program. In 1960, the NAD established the Junior NAD. The NAD publishes the *NAD Magazine*.
- Junior National Association of the Deaf—www.nad.org/JRNAD—Promotes scholarship, citizenship, and leadership skills in deaf and hard of hearing students from Grades 7 through 12. It publishes the *Junior NAD Magazine*.
- National Black Deaf Advocates—www.nbda.org—Promotes leadership, deaf awareness, and active participation in the political, educational, and economic processes that affect the lives of Black deaf citizens.

- National Council of Hispano Deaf and Hard of Hearing—www.nchdhh.org—Ensures equal access of the Hispanic deaf and hard of hearing community in the areas of social, recreational, cultural, educational, and vocational welfare.
- Intertribal Deaf Council—www.deafnative.com—Promotes the interests of its members by fostering and enhancing their cultural, historical, and linguistic tribal conditions.
- National Asian Deaf Congress—www.nadc-usa.org—Defines and addresses the cultural, political, and social issues experienced by Asians who are deaf or hard of hearing.
- Rainbow Alliance of the Deaf—www.rad.org—Assists in maintaining a society of deaf gay and lesbian people to encourage and promote the education, economics, and social welfare as well as to foster fellowship, defend rights, and advance social justice.
- USA Deaf Sports Federation—www.usadsf.org—Functions as the governing body for all deaf sports and recreation in the United States. Sponsors teams to the World Games for the Deaf and other regional, national, and international competitions.

SERVICES AND ORGANIZATIONS FOR THE DEAF

There are also statewide professional and parent groups that manage various services and organizations in the interests of deaf people, most of which include deaf and hearing members. Each state, the District of Columbia, Puerto Rico, and territory has a department of vocational rehabilitation. These departments have state coordinators of rehabilitation services for deaf people and provide job placement, vocational evaluation, and counseling services. The states also have state commissions or offices on deafness that provide advocacy, information gathering, referrals to agencies, interpreting services, and job placement. The following sample is a representative listing:

- Council of American Instructors of the Deaf (CAID)—www.caid.org—Established in 1821, promotes professional development, communication, and information among educators of deaf and hard of hearing individuals and other interested people. Along with the Conference of Educational Administrators of Schools and Programs for the Deaf, it publishes the *American Annals of the Deaf*. The *Annals* was established in 1847 and is the oldest educational journal in the United States.
- Conference of Educational Administrators of Schools and Programs for the Deaf (CEASD)—www.ceasd.org—Focuses on improvement in the education of deaf and hard of hearing people through research, personnel development, advocacy, and training.
- American Deafness and Rehabilitation Association (ADARA)—www.adara.org—Promotes and participates in quality human service delivery to deaf and hard of hearing people through individuals and agencies. It publishes the journal *JADARA: The Journal for Professionals Networking for Excellence in Service Delivery With Individuals Who Are Deaf and Hard of Hearing.*
- Alexander Graham Bell Association for the Deaf—www.agbell.org—Focuses on children with hearing loss, providing support and advocacy for parents, professionals, and other interested parties. The association publishes the journal *Volta Review.*
- Registry of Interpreters for the Deaf (RID)—www.rid.org—Certifies interpreters through its National Testing System, monitors professional self-regulation through its Ethical Practices System, and provides information on interpreting to the general public.

- American Society for Deaf Children (ASDC)—www.deafchildren.org—Supports and educates families of deaf and hard of hearing children and advocates for high-quality programs and services.
- Hands and Voices—www.handsandvoices.org—Supports families and their children who are deaf or hard of hearing and the professionals who serve them.

REFERENCES

Bell, A. G. (1883). *Memoir upon the formation of a deaf variety of the human race.* Washington, DC: National Academy of Science.

Bell, A. G. (1884). Fallacies concerning the deaf. *American Annals of the Deaf, 28*(2), 124–139.

Bender, R. (1970). *The conquest of deafness.* Cleveland, OH: Case Western Reserve.

Census Bureau. (2000). *Ancestry: 2000.* Suitland, MD: U.S. Bureau of the Census.

Census Bureau. (2005). *Population profile of the United states: 2005.* Suitland, MD: U.S. Bureau of the Census.

Gallaudet Research Institute. (2007). *National and regional summary report of data from the 2006–2007 annual survey of deaf and hard of hearing children and youth.* Washington, DC: Author.

Gannon, J. (1981). *Deaf heritage: A narrative history of deaf America.* Silver Spring, MD: National Association of the Deaf.

Moores, D. (2001). *Educating the deaf: Psychology, principles, and practices.* Boston: Houghton Mifflin.

National Commission on Excellence in Education. (1983). *A nation at risk: The imperative for educational reform.* Washington, DC: U.S. Department of Education.

Stedt, J., & Moores, D. (1990). Manual codes on English and American Sign Language: Historical perspectives and current realities. In H. Bornstein (Ed.), *Manual communication: Implications for education* (pp. 1–20). Washington, DC: Gallaudet University Press.

International Developments

"Globaleyes": A Partnership Between The Nippon Foundation (Japan) and the National Technical Institute for the Deaf at Rochester Institute of Technology (United States)

James J. DeCaro

IN 2001, The Nippon Foundation of Japan and the National Technical Institute for the Deaf (NTID) at Rochester Institute of Technology (RIT) came together and constructed a vision—a global network to improve the postsecondary education of people who are deaf. Recognizing that education, government, business, and industry are confronted with myriad challenges of globalization, these two organizations saw the need to form a collaborative that would address postsecondary education with "globaleyes." As a result, the foundation and NTID formed the Postsecondary Education Network International (PEN-International).

Internationally, there are a limited number of postsecondary education programs for people who are deaf or hard of hearing, particularly in developing countries. In an effort to address the postsecondary education needs of men and women who are deaf, The Nippon Foundation established a series of endowed scholarships in the United States for deaf men and women from the developing world. The foundation established these scholarships to provide people who are deaf with an education so they could return to their home countries, become role models, and serve as leaders in the deaf community of their respective countries. The scholarships were considered as much a long-term investment in the future of the countries' deaf populations as an investment in the recipients of the scholarships.

The actual outcome, however, proved to be quite different from the original intent. For the most part, scholarship recipients successfully completed their degrees but chose not to return home. Rather, they remained in the United States and pursued their careers. Although that path was of tremendous benefit to each individual scholarship recipient, it had little or no effect in the home country—except to propagate a "brain drain." That is, some of the best and brightest deaf people left their countries for a postsecondary education and never returned home.

This trend led NTID and The Nippon Foundation to partner in an effort to create a network that would improve postsecondary education, primarily in developing countries, so students could receive high-quality education at home that would allow them to enter society and the workplace to compete with their hearing peers. PEN-International established three operational goals to achieve this end in participating countries:

- Improve teaching, learning, curriculum development, and instructional development.
- Increase the application of information technology and instructional technology in the teaching and learning process.
- Expand career education opportunities for deaf and hard of hearing men and women internationally.

NTID AND THE NIPPON FOUNDATION

NTID and The Nippon Foundation were able to form this partnership because the mission, goals, and objectives of each organization were addressed by PEN-International.

NTID

For the past 40 years, RIT, through its college NTID, has been educating students who are deaf or hard of hearing on a campus that was designed primarily for people who are hearing. NTID is one of the eight colleges of RIT—a major national technological university. At RIT, approximately 1,100 deaf and hard of hearing men and women study and live with their 14,000 hearing peers. NTID supports close to 500 deaf or hard or hearing students who are mainstreamed with their hearing peers in the academic mainstream in one of the other seven colleges of RIT (close to 75% of these in science, technology, engineering, and mathematics curricula). The university has the largest number of mainstreamed postsecondary-level deaf or hard of hearing students in the world. To serve these men and women who are deaf or hard of hearing, the institute employs more than 120 sign language interpreters and more than 50 captioners. The other 600 students study within NTID for sub-baccalaureate associate degrees in paraprofessional fields with their peers who are deaf or hard of hearing. In effect, NTID serves as a national technical community college for these men and women.

For 40 years then, NTID has been honing pedagogy, support services, access services, and instructional technology for students who are deaf and hard of hearing in the educational mainstream and in self-contained classes and programs. Because a basic mission of NTID is "to share its knowledge and expertise through outreach and other information dissemination programs,"[1] it was determined that NTID should reach out to other countries around the world with proven strategies that could be adapted or adopted for use to improve postsecondary education in those countries.

The Nippon Foundation

As stated on their website (http://www.nippon-foundation.org.jp.eng/index.html), the Nippon Foundation was established approximately 40 years ago on the premise that the world is one family and that all mankind are brothers and sisters. At the time, the world was far from being one family. Instead, the world was in a rather precarious position where provocation by the Super Powers could lead to international incidents and conflict. Fear, not hope, dominated the world. But it was during this time that the late Ryoichi Sasakawa established The Nippon Foundation, with the overall goal of working for a better world.

---

1. See the NTID mission statement at http://www.ntid.rit.edu/president/mission.php.

The foundation envisions a world in which politics and ideology, religion and race are transcended—a world where we no longer suffer from hunger or disease. The foundation therefore set about working to remove barriers to full participation in society for all peoples, by enabling people who are now impoverished and physically and socially handicapped to be the arbiters and creators of their own lives. Since its founding in 1962, the foundation has dedicated itself to supporting primarily the efforts of those striving for independence.

Historically, Japan has very little experience with private philanthropy. Hence, The Nippon Foundation, as a nongovernmental organization, has taken the lead and the initiative in sponsoring numerous philanthropic projects and programs around the world. The foundation has attempted to help people to help themselves by supporting programs that enable those who are least able to become productive members of society. In this way, the foundation has contributed in part to the realization of a better and more prosperous world.

One of the prime working units of the foundation is the team that focuses on basic human needs such as agricultural technology support, leprosy eradication, the providing of prosthetic devices, disability-related support, and the like. Given the challenges that were arising in its scholarship program for deaf men and women from developing countries, the foundation determined to establish a program to improve postsecondary education in developing countries and cap its scholarship program for deaf men and women. The Nippon Foundation decided to undertake this effort so potential postsecondary education students would not feel compelled to leave their home country to receive a quality tertiary education.

A University/Foundation Partnership

Clearly, the mission, interests, and goals of The Nippon Foundation intersected nicely with the mission, goals, and skill set of NTID. As a result, in 2000, James J. DeCaro and a team of NTID colleagues developed a concept paper and presented it to The Nippon Foundation. The foundation was favorably inclined and requested a full proposal from NTID. The result was a university-foundation partnership—PEN-International—that was established at NTID in 2001. NTID provided the organizational skill and its 40 years of knowledge in the field of postsecondary deaf education, and The Nippon Foundation provided the funding for the program.

PEN-International was conceived as a collaborative and cooperative network of colleges and universities around the world that would provide postsecondary education for students who are deaf or hard of hearing. This network was conceived to propagate improvement of faculty teaching and the application of innovative educational and instructional technology in education. In effect, the program was established as a worldwide faculty training and development network that used innovative technology to addressed locally defined teaching and learning needs.

The PEN-International Vision

From its very inception, PEN-International has based all its efforts on four basic principles:

- The program exists as a collaborative that serves to address locally defined needs and priorities. The program does not presume to know what a participant institution or country needs.

- The political, religious, economic, geographic, and pedagogical traditions of a country mediate the length of time required to realize a needed change or intervention.
- Solutions to identified needs and priorities will be developed and implemented as a collaborative undertaking. Solutions will never be imposed.
- Solutions that have been implemented successfully in one country may or may not be appropriate for adaptation or adoption in another country.

These principles have proven to be useful and essential guiding tenets as PEN has developed the infrastructure for delivery of the training and as it has fostered development of training solutions themselves. It was essential that the program avoid at all cost the pitfall of functioning in a condescending fashion with developing countries. These countries may lag behind the developed world in terms of economic indicators, but they certainly do not lag behind in creativity and intelligence, and the desire to provide high-quality education for their citizens who are deaf. In fact, the developed world has a thing or two to learn from the developing world in terms of making do with limited resources.

The PEN Network

PEN-International selected a key partner institution in each country in which it works. The partner institution was chosen on the basis of the following four characteristics:

- The university had a program for the postsecondary education of deaf students.
- There was strong support from upper administration for the program for deaf students.
- The program for deaf students was recognized within the country as one of quality, and there was a strong commitment to continuous quality improvement.
- The program had as its goal preparing men and women who are deaf to enter careers that would allow them to participate in society and the workplace on a par with their peers who hear.

The PEN partner institution in each country serves as a major node of the PEN-International worldwide network. Each partner (node) is expected to work in collaboration with the other country nodes of the worldwide network and to coordinate activities through PEN-International headquarters at NTID. In addition, each major country node is expected to become a hub within its home country that is connected to other institutions in the home country to form a countrywide collaborative network or federation for improving the postsecondary education of men and women who are deaf. Each PEN worldwide node becomes the hub or center of excellence in its home country.

From Importer of Knowledge to Exporter

Once a partner institution was selected in each participant country, a needs assessment was conducted in collaboration with the partner to determine what issues were most in need of attention. On the basis of the needs assessment, a series of potential alternatives were presented for addressing the needs. Many of these solutions were based on the experience of NTID. The partner then worked together with PEN-International headquarters to determine what solutions could be adapted or adopted for use in meeting those needs. If none of the posited solutions were acceptable, PEN-International worked collaboratively with the partner to develop a solution custom tailored to its particular needs.

Depending on the solution selected, objective-based workshops and training were developed, and a cadre of faculty from the partner institution was brought to NTID for preliminary training. Training is always offered by skilled practitioners in the content area of the training—be they from NTID or elsewhere. Simultaneously, any technology that needs to be installed in the home institution is installed so when the faculty members return home from the training, they can use the skills and knowledge they have learned immediately. After the trained faculty members have applied the knowledge and skills they have learned for a period of time in their home institution, follow-up training is conducted by the same faculty members who conducted the initial training at NTID. The follow-up training is conducted on-site in the home country, by means of videoconferencing, or through a combination of both. In addition, all the materials used for PEN-International training at NTID, either by means of videoconference or on-site in the home country, are freely available to participants on the PEN-International Web site—usually in the language of the home country. Parenthetically, anyone who wishes can access these materials freely by visiting the Web site.[2]

In effect, PEN trains a cadre of faculty who import knowledge and skills that they can use to improve the education of men and women who are deaf. Through the initial training, subsequent application of the knowledge and skills learned, and the follow-up training, these faculty members become self-sufficient in the use of these skills. Once they have become self-sufficient, they are then expected to train colleagues at their home institution in the application of these skills and competencies.

However, the training cycle does not end there; once these faculty members are proficient at training their colleagues at their home institution, they are then expected to export what they have learned to other colleges and universities and to train faculty members who educate deaf students at those institutions. In effect, PEN-International propagates a training ripple effect. PEN-International provides support as this training is being conducted initially, but eventually, partners assume the full responsibility of exporting knowledge and skills within their home country.

Propagation of the Network

Although PEN is currently active in China, Japan, the Philippines, Russia, Thailand, Viet Nam, Hong Kong, the Czech Republic, and South Korea, PEN has focused over the past 6 years on its four initial partner countries—China, Japan, the Philippines, and Russia. In three of these countries (Russia, Japan, and China), a countrywide network is developing.

In Russia, the PEN node is Bauman Moscow State Technical University, which has now brought three other institutions together to form PEN-Russia. This network covers the breadth of the country: Novosibirsk State Technical University in Siberia, Vladimir State University outside of Moscow, and TISBI in Kazan. These four institutions have signed a formal agreement establishing PEN-Russia and have been able to use PEN-International's support for their efforts to leverage funding from their universities, municipalities, regional

---

2. For more information, see http://www.pen.ntid.rit.edu.

governments, and the Russian Federation for their efforts to improve the postsecondary education of deaf men and women.

In Japan, the PEN node is National Tsukuba University of Technology. The university has brought together 13 colleges and universities from across Japan to form what they call PEPNet-Japan (Postsecondary Education Network Japan). The network is modeled after the Northeast Technical Assistance Center of NTID—a grant-funded program of the U.S. Department of Education. PEPNet-Japan was established with initial funding from PEN and is now receiving the bulk of its funding from the government of Japan.

In China, the PEN node is Tianjin University of Technology, which has partnered with three other institutions to form PEN-China: Zhongzhou University, Beijing Union University, and Changchun University. These four institutions of higher education have created a videoconferencing capability with the support of PEN-International, and they are now using this technology for cross-university faculty training and to offer courses across the four universities to deaf students.

In the six remaining countries, the programs are still at the importer and self-sufficiency stages of development. Historically, PEN makes a comparatively large initial investment in a country. Over time, it is expected that institutional partners and the government of a country will assume the responsibility for the continuation of the program in the country. This expectation essentially has proven to be the case in the countries in which PEN currently works.

Challenging Sensibilities

Although the attitudes, philosophies, and pedagogical methods that prevail either in the United States or at PEN-International's host institution NTID may differ from those in partner countries, PEN is very careful not to impose those attitudes, philosophies, and pedagogical methods on the faculty it trains from partner institutions. For example, there are certain occupations that deaf people can access in the United States, and for which NTID students prepare at RIT, that are not available in some countries in which PEN works. In an effort to challenge the sensibilities of faculty from one country during a PEN training session at NTID, a deaf national female from that country who was studying in a major at RIT that was not available in the home country served as a teaching assistant for the PEN training. As a result, faculty members were presented with a conundrum—they were being trained in a skill set that they did not possess by a student from their country who could not receive such an education in her home country.

As another example, PEN-International works in countries that have differing philosophies with respect to communication in education; that is, some use an oral-auditory approach, some use sign language, and others use both. Although PEN-International's host institution NTID has a communication philosophy that is different from that of most PEN partner institutions, PEN is very careful not to impose the NTID philosophy on any of its partners. Rather, the approach that PEN-International takes is to challenge the sensibilities and the status quo at participant institutions. For example, PEN exposes faculty members from partner institutions to a variety of successful deaf role models who serve as trainers. These deaf role models use communication approaches ranging from those used by native ASL speakers who do not use speech to those who are predominately "oral." At PEN-International, there is a saying that is applied to trainers and trainees alike: "If they participate in a PEN-sponsored event and do not have their sensibilities challenged or do not feel uncomfortable, they have not learned."

Influencing Public Policy

In addition to having an effect on teaching and learning, PEN-International is also attempting to have a positive effect on educational policy in the countries in which it works. That effort is a very sensitive and diplomatic undertaking that requires the development of mutual trust and respect over time. In the end, how a recommendation for improvement is developed and stated is as important as the content of the recommendation itself.

For example, in China, PEN-International undertook a qualitative research study in an effort to collect and develop recommendations for the China Disabled Persons' Federation (CDPF) with respect to improving postsecondary education in the country. The study was conducted openly and with great care and is presented in detail in this volume. Those recommendations were presented to the CDPF, and officials of the CDPF, PEN-China, and the PEN-International home office have agreed on a set of training objectives to address one of the most pressing issues highlighted in the report—preparation of sign language interpreters.

CONCLUSION

The National Technical Institute for the Deaf at Rochester Institute of Technology and The Nippon Foundation have formed a productive and effective partnership that is having a positive effect on the postsecondary education of deaf men and women in the countries in which PEN-International is working. At a time when the world is shrinking but forces are acting to tear people apart, PEN-International has been drawing people from diverse cultures together to productively address the postsecondary education needs of men and women who are deaf. In effect, PEN has been attempting to use global eyes to improve the postsecondary education of men and women who are deaf.

Inclusion in an International Context

Merv Hyde

THE WORD *inclusion* in an educational context is itself somewhat of a paradox. It is frequently confounded by our concepts of earlier processes such as mainstreaming and integration. Although authors may disagree on the exact definition of each term and the distinctions among them, the following explanations reflect this writer's understanding of the consensus among most definitions:

- *Mainstreaming* was essentially a term that originated in the United States under legal challenges for the rights of minority groups and was regulated by the 1975 Public Law 94-142 and its reauthorization in 1997 and 2004. Mainstreaming was concerned with the placement of children with disabilities in a regular school setting. The term was influential and was adopted with various interpretations by other countries, many of which do not have the constitutional rights underpinning the original U.S. impetus for the mainstreaming movement.
- *Integration* implies that disabled people need to be integrated into mainstream society, but they, rather than society or a school system, are required to undergo more change. Definitions frequently consider the level or degree of academic, social, or personal integration that an individual may achieve and the circumstances that are required. Processes of identification, assessment, ascertainment, and reviews of the integration of children with a disability are typically found in associated education policy and practice.
- In contrast, *inclusion* takes as its starting point the fact that a just state of affairs is one in which people with a disability or difference are included in society and, in particular, in education. The required policy responses are broad and include a comprehensive focus on conditions for accepting individuals and groups and supporting the participation of children with a disability or difference in schools and their communities (Foreman, 2005).

SOME THEORY AND A FRAMEWORK

Inclusion is a term and a process that is relative in its interpretations and applications. The relativities involve the various historical, cultural, and pedagogical traditions; social structures; medical and technical resources availability; and the political, legal, and policy frameworks and economic priorities that a country embraces or within which an education system or school operates (Foster et al., 2003; Hyde, Ohna, & Hjulstad, 2006).

Inclusion may be seen as both a process of access, with associated considerations of the conditions for participation of students, and as a process of change in terms of the development of policy, practices, and attitudes. It is a concept that is deeply rooted in the philosophical and pedagogical traditions that we choose to express. The educational systems that we develop or elaborate may be characterized, more or less, by a cycle of differentiation and uniformity (Vislie, 2003; Wagner, 1994).

When they are most differentiated, education systems offer high degrees of specialization of services to individuals and to groups. Curriculum responsibility is devolved to local school or regional levels, and in some circumstances, also high degrees of privatization and choice. Reforms of differentiated service systems often involve some increased degree of centralization of legislation, policy, funding, or evaluation to establish central control and to ensure that available resources are distributed as equitably as possible and that desired outcomes are achieved.

When they are most uniform, education systems are characterized by central control of legislation policy, funding, guidelines for practice, central curriculum policy and content, and maintenance of certain pedagogic traditions. Reforms to more uniform systems usually involve attempts to decentralize some elements to allow for local variation in implementation and specialization (Vislie, 2003).

In practice, the process is always dynamic, with national and local systems of education moving between these two extremes of differentiation and uniformity, depending on changing political, social, cultural, or economic factors and influences. No single, effective definition of inclusion is therefore possible because each system may view inclusion differently. Differentiation allows the needs of each student to be considered or taken into account (e.g., students with a specific learning need). Uniformity allows for the rights, participation, and equity of all students. Both can, therefore, be at some level inclusive or exclusive in their policy and practice as well as in following their controls and pedagogical traditions. There would seem to be no utopian "school for all" possible because in each form of system there will always be some aspects of exclusion, for groups or individuals, wherever there is inclusion. Within the cycle between uniformity and differentiation, the individuals or groups included or excluded can change as the rules, structures, and attitudes change.

Within this broad framework, it is possible to describe or locate various countries and education authorities with respect to their policies, positions, and practices. By their histories, traditions, economic priorities, legal provisions, as well as social and cultural policies, we can see where they currently place themselves and where their values and their professional and social tensions may lie in the providing of education services and in the reform of those services.

Mitchell (2005) suggests that there are three conclusions that can be reached about inclusive education: (a) that inclusive education is seen by most as creating a single system designed to serve the needs of all students; (b) that inclusive education is based on both sociopolitical models and psycho-medical models; and (c) although many countries appear highly committed to inclusive education, their practice often falls short of their rhetoric and policies. In the remainder of this chapter, we will examine the broader applications and interpretations of inclusive education for students in a number of countries and then attempt to draw some conclusions that may assist policymakers and practitioners to reflect on their current provisions and consider approaches toward reform in deaf education.

SOME CONVENTIONS

Several international conventions and agreements contain guidelines that may provide us with structural contexts, or even imperatives, depending on how influenced we are by their proclamations. In particular, we should consider the perspectives of the Convention on the Rights of the Child (United Nations, 1989), the Salamanca Statement (United Nations Educational, Scientific, and Cultural Organization, 1994), the World Education Forum (United Nations Educational, Scientific, and Cultural Organization, 2000), and most recently, the United Nations Comprehensive and Integral International Convention on the Protection and Promotion of the Rights and Dignity of Persons With Disabilities that was adopted by the United Nations General Assembly in New York on December 13, 2006. That convention agreed that there should be the following:

- No exclusion from the general education system on the basis of disability;
- Access for disabled students to inclusive education in their local communities;
- Reasonable accommodation of the individual's requirements; and
- Required support within the general education system to facilitate effective education, including effective individualized support measures (United Nations, 2006).

This perspective seems clear enough, and it could have a major influence on the ways in which we provide education for deaf students. So what are the challenges to the implementation of this perspective? One could take issue with the term *disability* in any consideration of deaf people, deaf children in particular. Using the cyclical model described above, a predominant interpretation in this convention is toward uniformity through mainstream placement of deaf students in local schools with accommodations or adjustments to their needs. This interpretation is usually associated with policies that stress access, participation, and outcomes. Because access by itself is no longer a sufficient condition for evidencing inclusion, participation in social, educational, and community contexts becomes the objective. Even though it is agreed that inclusion is a process and not any single set of outcomes, some government education departments, as they attempt to mirror corporate structures in their operation, will try to measure outcomes in terms of student achievements in curricular learning, social learning, and personal development.

These terms and the policy objectives or "performance indicators" that usually accompany them are seen by many professionals working for deaf children and by some deaf groups as denying the linguistic rights of deaf children and of deaf people as a minority group. They challenge the disability perspective inherent in such conventions and policies. Critics (for example, Brennan, 2003; Padden & Humphries, 1988) argue that the psycho-medical model of deafness as disability actually restricts the access, participation, and outcomes that deaf children may receive. Failure to have effective national recognition of sign languages and the policies and practices that reflect such recognition is seen as a central criticism of such uniform approaches (Vonen, 2007).

Some stakeholders, however, especially many of the 95% of hearing parents of deaf children, government and social economists, and those associated with medical and technological progress, see that an approach to deafness wherein deaf people are "different" denies their preferred reality and their perspective of deafness as being an impairment that can be "habilitated," or at least one whose effect can be reduced. These stakeholders point to current high rates of early detection and diagnosis of hearing loss (now down to a few days after birth in many countries), high rates of early cochlear implantation, and successful auditory-oral outcomes as being portents of a different and, in their terms, a more inclusive future for deaf children and their families. However, McDonald (2006) cautions that "people's perceptions about the capacity of deaf babies to grow into happy, life-embracing deaf adults are shaped as much by all that they don't know as by the little that they do know" (p. 1).

Strong human value systems are inherent in these positions, as are apparent incompatibilities within these contrasting perspectives. Each country has a history of approaches toward the recognition of the rights and needs of people with a disability. This history typically follows a pattern that begins with early social, health, and educational responses involving charitable systems and moves toward more publicly funded government provisions. More resource-rich countries with longer democratic traditions have generally moved along this path more rapidly than poorer countries. Associated with this pattern has been the development of legislation, public policy, school systems, and community expectations. The balance between differentiation of needs or provisions for a particular group or individual and attempts at more uniform systems that champion equal access for all is an outcome of the political and social traditions of the countries involved and their response to international agreements and covenants. The following pages explore how a number of countries provide education for their deaf students.

The United Kingdom

In more recent times in the United Kingdom, this process toward more government involvement has resulted in a transition from the vestiges of the Warnock Report (Warnock, 1978) and the 1988 Education Reform Act and their processes of "statementing" the support needed by individuals with a special education need toward the path of full inclusion. Under the Blair government's New Labor initiatives, only a small minority of students continued to be educated in special schools. The Index of Inclusion developed by Booth and Ainscow (2002) and the Inclusion Charter (Centre for Studies in Inclusive Education, 2002) were influential in implementing this transition. This situation is not to suggest that the system in the United Kingdom is completely transformed or has resolved all the complexities but, rather, that the British government has placed itself at the forefront of international developments toward full inclusion through the implementation of such a uniform policy. This process has not pleased all those associated with deaf education in the United Kingdom, especially those individuals who had unhappy experiences in mainstream schools and those who express a view consistent with the politics of difference and of recognition (Taylor, 1994). Expressions of the politics of difference are found in the writings of Ladd (2003) and Kyle (2005), and there is support for the government's direction found among some parent organizations, some teacher associations, and the Royal National Institute for the Deaf. The policies of the British Deaf Association were unclear on this issue at the time of writing, but the organization has an active campaign directed at achieving bilingual education for all Deaf children in the United Kingdom.

In 2003, the British government officially recognized British Sign Language, an outcome that was significantly influenced by the work of the late Mary Brennan. She had for many years espoused a case for difference and differentiation based on the rights and needs of deaf

children for linguistic access to British Sign Language and for the development of a Deaf identity (Brennan, 1999). It is this issue of identity that demonstrates a tension between government moves toward full inclusion and those who would maintain separate programs for deaf
students or bilingual education programs. Such tension may be considered as a useful outcome and can result in a range of differentiated options being available for parents and deaf
people.

Australia

Australia is a nation of six federated states and two territories, each of which is responsible
for its education system, curriculum, and practice. Australia also has some private and independent schools for deaf children (see Power, this volume). These were originally developed
by charitable "missions" in each state, Catholic education authorities, and, more recently, by
parent and other organizations to create oral education alternatives when public schools
adopted communication philosophies involving signing.

The state systems have had official policies of placing deaf students in regular classes since
the 1940s. However, more recently, there has been evidence in most states of a change toward policies of inclusion with considerations of the accommodations that local schools should
make to include students with a disability, a learning difficulty, or a learning difference (these
terms are used in various state policies, not always distinctively). The Australian government
has no set national curriculum and does not provide specific directions to schools about the
nature of education services for students with a hearing loss. Each state has therefore developed its own set of policies and practices within national education curriculum guidelines
and has agreed common goals of schooling. Legislation is of a generic nature and is built
around principles of social justice, including access, participation, and equity of outcome. In
1992, the national government passed a Disability Discrimination Act, and each state has
separate anti-discrimination legislation. These laws are designed to be largely educative and
preventive in focus, but necessarily are protective of the rights of people with a disability or
cultural difference against forms of discrimination. Australia is required to comply with the
United Nations International Convention of the Rights of the Child and has significant national and state policies in the area of "multiculturalism." The National Language Policy (Lo
Bianco, 1987) includes the recognition of Australian Sign Language (Auslan) as a community language and recognizes the status of the Deaf community (Hyde & Power, 1992).

In a study involving deaf students and their teachers in all Australian states, Power and Hyde
(2002) and Hyde and Power (2004) reported that a significant majority (83%) of deaf students in Australia attend regular schools and are placed in regular classes with auditory-oral
conditions of communication. In attempting to measure the integration of these students in
their regular classes, they found that more than two thirds of the students were considered to
be performing at an academically "competitive" level (Mirenda, 1998) when compared with
their hearing peers, yet only one third of the deaf students were rated at the same level in
their social participation and development of personal independence.

The transition from policy to the practice of inclusion among Australian states remains
questionable, particularly because there is no clear research evidence with respect to the efficacy of the outcomes of stated inclusion policies for the students. This lack of evidence particularly applies to the research findings with respect to deaf students' social and personal

development in regular schools. Those measures of students' independence and participation in social and academic activities in schools that are available are usually determined from the perspectives of the schools and the teachers and make assumptions about the factors that are considered to be most relevant to the students themselves, an issue demanding intensive research (Hyde & Power, 2004).

Norway

European perspectives vary, but in education of deaf students, Scandinavian perspectives have had international influence in maintaining a focus on sign language use and on schools for the deaf. The case of Norway is illustrative. Norway's current ideology of inclusive education stems back to the 1960s and is best understood in the broader historical and social changes to its welfare state (Flem & Keller, 2000; Vislie, 1995). A reorganization of special education began late in the 1960s and was based on the principles of equality, integration, normalization, participation, and decentralization. New laws established the ideology of "integration" and what was called "adjusted" education. In the 1975 Integration Act, provisions relating to special schools and specific regulations for the administration of special education were eliminated (Flem & Keller, 2000). Since 1975, local municipalities have been responsible for the education of all students and for upholding their right to be educated in their local schools. The Act of Education of 1998, Section 1-2, emphasizes "adjusted" education as a legal right for all students (Kirke-, Utdannings- og Forskningsdepartementet [The Royal Ministry of Education, Research and Church Affairs], 1998). The national curriculum for compulsory education states that compulsory schooling is based on the principle of one school for all. "Compulsory schooling shall provide equitable and suitably adjusted education for everyone in a coordinated system of schooling based on the same curriculum" (Kirke-, Utdannings- og Forskningsdepartementet [The Royal Ministry of Education, Research and Church Affairs], 1998, p. 56).

The national discussion of integration and inclusion focuses on the concept of "the student's own environment." In an unusual policy decision, two apparently opposite interpretations were incorporated, one emphasizing the deaf student's "own environment" as being the local municipality school and the neighborhood as "home," and the other emphasizing the student's "own environment" as a place where there was access to and participation with other deaf students and adults using Norwegian Sign Language (NSL).

Students who had acquired NSL as their first language were given the right to receive their education through sign language. The National Curriculum introduced new syllabi for students educated according to Section 2-6: NSL, Norwegian for deaf pupils, English for deaf pupils, and Drama and Rhythmics for deaf pupils (Kirke-, Utdannings- og Forskningsdepartementet [The Royal Ministry of Education, Research and Church Affairs], 1998).

The Norwegian government enacted other initiatives to enhance the status and the competence of NSL use in schools and in families with deaf children. Some universities and university colleges developed programs to meet the regular teachers' needs for competence in NSL, and a similar program was established for hearing parents with deaf children. Parents are entitled to 40 weeks of training in NSL through the first 16 years of their child's life. Although the legislation gives all students in Norway the right to attend a school in their neighborhood, it also gives deaf students a right to education through the medium of NSL. The

student's level of hearing loss, whether moderate, severe, or profound, does not have any effect on the legal right to education under Section 2-6 in the Act of Education. However, deaf
students do not have a legal right to education within a school for the deaf. Students following the national syllabi for the deaf therefore have to alternate between two different schools:
the local municipality school and a school at a resource center for deaf students where they
spend time each year.

In 2001–02, approximately one third of deaf students attended their local municipality
school while the remaining two thirds went to special schools or classes for deaf students, either
within a regular municipality school or at a resource center. When a student is educated according to the legislative provisions for the deaf, the school receives additional teacher resources
to accommodate the need for communication in NSL. These resources can be used to provide two teachers for a classroom or to lower the class teacher-to-pupil ratio with a smaller
class size. These decisions are made at regional and school levels according to their traditions,
values, and objectives.

Two recent studies have examined the outcomes of these developments. First, Hyde, Ohna
and Hjulstad (2006) reported on learning and communication interactions in three classroom
structures: (a) two teachers, one with competence in NSL; (b) one teacher with an NSL interpreter; and (c) a single teacher who was competent in both spoken Norwegian and NSL.
A key finding of the study was that, in two of the class-teacher structures examined, there
was evidence of parallel discourses. Analyses of the interactive patterns and of language and
modality use indicated that the deaf student and his or her signing teacher or interpreter communicated independently of what the rest of the class was doing. This pattern resulted in the
deaf student's exclusion from some of the communication events in the classroom.

Hjulstad and Kristoffersen (2007) are conducting a 5-year study to examine the communication interactions of 24 deaf children ages 3 to 11 years, who are fitted with a cochlear
implant and are being educated in both rural and urban areas in Norway. The educational
placements of the students are mainly in local schools, but some are in schools or classes for
the deaf. Most have access to bilingual education. Hjulstad and Kristoffersen report a very
high level of heterogeneity among the classrooms, the communication environments and
resources, and the linguistic proficiencies of the students. Importantly, even though both languages (Norwegian and NSL) were found to be in use in the communication contexts observed, teachers often reflected a lack of understanding of the objectives and processes of
bilingual education, particularly where sign language use was seen as a consequence of "cochlear implant failure." These authors concluded by pointing to the great diversity among
the communication environments, local resources, teacher competencies, and student outcomes in the classrooms studied. Hjulstad and Kristoffersen proposed that there is little evaluation of outcomes and that, at present, there is no set of general principles or guidelines
informing schools and classrooms about facilitating a quality education for pupils with a cochlear implant, in either monolingual or bilingual programs.

Norway is an interesting and seemingly complex case. The education system for deaf students remains both centralized and uniform in its national legislation and policies, but quite
differentiated in terms of the interpretation of these characteristics at local levels, with elements of both of these dimensions evident in the findings of two studies cited.

Canada

The evolution toward inclusive education in Canada and the United States has a long history. Both countries have had major influences on policies and practices in other countries. In Canada, government legislation has evolved on a province-by-province basis around the national Federal Charter of Rights and Freedoms. Many aspects of Canadian legislation have been influenced by U.S. developments. However, historically, the principles of "normalization" espoused by Wolfensberger (1972) were most influential in Canada and around the world because he considered that the circumstances for disabled people should be as close as possible to the regular circumstances of society.

Current Canadian legislation and policy reflects a tension between (a) international covenants and national imperatives and (b) the legislation and the practices of the provinces. This tension has resulted in a number of court challenges, particularly to the interpretation of inclusion as *placement* (Mitchell, 2005). These challenges have been brought by advocacy groups and have the capacity to redefine the interpretation of inclusion in that country. The Canadian Association of the Deaf seems to have many policy positions, but not one specifically on inclusion of deaf students. The closest is a statement that "the centralized schools for the Deaf must be kept open as an alternative for the education and socialization of Deaf children" and that the regular schools where deaf children are educated should have access to their sign language (Canadian Association of the Deaf, 2007).

Another influential and enduring development from Canada is that it is the home of Auditory-Verbal International (AVI). This organization has continued to affirm a set of principles of auditory-verbal education established more than 30 years ago by Pollack (1970), and two of their principles are particularly germane to the debate about inclusion of deaf students in local schools. Principle 3 is to "guide and coach parents to help their child use hearing as the primary sensory modality in developing spoken language without the use of sign language or emphasis on lipreading."[1] Principle 10 is to "promote education in regular classrooms with typical hearing peers and with appropriate support services from early childhood onwards." Together, these principles firmly establish that normalization remains an objective and that the place of deaf students is in age-appropriate classes with hearing students. There is an obvious tension between these objectives of AVI and those of some deaf associations and school authorities in Canada. Some in Canada were also early advocates of bilingual approaches to education for deaf students as a way of presenting new models of inclusion (e.g., Ewoldt, 1996), although not without sustained and reasonable criticism of their own and others' assumptions and misassumptions about the application of Cummins's (1981) interdependence theory to bimodal bilingual education contexts (Knoors, 2007; Mayer & Wells, 1996).

Thus, Canada appears to be a country with some national legislation but provincial application and a diversity of programs structures for deaf students. Some criticism of interpretations of inclusion are still associated with placement.

---

1. Interestingly, this principled restriction of speechreading does not reflect the views of Alexander Graham Bell, founding father of the Alexander Graham Bell Association for the Deaf and Hard of Hearing, the planned merger partner of AVI.

The United States

The United States has a long history of inclusion, which stems back to debates between Edward Miner Gallaudet and Alexander Graham Bell at the end of the 19th century, about the educational placements possible for deaf students under their respective doctrines about communication (Bell, 1898/2005; Osgood, 2005). In many ways, that debate and their largely separate philosophies of communication and education still shows its influence today.[2]

The influence of national legislation has also been particularly great, as have been court cases and technological developments in amplification and in cochlear implantation. Legal challenges to U.S. education policies for people with disabilities began in the 1950s when, in a racial segregation case, the U.S. Supreme Court established that separate education was inherently unequal. The Supreme Court affirmed two principles that were to influence education for deaf students: that exclusion from public education was unacceptable and that it was inherently unequal.

What is now known as the Individuals with Disabilities Education Act (IDEA) was enacted by Congress in 1975 and called the Education for All Handicapped Children Act. This law mandated a free and appropriate public education for all students with disabilities. Schools must prepare an Individualized Education Program that details a child's current level of performance, the services that will be provided, the extent to which the student can participate in general education, and schedules of annual review. The Education for All Handicapped Children Act was amended and reauthorized as IDEA in 1997 and then again as the IDEA Improvement Act in 2004. These amended laws attempt to clarify the meaning of an "appropriate" education and link this concept to student outcomes.

There are tensions evident between the potential provided by this legislative process and the positions of Deaf associations, Deaf communities and the institutions that serve them. The position established by the National Association of the Deaf (NAD), for example, endorses the imperatives of the IDEA but states,

that direct and uninhibited communication access to all facets of a school's programming is essential for a deaf or hard of hearing child to realize his or her full human potential.

The inclusion doctrine is rooted in ideology and is frequently a blatant violation of IDEA as it disregards the language and educational developmental needs of the deaf and hard of hearing children. (National Association of the Deaf, 2008)

Successful inclusion programs must assist all students—deaf, hard-of-hearing, and hearing—to reach their potential in educational and social development. The students need active and regular interaction with one another to attain effective membership in school and classroom communities (Antia, Stinson, & Gaustad, 2002). Deaf students may experience negative attitudes from hearing peers in mainstream settings, even when they make sound academic progress. Hung and Paul (2006) found that the presence of deaf students in the same school with their hearing peers does not make a significant difference in changing the hearing stu-

---

2. It is of interest to note, however, that A. G. Bell affirmed strong support for the legitimate linguistic status of signed languages in a series of letters to the journal *The Educator* in 1898 (Bell Family Papers, U.S. Library of Congress) in which he also posited that deaf students so educated could reach similar levels of academic achievement to those of students educated orally. He differed from Thomas Gallaudet in that he believed that deaf children educated orally could more readily take their place in a hearing community.

dents' attitudes. However, providing meaningful forms of interaction, developing close relationships or friendships, and breaking down communication barriers all contribute to the creation of positive attitudes that can lead to the successful inclusion of deaf students.

Although the United States has a long history of providing education to deaf students, there is considerable differentiation within its history and current provisions. These differentiations show a continued presence of independent or private-school traditions, particularly those with an auditory-oral focus, and a continued commitment to state schools for the deaf. The presence of Gallaudet University, the National Technical Institute for the Deaf, and other college programs are further evidence of forms of differentiation. The powerful influences of medical, genetic, and other technologies is also evident in the changing demography of deafness and new balances among the relative influence of stakeholders, especially parents. Changing patterns of the incidence of deafness in the United States (a significant decline in the number of children born profoundly deaf compared with those with lesser levels of hearing loss) and the changing ethnic origins of deaf people (more than 21% having an Hispanic heritage) are further evidence of the pressures for change and differentiation of services (Foster & Kinuthia, 2003; Moores, personal communication, May 4, 2004). However, continued pressure for uniformity is also found in national testing of the achievements of all students and in the ranking of schools, consequences of the No Child Left Behind legislation of 2002. Unlike Australia, this form of national benchmark testing, with its intended political regulation, includes special schools and programs for deaf (and other "disabled" students) in its procedures and reporting functions.

Asia and South Asia

Asian and South Asian nations present a variety of approaches and challenges to inclusion. Even though most are signatories to the Salamanca Agreement (United Nations Educational, Scientific, and Cultural Organization, 1994) and subsequent United Nations conventions and the rights of individuals are usually enshrined in their constitutions, many of these countries have difficulty in deploying sufficient resources to support the realization of the potential of their disabled citizens. India is a case in point.

India is the world's largest democracy and the second most populous country. It is divided into 29 states and 6 union territories. State governments are responsible for the administration of their respective states while the central government is the highest political power in the country (Sharma & Deppeler, 2005). Although India has made impressive gains in economic development in the last few decades, more than 260 million people live below the poverty line.

India was a signatory to the United Nations Conference on the Rights of the Child of 1989, the United Nations Educational, Scientific and Cultural Organization (UNESCO) Jomtein Convention of 1990, and the UNESCO Salamanca Statement of 1994, which advocates education for all. As a result, the central government passed the Delhi Declaration on Education for All policy in 1994 (Singal, 2005), followed by The Persons With Disability (Equal Opportunities Protection of Rights and Full Participation) Act in 1995. Chapter 5 of this act states that the government will make provision for every child with a disability to have access to free education in an appropriate environment until the age of 18 years (Alur, 2006). The Indian eighth Five Year Plan 1991–1996 significantly increased the budget for disabled children for the purpose of promoting integrated education for children with a disability (Government of India, 1993).

In March 2005, the Minister for Human Resource Development restated the government's "zero reject" viewpoint for children with special needs, saying "It should and will be our objective to make mainstream education not just available but accessible, affordable, and appropriate for students with disabilities" (Alur, 2006, p. 15). However, development of education for individuals with disabilities in India, and for deaf children in particular, remains a substantial challenge for the provincial governments, who struggle with the many crises in health, unemployment, housing, and education associated with their large populations. As a consequence, services for deaf children and adults are often extremely differentiated and frequently are offered by nongovernmental organizations, charitable associations, and international aid projects, with support from governments to the extent that it is available within tight budgets (Parasnis, DeCaro, & Raman, 1996).

This pattern of (a) uniform national objectives, often reflecting international agreements and covenants, and (b) national philosophies expressing strong human values is common in many South Asian and Asian nations. The Salamanca Statement of 1994 and the United Nations Comprehensive and Integral International Convention on the Protection and Promotion of the Rights and Dignity of Persons With Disabilities of 2006 have been instrumental in leading national governments toward uniform approaches to inclusion of deaf students that also reflect their national values and current capacities. The differentiated range of government schools and programs available to deaf students and their families in many Western countries may not be an objective of some governments for some time, if at all.

A SCHOOL FOR ALL?

The framework of uniformity and differentiation established at the beginning of this chapter and the examples discussed suggest that, as far as deaf children are concerned, a "school for all" is not a definable construct. In any system, there will always be a degree of exclusion for some groups or individuals, even where inclusion is an avowed goal and policy. Because it was most often in deaf schools and programs that the features of Deaf culture were established and practiced for many Deaf people, the policies of inclusion and especially the "school for all" concept may appear most threatening or destructive of Deaf culture and community. Even if a school system and its local schools meet the principles of inclusion in supporting the access, participation, and outcomes for a deaf child, the acculturation of that child into a Deaf community may be limited at best if left until the postschool years.

Some countries have created programs to bring deaf students together from their local schools; these include "deaf weekends," Internet and video-streaming connections, and even mandatory periods to be spent in a deaf school or program each year. There are also blocks of time that parents can spend, or are required to spend, in deaf centers learning a sign language. Although not all of us would support the views of Tijsseling (2006), who suggests that the genetic relationship between a deaf child and his or her hearing parents is no more important than the natural relationship between a deaf child to a Deaf community, forms of contact are available to most schools to establish associations between deaf children who may be socially and culturally remote in inclusive education settings and the Deaf communities in those regions.

This contact remains a special challenge for nations or school programs that follow the United Nations Comprehensive and Integral International Convention on the Protection and Promotion of the Rights and Dignity of Persons With Disabilities of 2006 or the Salamanca Agreement of 1994. Alternatively, some countries interpret these conventions to mean that a deaf school or program is of itself an inclusive experience and that enrollment in a local school is a potentially excluding experience, if one changes (a) the assumptions behind inclusion—from going to one's local school to going to a deaf school—and (b) assumptions that reflect the values of Deafness and its linguistic, social, and cultural dimensions and differentiations.

These features of acculturation do not develop spontaneously unless there are sustained opportunities for deaf students and Deaf adults to come together, in the same way as there need to be structured, positive, and shared contexts for deaf and hearing students to come together in local schools. Many deaf children from hearing families may even need to be taught their national sign language, and having no access to it may be very excluding if the local school cannot provide it. Hence, enrollment in a local school could be a potentially excluding environment if it cannot provide an inclusive "Deaf" experience.

Although some countries develop a range of education options for deaf children (in reality, options for their parents to consider), this approach entails a significant financial and personnel resource base from the country involved. In addition, extensive efforts are necessary to ensure that all the options and their consequences are understood by and accessible to parents. Not all nations are able to fund such a range of options from within their contested national budgets.

Heterogeneity and the Need to Be Different

On the issue of deaf students having group characteristics that may be associated with inclusion, a number of studies have shown that different or, at least more differentiated, models of inclusion in practice are needed for deaf students (Hyde et al., 2006; Powers, 2002; Stinson & Kluwin, 2003). These models could better reflect the great heterogeneity among deaf students who are currently in regular classes and could more comprehensively encompass the needs of those students who could benefit psychosocially, communicatively, and culturally from the use of a sign language in regular classes. These possibilities do not necessarily suggest a form of "exclusion" but, rather, a structure of inclusion that respects the retention of certain individual characteristics. Knoors (2007) correctly suggests that there is no "best model" or one type of school suitable for all deaf students. Some students may thrive in local schools whereas others do well in schools for the deaf or in bilingual programs. He also suggests that we could be more flexible about what we consider to be bilingual conditions because "10% sign language and 90% spoken language is also bilingual" (pp. 245, 250).

It would seem that where countries have developed or adopted uniform approaches to legislation and policy with respect to education and inclusion of all students, sound arguments for retaining a sufficient degree of differentiation among programs for deaf students exist. A range of well-advised and comprehensively presented program options for parents would seem to be in best accordance with the evidence and experience that we have available to us. This observation is not to suggest that we do not need more research evidence; indeed, the opposite is true. We urgently need evidence of inclusion from the perspectives of the students themselves, both deaf and hearing.

A practice that seems to have become associated with inclusion more recently is the use of sign language interpreters to provide access for deaf students in local schools. Although at a policy level such access may be seen to be achieved if interpreting is provided, it is of concern that there is very little research evidence that this arrangement provides either equitable access to or participation in classroom communication with hearing peers and teachers in academic and social learning events (Hyde et al., 2006; Marschark et al., 2006). Indeed, it may be necessary for many of these deaf students to learn or be taught a sign language for use in regular class because one cannot assume that they have existing proficiency (Knoors, 2007). This approach, when adopted as a uniform response by school systems to families seeking local school placement for their deaf child, may not produce the inclusive experience that is assumed. Again, research evidence on this issue of policy and practice is urgently needed.

POLICY TO PRACTICE

In the literature and in practice in many countries, interpretations of inclusion within the contexts of place and process are typically confounded. Even when inclusion is strongly supported by national or state policy, or even legislation, as in many of the countries mentioned here, practices or outcomes in schools can remain substantially unchanged or demonstrate significant delays in their implementation. As Sowell (1995) suggested, policy issues can become ideological debates that present conflicting visions or the "vision of the anointed" (p. 241) that can prevail over others in determining policy, particularly visions that espouse "full" inclusion on only moral and rights principles. In consequence, we need to consider whether any particular approach to inclusion truly embraces diversity and differences, or merely tries to minimize them (Detterman & Thompson, 1997).

This chapter is not intended to be another exhaustive review of the international literature about inclusion of deaf students. It is an attempt to establish a framework for understanding the processes of inclusion and to see how different nations and education systems may position themselves within the framework by their polices and practices. Although the perspectives of African and Latin American countries are not described in the chapter, the framework discussed may well be applied to considerations of their situations.

REFERENCES

Alur, M. (2006, March 31). Inclusive education needs funds. *Times of India,* 15.

Antia, S., Stinson, M., & Gaustad, M. (2002). Developing membership in the education of deaf and hard of hearing students in inclusive settings. *Journal of Deaf Studies and Deaf Education, 7,* 224–229.

Bell, A. G. (2005). The question of sign-language and the utility of signs in the instruction of the deaf: Two papers by Alexander Graham Bell. *Journal of Deaf Studies and Deaf Education, 10*(2), 111–121. (Original work published 1898)

Booth, T., & Ainscow, M. (2002). *Index for inclusion: Developing learning and participation in schools* (2nd ed.). Bristol: Centre for Studies in Inclusive Education.

Brennan, M. (1999). Challenging linguistic exclusion in deaf education. *Deaf Worlds, Deaf People, Community and Society, 15*(1), 2–10.

Brennan, M. (2003). Deafness, disability and inclusion: The gap between rhetoric and practice. *Policy Futures in Education, 1*(4), 668–685.

Canadian Association of the Deaf. (2007). *Youth.* Retrieved August 27, 2008, from http://www.cad.ca/en/issues/deaf_youth.asp

Centre for Studies in Inclusive Education. (2002). *The inclusion charter.* Bristol, England: Author.

Cummins, J. (1981). The role of primary language development in promoting educational success for language minority students. In Charles F. Leyba (Ed.), *Schooling and language minority students: A theoretical framework* (pp. 3–49). Los Angeles: California State University Evaluation, Dissemination, and Assessment Center.

Detterman, D. K., & Thompson, L. A. (1997). What is so special about special education? *American Psychologist, 52,* 1082–1090.

Ewoldt, C. (1996). Deaf bilingualism: A holistic perspective. *Australian Journal of Education of the Deaf, 2,* 4–15.

Flem, A., & Keller, C. (2000). Inclusion in Norway: A study of ideology in practice. *European Journal of Special Needs Education*, 15(2), 188–205.

Foreman, P. (2005). *Inclusion in action.* Sydney: Harcourt.

Foster, S., & Kinuthia, W. (2003). Deaf persons of Asian American, Hispanic American, and African American backgrounds: A study of intraindividual diversity and identity. *Journal of Deaf Studies and Deaf Education, 8,* 271–290.

Foster, S., Mudgett-DeCaro, P., Bagga-Gupta, S., De Leuw, L., Domfors, L-A., Emerton, G., et al. (2003). Cross-cultural definitions of inclusions for deaf students: A comparative analysis. *Deafness and Education International, 5*(1), 1–19.

Government of India, Department of Education. (1993). *Education for all.* New Delhi: Author.

Hjulstad, O., & Kristoffersen, A-E. (2007). Pupils with a cochlear implant in Norway: Perspectives on learning and participation in research and practice. In M. Hyde & G. Hoie (Eds.), *To be or to become—Language and learning in the lives of young deaf children* (pp. 67–90). Oslo: Norwegian Government Printers and Skadallen Resource Centre.

Hung, H-L., & Paul, P. V. (2006). Inclusion of students who are deaf or hard of hearing: Secondary school hearing students' perspectives. *Deafness and Education International* [Special Issue], *8*(3), 88–100.

Hyde, M., Ohna, S-E., & Hjulstad, O. (2006). A comparison of the definitions, policies and practices associated with the educational inclusion of deaf students in Australia and Norway, *American Annals of the Deaf, 150*(5), 415–426.

Hyde, M. B., & Power, D. J. (1992). The use of Australian Sign Language by deaf people. *Sign Language Studies, 75,* 167–182.

Hyde, M. B., & Power, D. J. (2004). Educational inclusion of deaf students: An examination of the definitions of inclusion in relation to the findings of a recent Australian study of deaf students in regular classes. *Deafness and Education International, 6*(2), 82–99.

Knoors, H. (2007). Educational responses to varying objectives of parents of deaf children: A Dutch perspective. *Journal of Deaf Studies and Deaf Education, 12*(2), 243–253.

Kirke-, Utdannings- og Forskningsdepartementet [The Royal Ministry of Education, Research and Church Affairs]. (1998). *The national curricula for the compulsory education.* Oslo: Author.

Kyle, J. G. (2005). Living and learning bilingually—Deaf experiences and possibilities. *Deaf Worlds, 21,* 75–90.

Ladd, N. P. (2003). *In search of deafhood.* Clevedon, United Kingdom: Multilingual Matters.

Lo Bianco, J. (1987). *National policy on languages.* Canberra, New South Wales: Commonwealth Department of Education.

Marschark, M., Leigh, G., Sapere, P., Burnham, D., Convertino, C., Stinson, M., et al. (2006). Benefits of sign language interpreting and text alternatives to classroom learning by deaf students. *Journal of Deaf Studies and deaf Education, 11,* 421–437.

Mayer, C., & Wells, G. (1996). Can the linguistic interdependence theory support a bilingual-bicultural model of literacy education for deaf students? *Journal of Deaf Studies and Deaf Education, 1,* 93–107.

McDonald, D. (2006, November 16). Reaching across the hearing wall: Part one. Speaking out. *The Brisbane Line.*.

Mirenda, P. (1998). Educational inclusion of AAC users. In D. R. Beukelman & P. Mirenda (Eds.), *Augmentative and alternative communication* (2nd ed. pp. 391–424). Baltimore, MD: Paul. H. Brookes.

Mitchell, D. (2005). *Contextualising inclusive education: Evaluating old and new international perspectives.* New York: Routledge.

National Association of the Deaf. (2008). *Inclusion.* Retrieved November 7, 2008, from http://www.nad.org/site/pp.asp?c=foINKQMBF&b=180361

Osgood, R. (2005). *The history of inclusion in the United States.* Washington, DC: Gallaudet University Press.

Padden, C., & Humphries, T. (1988). *Deaf in America.* Cambridge, MA: Harvard University Press.

Parasnis, I., DeCaro, J. J., & Raman, M. L. (1996). Attitudes of teachers and parents in India toward career choice for deaf and hearing people. *American Annals of the Deaf, 141*(4), 303–308.

Pollack, D. (1970). *Educational audiology for the limited hearing infant and preschooler.* Springfield, IL: C. C. Thomas.

Power, D. J., & Hyde, M. B. (2002). The characteristics and extent of participation of deaf and hard of hearing students in regular classes in Australian schools. *Journal of Deaf Studies and Deaf Education, 7,* 302–311.

Powers, S. (2002). From concepts to practice in deaf education: A United Kingdom perspective on inclusion. *Journal of Deaf Studies and Deaf Education, 7,* 230–243.

Sharma, U., & Deppeler, J. (2005). Integrated education in India: Challenges and prospects. *Disability Studies Quarterly, 25,* 1.

Singal, N. (2005). Mapping the field of inclusive education: a review of the Indian literature. *International Journal of Inclusive Education, 9*(4), 331–350.

Sowell, T. (1995). *The vision of the anointed: Self-congratulation as a basis for social policy.* New York: Basic Books.

Stinson, M. S., & Kluwin, T. N. (2003). Educational consequences of alternative school placements. In M. Marschark & P. E. Spencer (Eds.), *The handbook of deaf studies, language and education* (pp. 52–64). New York: Oxford University Press.

Taylor, C. (1994). The Politics of Recognition. In A. Gutmann (Ed.), *Multiculturalism: Examining the politics of recognition* (pp. 25–73). Princeton, NJ: Princeton University Press.

Tijsseling, C. (2006). *Anders doof zijn: Een nieuw perspectief op dove kinderen* [Another way to be deaf: A new perspective on deaf children]. Twello, The Netherlands: Van Tricht Uitgeverij.

United Nations. (1989). *Convention on the rights of the child.* Retrieved November 7, 2008, from http://www.unhchr.ch/html/menu3/b/k2crc.htm

United Nations. (2006). *United Nations Comprehensive and Integral International Convention on the Protection and Promotion of the Rights and Dignity of Persons with Disabilities.* New York: Author.

United Nations Educational, Scientific and Cultural Organization (UNESCO). (1994). *The Salamanca Statement and framework for action on special needs education.* World Conference on Special Needs Education: Access and Quality, June 7–10, Salamanca, Spain. Retrieved November 7, 2008, from http://unesdoc.unesco.org/images/0009/000984/098427Eo.pdf

United Nations Educational, Scientific and Cultural Organization (UNESCO). (2000). *The world education forum: The Dakaar framework for action. Educaton for all: Meeting our collective commitments.* Retrieved November 7, 2008, from http://unesdoc.unesco.org/images/0012/001211/121147E.pdf

Vislie, L. (1995). Integration policies, school reforms and the organisation of schooling for handicapped pupils in western societies. In C. Clark, A. Dyson, & A. Millward (Eds.), *Towards inclusive schools?* (pp. 17–35). London: David Fulton Publishers.

Vislie, L. (2003). From integration to inclusion: Focusing global trends and changes in the western European societies. *European Journal of Special Needs Education, 18,* 17–35.

Vonen, A-M. (2007). Bimodal bilingualism in children—Similar and different. In M. Hyde & G. Hoie (Eds.), *To be or to become—Language and learning in the lives of young deaf children* (pp. 32–43). Oslo: Norwegian Government Printers and Skadallen Resource Centre.

Wagner, P. (1994). *A sociology of modernity: Liberty and discipline.* New York: Routledge.

Warnock, H. M. (1978). Special educational needs: Report of the Committee of Enquiry into the education of handicapped children and young people. London: Her Majesty's Stationery Office (HMSO).

Wolfensberger, W. (1972). *Normalization: The principle of normalization in human services.* Toronto: National Institute on Mental Retardation.

International Committee of Sports for the Deaf and Deaflympics

Donalda K. Ammons

HISTORICALLY, SPORTS have provided a rewarding reason for people from different countries to gather in unity. The same holds true for deaf people all over the world. The Deaflympics and World Deaf Championships are of special importance to the Deaf community in that they provide role models and are a source of social cohesion, perhaps especially for those countries that are turning more and more toward mainstreaming and inclusion in their educational systems. In addition to the benefits it provides in terms of physical fitness, Deaf sport is a catalyst for socialization among a low-incidence and geographically dispersed population under nonthreatening conditions. It is of particular importance for Deaf adults who spend most of their lives interacting in the absence of other Deaf individuals and signers (Stewart, 1991; Stewart & Ellis, 1999, 2006).

Emphasizing the need for lifelong physical activity, Stewart and Ellis (2006) state:

Deaf children need to learn about opportunities they will have as adults to participate as athletes, coaches, officials, volunteers, and spectators in local through international levels of competition in Deaf sport events. . . . [A] deaf student who is not taught the benefit of participation in Deaf sport activities may miss out on critical socialization and interaction opportunities during their adult years. (p. 79)

England and Scotland held the first international football (soccer) match in the 1890s, and, later, two neighboring countries—France and Belgium—joined them. Those early Deaf sport enthusiasts ultimately realized that to arrange an international event in a fair and honest manner, they needed a uniform set of rules and regulations. Thus, they saw a need for an international governing body of Deaf sports.

In 1924, two notable Deaf sports leaders—Eugene Rubens Alcais of France and Antoine Dresse of Belgium—helped establish a new governing body called the Comité International des Sports Silencieux (CISS). At that time, the goals of CISS were to establish mutual cooperation among deaf sports federations and to govern the newly established International Silent Games, held every 4 years. The names of these organizations have changed over time, and now they are known as the International Committee of Sports for the Deaf (ICSD) and Deaflympics, respectively.

STRUCTURE AND MEMBERSHIP

It is important to point out that Deaf people have always managed the ICSD organization. Jerald Jordan (1991), a former president of the Comité International des Sports des Sourds, wrote, "Nowhere in the Deaf community is the sense of Deaf people taking charge of their own lives as strong as it is in Deaf sports" (p. vii). At the time of the preparation of this manuscript, this author is the president of ICSD. The voting members of the executive committee are David Lanesman (Israel), vice president; Josef Willmerdinger (Germany), sport director; and three members-at-large—Dogan Ozdemir (Turkey), Siv Fosshaug (Switzerland), and Yang Yang (China). The nonvoting members of ICSD represent four regions within the ICSD structure: Peter Kalae (Kenya) for Africa, Chih-ho Chen (Chinese Taipei) for Asia-Pacific, Isabelle Malaurie (France) for Europe, and Maria de Bendeguz (Venezuela) for the Americas.

There are approximately 95 full members, who represent national deaf sports federations from all over the world. Associate membership is limited to deaf international single-sport governing bodies such as the Deaf International Basketball Federation and the World Deaf Golf Federation.

The ICSD is incorporated as a nonprofit organization in the state of Maryland and is in the progress of relocating the legal seat to Lausanne, Switzerland. It is staffed by two full-time and two part-time employees. The full-time executive director reports to the executive committee. In addition to the Deaflympics, the ICSD also supervises the Deaf world championships in various sports. A complete master calendar, with a list of events is available on www.deaflympics.com.

ORGANIZATION OF THE GAMES

The Deaflympics are typically organized by a national deaf sports federation, after successfully bidding to hold the games in their country. The federation then forms an organizing committee to specifically organize and manage the games on their behalf. This effort includes raising funds and seeking sponsorship support to ensure the games are held at an elite level, as required by the Deaflympics regulations. In some instances, governments have partnered with the national deaf sports federation, playing a significant part in the operation of the games. International, national, and local sports organizations are enlisted to assist with the running of the sport events, thus creating the need for a high level of sign language interpreting to assist communication between the deaf athletes and officials and hearing sport officials. In addition, visual presentation of information, through the use of video screens, captioning, and information boards, during the Deaflympics is crucial for both athletes and spectators.

In 2007, ICSD held the 16th Winter Deaflympics in Salt Lake City, Utah, the host city of three Olympic-style events: the Olympic Games in 2002, the Paralympic Games in 2002, and the Winter Deaflympics in 2007. Top-notch athletes from nearly 25 countries competed.

SCOPE OF ACTIVITIES

In 2006, ICSD supervised the organization of three world championships in cycling, golf, and orienteering. In addition to the Summer and Winter Deaflympics, 12 world championships have been scheduled for 2007 through 2009 (see Table 25.1).

The Deaflympics logo, designed in 2003 by graphic designer and Deaflympics silver medalist in cycling, Ralph Fernandez, is a positive and powerful symbol of the international deaf sports community. It ties together strong elements: sign language, deaf and international

Table 25.1. ICSD Activities 2007–2009

Date	Activity	Competition	Location
Feb. 1, 2007	16th Winter Deaflympics	Deaflympics	Salt Lake City, Utah, United States
June 22, 2007	World Deaf Basketball Championships	Deaf World Championships	Guangzhou, China
July 21, 2007	Dresse and Maere—Tennis Cup	Deaf World Championships	München, Germany
Aug. 11, 2007	World Deaf Swimming Championships	Deaf World Championships	Taipei, Chinese Taipei
Sept. 28, 2007	World Deaf Badminton Championships	Deaf World Championships	Muelheim/Ruhr, Germany
Nov. 8, 2007	World Deaf Futsal Championships	Deaf World Championships	Sofia, Bulgaria
Nov. 28, 2007	World Deaf Bowling Championships	Deaf World Championships	Mount Faber, Singapore
May 21, 2008	World Deaf Martial Arts Championships	Deaf World Championships	Toulouse, France
June 1, 2008	World Deaf Table Tennis Championships	Deaf World Championships	Sofia, Bulgaria
July 1, 2008	World Deaf Football Championships	Deaf World Championships	Athens, Greece
Sept. 14, 2008	World Deaf Wrestling Championships	Deaf World Championships	Yerevan, Armenia
Sept. 20, 2008	World Deaf Athletics Championships	Deaf World Championships	Barquisimeto, Venezuela
Sept. 30, 2008	World Deaf Golf Championships	Deaf World Championships	Perth, Australia
Sept. 5, 2009	21st Summer Deaflympics	Deaflympics	Taipei, Chinese Taipei

Figure 25.1. Official logo of ICSD.

cultures, unity, and continuity. The logo incorporates the four colors of the national flags of the world. The red, blue, yellow, and green represent the four regional confederations: the Asia Pacific Deaf Sports Federation, the European Deaf Sports Organization, the Pan American Deaf Sports Federation, and the Confederation of African Deaf Sports. The center of the logo represents the iris of the eye, which defines deaf people as visual people; they must use their eyes to communicate. The handshapes indicating "ok," "good," and "great," which overlap each other in a circle, represent the original sign for Deaflympics. Together, the handshapes represent the sign for "united" (see Figure 25.1).

The International Olympic Committee (IOC) has recognized ICSD since 1951, when it held a reception to honor ICSD's high standard of administration and sports activities. Then in May 1955, the IOC announced its unanimous recognition of the ICSD as an "International Federation with Olympic standing." With this recognition given, it was mutually agreed that the word "Olympic" and the five-ring emblems would not be used by the ICSD. In 1966, the IOC recognized ICSD with a prestigious award called the Olympic Cup that was created by Baron de Coubertin in 1906. Through this gesture, the IOC showed its high regard for ICSD services to sports. In 1981, Juan Antonio Samaranch became the first IOC president to attend the Deaf World Games (as they were known then). That year, the games were held in Cologne, Germany. The same year, an anti-doping policy was also implemented.

At their meeting in May 2001, the IOC Executive Committee voted to approve the change in the name of the quadrennial event from Deaf World Games to Deaflympics. With this new name, Deaflympics organizers have agreed to abide by the following IOC regulations:

- Deaflympics cannot use the term *Games* in connection with the events.
- The Deaflympics logo cannot be used to identify the ICSD.
- ICSD cannot put the Deaflympics logo on ICSD letterhead or any other printed materials.
- All members of ICSD shall abide by the stated restrictions.

THE ICSD AND THE INTERNATIONAL PARALYMPIC COMMITTEE

The ICSD has rights similar to the International Paralympic Committee (IPC), but it does not receive the same funding for its competitions. ICSD and IPC are listed as recognized federations of IOC and are under the Sport Department. The big distinction in this respect is that the quadrennial event—Summer and Winter Deaflympics—is governed by Deaf people and the ICSD whereas the Paralympic Games are administered by IOC Games Department.

The IOC Games Department has the critical responsibility for the oversight and coordination of the Olympic Games and the Paralympic Games. The Paralympic Games are held in the Olympic host city under the responsibility of the Olympic Games Organizing Committee 10 days after the Olympic Games.

The ICSD is aware that deaf sports was organized at an international level long before other disabled sports. Despite this fact, the organization sees a continued effort by national organizations for disabled sports around the world to pressure deaf sport federations to join ranks with them and consolidate resources. The pressure has not necessarily achieved its purpose because Deaf athletes do not see themselves as disabled athletes, and they have become empowered and resolute in safeguarding their self-determination. Maintaining this perspective, ICSD remains deeply committed to preserving the goals and principles of Deaflympics. Nevertheless, ICSD and the International Paralympic Committee signed a Memorandum of Understanding in November 2004, in a step toward creating a collaborative landscape in international competition.

One result of this pact has been that deaf athletes with additional disabilities may participate in various IPC events. Conversely, multidisabled Paralympic athletes with at least a 55dB hearing loss in the better ear will be able to compete in the Deaflympics and the Deaf World Championships. The agreement provides the National Olympic Committees and the National Paralympic Committees with better awareness and understanding of ICSD and Paralympics as two separate organizations that manage their own quadrennial events. The Memorandum of Understanding also stipulates that ICSD and IPC will

- mutually recognize and respect the autonomy of their organizations;
- cooperate in informing sports authorities of the international structures of both organizations; and
- cooperate in addressing conflicts between the affiliated organizations.

"This agreement illustrates our commitment to working together in sync," Donalda Ammons, interim president of Deaflympics, said. "It will ensure that these athletes have a global stage to display their sporting spirit and dedication."

FUTURE GOALS OF ICSD

ICSD will continue to uphold its mission, which is to cherish the value and the spirit of Deaflympics where Deaf athletes strive to reach the pinnacle of competition by embracing the motto *per ludos aequalitias* (equal through sports) and adhering to the ideals of the Olympics.

The ICSD mission statement contains the following objectives:

- To supervise the organization of successful Summer and Winter Deaflympics
- To promote and contribute to the development of sport opportunities and competitions, from grassroot to elite levels, for Deaf athletes
- To support and encourage educational, cultural, research, and scientific activities that contribute to the development and promotion of the Deaflympics
- To fully enforce a drug-free sport environment for all Deaf athletes in conjunction with the World Anti-Doping Agency

- To promote sports for Deaf athletes without discrimination for political, religious, economic, disability, gender, or race reasons

ICSD is committed to creating more and better athletes with higher standards for excellence, a significant level of international recognition, an increased and sound budget, and an efficient and effective organization. If deaf people are resolute in adhering to the ICSD mission and principles, the organization shall prevail with more and better recognition from the public domain and mutual respect among its members.

REFERENCES

Jordan, J. (1991). Preface. In D. Stewart (Ed.), *Deaf sport: The impact of sports within the Deaf community* (pp. vii–viii). Washington, DC: Gallaudet University Press.

Stewart, D. (1991). *Deaf sport: The impact of sports within the Deaf community.* Washington, DC: Gallaudet University Press.

Stewart, D., & Ellis, M. (1999). Physical education for Deaf students. *American Annals of the Deaf, 144*(4), 315–319.

Stewart, D., & Ellis, M. (2006). Revisiting the role of physical education for Deaf students. In D. Moores & D. Martin (Eds.), *Deaf learners: Developments in curriculum and instruction* (pp. 75–92). Washington, DC: Gallaudet University Press.

The World Federation of the Deaf

Roslyn Rosen

THE WORLD FEDERATION OF THE DEAF (WFD) is one of the oldest, if not in fact the oldest, international organization focused on advocacy of, for, by, and with Deaf people. The headquarters and legal seat of the WFD is currently in Helsinki, Finland. As of 2008, the WFD consists of 128 national organizations of the Deaf from six continents of the world; its membership base also includes associate members, international members, and individual members. This international nongovernmental organization represents approximately 70 million Deaf people worldwide. Approximately 80% of these 70 million live in developing countries, mostly in the southern hemisphere and parts of Asia, where their needs and desires are not known to or heeded by the authorities.

The WFD was established during the first World Deaf Congress in Rome in 1951, and it attracted attendees from 25 countries. In the ensuing years, the WFD has multiplied its influence; intensified its networks within and across organizations; and expanded its federation of Ordinary Members, or national associations of the Deaf, from Afghanistan to Zimbabwe. Each country is limited to one Ordinary Member, following the same principle as the organization and governing body of the United Nations (UN). An Ordinary Member is defined as a national organization of Deaf people with a clear majority of Deaf voting members, a governing board with a majority of Deaf people, and goals similar to those of the WFD.

The WFD is recognized by the UN as the sole spokes-organization on behalf of the 70 million Deaf and hard of hearing people of the world. In 1958, WFD was granted consultative status, B-category by the UN Educational, Scientific and Cultural Organization (UNESCO) and, in 1959, by the UN system and its agencies. The UN granted the WFD permission to share its logo (Figure 26.1), and to this day, the WFD is the only organization authorized to do so. The WFD cooperates closely with the UN High Commissioner for Human Rights and has representatives on the Panel of Experts on the UN Standard Rules for the Equalization of Opportunities for Persons with Disabilities. The WFD is also a key member of the International Disability Alliance.

The WFD provides information, training, and resources to the UN and its bodies as well as to its Ordinary Members and Deaf people in general to enhance knowledge and skills about Deaf people's human rights and empowerment. When necessary, the WFD uses special, legal, or administrative measures to ensure that Deaf people in all countries have the right to their own sign languages, education, organizations, and cultural programs. Key WFD priorities are human rights, sign language and culture, and equal opportunities in all spheres of life, especially in the developing countries. The WFD's philosophy is one of equality, human rights, and respect for all people, and it is inclusive in terms of race, nationality, religion, gender, abilities or disabilities, sexual preference, age, and any other human variations. The WFD supports and promotes in its work the many UN conventions on human rights, with primary

Figure 26.1. World Federation of
the Deaf logo.

focus on Deaf people who use sign language, their families, and the general public. The WFD works toward the goal of solidarity and unity to make the world a better place. As WFD President Emerita Liisa Kauppinen stated, "A society good for all disabled people is a society good for all people."

In its publications, communications, and relationships with other international organizations and professional groups, the WFD provides advocacy and expert advice on matters pertaining to Deaf people. The WFD advocates the human rights of self-determination and self-representation, as embodied in the statement and motto "Nothing about us without us." Over the years, the goals and priorities of the WFD have held steadfast and can probably be summarized in two words: equality and quality—both of which are contingent on the access to and achievement of human rights for Deaf people. The current emphases of the WFD can be summed up as follows:

- Advocate for human rights for all Deaf people, especially in developing countries.
- Advance the status of indigenous (national) sign languages, culture, and community.
- Advocate for equality and equality in life and the right to self-determination and self-representation.

WFD Deaf representatives in the 8th Ad Hoc Session, United Nations, New York City, are shown here with Don Mackay of New Zealand, United Nations Ambassador and Chair of the Ad Hoc Committee sessions. From right to left are WFD President Markku Jokinen, UN Ambassador Don Mackay, WFD President Emerita Liisa Kauppinen, and WFD Board Member Colon Allen.

- Upgrade education in terms of access and quality, and ensure Deaf people's involvement in the educative process.
- Improve access to communication and services.
- Promote the establishment of national Deaf organizations where none currently exist.

In 1991, the WFD established a Youth Section (WFDYS) for members ages 18 to 30. The WFDYS operates under the auspices of the WFD and works closely with the General Secretariat, yet retains its autonomy with its own board and priorities. The WFDYS has a representative on the WFD Board. It also operates summer youth camps annually or every other year.

OFFICIAL RELATIONSHIPS

The WFD works with several international organizations and has an especially close relationship with the UN. It is represented with the following groups:

- UNESCO
- UN Office of the High Commissioner for Human Rights
- UN Economic and Social Council
- UN Commission on the Rights of Persons With Disabilities
- World Health Organization
- International Labor Organization

The WFD maintains close working relationships with the International Committee of Sports for the Deaf (CISS/ICSD) and the World Association of Sign Language Interpreters (WASLI). It also works closely with the International Disability Alliance. WFD representatives attend the Congresses of other key international organizations, including the International Congress on Education of the Deaf, the Rehabilitation International, Deaf History International, the World Bank Global Partnership on Disability and Development, the Disabled People International (DPI), the World Federation of Deaf Blind, and the International Federation of Hard of Hearing.

ORDINARY MEMBERS

Each country is limited to one Ordinary Member to represent the nation in the WFD federation, the same way that the UN will recognize only one political national entity in its Assembly of Delegates. Although the WFD will adhere to the UN's list of nations, developing nations, and industrialized nations, it is not legally bound to UN definitions. For example, Macau and Hong Kong are currently Ordinary Members within the WFD, even though they are territories of other countries now and thus not bona fide members of the UN. When the local associations in Switzerland wanted to become an Ordinary Member, the WFD welcomed this initiative on the condition that they work together to create one national association of the Deaf (thus creating a national federation of three regional associations, each using a different sign language—Swiss Deutsch, French, and Italian)—which was accomplished.

The process to be approved by the WFD as an Ordinary Member requires that the proposing national association of the Deaf complete an application and attach its statutes, which attest that its goals are in line with those of the WFD and that the majority of its board and officers are Deaf. The Ordinary Member membership fees are different for developing and developed countries, with basic fees of US$50 or US$100 being waived frequently for the poorest Ordinary Members. The number of Ordinary Members tripled in two decades, during the terms of Presidents Yerker Andersson (working with then General Secretary Liisa Kauppinen) and President Kauppinen (1983–2003). The current list of the Ordinary Members and contact information can be accessed on the WFD Web site at www.wfdeaf.org.

WFD General Secretariat (Headquarters)

The WFD General Secretariat was established in 1951 in Rome, Italy, with the staunch leadership and support of the Italian Federation of the Deaf (Ente Nazionale Sordomuti, or ENS). The ENS president, Vittorio Ieralla, and Dr. Cesare Magarotto, a hearing son of Antonio Magarotto, one of the ENS founders, convinced the Italian government to support their efforts. Dr. Magarotto, who was fluent in several languages and who managed the ENS, served as the first general secretary of WFD (1951–1987). Under his leadership and the new board, the WFD General Secretariat established informative and advocacy networks, helped increase numbers of national associations of the Deaf and Ordinary Members, and published the WFD newsletter the *Voice of Silence,* now called the *WFD News.* (WFD currently also publishes periodical informational circulars for its membership.)

In 1987, when Dr. Magarotto retired, Dr. Liisa Kauppinen of Finland succeeded him as the WFD General Secretary (1987–1995). She worked out of the Finnish Association of the Deaf (FAD) headquarters building from 1987 to 1997. Like Magarotto with ENS, Kauppinen was the FAD executive director, and she managed both organizations at minimal cost to the WFD. The president of the WFD during Kauppinen's tenure was Dr. Yerker Andersson from the United States. When Kauppinen was elected president in 1995, she worked with the board on a visionary plan of action that would lead to the establishment of an independent WFD home office and its first paid full-time general secretary and staff.

An independent WFD General Secretariat was launched in 1996 in Ferney-Voltaire, France, just across the border from Geneva, Switzerland, in the International Disability Centre planned by the International Disability Foundation. Ms. Carol-lee Aquiline, then executive director of the Australian Association of the Deaf, was hired as the first full-time WFD General Secretary. After approximately 2 years, on recommendation by General Secretary Aquiline, and with the support of the Swedish Association of the Deaf, the board approved the relocation of the WFD General Secretariat and its operations to Stockholm, Sweden, with office space within the Swedish Association of the Deaf headquarters. The reason for the move was twofold: WFD needed financial and in-kind support from external sources (i.e., its Ordinary Members), and the General Secretariat needed community support and stimulation to operate. Later, when the Swedish economy started to decline, as was the case for many nations, the WFD office was relocated in 2001 to the FAD headquarters, the Lighthouse, in Helsinki, Finland, where it continues operations, with the generous support of the FAD. FAD also provides support with the staffing and in-kind services of WFD operations. However, because of the continuing financial issues and lack of support staff, Ms. Aquiline offered to resign from the office in 2003, thus enabling the board to establish plans for financial stability and resource reserves before appointing another general secretary.

In 2003, Dr. Kauppinen stepped down at the end of her term. The General Assembly voted Mr. Markku Jokinen (Finland) the succeeding President of WFD. When Dr. Kauppinen retired from FAD, Mr. Jokinen was appointed as the new executive director of FAD, wearing two hats. Even without a General Secretariat, the WFD, through its president, board, and volunteers, continues to provide information sharing, advocacy, training and support to its Ordinary Members, the UN agencies, and other international associations. The 2007 General Assembly approved Finland as the legal seat for the WFD.

REGIONAL SECRETARIATS AND NETWORKING

The WFD organizational infrastructure includes regional secretariats, each consisting of at least three Ordinary Members within a region. A regional secretariat may have a coordinator who usually wears various hats within the region or has a position within his or her Ordinary Member association or is supported by a regional grant-supported project. The regional secretariat collaborates with its member Ordinary Members and the WFD, engages in information sharing and gathering, and may send its representative to board meetings and WFD Congresses, as resources permit. Regional conferences are encouraged annually or every other year to facilitate training and information sharing. Goals, needs, and priorities are shared with WFD for board consideration and action as appropriate.

As is true for Ordinary Members, the officers of the regional secretariat must be Deaf and they must represent the Ordinary Members in their region. Otherwise, the regional secretariat is considered "interim" until Deaf leadership assumes the reins.

The current regional secretariats are as follows:

- South America
- Mexico, Central America, and the Caribbean
- Asia and the Pacific
- Eastern and Southern Africa
- Eastern Europe and Middle Asia
- Interim Regional Secretariat for the Arab Region
- Regional Cooperating Member European Union of the Deaf

Because at least three Ordinary Members are required to establish a regional secretariat, and because Mexico currently favors alignment with its neighbors to the south sharing common languages and cultures, there is no regional secretariat for North America.

Representatives of the regional secretariat are welcomed to board meetings. Regional caucuses are conducted during WFD Congresses and in each region between Congresses. Information and contact data for the regional secretariats are available on the Web site of the WFD at www.wfdeaf.org.

WFD CONGRESS

The first WFD Congress convened in Rome, Italy, in 1951, shortly after the UN was established. The last few Congresses have attracted 2,000 to 4,000 people from all over the world, including Deaf adults and youth, professionals, families, and business people. The 11th Congress, held in Tokyo in 1991, attracted a record number of 6,000 attendants. At each Congress, approximately 70% of the participants are Deaf.

The WFD Congress consists of two parts, a General Assembly and the scientific, cultural and special interest sections of the Congress. It tends to be a week long and concludes with an official Congress Resolution. The purpose of the Congress is twofold. The first purpose is to stress "that the only limitations to a Deaf person's achievement are those placed upon him by society—and what he himself accepts as his limitations. The second is that education, training, and the dissemination of information are essential to the removal of the barriers that have so far prevented Deaf persons from realizing their potential and the goal of full citizenship to which we aspire" (Crammatte & Crammatte, 1976).

Congresses continue to be a major forum for understanding human rights principles, sharing information, networking, and exchanging strategies for advocacy. Face-to-face communication in sign language boosts comprehension and empowerment for Deaf people. The WFD may also conduct special conferences between Congresses if resources permit or sponsors offer. In October 2005, the WFD, through the FAD, conducted an international conference "Our Rights—Our Future" in Helsinki, Finland, to train participants about advocacy strategies and to boost the ongoing work in the UN. Attended by 400 people from 70 countries, that conference helped to spread understanding about the roles that Deaf people can play in their own countries to support the passage of the UN International Convention on Human Rights for Persons With Disabilities.

THE GENERAL ASSEMBLY AND THE WFD BOARD

The highest decision-making body of the WFD is the General Assembly. The General Assembly convenes once every 4 years, usually 2 days before the beginning of each quadrennial World Congress of the WFD. Each Ordinary Member has the right to send up to two Deaf delegates to conduct WFD business during the General Assembly. The General Assembly is authorized by the WFD statutes to determine WFD policies and priorities, modify WFD statutes, act on audited and proposed budgets, and elect a board, which functions until the next WFD Congress. The board oversees WFD operations between Congresses and ensures that the spirit of the General Assembly, as embodied in its motions and directives, is followed, to the extent possible and as resources permit.

Before the amendment of the WFD statutes to require that Ordinary Member delegates be Deaf, many of the Ordinary Members included hearing members in their delegations. The "Deaf delegates only" amendment passed in 1991, and letters were sent to all Ordinary Members, advising them about the changed requirements for delegates. During the seating of the 1995 General Assembly, President Yerker Andersson had to ask hearing delegates to move from the assembly to the observation section, leaving their Deaf co-delegate alone in the General Assembly. The hearing delegates were visibly upset, and they expressed the concern that the Deaf delegates could not understand or function without them. The Deaf delegates, shaken at first, became acclimated to focusing and making independent decisions. They returned to their home countries feeling empowered with the ability to understand, to internalize, and to communicate the results of the Congress's deliberations. Although the WFD does encourage and cherish non-Deaf allies, it is committed to upholding the right and ability of Deaf people to avail themselves of self-determination and self-representation.

Table 26.1. Sites and Themes of WFD Congresses, 1951–2011

Year of Congress	Site	Theme
1951	Rome, Italy	—
1955	Zagreb, Yugoslavia	—
1959	Wiesbaden, Federal Republic of Germany	—
1963	Stockholm, Sweden	—
1967	Warsaw, Poland	The Deaf Among Hearing Persons
1971	Paris, France	The Deaf Person in the Evolving World
1975	Washington DC, United States	Full Citizenship for All Deaf People
1979	Varna, Bulgaria	The Deaf People in Modern Society
1983	Palermo, Italy	Deafness Today and Tomorrow: Reality/Utopia
1987	Espoo, Finland	One World—One Responsibility
1991	Tokyo, Japan	Equality and Self-Reliance
1995	Vienna, Austria	Towards Human Rights
1999	Brisbane, Australia	Diversity and Unity
2003	Montreal, Canada	Opportunities/Challenges in the 21st Century
2007	Madrid, Spain	Human Rights Through Sign Languages
2011	Durban, South Africa	—

The General Assembly also determines the site of the next Congress, based on bids by the Ordinary Members. Beginning in 1967, each Congress reflected a theme necessary or appropriate for the times, each of which was proposed by the host site and approved by the board (see Table 26.1).

In selecting the board, the General Assembly votes on a president, a vice president, and nine members from a slate of official nominations from the Ordinary Members. The General Assembly may also confer the ranks of President Emeritus, Honorary Board Member, and Honorary Member on deserving individuals. WFD board members serve a 4-year term, with the possibility of reelection. The board meets once a year and is responsible for conducting the business of the organization between conventions. It ensures that the spirit of the General Assembly, as embodied in its motions and directives, is followed to the extent possible and as resources permit. The board may appoint a management committee, which may meet once a year, between board meetings, as needed.

Because of the financial nature of the WFD, each Ordinary Member sponsors the travel expenses of its elected board member. However, this arrangement is problematic for developing nations, and the WFD has endeavored to broker agreements with the more wealthy nations to sponsor board members from developing countries in an effort to have appropriately diverse representation on the board in terms of region, gender, culture, goals, and needs. One of the long-term goals of the WFD is to raise and establish sufficient funds to pay these travel expenses. Because the WFD is dependent on the Ordinary Members to host the board meetings and the delegates' travel expenses, WFD holds board meetings to a minimum and has increased its use of technology to facilitate more frequent communications among the board members, mostly by means of e-mail and, probably in the near future, videophones and videoconferences.

LANGUAGES OF THE WFD

The official WFD languages are International Signs and printed English, and all communication at the meetings of the General Assembly are carried out through these two languages.

No interpreters are allowed unless a special invited guest speaker, who may be a representative of the UN or an allied organization, is not Deaf and is a nonsigner.

One of the issues that came up for debate during the 2003 and 2007 General Assemblies was whether the statutes should change the official language from "International Signs" to "International Sign Language" because International Signs meet the basic linguistic characteristics of a language. Each assembly referred this issue to its board and its experts for further study, expressing the concern that the designation of International Sign Language might prevent the providing of specific national sign language interpreters during important regional meetings in Europe. Although Deaf people can communicate with each other using basic signs, the WFD wanted to emphasize that sign language is not "universal."

Delegates new to the international scene may find it difficult to follow General Assembly deliberations, especially if they have neither working English nor basic expertise in International Signs. Thus, WFD established a 1-day, preassembly orientation and training session that includes a crash course on International Signs used for meetings. These signs include concepts such as government, approve and not approve, funds, people, terms of time, various action verbs, parliamentary procedures, human rights, and labels for officers and participants. It is truly amazing how relatively quickly one becomes acclimated to International Signs during international meetings.

During the scientific, cultural, and special interest sessions of the Congress, the official languages include International Signs, printed English, the sign language of the host Ordinary Member, and often, the printed spoken language of that country. Interpreters, not permitted during the General Assembly, are permitted during the Congress; the Ordinary Members may bring their own sign language interpreters, who often know English, to translate from spoken English into their sign language for their delegates. Earlier Congresses had all the sign language interpreters on the stage where one could observe the splendid array of variations, but recent Congresses, with growing numbers of participants from different countries in attendance, often have pockets of participants throughout the audience with their own interpreters close by. In addition, there are huge screens portraying the official sign language interpreters, the presenter, and sometimes the printed languages of English and that of the host nation.

When the WFD was first established in Rome, both Italian and English were used. Later, French was recognized as one of two official printed languages until 1991, when limited finances justified a statutes change to limit WFD to one printed language only—English. Ordinary Members may translate WFD materials and communications to their languages, with the national associations of the Deaf in Spain and France sometimes providing translations for developing countries sharing the same languages.

In 1975, the WFD published an book of International Signs, *Gestuno*. With the increasing advent and use of video technologies, WFD is producing more of its information as DVDs and VLOGs (video blogs) on its Web site. In 2007, the Norwegian Association of the Deaf collaborated with the WFD and others to produce a DVD on suggested International Signs for use in the WFD General Assembly.

CONGRESS RESOLUTIONS: WFD GOALS AND PRIORITIES

The WFD Board proclaims a resolution at the closing ceremony of each Congress that is based on discussions and recommendations made by the General Assembly and the Congress through its various scientific commissions and special interest committees. These resolutions encompass the WFD guiding principles and priorities for the next era. Over the years, resolutions have primarily reiterated the human rights of Deaf people everywhere to indigenous (native) sign language and culture; access to information and communications; education; and their own national organization, self-determination, and empowerment.

The past four Congress Resolutions have focused on Deaf people in developing countries, gender equity, responsibilities of industrialized countries to work with developing countries, and the role of emerging technologies, respectively. These resolutions have also emphasized diversity and equity across commonly oppressed human variations—women, senior citizens, youth, people with varying sexual orientations, and regional language variations. Resolutions have also addressed the need for geographical and gender balance on the WFD Board, including its various committees and delegations. (See the boxes below for the 2007 resolution.)

The World Federation of the Deaf (WFD), its Members and the participants at the 15th World Congress of the World Federation of the Deaf in Madrid, Spain, 16–22 July 2007,

Reaffirming that Deaf people are entitled to the same human rights as all social groups and that diversity is an intrinsic factor in the Deaf Community,

Recognizing the importance of children and youth; Deaf-blind; Deaf with disabilities; immigrants; Indigenous peoples; Lesbians, Gays, Transgenders and Bisexuals; people in rural areas; religious minorities; senior citizens; and all Deaf people as citizens of society with the same rights and obligations as other citizens,

Emphasizing that by adopting positive actions, equality among all will be accelerated,

Emphasizing that sign language is a human right for all members of the Deaf Community, including those who use assistive devices and implants,

Reaffirming that multilingual education in sign language gives Deaf and hard of hearing people the best opportunity to achieve full citizenship and enjoyment of all human rights;

Have agreed that WFD and its Members:

- Have an obligation to work together to promote government ratification and implementation of the United Nations Convention on the Rights of Persons with Disabilities thus assuring Deaf people full attainment of all human rights on an equal basis with other citizens.
- Must work together as a collective group, and those from developed countries must work in close partnership with those from developing countries.
- Must adopt measures to educate and to sensitize the Deaf Community about the diverse variety of peoples and cultures within the larger Deaf culture.
- Must promote gender-equality programs and policies to ensure the full development and empowerment of women, and adopt measures that combat violence and abuse against Deaf women.

continued

- Have a responsibility to preserve, promote and protect sign languages and cultural heritages; and to formulate language policies to empower sign language, including indigenous sign languages.
- Have an obligation to cooperate closely with schools and educational authorities to promote Deaf children's right to receive a multilingual/multicultural education and to implement training programs to develop healthy identities for all Deaf children, their families and CODA children.
- Should also protect the rights of children with cochlear implants and other sensory modification technologies to an education in sign language.
- Are responsible to sanction the employment of Deaf professionals in all fields that have an impact on the lives of Deaf people.
- Must promote the development of appropriate training programs and qualifications for sign language interpreters, and follow WFD principles of cooperation with interpreters.
- Must incorporate the principles of consistent application of universal design with technological innovations of new products and services.
- Must formulate a statement of Deaf bioethics concerns and priorities, and quality medical and surgical care for Deaf people, based on human rights principles.
- Have an obligation to establish mentorship and positive leadership programs for Deaf youth, and involve them actively in political decision-making and implementation.
- Have a responsibility to promote employment and self-sufficiency through Deaf economic empowerment.
- Are responsible to promote equal access to mental health services for all Deaf people.

Programs and actions developed by WFD and its OMs must take account of all Deaf people. Special attention should be given to education in both developed and developing countries in order to eliminate any further disadvantage that brings as a consequence unemployment, poverty, poor health and the lack of self-determination. Education for Deaf people, especially in developing countries, must be an initiative of Deaf persons from that country in order to include and impart their native sign language(s) and culture.

The linguistic and cultural rights of Deaf immigrants must be respected as well as assistance provided in learning the language and culture of their new country.

Sign language interpreters are a fundamental resource in achieving human rights and full access. The term sign language interpreter is a concept inclusive not only of hearing sign language interpreters but also Deaf sign language interpreters and interpreter guides for Deafblind people.

Technology and e-learning offer access to information, are vital for structured and informal learning, and promote independency. The principles of universal design will ensure full communication access and fulfillment of Deaf persons' human rights.

Equal and appropriate access to mental health services, through sign language and Deaf culture and by the provisioning of Deaf professional staff, is a basic human right of Deaf people.

In reference to the growing demographic of an aging population, attention must be given to programs and services for Deaf senior citizens.

continued

Sign languages serve as vital instruments to transmit culture and knowledge. The status and recognition of sign languages around the world will be strengthened through language policies, research and the preservation of and the teaching of sign languages. Sign languages should be a part of all national curricula.

The World Federation of the Deaf (WFD), its Members and the participants at the 15th World Congress of the World Federation of the Deaf agree to promote and implement this Congress Resolution to all governments and authorities, demanding respect for the realization of HUMAN RIGHTS THROUGH SIGN LANGUAGES.

MISSION, VISION, ACTION PLANS, STATUTES, AND POLICY PAPERS

During President Kauppinen's tenure, the 2003 General Assembly approved a forward-looking action plan titled *Charting the Future,* which defines a high quality of life for Deaf people by the year 2020 and delineates operational strategies. The document defines *equality and quality in life* for Deaf people and examines goals and objectives related to various strands of life such as access, education, employment, self-determination, and respect as well as the functioning of the WFD in terms of roles, staff, and resources. This strategic plan is used as a roadmap for priorities and operations for the WFD General Secretariat and the board.

The highest operational priorities for the WFD General Secretariat are as follows:

- To provide an effective link between WFD, Ordinary Members, Regional Secretariats, the UN and its agencies, other organizations, and national governments to achieve human rights for Deaf people globally
- To strengthen ties between and effectiveness of Ordinary Members and Regional Secretariats, thereby strengthening WFD and global capacity
- To provide capacity building and advocacy work to developing countries
- To strengthen the capacity of the General Secretariat to achieve Priorities 1–3, and the following goals: (a) education for all, (b) human rights and language rights, (c) financial strength, and (d) staff and resources.

The board has approved policy papers on specific issues, and these papers have been disseminated widely, affording Ordinary Members the language and support to attain attention and support for equality and quality in their lives. The topics include youth education, adult education, work in developing countries, sign language, and technology. Papers on bioethics, biotechnology, and cochlear implants also have been discussed by the board. The topic of cochlear implants has been deliberated within the board for several years, and the board supports the principle that sign language is an inalienable birthright and must be granted to all babies and youth, implanted or not. WFD also supports universal design, quality, and access in new technologies and information systems.

Sign Language as a Top Priority for WFD

WFD advocacy work and actions with the UN is inextricably linked to sign language as a fundamental human right. Furthermore, WFD holds that each country has the right to its own indigenous sign language, appropriate to its culture and customs. WFD finds funds to help associations of the deaf in undeveloped and developing countries to conduct sign language research and to develop curricula and training materials for teaching their sign language and for training interpreters, all in partnerships with experienced researchers and universities to gain credibility and government support. Training assistance and information sharing may be provided through national and regional conferences around the world.

In 1985, the governments of 12 countries recognized the legitimacy of their indigenous sign languages; 20 years later, at least 42 nations have some form of official recognition, ranging from inclusion in federal constitutions and laws to legal documents such as national policies and regulations.[1] This count includes the United States because laws such as IDEA and ADA recognize the right to sign language access and qualified interpreters.

Also important is that sign language is linked to culture and community. The concept of Deaf identity is bound to those three elements. Empowerment corresponds with one's self-esteem, knowledge, skills, and abilities to access information and to represent oneself or one's community in matters and decisions affecting Deaf people of all ages.

Education for All as a Top Priority for WFD

Equality and quality in education through sign language for all is a WFD mantra. Approximately 80% to 90% of Deaf people worldwide are illiterate or seriously undereducated. Less than 2% of the Deaf world population receives an education in sign language (http://www.wfdeaf.org/pdf/policy_adult_ed.pdf). Furthermore, Deaf girls and women may be denied any education. According to UN directives, bilingual education is a human right for cultural minorities and Deaf students. WFD policy papers focus mainly on children and include the right of Deaf adults to life-long learning and adult education. They also emphasize the importance of education and Deaf studies for families, professionals, and policy makers relative to Deaf people, sign language, culture, and community.

Position papers, articles, and lectures by WFD representatives advocate linguistic human rights of Deaf children in educational programs using at least two languages—the indigenous sign language and the spoken language (print form) in that country as used by their family and community. According to the 1987 Congress Resolution, "The distinct national Sign Languages of indigenous Deaf populations should be officially recognized as their natural language of right for direct communication. . . . Teachers of the Deaf are expected to learn and use the accepted indigenous Sign Language as the primary language of instruction" (World Federation of the Deaf, 1987). A position paper stated further. Like all children, "Deaf children must have equal and quality access to education. Sign Language (bilingualism) and visual strategies must be made available to Deaf people as a birthright" (World Federation of the Deaf, 2007). WFD papers present research on multilingualism and multiculturalism benefits over monolingualism in heightening skills in thinking, creativity, flexibility, and tolerance.

WFD representatives have lobbied and collaborated with various UN agencies and UNESCO to include sign language as a right for Deaf children in UN position papers and guidelines. There is a WFD representative on the UNESCO flagship initiative Education for All to ensure that inclusive education includes the Deaf child's bill of rights to standard and equal education in a visual and sign language environment with a critical mass of signing peers

1. For more information, see http://www.wfdeaf.org.

and professionals. Furthermore, WFD supports the inclusion of Deaf adults in the various facets of the educational process, as a cultural minority protected by specific UNESCO documents on Linguistic Rights of National Minority People with rights to use and to learn in their own language; to be taught by proficient language teachers; to be involved in planning curriculum and programs; and to be involved in the development, implementation, and monitoring of these programs.

WFD representatives have collaborated on a number of vital UN documents, including the following[2]:

- UN International Bill of Human Rights (1990) states that people with disabilities are entitled as members of society to equal access and services in education, health, employment, and social services and that equal responsibilities come with equal rights.
- UN Standard Rules on the Equalization of Opportunities for Persons With Disabilities (1993) recognizes the importance of creating universal standards for human rights for people with disabilities, including the need to consider sign language in the education of Deaf children, families, and communities.
- UNESCO Salamanca Statement on Special Needs Education (1994), Item 21, states the importance of sign language for Deaf students.
- UNESCO Universal Declaration of Linguistic Rights, Barcelona (1996), Articles 3, 5, 26, and UNESCO Education Rights of National (Cultural) Minorities, Hague (1996), Articles 1, 11, 12, 20, recognize the need and right of national minority people to use and learn in their own language; to be taught by linguistically proficient teachers; to be involved in planning curriculum and programs; and to be involved in the development, implementation, and monitoring of these programs.
- United Nations International Convention on Human Rights of Persons With Disabilities (2006) is a Human Rights treaty recognizing full and equal rights for all people with disabilities (discussed further in a following section).

In the WFD position papers, WFD delineates responsibilities for government, universities, and decision makers in each country to

- Legalize sign language and ensure quality lifelong education for all.
- Implement high standards and equal education policies or guidelines for Deaf people of all ages and to monitor programs.
- Provide resources to teach sign language and Deaf Studies to Deaf adults, families, professionals, interpreters, and service providers.
- Support professional development programs for Deaf people to become teachers, researchers, professionals, and administrators.
- Ensure full access to programs and media (signed and captioned), professional interpreters, and other needed support services.
- Support more research on strategies to teach indigenous sign languages and to assess fluency development.

---

2. See the United Nations Web site (http://www.un.org) for more information on these documents.

THE PINNACLE OF INTERNATIONAL ADVOCACY WORK: UNITED NATIONS INTERNATIONAL CONVENTION ON HUMAN RIGHTS OF PERSONS WITH DISABILITIES

The WFD invested 5 years of its resources in advocacy and networking with the UN, the International Disability Alliance and Caucus, and the WFD Ordinary Members to collaborate on and lobby for the passage of the International Convention on the Rights of Persons With Disabilities, which was finally adopted by the UN General Assembly in 2006. This landmark legislation is considered the "last frontier" in human rights for all. The UN has seven previous human rights treaties addressing the rights of women, children, minority cultures, immigrants and refugees, and racial diversity. The purpose of the 2006 convention is to promote, protect, and ensure full access and equal human rights for all people with disabilities on local, national, and international levels. It specifies the right to sign language and professionals fluent in sign language in several sections. The key sections of the convention that apply to Deaf people are as follows:

- Full access, including sign language, professional interpreters, and technology
- Independent living
- Freedom of expression and access to information in sign language
- Education—sign language and Deaf identity for Deaf students as well as qualified teachers who sign fluently
- Employment—no discrimination as well as equal pay and support
- Political and public life, involvement, and self-representation of disabled people
- Culture, recreation, and sports, including linguistic identity, sign language and Deaf culture

The WFD was a key player throughout the 5-year process from inception to passage. Dr. Liisa Kauppinen was often called to testify to the Ad Hoc Session Assembly, and she chaired sessions of the International Disability Caucus, which collaborated and compromised on mutually acceptable principles and language, a process that sometimes was very difficult. One issue of contention was related to inclusive education for all students; this topic required intensive discussions to craft the agreement that, for Deaf children, inclusive education must include a visually accessible environment, peers and qualified personnel who sign fluently, quality education with same standards for all, and Deaf studies.

The successful adoption by the UN General Assembly was the first step; the next step, which is still in progress is for the nations to ratify the document, to adopt these principles, and to implement them in their own countries.[3] WFD's focus has shifted to developing training, printed materials, and DVDs in sign language for the Ordinary Members to advocate for Deaf-appropriate implementation of the UN Convention in their countries.

An equally important highlight was the visibility of Deaf people throughout the process and the number of Deaf representatives of the WFD and Ordinary Members who attended the UN meetings. In the first session, only two Deaf representatives were involved, both representing the WFD. The WFD encouraged Deaf people to lobby their governments to appoint them as part of their national delegation as representatives of that government or as

---

3. Go to http://www.un.org/disabilities to check the progress of the ratification.

representatives of their association. It was a very expensive process because each representative had to bring his or her own interpreter. The UN recognizes six official spoken languages, but not yet International Signs.

Fifteen Deaf representatives (and their interpreters) from Australia, Chile, Colombia, Finland, Italy, Japan, Qatar, Russia, South Africa, South Korea, and Venezuela were present at the 8th (and final) Ad Hoc Session meeting at the UN in August 2006. Previous sessions also included representatives from the United States.

Access to Information: Interpreters and Technology

The WFD strongly promotes full and quality access to information through sign language interpreters and technology. The WFD Congress includes a scientific commission on technology and another on sign language and interpreting. The WFD uses networks of Deaf experts in communications and in technology to help develop policies and plans of action for the organization.

The WFD has encouraged the establishment of a professional organization of sign language interpreters, World Association of Sign Language Interpreters (WASLI). During the 2007 WASLI and WFD conferences in Spain, the WFD and WASLI signed a joint statement supporting advocacy for quality interpreting, the professionalization of interpreting, and close collaborations between both organizations on the national level.

Information technology has revolutionized communication processes for Deaf people all over the world. Key to this revolution is the Internet, a quickly growing means of information and networking for many Deaf individuals and associations. Deaf people in developed countries regularly use handheld devices to access and transmit information. The hope is that the digital divide between developed and developing countries will decrease over time. The WFD advocates for captions for all kinds of media at all times.

Cochlear implants and other auditory amplification devices have long been discussed within the WFD Board and Congresses. Some Ordinary Members (e.g., the British Deaf Association, the U.S. National Association of the Deaf) include their position papers on their Web sites. The WFD is working on a general policy paper on assistive technologies, biotechnology, and bioethics (genetics) to incorporate the overarching principle that Deaf people do not need to be fixed. They should have choices, but they all have the fundamental inalienable right to sign language and educational excellence.

Developing Countries

The WFD follows the UN definitions for developing and developed countries. A vast majority of Deaf people live in developing countries with very little or no resources, information access, language, education, jobs, or some combination of deficits. The WFD strives to elevate their awareness, knowledge, and status by helping them to organize their own national association of the Deaf. One of the highest priorities for WFD advocacy work and fundraising are projects and training for Deaf people in developing countries. The WFD collaborates with developed countries (mostly the Scandinavian nations) to use their governments' international funds to support developing countries (or regions) on access and empowerment projects such as sign language research, organizational leadership, and human rights strategies.

During the plenary session titled Commission on Developing Countries at the 2007 WFD Congress, a panel of representatives from the Balkan nations (Albania, Kosovo, and Montenegro) presented on needs and goals of Deaf people in unstable environments, especially emergency communications and ongoing equal access. The session concluded with recommendations on how to work with Deaf natives and organizations on their own initiatives and priorities.

DEAF WOMEN

Deaf women rejoiced in 2007 when their status was elevated from a special interest group to a Commission on Deaf Women at the WFD Congress in Spain. Deaf women have long been underrepresented and much oppressed and neglected in many countries. Previous Deaf women special interest groups have made several key recommendations for the WFD, including the need for greater representation and gender balance in the WFD as well as regional and national functions, support for equal status and treatment, and a clear statement of the WFD's position on gender equality.

The WFD Board has also made a concerted effort to expand the number of Deaf women on the board by filling vacant board positions with female representatives from previously unrepresented regions, whenever possible. The WFD also encourages each Ordinary Member to consider gender balance when sending representatives to conferences.

SYMBOL REPRESENTING DEAF PEOPLE

In the 1960s, the WFD General Assembly adopted a symbol, an ear with a slash through it, to denote being Deaf. The symbol was revisited in the 1995 General Assembly and deemed a negative representation of the Deaf person. Rather than focus on a defective ear, the delegates motioned for a replacement symbol to indicate that Deaf people are people of the eye and are visual beings with unlimited capacities. Accordingly, WFD conducted contests worldwide for a replacement symbol. Various and diverse drawings were submitted in 1999 and again in 2003; however, not one symbol leaped out as being the most logical one, as being internationally and culturally appropriate, or as being easily interpreted to mean Deaf people. Finally, rather than force a decision, the General Assembly agreed that individual OMs had the flexibility and power to select one that it deemed most appropriate and clear for its own country.

INTERNATIONAL DEAF WEEK

Since 1953, the WFD has encouraged all countries to celebrate an annual International Deaf Awareness Week. Although the WFD suggests the end of September for this celebration, each country is free to choose the week most appropriate for its region, culture, and programs. In recent years, the emphasis has shifted from Deaf awareness to Deaf action. The WFD encourages Ordinary Members to use this focus to promote and advocate for human rights, sign language, and quality access as well as to increase momentum for ongoing legislative campaigns on sign language and the Convention on the Rights of Disabled Persons. Ordinary Members vary in their political activities, conducting rallies, training, or festivals to draw the attention of politicians, government authorities, and the general public with respect to achievements and concerns of Deaf people. The WFD disseminates information packets for Deaf Week, encourages exchanges of ideas on its Web site, and subsequently publishes post-activity reports.[4]

RESOURCES ON WFD AND HUMAN RIGHTS

The following WFD official documents and fact sheets are available on the WFD Web site[5]:

- Policy on Education Rights for Deaf Children
- Statement on Adult Education
- Statement on the Unification of Sign Languages
- Position Paper on Technology and Accessibility
- Policy on WFD Work in Developing Countries
- Policy on Member Countries in Developing Countries
- Fact Sheet: Human Rights
- Fact Sheet: Sign Language
- Fact Sheet: Deaf in Developing Countries

The WFD produces a variety of regular publications. The WFD circulars are published two or three times a year; *WFD News* is published once annually and summarizes the organization's achievements.[6] In addition, the organization publishes proceedings of each of the WFD Congresses. It has also published *WFD Report 2003–2007: Charting the Future*, a single document that considers work to be done between congresses.

Other helpful documents provide important information with respect to the efforts of the WFD and its members. Some of these are listed here:

- Joutselainen, Marjo, *WFD Survey of Deaf People in the Developing World,* World Federation of the Deaf, 1991.
- UNESCO, *The Hamburg Declaration on Adult Learning and Agenda for the Future,* CONFINTEA V, Hamburg, Germany, July 1997.
- UNESCO, *The Salamanca Statement and Framework for Action on Special Needs Education,* adopted by the World Conference on Special Needs Education: Access and Quality, Salamanca, Spain, June 1994.
- United Nations, *The Charter of Fundamental Rights*, Articles 21, 24, 26, and 28, September 2000.
- United Nations, *UN Convention on the Human Rights of Persons with Disabilities,* 2006.
- United Nations, *Convention on the Rights of the Child*, adopted by the UN General Assembly 1959 and 1989.
- United Nations, *Declaration on the Rights of the Child*, adopted by the UN General Assembly February 22, 2001, particularly the section "Children with Disabilities."
- United Nations, *Declaration on the Rights of Persons Belonging to National or Ethnic, Religious and Linguistic Minorities*, adopted by the UN General Assembly December 18, 1992.

---

4. See http://www.wfdeaf.org/news.aspx#50 for examples of how various countries celebrated Deaf Week in September 2007.

5. Go to http://www.wfdeaf.org/documents.html.

6. Go to http://wfdeaf.org/news.aspx.

- United Nations, *The Standard Rules on the Equalization of Opportunities for Persons with Disabilities,* particularly Article 6.1–6.9, adopted by the UN General Assembly December 20, 1993.
- United Nations, *Universal Declaration of Human Rights*, adopted by the UN General Assembly December 10, 1948.
- World Federation of the Deaf, *Report on the Status of Sign Language,* WFD Scientific Commission on Sign Language (T. Supalla, R. Bergmann, C. Denmark, M. Jokinen, O-I Schroeder, and M. Suwanarat), 1993.

Finally, the following Web sites contain useful information that is related to the work of the WFD:

- International Committee of Sports for the Deaf—www.ciss.org
- United Nations—www.un.org
- United Nations Educational, Scientific and Cultural Organization (UNESCO)—www.unesco.org
- UN Enable—www.un.org/esa/socdev/enable/conventioninfo.htm
- World Association of Sign Language Interpreters (WASLI)—http://www.wasli.org

REFERENCES

Crammatte, F., & Crammatte, A. B. (1976). Full citizenship for all deaf People. *Proceedings of the VII World Congress of the World Federation of the Deaf.* Silver Spring, MD: National Association of the Deaf.

World Federation of the Deaf. (1975). *Gestuno: International Sign Language of the Deaf.* Carlisle, UK: Author.

World Federation of the Deaf. (1987). Congress Resolution. *1987 World Congress of the Deaf in Helsinki, Finland.* [Videorecording]. Washington, DC: Gallaudet University Department of Television, Film, and Photography.

World Federation of the Deaf. (2007). Education rights for Deaf children. Retrieved February 25, 2009, from http://www.wfdeaf.org/pdf/policy_child_ed.pdf

Concluding Observations

Donald F. Moores and Margery S. Miller

A BOOK of this nature addresses enormous complexity. It presents and analyzes social, political, and educational realities that deaf people around the world encounter in diverse societies at various stages of development and evolution and while operating under quite diverse philosophies. The authors of the different chapters have presented their information clearly and graphically, enabling the reader to gain not only an appreciation of the uniqueness of the lives of deaf people in individual countries but also develop an understanding of areas of commonality. We have identified four major themes and want to highlight them briefly.

First, there is a sense of confidence and empowerment of deaf people around the world and a global awareness, a belief that there are shared experiences regardless of race, gender, nationality, or educational level. This belief is exemplified by the World Federation of the Deaf (WFD) and The International Committee of Sports for the Deaf. Each organization is run by and for deaf individuals and has a global reach. The WFD advocates for human rights, education, and recognition of national sign languages, and the International Committee effectively brings deaf people together from across the world in an atmosphere of sharing and respect.

A second theme is that large numbers of deaf people around the world have experienced significant improvements in their lives. Educational opportunities through the university level and subsequent career opportunities have opened up in unprecedented volume in the past generation, leading to growing numbers of deaf professionals in many countries. The process has been facilitated by legislation, improved technology, official recognition of sign languages in many countries, and a growing awareness of deafness and deaf individuals. In countries struggling to rid themselves of poverty and the residual effects of colonialism, serious efforts are being made to meet United Nations mandates to address the needs of all citizens, including those who are deaf.

The authors also stress a third theme, calling attention to the fact that for more than a generation, deaf leaders have argued that we must move past a medical, deficit, or pathological model of deafness, one that implies that deaf people are deficient and in need of a "cure." And if a "cure" is not possible, this model advocates that deaf people should be trained to exhibit "normal" behavior by speaking instead of signing. Although there has been growing acceptance of a social-cultural model of deafness and of deafness as a normal part of the human condition, we must admit that the medical model predominates in much, if not most, of the world. This medical mind set has been strengthened over the past generation by the rapid expansion of cochlear implants and a steady decline in the ages in which the surgical procedure occurs, to the point where it is now common with toddlers and infants. All too frequently, cochlear implants have been advertised as a universal cure for deafness instead of as an aid that is appropriate for some individuals.

Finally, a fourth theme, a move toward educational inclusion, is evident. Taking various forms across the world, educational inclusion of deaf children has assumed global dimensions to such an extent that we have devoted a separate chapter to it in this volume. Although not often expressed in such terms, to some extent it is an educational manifestation of a pathological model of deafness in that it implies that it is preferable for deaf children to be educated with hearing children instead of with other deaf children and, by extension, to be taught by hearing teachers rather than by deaf teachers. The assumption is that educational outcomes in the form of academic achievement will be better, and little attention is given to social-emotional considerations. Typically, if deaf children are in inclusive situations, they receive special services and are visited once a week or so by an itinerant teacher, who is almost invariably hearing. In fact, on most occasions, there is little or no contact with deaf adults or deaf role models. Unfortunately, the confidence and empowerment felt by deaf adults mentioned above in economic and social areas has had little influence on educational programs for deaf children, which are controlled by hearing people in every country in the world. In 1864, the U.S. government established what is now Gallaudet University as the first liberal arts college for deaf students in the world. A century and a half later, it remains the *only* college for deaf students in the world. We are not aware of any serious thought being given to establishing a similar college or university in North or South America, Asia, Europe, or Africa. That fact, in itself, should speak volumes. We hope that ways will be found for the current generation, and future generations, of deaf children to enjoy access to and membership in a vibrant Deaf community.

Contributors

C. Tane Akamatsu
Psychological Services
Toronto District School Board
Toronto, Ontario, Canada

Yasser A. Al-Hilawani
Department of Educational Psychology
Kuwait University
State of Kuwait

Jesús M. Alvarado
Department of Methodology of the
    Behavioral Sciences and
Institute for Biofuntional Studies
Complutense University
Madrid, Spain

Donalda Ammons
International Committee of Sports for the
    Deaf
Lausanne, Switzerland

Ana Paula Berberian
Department of Speech Language Therapy
Tuiuti University
Curitiba, Brazil

Mary Anne Bibby
Faculty of Education (Professor Emeritus)
University of Alberta
Edmonton, Alberta, Canada

Sung-Kyu Choi
Department of Special Education
Daegu University
Daegu, Gyeongsan City, South Korea

Ian Cocks
Ministry of Education
Special Education
Christchurch, New Zealand

Edward Corbett
Ohio School for the Deaf
Columbus, Ohio

James J. DeCaro
PEN-International
National Technical Institute for the Deaf
Rochester, NY

Goedele De Clerck
Comparative Science of Culture
Ghent University
Ghent, Belgium

Shai Ezrachi
School of Education
Tel Aviv University
Israel

Ana Cristina Guarinello
Department of Speech Language Therapy
Tuiuti University
Curitiba, Brazil

Klaus-B. Günther
Department of Rehabilitation Science
Humboldt University
Berlin, Germany

Johannes Hennies
Department of Rehabilitation Science
Humboldt University
Berlin, Germany

Valeria Herrera
Dirección de Postgrados
Universidad Metropolitana de Ciencias
    de la Educación
Santiago, Chile

Manfred Hintermair
Department of Special Education
University of Education
Heidelberg, Germany

Merv Hyde
Centre for Applied Studies of Deafness
Faculty of Education
Griffith University
Brisbane, Australia

Janet R. Jamieson
Department of Educational and Counselling
    Psychology, and Special Education
University of British Columbia
Vancouver, British Columbia, Canada

Kathryn Johnson
Department of Special Education
St. Cloud State University
St. Cloud, MN

Nassozi B. Kiyaga,
Deaf Link Uganda
Wandegeya-Kampala
Uganda

Jim Kyle
Centre for Deaf Studies
University of Bristol
Bristol, United Kingdom

Paddy Ladd
Centre for Deaf Studies
University of Bristol
Bristol, United Kingdom

Venetta Lampropoulou
Deaf Studies Unit
Department of Primary Education
University of Patras
Patras, Greece

Raymond LeBlanc
Atlantic Provinces Special Education
    Authority
Halifax, Nova Scotia, Canada

Richard Lytle
Department of Education
Gallaudet University
Washington, DC

Lucas Magongwa
Centre for Deaf Studies
University of the Witwatersrand,
    Johannesburg
Gauteng, South Africa

Fred R. Mangrubang
Department of Education
Gallaudet University
Washington, DC

Giselle De Athayde Massi
Department of Speech Language Therapy
Tuiuti University
Curitiba, Brazil

Connie Mayer
Faculty of Education
York University
Toronto, Ontario, Canada

Christine Miller
Ministry of Education
Special Education
Auckland, New Zealand

Margery S. Miller
Enrollment Management
Gallaudet University
Washington, DC

Ownali N. Mohamedali
Department of Library and Information
   Studies
The University of the West Indies
Mona, Jamaica

Donald F. Moores
Department of Exceptional Student and
   Deaf Education
University of North Florida
Jacksonville, FL

Tova Most
School of Education and Department of
   Communication Disorders
Tel-Aviv University
Tel-Aviv, Israel

Patricia A. Mudgett-DeCaro
Educational Consultant
Rochester, NY

Ingrid Parkin
Director of Deaf Education
Deaf Federation of South Africa
Johannesburg, South Africa

Desmond Power
Centre for Applied Studies in Deafness
Griffith University
Gold Coast
Queensland, Australia

Aníbal Puente
Department of Cognitive Processes and
Institute for Biofuntional Studies
Complutense University
Madrid, Spain

Gunilla Preisler
Department of Psychology
Stockholm University
Stockholm, Sweden

Roslyn Rosen
National Center on Deafness
California State University, Northridge
Northridge, CA

Ana Paula Santana
Department of Speech Language Therapy
Tuiuti University
Curitiba, Brazil

Claudine Storbeck
Center for Deaf Studies
University of the Witwatersrand,
   Johannesburg
Gauteng, South Africa

Marian Valmaseda
Guidance Education for Deaf Students
Community of Madrid
Madrid, Spain

Madan M. Vasishta
Department of Administration and
   Supervision
Gallaudet University
Washington, DC

Amatzia Weisel
School of Education
Tel Aviv University
Israel

Jun Hui Yang
School of Education and Social Science
University of Central Lancashire
Preston, United Kingdom

Index

toring issues and, 64; national education planning and, 60–61; National Plan for the Education of Children and Young People who are Deaf or Hearing Impaired in Aotearoa/New Zealand and, 60; placement trends and, 65–66; postsecondary education access and, 61; preschool programs and, 58; regional services and, 59; resource accessibility and, 56–57, 63–64; school programs and, 58; special personnel and, 55–56; teacher training and, 61–63; Total Communication and, 56; World War II era and, 55

New Zealand Disability Strategy, 61
New Zealand Federation for Deaf Children, 60
New Zealand Sign Language (NZSL), 53, 56–65
Nguni people, 133n2
Nie, 37–38
Nigeria, 145–153
Nigerian Educational Research Council, 152
Nippon Foundation of Japan, 345–351
Niv School for the Deaf, 102
Nixon, Cathy, 3
No Child Left Behind, 89, 334, 339, 361
Nordén, K., 231, 234, 242
Northern Cochlear Implant Trust, 57
North Korea, 88
Norway, 207, 357–358
Norwegian Sign Language (NSL), 357–358
note-taking, 9
Nova Scotia, 285–290, 296, 298
Novosibirsk State Technical University, 349
Nucleus implant, 6, 115
Nunavut Territory, 284
Nuns, 73, 134–135, 302
Nurse, D., 147
Nuthall, B., 56

Oakland, T., 89
O'Donoghue, G. M., 249
Office of Special Education, 19–20
Ohlwein, S., 182
Ohna, E. S., 189
Ohna, S.-E., 352, 358
Old French Sign Language, 334
Olympics, 11, 30
One Child Policy, 29, 36
Ontario, 286–288, 292–299
Opium War, 17

oralist instruction: Australia and, 6–7; Brazil and, 275, 278; Canada and, 287, 292, 297–299; Chile and, 307–309; China and, 18–21, 24, 36; Flanders and, 157–159, 162–163; Germany and, 178–181; Greece and, 197; Israel and, 102–103; legal issues and, 265–266; pure, 6–7; Singapore and, 70–74; South Africa and, 134–136; sub-Saharan Africa and, 147; Sweden and, 231–234, 242; Systematical Language Construction and, 181; United Kingdom and, 262, 265–266; United States and, 335
Oral School for the Deaf, 70
Örebro University, 238
Organization for Cooperation and Economic Development (OECD), 304
Osberger, M. J., 249
Osborne-Clark v. Inland Revenue, 265
Osgood, R., 360
Osman, M., 81
overinoculation, 19
Oviedo, A., 213
Ozdemir, Dogan, 369
Ozolins, U., 10

Padden, C., 354
Padeliadou, S., 197, 200, 208
Paget-Gorman System, 135–136
Pakeha, 53, 58
Pakistan, 69
Palatidou, Helen, 195–196
Pan American Deaf Sports Federation, 371
Panara, R. F., 148
Pang, Y., 26
Paralympics, 27, 30, 369, 371–372
Parasnis, I., 362
Parfkin, Ingrid, 133–144
Park, J. Y., 89–91
Parkes, R., 249
Parsons, M., 54–56
Partners in Education (PIE), 21–23, 29, 30
Partners in Excellence for International Development, 22
Pasifika, 53, 63
paternalism, 12
Patras, 201–202
Patterson, P. J., 317
Pattison, John, 4